THE LIBRARY
A FRAGILE HISTORY

ANDREW PETTEGREE AND
ARTHUR DER WEDUWEN

BASIC BOOKS
NEW YORK

Basic Books
Hachette Book Group
1290 Avenue of the Americas, New York, NY 10104
www.basicbooks.com

Printed in the United States of America

Originally published in 2021 in Great Britain by Profile Books Ltd.

First US Edition: November 2021

Published by Basic Books, an imprint of Perseus Books, LLC, a subsidiary of Hachette Book Group, Inc. The Basic Books name and logo is a trademark of the Hachette Book Group.

The Hachette Speakers Bureau provides a wide range of authors for speaking events. To find out more, go to www.hachettespeakersbureau.com or call (866) 376-6591.

The publisher is not responsible for websites (or their content) that are not owned by the publisher.

Typeset in Garamond by MacGuru Ltd.

Library of Congress Control Number: 2021945164

ISBNs: 978-1-5416-0077-5 (hardcover); 978-1-5416-0078-2 (ebook)

TR

10 9 8 7 6 5 4 3 2 1

Dedicated to the memory of
Felicity Bryan
(1945–2020)

CONTENTS

You have before you a short work on libraries, that is to say, on books. What subject could be worthier for those of us who constantly use them?

Justus Lipsius, *De Bibliothecis* (1602)

CURATING THE RUINS

For the Dutch scholar Hugo Blotius, appointment as librarian to Holy Roman Emperor Maximilian II in 1575 should have been the crowning achievement of his career. Yet when Blotius arrived in Vienna to take up his new responsibilities, he found a scene of devastation. 'How neglected and desolate everything looked,' he wrote, plaintively:

> There was mould and rot everywhere, the debris of moths and bookworms, and a thick covering of cobwebs. The windows had not been opened for months, and not a ray of sunshine had penetrated through them to brighten the unfortunate books, which were slowly pining away: and when they were opened, what a cloud of noxious air streamed out.[1]

This was the emperor's court library, the Hofbibliothek, a collection of 7,379 volumes (Blotius's first task was to make a catalogue); and it was situated not in the imperial palace but on the first floor of a Franciscan convent, a place of refuge for an orphaned collection which clearly played no part in the emperor's cultural programme.

When Blotius arrived in Vienna, it was over a hundred years since the invention of printing, a technological marvel that would bring the joys of book ownership within the reach of many thousands of Europe's citizens. Yet, in the midst of this great flourishing of literary culture, one of the principal libraries of Europe had become a dusty mausoleum. This was not an isolated example. The famed library of Matthias Corvinus, King of Hungary, one of the wonders of the first great age of book collecting, was completely destroyed; the rare and precious books of Cosimo de' Medici in

Florence had been absorbed into other collections. The spectacular collection of Fernando Colon, son of the explorer Christopher
Columbus, was intended to rival the fabled ancient library of Alexandria; but it too was also largely dispersed, ravaged by time, the
disapproval of the Inquisition, and the depredations of the King
of Spain.

The library of Duke Federico of Urbino, a collector so grand
that it was said that he would allow no printed book to pollute his
wondrous manuscripts, also fell into neglect. When the famous
library scholar Gabriel Naudé visited in the 1630s, he found Duke
Federico's library 'in such a deplorable state that the readers despair
of finding anything there'. Naudé was a young man on the rise,
the author of one of the first guides for book collectors, aimed
squarely at the elite buyers who might offer him a comfortable post
building them a library (which they duly did).[2] What Naudé did
not discuss in his writings was the uncomfortable truth of libraries
throughout the ages: no society has ever been satisfied with the
collections inherited from previous generations. What we will frequently see in this book is not so much the apparently wanton
destruction of beautiful artefacts so lamented by previous studies
of library history, but neglect and redundancy, as books and collections that represented the values and interests of one generation
fail to speak to the one that follows. The fate of many collections
was to degrade in abandoned attics and ruined buildings, even if
only as the prelude to renewal and rebirth in the most unexpected
places.

If we leave Naudé scrabbling around the faded glories of Italy
and scroll forward 400 years, we find the library still going through
an existential crisis of relevance, even if a collection of 7,000
volumes is a less remarkable achievement. Today, public libraries
face falling budgets and the maintenance costs of old and decaying
buildings, at the same time as demands for new services and declining interest in their legacy collections. During our research for this
book, we witnessed at first hand the struggle over the Durning
Public Library in Kennington, which Lambeth Council planned
to turn into a community resource (council-speak for defunding it
and allowing it to be run by volunteers). This ran into determined

resistance from a group of local residents campaigning to keep it open. Does the campaign represent public-spirited altruism that we should applaud – or is it a nostalgia for a world that has now disappeared and will never return? The educated and affluent part of our community takes it for granted that public funding of the arts and the facilitation of recreational reading is part of the core functions of government. But the public library – in the sense of a funded collection available free to anyone who wants to use it – has only existed since the mid nineteenth century, a mere fraction of the history of the library as a whole. If there is one lesson from the centuries-long story of the library, it is that libraries only last as long as people find them useful.

In other words, libraries need to adapt to survive, as they have always adapted to survive, a feat very successfully accomplished in recent years in France, with its network of Médiathèques, albeit with a huge commitment of public funds. University libraries, responding to student demand, are now social hubs as much as places of work, the cathedral silence that once characterised the library a thing of the past. In this, libraries actually hark back to an earlier model, pioneered in the Renaissance, when libraries were often convivial social spaces, in which books jostled for attention alongside paintings, sculptures, coins and curiosities.

This history of libraries does not offer a story of easy progress through the centuries, nor a prolonged lament for libraries lost: a repeating cycle of creation and dispersal, decay and reconstruction, turns out to be the historical norm. Even if libraries are cherished, the contents of these collections require constant curation, and often painful decisions about what has continuing value and what must be disposed of. Very often libraries flourished in the hands of their first owner, and then wasted away: damp, dust, moths and bookworm do far more damage over the years than the targeted destruction of libraries. But while growth and decline are parts of the cycle, so too is recovery. In 1556, the University of Oxford, its book collection despoiled, sold off the library's furniture. Fifty years later Sir Thomas Bodley established the greatest university library of the next three centuries. Fire ravaged libraries with remarkable frequency, only for the collections to be rebuilt, more easily with each passing generation as the number of books available on the open market multiplied.

This is a story, then, of many unexpected twists and turns. What makes a library is, to a great extent, something each generation must decide anew. Some of those we discuss here are personal, workaday collections, reflecting the personal taste of an individual, while others are vast endeavours, established as monuments to national civic pride or even pursuing the Alexandrian notion of collecting the sum of human knowledge. Some were housed in richly decorated palaces and others, like that of Erasmus, had no home at all, being carted from house to house after their itinerant owner. Just as the books themselves have followed unexpected courses, flowing from collection to collection in the wake of war, social upheaval or light-fingered bibliophiles, the evolution of the library is far from linear.

Books on the Move

After the splendours of the great library at Alexandria, an inspiration for each subsequent generation of collectors, the muted contribution of the Roman Empire to the history of the library is something of a surprise. It was as if this military people could understand the purpose of an aqueduct, but could not quite work out what a library was for. Many great Roman libraries arrived in the baggage train of conquering generals: the great library of the Greek philosopher Aristotle found its way to Rome in this way. In this robust approach to intellectual property the Romans would find many imitators. In the first decade of the nineteenth century, Napoleon employed the author Stendhal to cherry-pick the libraries of Italy and Germany on behalf of the French national library.[3] Two centuries previously, in the Thirty Years' War, the Swedes had created an efficient bureaucratic process for appropriating the libraries of captured German cities. Transported back to Sweden, many of the books are still in the university library of Uppsala; the French Bibliothèque Nationale, in contrast, was obliged at the Congress of Vienna to repatriate Napoleon's trophies, something that caused no little indignation, given the amount they had spent on having the books rebound.[4]

The most substantial legacy of Rome, none of whose libraries survived the fall of the western empire, was the gradual transition from papyrus scrolls to parchment books as the medium of storage. Parchment, made from animal skins, was a much more resilient surface, and it was on parchment that the learning of Rome lived out the next millennium in the monasteries of the Christian West. This thousand-year supremacy of the manuscript book provides us with some of the most hauntingly beautiful products of medieval culture: today, these manuscripts are the most treasured possessions of the libraries where they have found their final homes.[5] By the fourteenth century, the works of monastic scribes and illuminators were increasingly reinforced by a secular market for beautiful books, as these became one further way for the leaders of European society to display their cultural sophistication.

Muslim caliphs in Baghdad, Damascus, Cordoba and Cairo also assembled libraries, famed throughout the Islamic world for their size. The caliphs attracted the best calligraphers to furnish these collections, and enticed scholars to visit them, enriching the courts with their rhetorical talents. In Persia, India and China the collecting of fine manuscripts, embellished with elegant decorations, lavish colours and superb calligraphy, was a favoured pastime of princes and emperors.

Thus, when in the mid fifteenth century Johannes Gutenberg and others began experimenting with a mechanical process for supplying the ever-increasing number of books required by churches, scholars and discerning collectors, they had a lot to live up to. Gutenberg's printed books dazzled the first generation of readers with their technological intricacy, but it still proved difficult to persuade established collectors that drab black-and-white texts were an adequate substitute for their beautifully illuminated manuscripts. Nor was it very clear how these thousands of printed texts could be brought to a market spread around Europe, something that caused some heartache to early investors in the medium. But once these teething problems were solved, the printed book brought the possibility of building a library to ever greater numbers of potential customers – even as it limited the appeal of book collecting as a form of aristocratic display.

Print also represented a decisive fork in the road in one other respect, for the vibrant manuscript cultures of Africa, the Middle East and East Asia did not follow Europe in embracing the mass production of print. The Ottoman Empire largely eschewed print altogether. The unhappy Venetian who presented to the Sublime Porte the first printed copy of the Qur'an was condemned for blasphemy. China, despite remarkable early experiments with woodblock printing, did not embrace metal type, for principally technical reasons. These cultures generally stayed loyal to woodblock or manuscript bookmaking, though not before they had shared with the West one further remarkable gift: paper. Made from cloth rags, paper was a far cheaper medium than parchment, and exquisitely well suited for partnership with the printing press. But without the multiplying capacities of print, book collecting outside of Europe and European colonies remained largely an elite privilege. For the next three centuries the vast proliferation of libraries, public and private, serving ever-expanding circles of readership, remained predominantly a phenomenon of Europe and its global diaspora.

This growth of book ownership was driven forward by a steady growth in literacy. At first, this was largely a case of professional necessity, evident among those who had to read for their work: merchants, clerks, lawyers and officials, medical doctors and priests. Print offered these emerging, aspirational professional classes the chance to own and collect books. Soon they were accumulating libraries of a size – several hundred items – that would only have been possible in the manuscript era for those at the apex of society. This democratisation of luxury, making widely available what was once rare and precious, is a recurrent phenomenon in every era of human history, but it has often had painful consequences for book collecting. An aristocrat could hardly expect the same reception for their collection of 300 texts when the local cloth merchant had as many: better to buy a sculpture, a painting or a lion. Emperor Maximilian II sent his books off to the attic because they no longer featured in this lexicon of conspicuous display.

Print and Power

Resentment of this democratisation of luxury, and the intrusion of more plebeian collectors into the refined world of books, continued for the best part of three centuries. The desire to accumulate knowledge competed with the desire to control access to it, or use it to somehow 'improve' its readers. This was most obviously manifested in disapproval of the reading tastes of these new readers: from the sixteenth-century war on chivalric fiction, to criticism of the novel, to disapproval of female reading tastes and particularly female authorship. Sir Thomas Bodley's great work in the re-foundation of the University of Oxford library is rightly celebrated, but he was adamant that he would not tolerate 'idle books and riffe raffes' in the collection: by which he meant texts in English rather than Latin. When Oxford received, by donation, a copy of the famous First Folio of Shakespeare's plays, they sold it a few decades later. In 1905, a copy was bought back for the university, at enormous public cost, to prevent it from falling into the hands of the American collector Henry Folger.[6]

With each century, new readers were brought into the compass of book ownership, and the same battles were repeatedly replayed, marking out the library as a political space. Should readers in the new nineteenth-century public libraries have the books that they desired, or books that would make them better, more cultured people? This raging debate was still echoing deep into the twentieth century: in the lists of 'recommended' texts issued for public libraries in America; in the prejudice against fiction in general, tolerated only in the hope that it would lead readers to more demanding literature (it did not); and in the anathematising of certain genres, such as romance. In the first half of the twentieth century in provincial England, Boots Booklovers Library provided a refuge for respectable women who sought such guilty pleasures. Even as late as 1969, the former director of the library service in the London Borough of Haringey could write mournfully: 'There is nothing more deadly to a public library service than pandering to a taste for "light" fiction.'[7]

In the fifteenth century, hostility towards the depreciation of what had previously been an elite currency – books – greatly complicated the history of the library. The first consequence of the temporary retreat of kings and princes from the building of libraries was an era of tribulation for institutional collections. The first great institutional libraries, like the Biblioteca Ambrosiana in Milan, were often based on the donation of a distinguished private collector; or, in the case of university libraries, the accumulation of multiple smaller donations. Hardly any institutional library before the nineteenth century had a budget for the acquisition of new books, so donations were essential for growth (even if this meant receiving multiple copies of the same worn-out class texts).

The fate of these collections demonstrates that the history of the library is not a story of relentless progress. During the two centuries after the invention of printing, most institutional collections went into decline. In universities, the repudiation of the medieval curriculum made much of their stock redundant. The conflicts of the Reformation era, and the division of Europe's libraries into contesting Protestant and Catholic blocs, led to the painful examination of existing holdings for heretical content. The complete closure of the English university libraries was drastic and unusual: elsewhere institutional libraries simply faded away. In Copenhagen in 1603, the university library possessed a paltry 700 volumes, and with the exception of Leiden, none of the new Dutch libraries fared much better. It was not unusual for professors to accumulate personal libraries three or four times the size of the university collection – a reversal of roles inconceivable today.[8]

Indeed, for much of the sixteenth and seventeenth centuries the history of the library was driven forward largely by personal collecting. Books became simultaneously more affordable and more necessary to the professional life of lawyers, doctors and ministers of the church. By the mid seventeenth century, many could boast collections of over a thousand books. In contrast to the rapacious Renaissance book hunters of the manuscript era, who plied their trade in remote monasteries and religious houses, these men found books relatively easy to come by. Their correspondence is full of chatter about books: lending books back and forth, exchanging news about new titles, passing on their own newest publications (many collectors were also authors) or recommending books written by their friends. This was an era in which books were valued not just for the knowledge they contained, but as a commodity: innovations in the market such as book auctions meant that collectors could continue buying, secure in the knowledge that on their death their families would be able to realise something close to the real value of the collection. The result was a virtuous circle in which collectors could indulge their passions, while also doing something that passed for inheritance planning.

Histories of libraries have thus far concentrated disproportionately on the world's great libraries, particularly those that have survived the ravages of time and lived on through the ages. One can well understand why: they are the charismatic megafauna of the library world, often occupying striking or historic buildings. Who can resist an example of eighteenth-century Austrian baroque, the quintessential cathedral of knowledge? But these were less temples to learning itself than buildings that were created to make a statement, whether the civic pride and values of a new elite (the Boston or New York Public Library) or the evangelical fervour of a missionary faith (the Jesuit libraries of the seventeenth and eighteenth centuries). Other libraries memorialised the success of the king's favourite raised above his peers (the Bibliothèque Mazarine in Paris) or the imposition of western culture in the non-European world (the Imperial Library in Kolkata, now the National Library of India).

This was the library as a symbol of power: a statement of what a nation or a ruling class stood for. Inevitably, when this power was challenged these monumental buildings bore the brunt of the cultural or intellectual insurgency. In the German Peasants' War of 1524-5, the rampaging armies made monastic libraries a deliberate target, a symbol of their detestation of their clerical landlords, who appeared to show greater devotion to their treasures and their incomes than to the humans from whom they extracted service and painful rents. Four hundred years later, in the wars of the twentieth century and since, libraries remain vulnerable for their cultural capital. In Sri Lanka, the public library of Jaffna was one of the largest libraries in Asia, and the pre-eminent repository of the written record of Tamil culture. On the night of 31 May 1981, the library was razed to the ground by a Sinhalese crowd, one of the principal examples of ethnic biblioclasm of the twentieth century.[9] A similar melancholic drama was played out in Sarajevo in 1992, when the Bosnian state library was deliberately targeted by the Serbian militia attacking the city. The entire collection of 1.5 million books and manuscripts was consumed in the resulting inferno.

The Perils of Modernity

Between 1800 and 1914, the population of Europe increased from 180 to 460 million. In the United States, growth was even more spectacular, from 5 to 106 million. Much of this population growth was fuelled by immigration, providing a workforce for the new industrial economy. Integrating these new citizens into the social fabric required, above all, a vast increase in educational provision. This stimulated a concerted drive towards compulsory education, at least for early years learning. By the early twentieth century, western societies were approaching universal literacy for both men and women. This permitted a parallel impetus towards a radical idea: a network of public libraries, free to all, catering to the reading needs of the broad mass of the population.

This bold vision took a long time to achieve. In the United States, the densely settled New England states led the way. In Britain, the critical moment was the passage in 1850 of the Public Libraries Act, empowering local authorities to establish libraries in their town or borough. The impact was, on the face of it, remarkable. By 1914 there were over 5,000 library authorities established in Britain under the terms of the 1850 Act, collectively circulating between 30 and 40 million volumes a year. By 1903, the United States boasted at least 4,500 public libraries, with a total book stock of some 55 million volumes. This growth would continue: by 1933, Germany had over 9,000 public libraries, while the collective book stock of American libraries then exceeded 140 million books.[10]

Behind these impressive statistics lies a more difficult struggle than this upward trajectory would suggest. In the nineteenth-century industrial world, where many still endured poverty, poor housing and appalling working conditions, not everyone believed that libraries were a priority for public funds. In Britain, where the establishment of a local library board required a taxpayer levy, the take-up rate was initially sluggish. Even when a library rate was proposed, hostile campaigning, often underwritten by the powerful brewers' lobby, could ensure that it was defeated. But for the impetus provided on both sides of the Atlantic by the Scottish-American steel magnate, Andrew Carnegie, the spread of this network of libraries would have been far less rapid. It is on such individual passions and obsessions as well as on vast global changes that the history of the library hinges.

Communities were certainly proud of their new libraries, often provided with a prime location in the centre of town. Yet when the ribbon was cut and the band had played, serious questions still had to be addressed. Who was the library intended to serve? Should children be admitted? What of those who saw the library mainly as a warm place to shelter while leafing through a newspaper? The issue was complicated by the fact that neither Andrew Carnegie, whose fortune funded a swathe of civic libraries across America and the United Kingdom, nor the British Public Libraries Act made provision for the purchase of books. These decisions lay in the hands of the library committee, usually dominated by the same local worthies who had previously populated the more exclusive subscription libraries.

The decisions these guardians made regarding access and library stock set off a new round of culture wars. Technological revolutions in the nineteenth-century print industry had greatly extended the range of reading matter that could be placed in the hands of neophyte readers. Publishers quickly developed a literature specifically aimed at this fresh market of the newly literate: books designed not to improve or educate, but to entertain. But if these tales of adventure, gore and criminality, with few pretensions to literary merit, caused horror in the traditional book trade, publishers had only themselves to blame. Their cosy understanding with commercial circulation libraries, most notably Charles

1. The mockery of plebeian reading tastes has been a ubiquitous feature of library history. As in James Gillray's *Tales of Wonder!* (1802), the object of this mockery was often the reading tastes of women, and their taste for light fiction of the sort few librarians took seriously before the twentieth century.

Edward Mudie's library empire, had kept the price of new books unnecessarily high, excluding all but the prosperous middle classes from new literary fiction.

For librarians and those who populated the higher reaches of the literary establishment, the story papers and yellowbacks represented a significant basket of deplorables, though it was more difficult to work out precisely what belonged in the basket. Low-life tales of the criminal underworld were obviously bad, but then detective thrillers were fast becoming one of the glories of twentieth-century fiction. Leaders of the library profession did their best to steer librarians through these turbulent waters by issuing regular lists of approved titles. Often the passage of time canonised a work such as Stephen Crane's *The Red Badge of Courage*, thought too dangerous on first appearance. It was left to the library assistant on the front desk to answer difficult questions about why a looked-for title was not available.

Critics of the new reading public received unexpected support from many of the twentieth century's literary elite. Aldous Huxley, George Moore and D. H. Lawrence all deplored the reading preferences of the great unwashed. In particular, D. H. Lawrence (who had read too much Nietzsche) was, like T. S. Eliot, an enemy of mass education: 'Let all schools be closed at once ... the great mass of humanity should never learn to read and write.'[11] Ironically, Lawrence first came across Nietzsche in Croydon Public Library, one of many institutions animated by the desire to make the fruits of learning available to a mass readership.

This disdain for new readers did little justice to the seriousness of the engagement with literature of at least a portion of this new reading public. When the journalist and social commentator Henry Mayhew examined the bookstalls of mid nineteenth-century London, he found working men already regular customers. Their preferences were largely for established classics of the English literary canon: the novels of Goldsmith, Fielding and Sir Walter Scott, Shakespeare of course, the poems of Pope, Burns and Byron.[12] Dickens made a fortune by understanding the temper of this expanding market and in due course the publishers cashed in with series of 1-shilling reprints of out-of-copyright materials.

What these readers lacked was not ambition or intellect, but time. This helps to explain why nineteenth-century legislation for shorter working days helped boost the library movement, and why libraries were also more intensely frequented in times of war and economic depression. Wars inevitably closed down other opportunities for recreation, leading to an increase in the demand for books, both from troops in the field and on the home front. While libraries were all too often on the frontlines of the industrial warfare of the twentieth century, war did a great deal to inculcate the habit of reading: the raw material without which the library cannot survive.

The history of the library, it turns out, is a story with many such paradoxes, false dawns and a laborious struggle to foster a reading public. Now we talk of its very survival, even though the death of the library has been predicted almost as often as the death of the book. Yet when, in the spring of 2020, a global pandemic forced all libraries to close their doors, the sense of loss was palpable. We should not romanticise libraries, not least because their owners seldom did. For much of their long history, libraries were primarily an intellectual resource and a financial asset. Only the very rich could afford to treat their libraries as shiny toys with which to impress their friends, passers-by and, more incidentally, posterity. The physical remains of these display libraries should not beguile us into confusing the impressive facade for the substance: the numberless collections of books assembled in private homes did every bit as much to sustain a vibrant book culture as institutional libraries. That, as we have seen repeatedly in times of loss and tribulation, is likely to remain the case. It is also the reason why, in the endless cycle from destruction to greatness, libraries have always recovered: it is in our nature to leave our own stamp on society. It is by no means clear, however, that what we preserve for the future will be similarly valued by our descendants.

PART ONE

INCEPTION AND SURVIVAL

CHAPTER ONE

A CONFUSION OF SCROLLS

On 16 October 2002, an impressive cast of world dignitaries gathered in the Egyptian city of Alexandria for the formal opening of one of the most remarkable cultural initiatives of the modern age: a new waterfront library resurrecting one of the wonders of the ancient world. Thirty years in the making, its genesis dated back to a visit to Egypt by American president Richard Nixon in 1974, during which the ill-starred president asked if he could be shown the site of the fabled library of Alexandria. Embarrassment ensued, since no one knew exactly where it might be: along with the buildings and its multitude of scrolls, even the place on which the ancient library stood had vanished into the sands of time.

Nixon would resign two months later, but local academics sniffed an opportunity. Frustrated by Alexandria's loss of influence to Cairo as a consequence of Gamal Abdel Nasser's Pan-Arabism and anti-colonialism, they saw the chance to revive a cultural icon, and with it Alexandria's place in the intellectual world. The appeal to universal civilising values embodied in the ancient library secured the influential support of UNESCO, leading in 1990 to the portentous Aswan Declaration, which committed the governments of Europe, the United States and the Arab world to building a new library as a monument to the 'quest for universal knowledge'. Saudi Arabia and the Gulf States pledged substantial sums, only to be trumped by Saddam Hussein, whose pledge of $21 million secured for Iraq the place of honour at the 2002 ceremonies.[1]

With so much international enthusiasm, it seemed almost impolite to question the wisdom of building a library in a run-down Egyptian port with no discernible need for such a facility. Certainly there would have been other ways to spend a grand total of $210 million that would improve the lives of Egyptian citizens. In the twelve-year period between the Aswan Declaration and the library's grand opening it was not difficult to find critics of 'Mubarak's new pyramid', painstakingly erected in a nation with widespread illiteracy and a far from unblemished record with regard to intellectual freedom. Much of the pledged help came in the form of donated books, including half a million in French, many of which were functionally useless and had to be discarded. The decision of Alexandria University to sell much of its own collection in anticipation of these new riches proved woefully premature.

In the twenty years since its opening, the new library of Alexandria has struggled with an insufficient acquisitions budget, disaffected staff and accusations of corruption, not to mention the upheaval of the Arab Spring and its aftermath. But regardless of whether you see the new library of Alexandria as a quixotic monument to the tortured politics of international cultural diplomacy, or the visionary celebration of a unique experiment in the history of human knowledge, it certainly points to the distinguished role of the ancient library of Alexandria in the history of libraries. Part fable, part historical reality, the ancient library of Alexandria has been a powerful symbol of intellectual aspiration throughout the history of book collecting. When the libraries of Rome burned to the ground in the heyday of the Roman Empire, it was to Alexandria that Emperor Domitian sent his scribes to create new copies for his library. When Fernando Colon decided to assemble a library encompassing all the world's knowledge in the sixteenth century, it was Alexandria he claimed as his inspiration.[2] Renaissance champions of scholarship evoked Alexandria as regularly as have the new barons of the digital age. The progenitors of Amazon, Google and Wikipedia can all, in this sense, lay claim to Alexandria's mantle.

The foundations of western civilisation owe so much to the inspiration and achievements of Greece and Rome that it is no surprise that we look there for models of library building and the roots of our culture of collecting. This expectation is, to an extent, justified. The Greeks required, and devised, the means to capture the intellectual achievements of the age of Aristotle, and

the Romans appropriated this cultural legacy with their customary ruthless efficiency. But even the Romans, with their apparently
limitless resources for major infrastructure projects, struggled to
resolve the problems that would bedevil the history of book collecting for the next two millennia: the provision of reliable texts
and the principles governing who had access to them; the optimum
means to store knowledge; and most of all how to establish stable
collections that would pass down through the generations. All of
this somehow eluded these most gifted architects of civilisation.
Later scholars would take from Greece and Rome an inspiring
vision of the empowerment of knowledge, and the potentialities
of collecting – as well as a lesson in how easily attempts to embody
this vision could turn to ashes.

Behold Alexandria

The Greeks were not the first to create libraries. The rulers of the
Assyrian Empire of Mesopotamia (present-day Iraq) gathered
considerable quantities of documents, all carefully inscribed in
their distinctive cuneiform script on to clay tablets. These baked
clay tablets survive remarkably well, since they are virtually imper-
vious to damp or fire; but they were enormously bulky to store and
too ponderous to move around easily. These cuneiform libraries
were located in royal palaces or temples, and intended exclusively
for the use of scholarly staff and royal owners. They were not open
to the public, as was made clear by this inscription at the end of
one such text: 'One who is competent (or knowledgeable) should
show this only to one who is also competent, but may not show
it to the uninitiated.'[3] In any case, in societies where literacy was
confined to the ruling class, and their officials and spiritual guides,
few would have aspired to access these early monuments of written
culture.

Some of these elite libraries were quite considerable. Collections of 700 or 800 items have been excavated, and the royal
libraries of Nineveh stored 35,000 tablets. All of these libraries
were destroyed when the Assyrian Empire was conquered by the
Babylonians in 614–612 BC. The Babylonian libraries faded from

view more gradually, rendered redundant by more functional alphabetical writing systems, and new media more convenient than clay tablets: parchment and papyrus. The discovery of the papyrus plant, and its excellence as a writing medium, was an essential requirement for the translation of the emerging Greek culture from an oral to a written form: papyrus grew abundantly in the Nile delta, and the techniques of splitting the reed stalks and weaving them together as writing sheets were easily mastered. Papyrus became the pre-eminent writing medium of the ancient world, exported from Egypt to Greece and later Rome, and made possible the extraordinary experiment in knowledge acquisition that became the library at Alexandria.

By the fourth century BC, Greece was a highly literate society, at least at the elite level.[4] A flourishing commercial book trade ensured that the milestones of literature and texts taught at schools were fairly freely available, and those with an occupational need for books (always in this period papyrus scrolls) could find them easily enough. Aristophanes mocked Euripides as a journeyman writer who 'squeezed [his plays] out of books'.[5] By 338 BC, Athens was sufficiently concerned about the poor copies of plays in circulation that they established an official archive of authoritative texts. The philosopher Aristotle, who tutored the young Alexander the Great and deserves credit for infusing the young warrior with a similar love of book learning, assembled a personal collection of considerable size. His books would eventually make their way to Rome, removed in 84 BC from the conquered city of Athens by the victorious general Sulla, though not before this remarkable personal library had helped inspire the organisation of the new institution in Alexandria.

The planting of a Greek city on the northern coast of Egypt played a key role in the expansive imperial vision of Alexander the Great, though he did not live to see the creation of the great seaport or its library. This was the achievement of the first two Ptolemaic kings, the dynasty born of Ptolemy the First, who secured Egypt when Alexander's empire was carved up among his leading generals. The library of Alexandria was first and foremost a scholarly academy: the rapidly developing collection of texts was essentially their research archive. Scholars who agreed to join the community in Egypt received benefits few academics could even dream of: a lifetime appointment, with a handsome salary, exemption from tax and free food and lodging. Among those tempted by these blandishments were the scientists Euclid, Strabo and Archimedes. From these names we can judge that the Ptolemies furnished their library not only with the classics of literature, but serious texts in the fields of mathematics, geography, physics and medicine. The pace of acquisitions was dazzling. Agents travelled throughout the Greek territories purchasing books on an industrial scale. Less creditably, scrolls were forcibly removed for copying from any ship entering the port. Many ships' captains would have needed to continue their journey before the originals were returned.[6]

We will never really know how many texts were accumulated by this library: scholars have spoken of 200,000 or even half a million scrolls. Whatever figure we choose, this was a library of a size that would never again be achieved until the nineteenth century. A collection of this magnitude necessarily required careful organisation. Scrolls were stored in recessed alcoves, where they could be stacked in organised groups. The sheer size of the Alexandrian library demanded far more systematic cataloguing, with books split between many different chambers. The texts were stored alphabetically, though presumably also organised by genre, the leading principle of classification in every institutional library thereafter. A feature of the Alexandrian library was the high quality of the scholars recruited as librarians. One, Callimachus of Cyrene, completed the first ever bibliographical dictionary of authors. Like so much connected with Alexandria, this has not survived. The scholars of Alexandria also took advantage of the inevitable presence of many duplicates to attempt to establish authoritative editions of the major texts, a quest that would be resumed in the Renaissance with the exhumation of classical texts from monastic libraries.[7] In Alexandria, as also in the Renaissance, this endeavour inevitably spawned another critical genre, the scholarly commentary.

When Rome seized leadership of the ancient world, the Alexandrian Academy would recede in importance. What became of the contents of the library is one of the great mysteries in the long history of libraries. In Plutarch's *Life of Caesar*, the destruction of the library is presented as a tragic by-product of the campaign of Julius Caesar to secure Egypt for his lover, Cleopatra. When Caesar ordered the burning of the Egyptian navy in the harbour, the fire spread to a dockside warehouse, consuming many books. These were likely to have been new acquisitions awaiting cataloguing, rather than the main library: as we have already seen, Emperor Domitian relied on Alexandria to restock Roman libraries lost in the fire of AD 79. A more plausible explanation sees the destruction of the library as a consequence of the Egyptian campaign of Emperor Aurelian in AD 272, when the palace quarter of Alexandria was laid waste. The polemical contribution of the relentlessly anticlerical eighteenth-century English author Edward Gibbon, who blamed the loss of the library on the campaign against pagan structures waged by the Christian Emperor Theodosius in AD 391, can largely be disregarded; likewise the suggestion that the books were destroyed on the orders of Caliph Omar after the Arab conquest of Egypt in the seventh century.[8]

The truth is that none of these explanations need be true. The major disadvantage of papyrus, otherwise an excellent medium for information storage, is its susceptibility to damp. Even in a well-curated collection, texts need to be recopied after a generation or two. The sheer size of the Alexandrian library militated against its survival. As with so many of the libraries we will meet in this book, neglect was a much more potent enemy than war or malice.

Rome

The contribution of Rome to the foundation of western civilisation – roads, aqueducts, the postal service, a host of administrative systems and legal codes – is so profound, that it is natural to expect a major contribution also to the development of the institutional library. In fact, in this respect at least, Rome fell short. The government of a large empire certainly generated an enormous amount of wealth and required considerable development in the bureaucratisation of administration. A vibrant commercial book market facilitated the accumulation of significant collections of books. Statesmen, authors and philosophers all gathered great libraries, often in each of their several residences. But for all that, Rome boasted nothing that we would recognise as a public library.

By far the most prominent and visible libraries in Rome were those established by the emperors, beginning with Augustus. This built on a scheme first conceived by Julius Caesar, thwarted by his assassination, to include libraries in his plan for 'adorning and building up' the city of Rome, a phrase which hints at the true purpose of these collections. Emperor Augustus placed libraries in the Temple of Apollo, establishing a widely imitated practice of dividing the Greek and Latin texts into separate collections. Most imperial libraries, like those of Augustus, were situated in a palace or temple. Libraries were seldom, if ever, housed in a separate building.

The establishment of such libraries greatly excited Rome's poets, who heaped praise on Asinius Pollio, the friend of Julius Caesar who would bring his plan for a library to fulfilment. According to Pliny the Elder, Asinius was 'the first to make the genius of man public property', a phrase echoed by Suetonius when he described the library as 'open to the public'.[9] We have to be careful with these phrases: authors in Rome, from Cicero to Pliny, were almost by definition members of the elite, and the public they had in mind was composed of people like themselves. When Pliny the Younger capped a successful public career by establishing a library in his home town of Comum, the opening was not accompanied by celebratory games or gladiatorial contests of the sort likely to engage the local population. Pliny's speech at the dedication of the library was given to a far more select audience in the council building. Here the library was primarily a monument to its founder. The role of the townspeople was largely to admire the library as they walked past, and thus recall the brilliant career of their most prominent local son. As we will see, this was not so very different from the motivation of many generous philanthropists in the nineteenth-century United States when they gave their home town a public library (often adorned by classical colonnades in the Roman style).[10]

The imperial libraries were, nevertheless, important public institutions. They served as venues for gatherings of prominent citizens who would frequently be treated to poetic declamations. They also played a role, by their choice of texts, in establishing a canon of admired authors. The most distinguished would sometimes be honoured by a bust in the library; those overlooked fretted about how their masterworks could be insinuated into the collection. Emperors were also not slow to intervene in banning the circulation of disapproved texts, or works thought to be personally embarrassing, as Augustus did in the case of three pieces of juvenilia written by his ancestor Julius Caesar. In one particularly egregious case, Emperor Domitian ordered not only the execution of the author and bookseller of an offensive text but also the crucifixion of the unfortunate enslaved scribes responsible for producing the actual copies.[11]

A far larger number of people would have attended events in the imperial libraries than the much more restricted circle who needed access to the texts. Active users would have been limited to a small number of imperial officials, favoured poets and members of the Roman legal establishment and ruling classes. The library, like access to the imperial households, was an important part of the nexus of patronage, and the example set by the emperors in this regard was imitated by statesmen and generals such as Sulla, who returned from campaigns bearing valuable collections of books. The great library of Lucullus, booty from the Mithridatic War, became a magnet for Greek scholars in Rome. Even Cicero, who had significant collections of books at all of his residences, found it opportune to consult in the library of Lucullus texts that he did not own himself.[12] By opening their collections to visitors, ambitious public figures could simultaneously consolidate their reputations as men of letters while building a personal following. In the case of statesmen and generals, this did not necessarily involve an intimate acquaintance with their own books. Seneca considered a library a necessary part of a stylish home – but he also complained of the overabundance of unread books that this collecting generated. According to the waspish Lucian of Samosata, in the second century many politicians acquired a library purely to win the favour of Marcus Aurelius, a notably bookish emperor.[13]

The Avoidance of Grief

Books served many purposes in Rome, not always having much to do with reading. For all that, the accumulating wealth of learning made its way through radiating circles of readers on to the shelves of many private libraries. We see this not only in the libraries of distinguished scholars like Cicero, Pliny, or the great Greco-Roman medical authority Galen, but in the extraordinarily rich library excavated from the ruins of a private house in Herculaneum entombed after the eruption of Vesuvius in AD 79. In this expansive villa, archaeologists discovered a small storeroom containing 1,700 scrolls. These were not administrative or estate records, but a collection of Epicurean philosophy.[14] From circumstantial evidence it has been established that this collection belonged originally to Calpurnius Piso Caesoninus, father-in-law of Julius Caesar, who was the patron of Philodemus of Gadara, the philosophical writer whose works were so generously represented in this collection. Most of the writings were over a hundred years old when the villa was buried in the eruption. The room in which they were stored would have been too small for reading: doubtless they were brought to a well-lit chamber elsewhere in the house by the enslaved worker charged with curating the collection.

Creating and maintaining a library of this size would have been an expensive undertaking. While texts were easily accessible in the markets of Rome, concerns about their accuracy impelled serious collectors to employ their own scribes to make copies of trusted texts on their behalf. Access to texts required the mobilisation of well-placed friends; Cicero relied on the library of Atticus, a well-connected patrician deeply engaged in the Roman publishing industry. Even if a friend could be prevailed upon to furnish the text, copying was expensive, since a slave trained as a scribe was hard to find. One could buy a small library for the price of an enslaved scribe capable of writing both Greek and Latin.[15] For this reason, if we set aside the show collections of retired generals and the main imperial libraries, the more serious collections were usually those assembled by professional men such as Galen, the lawyer Cicero, or men who combined a career in public life with philosophical enquiry, such as the Elder and Younger Pliny.[16] In these lives, books played an indispensable part. Galen's library is known to us through his plaintive treatise written after the fire in the Temple of Peace in AD 192 where much of his collection was stored.[17] This work, the evocatively titled *On the Avoidance of Grief*, painfully recreates the process by which Galen had built his collection: consulting texts in numerous Roman libraries, sometimes making copies, sometimes epitomes and compilations of texts. The flexibility of the compilation, the ability to create bespoke texts from segments of other works, was one of the key features distinguishing the manuscript book world from the age of print, where the order and nature of texts was established before they came into the hands of the purchaser. This loss of autonomy in the creation of books would be one of the major sources of regret among established collectors in the transition from manuscript to print in the fifteenth century.[18]

Some books had to be purchased, and others arrived as gifts; some works came to Galen in exchange for his own voluminous works (these on their own were enough to fill 700 scrolls). This pattern of collecting could also describe the experience of professional men eager to build a library at any point between the sixteenth and the nineteenth century.[19] Exploring every avenue to obtain books, perhaps even strategically forgetting to return books loaned by friends, helps explains why so many doctors, lawyers, ministers or professors in this later era of book collecting could build very considerable libraries, often with only a fraction of the financial resources on which a man like Galen could draw.

The literary output of the Roman Empire, along with the inherited culture of Greece, would shape western civilisation; if, that is, it could be preserved. None of the imperial libraries, and certainly none of these personal collections would survive the ravages of time, except for the library of Herculaneum, preserved by the calamity that destroyed both this coastal resort and the neighbouring Pompeii. But even with this imperfect historical record, and recognising how little we know about how Romans read or stored their books, this early period of library formation lays bare many of the dilemmas of collecting that would shape the library world in the succeeding two millennia.[20] What was a library: were books for display or working tools? Should collectors aim to emulate the universalist library of Alexandria, or the more focused collections of Galen or Cicero?

What, crucially, was the public for a public library? Was the key motivation for building a library accessibility, or the demonstration of elite power? Should the library be a place of sociability or silence, a meeting place or a place of study? In Roman libraries, it seems quite frequently to have been the case that the scrolls were stored separately before consultation in a study or a more public gallery. Certainly, on the few occasions when contemporary accounts give us a glimpse of the workings of the imperial libraries, there is little sign of space set aside for quiet perusal of the library's riches. The Romans promoted important innovations in indexing and cataloguing; they sold books at auction, a practice which, when reinvented in the seventeenth century, completely transformed the process of building a library. They also faced the problem, common to all ages of collecting, of what to do with redundant texts; should they be stored for future generations as memorials of previous historical eras, or cast out to make room for new books? In the age of the papyrus this was a particularly urgent question, since neglect would eventually imply extinction. With papyrus, one did not have the luxury of the age of paper or parchment, of allowing books to slumber unread on the shelves for centuries without the need for further curation. Even when one welcomed a flourishing book market, how should the circulation of information be controlled? We have seen that the Romans would take decisive and sometimes cruel steps to remove seditious or embarrassing literature from the market-place: it did not need the invention of printing to convince authorities of the potential dangers of unfettered access to texts.

The Romans faced all these issues and more. Despite the glamour of the imperial libraries, the Roman Empire points to private collections as the natural locus of the library, and principal vectors of public discourse; largely because the public admitted to allegedly public libraries was so shallow and narrow, as it would continue to be, right through until the end of the nineteenth century. Collectively, the libraries assembled in villas and town houses in Rome and scattered through the empire offer a more promising road map to the future of book collecting than the imperial libraries or, it must be said, the semi-mythical beast that was the library of Alexandria.

Finally, we must pay tribute to two unsung heroes of the Roman book world: the enslaved scribes who ensured that texts would be preserved through their copying, and the Christian Church, initially reviled, but ultimately the salvation of Roman culture. In the first centuries after the birth of Christianity, Romans became accustomed to the spectacle of watching Christians being torn apart by wild animals in the Colosseum; many others died a less theatrical but equally painful death. So it is a neat irony that ultimately the fruits of Roman learning would depend on the resilience of the Christian faith for their survival. For while the Vandals, Goths and Ostrogoths feasted on the wreckage of Roman civilisation, its culture would find its ultimate refuge in that quintessentially Christian institution, the monastery. Here, the works of Cicero and Seneca would nestle peacefully among Christian texts, temporarily safe from the ravages of time and plunder, to take their place as cornerstones of library culture after their rediscovery in the Renaissance. This was but one of many examples we will see of the operation of a whimsical lottery that ensured that some texts would survive, poked away in some Bavarian monastery, while others would be lost for ever. That was the fate that awaited the intellectual harvest of this most remarkable civilisation as the tides of history swept away the glories of Rome.

CHAPTER TWO

SANCTUARY

In the middle of the fourteenth century, the writer and poet Giovanni Boccaccio paid a visit to the Italian monastery of Monte Cassino. Located on an imposing Apennine hilltop, some 80 miles south-east of Rome, this monastic complex resembled a fortress, commanding strategic views over the Latin valley, one of the chief routes from Rome to Naples. Within the protection of its thick walls, Monte Cassino housed a great treasure: an extraordinary collection of ancient manuscripts. To Boccaccio, a devoted student of the Roman classics, making the formidable ascent to the hill was the stuff of dreams. The humanist scholar Benvenuto da Imola, who heard the story first hand from the poet himself, wrote that upon arriving, Boccaccio 'modestly asked a monk – for he was always most courteous in manners – to open the library, as a favour, for him'.

> The monk answered stiffly, pointing to a steep staircase, 'Go up; it is open'. Boccaccio went up gladly; but he found that the place which held so great a treasure, was without door or key. What he found, when he pushed through the open doorway, shocked him to the core. He entered and saw grass sprouting on the windows, and all the books and benches thick with dust. In his astonishment he began to open and turn the leaves of first one tome and then another, and found many and diverse volumes of ancient and foreign works. Some of them had lost several sheets; others were snipped and pared all round the text, and mutilated in various ways. At length, lamenting that the toil and study of so many illustrious men should have passed into the hands of [the] most abandoned

wretches, he departed with tears and sighs. Coming to the cloister, he asked a monk whom he met, why those valuable books had been so disgracefully mangled. He answered that the monks, seeking to gain a few *soldi*, were in the habit of cutting off sheets and making psalters.[1]

As with Hugo Blotius's description of his arrival in the Hofbibliothek, we may suspect an element of exaggeration in this account of Boccaccio's visit. Just as the emperor's new librarian was keen to play up his own great achievement in reordering the library, so too the humanist scholars of the Renaissance were eager to contrast their own bold new intellectual agenda with the obscurantism of the established medieval institutions. This somewhat mean-spirited account, written during the 1370s, does little credit to the fortitude of the monks of Monte Cassino, whose home had recently been devastated by an earthquake. Many of the monks had been expelled, replaced by a garrison of soldiers fulfilling their part in the political game of chess played by the Pope and the crowns of France and Aragon for control of southern Italy. Some of the choicest pieces in the library, including presumed lost manuscripts of works by Tacitus and Apuleius, had already been removed in the preceding decades by other illustrious visitors, and found their way to the private libraries of abbots, diplomats and scholars.

We can learn much from the turbulent history of the monastery at Monte Cassino. It was founded in the third decade of the sixth century by Benedict of Nursia (later St Benedict), as one of the first of many monastic communities to emerge from the ruins of the Roman Empire. Within fifty years, the monastery was razed to the ground by invading Lombards; resurrected, it was destroyed again by Saracens at the end of the ninth century. A period of renewal between the eleventh and thirteenth centuries saw the monastery amass immense riches as a pilgrimage site and centre of feverish literary production. In 1239, Emperor Frederick II expelled the monks, after which followed a series of unfortunate events that culminated in the reduction of the monastery to the decaying shell that Boccaccio encountered a hundred years later.[2]

Through all vicissitudes, the monks of Monte Cassino had

accumulated and lost, several times over, an unrivalled library of manuscript books. In the centuries that followed the collapse of the Roman Empire, book production and book collecting took place largely within the domain of monastic communities, established throughout Europe by missionaries of Jesus Christ; through their careful curation of the written word they played a vital role in the survival of the western world's heritage of books. By establishing small and often isolated bastions of spiritual contemplation, these evangelists provided a safe haven where scripture was copied, over and over, as an act of pious devotion. Many monasteries also played an important role in salvaging the remains of Roman culture by copying manuscripts containing the works of classical authors; indeed, this is how virtually all classical texts have come down to us today.

As the safe harbours of books, monasteries were also responsible for the survival of the library. This, as the case of Monte Cassino shows, was a story of triumph as much as heartbreak. In the millennium between 400 and 1400, periods of prosperity interspaced by spasms of political instability ensured that monasteries were rich targets for the next round of invaders, whether they were Saracens, Danes, Saxons or Magyars.[3] Yet the virtues instilled in monastic communities required a steadfast devotion, even in the face of the greatest adversity. If one monastery fell, it would be replaced elsewhere; and when books were torn, burned or abandoned, they could be made anew. So Monte Cassino would also rise from its fourteenth-century ruins, surviving intact until its destruction during the Second World War. Even that calamity was not terminal; the monastery of Monte Cassino lives on, a beacon for pilgrims and booklovers still.

Behold the Codex

Despite their role as protectors of the classical inheritance, the Christian orders were far from innocent in the cycles of violence that often led to the destruction of libraries. Benedict and his followers established the monastery at Monte Cassino within the remains of a temple dedicated to Apollo, the altar of which they had smashed. As pagan temples crumbled throughout the twilight days of the Roman Empire, so Christian churches and convents replaced them. In this process the young zealots of the Christian Church trampled underfoot many books, as Roman temples also functioned as libraries. The final great persecution of Christians, which took place between 303 and 312, had specifically targeted Christian books and libraries, along with their owners; now the Christian God would be honoured in a purified space.

Libraries played an important part in the lives of the earliest Christian believers. The apostles and their followers, many of whom led itinerant lives, had small travelling book collections: Paul asked Timothy to 'bring the books' which he had left at Troas.[4] These were by all accounts practical libraries, made up predominantly of the books of the Old Testament and of the writings which were later to be canonised as the New Testament.[5] The copying of scripture, old and new, was undertaken by believers throughout the Roman Empire, as essential tools for preaching and evangelising. Making copies of revered texts was also an act of prayer: as believers sought to live by scripture, they internalised the holy books through a form of meditation achieved through a constant recitation of the texts. In some of the earliest Christian monasteries, founded in the Egyptian desert during the dying days of the Roman Empire, the process of copying scripture was a commonplace meditative activity.[6]

The production of books gathered pace with the foundation of monastic institutions across the Mediterranean basin. John Cassian, founder of a monastery near Marseille around 415, included the manual copying of books among the useful labours to be undertaken by monks in order to focus spiritual contemplation: because 'a monk who works is troubled by only one devil, while an idle monk is troubled by many'.[7] The rise of institutionalised monasticism, which enshrined the duties of an austere life devoted to prayer, called for discipline. As Cassian was writing, the young church was riven by doctrinal divisions; there was an ever-present danger that the monasteries could descend into hotbeds of heresy if the monks were allowed to waste away their leisure time with theological debate.

2. A miniature depicting St Benedict of Nursia handing down his Rule to his followers, in a copy of the Rule written around 1130. Although libraries were not mentioned in the Rule, the emphasis placed on individual reading ensured that western monasteries were active producers and collectors of books.

Cassian's talent for organisation and discipline inspired others to emulate him, including Benedict of Nursia. At Monte Cassino, Benedict composed his famous Rule, dictating how monks in Benedictine houses should order their day and regulate their lives. The Rule of Benedict, which would be used as the basic model of organisation for monastic orders throughout the medieval era, set aside ample time for reading, under the rubric of 'daily manual labour'. Every day the brothers were to read from scripture, communally and in private, for several hours. On Sundays, even more time was given over to reading, but 'if somebody is so careless or lazy that he is unwilling or unable to meditate or read, let him be given some work to do so he will not be idle'.[8] Although Benedict's Rule never mentions writing, it implicitly encouraged the copying of books as a virtuous and valuable activity, for the monks required many books; to share over evening readings as well as to take to their individual cells for study.

One contemporary of Benedict, a Roman nobleman named Cassiodorus, was more explicit in his encouragement of book production. Around 538, Cassiodorus retired from service as secretary to the Ostrogothic King Theodoric, and founded a monastery in southern Italy, the Vivarium. Cassiodorus instilled in his brethren the importance of the meticulous copying of books, urging scribes to pay particular attention to accuracy. Although the central purpose of his monastery was the faithful multiplication of Christian literature, the monks of the Vivarium also copied classical works. In this Cassiodorus was different from some of his contemporaries. Isidore of Seville, the encyclopaedic scholar, would warn: 'Let the monk beware of reading the books of gentiles and heretics. It is better for him to be ignorant of their pernicious doctrines than through making acquaintance with them to be enmeshed in error.'[9]

The Vivarium collapsed after the death of Cassiodorus, but its principles were passed on to others. Even Christians who, like Isidore, found themselves hostile to pagan literature, were caught in a dilemma.[10] Christians in the remnants of the western Roman Empire could not sever the connection with their *lingua franca*, the Latin language. The monasteries had to follow the model of classical education, since there was no plausible alternative. Abbots, scholars and monks might be distrustful of the polytheistic religion, loose morals and flowery oratory of the classical authors, but they required the Roman rhetoricians, philosophers and historians to teach their brothers to read and write. The style of ancient Rome also infused the writings of the great Church Fathers, like Ambrose and Augustine, who relied heavily on the classical rhetoric of Cicero.

The debate on the copying and collecting of pagan literature unrolled in tandem with another crucial development of the period between the third and sixth centuries AD. The transition from the papyrus scroll, the preferred medium of ancient writing, to the parchment codex, with separate pages sewn together (a book), would transform the library. Parchment was not a new invention.

The treatment of animal skins to make sheets for writing was a long-established practice. The name derived from the Greek city of Pergamum, which is credited with having developed the technique of soaking, scraping and stretching skins to create a surface for writing. Yet parchment was not widely used in the ancient world, relied upon only during shortages of papyrus. In an era of abundant and cheap papyrus, this is understandable: parchment took longer to prepare and was far more expensive: a substantial parchment book would require the skins of more than a hundred calves, goats or sheep. But it did have two advantages: it was durable and would not degrade in climates colder than that of the Egyptian Nile delta, and one could write on both sides of the sheet, instead of the single side of papyrus.

It seems that the fall of the Roman Empire disrupted significantly the supply of papyrus throughout the Mediterranean world; parchment became the standard replacement. As the material of the book changed, so did the form. The codex, sheets or tablets laid on top of one another and sewn or stitched together at one edge, was also an older medium. Codices were available in ancient Rome but used almost exclusively as notebooks or as exercise boards in schools. At some time in the third century, codices began to replace scrolls as the normative way to preserve a body of text; it was clear that this transformation was tied up with the Christian movement, whose early texts were almost universally produced as codices. By the sixth century, the codex was triumphant and remained the standard form of the book until the present day.

The advantages of the codex over the scroll are profound: a codex can be opened at any point of the text with ease, whereas the scroll requires a serious effort, with both hands, to find one's place. Codices could also accommodate more material: a parchment codex could carry the entire text of the Old and New Testament, whereas a scroll would usually hold only a single book from the Bible. Storage was also an issue. Stacking large numbers of scrolls in a way that enabled an individual text to be easily identified was always difficult. The codex, especially when bound between wooden or leather covers, had a sturdy individuality, though it would be a considerable time before owners fixed upon what we think of the natural way of displaying books, standing them upright in serried ranks on shelves. For the millennium after the collapse of the Roman Empire, books were mostly laid on tables, or stored in chests.

The abandonment of papyrus and the replacement of the scroll undoubtedly involved a considerable measure of loss of the inherited cultural tradition. All literature had to be recopied from rolls to codices, a process that took place largely in the Christian monasteries. Here the hierarchy of importance, what should be copied and what should be left to rot, depended on the character of the abbot in charge. Even if a text was marked for preservation, it would not necessarily be safe for long. The period between the sixth and the eighth centuries was the great age of the palimpsest: a parchment manuscript where the original text had been scraped or washed off, in order to free up valuable writing material.[11] The obliteration of classical texts was not necessarily an act of hostility to the august literature of Rome: many more Christian than pagan texts were destroyed in this manner. Parchment was too precious to carry an obsolete text; and in an era when the very act of writing was a pious activity, even the reuse of a Christian book was of no concern, only a necessary task to fulfil the spiritual needs of a community working towards salvation.

Scriptorium

The first generations of monasteries were not particularly wealthy institutions. Founded by a handful of monks, most monasteries developed out of little more than what the monks themselves could build and cultivate. Their lives were hard, their diets spartan. The monastic life was devoted to prayer and spiritual contemplation, but this was undertaken concurrently with back-breaking labour. The *Dialogues* of Pope Gregory I (*c*.540–604), which mention valuable labours that can be undertaken by monks, include an extensive list of manual works: building, baking, cleaning, gardening, and, of course, tilling the land.[12] Literary production may have been revered as a pious activity, but in practice it was a task that could, in the first years of the monastery, be reserved for the infirm.

Over the course of the seventh, eighth and ninth centuries, changes were set in motion that would alter the status of the monasteries from isolated retreats to centres of religious, pedagogical and cultural authority. The first factor that prompted this transformation was the feverish missionary activity undertaken by monks to convert those areas of Europe that were not incorporated into the Christian Church. This was a process that was sometimes undertaken from Rome, as when Gregory I sent Augustine to England to Christianise the Anglo-Saxon King Aethelberht of Kent, but the main impetus came from Ireland and western Scotland. From around 600 onwards, Celtic missionaries fanned out across Britain, France, Germany, Switzerland and Italy. They converted local rulers, extracted promises of land, and founded small communities of learning before moving on. One of the accomplishments of this strategy was the emergence of networks of religious houses, united by a shared founder and culture, and bonded through the fraternal exchange of news, resources and books. Some monasteries, like St Gallen in Switzerland, on the south-west shore of Lake Constance, became central nodes in this expanding network, frequented by monks and other travellers.[13]

The sprawling network of monasteries that emerged during the seventh and eighth centuries was underpinned by the circulation and production of books. St Boniface, an English monk who proselytised in Germany and the Low Countries, travelled with a substantial library. When he was murdered in Frisia, his assailants stole several chests of books from Boniface's party, which they then destroyed. The missionaries' need for literature, not least to establish the liturgical order, was initially met by their former communities in Ireland, Scotland and England; once they had grown in size, the new institutions founded on the continent could also play a role in circulating the stock of Bibles, missals and prayer books. Some monasteries, like Lindisfarne and Jarrow in England, Murbach in Alsace, Fulda in Hessen and St Gallen in Switzerland, would turn into important centres of book production.

The fortunes of the flourishing new monasteries were heavily dependent on political support. The missionaries who travelled through the realms of Merovingian France found local rulers who welcomed their endeavours, not only out of Christian piety.[14] Noble power brokers often reserved the right to appoint abbots at the monastery which they sanctioned; while the donation of land to the monasteries would create a loophole to exempt them from taxes demanded by the sovereign. Monasteries and convents became the favoured destination for surplus sons and daughters who might threaten the integrity of the family inheritance, and at the same time provided a means to extend a family's influence within the growing ecclesiastical power structure.

It was under the patronage of Charlemagne (742–814) that the monasteries assumed greater political importance and took on a more active role as book producers. Over the course of his long reign, Charlemagne unified much of western and central Europe. This was a military as much as an administrative endeavour. The great ambition of Charlemagne, the first emperor in the West since the fall of Rome, was to reform the disparate territories and peoples under his Christian rule, uniting them in administration, law and faith.[15] This extraordinary undertaking required a ruler with the administrative talent and vision of Charlemagne, yet it could not have been achieved without the ecclesiastical network of monasteries.

The Christian Church was the common denominator in Charlemagne's empire, and Latin was the only tongue that could unite it. One of Charlemagne's primary concerns was the accuracy of language and its proper usage by his clergy, administrators and subjects. This was not the pedantic hobby of a linguist: the emphasis on correctness was of vital importance for church dogma and the precise performance of ecclesiastical rituals that underpinned Christian worship. Efficient governance also relied on effective communication; in Charlemagne's vast empire, communication became increasingly written, which prompted demand for a standardised language.[16] In 784, Charlemagne wrote to all monasteries and bishops in his realm, stating that he 'deemed it useful that the bishoprics and monasteries should devote their efforts to the study of literature and to the teaching of it'. He praised the zeal of the monasteries but noted that letters which he received from them often revealed their poor command of Latin. In a decree issued five years later, Charlemagne specifically addressed the need for proper schools, where boys could learn to read, and the need for monasteries to prepare better books, 'because often some desire to pray to God properly, but they pray badly because of the incorrect books'.[17]

The proliferation of such 'incorrect books', in Charlemagne's eyes, provided the impetus for an intense period of book production and circulation, unlike anything that Europe had seen since the days of the Roman Empire. The focus of this heightened activity was, given the intentions of the movement, largely focused on Christian texts, ranging from works by the patristic authors to a large body of corrected liturgical handbooks, lives of the saints, sermons and parts of the Bible. The copying of some pedagogical, moralistic and historical works from classical Rome and Greece was also seen as a beneficial activity, though some writers, like Virgil, Cicero and Aristotle, were favoured over their contemporaries.[18] Most popular of all were the school books of late Roman authors like Aelius Donatus and Martianus Capella, which dominated the curriculum of Carolingian education.

It was appropriate that Charlemagne, who busied himself so greatly with the correctness of literature, should also come into the possession of a rich collection of books. Some of these were made for him by monasteries or by talented scribes at court, and included sumptuous books: the *Godescalc Evangelistary*, a liturgical work made for Charlemagne's court chapel, was written on purple-dyed parchment using gold and silver ink.[19] Many other similarly magnificent books, which had their bindings decorated with jewels, gold and silver plate, were made for the emperor to present to loyal dignitaries, much as they would offer him gifts of jewellery, horses or land.[20]

The beauty of these books and the impressive care that was lavished on their illumination, binding and decoration, was not representative of most books produced during the Carolingian renaissance. The average monastic book was a functional object, destined for intensive use. These unassuming works were the staples of the monasteries, and they would remain so after the Carolingian empire was divided, and ultimately crumbled. It was to his credit that Charlemagne did not concentrate book production around his own court but allowed it to remain common practice in the monasteries, ensuring that the habit of scholarship and scribal activity would outlast the period of political instability that followed Charlemagne's death.

The organisation of monasteries and nunneries into separate orders, with houses spread out across the continent, provided a natural network for the circulation of texts. Indeed, the lending of books from one monastery to another was one of the principal means by which books could be acquired.[21] A book would be borrowed and copied; or a monastery could send one of their members to another house to copy the work in situ. Sometimes monasteries could agree to exchange a significant selection of their books for copying. One can understand that this last option was least desirable in an era of frequently disrupted and uncertain travel. To ensure their safe return, some monasteries put their volumes under anathema, threatening unfaithful borrowers with excommunication. The secretary of the Cistercian abbot Bernard of Clairvaux (1090–1153) worked under the shrewd principle that if he loaned a book from his collection, he would require the borrower to return the original as well as one copy; this extra copy he could then barter for other books.[22]

The importance of books for the monastic life was symbolised by the introduction of a new term in the history of the book: the scriptorium or writing room. This inevitably calls to mind a large room filled with silent, hushed monks, bent over enormous tomes: certainly no medieval monastery in film or fiction is without such a place. There were indeed monasteries which had separate, dedicated rooms for the production of books: at one time in Fulda, some forty monks were employed at the scriptorium. Yet in many monasteries, scribes would be working in general workrooms, or, indeed, in individual cells. In the twelfth century, the fifth prior of the Grande Chartreuse, the head of the Carthusians, specifically enumerated writing materials as an indispensable tool for a monk to have in his cell.[23] Some scribes would be employed full time, writing up to six hours each day, and it is from such monks that we often find annotations or marginalia on medieval manuscripts that betray the physical demands of the work: 'St Patrick of Armagh, deliver me from writing', or 'O that a glass of good old wine were by my side'.[24] Working on a substantial commission on the orders of the abbot, one can perhaps understand such sentiments; yet many monks would be copying books for their own needs, for their brethren or for family members outside the institution.

In many institutions, writing and book copying became a normal part of the daily round, and for some, the core of their religious life. We know of over 400 women scribes active in medieval German convents, some of whom were experts, much in demand for significant projects, and others who might in their lifetime produce only one or two works, mostly for their own spiritual needs.[25] The production of books could be intensely personal, yet also collaborative and communal. It might take a scribe a year to write a book; a team of scribes, working on different quires, could take much less. Some works, like chronicles, or institutional histories, would be augmented and expanded every year.[26] Outside the largest institutions, where the number of scribes would allow for some to acquire specialist skills, it became common to hire in illuminators to decorate a particularly sumptuous work.

Most of all, monasteries produced books to fulfil their needs: those of the community as a whole and those of individual members. This naturally circumscribed the size of many monastic libraries, and, together with the sheer cost of parchment, helps explains why few medieval monasteries had libraries larger than 500 or 600 volumes. St Gallen possessed around 400 books in the late ninth century; Cluny, one of the richest monasteries in Europe around the twelfth century, had some 570 volumes. Before the thirteenth century, the norm for most monastic libraries was probably not much larger than around 100 or 200 books. Some monastic library collections were so small that the monks had no need to produce a catalogue of the books in their possession: books are sometimes found only in inventories as valuable possessions, along with furniture, goblets and silver plate.

The size of libraries would, of course, fluctuate. Monastic book collections were practical resources, intended for intensive use: worn-out books would need replacing on a regular basis. Other, more malign forces could also shape the fortunes of libraries. In the ninth century, St Gallen suffered plunder from Hungarian invaders, and was struck by fire, another ever-present danger. A visit from a political patron, like Emperor Otto the Great, could lead to a generous donation, or disaster: the ruler might be so impressed by the monastic books that he requisitioned them for his own pleasure.[27] The English monasteries, which had provided so much copy for continental houses, were plundered repeatedly during the ninth century by Vikings; so too were many monasteries in France. In all these cases, the destruction of a library might take a day, but its replenishment and slow recovery would occupy the better part of a century.

Niche, Chest and Chain

The development of the library as a monastic space was a gradual process. In many monasteries, a separate library room never came into being. From the earliest times, monasteries made generous use of wall niches for storing books.[28] These would be insulated from stone walls by a wooden lining to preserve the books from damp; the great enemy of books, particularly in unheated stone buildings. This was a practical arrangement, to befit a community constantly engaged with books. The reality of monastic book collections was that they were spread out throughout the complex, depending on the function of the books.[29] The most regularly used items, the mainstay of every monastery, were located in the sacristy or chapel: the liturgical books, missals, gospels, graduals, antiphons and psalters. These would generally include the largest and most lavishly illuminated works owned by the community, those that celebrated God's glory through their aesthetic magnificence in the central act of communal worship. We have to bear this in mind when humanist visitors expressed their disappointment at the books in the library: by its nature, it would have been a reference collection of books no longer in regular use.

The chapter house was often the location for books used as communal reading material. This was the place where the community gathered for formal meetings, so typical books found here included monastic rules, martyrologies and lives of the saints.

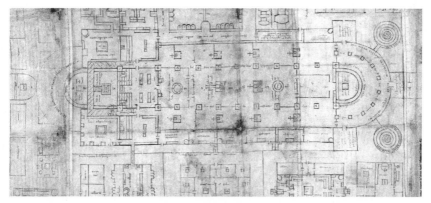

3. An early ninth-century plan of the monastery of St Gallen,
which envisions (in the bottom left of the image) a library room
above a scriptorium. Although the plan was not realised, the
inclusion of the scriptorium and library suggests that both were
emerging as distinct spaces within monastic buildings.

Some sermons or patristic texts might also be kept in the refec-
tory, where they were easy to hand out during mealtimes. This was
a time usually reserved for communal reading. The cloister, where
supervised private reading might take place, could hold a chest
or cabinet of books, the *armarium*, the keys to which were in the
possession of the librarian. In Dominican convents the librarian
was instructed to house these books in a wooden cabinet, divided
by several compartments so that the books could be classified
according to subject.[30] Such cabinets would generally hold books
of common use to all members of the monastery. Bernard of Clairvaux determined that in his Cistercian monasteries, 'the book for
Holy Mass, the Gospels and Acts of the Apostles, the Prayer Book,
the Antiphonary, the Psalter, the Rule and the Calendar' would be
freely at the disposal of all monks.[31]

In Tegernsee Abbey in Bavaria, monks had the pleasure of
reading in a communal heated chamber in the evenings.[32] More
commonly, monks and nuns would do much of their reading in
individual cells, and it was here that they took books from the
communal *armaria*. They would also be allowed to keep books
that they made themselves, that they received as gifts, or that
they brought with them when they entered the monastery. These

personal libraries might, in the thirteenth and fourteenth centuries, comprise ten or twenty volumes. All these books would, on the death of the owner, be donated to the monastery, thus enlarging the communal collection.

It is clear that the storage strategies adopted by monasteries were primarily concerned with ease of access. It was only those monasteries with a substantial collection of books beyond those required for the immediate spiritual needs of the monks that had to concern themselves with a separate library. This would typically be the destination for books on history, philosophy, medicine or science that would not be suitable for the eyes of every monk. Housing these books in a closed-off room, under the supervision of a librarian, was a natural solution. A library room of this sort was often located above the sacristy or the scriptorium; the earliest reference to this arrangement comes from ninth-century St Gallen; others can be dated from the twelfth century onwards. In this library room, the books would still generally be kept in locked cabinets or chests.

The most progressive experiments in creating designated library space took place outside the monasteries. From the twelfth century onwards, the monasteries gradually lost their hegemony over the production, circulation and collecting of books.[33] A serious challenge emerged from new institutions: cathedral chapters, schools and universities, established in the expanding towns of Italy, France, Germany and England.[34] The increasing concentration of clergymen, nobles and merchants in urban communities transformed the landscape of learning in medieval Europe. The cathedral chapters and their colleges, which grew into the first universities, benefited greatly from donations, from former students as much as local lay folk, anxious for their future salvation. At the same time that cathedrals and their schools attracted ever more ecclesiastical and secular patronage, the accumulation of wealth in the monasteries came under criticism from within the church itself, leading to the foundation of new mendicant orders dedicated to the original vision of monastic poverty. This movement too siphoned off resources from the monasteries and their scriptoria.

While many monastic book collections stagnated, the new

institutions flourished. Within fifty years of the establishment of a library for the cathedral of Salisbury in 1075, this collection boasted over a hundred volumes, many made at its own scripto-rium.[35] By the fourteenth century, the best university libraries were outclassing those of the monasteries. The College of the Sorbonne in Paris acquired over 2,000 volumes between its foundation in 1257 and 1338. In the early fifteenth century, the university college at Erfurt received over 600 manuscripts in one donation, which put it on an equal footing with some of the greatest monastic col-lections.[36] The colleges founded at Oxford were generally endowed with substantial libraries by their benefactors; indeed, founders of colleges were virtually obliged to make adequate provision for a library.[37] Around 1350, Merton College had some 500 books. Some fifty years later, seven large donations enriched the collections of several Oxford colleges by another 2,000 volumes. Colleges also acquired books as unredeemed securities when they loaned money to indebted scholars.

Although the university colleges were rapidly becoming richer and intellectually more influential than the monasteries, their scholars continued to honour core principles of monastic book collecting. Some Oxford colleges had two book collections: one which was confined in a room for use by the fellows, and the other which was distributed among the fellows for periods of a year or longer. Generally, the books destined for distribution were texts of canon or civil law, the works of Aristotle or editions of the Church Fathers. The founder of All Souls College had provided 101 volumes of nine key textbooks, eighty-three of which were for distribution, and the other eighteen for the main library.[38]

In the separate library rooms of the colleges, a profound shift took place: the scholars abandoned the sturdy storage of the monas-tic chest and moved towards libraries where scholars could work with the books. The new norm became a series of lecterns with benches for seating, placed in a row in the body of the room. The most sophisticated lecterns were those which combined a reading platform and additional horizontal shelves above or below to store books. The college library of the Sorbonne had twenty-eight lectern desks of this sort. The room in which they were placed was

lit by nineteen windows, of vital importance to the working scholars, who were not permitted to bring candles into the library.[39]
This was a critical development: books were now displayed openly
rather than safely locked away in chests or cabinets. Readers could
consult many texts in a short space of time, essential for the sort
of textual work we associate with the advance of learning. But it
also meant books could go missing with greater ease: by 1338, over
300 of the 2,000 volumes in the possession of the College of the
Sorbonne had already disappeared.

Monasteries, as closed communities, could control access to
their libraries relatively easily; the monks in the community would
be known, and seldom left the confines of the monastery. Yet in the
urban institutions, the city chapters of the religious houses, cathedrals and churches, and especially the new universities and colleges,
visitors would be more frequent and less familiar. The solution,
expensive but regarded as increasingly necessary in the institutions
with larger libraries, was to put the books under restraint. Books
were fitted with iron chains, anchoring them to their lecterns or
shelves. The first general use of chained books seems to date from
the thirteenth century, at the Sorbonne. Gerard of Abbeville, who
in 1271 donated 300 volumes to the college, asked that they be
carefully preserved and chained.

Chains had obvious disadvantages: what if one wanted to
consult multiple texts that were not chained to the same lectern?
As libraries grew in size and complexity, many institutions avoided
chaining their books, and private owners seldom contemplated
such a grandiose form of security. Still, the chained library proved
remarkably enduring in cathedral, church and college collections.[40]
Fresh chains were still being purchased in some libraries as late as
the middle of the eighteenth century. Merton College, Oxford, did
not unchain its books until 1792. When they were first attached to
the lecterns in Oxford and Paris in the thirteenth and fourteenth
centuries, the chains seemed a reasonable precaution, and a proper
recognition of the value of the books as an intellectual resource.
Readers could now enter a library with reasonable assurance that
the desired text would not have been removed; they would find it
there, available on a desk, whenever they wanted. To the scholars

4. Books chained to a lectern at the library of Hereford Cathedral. As libraries outgrew chests, this was seen as an adequately secure replacement. This arrangement was less convenient for users, while the most dedicated thieves still found ways to cut chains and disappear with the volumes.

of the new academe, this ease of access was in marked contrast to the closed doors of the monasteries, where one had to rely on the whims of the abbot in charge. While the two worlds may not have been so different in practice, in the busy urban centres of Europe intellectual resentment of the monasteries, those seemingly ancient and declining custodians of learning, was on the rise.

A Better Class of Thief

As money flowed into the cities, many monastic orders followed; by the fifteenth century, there would be more urban than rural monastic houses. This movement only exacerbated the plight of the formerly great houses, which were now less attractive as a focus for pious giving and even more vulnerable to the opportunistic greed of bishops or sovereign rulers. The deterioration was so pronounced that in the thirteenth and fourteenth centuries, some of the great Carolingian monasteries like St Gallen and Murbach had few monks left who were able to write; all books produced at their monasteries were made by hired lay scribes. A sixteenth-century catalogue of the library of Fulda reveals that almost no books were added to the collection between the tenth and the sixteenth centuries.[41]

Many monasteries lost considerable quantities of books, with those in or close to urban centres suffering the worst damage. By 1400, the Capitular library of Verona had lost more than three-quarters of the manuscripts which had been present in its collection four centuries earlier.[42] Indeed, it was on the Italian peninsula that the book collections of the monasteries were devastated first, for here the monks had to contend with the emergence of a rapacious new breed of book collector, represented by the likes of Giovanni Boccaccio. From the late thirteenth century onwards, the Italian city-states became home to the first generations of humanist scholars. Humanism was first and foremost a literary activity, based on the study and imitation of classical literature. It was, in its first iteration, an activity dominated by men associated with government and the legal professions: diplomats, secretaries and notaries, to whom command of oratory and an elegant script were essential requirements for a flourishing career.

The rediscovery of the classics by this class of scholars would play a major role in the blossoming of the Renaissance. Classical literature would profoundly shape tastes in art and architecture, as well as exercising considerable influence over developments in engineering, science, politics and warfare. The heart of the humanist movement would, however, remain literary. The collation of manuscripts in the search for the most authentic and complete copy of an individual work was the lifeblood of the humanist scholar. This was an activity that required deep familiarity with a common corpus of widely diffused works, but also knowledge of where the gaps were: which texts known from other sources remained lost or incomplete. Among their other many services to the revival of classical learning, these scholars provided the expert guidance which would allow the creation of the first great personal libraries that would alert Europe's princes, dukes and rulers to the possibilities of serious book collecting.[43]

The first luminaries of the Renaissance, including Petrarch, Dante and Boccaccio, knew that the monasteries provided a rich source of classical material. When the book hunters began a systematic search of these libraries, they invariably railed against the conditions they found in the decaying monastic houses. They expressed little gratitude that these communities had provided sanctuary to classical texts for almost a millennium. The most successful book hunter of the period was a brilliant papal secretary, Poggio Braccciolini (1380–1459), who took his explorations for manuscripts beyond the Alps into the monastic heartlands of France, Germany and Switzerland. Here Braccciolini was responsible for the rediscovery of lost works of Lucretius, Cicero, Vitruvius, Quintilian and many other authors. He corresponded extensively with his friends about his discoveries, most diligently with Niccolò de' Niccoli, an avid Florentine book collector. Their surviving letters provide invaluable insights into the mind-set of these deeply learned but acquisitive scholars.[44]

In 1416, Braccciolini found his greatest haul, the one that cemented his reputation, when he and his two friends, Cincius de Rusticis and Bartholomeus de Montepolitiano, were at the Council of Constance. They visited the nearby monastery of St Gallen, where, in the words of de Rusticis, they found 'countless books ... kept like captives', and a library 'neglected and infested with dust, worms, soot and all the things associated with the destruction of books'. The visiting scholars (or so they claimed) burst into tears and could scarcely conceal their anger. 'There were in that monastery an abbot and monks totally devoid of any knowledge of literature. What barbarous hostility to the Latin tongue! What damned dregs of humanity!'[45] Such rhetoric permeated the circle of the book hunters. A friend of Braccciolini, who had received a copy of the complete text of Quintilian that Braccciolini had acquired at St Gallen, lauded him for freeing the work 'from a lengthy and cruel prison sentence among the barbarians'.[46]

The complete Quintilian was the greatest treasure from a substantial haul: Braccciolini and his friends also retrieved works by a dozen other classical writers. The foray at St Gallen would be the first of many for Braccciolini, as he talked his way into monasteries and copied or bought books from their libraries. He, like other Italian humanists, took advantage of the natural generosity of monks sharing their treasures with erudite visitors, often in ways that were unscrupulous or downright dishonest. Bracciolini did not always leave with armfuls of books; his sojourn in England in particular was a great disappointment. On 13 June 1420 he reported to Niccoli that 'I have obtained the catalogues of several monasteries which are considered famous and old. There is nothing of value in any of them.' Five months later Bracciolini once again despaired of the English 'barbarians, trained rather in trifling debates and in quibbling than in real learning'. 'There were a few volumes of ancient writings' that he had seen, but 'we have [them] in better versions at home'.[47]

Although the monks north of the Alps were, in the minds of the book hunters, the most offensive of a disdained breed, they also heaped opprobrium upon their Italian compatriots, who dishonoured the traditions of Rome by their ignorance. When Bracciolini learned that a humanist collector had bequeathed his library of Greek books to a monastery, he derided him for giving such prized items to 'those two-legged donkeys who do not even know a word of Latin'.[48] He also complained about the 'barbarians' at Monte Cassino, who according to him were only interested in money rather than in providing him access to their text of Julius Frontinus. Even those monks who themselves had an interest in classical writings were not worthy of Bracciolini's attention, unless they were like the monk from Cluny, who was helping Bracciolini acquire a copy of Tertullian from his monastery and therefore did 'not seem in the least bad'. However, he was still a monk.[49]

It is clear that Renaissance book hunters were not kind about their medieval predecessors – especially if the monks would not be bullied into handing over their choicest manuscripts. For this ardent, impatient new type of collector, the monastic library was a symbol of all they were not, and all they did not want to be. But these fastnesses of written culture left behind several principles of lasting importance for the development of the library: the library as a sanctuary and storehouse of culture; the fixity of stock; the role of the Christian Church in the recovery of the antique; the library as a place of work and silent contemplation. All this was distinctly uncongenial to the Young Turks of the early Renaissance, impatient and urbane, looking for personal advancement in the glittering new courts of the Italian city-states and the emerging monarchies. But these sober medieval principles, though temporarily unfashionable, would continue to play a large and underappreciated role in the history of the library.

CHAPTER THREE

LITTLE MONKEYS AND
LETTERS OF GOLD

A student away from home with money in their pocket is a recipe for parental anxiety, something as true in the thirteenth century as it is today. Still, one has to spare a thought for the French father who had invested half the family income in sending his son to study at the University of Paris. Part of this generous allowance was intended for the purchase of necessary books, but the father had not allowed for his son's bibliophilic tendencies. Instead of the workaday texts, freely available from the bookshops of the university quarter, the young man had sought out fancy manuscripts lavishly decorated in gold leaf and witty marginal embellishments – or, as the enraged father would have it, books made with 'little monkeys and letters of gold'.

This anecdote was told some time around the year 1250, by a lecturer in law at the University of Bologna in northern Italy. Intended as a cautionary tale against the moral hazard of choosing the temptations of sophisticated Paris over the austere regime of its distinguished southern competitor, it also provides us with evidence of the development of an efficient commercial book market outside the monasteries and convents.[1] A young student of theology or law was expected to own books – either those he copied out himself, or those bought from stationers associated with the university. This was so common that students with money to spare might seek to distinguish their small working collection with a touch of decorative flair.

That students could aspire to small book collections of this sort was one consequence of the gradual industrialisation of book production. The thirteenth and fourteenth centuries experienced a transformation in the scale of production of manuscript books as scribal workshops in the cities of France, the Low Countries and Italy turned bookmaking into a commercial enterprise that outstripped the great monastic scriptoria. Instead of monks crafting books to edify their community and satisfy their spiritual needs, the secular workshops in the cities were filled with lay scribes working at the orders of a merchant–stationer. Although the stationers who ran these commercial workshops might be deeply learned and indeed pious men, for them this was a trade, not unlike that of the merchant who dealt in cloth or wine.

The rise of these lay scriptoria was prompted by an increasing appetite for the ownership of books, whether for work, study or the lavish display of wealth. It is important to realise that the invention of printing did not create this demand; instead, the market was fuelled by universities and schools, movements of popular lay devotion and the steady growth of cities, where a bourgeois class emerged as a significant economic and political force to challenge that of the nobility and the church. The mass production of student texts and pious literature, not least the ubiquitous Book of Hours, was a harbinger of a massive increase in book ownership that in turn prepared the way for experiments with the printing press in the middle of the fifteenth century.[2]

The mass production of manuscript books in urban scriptoria did not lead to a sea of indistinguishable products. On the contrary, it was in the century before printing that books attained their greatest status as objects of aesthetic brilliance, customised to the wishes of the owner. Beautiful books, lavishly rubricated with vermilion, lapis lazuli and verdigris, decorated with gold leaf and bound in bejewelled covers, had been a mainstay of the libraries of European monasteries and courts since the age of Charlemagne. Yet it was in the workshops of Paris, Bruges and Florence that the art of bookmaking reached its apogee, driven by specialisation, the division of labour and the deep pockets of the nobility. Some workshops employed illuminators who were masters of their art, famous painters who could charge exorbitant fees. This was a brief age in which books were an expression of the highest form of visual art, and where the price of a book might match or even outstrip the value of other possessions in the home.

The possibilities of display afforded by this new type of book, portable, often devotional in content and aesthetically dazzling, appealed greatly to the noblemen and women who populated the courts of Europe. Books became ubiquitous objects in noble households, as emblems of piety, gifts to be exchanged with other households or texts for communal reading. They also served a political purpose, when princes commissioned new texts to justify their claim to a throne or memorialise their achievements. Surrounding oneself with books became as important as displaying valour at a joust. Serious collectors were soon building the first great secular libraries in Europe since the fall of Rome, rivalling monastic collections in size and importance.

The Book Factory

It is easy to see why a young student, keen to impress his new friends, might fall for the trappings of 'letters of gold'. Most university texts were plain and unillustrated notebooks. They contained copies of lectures by professors reciting Aristotle, Thomas Aquinas or volumes of canon law, interspersed with commentary. Although they may not have been much to look at, these were valuable texts, the entry point for a young student to a glittering career as scholar, lawyer or secretary.[3] The provision of these texts became a pressing concern as universities grew throughout thirteenth-century Europe, most prominently in northern Italy, France, England and Spain.

As these institutions developed into important training centres for Europe's emerging professional class, they attracted a new type of artisan, the stationer, who made his business selling parchment, pens, inks and books. Stationers' workshops also became the locus of an innovative form of book production, the *pecia* system.[4] The *pecia* model allowed for a single text, generally a key textbook, to be reproduced simultaneously in parts. Whereas an entire book might take half a year to transcribe, stationers divided a text into standard quires, often eight pages long, which students could rent out for a short period of time. A student could then copy the section they required that week or month, before returning to the stationer for the following section. The system spread the cost and time required to copy a work, and allowed a single text to be available to many students at the same time. Students who did not wish to copy out their own *peciae* could buy copies directly from stationers, who had them copied by professional lay scribes. The system worked especially well for the university market because the curriculum was limited and traditional: in 1275, when the system had developed substantially, the Parisian *pecia* stationers supplied a maximum of 138 texts.[5]

The *pecia* system originated in Bologna in the early thirteenth century and was soon put into place at other universities throughout Europe. Fearful of the influence of the stationers on the prices of key texts, universities ensured that the price of *peciae* remained low. This was a noble gesture to the many students with limited financial means, but it also meant that stationers could not survive on *peciae* alone. In consequence, these university-affiliated workshops were allowed to take work on the side. This was a crucial provision, one that prompted the development of a broader, non-academic market for books. Stationers who sold plain student texts for a pittance realised that a very different clientele, the nobility, might pay a hundred times the price for an altogether different sort of book.

This was a phenomenon that emerged most prominently in Paris.[6] Already in the late thirteenth century, the making and decorating of books were recognised trades in the French capital, famous not only as the home of the most distinguished university north of the Alps, but also a major centre of trade; it was also home to the judicial and legal apparatus of the French crown. The trade was concentrated in two distinct districts: the university quarter on the left bank of the Seine, and the area around Notre Dame. The most enterprising stationers on the left bank, like Geoffrey de St Leger, attracted patrons that included two queens, Clemence of Hungary and Jeanne of Burgundy. Thomas de Maubeuge, a colleague working in the Notre Dame quarter, supplied books to Jeanne's mother, Countess Mahaut of Artois (1268–1329): these included lives of saints, missals, breviaries, a Bible and collections of pious stories. This selection reflects the need for great noble households to own traditional Latin liturgical works for use in their chapels. Yet Mahaut also commissioned books in French, most notably histories, prose romances and prayer books. Over time, the booksellers around Notre Dame came to specialise in French-language books of this nature, commissioned by the wealthiest and most powerful figures of the realm for their personal collections.

Noble patronage and courtly life set the standard for the production of books beyond the academic and monastic world. The growth of courts as administrative centres stimulated literary activity: administration required literacy and penmanship, and it is no surprise that many of the secular histories, romances and poems produced during the thirteenth and fourteenth centuries came from the pens of secretaries and officials attached to courts in France, Burgundy or England. One of the most famous was Jean Froissart (*c.*1377–1405), a cleric who became historiographer and poet to several distinguished courts, including that of the Queen Consort of England and the dukes of Brabant and Blois. Froissart's chronicle of the Hundred Years' War would become one of the most popular historical texts of the fifteenth century, and it survives today in more than a hundred richly illuminated copies. Courts were important as places where such wealth and sophistication could be displayed. To a prince, it was worth having beautiful books if there was an audience to impress and courtiers who wished to imitate their patron. Creating a courtly library was a public act; not necessarily because the books were on permanent display or for public use, but because the acts involved in creating books, composition, copying, illumination and presentation, all took place under the patronage of the ruler and their family. Books were also enjoyed as part of the rich traditions of storytelling, singing and musical performance that were so vital to court life. Courts would employ gifted orators and troubadours to tell tales, or to read for them, edifying or entertaining not only the ruler, but his entire entourage.[7]

The medieval court lived a peripatetic lifestyle, and a prince's book collection was constantly on the move. As a result, most books were still kept in chests: secure and easily transported. A collection was often spread among several castles or kept in the hands of multiple members of the ruling family. Books were also cycled in and out of the library, because like all precious objects they could be used as security for loans or gifted to retainers or fellow princes. Many books entered a courtly collection as gifts, presented by authors or scribes. Other items were specifically acquired by a prince to give away. In this, books were but one of the many sumptuous objects that graced courts, alongside paintings, silverware, robes, clasps, brooches and tapestries. It is no wonder that many books themselves were bejewelled on their covers, or bound in the richest velvet, to match the brilliant display of other objects admired at court.

The most lavish book owned by the noble classes was also one of the most ubiquitous: the Book of Hours, which originated in the expansion of lay devotion promoted by the Catholic Church since the Fourth Lateran Council of 1215. Growing numbers of lay people aspired to the pursuit of a religious life without the repudiation of worldly possessions required by the monastic life. The Book of Hours provided a means to access some of the spiritual routines of the clergy, by assembling a selection of popular prayers, hymns and meditations arranged around the traditional hours of liturgical service in use in monasteries. While monks and nuns relied on a complex and dynamic liturgy that required large breviaries and missals, the lay person had in their Book of Hours a simpler collection that could be recited over and over again. Although the content of a Book of Hours was inherently flexible, most included some combination of a religious calendar, brief gospel lessons, psalms, the office of the dead, and prayers to the Virgin Mary and a selection of saints.[8] These traditional meditations were all in Latin, rather than French, usually the preferred vernacular of court literature: but even if the owner had limited or no working knowledge of Latin, that did not prevent one from learning all the prayers in one's Book of Hours by heart.

We have entered a critical period in the history of the book, when books became much more common, and bookmaking hugely more efficient. This coincided with a gradual rise in lay literacy rates, but most new book owners were not yet book collectors. The

Book of Hours might be the only book in the house, used daily, and kept at the bedside or on a prominent table. The *peciae* for which students paid their necessary few pennies would most likely have been discarded as soon as their university days were behind them, or (illegally) sold on to an incoming student. These were not libraries. When it came to building a library collection, the new bookmaking capacities of medieval craftsmen were still largely at the disposal of the traditional book-collecting classes of medieval society, rulers and their families, the nobility and the leaders of the church. What had changed was the ability of those at the apex of society to build larger collections.

In the early fourteenth century, royal women like Blanche of Burgundy played a prominent role in cultivating the popularity of the Book of Hours as an object of courtly fashion. Personalisation was a crucial factor: Blanche commissioned one Book of Hours which included twenty-five pictures of herself among the splendid miniatures that were integrated into the text.[9] Personalised illustrations were a key component of any luxury Book of Hours: ranging from the ubiquitous coats of arms to full-page portraits of the owner and their family, often shown kneeling in prayer. These delicate and sumptuous miniatures ensured that such books were prized possessions, passed down to children or other family members within the ruling dynasty.[10]

Spurred by the ownership and display of pious literature, it was often through women that many courts acquired a bookish atmosphere. When the ladies of court offered their patronage to renowned poets and artists, their husbands began to take note. The greatest collectors of the age were undoubtedly King Charles V of France (1338–80) and his three brothers, Duke John of Berry, Louis of Anjou and Philip the Bold of Burgundy. The Duke of Berry had no fewer than eighteen Books of Hours, including examples recognised as the most beautiful of the age. Philip of Burgundy possessed around seventy manuscripts, mostly a mixture of histories and romances, equally richly illuminated.[11] By 1400, a collection of this size and quality was already significant, but it paled in comparison with the 910 volumes in the library of Charles V, established in the newly converted Louvre.

It is telling that these extraordinary collections were built up while the population of France suffered the deprivations of the Hundred Years' War.[12] After the death of Charles V, the war also caught up with his collection: when Paris fell into English hands in 1420, it was an English duke, John of Lancaster, who acquired the great library. The duke later transported the collection to London, where it was dispersed upon his death in 1435.[13] The occupation of Paris introduced many of the English elite to the delights of its stationers' workshops. In 1430, John of Lancaster and his wife, Anne of Burgundy, would present to the young King Henry VI of England a magnificent Book of Hours produced in Paris, featuring over 1,200 decorated medallions that embellish the margins.[14] A brother of John of Lancaster, Humphrey of Gloucester, also acquired a distinguished manuscript collection of Latin scholarly works and French literature. In two bequests, Humphrey donated his scholarly manuscripts, 281 books in all, to the University of Oxford, to serve as the foundation of a central university library. The grateful university commissioned the construction of a library hall above the Divinity School to house the manuscripts.[15] For several decades, Humphrey's library took pride of place in Oxford; as we shall see, it was to meet an unhappy end only a century after its creation.[16]

Despite the patronage of an occupying force, which could afford to spend its loot to commission lavish books for their homes across the Channel, the Parisian trade suffered from the ravages of war. As Paris lost its prime position as an international supplier of books, commercial bookmakers fled to other university towns and centres of commerce and power.[17] This particularly benefited Flanders and Brabant, in the territories of the Burgundian dukes, whose power struggles with the French crown had made them crucial allies of England in the Hundred Years' War.

Cities like Bruges and Ghent, key entrepôts in the northern European trade, became the new home of luxury manuscript production. Workshops in these Flemish cities were to provide the Burgundian dukes and the highest nobility of the realm with dazzling libraries. The son of Philip the Bold of Burgundy, John the Fearless, owned some 250 manuscripts; his successor, Duke Philip the Good (1396–1467), would expand the ducal collection to close to 900 manuscripts, almost all of them newly made books, written in French, the language of the court.[18] Most impressive was the number and the quality of the miniatures and illuminations in Philip's library, which was quickly recognised as one of the cultural jewels of Renaissance Europe. The collecting of illuminated manuscripts became a necessary fashion at the Burgundian court.[19] The Flemish boom in luxury manuscript production continued into the 1480s, two decades after Philip's death. No other collectors could match the quantity of commissions of the duke, but the greatest noblemen, like Lodewijk van Gruuthuse, were able to acquire collections of 200 richly illuminated manuscripts.

The high standard of Flemish manuscript production was internationally renowned: Books of Hours from Bruges were exported to courts as far away as Lisbon. When King Edward IV of England was in exile in Holland and Flanders, a guest of Lodewijk van Gruuthuse, he ordered a significant number of Burgundian manuscripts: when he regained his crown, he dispersed £240, a small fortune, for books bought during his stay in the Low Countries.[20] The artisans of Flanders and Brabant also began to cater for a different clientele. For the aspiring urban elite, who wished to imitate the book ownership of the high nobility, stationers developed new, mass-produced Books of Hours. These did not feature the lavish, integrated and personalised miniatures, or copious marginal embellishments, but pre-made sets of page-size illustrations, which would be tipped into the Books of Hours as separate leaves.[21] Although such standardised items would never match those that graced the court of the Duke of Burgundy, these colourful Books of Hours still gave the impression of luxury. They would be a considerable expense for many households: the Book of Hours owned by the York baker Thomas Overdo in 1444 was valued at 9 shillings, approximately the price of a cow.[22] Many surviving Books of Hours of this sort reveal copious personal annotations and prayers, evidence of treasured use for several generations. These were clearly cherished possessions; for many, the first and only book in their homes.

Renaissance Calling

The impressive collections of books gathered by the princes of northern Europe were for public display, but not for public use. Although the vast expenditure lavished on manuscripts relied on princely revenue, sometimes gathered from taxation, this did not engender a culture of public availability. Upon the death of a prince, his books were inherited by his successor, or distributed among his relatives. For the purposeful construction of libraries, accessible to a wider public, we have to cast our eyes south, to the Renaissance city-states of Italy. Here an altogether different cast of book owners was shaping a competitive world of collecting, one that soon gained the attention of the bankers, merchants and mercenary generals who fought for power in the deadly game that was Italian politics.

The pace of Italian book collecting, as we have seen, was set by humanist scholars. The humanist movement revolved around books, and it established book ownership as a marker of cultural refinement. It required participants to seek out books from friends and correspondents, to copy them and most of all, to study them. These activities were undertaken to reconstruct a body of the writings of antiquity as comprehensive as possible. Although religious works, especially Bibles and patristic texts, had their place in these collections, they exhibited fundamentally different collecting priorities from the French or Burgundian princes. The collections curated by Italian scholars were largely made up of works in Latin, while some connoisseurs also sought out manuscripts in Greek.

The importance attached to books in this scholarly programme was most obvious in the emergence of private studies, specific rooms set aside for a book collector's literary activities.[23] To own a *studio* – derived from the Latin *studium*, describing a monk's cell – was to lay claim to the highest form of devotion to letters. In the fourteenth and fifteenth centuries, it was a rarity to have a separate space in one's house dedicated to one's personal use. To have a room of this sort filled with books, a desk and some writing equipment, was the apex of civility. Benedetto Cotrugli suggested that the sophisticated merchant would have a separate study from his common business office; ideally the study was located close to the bedroom, so that one could study in the early or late hours of the day.[24] One did not need to have a massive library to value a space for books. One humanist scholar wrote to a friend that in his country villa, 'I do not have a library here like that of the Sassetti or Medici [banking families], but I do have a little shelfful of corrected texts, which I treasure more than any rich ornament'.[25]

The emergence of private studies marked an important step in the developments of library space. Some studies were box units constructed within an existing room: a small wooden compartment, with a built-in desk, a cupboard for books and writing materials, and a seat. Over time this box gave way to a room in the house, set aside for reading and suitably equipped, sometimes with an ingenious revolving desk or book-wheel, which allowed the user to consult multiple books with great ease. The study might also be equipped with shelves. These allowed books to be on display, and also gave the study a sense of greater permanence, given that it was much more troublesome to move shelves of books than if they were kept in a chest. Not all collectors thought that this was an appropriate development. Leonello d'Este, Marquess of Ferrara, advised that one should:

> Keep books free of household dust, as people do who shut them up in cupboards or chests, and never take them out to read or put them back except one at a time – which is to keep them inside a private and secret library – not an open one and for one's friends. Household dust sticks stubbornly to books soiled just in the course of being taken out and put back, no matter how often the floor of the room is washed – which is why washing one's hands counters the trouble to begin with, and which ought to be seen [to] even more carefully ... Also some people shut them up behind glass or canvas panes, on account of the dirt, and to protect them from too much direct sunlight and dust in the air.[26]

These were admirable conditions to keep books in a pristine state but ran counter to the notion that the study was a place of active consultation. Here the owner's intellect was stimulated not only by being surrounded by books, but other objects, including busts, vases, coins and a great variety of curiosities, especially antiquities. Furthermore, while the study provided a private space of quiet reflection, the culture of collecting and scholarship was inherently social. Collecting the best books required an extensive network of like-minded friends: we have already met Poggio Bracciolini and Niccolò de' Niccoli, who corresponded extensively about their quest for lost manuscripts.[27] While Bracciolini was a notorious book hunter, it was Niccoli who was the collector, building one of the finest libraries of his day without leaving Florence. Niccoli devoted his life and his entire fortune to his library, assembling some 800 manuscripts. Far from keeping these books out of the public eye, he freely invited scholars, friends and interested citizens to study, discuss and admire his books; he even lent them out, to the extent that 200 of his books were out of his home at his death in 1437.

Although there were few who could match Niccoli's generous lending, it was expected that humanist scholars would open up their libraries to others.[28] This was one of the crucial tenets of book collecting that the scholars passed on to their patrons, the political and ecclesiastical elite. The humanists could point to many examples from classical Rome that indicated the lengths to which Roman generals and emperors had gone to amass great public collections. That these libraries were circumscribed by a limited notion of openness we have already seen, but to the Italian princelings, who believed their world to be Rome incarnate, the building of impressive libraries was a challenge that they readily accepted.[29]

Scholarly collectors themselves copied many of the books to be found in their libraries. Niccoli in particular was renowned for his innovative humanistic script, which would later inspire the design of italic or cursive type. This allowed the pen to move more rapidly over the page, creating greater efficiency in copying. In contrast, the great princely and ecclesiastical collectors had their manuscripts written for them, increasingly not only by scholars but by armies of scribes working in stationers' shops. To satisfy the literary desires of the popes, cardinals, bishops, generals and statesmen who had begun to take a serious interest in book collecting, there emerged a new class of book dealers, the *cartolai*. Originally sellers of parchment, these were artisans who combined the function of stationer, binder, bookseller, bibliographer, publisher and literary agent. They acted as middlemen between scribes and clients, but also dabbled in production, employing scribes and illuminators to work on substantial projects. Only the Italian cities provided the affluent clientele, and the concentration of available skilled workers, that could create an organised trade in books on this scale. The book market became most advanced in those cities where humanists abounded: Florence, Naples, Rome, Venice and Milan. These were not cities associated with the earliest universities of Italy, but great commercial and political centres. By the middle of the fifteenth century, they were also cities that had an international reputation for the trade in fine books: here foreigners might come to live for several years, commissioning and collecting books, both for themselves, and for benefactors and institutions back home.[30]

The best *cartolai* were to be found in the Republic of Florence; and among them, the most prolific was Vespasiano da Bisticci.[31] Born around 1420 in a village outside Florence, Vespasiano became a stationer by training with an established binder and book dealer, Michele Guarducci. Despite an absence of a formal classical education, Vespasiano emerged as the most prominent supplier of manuscripts to clients within and beyond Florence. Whereas many *cartolai* dealt only in second-hand books, Vespasiano had books produced on a massive scale, employing up to fifty scribes on important commissions from princely customers. Vespasiano's easy manner among the richest class of collector, together with a shrewd eye for business, led to a flourishing career. A part of his success lay in sensing that not all collectors wanted, or could afford, the same sort of book. Vespasiano's workshop was responsible for some spectacular luxury artefacts, completed with magnificent frontispieces and marginal illumination throughout, bound in the finest calf or goat skin, but not necessarily with an accurately transcribed text. For other clients, Vespasiano offered more utilitarian books, lacking illumination, perhaps graced only by simple coloured initials, but with emphasis on scribal precision.

The prices charged by Vespasiano meant that only the most

affluent could afford to buy often at his shop, even of the cheaper kind of book. The rent on Vespasiano's shop was 15 florins a year, approximately the same price as one of his mid-range products.[32] A leading illuminator might make 60 florins a year; a *cartolai*'s apprentices might make only 10 or 15. A lavish frontispiece might increase the cost of a book by 25 florins: the pigments required for the colours were ruinously expensive. Some of the richest bindings, inlaid with gold and silver and studded with precious stones, could cost over 100 florins. In 1483, the Chancellor of Florence, one of the highest civic officials in the city, was paid only 432 florins.[33] Although this was naturally a salary that would be supplemented by many other streams of income, it makes clear that collecting even a small library was a formidable endeavour even to those of substantial means. Yet if a collector wanted to open his collection to the public, he could not afford his books to look inexpensive: he had to invest in the finest copies, decorated with his coat of arms and numerous illuminations, if only to impress upon his visitors the patron's respect for learning and love of books.

In 1478, Vespasiano retired from business and retreated to a family dwelling in the countryside. Here he wrote a series of biographical sketches of the illustrious men of his era, many of whom had been his clients; most were Italians, but they also included a couple of Englishmen, the Earl of Worcester and the Bishop of Ely.[34] In this wonderfully rich account, describing some hundred rulers, cardinals, bishops, statesmen and famous writers, Vespasiano dwelt lovingly on the book-collecting habits of his subjects. This was a topic on which he was naturally well informed, but Vespasiano also makes clear that building a library was one of the chief virtues of a ruler, cardinal or bishop, on a par with martial courage, wisdom, generosity and loyalty. Duke Federico of Urbino (1422–82), a hardened general and great patron of the arts, had a wish to create, as Vespasiano writes, 'the finest library since ancient times. He spared neither cost nor labour, and when he knew of a fine book, whether in Italy or not, he would send for it.' He employed some thirty to forty scribes in Urbino, Florence and other cities, commissioning lavish manuscripts of all the classical writers. His two-volume Bible was 'illustrated in the finest possible manner and bound in gold brocade with rich silver fittings'. His works of Aristotle and Plato were written on 'the finest goat-skin'; many books were bound in scarlet and silver.[35]

It is telling that his substantial collection, rumoured to be one of the largest in Italy, was kept in a locked ground-floor room in his palace at Urbino. Federico did not consult his books here; instead he took them to his magnificent panelled *studiolo*, different from most studies, as it functioned as a small intimate reception room, designed for elegant conversation and musical entertainment, where he could share his treasures with visitors.[36] This replicated the arrangement followed in Roman villas and provides the distant precursor for the system of stack storage in modern institutional libraries.

Vespasiano, in line with the humanist ideal, had an expectation that his wealthiest customers would make their collections accessible to the public. But although he frequently mentions in his biographical portraits that his clients had this intention, he was seldom able to record that this actually happened.[37] There was one patron, though, who did achieve remarkable success: Cosimo de' Medici (1389–1464), one of the richest bankers in Italy, and de facto ruler of Florence. Vespasiano was an intimate of Cosimo from a young age, and the banker's *cartolai* of choice. Their paths first crossed after Cosimo, returning from a period of exile, sought to rekindle the affection of the people of Florence. Cosimo became the patron of a dilapidated monastery in the city, San Marco, which had recently been granted to a new brotherhood.[38] When the friars arrived to take possession, they found crumbling buildings, devoid of furniture, sacred vessels or books for the liturgy. Cosimo commissioned Michelozzo Michelozzi, one of the greatest Italian architects of his day, to rebuild the entire monastery, including a separate library hall, which was finished in 1444. The library, which Cosimo envisioned as a resource for all literate citizens of the city, was built to imitate a church, with three aisles and vaulted arcades. Sixty-four cypress reading desks occupied the two side aisles, under the vaults.

San Marco now had a library, but no books. Helpfully, an opportunity arose which allowed Cosimo to fill the library with a

5. The interior of the library of San Marco, Florence, designed by
Michelozzo. The central corridor was flanked by rows of lecterns,
lit by individual windows. Cosimo's gift to the people of Florence
augmented its reputation as a centre of classical learning.

superb collection. In his will, the great collector Niccolò de' Niccoli had determined to leave his library as a public collection. He had tried to provide funds to fulfil this desire, but was nearly bankrupt on his death, so he granted possession of his library to a board of trustees which included Cosimo and his brother Lorenzo. In 1441, the other trustees allowed Cosimo to place the books in the library of San Marco, on the condition that Cosimo would redeem Niccoli's debts. This was easily done, given that over half of the debts were owed to the Medici family. In one fell swoop, Cosimo had acquired one of the most valuable libraries in Italy, comprising some of the best copies of classical works in Latin and Greek.

The San Marco library would open with 400 volumes chained to the sixty-four reading benches. Access was restricted to literate male citizens of the city with scholarly interests, but this may have encompassed up to 1,000 men in fifteenth-century Florence. Over the course of eighteen years, Cosimo would add more than 120 books to the library, many of them furnished for him by Vespasiano, who had been tasked with providing a more comprehensive selection of religious manuscripts. Cosimo was a model customer: in addition to actually paying Vespasiano for his books (something that not every great collector would do), he paid him a commission of 400 florins.[39] Even after this expense, Cosimo did not limit his library building to San Marco alone: he also paid for an entire library for the Badia monastery at Fiesole, on the outskirts of Florence. This commission too fell to Vespasiano, who claims that he engaged forty-five scribes to complete 200 volumes for the library in the space of twenty-two months.[40]

After Cosimo's death in 1464, the Medici continued to wield power in Florence, but the family's passion for public libraries dissipated. While some citizens of Florence, like Lorenzo da Bisticci, a nephew of Vespasiano, donated books to the San Marco library, Cosimo's successors became more interested in amassing a great private collection. Lorenzo the Magnificent (1449–92), Cosimo's grandson, did not collect for the citizens of Florence or the monks of Tuscany, but for himself, some 1,000 manuscripts in all.[41] One of his prize possessions was a missal, bound in solid silver and crystal, valued at 200 florins. This was the collection of a prince, rather than an astute financier bent on bolstering his civic reputation, and a revealing testament to the transformation of the Medici, from bankers to political behemoths.

Universal Values

Princes of the calibre of the dukes of Burgundy or Lorenzo the Magnificent built libraries because this was an endeavour that was befitting their status. Books were expensive and precious objects, and collecting a large number of books was an exclusive activity. As a proportion of the population, those who engaged with books on a daily basis were relatively few in number, and mainly drawn from the class of court officials, clergymen, physicians and scholars. To a prince, curating a great book collection was a means to draw these individuals to one's court and into one's favour. One did not have to be a learned prince to appreciate the value of a library, or be literate to understand the mystical power of books.

In all these respects, the great libraries of fourteenth- and fifteenth-century Europe were similar to those found in other parts of the world. The emirs and sultans of Persia and the caliphs of Baghdad, Cairo and Cordoba all assembled collections of books, and surrounded themselves with great artists and scholars. The greatest cities of Andalusia, Egypt, the Levant and Mesopotamia nurtured brilliant scribes who were as talented as those working around Notre Dame or in the workshops of Bruges. Calligraphy, illumination and painting ranked among the highest art forms in the Islamic world. Richly decorated books, produced with painstaking effort, were a staple of elite collections, which included works in all disciplines: naturally in theology, but also science, mathematics, astronomy, and compendious encyclopaedias, filled with all the knowledge of the world.[42] Like similar libraries in Europe, access was generally restricted to the ruler and his entourage.[43]

The establishment of theological schools and academies in cities like Damascus also incubated a commercial book market, in which stationers, scribes and scholars, who might be one and the same individual, supplied texts to students. Their services were also available to other scholars, to court officials and of course to the

Abbasid, Fatimid or Mamluk elites. One of the most remarkable centres of book collecting was the city of Timbuktu, an important trading centre on the banks of the river Niger. Between the fourteenth and the sixteenth centuries, this was renowned as the home of the most learned Islamic scholars, whose rulings on sacred law were held in high regard by communities spread across North Africa.[44] Many of these scholars owned libraries, consisting of manuscripts of Islamic theology, law, history, science and medicine: these were important markers of erudition, and an indispensable foundation for their legal authority. Some of these collections were composed of hundreds of volumes. In a city overflowing with scholars, but with limited capacity to produce books locally, libraries were their owners' most valuable possessions.

Timbuktu's days of scholarly glory were effectively ended after a devastating Moroccan invasion in 1591. Its scholars were killed, taken captive or exiled, while the book collections of the city were dispersed or fell into disuse. Similar misfortunes befell other great collections in the Islamic world, not least the thirteenth-century Mongol razing of Baghdad and the destructions of Christian Reconquista in Muslim Spain. An unfortunate consequence of this erasure of Islamic libraries from the medieval era is that verifiable details on the scope of these collections are extremely hard to uncover. Figures cited in later accounts offer estimates of hundreds of thousands or even millions of books, reminiscent of the panegyric heaped upon the holdings of the ancient library of Alexandria.[45] Reliable information on the great court libraries of Cairo and Baghdad remains elusive, as it does for the medieval book collections of China, Korea and Japan. Here too, emperors, shoguns and warlords are known to have acquired substantial libraries, largely as a resource for the scholars and administrators associated with the court.[46]

What is established with greater certitude is that Chinese and later Arab society contributed a crucial innovation to the development of the library with the art of making paper. In East Asia, sheets of paper were made from plant fibres, like bamboo, and used for both scrolls and codices. This technology spread during the first millennia to the Islamic world, where textile rags became the common resource with which to produce paper. The manufacture of paper was far cheaper and more efficient than the production of parchment from animal skins: all that paper-mills required were a steady supply of linen, cotton or hemp rags and a source of running water to power the hammers that reduced the rags to pulp.[47] By the thirteenth century, the first paper-mills were established in Italy and Spain, and later in France, Germany and the Low Countries. It was immediately clear that paper would provide a far cheaper and more abundant writing material; it was nevertheless less durable than parchment, and in both the Arab world and medieval Europe, used initially for note taking and administration rather than bookmaking. The impact of paper on book production would only become apparent in the fifteenth century.

Another critical technological development that took place in China was the introduction of woodblock printing, an art that also spread quickly to Korea and Japan. The impression of wood-carved texts and images became common around the seventh century, and this remained the predominant form of printing in East Asia until the nineteenth century. Given the rich complexity of the Chinese, Korean and Japanese alphabets, with their thousands of characters, woodblocks remained far more widely used than ceramic and metal types.[48] Until the modern era, the art of printing remained largely at the behest of the great imperial courts, or for use by Buddhist monasteries and temples, where the act of copying prayers and scripture using woodblocks was a spiritual activity. That Buddhist monasteries could amass extraordinary collections was confirmed in the early twentieth century, when a 'library cave' was discovered in Dunhuang, western China, as part of a vast underground monastic complex. Sealed since the eleventh century, the cave held around 40,000 manuscripts, most of them Buddhist texts, but also a rich variety of works in other genres, from Greek classical philology to medicine, revealing the scholarship and intellectual curiosity of this monastic community strategically located at a crucial junction of the Silk Road.[49] After the opening of the cave, thousands of manuscripts were sold to Western and Chinese visitors: today the remnants of this remarkable collection are found throughout the globe.

The Dunhuang cave also demonstrated the extent to which the handwritten book remained the staple of library collections in large parts of Asia. In the Islamic world, print was also largely rejected, and calligraphy remained celebrated as one of the finest visual arts, and a suitably refined medium through which to honour the word of God. There is indeed little evidence that the technology of moveable-type printing passed from China to Europe, and Johannes Gutenberg's invention during the middle of the fifteenth century was certainly arrived at independently of developments elsewhere.[50] It was European printing technology that would have the most radical impact on the production and distribution of books, and change for ever the face of library building. Some of the universally shared foundations of library building, found in the medieval period across Europe, the Islamic and East Asian worlds, would be uprooted. This would pose unexpected challenges to the library, as the creation of a mass market for books manufactured with the new technology of printing would bring the joys and tribulations of book ownership to a new generation of European collectors.

PART TWO

THE CRISIS OF PRINT

CHAPTER FOUR

THE INFERNAL PRESS

On 12 March 1455, Aeneas Piccolomini, the future Pope Pius II, wrote to Cardinal Juan de Carvajal in Rome with extraordinary news. In Frankfurt he had seen pages of a Bible produced by a 'miraculous man'. This man had over 150 of these Bibles available for sale, an exceptional quantity for a single individual to possess. Piccolomini warned his patron that they were already selling out, and he apologised for not being able to acquire a copy for the cardinal, all the more so since the pages were 'exceedingly clean and correct in their script, and without error, which Your Grace could read effortlessly even without glasses'.[1]

Piccolomini was describing the book that we now know as the Gutenberg Bible. The 'miraculous man' was Johannes Gutenberg, the goldsmith of Mainz responsible for the invention of printing with moveable metal type. Although the invention would bring Gutenberg little fortune, it had a transformative impact on the future of the library, one that would shape for ever how libraries were built, and who was able to collect books. None of this, however, was immediately evident. The production of manuscript books increased in volume for at least two decades after the invention of printing in the middle of the 1450s. The birth of print did not cause the collapse of manuscript culture; manuscript writings, in many forms, would continue to play a major part in the work of government, in the provision of news and in the literary world, for many centuries. However, print did cast a shadow over the commercial manuscript book production that had emerged in France and Italy since the thirteenth century. As the new medium of print matured, other readers, for whom the services of a workshop like Vespasiano's were too expensive, could aspire to become collectors.

Ownership of a library no longer marked a man out as a member of the European social and political elite.

This, indeed, may have been the most immediate impact of the invention of print on libraries. For a century or more, the collecting of books lost allure for the leaders of European society. There were other ways to spend the money required to build a collection on the scale of the dukes of Burgundy and the Medici: tapestries, statues and paintings to commission, and wars to be fought. These endeavours, unlike book collecting, remained securely in the realm of princes. The great libraries of the manuscript era found themselves suddenly friendless, and many fell into disrepair. Ironically, given the contempt with which they were viewed by Renaissance intellectuals, the survival of libraries was reliant once again on the monks and friars who had sustained the book world through the medieval era. Yet in the early sixteenth century, with the onset of the Reformation, the monastic way of life would be severely challenged, and with it, the assiduous collecting of the monks and nuns. While print gradually cleared the ground for the rise of a new breed of collector, the institutional libraries of the court, the university and monastery, would be temporarily eclipsed.

The Work of the Books

Less than a year after Aeneas Piccolomini marvelled at the wonders of the Gutenberg Bible, its printer was in deep trouble. Gutenberg was embroiled in a court case with his erstwhile partner, Johann Fust, who had provided much of the finance for the 'work of the books', and who accused Gutenberg of owing him 2,026 guilders, enough money to buy twenty large houses in Mainz. Although the legal wrangle would ultimately demonstrate that Gutenberg owed only about half this amount, this debt was enough to ruin him financially.[2] The stark warning that a successful printer had to keep a shrewd eye on his purse would be lost on many of Gutenberg's successors in the trade.[3] In the fifty years after Gutenberg printed his Bible, at least a thousand printers would at some point establish premises in one of 240 towns scattered around Europe. Many of them were active for only a few years; few found riches.

Technological curiosity was a significant factor in accelerating the spread of printing. Contemporaries were amazed by the reproduction rate of the printed book: while a scribe might take a year to produce two substantial folio manuscripts, a team working on a press could produce 1,000 copies of the same work in around eight to ten months. Yet a press did not churn out copies of a book on a daily basis: crucially, printing was done by the sheet. After setting up the metal type in a frame, the printer would print a certain number of copies of one sheet; then the frame would be broken up, the type washed, and re-set for the next sheet, and so on. A book could thus be on the press for six months, and the printer would not have a single product to sell, given that the book was never ready until the final sheet had been printed. Through all this time, the printer would have to bear the costs of the supply of paper, the wages of the compositor and pressmen and storage costs.

The invention of printing also upset the traditional rhythms of trade in the book world. A scribe would ordinarily have a customer in mind when producing a book; indeed, most scribes would have been commissioned directly by a client. When the book was finished, the scribe could be paid and the transaction was concluded. The printer, although he may have had a few customers in mind, had to speculate how many buyers might be found for 300, 500 or 1,000 copies, and where those buyers might be. Several hundred buyers would rarely be found in the same city: the market for a substantial Latin edition might well be dispersed around Europe. Underestimating demand would rob the printer of additional profit; overestimating demand was financially lethal, as investment had been sunk into unsaleable printed sheets.

These were tough lessons, learned the hard way by many pioneers of the press. These new problems of finance and distribution were of little concern, however, to those who stood to gain most from the invention of printing: those who bought books. The enthusiasm shown for the new printed books by monks, friars and priests, the largest traditional segment of book users and buyers, was remarkable. The invention of printing had coincided with a widespread movement of spiritual renewal, one that saw monasteries, rural and urban, eager to build or replenish their book collections.[4] Printing seemed like a divine invention, bestowed upon the world at the time when it was needed most. In the words of the Bishop of Brescia,

> Merciful God instructed our contemporaries in a new art. Thanks to typography ... three men working in three months have printed 300 copies [of a folio commentary by Gregory the Great], a feat they could not have accomplished in their entire lives had they been written with a pen or stylus.[5]

It was natural for clergymen to admire products from the new presses, because the first printers were very careful to imitate manuscript books in shape, style and content. This was not a coincidence: some of the earliest printers had been scribes themselves, or were fully immersed in the manuscript book trade; but it also makes clear that the first printers were not trying to revolutionise the book world.[6] For this reason, monastic scriptoria did not see the new art as a challenge to their activities. In fact, in the first years of printing, the scriptoria were kept busier than ever. The first books generally required finishing by hand, with the insertion of handwritten initials, red lettering and illumination.

Some monastic communities were so taken by the concept of the press that they established their own. In the early 1470s, Melchior of Stanheim, abbot of the Saints Ulrich and Afria monastery in Augsburg, tried to persuade his fellow brethren that printing books 'would be useful labour for [them] against idleness'. Abbot Stanheim also argued that a local press would invariably see 'a large number of books enter the library'.[7] He was not the only enthusiast. Printing houses would appear in monasteries and convents throughout Germany, but also in Sweden, Italy, England and Spain. As Abbot Stanheim's comments suggest, the first thought of the monastic community was generally itself and the other houses in its order. It made sense to keep a printer close by if the order required a new missal or breviary, a substantial and complex project that required strict supervision by clergymen.

To monks, like many other contemporaries, the press was seen as a mechanical extension of the activities of a scribal workshop.

6. The first printed books were designed to imitate, as closely as possible, their manuscript predecessors. This copy of the Gutenberg Bible has two coloured initials: like all other decorations, these would have been added by hand.

For some tasks, printing functioned very efficiently: Johann Luschner, invited to take up printing in the Benedictine monastery at Montserrat in Catalonia, produced 190,000 indulgence certificates on behalf of his patrons.[8] Printing these little sheets of paper was far easier than copying the same quantity by hand; for more substantial projects, the business case was not always straightforward. The monastery of San Jacopo di Ripoli in Florence, which acquired a press in 1476, laboured for thirteen months to produce 400 copies of Boccaccio's *Decameron* – and then struggled even longer to sell them.[9] The Ripoli monastery press had more success with other titles, mostly staples of pious devotion and classical learning, almost all of which were sold to other monastic houses.

By the 1490s, the early monastic printing houses had mostly closed, either because the printers associated with them lost patience with their hosts, or because the monks themselves lost interest. It turned out that it was easier to fill a monastic library by buying the books that one needed from bookshops in Europe's great cities, then to have hundreds of books printed locally, and then seek to sell or barter those for other works required for the monastic library. This change took place at the same time as the price of books was decreasing considerably. The first printed books had not necessarily been much cheaper than similar manuscript books – the Gutenberg Bible was an extraordinarily expensive work, and for that reason only affordable for princes, bishops and monastic institutions. Yet forty years later, in 1491, the Augustinian canon Wilhelm von Velde of Frankenthal could claim that:

> An astonishing number of books was made in our lifetime, and new ones are being added every day. Not only are they produced by teacher's dictation and by handwriting as in the past, but also by printing, which is an astonishing new art ... Books are so cheap these days that you can buy one for the same price that you otherwise would once have paid for listening to or reading.[10]

This rather elliptical remark refers to the widespread practice, at court and in the monastic houses, of having books read aloud as entertainment or spiritual nourishment. The much greater number of books available by the sixteenth century certainly reduced the necessity, if not the pleasure, of sharing the same text communally, a medieval practice that would eventually be recreated by the birth of radio and television in the twentieth century.

The sheer quantity of new books in circulation certainly drove down prices by the 1490s.[11] By 1500, 9 million copies of printed books had been turned off the press, and more were printed each year. In some sectors, the market was already saturated. Monasteries had feasted on the glut of new books, but there was a limit to how many customers one could find for large tomes of theological commentaries and canon law.

Prices had also been driven down because paper rather than parchment had now become the preferred medium of book production. This transformation was one borne of necessity, as the supply of parchment could never feed the insatiable demand of the presses. The thirty copies of the Gutenberg Bible printed on parchment required the skins of at least 5,000 calves.[12] The production of paper, still an expensive commodity, could be scaled up more easily than parchment, and the invention of printing saw the proliferation of paper-mills throughout Europe. The librarian of the Benedictine monastery at Tegernsee in Upper Bavaria could rejoice after acquiring a three-volume edition of Ambrose for only 3 florins, roughly the same amount as earned by the monastery from selling thirteen sheets of prepared parchment.[13]

Around the same time, a ruling was promulgated in Cambridge that books on paper could not qualify as a pledge for loans, unlike parchment books.[14] This was one of the first signs that the invention of printing might have some adverse effects on the status of books and libraries. Printing was undoubtedly a boon for scholars like John Veysy, a fellow of Lincoln College, Oxford, who was able to collect, with relative ease, some eighty-five books in the 1470s and 1480s; or Hans Urne, provost of the cathedral of Odense, who could leave to his friends and family 268 books at his death in 1503.[15] It proved more damaging for the communal college libraries, carefully built up by the pious donations of scholars over the course of two centuries. As books became cheaper and more abundant, scholars had less need for the resources of communal collections; their donations, in consequence, dried up. The library of Merton College, Oxford, was still virtually devoid of printed books in 1540, ninety years after Gutenberg's triumphant experiment.[16]

Crying in the Wind

The men who learned Gutenberg's art fanned out from Mainz to all corners of Europe. The rugged artisans who could work the new presses were besieged with invitations and commissions from abbots, bishops or magistrates to dignify their city, diocese or monastery with the new art: from Malmö to Lisbon, no self-respecting civic elite wished to be left behind once they had handled examples of these new technological marvels. This age of rapid expansion lasted less than forty years. As debts and disappointments accumulated, printers huddled together for security in the largest mercantile cities of Europe, especially those that had a pre-existing commercial book trade. Here they could find an established community of booksellers and buyers, as well as merchant investors used to the concept of risk capital: these merchant publishers also had access to the necessary logistical infrastructure to distribute books throughout the continent. It was therefore little surprise that Paris would be the great centre of printing in northern Europe; in the south, Venice became the main print emporium, the home to 150 printers at some point before the end of the fifteenth century.

The veritable flood of printers in Venice touched a raw nerve with the Dominican friar (and scribe) Filippo de Strata. In 1473, only four years after the first printer arrived in Venice, de Strata petitioned the Doge of Venice (unsuccessfully) to put a halt to this abominable new trade:

> They shamelessly print, at negligible price, material which may, alas, inflame impressionable youths ... They print the stuff at such a low price that anyone and everyone procures it for himself in abundance ... The printers guzzle wine and, swamped in excess, bray and scoff. The Italian writer lives like a beast in a stall.[17]

De Strata was a well-known and widely travelled preacher; his highly invective style, mirroring that of a fiery sermon, infuses the text. De Strata could disguise the special pleading of the scribe facing a more efficient competitor by invoking the same xenophobic sentiment as Poggio Bracciolini and his humanist friends a century earlier: in Italy, printing was identified as a German invention, largely practised in its early years by German immigrants. The idea that barbarians could contribute anything of worth to letters was absurd; that elegant Italian writers now had to rely on the print shop to circulate their writings was a disgrace.

Many of de Strata's other arguments centred on the moral vices encouraged by the press, chiefly the printing of lascivious poetry for 'impressionable youths'. That the new presses served only to churn out rude songs was most certainly incorrect (printing, as we have seen, served mostly a pious clientele) but it was a standard duty of the preacher to warn his flock against vice. The same arguments would be resurrected in the eighteenth and nineteenth centuries about the dangers of industrial workers and women idling their time away by reading fiction.[18] De Strata also took issue with the undignified mechanical operation of the printing house. Printing was a loud, sweaty and oily business, requiring immense strength from the pressman pulling the press, and the constant reapplication of ink; bookmaking now required far more manual labour than delicate calligraphy.

De Strata railed against printing, but many of his arguments might also have applied to the commercial manuscript workshops. Not all scribes were pious monks, nor did they write exclusively devout books. The notion that illiterate printers would corrupt literature by reproducing errors in hundreds of books could equally be applied to hasty and careless scribal work. Those buyers who bought a book for its text do not seem to have minded whether it came from a press or pen. In the first decades after the invention of printing, booksellers happily sold printed and handwritten books in the same shops. Inventories of possessions from this period do not necessarily make distinctions between them.

Filippo de Strata's petition went unheeded, but the friar would not give up. On several further occasions he would urge the government of Venice to step in and regulate the print trade. Evidently the Doge found little of value in these arguments – on the contrary, print had brought both business and prestige to Venice. Perhaps the only point on which de Strata would be proved correct was the low price and widespread availability of print. It is no coincidence that around the same time as he wrote his petitions (*c.*1480), commercial manuscript production was entering a downward spiral. Vespasiano da Bisticci, the great manuscript dealer of Florence, retired in 1478. He professed not to admire printing, and remarked that the library of Federico of Urbino, one of his best clients, did not include a single printed book, or 'it would have been ashamed in such company'.[19] This was disingenuous, for in fact, Federico did own printed books, and Vespasiano himself used printed books as exemplars for his handwritten products.[20]

There were few great collectors who actively disdained printed books. Nevertheless, the growth of printing did dim the appeal of library building for the ruling classes. Apart from their drop in value, the fact that books were now so freely available also reduced the intimate bond between a connoisseur and the handwritten text acquired through a laboriously built network of personal connections. The books commissioned from a workshop like Vespasiano's were tailored to a patron; even if his scribes had written the same books a dozen times over, the buyer could feel that he was purchasing a bespoke product. In many respects, too, print was inherently inflexible compared to manuscript book production. It was the printer who decided how to arrange the book and lay out the text; with a manuscript, one could shape a text arranged according to one's wishes, with excerpts from different authors, and a personalised illustrative scheme. Manuscript books, if one had the resources, could be vibrant and colourful objects. Although printers experimented with double or even triple colour printing, most books were printed only in black ink.

As more people amassed collections of books, the great libraries of the manuscript age lost their lustre. The San Marco library in Florence, assembled by Cosimo de' Medici, entered a period of decline, with the loss of manuscripts, dismembered or stolen. Later Medici rulers, like Cosimo I, the first Grand Duke of Tuscany, also removed some of the manuscripts to their own collections.[21] While the library had been erected to provide a valuable source of classical and religious literature for the citizens of Florence, by the middle of the sixteenth century it seems that the citizens, the duke and the friars had lost interest in maintaining such a resource. In Venice, Cardinal Basilios Bessarion donated his magnificent collection of more than 600 manuscripts, including many rare Greek texts, to the city in 1468 to provide the basis for a public library. Although this was received gratefully, the books sat disregarded in crates in the Doge's palace for the best part of a century before a building was erected to house them.

Outside of Italy, there was one collector who, decades after the invention of print, was still assembling an enormous manuscript library. At the time of his death in 1490, books were still being prepared in Florence to be dispatched to Matthias Corvinus, King of Hungary, for his great library in Buda.[22] As an admirer of the artistic achievements of the Italian Renaissance, Corvinus hoped that a distinguished library, filled with classical and humanist books written in Italy, could give Buda, his capital, something of the status of the great Italian cities. Corvinus acquired some 2,500 volumes, many commissioned specifically by him at great expense. The finest books were exhibited on exquisite tripods of gold, jewels and snakeskin. Italian scholars, upon hearing of the size of his library, wrote panegyrics on the wisdom and generosity of the king. In Hungary, praise was rather more hesitant. When Corvinus died, it became clear how much resentment had built up over the king's lavish expenditure on his library. The books remained in Buda, until Ottoman forces conquered the city in 1526, taking back to Istanbul many of the volumes, while soldiers ripped off the rich bindings of others, trampling over the sorry remains.

Today the library of Matthias Corvinus has a near-mythical status. If it had not been lost, however, it is unlikely that its reputation would have stood so high; it seems that in the years of the most frantic collecting, unscrupulous dealers has passed off on Corvinus texts that were neither accurate nor particularly distinguished. It is telling that although contemporaries in other European countries despaired of the despoliation of Hungary and its famous library, no ruler tried to emulate the collecting practices of the Hungarian king. The ducal library of Burgundy had been a prized cultural symbol of the lustre of the court. Yet after the death of Duke Philip the Good in 1467, his successors did not embrace the opportunities afforded by the invention of printing to expand the collection in any way. When Philip's great-grandson, Duke Philip the Fair, died in 1506, he owned barely any printed books.[23] He was not alone in his aversion to print; as usual, the grandees of the realm followed their sovereign in fashion and taste. In 1528, one of the leading noblemen of the Habsburg Netherlands, Philip of Cleves, possessed a library of 175 volumes, of which only five were printed books.[24] Others, like Charles, Duke of Croÿ, actually sold off the large part of their manuscript book collections, seventy-eight richly illuminated volumes in all.[25]

The seventy-eight books of the Duke of Croÿ were bought by Margaret of Austria (1480–1530), governor of the Habsburg Low Countries and brother of Duke Philip the Fair. She was one of the few among northern Europe's elite who continued to collect actively, building a library of close to 400 volumes, almost all manuscripts. Margaret endured a turbulent life: she lost her mother and brother at a young age, was spurned by the Dauphin of France, before being twice widowed by the age of twenty-five. Growing up alone in a rapidly changing world, a courtly library of manuscripts represented a place of refuge among the past glories of Burgundy. She paid the Duke of Croÿ an extraordinary sum for his manuscripts, roughly the same price as if they had been commissioned for her, because the production of new deluxe manuscripts had now effectively ended.[26] Instead, Books of Hours, for a time the most luxurious of manuscripts, were now affordable to anyone aspiring to respectability. The scale of this trade had become immense: in 1528, the warehouse of one Parisian bookseller, Louis Royer, contained 98,529 printed Books of Hours.[27]

To the princes and monarchs of Europe, libraries may have lost their splendour, but that did not necessarily mean that they stopped acquiring books. Books continued to come their way, not least as gifts from authors, hoping for advancement or a lucrative position as court poet or historiographer. The astrologer William

Parron presented copies of his prognostications to King Henry VII of England on numerous occasions.[28] It is noteworthy that when he did so, he did not offer one of the hundreds of printed copies of his work produced by London printers, but a richly illuminated manuscript copy. It seems that 'the most noble and heavenly art of printing', as Parron described it himself, was not yet deemed illustrious enough for a king.

Henry VII's son and successor, Henry VIII, had a fundamentally different relationship with books. As a young man, Henry VIII was well read, interesting himself greatly in Catholic and Protestant debates. To him, books were of practical use; they had little value as artefacts for display. The book collection of the king was dispersed throughout many residences – Richmond, Westminster, Greenwich, Hampton Court, Windsor and New Hall – and kept there in closed chests, ready to be hoisted up on carriages and wagons should the king have need for them.[29] In the later years of his life the king seems to have lost interest in these books; some of the chests were entirely forgotten, and rediscovered only in the early seventeenth century. Richard Bancroft, Archbishop of Canterbury, appropriated some 500 volumes for himself, many of which he had rebound and stamped with his own coat of arms. Given that Henry VIII procured his books predominantly as consequences of his own acts of brutal realpolitik, it may seem that justice was served. The dissolution of the monasteries provided a steady stream of books, as did the libraries of his many queens and the even more numerous sequestrations of the estates of courtiers who were convicted of treason.[30]

Henry VIII and his successors could acquire far larger numbers of books than his predecessors could ever have dreamed of. Yet they no longer sought out books, like Edward IV, marvelling at the Flemish manuscripts he saw in exile in Bruges, who spent a fortune he did not have on acquiring a library of fifty or a hundred books. While the invention of printing heralded a new age for the library, filled with possibilities, it also condemned to obscurity and neglect the collections of an era left behind. It would take the best part of a hundred years before the comparative rarity of manuscript books would make them once more treasured objects of desire.

CHAPTER FIVE

COMING OF AGE

In the autumn of 1506, Johannes Trithemius turned his back on the love of his life. For twenty-three years, Trithemius, a rising star of the Benedictine Order, had been the Abbot of Sponheim, a small religious house south-west of Mainz. Trithemius was a reforming abbot, keen to impose order not only on the monks under his direct control, but also on other houses in the region. In his years at Sponheim, he had achieved much: an orderly monastery, and a rising reputation among Europe's humanist scholars. These talents he could take with him, but his greatest creation was left behind at Sponheim: for here, Trithemius had created a stupendous library, one of the last great monastic libraries of the medieval era.

When Trithemius arrived at Sponheim, its library apparently held only forty-eight books. The library he abandoned in 1506 was now one of the largest in Europe, containing a reputed 2,000 volumes.[1] This was a collection worthy of a Medici, or a Duchess of Burgundy, and it bears examination how a priest in holy orders could pull off so audacious a feat. All great collectors are ruthless, and the greatest weapon in Trithemius's armoury was his right of visitation to other local houses. Many had accumulated books beyond the requirements of the monastic round, on music and poetry, history, medicine or philosophy. A quizzical raised eyebrow from Abbot Trithemius and the monks were only too keen to press such incendiary cargo into his willing hands. As the years went by, and tales of the miracle of Sponheim spread through the humanist networks, visitors, among them scholarly grandees like Conrad Celtis, Johannes Reuchlin and Jacob Wimfeling, arrived with their own gifts of books.

Trithemius had one other mighty weapon at his disposal: the

labour, not always willing, of the monks under his charge. Trithe-mius never forgot the derelict state in which he found Sponheim in 1482. As the buildings were rebuilt, so too would be the pious spirit of the brethren, not least through the ceaseless copying of books. In 1492, Trithemius, not a modest man, celebrated these achievements with a triumphant pamphlet, *In Praise of Scribes*.[2]

This much misunderstood work is often seen as the last gasp of the print-hating defenders of the old order. Yet Trithemius was no Filippo de Strata, fulminating impotently against the corrupt-ing influence of the new printed books. Although Trithemius remarked, correctly, that parchment made from animal skins would endure longer than paper, he was no enemy of print. Already by 1492, he was a much published author, his reputation made by the new printed books as much as by the praise of friends. So it was entirely in character that Trithemius arranged for a printed edition of his encomium to the art of the scribe, and this neat printed pam-phlet was a great success. One thousand copies were printed (a large edition for this date) and at least thirty copies can still be located in libraries today.[3]

Trithemius's point was not that print was bad, but that copying was a good and worshipful activity. 'These things that we copy we impress most deeply on the mind.' If the scribes of Sponheim paused to rest their sore fingers and read the abbot's new book, they would have seen themselves described as heralds of God: the scribe 'enriches the church, maintains the faith, destroys heresies, repulses vice, inculcates morality and increases virtue'.[4] Not all were convinced, and when Trithemius left for a trip to Berlin in 1505, the weary monks rebelled against his authority. Not all shared his devotion to labour, or his bibliomania, building, as Trithemius perhaps incautiously expressed it, 'on the model of the ancients (even the pagan ones)'. So much for putting heresy to flight. By the time Trithemius returned to Sponheim in 1506, the situation was past saving, and the bruised and resentful abbot took himself off to continue his writing projects elsewhere. These, sadly, did not burnish his reputation. Deprived of his great reference library, he relied too much on an ageing memory and his still vivid imagina-tion; later generations of scholars forgot the great library builder and instead poured scorn on the inaccuracy of his historical writings.[5] It was a sad end for a gifted, driven man, though the fact that his books continued to be reprinted for over a century, in defiance of learned opinion, ensured that his name would not be forgotten.

For us, the great library at Sponheim offers a snapshot of the book world at the junction of manuscript production and the new potentialities of print. In the great library assembled by Trithemius the books copied by the monks mingled with the print and manuscript texts brought from elsewhere. The two forces were not necessarily in collision, and for many years after, scholars and collectors would continue to augment libraries mainly composed of printed books with manuscript texts, either copied by themselves, or bought in the second-hand trade.

That a collection of 2,000 books could be assembled in an undistinguished German monastery is remarkable in itself, and religious houses would continue to play a major role as centres of collecting for the next three centuries, through all the vicissitudes of the Reformation and the ensuring religious conflict. For the moment, though, the centre of gravity was shifting. The future of collecting lay ever more clearly with the new world of print, its enormous abundance and the newly emboldened scholars working outside the institutional church. The impatient collector with money to burn could now build a quite astonishing collection in a remarkably short space of time. Even a scholar of more modest means could assemble a working collection with a fraction of the effort and heartache of a century before. In the rest of this chapter, we will explore this new world of collecting through two of its most remarkable figures, who held contrasting attitudes to the buying of books. One will be Desiderius Erasmus (1466–1536), the greatest author of the day, and the proprietor of a surprisingly modest library. First, though, we will set sail with Fernando Colon (1488–1539), the son of Christopher Columbus and the greatest collector of the age. It was Colon who came closest to recreating the universal library, the mirage of Alexandria that continued to inspire and haunt those engaged with the collecting of books. That he ultimately failed should not detract from the originality of the remarkable library he created by the banks of the Guadalquivir in Seville.

New Worlds

Fernando Colon and Desiderius Erasmus were separated by so much – geography, education and life experience – that it was a neat twist of fate that the two should be brought together by the love of books. They met once, in 1520, when Colon was serving the Holy Roman Emperor as a diplomat, and Erasmus was at the height of his fame. For Colon, this meeting was the vindication of a long struggle for recognition and survival. He spent much of his childhood waiting anxiously for news of his father's voyages, and when the father returned in triumph, Colon was brought to live at court. When later voyages failed, he felt directly the chill of disfavour, and would spend one uncomfortable year together with his father, abandoned on a wrecked vessel in the Caribbean, despairing of rescue.[6] Erasmus's upbringing, consigned to a joyless monastery, was less adventurous but equally hard.

As an adult, Colon would impress with his talent as well as his resilience. With the accession of Charles V, King of Spain (1516) and Holy Roman Emperor (1519), Colon was at last able to move on from defending his father's complex financial legacy and build his own career. Charles V was taken by this young man with the interesting past and impressed by his versatility, always a useful quality in a Renaissance court: the emperor would make use of him as an administrator, diplomat and surveyor, conducting the first thorough mapping of Castile.

Colon took his first plunge into the international book market in Italy in 1512, during a long and tedious attempt to rescue the fortunes of his older brother after a marital catastrophe. Rome provided an education in the art of book collecting, and it was here that Colon established the basis of the superb collection of woodcuts and engravings that would accompany his book buying.[7] But it was the emperor's diplomatic business that gave him the opportunity to explore at length the major emporia of northern Europe: first Antwerp, the great metropolis of the Low Countries, then Aachen for the imperial coronation, and a long sortie down the Rhine. He bought in Mainz, the birthplace of print, and in Strasbourg and Basel. It was in Germany that he was able to sample the books of the next great controversy convulsing Europe, Luther's battle with the Catholic Church. Although his own allegiance to Catholicism never wavered, Colon bought freely the books published on both sides of the debate. His extensive collection of Luther's works would later cause his heirs some embarrassment, and would be culled from the library by the Spanish Inquisition.

It was on this tour that Colon met Erasmus, at this point a tepid admirer of Luther's courage, if not his more trenchant denunciations of the papacy. Colon bought no fewer than 185 books by Erasmus, the only author honoured by a separate section of the library when they reached their destination in Seville. However, it would be some time before Colon would see them there: for now, he was en route to Venice, the beating heart of the international book world. In seven months he hoovered up 1,674 books. These were consigned to a merchant for shipping back to Spain. Colon meanwhile was on his way back to the Low Countries, then Nuremberg and once again Mainz, German cities that offered up another thousand titles.

It might be thought that buying on such a scale could only be indiscriminate, but Colon was certainly following a plan, albeit an ambitious one. Colon was determined that his library in Seville should encompass the world's learning, a task that he believed print had now brought within the bounds of possibility. Colon had his father's imagination allied to a more practical spirit: he was at heart a civil servant, bringing order to the emperor's affairs and to his own growing library. At an early stage, he began his *Abecedarium*, an alphabetical list of the authors and titles of books in his collection. This precocious application of alphabetical logic was greatly admired, but as a means to organise a library collection it found few followers. Most collectors at that time would still follow the principle established by medieval libraries, and canonised by the Frankfurt Book Fair catalogues, of ranging books according to their scholarly faculties. Theology would be placed first, then jurisprudence and medicine, with literature, philosophy and science normally consigned to a compendious miscellaneous category. This would remain the predominant mode of organising books and catalogues into the eighteenth century, though with some expansion of the list of categories.

In addition to the *Abecedarium*, Colon found time for a separate cataloguing enterprise, offering a detailed note on each of his purchases, including where it was printed, where he had bought it and how much he paid. This detailed record allows us a view of the workings of the international book market of unprecedented subtlety. For most of his life, the emperor was at war with France, so the great book market of Paris was out of bounds for Colon. He nevertheless accumulated a collection of almost 1,000 Parisian imprints, purchased in thirty-five cities around Europe. A visit to Lyon during a rare interval in the Habsburg–Valois wars harvested 530 books, printed in forty-five cities, from Wittenberg and Leipzig to Rome and Palermo; conversely 250 Lyon imprints were among the books he bought in twenty-five other places, including Nuremberg, London and Seville. Paris and Lyon were great commercial cities, and established centres of the international book trade. But in 1535, when Colon made his last great book-buying tour, he was able to buy 434 books, from thirty-five different cities, in the small French town of Montpellier, a place that had a distinguished university, but at this point no printing press.[8] The smooth sophistication of the international trade in books was such that purchasers who did not enjoy Colon's opportunities to travel could be confident that the world's emporium would be available at their local bookshop.

Colon's systematic register of every purchase also allows us to reconstruct the fruits of his Venetian buying spree, since the books themselves never made it to Seville. The ship dispatched with the books succumbed to the notoriously fickle winds and tides of the Mediterranean, and the entire cargo was lost. This Venetian collection was to have been the glory of Colon's library, a consignment which itself was larger than most libraries of the age. Gone were not only these magnificent volumes, but the 2,000 crowns donated by the emperor that Colon had invested in them. Yet printed books, though expensive, were easily replaced. What marks out Colon's collection from that of other great libraries of the day is his interest not only in the milestones of scholarship, but in the ephemeral literature of the day: pamphlets, songs, cheap works of devotional literature and other practical books.

There is no obvious reason why Colon, an autodidact proud of his hard-won learning, should have collected this cheap print so assiduously. There was no encouragement to do so from the libraries of the great collectors that Colon was determined to emulate and surpass. Perhaps we should look for the clue in a critical moment in his father's career. When Columbus struggled back from his first voyage, his ship, the *Niña*, was scarcely seaworthy and without most of the crew, yet he had very little to show for his epic feat of navigation. There was little gold, and none of the famed riches of the Indies. The discovery of a western passage to Asia, the voyage's main purpose, had patently failed. Columbus realised his vulnerability, and that the fickle favour of his royal patron would not necessarily survive this underwhelming balance sheet, all the more so since, having made landfall in Lisbon, he faced incarceration by the King of Portugal. Columbus dashed off an open letter, reframing his tortured passage as a triumph for Spanish arms, new lands captured and claimed for Spain, renamed in honour of Ferdinand, Isabella, Christ and the Virgin Mary. These were territories filled, according to Columbus, rather in defiance of the evidence, with unimaginable goods and wonders, pregnant with possibility.

This letter, swiftly published in pamphlet form, saved Columbus and the fortunes of his family. As he penned it, Columbus was unaware that a second vessel from his fleet, the *Pinta*, had survived to make landfall in Spain. Its captain, Martín Alonso Pinzón, was on his way to court to claim the triumph. But Ferdinand and Isabella kept faith, and Pinzón was not received. As Columbus's announcement of the new territories claimed for Spain, *De insulis nuper in mari Indico repertis*, ricocheted around the print capitals of Europe, the status of Columbus as the admiral of the New World was assured, and with it the future of his family.[9] Colon, of all book collectors, had reason to understand the power of the pamphlet.

Erasmus

When Colon met Erasmus in 1520, the great humanist was at the height of his fame, as a scholar, an author and a wit. The triumphs of 1516, Erasmus's controversial translation of the Greek New

Testament and his edition of Jerome, had cemented his reputation as the international champion of the Renaissance. He was also a highly versatile writer: while the *Enchiridion militis christiani* (Handbook of the Christian Soldier) revealed him as a religious author of high seriousness, his bestselling titles were the *Moriae Encomium* (In Praise of Folly), a playful exercise in humanist wit, and the *Adages*, a collection of epigrams and paradoxes that Erasmus revised continuously throughout his career. By 1520, over 600 editions of his works had been published in almost all the major printing centres of northern Europe: he was by some distance the bestselling author of his day.

Erasmus had shown that it was possible for a talented author to make money in the new industry of printed books, and could have made more. He was wooed by both Emperor Charles and Francis I of France, who competed in this, as in so much else, to have him as the adornment of their court. All of this, one would have thought, would have enabled him to build a stunning library, but in fact the opposite was the case. When Erasmus died in 1536, the collection he had left behind could be fitted into three packing cases, a mere 500 titles.[10] This was not wholly unsubstantial, but eighty years after the invention of print, a bookish merchant or lawyer could assemble a collection of this sort: and Erasmus was the most famous man in Europe, who inhabited, even reshaped the book world, and understood the business of books intimately.

Why did Erasmus, of all people, pass up the opportunity to build a library? Perhaps it was because, when he abandoned the monastery to which he had been unhappily consigned as an orphaned youth, he became a citizen of nowhere. The success of his early writings brought many invitations to visit, a blessing to a man with no family money to fall back on, but a curse for a serious collector. Despite longer periods in Louvain, where he helped to found the Trilingual College at the local university, and Basel, where he was close to Johann Froben, the favoured publisher of his mature years, Erasmus never owned a home of his own. To a man used to travelling light, books were a further burden that presented major logistical difficulties when he moved on.

Friends were prepared to help out, up to a point. When Erasmus was on the road, or between homes, his long-suffering friend Pieter Gilles, the town clerk of Antwerp, was prepared to give his books a home. Once Erasmus was settled, he would have the books sent on, relying on his last host to make the arrangements, or contracting with a local bookseller to organise carriage. This was not always fail-safe. Staying with Thomas More at Mortlake, Erasmus complained that his books had not yet found him; and often, as soon as they arrived, he was on the move again.

Only in 1521, when Erasmus settled with some degree of permanence in the comfortable home provided for him by Froben in Basel, could he think seriously of building a library. Yet even now, housed and financially secure, his book buying was curiously restrained. Far more books came to him as gifts rather than purchases; almost the only references in his correspondence to book buying are for the Greek titles he needed that were not widely available in northern Europe. What concerned him most was access to texts, and if he had easy access to a copy, through friends, or there was a copy he could lift from Froben's shop, then he had no reason to buy the work. He was not concerned with ownership. Through Froben, and his contacts in the Basel book world (one of the leading centres of scholarly publishing), Erasmus could source most of what he wanted. Other texts came to him through friends, or as gifts from younger scholars keen to make an impression.

Scholars are not always the most hospitable, particularly if they are working to deadlines. Erasmus understood intimately the rhythms of the international trade, centred on the Frankfurt Fair, already in the sixteenth century the critical biannual meeting of publishers from all over Europe to exhibit their new titles and make bargains (as it still is). In the weeks before Froben's carts set off to Frankfurt, Erasmus was often working flat out to get a new text finished, so he much preferred to be sent books than to have their authors hanging around the house. One who despite this wormed his way into Erasmus's good grace was the young Polish scholar Johannes à Lasco (Jan Łaski). The scion of a distinguished noble family, the young humanist was in the position to offer Erasmus an advantageous bargain. He would buy Erasmus's library, but allow the great man continued use of it for the remainder of his life. It did not take Erasmus long to accept: money in hand meant a great deal to him, and à Lasco was prepared to defer the pleasure of ownership for the honour of doing Erasmus a service.

There was, of course, much that could go wrong with such an arrangement. Books continued to arrive, and Erasmus began to think that he had willed away his library too cheaply. Perhaps because of this he did not scruple to continue making gifts of books from his collection which were technically no longer his to give. Erasmus never catalogued his books; the collection was small enough for him to remember where everything was to be found. There is, however, a title list made after his death to accompany the books on their long journey to à Lasco in Poland. From this we know that of the 500 books consigned to the road, 100 were his own works (though Erasmus, curiously, did not own a copy of everything he had published). A quarter of the rest were titles from the Froben press, presumably obtained free of charge. The remainder were the basis of a standard scholarly working collection, along with a few smaller books, presumably ones that, for one reason or another, Erasmus had passed over when he was looking for something to press into the hand of a young admirer to get them out of the house.

Post-mortem

By 1536, 15,000 books had been purchased to grace Colón's new library, which had, as a nice modern touch on its owner's part, shelves. Vertical shelving seems to us so much the obvious, logical way to store books, that it is hard to see why it took so long for this to become standard practice. The libraries of the Renaissance had preferred inclined desks or tables where each book would be displayed separately, while many owners still stuck to the traditional chests. Few had enough wall space to accommodate shelving, and even those who accumulated several hundred books could trust to memory to find the required text in one of their chests. Chests could also be far more easily moved from room to room, or house to house. Colón's decision was partly dictated by the size of his library. With a collection so vast, shelving, and a shelf order, was a necessity if books were not to be permanently lost. A further attraction to the self-designated heir to Alexandria was that this represented a return to the archiving practice of the ancients, with the vertical books in place of the heaped scrolls.

The plans were made and the building secured, a gracious site on the waterfront. But if Seville, as the major entrepôt of the American trade, was to Colon the new centre of the world, it was nevertheless not an ideal place for a major scholarly library. The city was only a destination for those on their way to the Indies or the Americas: many of those who passed through would never return, and few would be scholars interested in his books. Seville could not easily be included in the itinerary of a bookish traveller on their way to Paris or Venice, in the same way that they could try knocking on Erasmus's door in Basel, or visit Sponheim.

In the absence of the remedies available to modern medicine, everyone in the sixteenth century would experience intimations of mortality. Faced with the recognition that his own time was short, Colon embarked on feverish plans for the perpetuation of his grand design. Although fantastical in their ambition, his instructions do demonstrate how well he understood the contemporary book world. Each year a bookseller in five cities – Rome, Venice, Paris, Nuremberg and Antwerp – was to dispatch 12 ducatos' worth of new publications to Lyon. There a sixth bookseller would expend an equivalent amount, and then ship the entire consignment to Medina del Campo, the great fair town of Spain, from whence the books would be transported to Seville. Each sixth year a member of the library staff would embark on a pilgrimage around a sequence of smaller cities: nothing was to be missed. Most remarkably, the booksellers were instructed to follow Colon's own strategy, of privileging pamphlet literature in their purchases. Only when all had been collected that could be, would the remaining funds be spent on more substantial books. Here Colon was ensuring that his primary aim should be accomplished, that the library should encompass 'all books, in all languages, and on all subjects, which can be found within Christendom and without.'[11] This was very radical: well into the eighteenth century, libraries, personal and institutional, would continue to privilege books in Latin and the other scholarly languages. Some actually banned books in the common tongue: most books in the local language were destined for reading and disposal, rather than collection. Here, especially, Colon was a man ahead of his time.

Colon's heirs also had to face the fact that western Christendom was not an undivided family, but two opposed traditions, making war on each other's books. Since he died without direct heirs, the library descended to a nephew, who showed no interest in shouldering the burden laid upon him. The books were transferred to the monastery of San Pedro, and thence, after an extended legal battle, to Seville Cathedral. This was far from a safe haven. A cathedral has other priorities, and the only logical place of storage was a loft or the crypt. Colon's books could still have been fetched for a consultation from this new location, but not before the Spanish Inquisition, which did not share Colon's eclecticism, had removed anything suspect. The Spanish crown took its pick of the manuscripts and folio volumes, and today there remain only 4,000 titles, now adequately housed and available for use in Seville. Ironically, this includes a large number of the French-language pamphlets gathered up by Colon in his last major buying spree in 1535–6. Too cheap to be worth stealing, too orthodox to merit destruction by the Inquisition, miraculously they have lived on through the centuries, until rediscovered and re-catalogued. Often these turn out to be the only surviving copy of these small Catholic devotional works.[12] This, at least, is a legacy worth cherishing.

Although Erasmus was far from matching Colon's great vision, it did not take long for his equally careful plans for the disposal of his books to come unstuck. In the eleven years since contracting his bargain with Erasmus, Johannes à Lasco's circumstances had changed in a material way. The young humanist was now on a journey towards Protestantism, exposing a rift with his rich but traditionally Catholic relatives. À Lasco now had no money for books, and more pressing concerns than fame as a humanist scholar. In 1539, he too embarked on a peripatetic career: first in Germany, where he was appointed as superintendent of the local churches in Emden and East Friesland, then to London as first superintendent of the newly established Dutch and French refugee congregations.[13] Expelled with his flock with the accession of Mary Tudor in 1553, à Lasco spent three years wandering around Germany and the Baltic, before returning to his homeland, dying in Poland in 1560.

These were hardly optimal conditions for the curation of a distinguished library, and à Lasco made little attempt to keep Erasmus's books together. When part of the library was sent to him in Germany, this was so that he could raise money by selling it. Not that this proved particularly easy to accomplish. Most of the theological staples in Erasmus's collection were widely owned and easily accessible, and there appears to have been little appetite to buy them because of their distinguished provenance. Erasmus's reputation was in something of a decline in the mid sixteenth century, his ecumenical spirit out of alignment with the polarised religious politics of the age. It is possible that some who bought books from his library may have carefully removed any signs of his ownership, an act of oblivion scarcely conceivable to us today. In consequence, of the 500 books enumerated in the list that accompanied his books to Poland, only twenty-five can be definitively identified today as part of Erasmus's collection.[14]

Finally, what of Trithemius's labour of love, the library at Sponheim? Sadly, this fared little better than the libraries of Erasmus and Colon. Dispersal began almost as soon as the gates banged shut behind the former abbot. The monks had little interest in cherishing this memorial of many cold, shivering years of hard labour, and whether by sale or attrition, most of the books were soon gone. When the monastery closed its doors in 1564 only a small residue remained. At least some of the new owners cherished their prizes: manuscripts clearly associated with Sponheim can now be found in at least sixteen major collections.[15]

This, as it turned out, would be an everyday story of library history. One man's passion project would be nothing but a burden to those to whom the responsibility of curation was passed on. At least in the age of print, no failure was ever final. Libraries abandoned or dispersed, burned down or looted, could be regenerated with astonishing speed. That was the miracle of print: the ever-accumulating mountain of books was available, sometimes at knockdown prices, for anyone with the energy and determination to build libraries. For the moment this would be largely private citizens rather than institutional collections. For the next two hundred years, the fate of the library would lie in the hands of generations of scholars, civil servants, lawyers, physicians and merchants, who collected books for work, and increasingly for pleasure. This was the age of the professionals; and it was they who would shape the future of the library.

CHAPTER SIX

REFORMATIONS

The Protestant Reformation represented a critical moment for the history of the library. Martin Luther's impassioned protest against the papacy was accompanied by a torrent of print, stimulating an astonishing public interest in Luther's bold repudiation of the church and transforming the book trade. In the decades after 1517, when Luther posted his Ninety-Five Theses on the door of the All Saints' Church in Wittenberg, presses were established in many places previously unable to sustain an active printing industry. Much of this was a direct result of the revolution in communication that had made Luther the talk of every town. The former monk was a pioneer of the printing press: Luther appealed directly to a broad public by writing short pamphlets, in the vernacular German tongue, that addressed crucial issues of theology succinctly. Luther was a prolific writer, and as his pamphlets spread rapidly throughout the Holy Roman Empire, he found many supporters who were also eager to take up their pens; and printers, ready to feed the seemingly insatiable demand for all things Luther.[1] Members of the publishing industry who could not take advantage of this new market suffered greatly. In 1521, the printers of Leipzig, Germany's greatest centre of printing before the Reformation, were faced with bankruptcy when Duke George of Saxony forbade them from publishing Luther.[2] By the middle of the sixteenth century, little Wittenberg had become the most important centre of printing in all of Germany.

The Reformation gradually changed the nature of the book: it became cheaper, shorter and less scholarly. This transformation encouraged many people who were not habitual buyers of books to build their own collections. Once individuals became used to visiting bookshops and reading pamphlets, they would often return for more, and soon they too had small libraries, stacked with as many German texts as traditional Latin tomes. Although Luther's pamphlets were too small to merit the expense of binding on their own, once they were bound with twenty or thirty others, they made an impressive volume; indeed, this is how so many of them have come down to us today. Yet while many more people were introduced to the pleasures of book ownership thanks to Luther's movement and its subsequent offshoots, we should not forget that in many other ways, the Protestant Reformation was a calamity for Europe's libraries.

The Reformation shattered the unity of western Christendom. Those loyal to Rome denounced Luther and his followers as heretics; Luther, meanwhile, gradually broadened his attack to encompass the whole institutional structure of the Catholic Church. The sacramental underpinnings of the church were called into question, along with its theological precepts and written heritage. To Protestant reformers, this made huge numbers of books, a large proportion of the accumulated European book stock, redundant; while the new products that emanated from the print shops of Germany, Switzerland, and later England and the Netherlands, were anathema to the Catholic world. As European territories divided along confessional lines, in many parts of the continent the result was quite devastating; Europe's libraries would feel the effects of the schism for the next two centuries.

Fanning the Flames

In 1520, when Pope Leo X announced the formal condemnation of Martin Luther, it was also decreed that Luther's erroneous books should be burned. Luther pre-empted this sentence by burning the Pope's bull of condemnation. The bull was flung into the fire in Wittenberg, along with a handful of pamphlets written by his opponents and critical texts of the institutional church, such as volumes of canon law. This began a tit-for-tat struggle, with books stoking the fires of controversy throughout Europe. Sometimes unfortunate authors or printers were consigned to the flames along with their books; on other occasions, books were burned by the public executioner as a proxy for their absent creators, occasions that could all too often degenerate into farce when onlookers tried to rescue the texts from the flames.

This exchange, from which neither side emerged with much credit, established a standard for the destruction of disapproved texts that would continue to haunt European society down to the twentieth century. The condemned books were mostly newly written texts, but even the accumulated stock of Europe's libraries would not be safe from the passions unleashed by the collapse of the accustomed religious order.

A first indication of the trials ahead came in 1524, when Germany's rural population rose in revolt. The principal cause of the so-called Peasants' War was the hard conditions of life in the German countryside; hated landlords were the rebels' first target. Many of these landlords were members of the clergy: either rich cathedral chapters, or the monastic orders, which over the centuries had accumulated thousands of acres of farming land as a result of pious bequests from citizens anxious for the fate of their eternal soul. Church institutions took a pragmatic view of their responsibilities as landowners, and were not noticeably more gentle than their neighbours in the nobility. Many German peasants still lived in a state of vassalage, obliged to perform labour for free, and were constrained in their choice of where they could sell their goods. To many country folk hearing second hand of Martin Luther and his radical interpreters among the clergy, the Reformation's teachings offered them the hope of a new world.

As the peasant bands massed, obvious targets were the unprotected monasteries scattered around the German countryside.[3] Their libraries had expanded rapidly since the invention of printing, as the monastic houses had taken advantage of the easy availability of texts to build their collections of liturgical and scholarly works. So when the peasants broke down the doors, they ransacked not only chapels, grain stores and kitchens, but libraries and scriptoria too. Often this was the result of uninhibited rage, especially when fuelled by loot from the wine cellars. Many monasteries were entirely burned down; in Thuringia alone, seventy were completely destroyed, and the books perished in the flames.

Some of the destruction went hand in hand with plunder. Peasants looking for valuables ripped silver clasps and bindings from richly decorated books before throwing the mutilated volumes aside. At the Cistercian monastery at Herrenalb in Schwarzwald, so many books and manuscripts were torn apart that one could not enter the monastery without stepping on the trampled remains.[4] One looter gathered up books to sell them to stall holders for use as wrapping paper. In Ittingen, a farmer beat up the prior and then used the missals as kindling so that he could 'boil fish' for his dinner.[5] Others in the peasant bands, most likely radical preachers, stole books to add to their own collections. The monastery at Frankenthal lost its copy of the 1493 *Nuremberg Chronicle*, only to have it returned by the nobleman Schenk Everhard zu Erbach, who recovered it at the battle of Pfeddersheim.[6]

In the aftermath of the war, every pillaged monastery recorded damages to its book collections. Maihingen lost its library of 3,000 volumes; Auhausen lost 1,200; Ochsenhausen recorded losses worth 3,000 florins, as did Reinhardsbrunn. Books and manuscripts accumulated over many centuries, some as old as the ninth century, were the collateral damage of this settling of ancestral scores. Yet sometimes the intruders' motives were more calculated. The insurgents saw the opportunity to destroy institutions whose ruthlessness as landlords accorded so poorly with the life of contemplative prayer to which monks had ostensibly devoted themselves. Their libraries often contained the monasteries' collections of charters and deeds that gave proof of their rights to property and feudal service. At Weisenburg, the peasants celebrated by burning a wagon of archival papers at the market square, whereas those at Reinhardsbrunn ensured that all fragments were consumed by the flames in a bonfire held in the cloister's court. In Bamberg, when the peasants attacked the episcopal palace, 'they tore up books, registers and letters, especially those of the fiscal office [along with] many judicial acts and registers'.[7] The deliberate destruction of archival documents helps explain why the peasant bands also targeted the much smaller personal libraries of noblemen, or abbots and bishops, which contained many legal papers. In Bamberg alone, twenty-six noble families made claims for damages to their libraries.

The Peasants' War was the most extreme example of the devastation unleashed by the Reformation, but its fury was brief. Far more influential, in the long term, was the confiscation and dispersal of libraries that followed the dissolution of ecclesiastical institutions in Protestant territories. As German princes, dukes and city-states abandoned the old religion, they appropriated monastic houses and ecclesiastical property. The buildings could be turned to new use, coin could be added to the state coffers, but the large quantities of books posed an altogether different problem. In 1524, Martin Luther had advised that former monastic book collections could be used to establish school libraries, or Protestant church libraries, but warned that these collections would first have to be picked over carefully to remove authors and titles that had no place in the new reformed institutions. If this investigation was undertaken assiduously, as it was in the Swiss city of Zurich under Huldrych Zwingli, there might not be many books left. According to the Reformer Heinrich Bullinger, the library belonging to the great church of Zurich was examined 'for good books', after which the rest was sold to market vendors, apothecaries and bookbinders.[8] There was so much material for the local bookbinders that a century later some of them were still using material removed from the church library in 1525. Illuminated manuscripts from Zurich found their way to the goldsmiths too, who could reuse the gold leaf.

In Basel, which adopted the Reformation four years after Zurich, most monastic books were deposited in the local university library. This was a temporary solution, and for the next hundred years the regents of the university sold off large numbers of Catholic works deemed to be useless to Protestant scholarship. Around 1600, the university was still selling off vellum manuscripts from monastic libraries, but the regents instructed their librarian to cut out random leaves, and jumble others together, so that if the manuscripts ended up back in Catholic hands, they would no longer be of much use.[9] The fight against Catholicism could be fought on many fronts.

7. The Reformation was a disaster for the library culture of Europe, not least through the destruction of monasteries in Protestant countries. The historic libraries of the monasteries usually perished with their institution, leaving only an empty shell in its wake, as in the cloister of Koningsveld, near the Dutch city of Delft.

Similar processes of dissolution and confiscation would continue for many years. Not all territories embraced the Reformation immediately, but when they did, an example had been set by their predecessors: to seize all monastic possessions, including their significant stocks of books. The more meticulous rulers, most notably the rich city-states of the Holy Roman Empire, would make repeated efforts to transform the confiscated libraries into new institutions. Elsewhere in Europe, the appropriation of monastic property seldom resulted in library collections of genuine utility to the local population.[10]

Stripping the Shelves

In England, the dissolution of the monasteries followed a different trajectory from that in the German Empire or the Swiss Cantons. Here an entire way of life was obliterated, along with the literary record so carefully curated over many centuries. The effect on the cultural heritage of a nation – until this point a sanctuary of ancient learning – was profound and long-lasting. There was initially no indication that this would be so. King Henry VIII was one of Martin Luther's most prominent critics, and he was hailed by Catholic Christendom as a defender of the faith. The first books to be burned in England were Lutheran works, which may well have kept feeding the flames were it not for Henry's determination to seek a divorce from his first wife, Catherine of Aragon.

The Act of Supremacy of 1534 acknowledged King Henry as head of the Church of England, and granted him the power to dissolve monasteries, priories and convents, and appropriate their income. Ultimately, some 800 institutions were closed, commencing with the smallest and poorest houses. A popular Catholic uprising in 1536, the so-called Pilgrimage of Grace, only made Henry and his advisers more certain that the monasteries were a hotbed of dissent, and further dissolutions followed. By the middle years of the 1540s, the process, swift and ruthless as it had been, was complete.

The dissolution of the monasteries instigated the largest transfer of land in England since the Norman Conquest of 1066. This was a massive undertaking, spearheaded by royal commissioners who toured the monastic houses and the administrators who kept the books at the Court of Augmentations, the financial institution founded to administer all dissolved property. The first commissioners made the rounds in 1535 to begin the process of appraisal and the supervision of the sale of monastic goods. It is striking that this initial commission never even mentioned books, bizarrely so, since at this point the monastic libraries contained the largest collections of books in the country.[11] The Benedictine monastery at Bury St Edmunds possessed around 2,000 volumes, a fine mix of printed books and manuscripts; Canterbury priory had a similar number, with another 1,800 volumes stored in the Canterbury abbey library.[12] Yet to the Court of Augmentations, working with hard-nosed efficiency, these books had little value. Although we can track the fate of every piece of silverware, every bell and every lead roof, libraries are only mentioned in the assessment reports for the value of their wooden furniture.

The commissioners had a natural interest in the manuscript charters and muniments of monastic houses, which they needed to document their estates and privileges. The fate of the remaining papers, manuscripts and printed books was mixed. Many were left in situ, others carted off, some vandalised. Their future often depended on the new owner of the monastic house. Many opportunistic noblemen purchased the former buildings from the crown during the 1540s, so the former libraries also came into their possession.[13] The Welshman John Prise, for example, fashioned his country house out of the monastic buildings of St Guthlac in Hereford, and filled its library with the spoils of religious houses in the west of England. Over time, the fine pickings from the monasteries attuned noblemen to the delights of manuscript collecting. We can identify in this period the early traces of the commercial exchange of manuscripts among collectors that would ultimately blossom into a significant branch of connoisseurship.[14] Yet not all new owners of rare manuscripts recognised their cultural value. Fragments of the Ceolfrith Bible, one of the three earliest English Bibles in existence, were found at Kingston Lacy House in 1982, wrapped around estate documents.[15] Sir William Sidney used leaves from prayer books and service books from Robertsbridge Abbey to bind the account books of his iron works.[16]

Liturgical books belonging to the monasteries were valued greatly, but only for the potential to salvage gold, silver and semiprecious stones from their bindings. Beyond this decoration they were of little intrinsic value to their new owners, so they were invariably thrown away or sold in bulk. In 1549, the Protestant scholar and clergyman John Bale wrote despairingly that:

A great number of those who purchased those superstitious mansions [monastic properties], reserved of those library books, some to serve their jakes [lavatories], some to scour their candlesticks, and some to rub their boots. Some they sold to the grocers and soap-sellers, and some they sent overseas to the bookbinders, not in small number, but at times whole ships full, to the wonderment of foreign nations.[17]

Bale would later reflect on these 'uncircumspect and careless days [when] there was no quicker merchandise than library books'.[18] Men like Bale did not condemn the act of dissolution, but were frustrated by the manner in which the written heritage of England had been dispersed so wantonly. In their quest to justify the emergence of the independent Church of England, Protestant scholars sought for evidence among the monastic manuscript collections of the Anglo-Saxon origins of an ancient national church, free from papal deviancy. Bale argued that 'in all ages have there been some godly writers in England, which have both smelled out and … detected the blasphemous frauds of this Antichrist [the Pope]'.[19]

Other scholars were concerned with material that would help decipher the history of England and its antiquities. In 1533, the antiquary John Leland had received a royal commission to undertake a tour of monastic libraries to ferret out works of importance to the history of the English realm. In some houses he marvelled at the wonders laid out before him, manuscripts presumed lost brought for his inspection. Yet he also played a role in reaffirming suspicions that the monasteries were idle places, filled with illiterate monks, and poor custodians for books, let alone precious texts. Describing the library of the Oxford Franciscans, Leland remarked: 'Good God! What did I find there? Nothing but dust, cobwebs, bookworms, moths, in short filth and destitution. I did find some books, but I should not willingly have paid threepence for them.'[20]

Like all antiquarian collectors, Leland had a discriminating understanding of what was valuable, and he was entirely unsentimental about the bulk of the books he encountered. Thus, when the dissolution of the monasteries was in full swing, Leland knew where the treasures were to be found, and which libraries could be left to be dispersed to the four winds. In 1536 he reported to Thomas Cromwell that foreign scholars were entering dissolved monasteries to despoil and steal books, and he urged the chief minister to allow him first rights of salvage.[21] Leland subsequently retrieved hundreds of manuscripts and books, some of which were placed in Henry VIII's royal library, spread among the palaces of Westminster, Hampton Court and Greenwich. Others he kept for himself, including many books belonging to the monastery of Bury St Edmunds.[22]

The accession of Edward VI in 1547 accelerated the destruction of former monastic book collections. In 1550, an Act was passed 'against superstitious books', which called for 'all books called antiphoners, missals, grails, processionals, manuals and primers [books of hours] ... heretofore used for service of the Church' to be 'utterly abolished, extinguished and forbidden for ever to be used or kept in this realm'.[23] While the first phase of the Reformation had made the former monastic collections generally redundant, the 1550 Act made the very possession of the same books illegal. This destroyed their monetary value on the open market, and ensured that former monastic books could only be traded in for waste paper or parchment.

The passing of the Act against superstitious books led to widespread devastation of surviving Catholic works, extending far beyond the realm of the monastic houses. Even the books of the late King Henry were not safe: in 1551 a commission sorted through the royal collection to look for missals, antiphons and other devotional works to strip the 'garniture of the same books, being either of gold or silver' and to remove the books from the collection.[24] The Act also applied to parish libraries, many of which had book collections dating back to the fifteenth century. One clergyman in Cartmel, Lancashire, noted dryly in a memorandum that 'I burned all the books'.[25] This wave of destruction may have encompassed many more books than intended: it is understandable that not everyone tasked with book burning could tell the difference between secular manuscripts of historical importance and works of Catholic theology.

Many church libraries suffered multiple book burnings. To propagate the Reformation, royal injunctions in the 1530s and 1540s had specified that each parish was to acquire at least one Protestant Bible, as well as the *Paraphrases* of Erasmus. These, and other Protestant books bought for parish churches, were prime targets when Edward VI was succeeded by his Catholic half-sister, Queen Mary, in 1553. This reversal of fortunes was a disaster for institutional book collections in England, not least the college libraries of Oxford and Cambridge.

Universities across Europe underwent intense scrutiny during the upheavals of the Reformation because of their important role as educational institutions for the clergy. This ensured that with the introduction of the English Reformation, its reversal under Mary, and reinstatement under Elizabeth, the old syllabus and familiar texts of both universities came under critical inquiry. Oxford and Cambridge underwent three visitations, one each during the reigns of Henry, Edward and Mary. These were not as destructive as the dissolution of the monasteries, but nevertheless instrumental in reshaping the book collections of the colleges, many of which dated back several centuries.

In 1535, a review of the university curriculum prompted a royal ban on a number of medieval scholastic texts, including the works of Duns Scotus, which had been a mainstay of academic learning. Richard Layton, the dean of York, wrote with pleasure to Thomas Cromwell that 'Dunce' was now 'utterly banished'. At one college, Layton 'found all the great quadrant court full of the leaves of Dunce, the wind blowing them into every corner'.[26] More books were removed in 1549, while an extensive visitation took place in 1557, during Mary's reign. To assist this inspection, all colleges were instructed to draw up lists of books in their possession. Given that the mere ownership of Protestant books was now unlawful, none of the colleges listed any. Today no Oxford colleges own any Protestant books acquired before the reign of Elizabeth, which makes it likely that some made sure these disappeared before the visitors arrived.[27]

Comparing the size of libraries before and after these repeated inquests makes clear how the libraries suffered. In 1529, the university library of Cambridge possessed a collection of between 500 and 600 volumes; in 1557, after the final visitation, only 175 volumes remained.[28] It would not increase in size again until the 1570s. Oxford's famous university library, the pride of which were the 281 manuscripts donated by Duke Humphrey of Gloucester in the middle of the fifteenth century, suffered even worse depredations. Several rounds of book removals ensured that the library, kept in a purpose-built hall dating to the 1480s, was left almost devoid of books. In January 1556, the university set up a committee to sell off the library furniture. Only three of the original 281 books donated by Duke Humphrey are still in Oxford today.

The experience of the university libraries in the turbulent middle decades of the sixteenth century also stunted the expansion of the collections afterwards. Why would colleges spend money on books when the books might be confiscated or burned after the next reversal of royal policy? Trinity College, Oxford, spent more on feasting the Bishop of Worcester on 2 August 1576 than they spent on their library in the previous forty-five years.[29] Donations of books, the main motor of growth for institutional collections until the nineteenth century, also dried up, which meant that, decades into Elizabeth's reign, many colleges still did not have any Protestant books at all. Many colleges, as well as the central libraries of both universities, were greatly diminished compared to a century earlier. Oxford would have to wait until the arrival of a visionary library builder, Sir Thomas Bodley, at the end of the sixteenth century, to undo the damage that had been inflicted.[30]

Expurgation

Even in those parts of Europe loyal to the old church, the extent of the calamity brought about by the Reformation was fully apparent. The evangelical rebellion presented loyalists with a crisis of authority, and questioned the validity of the inherited learned tradition. Those who remained staunch in their allegiance did what they could to bolster the church, but it took a major effort to steady nerves and draw a firm line around theological orthodoxy. This work of renewal took shape in the Council of Trent (1545–63), which in twenty years of deliberations laid down firm guidelines for the institutional future of Catholicism. This involved direct intervention in the book industry, permanently changing the European book market, and having lasting effects on the development of libraries across the continent.

It was by no means guaranteed that the Catholic Church would take a sustained interest in the censorship of print. The first instruments of control in the book trade had been introduced at the insistence of printers and booksellers, when, anxious to protect their investments, they petitioned for privileges to secure protection against competing editions of their books. This was especially important because printing was a new trade, and in many places in Europe not subject to traditional guild regulations. As Erasmus pointed out 'while not everyone is allowed to become a baker, no human being is prohibited from trading books'.[31] Although the papacy had issued a bull as early as 1477 against printing books that opposed key tenets of church doctrine, until Luther appeared on the scene, active enforcement remained at the behest of local authorities.

It was in the Netherlandish territories of the emperor, Charles V, that the reaction to Luther's message was fiercest. Charles was adamant that the heresy should not flourish in the Netherlands, his ancestral homelands, after he had failed to stop its spread throughout the German Empire. On 20 March 1520, three months before the papal bull appeared, the emperor ordered that all Lutheran books in the Low Countries should be 'reduced to ash'. After the formal excommunication of Luther in 1521, Charles issued further edicts targeting the book trade. All Lutheran works, in print or manuscript, were to be burned in public. After the proclamation of one edict in March 1521, 400 books were consigned to the flames in Antwerp, most of which had been confiscated from booksellers; the rest had been surrendered by anxious citizens from their own collections.[32] Despite this show of force, reports indicate that the ceremony was noisily mocked by watching citizens: one account noted that some citizens, clearly enamoured of the Lutheran movement, clamoured for the heretical books to be sold to raise funds to finance a bonfire of clergymen in Rome.

In the first days, such humour was widespread, but the burnings persisted. On 1 July 1523, two Augustinian friars were added to a bonfire of books. Several printers would also pay with their lives over the next decades for producing Protestant texts. The wave of repression hit the book community hard. When any suspect individual was arrested and underwent questioning, the interrogation naturally included questions concerning the possession of heretical books. The inquisitors identified books as crucial factors in the spread of heretical beliefs; but the books also offered a means to discover networks of Protestants, as they implicated booksellers and pedlars who could then be interrogated to discover the identities of their customers.[33] Bookshops were raided and stock inspected, especially for books that clearly revealed their origins in dangerous Protestant printing centres like Wittenberg. To circumvent this, printers took to falsifying the place of publication on the title pages of their books, or anonymising them altogether. Over time, the hardening of religious fault lines ensured that books from suspect printing centres would be anathema in other markets. This had a huge impact on the international supply of books. In Spain, which had always been reliant on substantial imports, books were initially free from excise duty. By 1558, however, anyone importing vernacular books without permission was threatened with the death penalty.[34]

Italy was one of the major centres of the European book trade, and these convulsions would radically reshape its publishing industry. This was a slow-building crisis: many Protestant books continued to circulate in Italy long after booksellers in the Low Countries had to fear for their lives. In 1540, Cardinal Morone's vicar described Modena as 'sullied, infected by different contagious heresies like Prague. In shops, street-corners, houses etc., everyone … argues about faith, free will, purgatory, the Eucharist and predestination.' Uneducated people could be seen 'theologising out of all proportion', according to another commentator.[35] Protestant sympathies flourished in Italy until around 1542, when it became clear that there was no chance for the Protestant and Catholic churches to be united, and several leading Italian theologians, like Bernardino Ochino, fled the country for Calvinist Switzerland. The response of the Catholic Church stiffened. While the Council of Trent was underway in 1559, Pope Paul IV issued the first papal *Index Auctorum et Librorum Prohibitorum* (Index of prohibited authors and books). This would be the first in a long series, complemented by separate indices issued by the Catholic universities of Louvain and the Sorbonne in Paris, as well as the Spanish Inquisition.[36]

The indices would become the most significant impediment

to the circulation of texts and the collecting of books. The lists included the names of authors whose works were entirely forbidden, books which were deemed heretical, as well as specific editions of orthodox texts condemned because they had been corrupted by heretical commentaries. The first Roman index also included a category of heretical printers, sixty-one in all, whose entire output, regardless of content, was suspect. Good Christians were supposed to surrender copies of these books from their libraries, while the production, sale and ownership of all texts listed in the index was strictly forbidden.

Publication of the first papal index was accompanied by substantial book burning, but mostly in Rome itself. Many secular authorities elsewhere in Italy were hesitant to put the full force of the index into effect. In Florence, Duke Cosimo de' Medici forbade the monks of San Marco from burning any books in their library which his predecessors had donated. Future indices relaxed the most sweeping prohibitions and placed more emphasis on the capacity of local inquisitors and bishops to grant exemptions for certain individuals to own dangerous books. Expurgation of texts was also considered, because that made large texts permissible by removing the few doctrinal errors they contained. The publication of some of Erasmus's works in Italy would be permitted after special expurgated editions were prepared, but this proved such an immense task that ultimately the papacy allowed collectors to expurgate their own copies.[37] Many copies survive today with large segments of texts crossed through or otherwise defaced. Between 1597 and 1603, the Inquisition carried out a survey of all books in Italian monasteries, to purge them of forbidden books. This systematic investigation of some 9,500 libraries provides a vivid demonstration of how entrenched library culture had become even in the smaller, poorer religious houses, as well as the new-found power of the church to shape the development of institutional book collecting.[38]

The influence of the indices was felt throughout the Catholic world including in the newly colonised Spanish possessions of Mexico, Guatemala, Nicaragua and the Philippines.[39] Despite local initiatives to circumvent the most stringent guidelines, the

8. An edition of the *Index librorum prohibitorum* (1758), a cornerstone of the Catholic response to the threat of Protestantism. The frontispiece of the book shows a pile of heretical books in flames.

indices also had a devastating impact on the book trade in Venice, Italy's principal mode of contact with the transalpine book market. The updated 1564 index prompted a period of intense persecution of heretical books.[40] But the most significant impact on the international trade came from the ban on the import of books published in Protestant centres of print. This meant that Italian publishers attending the major international book fairs could not take these books in exchange for their own publications, undermining the viability of the wholesale trade. By the early decades of the seventeenth century, the Venetians, until this point the largest contingent of foreign visitors, had virtually vanished from the Frankfurt fair, cutting off their access to the scientific and scholarly books produced by the northern centres of publishing.[41]

The uncompromising reaction of the papacy to the Reformation meant that libraries were devastated in unexpected ways. Jewish libraries were one victim of the repressive atmosphere of the second half of the sixteenth century. There were significant Jewish communities in Italy, most notably in Venice, which had become the global centre of Jewish book production in the sixteenth century. The Jews were identified as an unorthodox presence in the midst of Catholicism, and an easier target than the militant German Protestants beyond the Alps. A papal order of 12 August 1553 condemned the Talmud, one of the crucial sources of Jewish sacred law and theology. Burnings took place throughout Italy, and as far away as the Venetian territories in the eastern Mediterranean: many thousands of books were destroyed, most taken from Jewish homes and bookshops. Christians were also forbidden to possess or read the Talmud, or to help Jews publish their sacred texts, on pain of excommunication. In 1559, the great Hebrew school at Cremona was raided, and some 12,000 volumes were burned. Persecutions continued in Venice too, where tensions with the Ottomans persuaded the Venetians that local Jews were Turkish agents. In 1568, some 8,000 volumes were consigned to the flames, and others forcibly exported.

These waves of destructions severely curtailed the Jewish book trade, and Jewish book dealers prudently abandoned Venice for safer locations, most notably Amsterdam and Poland–Lithuania.

For Catholic printers, the bonfires also created new opportunities. The concluding decrees of the Council of Trent called for the revision of the Roman breviary, missal and catechism: all texts central to Catholic liturgy and devotion, which were in demand across the Catholic world. The Aldine press of Venice produced 20,000 copies of the *Officium Beatae Mariae Virginis*, a Book of Hours, in 1572 alone.

Commercial incentives were important to keep printers and booksellers content. Far less respect was paid to libraries, especially those, like the Hebrew school at Cremona, that were associated with religious divergence. Their fate often depended on the twists and turns of a fickle and turbulent political environment. The library of Philippe Duplessis-Mornay, an important Protestant writer, statesman and founder of the Huguenot Academy at Saumur, stands as an example for many. In 1621, King Louis XIII of France dismissed Duplessis-Mornay from his duties and royal troops ransacked his castle. His magnificent library was plundered, all silver clasps removed from their bindings, and many of the books thrown into the moat. A Catholic civil servant gleefully described how:

> These books, full of heresies and blasphemies, were in part thrown into the river Loire, in part burned, flung and scattered both around the castle and in the streets ... which were so covered in them that all one could see was books and papers. So they were all left to the mercies of those who followed the court and all the inhabitants ... This scattering of the books has given great heartache to Plessis-Mornay and great terror and rage to the Huguenots, and to Catholics a great joy.[42]

Institutional libraries, or semi-public libraries like that of Duplessis-Mornay, suffered so greatly because they were easy targets. Repressive action against small personal libraries, behind thousands of closed doors, was more difficult.[43] Institutional libraries were targeted by Protestants and Catholics alike, because both recognised the symbolic capital invested in them. These libraries functioned as archival storehouses, as repositories of knowledge and as meeting places. They gave shape to competing churches and fostered the spiritual health of their members. To destroy these institutions was to take one further step towards restoring unity in Christendom, the ultimate goal of every denomination, yet not all destruction needed to be as overt as book burnings. Locking up a library, reducing its contents to waste paper, or expurgating texts: these were the varied tools used to limit access to undesirable literature. In time, the missionary zeal of the separated Protestant and Catholic churches would inaugurate a new age of library building, with impressive results, but in the first two generations of the Reformation this was still some way in the future. To those who lived through the sixteenth century, theirs was an age in which great libraries found more enemies than friends.

PART THREE

THE NEW COLLECTORS

CHAPTER SEVEN

THE PROFESSIONALS

By 1550, one hundred years after the invention of printing, Europe was awash with books. More books had been created in the last hundred years than in the whole history of mankind to this point. So it is the greatest irony that the future of the library, as an institution and social construct, looked decidedly bleak at this point in history. Europe's rulers had more pressing concerns than to curate a library, and the major collections of the manuscript era had been dispersed or destroyed. The library of Fernando Colon, the first attempt to create a universal library in the new age of print, was shuttered and empty. In many parts of northern Europe, monasteries, the sanctuary of books through the darkest days of the first millennium, were ransacked and abandoned, their books scattered or destroyed. Even in Catholic Europe, where the role of monasteries was still respected, the traditional institutions faced fresh challenges from new, mobile orders such as the Jesuits. Even worse, the challenge to the traditional university curriculum posed by humanism and the Reformation seemed to render much of the content of existing libraries redundant.

It would be some time before institutional libraries found their role in this new world; in some parts of Europe, France for instance, universities did not build significant collections until the nineteenth century. But as ever, faced with disengagement on one front, libraries found a new role, as Europe's rising class of professionals eagerly embraced the opportunities of book ownership. It was here, in the personal collections of lawyers, civil servants, doctors, professors and ministers of the church, that the new products of Europe's buoyant book market found the warmest welcome.

These were men for whom the pleasures of book ownership were often a new experience. A century before, doctors and lawyers had not had the connections and the resources to build a collection of manuscripts; perhaps a volume of 'recipes' for a doctor, and a text of Justinian for the lawyer, but nothing approaching a library. Now the wonders of the new age of print were brought to their doorstep. This brought a transformation in the locus of the library. The creation of libraries became an urban phenomenon: these new classes of book owners were largely city dwellers. Sometimes the building of a library was the by-product of other intellectual concerns: the new obsession with archiving family papers, correspondence and financial documents, or the fascination with exploring the wealth of the classical and natural world reflected in the rage for cabinets of curiosities.[1] All of this required more space, and the laying out of additional funds.

This recalibration of the library, through the creation of thousands of personal collections, brought new challenges. Crowded together in the towns where they plied their trade, the new book owners had no dusty castle or monastic scriptorium in which to keep their books. Storage and display in family homes required new and urgent architectural solutions. Nevertheless, between 1550 and 1750 a library became ubiquitous in the home of the urban professional. This was the library's new sanctuary, and it would revolutionise the book world.

Market Forces

Most of those who built collections of books in the manuscript age relied heavily on the major centres of quasi-industrial production in Italy (Rome and Florence) or northern Europe (Paris and Bruges). In principle, manuscript books could be made anywhere, but the creation of a substantial collection required both money and access to a critical mass of texts. Many of the spectacular manuscripts that made their way to England in the fifteenth century came in the luggage of collectors who had visited Italy; Netherlandish workshops furnished others.[2]

By 1550, the world of print had built a whole new distribution network, cycling printed books from all of Europe's major centres of production through the international market. The effect of this in a place like England, in other respects very much on the periphery of Europe's book world, was startling. The printing industry remained comparatively small and wholly orientated to the domestic market, turning out a range of almanacs, ordinances for the crown and vernacular devotional works. When it came to any substantial Latin texts of jurisprudence or scholarship, London publishers could not compete with Paris, Lyon, Cologne or Basel. But as long as the books could be imported, English collectors hardly cared, and the booksellers of London, Oxford and Cambridge were perfectly happy to take the profits in supplying their needs.

Looking at the surviving documentation, it becomes very clear that English collectors could gather very substantial libraries without ever risking the perils of crossing the English Channel. We see this in the hundreds of inventories that have survived in the post-mortem documentation of property left in the sixteenth century. David Tolley, a physician, had built a library of some sixty-eight books at the time of his death in 1558. These were all in Latin and all printed on the continent. Thirty years later, Thomas Lorkin, a practising physician and Regius Professor of Medicine at the University of Cambridge, had built a collection of 589 books, including the newly fashionable chemical medicine of Paracelsus as well as a selection of the classics. A notable feature of these libraries is their range: Cambridge testators between them owned books by over 350 different medical authors. This was an age in which people worried incessantly about their health; most book owners, whatever their profession, owned at least a handful of medical books.[3]

Those who lived in sixteenth-century Oxford and Cambridge probably accumulated disproportionately large libraries, but this steady upward trajectory is clearly characteristic of English collecting more generally. The undistinguished Mr Mote, who died in 1592, had an extraordinarily fine collection of 500 books, and the London grocer Edward Barlow, his near contemporary, almost 200, most of his books being medical texts to support his apothecary shop.[4] The bibliophilic Thomas Barker, who arrived as a student in Cambridge in the Easter term of 1549, during the short reign of Edward VI, died within two months. Yet he left a library of seventy-five books, including a Greek dictionary, the works of Hippocrates and the *Moriae Encomium* of Erasmus; he was one of thirty-one Cambridge testators to own this book.[5] His scanty possessions otherwise comprised only his clothing, and a large chest with lock and key, presumably to house his books.

Most of these owners were either scholars, or professional men with a university education. But merchants, too, delved into the world of learning, especially when, like the aspiring author Gerard Malynes, they had a point to make and were prepared to take to print to make it. The books he published in an attempt to influence government policy on international trade were stuffed full of references to the medieval jurists, as well as a range of classical authors. He had wide acquaintance with the works of Aristotle, as well as the geographers Ptolemy and Strabo, and the Roman historians. He had read Thomas More's *Utopia* and Chaucer as well as the voyages of Drake and Cavendish, and was aware of Copernicus, but like most contemporaries dismissed his theories as 'imaginary mathematics'.[6]

This was truly a new age in terms of collecting: compared to the manuscript era of the fifteenth century, these are remarkable libraries. But move forward another hundred years, hop across the English Channel, and we will see libraries of an entirely different order. By the middle of the seventeenth century a new power had risen on the ruins of the Habsburg possessions of the Netherlands, the Dutch Republic. This was Europe's most urbanised state, with the most literate population and a buoyant economy. It had also, to the frustration of the established giants in France, Italy and Germany, become the centre of the international book market. Books from all over Europe arrived in Amsterdam to feed the hungry domestic market, and for onward dispatch to England and Scotland. Leiden, Europe's most glittering new Protestant university, became a major centre of scholarly publishing. Thanks to its advanced system of internal transportation, the newly completed canal network, books could be printed almost anywhere

9. The Dutch theologian Jacobus Taurinus (1576–1618) stands proudly in front of his library. In the seventeenth-century Dutch Republic, it was not unusual for ministers to own hundreds, if not thousands of volumes. These libraries were often larger than the local institutional libraries, and functioned as private as well as communal collections.

in Holland and swiftly supplied to their customers. Per capita, the Dutch bought, published and read more books than in any other part of Europe, and they created some of the most exquisite libraries.[7]

The collectors of the Dutch Republic deviated sharply from the patterns of the late Middle Ages. There was not much in the way of a local nobility, and what there was had little influence. This nation of traders and fishermen soon spawned a sophisticated professional class of well-educated lawyers, physicians and state officials, and most of them collected books. These collections were initially a professional tool, as in England. But men of this stamp did not abandon the classical learning of their days in high school and university. The Dutch Republic witnessed a new efflorescence of the classics, the publishers of Amsterdam and Leiden turning out new editions of the Greek philosophers and Roman historians and rhetoricians almost annually. This market demanded multiple editions in all sizes: stately folios for the library, substantial quartos for study and tiny pocket editions to carry in their travel bag or read on the barge, a curiously democratic form of transport where the lawyer would rub shoulders with the farmer or the midwife.[8]

This new professional elite assembled collections of an astonishing size. Daniel Heinsius was one of the leading scholars of the Republic and his collection of 4,000 books was not especially remarkable, though the 15,000 guilders (the equivalent of thirty years' annual salary for a minister) for which it sold at auction in 1656 was a record for the mid seventeenth century. More surprising was that his son Nicolaas Heinsius could create a new collection three times this size in the next twenty-five years. Its auction in 1682 raised 24,708 guilders, and no wonder: this collection of 13,000 books was at this time as large as the libraries of all five Dutch universities put together.

In many ways most astonishing was the collection of Cornelis Nicolai, the son of a burgomaster of Amsterdam. Although Nicolai was only twenty-four at the time of his tragically early death in 1698, he had still amassed a collection of some 4,300 books worth 11,000 guilders. These were men deeply embedded in the networks of the international scholarly elite, yet men who collected purely for professional reasons also assembled collections that a century before would have been unthinkable. We can reconstruct the collections of at least 340 men who earned their living as doctors or lawyers in the seventeenth-century Dutch Republic.[9] Their collections ranged in size from the modest 265 books owned by Isaac van Bebber, who practised medicine in Dordrecht, to the 3,572 books owned by Abraham van der Meer in The Hague. The average size of these collections was around 1,000 books.

These were learned men: 75 per cent of the books owned by the lawyers and doctors were in Latin or Greek, a higher proportion, indeed, than the books owned by ministers of the church. The Leiden brewer Johannes de Planque left a collection of more than 1,000 books at his death in 1698; there were many more vernacular books in this collection, and many more books in small formats, but this was nevertheless still a remarkable library. This was a world where a library of 250 books, which would have been quite special a hundred years before, was now unremarkable; and this applies not only to the Dutch Republic, but other busy urban communities, in Germany, Switzerland, France and Italy, as well.[10] This transformation owed a great deal to a remarkable innovation in the book market, almost as significant for the development of libraries as printing itself: the book auction.

Under the Hammer

Books had been sold at auction with the furniture, clothing and other possessions of deceased householders since the fifteenth century.[11] But the Dutch were the first to separate out the sale of books and put the trade entirely in the hands of the book industry. Equally important, from an early date every auction was accompanied by a printed catalogue, with each volume carefully listed as a separate lot. The first such catalogue was for the auction of the books of Philip van Marnix, companion of William of Orange and hero of the Dutch Revolt, who died in 1598. Thereafter the printed catalogue became a ubiquitous aspect of book auctions; in some Dutch cities a printed catalogue was made a legal requirement. There were at least 4,000 book auctions in the Netherlands in the seventeenth century, and catalogues survive for at least half of these. They are a goldmine of information on the ownership and sale of at least 2 million books. Here, and elsewhere in Europe where auctions were adopted, they had a profound impact on the book market, and one very much to the advantage of collectors. Crucially, you no longer had to visit the bookshop to make purchases. The printed catalogues were distributed widely, often outside the borders of the Dutch Republic; collectors would bid through friends, or by letter.[12] The catalogues had a long afterlife, as even if they did not bid, the owners of libraries could use these catalogues to shape their future collecting, marking the books they desired or already possessed. For the serious collector, the most prized copies were those marked up with the prices raised at the auction. It is significant that of the 2,000 surviving Dutch catalogues, fewer than 10 per cent are today in a Dutch library; the rest were scattered round the continent, where they had been dispatched to connoisseurs and librarians to keep them abreast of the market-place.

Booksellers had initially not welcomed the new book auctions, until they realised how much opportunity it provided for them to make money. Booksellers assessed collections, compiled the catalogues and sold them in their shops, taking 5–15 per cent commission on sales. They even, less creditably, infiltrated some of their own slow-moving stock into the sale, where it could be passed off as part of the distinguished library going under the hammer. This process was widely deplored, frequently prohibited, but thought to be ubiquitous.

Auctions helped collectors build their libraries more quickly, and with a clear conscience. Collectors are always greedy, sometimes unscrupulous and often selfish. Auctions not only provided huge new opportunities to buy, but also allowed collectors to salve their conscience with the thought that their heirs could easily realise the value of their books after their death. This was indeed the case. Books seem to have held their value remarkably well, and often sold for much the same prices for which they were purchased twenty or thirty years before.[13] Sometimes they would go for a higher price, particularly if the owner had had them elegantly bound. A doctor or minister could invest in a desired title, secure in the knowledge that his grieving widow and children would quickly recover the money spent: all the more so as auctions were strictly cash sales, so the family got the money quickly. There were none of the otherwise crippling problems of collecting money owed in an industry that functioned very largely through credit and debt, a problem that bedevilled many apparently well-established publishers.[14] Books were a necessary part of professional lives; they could also be seen as prudent pension planning.

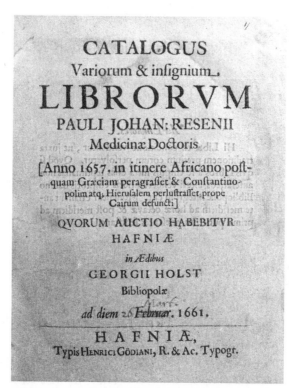

CATALOGUS
Variorum & infignium
LIBRORVM
PAULI JOHAN: RESENII
Medicinæ Doctoris

[Anno 1657. in itinere Africano poft-
quam Græciam peragraffet & Conftantino-
polim atq; Hierufalem perluftraffet, prope
Cairum defuncti]

QVORUM AUCTIO HABEBITVR
HAFNIÆ

in Ædibus
GEORGII HOLST
Bibliopolæ
ad diem 26 Februar. 1661,

HAFNIÆ,
Typis Henrici Gödiani, R. & Ac. Typogr.

10. Printed auction catalogues, like this Danish example (1661), were
a useful tool for auctioneers and book buyers alike. They facilitated
the dispersal of personal libraries, and consequently the catalogues
are often the only trace that we have left of the collections that graced
thousands of homes in the seventeenth and eighteenth centuries.

This was a pragmatic market. Scanning the prices paid, there
seems to have been no real premium for the fact that the book
came from a distinguished library. The one exception was the
books of the leading philologists and scholars, like Daniel or Nicolaas Heinsius, where a purchaser might find valuable marginalia.
Otherwise books did not accrue extra value if they were particularly old, or almost new. Professional collectors wanted the text in
an edition of appropriate size and quality; the birth of an antiquarian market, when books from the first age of print were collected
for their significance in the history of printing, was still to come.
Around 1700, on a slow day in the auction house, you might still
pick up a couple of undistinguished fifteenth-century books for
the price of a jug of ale.[15]

Auctions lubricated a book market which, to this point, had threatened to be buried under a mountain of unsaleable stock. It also gives us a window on to a part of the book world that would otherwise be largely hidden. In these catalogues we have a mass of information on how the newly prosperous inhabitants of this precocious urban society conducted their affairs, expanded their intellectual horizons and occupied their leisure hours. This was a society that, if not exactly embarrassed by their wealth, knew that calamity could strike at any moment. Their books, mixing professional tools with books of religious consolation and medical remedies, reflected a pragmatic mixture of hope and anxiety in the face of life's unpredictable misfortunes.

Preaching and Its Profits

Among the new generation of collectors, we must not ignore one very important component of this new buying public: ministers of the church and university professors (often overlapping categories as the universities were still largely religious institutions). These collections often ran to several hundred, and sometimes more than a thousand books, provoking the obvious question of how ministers were able to afford them. Clerical salaries in the Dutch Republic were not all that generous: one, sadly anonymous minister, published a plaintive pamphlet in 1658, carefully enumerating his outgoings for food, clothing and other domestic needs. At the end of this extraordinarily detailed calculation, virtually nothing was left for newspapers, writing paper, pens, ink and books: just 25 guilders a year. This might buy you forty pamphlets and a book of psalms, or three decent folios.[16]

The pamphlet struck a sufficient chord with the clerical brotherhood that it demanded an almost immediate reprint, but the truth was that a minister's income was seldom limited to their salary alone. Parishioners might bring gifts of food or livestock; a market garden or smallholding might reduce outgoings for meat, milk, butter and vegetables. Ministers were also provided with free accommodation, which might be a generously sized town house. The most able ministers could take in students from the local grammar school or university as boarders, and even offer private tuition. This was a privilege so notoriously abused by university professors that they sometimes had to be admonished for ignoring their lectures to teach these more lucrative tutorials. City preachers were in any case paid well above the basic salary, and if they coupled these responsibilities with some work lecturing in the local university they might earn well over 1,000 guilders, double the normal clerical stipend.

Ministers were also often authors, and so familiar visitors in the print shops. Many books came to them as gifts, or as thanks for services rendered, proofreading sheets in unfamiliar languages or persuading a friend to offer their text to a particular publisher. Authors very frequently received copies of their own books in lieu of royalty: these could be exchanged with the books of friends.

When we layer on these extra sources of income, a library of 1,000 or more books becomes more understandable. But this was still an extraordinary advance on the clerical collections of the first generation of print. When Johannes de Platea, canon of cathedral chapters in Mechelen, Bruges and Den Bosch, died in 1489, he left sixty-nine books, consisting of fifty-nine manuscripts and only six printed books (the other four cannot be clearly identified). De Platea was a senior official at a wealthy diocese: the libraries of other canons dying in the 1470s and 1480s number thirty-five and twenty-six books.[17] All of these were senior clerics attached to a cathedral: many parish priests would probably have had access to no books other than the Mass books in church. In the early days of the Reformation, a time of febrile publishing, the library of Huldrych Zwingli, the leading figure of the Protestant Church in Zurich, amounted to no more than 250 titles, though admittedly his collecting was cut short by an ill-judged sortie on to the battlefield at Kappel, where he was killed. A not inconsiderable part of this library consisted of the works of Martin Luther, obtained so he could refute them.[18] Even Conrad Gessner, the creator of the first published survey of the history of book publishing, the *Bibliotheca Universalis*, owned only around 400 books. This tight-knit Zurich circle borrowed books from each other: 100 titles in Gessner's own copy of the *Bibliotheca* are annotated with the names of owners who loaned him crucial texts.[19]

In the Dutch Republic, a hundred years later, this was very different. Abraham Heidanus, professor of theology at Leiden and a leading controversialist, left a collection of 3,700 books, sold at auction for 10,000 guilders, twenty times the base ministerial salary. André Rivet, despite a varied and peripatetic career, assembled a collection of 4,800 books, which raised 9,100 guilders at auction in 1657. These were major public figures, and Rivet, who served a term as court preacher to Prince Frederick Henry of Orange, earned a suitably princely salary. But a collection of 1,000 books or more was relatively commonplace. A recent investigation of some 450 ministerial collections sold at auction in the seventeenth-century Dutch Republic finds an average size of 1,144 books.[20] Obviously, these were the collections sufficiently distinguished to merit a separate sale and a printed catalogue, but this sample represents something close to 10 per cent of all the ministers serving in the Dutch Reformed Church during the course of the century. Many ministers would have had far fewer books: but few would have been without a working library of some sort.

What, for instance, are we to make of Johannes Lydius, minister of Oudewater, a relatively small community in south Holland? Lydius had made a disadvantageous marriage and had three children to support: in his correspondence he bitterly lamented that he could not afford more books. He still put together an impressive collection of 1,747 titles. His resentment can only be explained by the fact that his brother Balthazar and nephew Jacob each had magnificent libraries of more than 5,000 volumes.[21] Lydius, despite his self-proclaimed poverty, clearly had access to that web of connections that allowed ministers to accumulate such fine collections: exchanging new publications, passing on recently published pamphlets, bidding for each other at auction. Rivet, operating at the top of the market, could prevail upon the Elzeviers of Leiden and Amsterdam, by this time one of Europe's leading publishing houses, to attend auctions on his behalf, and friends abroad performed similar services. This deep connection with the world of books helps explain why ministerial libraries were, on average, slightly larger than those of the other learned professions, despite a lower income.

A Place of Their Own

In the 1580s, Claes Cornelisz was one of Leiden's five apothecaries, and he made a good living. After his death in 1586 and that of his wife the following year, an inventory was made of their possessions. This reveals that the family owned sixty-five 'large and small, good and bad' books, all kept in an Oriental chest in the attic of their home. In the shop itself there were eight medicinal books, an unknown chained book and a Greek grammar; in the living room of the house there were several herb books and Cicero's *De officiis*.[22] This medieval practice of storing books in a chest proved surprisingly tenacious, though the books were not always consigned to the attic. In households where books did not have to be consulted daily, solid wooden chests offered maximum protection for what were precious possessions; often they shared space in the chests with important documents, account books and other valuables. Collections of 200 books could comfortably be stored in this way, and the provision of additional chests allowed for some rudimentary classification. It was also very common, as in the house of Claes Cornelisz, for books to be spread around several rooms. The most frequently used might never have a more permanent place of storage than a convenient tabletop.

Once collections grew from the low hundreds towards 1,000, this was clearly no longer an appropriate way to store books, particularly if they were in regular use. A collection of 1,000 or more was also a powerful statement of one's wealth and intellectual credentials, but only if the books were visible. The first to confront this issue was that generation of sixteenth-century scholars and intellectuals who became self-conscious collectors: not just of books, but of coins, medals, statuettes, shells, dried plants, stuffed animals, stones and minerals. Books were rarely the main point of such a collection, but necessary as a reference tool in building a distinguished cabinet of curiosities. This was certainly the case with Ulisse Aldrovandi (1522–1605), professor of natural philosophy and natural history at Bologna, and one of the foremost collectors of his day. Aldrovandi created a museum of natural history that became a popular destination for travellers in Italy. To support his work, Aldrovandi also gathered together one of the greatest libraries of his age. At his death he owned 3,598 volumes, including 992 volumes of folios. He had two library rooms, only accessible from his museum room, for which he had appropriated the main reception room in the house; their role was to provide a private haven from visitors in a house which had become a public exhibit.[23]

We can say frustratingly little about the physical space the pragmatic professional men of the Dutch Republic allocated to their libraries. We have little in the way of architectural drawings; it is hard to know how far the gracious houses of the Herengracht, in Amsterdam's new canal quarter, made provision for books. Books are not a conspicuous feature of the elegant interiors pictured in Dutch paintings; we have pictures of the scholar in their study or the student in their garret, with a few books tumbled about, but no clue how 1,000 volumes would be stored. Doctors and lawyers would not have needed a book-lined study to impress their clients, since they would normally have attended on them in the clients' own homes. Most likely a writing desk or bureau was set up in one of the public rooms, or the dressing room of the mistress of the house.

Where ministers were concerned, we can be reasonably confident that shelves had superseded book chests as the preferred method of book storage. A whole series of engraved portraits of leading figures in the Reformed Church show them standing in front of a well-ordered bookcase. Of course, this was a figurative claim to learning rather than a photograph, and the engravings are suspiciously uniform in their design. A conspicuous feature of these pictures is the presence of a curtain half drawn back to reveal the books. This curtain seems to be a feature of the transition from chests to shelves. Removed from the security of the chest, the curtain offered some protection from dust and wandering fingers. It was not uncommon to protect a cabinet of curiosities in the same way.

The parochial house often provided room for more books

than a minister would be able to afford. There was also the opportunity to store books in the church itself. A Lutheran diarist in the Thirty Years' War recorded his distress when a marauding Swedish army passed through his town. The inhabitants had taken refuge in the woods, but when they returned the pastor found that the Swedish army chaplain had made off with thirty-two valuable books from his collection, housed in the church vestry.[24] Schoolmasters also commonly kept a small stock of texts to sell to pupils in the schoolhouse, and probably their own working library as well. The rectors of the Dutch Latin schools built substantial collections: 1,900 books in the case of Paulus Junius, rector of the Leiden Latin school. On his death the books sold at auction for 4,500 guilders.

Overall, these scattered scraps of evidence suggest that the scholars and professional men who required many books still had to improvise solutions for their storage, balancing accessibility and security. Among the most inventive solutions were those adopted by the English philosophers Thomas Hobbes and John Locke, who both found ways of outsourcing the housing of their working collection.[25] Hobbes spent much of his life in the service of the Cavendish family of the Earl of Newcastle, successively as tutor, family adviser, librarian and elderly retainer, an arrangement that worked for all parties. Hobbes brought intellectual kudos to his aristocratic hosts, who built a substantial library of 2,000 books for Hobbes's use in their house at Hardwick Hall in Derbyshire. Locke, too, found his career as an aristocratic client, first as personal physician to the later Earl of Shaftesbury, a leading Whig politician, later as his intellectual apologist. In consequence Locke would share Shaftesbury's fall from grace, with five years of exile in the Netherlands. On his return in 1688, Locke took rooms with friends in Essex, apparently as a paying guest. Perhaps not wishing to concede that this was a permanent arrangement, the Marshams did not provide shelving. The books remained in chests in Locke's work room and in the attic for the rest of his life.[26]

Legacy

Gian Vincenzo Pinelli was one of the great collectors of the six-teenth century, so it is rather unfair that his library should today be remembered less for its contents that for the chaotic nature of its post-mortem dispersal. A polymath with an expertise in botany and mathematics as well as a keen artistic eye, Pinelli built during his lifetime a collection of over 6,000 books and many precious manuscripts.[27] His fame reached across Europe, and it is a testa-ment to the efficiency of his network of correspondence that Pinelli was able to build his library without leaving the safety of his own home. This also makes it less surprising that his biography, probably the first to be written of a distinguished book collector of the print era, should be published not in Padua, where he lived and died, but in the German city of Augsburg.[28]

Pinelli intended that on his death his books should be the foun-dation of a new library close to the family seat at Giuliano outside Naples, an eternal testament to his learning, and a major resource in a part of Europe not particularly well stocked with libraries. Alas, none of this would come to pass.[29] Like Fernando Colon, Pinelli's heir was a nephew and, also like Colon, the nephew would prove to be no help in carrying out his uncle's great endeavour. Even before the books could be crated for transportation to Naples, the Venetian authorities intervened to remove some manuscripts which, they claimed, contained state secrets. The books were then allowed to depart, packed into 130 chests divided between three ships, only for one to be intercepted by Turkish pirates. Disap-pointed that their booty was nothing more than printed sheets, they tossed several of the crates overboard. Eventually the books reached Giuliano, but the heir died shortly thereafter. The books disappeared from view, but not from the intelligence network of Cardinal Federico Borromeo, eager to find distinguished manu-scripts for his new public library in Milan. An agent dispatched to secure them found the remaining stock much degraded by water damage. A farcical sale overseen by a judge to ensure fair dealing for the litigious relatives brought no clear conclusion, and it was only after further negotiation and some double dealing by a local bookseller that Borromeo could make his bargain. What remained serviceable was put back into its boxes to join the stock of the Ambrosiana library in Milan.

In 1601, when Pinelli died, his was the greatest private library in Europe. That a man of his distinction could not crown his life's work by determining its post-mortem fate boded ill for humbler collectors keen that their library should become their memorial. Broadly speaking, collectors could choose between four strategies for the disposal of their books. First, and most expensive, they could establish their books as a public collection, with a sufficient endowment to provide suitable accommodation and maintenance. This was very rare, and could often end in catastrophe, as we have seen with both Pinelli and Fernando Colon, though it did not stop collectors from attempting it.[30]

More affordably, collectors could leave their books to an existing library. Sometimes this worked, though proud owners would all too often impose conditions that were too expensive to meet, such that the books should be housed together, or new rooms built to display them. Ulisse Aldrovandi of Bologna was one who just about managed it: having left his books to the city, they were moved after a twelve-year delay to new quarters in the public *palazzo*.[31] Aldrovandi was Bologna's leading public intellectual, and an adornment of a distinguished university which at this point was losing ground to rivals in northern Europe, so naturally the city fathers wanted to keep alive the memory of such distinguished scholar. William Harvey secured the future of his collection in the library of the Royal College of Physicians by including the gift of his patrimonial estate at Burmarsh as an endowment for a new library building and the upkeep of the collection. Unfortunately, the library was burned to the ground in the Great Fire of London (1666), taking Harvey's collection with it.[32]

The third and most obvious strategy was to leave the collection to one's family or friends in the hope that they would cherish it. Often they did not. John Locke repaid the generosity of the Marshams with the gift of half his collection. Sadly, they proved not to be bookish, and the portion of the library left to the family was dissipated by successive generations, most dramatically when, as reported in the *Critical Review*:

> About the year 1762, when the late Lord Marsham married his second lady, his lordship thought proper to remove the useless volumes of ancient learning, part of the library which had been bequeathed to the family by John Locke, and the manuscripts of Dr Cudworth, to make room for books of polite amusement.[33]

The *Critical Review* damned Lord Marsham as 'the right honourable Goth', though his family had provided houseroom for the books for the best part of a century, and one can see why polite amusement might have its attractions. The other half of Locke's library, left to his friend Peter King, moved from house to house of the soon ennobled family, and eventually to the Torridon estate at Achnasheen in the Highlands of Scotland, where it would not have received many scholarly visitors. From here the books most clearly identified as belonging to the Locke library were sold to Paul Getty, on whose death they were donated to the Bodleian Library in Oxford.

Lastly, one could simply realise the value of the books, either during one's lifetime or by leaving the task to a grieving widow or children. This worked well in the Dutch Republic, where a public auction ensured fair dealing, but less well where auctions were less well established, and booksellers could offer a fraction of the library's value to take the collection off the hands of its owners. Faced by this litany of ill-fortune, one can see how clever Erasmus had been to secure both the value and the use of his books, even if his library was also soon dispersed in the hands of its new owner.

The essential problem was one that has not changed through the history of collecting, from Alexandria to the present: no one cares about a library collection as much as the person who has assembled it. Only the library's creator records the place of a fortuitous purchase, the identity of kind donors, or remembers how a particular text changed their lives or opinions. Only they experienced the joy of tracking down a long-desired edition, and the network of friends that helped in the quest.

Shorn of these personal connections, the books retained their financial but not emotional value. Sometimes the heirs already had a portion of the same texts, or wanted to take their own collection in a different direction. Institutional libraries had their own space problems, and for librarians who would much have preferred to be professors, the work of receiving and examining gifts greatly outweighed the benefits of new accessions. It required a librarian of the energy of Thomas Bartholin of Copenhagen to see the potential in such donations. In 1675 he was able to oversee an auction of over 3,000 duplicates from collections offered to the university library by civic-minded Copenhagen residents, which raised a considerable sum with which to buy new books. Sadly, Bartholin, an eminent scholar in his own right, did not have the problem of deciding what to do with his own distinguished library, since the whole collection was lost when his house burned down, an event which at the time was regarded as a national scientific catastrophe.

Fire, neglect, assault by pirates, ungrateful heirs, careless nephews: the transition of a library from working tool to intellectual monument was strewn with so many pitfalls that it is no wonder that few collections survived to memorialise a stratum of collecting that was, at the time, essential to the history of the library. Historians necessarily privilege that for which they have evidence, and in the case of libraries it is often the most static collections that attract the most attention, preserved as much through lack of use as through being particularly cherished. This may help explain why royal collections and books of the nobility loom so large in the history of collecting in the pre-modern era.[34] Large estates and generously proportioned baronial houses provided plenty of space where books could be stored and often then forgotten. From the seventeenth century onwards the English nobility were engaged on a systematic programme of remodelling the houses and gardens of their country estates, a practice which now routinely included the incorporation of a library close to the ground-floor state rooms. Books with rich ancestral armorial stamps and expensive bindings would become a valued feature of these expanding collections, and aristocratic patronage of the auction room became a major stimulus to the booming antiquarian market in the eighteenth century.[35]

In contrast, the death of a doctor or lawyer, even one enjoying a reasonable affluence, often uprooted the whole family; this was certainly the case with the wife and children of the clergy who would be obliged to leave the parish rectory. Even if the family were able to remain, the heirs might be less tolerant of the professional clutter of an occupation that they had chosen not to follow. So most of these professional libraries were broken up, dispersed or sold without much ceremony and without leaving a record. If they were sold to a bookseller to add to general stock, they would have disappeared altogether. It is only thanks to the printed auction catalogues that so many collections can now be reconstructed; collections, it must be said, much more heavily used than the inherited library of many a noble house. Yet what these printed catalogues, themselves often extremely rare, reveal to us is a critical moment in the history of collecting, when private individuals of less than extraordinary wealth assembled libraries that were bigger than many of the institutional collections of their day. In the process, they preserved the library as a concept for the generations who would follow.

CHAPTER EIGHT

IDLE BOOKS AND RIFF RAFF

In 1598, the University of Oxford received an extraordinary proposal. Sir Thomas Bodley, a retired diplomat and Oxford alumnus,
offered to restore the dilapidated university library, entirely at
his own cost. He promised to make the library 'handsome with
seates and shelfes and deskes and all that may be needful to stirre
up other mens benevolence, to helpe furnish it with bookes'.[1] The
library hall had stood vacant for several decades, its books removed
during the upheavals of the Reformation, its furniture sold off in
1556. When Bodley turned his attention to the library, it was in use
only as a lecture hall.

Over the course of fifteen years, until his death in 1613, Bodley
would oversee the transformation of Oxford's library from this
empty shell to the finest institutional library in Europe. First the
building itself had to be repaired, not least its roof. By June 1600 the
hall was fitted out with oak bookcases with integral reading desks.
On 8 November 1602, the library was inaugurated with a collection
of over 2,000 volumes. By 1605, when the first published catalogue
of the collection appeared, it had 5,600 volumes; fifteen years later
the collection had quadrupled in size, to 23,000. This extraordinary growth was the result of Bodley's uncompromising ambition,
combined with impeccable scholarly and political connections.
He solicited donations from his network of fellow statesmen and
diplomats, and his friends gave liberally, among them Sir Walter
Raleigh, who would soon be languishing in the Tower of London,
and Robert Sidney, the Earl of Leicester. The Earl of Essex gave
books instead of money, as he had recently acquired 252 volumes
from the library of a bishop in Faro, Portugal, that he had plundered on his return from naval engagement against the Spanish

crown. Bodley contributed most of the funds from his own deep
pockets, padded by the fortunes of a wealthy Devon widow who
had succumbed to his charms some years earlier.[2]

The fact that Bodley could raise the status of Oxford's library
so rapidly is also indicative of the poor conditions of university
libraries throughout Europe. Most universities were founded
without a library. Some, like Louvain and St Andrews, had several
college libraries, but lacked a central university library for almost
two centuries after their foundation. The Sorbonne at Paris had
no central library until 1762, 500 years after it was first established.
Others, like Oxford, assembled a library in the medieval period,
but saw their libraries damaged, confiscated or destroyed in the
early upheavals of the Reformation.

The convulsions of the sixteenth century left a lasting impression. In 1605, Francis Bacon thanked Bodley for building 'an ark to
save learning from the deluge'.[3] Scholars on the continent, Catholic and Protestant, felt similarly, and by around 1600, universities,
new and old, began to acquire libraries. Yet the purpose of these
institutional libraries, what books would be in them, and, crucially, who would pay for them, were contentious issues, in many
cases inadequately resolved. In 1710, the German scholar Zacharias
von Uffenbach observed that 'Large works, those that not everyone can buy, should be bought [for university libraries]; the little
books anyone can collect as they wish'.[4] This was a widely shared
view. As we have seen in the last chapter, professors were part of a
new book-buying elite and enjoyed building their own substantial
libraries: in many towns the libraries of professors would be much
larger than the library of the university. The rise of a lively auction
market ensured that many collectors sold their libraries, rather
than donating the books to their local institution. Yet even when
they did bequeath their books, it was never guaranteed that any
would be consulted by future readers. Changing university curric-
ula and new models of thought were as great a threat to the success
of a library as was destruction by fire or sword. How universities
chose to navigate these issues would have a lasting influence on the
future of the institutional library.

Kindling a Flame

Thomas Bodley was without doubt a visionary. A child of exile during the reign of the Catholic Queen Mary, he had seen many scholars scattered to the winds, their libraries confiscated or abandoned in their haste to depart. He enjoyed a superb education in Geneva and Oxford that had instilled in him the value of books, but he also understood that libraries could not survive if one did not plan for their future, so that the initial enthusiasm did not die with its founder. Bodley, it seemed, had learned the lessons from the failures of earlier collectors: he ensured that his library would be provided with a substantial endowment, of land and property rents, to acquire books. This was key if the library was to remain supplied with the latest scholarly publications; he was rightly convinced that it was the absence of this provision that had caused so many ambitious library projects to atrophy.

A second key provision was the prohibition on borrowing books from the library. University libraries regularly struggled with the loss of books, often taken home by professors, sometimes by visitors. Once the books left they rarely returned. Oxford's blanket ban on lending was maintained after Bodley's death and upheld even in the face of requests to borrow books from both King Charles I and the Lord Protector, Oliver Cromwell. Bodley also insisted that the Bodleian Library should welcome readers, and not only those from Oxford. This was perhaps the most significant aspect of Bodley's vision. Thus far, university or college libraries had largely been for the use only of the scholars employed at that institution. Some distinguished visitors might be granted access, but always by invitation only. Bodley inverted this rule, and although he cautioned against letting new undergraduate students into the library, visiting scholars were welcome to use the library's resources.

Within the first year of the Bodleian's establishment, it welcomed a remarkable 248 visitors, including scholars from France, Denmark, Silesia, Prussia, Switzerland and Saxony. Over time their number would grow, especially to consult the Bodleian's substantial collection of manuscripts. Bodley rightly considered that manuscripts, rather than printed books, would be the greatest attraction of the library. Manuscripts were essential for the work of theologians and humanist scholars, but were naturally much rarer. Few libraries had large collections, and access was tightly controlled, but the status of the Bodleian ensured that it received significant bequests of manuscript collections, such as that from Archbishop William Laud, who gave 1,300 manuscripts to the library between 1635 and 1640.[5] Such large donations were supplemented by the Bodleian's generous acquisitions budget. Within half a century it had an unrivalled collection of Oriental, Anglo-Saxon and northern European manuscripts.

Few of the foreign visitors left their impressions of working at the Bodleian. Although more than one noted the absence of Oxford's resident scholars from the library, on the whole visitors had little to complain about: the hours were extremely generous, the library being open for an unprecedented six hours each day at a time when most other institutional libraries, if they were open at all, offered readers only four hours a week. Bodley was adamant in his instructions that the library should never be closed, and this too was followed to the letter.

Bodley envisioned that his library should be composed of serious books, ordered according to the traditional hierarchy of university faculties: theology, jurisprudence, medicine and the higher arts (philosophy, history, logic, grammar and mathematics). He also saw the value in buying books in what were, at the time, little-known foreign languages: his first commission to two London booksellers included works in Hungarian, Persian and Chinese. But, nonetheless, Bodley did not want to clutter the shelves of the library with what he viewed to be 'idle books and riffe raffes' – by which he meant books in the English language.[6] Almanacs and other ephemera, as well as play books, were not to be accessioned. He conceded that some of the milestones of European literature, like *Don Quixote*, could be bought, but certainly not Shakespeare, then at the height of his activity.

Ultimately, Bodley did not get his way, and the embargo on buying English books was not continued after his death. Indeed, had it been continued, it would have made one of Bodley's other achievements rather pointless: he had extracted from the

Stationers' Company, the cartel of London publishers that dominated the English book trade, an agreement to send one copy of each of their new books to the library. Another early rule, the exclusion of junior members of the university, was also abandoned after Bodley's death. A more lasting principle that Bodley introduced was a rule of silence – perhaps the first modern instance of this, and very different from the noisy conviviality of the Renaissance court libraries. By 1711 the rule of silence had been adopted more generally, most fervently in Amsterdam, where the user of the library was greeted by this severe warning in verse:

> You learned sir, who enter among books,
> don't slam the door with your tumultuous hand;
> nor let your rowdy foot create a bang,
> a nuisance to the Muse. Then, if you see someone
> seated within, greet him by bowing,
> and with a silent nod: nor waffle gossip:
> here it's the dead who speak to them who work.[7]

Bodley was assembling a modern collection that drew heavily on the scholarly culture of humanism, but sober Protestant that he was, his vision of the library also owed a great deal to the medieval scriptorium. There was the silence, and the provision of individual work benches. More punishingly, there was the cold. The strict embargo on kindling 'any fire or flame' (still recited aloud by new readers to this day), made work conditions gruelling in winter, and probably contributed to the deaths of some of the more determined readers; but it did save the Bodleian from destruction by fire, a fate common to many libraries in northern Europe (and later Harvard, in North America).[8]

Thomas Bodley was only the first of many powerful personalities associated with the library: his first librarian, the theologian Thomas James, was almost as influential. James had taken on the assignment as Bodley's librarian in order to conduct his own research on patristic texts, but he seriously underestimated Bodley's ambition, as much as the incessant demands with which he tormented his librarian.[9] The large number of visitors and the endless flow of new books left James little time for his own work. He was also responsible for the first comprehensive catalogues of the collection, an aspect of the librarian's work in which he excelled. The two catalogues that he produced appeared in print in 1605 and 1620. Although they were not the first printed catalogues of library collections in Europe, those of the Bodleian would resonate through the European book world, influencing the contents of libraries throughout the continent for the next two centuries.

To this point, England was a substantial net importer of books, yet by 1606 a copy of the first catalogue had already found its way to the small town of Freiberg in Saxony, its binding stamped with the local coat of arms.[10] These Oxford catalogues were used by many other institutions and private owners to shape their own collecting. The third catalogue, published in 1674 by librarian Thomas Hyde, was printed in two folio volumes, replete with numerous cross references; this was a masterpiece of bibliography as well as testimony to the continued rapid growth of the collection.[11] Numerous other institutions used a copy of this 1674 edition as their own catalogue, including some of the Oxford colleges, the University of Cambridge and the Mazarine library in Paris.[12] Private collectors who did the same included the philosopher John Locke, who used interleaved sheets to note the books that he owned which were not in the Bodleian. Of the 3,641 books he is known to have possessed, 3,197 were also available at the Bodleian.[13] The requirement that any newly registered reader should purchase a copy certainly helped sales, but the European-wide reach of the catalogue, was, for the time, unique.[14]

Ironically, at precisely the time when the 1674 catalogue inspired collectors across Europe, Bodley's library lost some of its momentum. Despairing of ever receiving the increased salary promised him for compiling the new catalogue, Thomas Hyde turned increasingly to his own scholarly endeavours. Scholars even took the opportunity to remove some books from the library to their own chambers, where a cheerful fire could accompany their reading. Inevitably, some never made their way back, vindicating the founder's stern injunctions.

Luckily, by the end of the seventeenth century the collections of the Bodleian had swelled to such a size that the occasional loss of books could never dent its reputation. Thanks to the liberal endowment of its founder and the determined work of its librarians, the Bodleian had acquired a place in the European culture of scholarship unknown for a British institution since the destruction of Lindisfarne Abbey in 793. The seventeenth-century Dutch scholar Johannes Lomeijer described the Bodleian as 'a library which has thrust its head above all the rest like a cypress among trailing hedgerow shoots'.[15] As long as its curators continued to acquire new books, and maintain its generous policy of access, readers would flock to the library. Without doubt the Bodleian occupied a central role in Europe's growing network of institutional libraries, none of which, despite attempts at imitation, could live up to the standards set in Oxford.

Chasing Donors

At the beginning of the seventeenth century there were close to a hundred universities in Europe and another thirty-five would be founded before 1700. The religious divisions which had riven Europe in the previous century became a force for the reinvigoration of academic scholarship. Every small Calvinist or Lutheran territory wished to have its own university, to train a loyal and doctrinally sound class of ministers and civil servants, and hopefully attract talented foreign co-religionists. New universities were also founded as institutions to propagate the counter-Reformation, especially by the energetic Jesuits.[16] Academic culture flourished, even if the growth of university libraries was remarkably haphazard.

The convulsions of the Reformation ensured that older universities in newly Protestant territories, like Basel, received many books from former monasteries and churches. The university library of Leipzig grew from 600 to 4,000 volumes after the Duke of Saxony embraced the Lutheran faith in 1539 and ensured that books from monastic libraries made their way to the university. Newly established universities, like those in the Dutch Republic, tended to rely on donations from benefactors, as monastic books had already been reassigned to the first generation of town libraries.[17] The University of Helmstedt, in northern Germany, founded in 1576, was presented with the library of the local duke in 1617, comprised of some 5,000 printed books and manuscripts. Most of these volumes had been appropriated by the duke from dissolved convents, yet the duke had little personal interest in the books. Moving them to the university freed up space at court for other trophies. There is little indication that these former monastic collections, dominated as they were by Catholic theology, were much used at Helmstedt either.[18]

Older universities, generally those founded before 1500, tended to have a collegiate structure. This was detrimental to the formation of a central library, for the simple reason that most colleges had a library of their own. For the most part these college libraries functioned as extensions of multiple personal libraries, and were prized community resources, available only to the scholars of the college. Early universities recruited significant numbers of foreign students, often organised into 'nations'. Sometimes these nations too had their own libraries: in Padua, the library of the *Natio Germanica* had 5,400 books by 1685.

The University of Louvain, the oldest university of the Low Countries, was home to forty colleges and student groups, almost all of which had small book collections. Notwithstanding, there was demand for a central reference library: Justus Lipsius, a celebrated professor at Louvain, wrote an entire book praising the libraries of antiquity to nudge a rich Habsburg nobleman, the Duke of Croÿ, into donating his collection of books to the university.[19] This elaborate literary hint, though a milestone of scholarship on the history of libraries, failed in its main purpose, and when the duke died, his heirs decided to sell the collection. It was only in 1636, three decades after Lipsius's valiant effort, that Louvain was finally able to open a central library after two local scholars had bequeathed their substantial collections to the institution. These two donations were supplemented by smaller gifts from Louvain's professoriate and professional class. In 1639, when a catalogue was published to celebrate the inauguration of the library, the donors were lauded with the inclusion of the donor's name after each entry.[20] Honouring donors in this fashion was a widespread practice, as the munificence of benefactors might inspire or shame others into similar gifts. Thomas Bodley had a benefactors' register installed at the entrance to the Bodleian, illustrated with the coat of arms of each donor.[21] In Louvain's case, the practice of noting the name of the donors in the individual catalogue entries also exposed the fact that some professors had contributed the bare minimum of a single inexpensive book.

Building a library by bequest was a slow process. Logistically, it was also problematic, especially if the library was fortunate enough to receive a very large donation. In 1715, King George I of England bought the library of the late Bishop of Ely, John Moore, to give to the University of Cambridge as a token of gratitude for its loyalty during the Jacobite uprising. One might expect that the university would have been delighted: instead, the collection, over 30,000 volumes strong, 'lay around in heaps, uncatalogued and pilfered for a generation'. Only in 1758, more than forty years after the donation, were the books organised and placed in a purpose-built room.[22] Most remarkably, it was only with the gift of Moore's library that the university library acquired some of the seminal scientific works of the age, including a copy of Isaac Newton's *Principia* and his *Opticks*. Shakespeare's collected works also first entered the library with the Moore collection.[23]

The fact that Cambridge university library did not own the most celebrated works of its own scholars was a common phenomenon. The only way in which university libraries could grow sustainably was with an acquisitions budget that allowed the latest works to be added to the collections, as Bodley had recognised. Sadly, such budgets were rare, even at some of the greatest academic institutions. The University of Leiden was an exception. Founded as a bastion of Calvinist scholarship during the Dutch Revolt, the university was liberally funded by the States of Holland. In the early seventeenth century, its librarian, Professor Daniel Heinsius, was initially given free rein to purchase books for the university. In May 1615 he was reprimanded by the curators for spending more than 1,300 guilders on books within the year, including 'various French books ... unnecessary and not useful for the library'. Henceforth he was given no more than 400 guilders per annum.[24]

This was still a substantial budget, one of which many libraries would have dreamed. If spent well, this could provide for around 100 to 200 new titles every year. At Leiden, however, much of the budget was reserved for manuscripts, recognised as critical to a university's international reputation. In the 1620s the university dispatched its professor of Arabic, Jacobus Golius, on a four-year leave of absence in North Africa and the Levant, to study and procure Oriental manuscripts. Golius returned triumphant, with 230 works for Leiden. This great acquisition, like others at Leiden, was publicised widely. Leiden had been the first university to publish a printed catalogue of its collections, in 1595. An engraving made of the library in 1610 as promotional material was widely circulated and frequently reproduced.

This publicity campaign made Leiden an obligatory destination for any scholar or young nobleman on a grand tour. Yet many visitors, having read travel guides that extolled the virtues of the library, were disappointed when they visited. William Nicholson, an English student at Oxford, commented in 1678 that the university library in Leiden was 'very inconsiderable were it not for the manuscripts'.[25] These manuscripts could only be consulted under supervision of the librarian, who was not always to be found. Even if he was, one was not assured of success: when a Swedish librarian from Uppsala visited Leiden in 1769, he was not allowed to see the manuscripts on the pretext that permission was required from the curators of the university. 'I became angry, and yet at the same time simply had to laugh at the absurdity of the regulations,' he reflected: a brave defiance, but a poor substitute for actually examining the university's treasures.[26]

In some ways, the Swedish visitor was lucky to be granted access to the library at all. Although Leiden had opened its library with relatively generous terms of access, these were pared back within a few years. For several decades, university students were not allowed to enter the library, and when access was restored to them in 1630, this was for only four hours a week, divided between two afternoons. These opening hours remained practically unchanged until the early nineteenth century, and they were similar to those of many other universities across Europe. In Tübingen, although

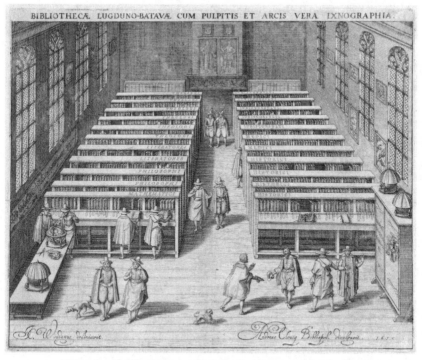

BIBLIOTHECÆ LUGDUNO-BATAVÆ CUM PULPITIS ET ARCIS VERA IXNOGRAPHIA.

11. This graceful depiction of Leiden's university library (1610)
was widely disseminated, greatly enhancing the reputation of
Leiden's collection. Its policy of access, however, was not as
congenial as the engraving suggests. The standing lecterns would
also have been less comfortable than Bodley's seated desks.

students were allowed to enter the library accompanied by their
professors, there were no established opening hours at all. Borrowing rights were almost always severely restricted. Professors
were generally allowed to take books home, but students rarely so.
Access to university libraries was further complicated by the lack
of suitable accommodation for the collection. Few institutions
possessed the Bodleian's luxurious bookcases with reading desks.
University libraries were often housed in a lecture hall, a church,
chapel, the university printing office, or, most discouragingly,
an attic.[27] These ubiquitous constraints make it clear that most
universities did not consider their libraries a necessary resource
for their students: instead, universities seemed to think of the
students only in terms of potential damage to the collection,

ironically so, given how little concern many university librarians showed for their duties.

This caution and conservatism would, in the long term, prove detrimental to university libraries: more so, indeed, than having their members wander off with a few books. A reliance on bequests resulted in randomly formed collections with awkward gaps and increasingly redundant scholarship. Limited access ensured that many professors and students took little interest in their local institutional library, choosing instead to build their own personal collections. In the Dutch Republic, no university library had more than 10,000 volumes before 1700. Harderwijk, the youngest university of the Dutch Republic, did not even have 500 books forty years after its foundation. Between 1671 and 1690 only eleven books were added to the library.[28] In the German territories, Marburg, Kiel, Wittenberg, Duisburg and Greifswald all had libraries with fewer than 5,000 books.[29] Tübingen university library was so insignificant that when Duke Maximilian of Bavaria occupied the town in 1634, and shipped to Bavaria the entire court library of the dukes of Württemberg, he left the university library unscathed.[30]

In contrast, we know of many professors who owned libraries of 10,000, 18,000 or even 22,000 books around the same period.[31] While the university library of Groningen had just over 4,000 books, its most bookish professor possessed more than 11,000. Two German scholars who visited the university library wrote that it was 'very neglected and wild' (1710) and 'miserable' (1726).[32] Even in Göttingen, home to one of the largest university libraries in Europe, as late as 1770 a professor mused whether it was strictly necessary to keep the university library open when private collections could be such a satisfactory substitute.[33]

Such attitudes, widespread as they were, were especially damaging because it was often a university professor who doubled as the librarian. Given that access was generally restricted to professors, this seems sensible enough, but few professors were anywhere near as dedicated as Thomas James. In some institutions, the post of librarian was essentially a sinecure, a transitional office for those waiting for a promotion. The professionalisation of librarianship in universities would not occur until deep into the nineteenth century. Those scholars who aspired to a career as full-time librarians, like the Frenchman Gabriel Naudé, sought a place in the great courtly and princely libraries.[34] In universities, their talents were wasted. The Scottish minister John Dury wrote disparagingly of the 'Librarie-Keepers, in most Universities that I know,

> nay indeed in all, their places are but Mercenarie, and their emploiment of little or no use further, than to look to the Books committed to their custodie, that they may not bee lost; or embezeled by those that use them.[35]

Franeker University, in Friesland, went through twenty-one librarians in the first 120 years of its existence. In 1698, the German scholar Johann Mencke was shown around the library of Franeker by Professor Jacobus Rhenferd, who had few good words to say about the librarian.

> Because he [Rhenferd] had the key to the library he brought ourselves up there, and he showed us many surprising and precious books, though he complained that such a person was made librarian who was not educated, and yet given an annual salary of 500 guilders, which could be better applied to the library. Also the 200 guilders, which was used for the catalogue, was an unnecessary expenditure, as the catalogue although magnificently printed, was so poorly made that one might not show it to anyone.[36]

With poor standards of librarianship, thefts followed. More than a hundred folio volumes were stolen from the library at Franeker in the 1640s, including fifty-six that had been fastened with chains precisely to prevent such thievery.[37] At least 1,000 books were stolen or lost from the collections of the University of Utrecht within half a century of its foundation. These sad episodes only reinforced the university curators in their view that access should be restricted to professors, and that students should not be trusted with books; even though, more often than not, it was in fact the professors who had run off with the books.

The greatest drag weight on the development of university libraries was, somewhat paradoxically, an overabundance of books available in the general market. If it was relatively easy for a professor to build a substantial personal library, then he had little need for a large university library. A lively auction market also diminished the incentive to donate one's personal library to the university. Better to raise a neat sum in the salesroom, safe in the knowledge that one's books would find new owners who would cherish them.

This was less true of institutions far removed from the heart of the European book trade, where the absence of an auction market encouraged more traditional acts of library philanthropy. In the new Baltic domains of the Swedish Empire, universities were planted as cultural bulwarks of the state. University libraries, in Uppsala and Lund, in Turku, Finland, and Tartu, Estonia, were established with large donations from the Swedish crown. A substantial university collection was absolutely vital in a town like Tartu, far removed from major book centres, where the library could play an important role as a resource for members of the professional classes beyond the university community. Tartu University had first opened in 1632 but closed again two decades later after a Russian invasion. When it reopened in 1690, King Charles XI donated 2,700 books, a very modern collection, which included works on Newtonian physics and Cartesian philosophy that would not have featured in many other university collections. The library was open to all students, who could even borrow books. Thanks to the survival of a borrowing register, we know that at least a hundred books a year were loaned out.[38] Tartu, even if it did not survive the ravages of the Great Northern War (1700–21), enjoyed brief but spectacular success.

The Danes, the greatest rivals of the Swedes, also shared a profound appreciation of their great institutional library at the University of Copenhagen. In 1603 the university library was a moribund collection of some 600 antique texts, but by the 1680s, after numerous donations by professors, ministers, jurists and local citizens, the library had grown to one of the largest institutional collections in Europe. Some of the donors had no affiliation with the university, and gave to the library simply out of local patriotism, to build as distinguished a collection as possible in a country not well provided with institutional libraries. The library responded to this generosity by printing catalogues of donations from various benefactors, even if it later sold on some of their books. When the library burned down in the Great Fire of Copenhagen (1728), 30,000 volumes burned with it, the result of almost a century of civic activism.[39] The attention lavished on university libraries in the Baltic offered one path to renewal for institutional book collections. Even in those towns with a small and generally unloved university library, there was a sense that a self-respecting community should have a library within its midst, even if most members of that community did not use the collection in any meaningful way.

The Return of the Riff Raff

Universities often secured from the town council or ruler a commitment that they would receive gratis any publication produced by local printing presses. This deposit right was, as one can imagine, deeply resented by publishers, who rarely gave up free copies without a fight. This forced universities to police the rules themselves, which they did reluctantly. This was due less to a desire to maintain good relations with local printing houses, although those were important, than the fact that most universities had little interest in what the presses were producing. The riff raff that Thomas Bodley had warned against – popular literature, almanacs, newspapers, school books and poetry – was the backbone of the printing industry, but most university librarians agreed with Bodley that such ephemeral works, generally printed in the local vernacular, had little place in an institutional collection. Some universities were so lax that they even neglected to collect a copy of the dissertations defended by their students. The Bodleian and Cambridge university library regularly gave away or sold off items that came into their possession thanks to their deposit right, formally acquired in 1665.[40]

University collections could have grown much more quickly if they had relaxed their policy on acquiring riff raff books. Instead they collected large tomes of redundant scholarship, which, as we have seen, often sat unread in locked churches and attics. While the local presses turned out ever more books, institutional collections turned up their noses at the opportunities afforded by a diverse range of titles available in the market. There were some private collectors, like the diarist Samuel Pepys, who pursued a different path and embraced printed material of all shapes and sizes. Pepys described his collecting habits, which included newspapers, ballads and other ephemera, as 'for the self-entertainment onely of a solitary, unconfined enquirer into books'.[41] His collection, donated to Magdalene College, Cambridge, by his nephew, remains today one of the finest libraries of seventeenth-century ballads, some 1,800 in all. That a collection of this sort was preserved was undoubtedly thanks to Pepys's distinguished political career. Another fastidious collector of ephemera, the antiquarian Anthony Wood, was a devoted Oxonian who spent much time at the Bodleian, and whose collections have, ironically, ended up in the same institution.

Wood, born in Oxford in 1632, remained in the city for his entire life. After studying at the university, he would make its history the main object of his study. His *Historia et antiquitates universitatis Oxoniensis* (1674) won him instant fame, allowing him to embark on other projects, including the *Athenae Oxoniensis*, a biographical bibliography of Oxford notables. This gave him a position of some influence in the Oxford community, and many authors attempted to influence his judgement (and to secure their own inclusion in the book) with gifts of books, often including their own works. This helps to explain why Wood, who had little regular income, was able to assemble a library of some 7,000 items during his lifetime.[42] He did not attempt to create the sort of formal library to which institutions, or its professors, aspired. Rather Wood's buying, which he did on an almost daily basis, reflected a fascination with the sort of ephemeral materials, pamphlets and broadsheets that libraries had no wish to acquire. These Wood collected for his own amusement, personal curiosity and to indulge his interest in current events.

Wood's policy of library building would have horrified Bodley. Some ephemeral material in his collection came to him free from acquaintances; other sheets and notices he simply appropriated from coffee houses or the university notice-board. Sometimes he added a helpful annotation on the poster or pamphlet to explain where he obtained them. One notice was 'stuck up on all the common places in the university', another 'stuck up on every corner in Oxon'. An advertisement that caught his eye 'was dispersed in every coffey-house in Oxon'; Wood removed this copy despite a further manuscript note, from the coffee house patron, that 'the reader is desired not to take away this paper'. Occasionally published material was simply offered to him on the street, such as the catalogue of a sale of books 'put into my hand at Trin Coll gate, Apr. 13 1685', which joined a valuable collection of 200 similar book catalogues in his library.[43]

Wood's library was entirely for his own use: necessarily so, since he allowed no visitors to visit the attic rooms where he worked, slept and kept his books. But the collection was certainly punctiliously curated. Whenever he had a little spare money, a carefully selected collection of pamphlets or notices would go off to the binders. It is only thanks to Wood that we have access to much material that was not otherwise systematically saved, such as published lecture lists, notifications and ceremonial pronouncements of the University of Oxford. Wood owned 171 almanacs, some of which (as was commonly the case) served as his diary. His keen interest in contemporary politics is reflected in long series of newspapers, from the Parliamentarian period onwards, including a thirty-year run of the *London Gazette*. The temptation to dispose of these early papers, to make room on his shelves for more current material, or new acquisitions in his collection of history and theology, must have been strong. The cost of extra shelving for the crowded attic must also have been a concern. But like all true collectors, Wood was a hoarder, and the 112-page shelf list he compiled of his library in 1681, divided into categories of his own devising ('Travels of various men', 'military matters', 'husbandry & gardening') meant that it was all at his fingertips: a private encyclopaedia of the world's wisdom and follies. This rich collection of print, a goldmine of information for politics and daily life in seventeenth-century Oxford, was given by Wood to the Ashmolean, the university museum. There it rested until, in 1860, it entered the hallowed space of the Bodleian.

CHAPTER NINE

MISSION FIELDS

Over the course of history, and particularly in the last hundred years, wars have taken a heavy toll on libraries. In most cases libraries and their books were collateral damage: carpet bombing leaves little room for discriminating choices. But there is no doubt that libraries have sometimes been sought out as deliberate targets: as symbols of a hated power, or repositories of a culture marked for eradication. For lovers of books, these orgies of destruction, in which libraries are perceived as helpless victims, are tragic and senseless. Far less attention has been paid to the role of libraries as agents of conflict. Libraries and their collections could play a critical role in incubating the ideologies that have set creed against creed, nation against nation, even neighbour against neighbour. At the same time, both within Europe and throughout its newly acquired colonies, books and libraries have frequently been the advance guard in campaigns to impose on a population a new kind of society, promote a new religion, or win back territory lost to a rival ideology. These libraries were ideological weapons with a specific mission: boldly planted in hostile or (from the point of view of colonisers) uncharted territory, libraries became intellectual castles and fortresses, and an encapsulation of the values of the settlers who had crossed the seas to seize and subdue.

As Europeans expanded their control over vast swathes of the globe, they often attempted to create microcosms of European society, erecting European-style buildings, wearing European clothes, importing European models of education. The first convict ships sent to Australia carried with them a printing press. However, as they had not managed to persuade a printer to join the perilous voyage, for some years the press lay dormant. But within thirty years the new colony had a newspaper and bookshops, and soon circulating libraries: all accoutrements of polite English society imported from a homeland half a world away.[1]

The first library carried to Spanish America was, appropriately enough, a chest of books that accompanied Fernando Colon on the voyage with his father. More ostentatious structures were soon established by the colonising religious orders. Books, sometimes translated into the indigenous languages, were a potent weapon in their efforts at conversion. Even those who had rejected European society, like the Pilgrim Fathers, clung to books and libraries as essential markers of their civilisation.

The new settlers planted books, libraries and eventually domestic printing in almost all the places where Europeans asserted right of abode and rulership. Most of the books were imported from the home country: the demand for books to fill the new libraries far exceeded the small capacities of the printing presses they carried with them, which continued to be the case until the end of the eighteenth century. But these colonising missions found an equally contentious theatre in Europe itself, one rather neglected in the narrative of library building: the contested spaces in northern and central Europe where Protestants and Catholics fought for supremacy. Here, in lands somewhat removed from the main centres of European print culture, the libraries erected were statements of purpose and celebrations, often prematurely, of victory. Inevitably, whenever the balance of power shifted, the libraries were regarded as legitimate targets. Libraries were looted or dismantled to delegitimise the claims of the rival, and carried off as booty to decorate a different library in the conqueror's homeland.

All of this paid homage, albeit in a painful way, to the power of books. None of the protagonists questioned the ability of books to create a new people, to shape lives and banish doubt. That was why books often suffered a similar fate to human missionaries subjected to ritual humiliation and put to death, when their claims to sacral power were contested.

The Monks of War

'Our world has lately discovered another, not less large, populous and manifold than itself ... I very much fear that we shall have greatly hastened the decline and ruin of this other hemisphere by our contagion.' This was Michel de Montaigne, writing in 1588, but by this point the damage had been done. When Christopher Columbus returned from his first voyage with tall tales and curiosities but little of the fabled wealth promised, his greatest achievement was to recast the voyage as a patriotic triumph. He laid at the feet of his royal patrons the glorious vision of a new empire. It was only when Hernán Cortés had bludgeoned his way through the Mexican interior to the dazzling city of Tenochtitlan that hopes of unlimited plunder were reignited. When the Spanish received lavish gifts of gold and jewellery from the Aztec ruler Montezuma, his death warrant was as good as sealed.

Among the treasures laid out by Montezuma for his guests were a number of books. These were the first casualties of the conquest. The Spaniards recognised that they were in the presence of a sophisticated civilisation. The Aztecs and the Mayans in particular could boast major achievements in the fields of mathematics and astronomy. Tenochtitlan, now the site of Mexico City, was an architectural marvel, and probably larger than any contemporary European city. The subjugation of such an advanced society required a systematic destruction of its books and archives, partly to demoralise a potentially potent military foe, but also to eradicate the worship of what the Spanish identified as false gods. Poring over these multicoloured scrolls of deerskin or screenfold panoramas inscribed on tree bark, Spanish suspicions were exacerbated by the fact that Aztec writing used a pictographic system, easily denounced as witchcraft. Only the Mayans had a recognisably alphabetical system of writing.

The consequence of this brutal assertion of power was the destruction of a large proportion of the cultural heritage of Mesoamerican civilisations. Shortly after his arrival as the first bishop of Mexico City, the Franciscan Juan de Zumárraga ordered a public burning of Aztec manuscripts. A group of Tlaxcalan warriors, Spanish allies against their ancestral foes, destroyed the irreplaceable Aztec archive at Texcoco. In 1562, Bishop Diego de Landa placed forty of the key texts of the Mayans on a pyre at Maní. According to his own account: 'As they contained nothing but superstition and lies of the devil, we burned them all, which impressed them greatly and caused them much pain.'[2]

These acts were all the more tragic because they were committed by men who were inherently bookish. The first generation of Franciscan friars would play a major role in creating the essential tools for learning the indigenous languages. In 1547, Andrés de Olmos published a grammar for learning Nahuatl, and Alonso de Molina published a bilingual Spanish and Nahuatl dictionary in 1555.[3] These were part of a steady flow of manuals, catechisms and grammars, published in a dozen of the local tongues. It is reckoned that some 30 per cent of the books published in Mexico in the sixteenth century were in the local languages.[4] The warrior bishop Juan de Zumárraga was at the heart of this printing campaign, having arranged for a printing press to follow him to Mexico from Spain. One of the first books to be printed in Mexico was a brief summary of the Christian faith that he himself had written.[5] Zumárraga was also instrumental in the foundation of the college of Santa Cruz, where talented boys from the indigenous population could be trained for service to the church. This would lead in 1551, three years after Zumárraga's death, to the establishment of a university in Mexico City, teaching the full European curriculum, with all the traditional faculties.

All this required books and the creation of libraries, a task for which the single local press in Mexico City was scarcely sufficient. Apart from publishing the bilingual primers for training converts to Catholicism, much of the press time was given over to supporting the business of government, turning out ordinances and books of local laws.[6] The sorts of books that made up the staples of scholarly and institutional libraries in Europe would not have found a sufficient market in the Americas to justify a local edition.

From the very beginning, therefore, large numbers of books were imported. Bishop Zumárraga, not surprisingly, owned a considerable personal library of at least 400 books, which on his death he left to the convent of San Francisco de México; others he gave during his lifetime to the college of Santa Cruz. Almost 400 of the sixteenth-century works accumulated by the college of Santa Cruz are now in the Sutro library in San Francisco, California. Examination of these texts reveals a broad collection of European classics of the sort that would grace any scholarly collection, including works by Aristotle, Plutarch and Flavius Josephus. They emanated from Paris and Lyon, Antwerp and Basel, as well as the publishing centres of Italy and Spain. Of the books known to have been owned by Zumárraga, five were printed by Johann Froben in Basel, the major scholarly publisher in a city tainted by Protestantism.[7] An analysis of the library of the monastery of San Francisco of Guadalajara, now in the public library of that city, reveals 479 fifteenth- and sixteenth-century titles, a mixture of classical texts and Spanish religious and mystical authors. Again Lyon was the greatest source of books, including a surprising number printed by Jean Crespin, who would go on to print for Calvin in Geneva.

The prominence of Lyon reflects the close business relationship between Lyon printers and the Spanish market: these books, along with those from Paris and Antwerp, would no doubt have been transported through Seville, from where the family Cromberger had been granted the exclusive right to supply books to the Americas. Cromberger had been intimately involved with the Mexican mission since the beginning, and had provided both the press and the printer for Zumárraga's new enterprise. The monopoly of supply was a reward for this investment, but also provided the opportunity for the cargo to be closely inspected for orthodoxy before dispatch overseas.

This preventative censorship was, as it turned out, far less effective than the friars might have hoped. Thrown into unfamiliar communities, or isolated on huge estates with few European peers in reach, for the planters books were even more of a necessity than in Europe. These new citizens desired books of a rather different type than those that populated the ecclesiastical libraries, not least the chivalric novels that had fired the imagination of these adventurers. In principle, such literature was banned from the colonies, but it still found its way on board in large quantities. A large part of the first edition of *Don Quixote* (1605) made its way to Mexico. In Peru, too, the growing class of lawyers, clergy and royal officials provided a healthy market for the local booksellers in Lima, all of whom secured their stock from Spain.[8] Predictably, the senior clerics built the largest libraries. Francisco de Ávila, canon of the cathedral of Lima, had assembled a collection of some 3,108 volumes by his death in 1647, which was easily the largest collection in the Americas, and would, indeed, have dwarfed many institutional libraries in Europe. The enormous number of European books available on the market in Peru can be demonstrated by the inventory of the Franciscan convent of Arequipa, founded in 1648. By the time of its dissolution, the convent had gathered a collection of 15,000 volumes, mostly dating from the sixteenth and seventeenth centuries.[9]

If Spanish America was the domain of the Dominicans and Franciscans, Portuguese Brazil was the kingdom of the Jesuits. The result was an extraordinary efflorescence of book culture and libraries. Although this had not been the original intention of Ignatius of Loyola, the founder of the order, education quickly became central to the Jesuit mission, and increasingly defined the identity of the order.[10] All Jesuit colleges were expected to have a library, and 'keys should be given to those who, in the opinion of the rector, ought to have one'.[11] In addition to this institutional library, Loyola recognised that teachers might need their own collection; these would usually be donated to the library on the instructor's death or departure. A well-ordered library also required a capable librarian, and here Loyola was rather ahead of his time. In many universities, the position of librarian was regarded as a sinecure, an acceptable salaried position to enjoy while one waited for something better. Jesuit librarians, in contrast, were kept busy ordering and cataloguing, managing loans and creating bibliographical registers: it was an important and respected vocation.

The Jesuits had arrived in Brazil by 1549, and colleges were established in six of the major settlements. The King of Portugal supported the venture with gifts of books. A seventeenth-century inventory of the library at Salvador da Bahia identified a collection of 3,000 books, 'by any type of writer one would want and is cared for and skilfully protected by a diligent and capable librarian'.[12]

Salvador da Bahia also became a distribution centre for the building of library collections in up-country settlements. Any priest starting a school could contact Salvador da Bahia secure in the expectation that a chest of books would quickly be dispatched. By the time of the expulsion of the Jesuits from Brazil in 1759, their Brazilian libraries collectively owned 60,000 books, with Salvador da Bahia the largest library owning 15,000 items. The suppression of the order dealt a devastating blow to the Brazilian educational system, and indeed to that of Spanish Peru, where the Jesuits were also active.

How successful were these efforts at winning hearts and minds? For much of the seventeenth century the Portuguese were fighting a complex two-front battle: for the loyalties of the indigenous peoples, and to repel Dutch efforts to conquer Brazil. When the Dutch applied their superior economic resources and naval strength to wresting Brazil from Portuguese control, no one in Europe would have wagered against them. For twenty years they occupied strategic ports, including the major city of Recife, before two catastrophic battles against local armies dealt their authority a fatal blow. The Dutch, it must be said, were not natural missionaries. Although a printing press was sent to Dutch Brazil in 1643, there was no one in the colony capable of using it, which militated against the sort of religious engagement into which the Spanish and Portuguese had put such energy. The well-meaning attempt to distribute a trilingual catechism in Dutch, Portuguese and Tupi ended in farce. Printed in Enkhuizen in 1642, it was shipped to Brazil despite doubts about the quality of the translation. Three years later, 2,951 copies out of the 3,000 printed were still rotting in the warehouse at Recife, along with a further 5,000 volumes of Dutch devotional classics.[13]

Thanksgiving

In 1620, when the Pilgrim Fathers set sail from Leiden, en route to Massachusetts, their rejection of the European world they had left behind was very partial. Books, in particular, were an essential accoutrement of the new life they had chosen: indeed, it was often these books that had led them to separate from the Church of England. Seeking to dissuade his friend John Winthrop from joining the Massachusetts project ten years later, Robert Ryece warned him, 'how hard will it be for one brought up among books and learned men to live in a barbarous place where is no learning and less civility'.[14] The colonists' response was to take their civilisation with them, in the form of books. Books were the bread of life, and would be hardy survivors of the first starvation winter that claimed the lives of so many of the settlers.

The Pilgrims brought with them an extraordinary quantity of books, stocks that were gradually replenished by relief ships and trading vessels over the following years. At the death of their owners the books were inventoried along with other possessions, so that they could be recycled to new owners in the community. Careful study of these documents reveals collections of quite startling size.[15] Chief among them was the library of William Brewster, one of the leaders of the community in Leiden and again in Plymouth. The 350 books listed on his death in 1644 included staples of Latin Protestant learning: Calvin, Beza and the Latin Bible of Tremellius and Junius. As remarkable is the large number of English pamphlets, many of them printed on the dissident presses in Amsterdam, Middelburg or Leiden, including Brewster's own.[16] Generally, such lists specified individually only the books with the largest value, the Bibles and books in large formats. The smaller books are dealt with in more summary fashion: 'five small stitched books', 'smalle books unbound', 'five small books were in the kitchen', 'three and fifty small books' and 'divers other Dutch books'.[17] The reason why the description of Brewster's books is more detailed, listing every book separately, is most likely because he died at a point where the book stock of the colony was much smaller than it was twenty years later when the next large library, that of Ralph Partrich, came on the market.[18] For this reason, Brewster's smaller books would also have been likely to secure higher prices; his grateful fellow Pilgrims no doubt also welcomed a comforting reminder of his contribution to the settlement. In societies such as this, clinging to the edge, as they saw it, of the known world, books were valued for their totemic value as well as for their texts.[19]

1. A modern tribute to an ancient fable: the interior of the library of Alexandria, pictured in 2018. The library's fine interior is not matched by the rather more jumbled contents of its holdings.

2. The reconstructed facade of the Roman Library of Celsus (Ephesus, modern Turkey), one of the few extant library buildings from the ancient world. The library served as a repository for scrolls as well as a mausoleum. In the Roman Empire, libraries often functioned as monuments that celebrated the achievements of their founder and their family. In this, the library was just another means with which to bolster a political reputation.

CODICIBVS SACRIS HOSTILI CLADE PERVSTIS
ESDRA DŌ FERVENS HOC REPARAVIT OPVS

3. A miniature depicting Ezra the scribe in front of a book cupboard (armarium), from the Codex Amiatinus (early eighth century). For much of the first millennium after the fall of Rome, book chests and cupboards remained the standard means to store and organise a library.

4. The author hard at work, in front of a lavish collection of books, protected by curtains. This miniature of Vincent of Beauvais appeared in a copy of his *Miroir historial*, written in Bruges around 1478–80, presumably for the English King Edward IV, whose coat of arms is placed five times in the border.

5. The Book of Hours was the most popular type of literature in late medieval Europe. In the workshops of France and the Low Countries it found its most exquisite form, with richly illuminated miniatures and decorated borders, as in this fifteenth-century copy.

6. The warrior bibliophile. In this portrait of Duke Federico of Urbino and his son Guidobaldo (*c*.1475), the duke has his attention fixed on one of the valuable manuscripts from his collection, while decked out in martial finery. Having spent a fortune on his library, the collection would be a sad ruin a century after his death.

7. This portrait by Parmigianino (*c.*1523) is one of many examples of Renaissance portraits in which the sitter grasps a richly bound book, a symbol of his wealth as much as his intellectual ambition.

8. Desiderius Erasmus, pictured by Quentin Metsys (1517), in front of
an untidy cupboard of books. Although his life revolved around books,
Erasmus was remarkably nonchalant when it came to assembling a library.
For Erasmus, access to texts was far more important than owning them.

9. A trade card for Liebig's beef extract (1912), featuring a highly fictionalised travelling book merchant. The expansion of the book trade in the sixteenth and seventeenth centuries brought the pleasures of book ownership to many more people, as bookshops and itinerant pedlars proliferated around the European continent.

10. Duke Humphrey's original bequest to the University of Oxford suffered from the ravages of the Reformation, before his library hall was restored by Thomas Bodley. The large lectern bookcases ensured that this was an amenable place to work, except in the depths of winter, when the absence of heating hastened the demise of the most determined scholars.

11. The university library of Göttingen, one of the largest institutional libraries in eighteenth-century Europe. The space for conversation makes clear that libraries continued to be places of social interaction as much as study: perhaps another reason why one Göttingen professor suggested that a university library was not so necessary a service after all.

12. The interior of the library of the monastery of San Francisco in Lima, Peru, founded in 1673. In Spanish South America, dominated by the Catholic orders, monasteries fulfilled a prominent role as centres of education, research and book collecting.

This pragmatic recycling of books left by the deceased was stoically accepted in all of the early settlements. When in 1621 the Virginia Company wrote to the struggling colony about supplying a new minister, they did not intend to equip him with a library: 'As for books, we doubt not that you will be able to supply him out of the libraries of so many who have died.'[20] Those returning from the colonies to England were also encouraged to leave their books behind, where, as John Smith put it, 'we have so much need of them'. Smith, zealous writer of religious tracts and author of the milestone translation of the Bible into Algonquian, was a great snapper-up of other men's libraries; in New England, the natural acquisitive urge of the collector could legitimately be defended as God's purpose.

All told, we have 510 surviving inventories for men and women dying in the Plymouth colony between 1631 and 1692. More than half record some books, including fifty-one that list a Bible and unspecified other books, and thirty-nine that list only a Bible and the psalms. Where we have more detail, we see exactly the sort of names that one would expect: the fathers of the continental Reformed movement, John Calvin and Zacharias Ursinus, and English Puritan authors (also popular in Dutch translation, so very familiar to those coming from the Low Countries). If this seems terribly earnest, with none of the rousing tales so beloved of the conquistadores, it was partly because the Pilgrims were earnest folk; recreational books were likely to have been in the parcels of small books not spelt out in the inventories. Brewster owned William Camden's *Britannia*, which would have helped while away some evening hours, as well as Francis Bacon's *Cases of Treason*, and a copy of *The Prince* by Machiavelli; not exactly light reading, but more than useful when navigating the colony's sometimes turbulent politics.

All of these were personal collections, though one would imagine that collections the size of Brewster's would have served as a community resource in small settlements as tightly knit as this. Throughout the first century of colonial America, the most important collections were those assembled by the leading preachers. Lay members of the congregation had to fend for themselves

on the increasingly active Boston book market. An attempt was
made to establish a town library in Boston in 1656, but this was
conceived as a collective resource for the town's ministers rather
than as a source of recreational literature for the congregation.
This was a colony still dominated by the values of mission, which
helps explain the particular importance of the legacy left in 1638 to
the newly founded teaching college in Cambridge, Massachusetts,
by the Charlestown minister, John Harvard.

Harvard's legacy came with an endowment sufficiently large
to justify the renaming of the college in his honour. By the end of
the seventeenth century, Harvard College could boast the largest
library in North America. The collection grew steadily though
entirely through donation, since the college, in common with
almost all institutions of higher education before the modern
era, did not allocate funds for the buying of books. A large gift in
1678 from Reverend Theophilus Gale, an independent minister
in London, increased the library by a third. The gift of Sir John
Maynard in 1698 was so considerable that it led to a sale of duplicates. By the first decades of the eighteenth century, the collection
had grown to around 3,000 volumes, far exceeding the capacities
of its original housing in the old college.

In 1723, the college commissioned the publication of a printed
catalogue.[21] The initiative for this came from friends in England,
and perhaps it would have been better had it also been printed in
London. Instead, the trustees commissioned the work from the
local Boston printer, Bartholomew Green, who had little experience with Latin printing. He chose the cautious format of quarto
in half sheets, a laborious and time-consuming process, both for
the printer and the binder. Four hundred copies were printed, 100
made available for sale by the bookseller Gerrish, who had supervised the project, and 300 to be distributed by the college gratis to
alumni and potential donors: 100 were immediately dispatched to
England to encourage further gifts. Overall, the prosperous pious
merchants who received the catalogue were disinclined to donate.
They were more struck by the size of the collection than conscious
of gaps, and thought Harvard could well fend for itself: 'saying
how rich, how numerous you are, and able to buy what you want

of yourselves, etc.'[22] None of these donated copies of the catalogue can be identified today: their recipients seem to have discarded them quite rapidly.

Nor were these potential patrons particularly impressed by what they had heard of the curation of the collection. As Thomas Hollis wrote frankly to Benjamin Collins in 1725, while the catalogue was circulating in London:

> Your library [Harvard] is reckoned here to be ill managed by the account I have of some that know it. You want seats to sit and read, and chains to your valuable books like our Bodleian Library, or Sion College in London. You let your books be taken at pleasure to men's houses, and many are lost. Your (boyish) students take them to their chambers and tear out pictures and maps to adorn the walls; such things are not good.[23]

In the end, Harvard may have reason to be grateful for these sloppy boyish students, since in 1764 Harvard Hall burned down and the library was completely destroyed. More than 5,000 volumes were lost; only those in the hands of borrowers could be recovered. This time, English donors were more generous. A new catalogue published in 1790, at the birth of the new independent nation, listed close to 9,000 titles. Striking here is the large number of pamphlets: not surprising, perhaps, in view of the role of pamphlet propaganda in the recent revolutionary events, but still unusual in university libraries.

Put to Proper Use

When it was first established in the sixteenth century, the Jesuit order undertook a series of spectacular missions to enhance the global reach of the Catholic faith, in Japan and China, Brazil and the Indian archipelago. Taking advantage of the vogue for travel writing, these adventurous and exotic trips were eagerly publicised by the order, and are staples of library collections today.[24] This should not, however, disguise the fact that the core mission, for

which the order was given unprecedented freedom of action by
a series of supportive popes, was always the re-evangelisation of
Europe. The first Jesuit college was established in Messina, on the
island of Sicily, in 1548. In the course of the century a network
of more than 200 colleges would spread through the Italian peninsula, Spain and northern Europe. Libraries formed an essential
part of each project; as Peter Canisius would rhapsodise, 'Better a
college without a church of its own, than a college without a library
of its own'. Canisius was the first Jesuit author to publish a book,
and can perhaps be forgiven this rhetorical flight. Juan de Polanco,
secretary of Ignatius of Loyola, put the matter more plainly: 'For
the houses of study purchasing of books is as essential as the buying
of food. A book is a tool in the service of God.'[25]

The Jesuits reached a critical new juncture in the 1560s, with
the establishment of a mission to Poland. In the sixteenth century,
Poland enjoyed a reputation as a land of unusual religious freedom,
home to fugitive sects of many denominations, as well as Catholics, Lutherans and Calvinists. But contemporaries also recognised
its critical role in the politics and economy of the continent, a hub
of Baltic trade, and a redoubt of western Christendom on the borderlands with Russian Orthodoxy. The arrival of the Jesuits was
thus an event of geopolitical significance: a bold thrust to reclaim
this ancient kingdom for Catholicism.

Crucial to this strategy was the foundation of the Jesuit college
in Braniewo in 1565. The brainchild of Cardinal Stanislaus Hosius,
generously supported by both Pope Gregory XIII and the papal
nuncio Antonio Possevino, the college occupied a strategic location
near the Baltic coast, sandwiched between the two major German
trading posts of Danzig and Königsberg. Königsberg in particular
was a Protestant stronghold, the location of the most easterly Protestant university and a major centre of German-language printing.
The new Jesuit college was planted in clear and open rivalry with
this powerful institution, a magnet not only for Polish students
seeking a Catholic education, but also students from Lithuania,
Ruthenia, Russia and the northern Lutheran stronghold, Sweden.
Its major goal was to train missionaries for the assault on Protestant Europe: its philosophy school was nicknamed the 'Swedish

seminary'. So great was the fear of Braniewo, that in 1613 Swedish students were forbidden to study there on pain of death.

The flow of students from Sweden receded, but at its peak, the college enrolled 300 candidates a year. Naturally this required a substantial library, and between 1565 and the second decade of the seventeenth century, a very considerable collection was accumulated. Among the 2,600 titles, local authors of the Polish counter-Reformation were available along with the Church Fathers and the classical authors. It seemed only a matter of time before Braniewo would be recognised as one of the leading universities of Catholic Europe. This was the library as tool of conversion and conquest, a crucial weapon in the battle for hearts and minds in Europe's most complex religious battlefield. Unfortunately for the Jesuit librarians charged with making this vision tangible, they came up against an equally doughty warrior for God: the lion of the north, Gustavus Adolphus, King of Sweden, a devout Lutheran, and ambitious to build a Swedish empire in the Baltic.

In 1621, Gustavus Adolphus had conquered Riga, now capital of Latvia, but then a Protestant city under the suzerainty of the Polish crown. The Jesuit library there was a first target, surrendered without much regret by the Protestant magistrates. One thousand books were packed up and taken off to Sweden. In 1626, the chapter library in Frauenburg (Frombork) suffered the same fate, and then the Jesuit college at Braniewo. The books were carefully boxed and crated, and dispatched across the Baltic to their new home. To receive all these treasures, a central clearing station was established in Stockholm, under the leadership of the royal librarian, Johannes Bureus. Books received were sorted and then dispatched either to the royal collection or other Swedish libraries. The best collections, including Braniewo and Riga, were reserved for the university at Uppsala. For the university library, this was very much business as usual: it had been established with a donation of 4,500 books from religious houses plundered during the Reformation. Now it could feast on the property of new enemies. The new quarters established to hold this cascade of fresh accessions reflected the peculiar spirit of the times. The library in Uppsala was organised on two floors: the upper floor contained the teaching books of the university, including Lutheran theology. The lower library contained books variously described as Catholic, Calvinist or Jesuit: it was here that the booty of Germany came to rest.[26] Good books and bad books; of course scholars needed both if they were to strengthen their defences against the enemy, but it was right that only those sufficiently strong to resist their blandishments should have access to the Jesuit books. The two floors were reached by separate doors on external staircases. Only those of ironclad faith would be trusted with the key to the lower floor.

With the fruits of Swedish military might, Uppsala was soon in possession of the greatest university library in the north, particularly with the competition of Braniewo extinguished. But it was far from being the only client for the books brought from Swedish conquests in Germany and Poland. There were now two further Swedish universities, at Tartu, now in Estonia, and Turku, in Finland. The grammar schools at Västerås and Linköping also received their share of the spoils, as would, in due course, the cathedral library at Strängnäs.[27] These were not, in the eyes of their new Swedish owners, acts of pillage, but a hostage rescue. The Jesuits had held these books prisoner: now they were released from bondage. In the words of Swedish Archbishop Laurentius Paulinus Gothus in 1642:

> In this war, where God at times graciously helps us to take our enemies' renowned colleges and glorious libraries, which [the Jesuit order] misuse in the oppression of the true religion, but here could be put to *genium usum* [proper use] again, which is to the glory of God.[28]

The Swedish system of library building was documented in an instruction issued by the Swedish chancellor, Axel Oxenstierna, in 1643, though in truth this only formalised arrangements that had been in place for a generation. According to these instructions, in each new captured city the officers of the Swedish army were to seek out any local inhabitants who could advise on any significant local archives, documents or libraries. Once identified, these properties were then to be packaged into chests and shipped back to Sweden.[29]

The year 1642 brought a new harvest from the Capuchin monastery and Jesuit college in Olmütz (Olomouc) in Moravia, and in 1648, when negotiations for the peace settlement to end the Thirty Years' War were already reaching their conclusion, the Swedes helped themselves to the famous library of the Strahov monastery in Prague. Only determined resistance from the local population, which prevented the Swedes from crossing the Charles Bridge, saved the library of the Jesuit university in the lower town. In 1646 the university library at Turku received a magnificent donation of more than 1,092 titles, including 248 folios, from Christina Horn, wife of the Swedish general Torsten Stålhandske. General Stålhandske had received the library as war booty following the Swedish conquest of Jutland (in Denmark) in 1644. Its original owner was Martinus Matthiae (1596–1643), bishop of Aarhus. The widely travelled Matthiae had assembled his collection in Paris, Louvain, Antwerp, Amsterdam and Leiden as well as Wittenberg; now it was housed in a Swedish university library. Even fellow Lutherans were not safe from the voracious Swedish appetite for other people's books.

We know of the Horn bequest only from an early printed catalogue of the Turku library collection published in 1655; the whole library was lost when the city was destroyed by a disastrous fire in 1827. More of the war booty appropriated by the Swedes was lost in another devastating fire that destroyed the Swedish royal library in 1697. Such fires were less an act of a vengeful providence than inevitable events in towns still largely built from timber, particularly in the north where fires had to be lit throughout the cold winter months. The books of Riga and Braniewo, sent to Uppsala, survived rather better, and can still be clearly identified on the shelves of the university library. Recently the library has permitted librarians from Poland and Latvia to come and make catalogues of their former Jesuit libraries, though they seem less inclined to return the books themselves.[30]

The conclusion of the Thirty Years' War did not bring an end to this predatory collecting. An example – of both the continued despoliation of libraries and the extraordinary resilience of the Jesuit missionaries – can be found in the Jesuit college in Vilnius, founded in 1569 at the request of Catholic members of the Lithuanian nobility. In this eastern stronghold of Catholicism it thrived, and eagerly embraced an apostolic mission to the east. This was greatly enhanced by the gift, in 1572, of the extraordinary library of King Sigismund Augustus (1520–72), reputed to be of 4,000 books, and in 1575, by the provision of funds to establish their own printing house.[31] For the next hundred years this would be one of the most important presses in the Polish–Lithuanian Commonwealth, turning out a steady stream of pedagogic and devotional works in both Latin and Polish. The earliest surviving work in the Lithuanian language published on Lithuanian soil was the product of this press, not surprisingly a catechism.

Vilnius escaped the worst of the destruction during the Thirty Years' War, but the end of the war ushered in a still darker period for Poland–Lithuania, known as the Deluge. While the Swedes occupied Warsaw and most of Poland, Russian armies invested Lithuania and occupied Vilnius, with predictable results; it was looted again by Swedish armies during the Great Northern War (1700–21). In 1710, a weakened population fell victim to one of the last outbreaks of bubonic plague in Europe. At least 35,000 died, half the population of the city. All of this, together with a series of disastrous fires between 1715 and 1749, reduced Vilnius to a shadow of its former self. The academy struggled to survive, its library a natural target for plunder, not least after the spectacular donation of the *Bibliotheca Sapiehana*, consisting of 3,000 books from libraries of the chancellor of the Grand Duchy of Lithuania, Lew Sapieha (1557–1633) and three of his sons.[32] Even so, by the time of the institution's definitive closure with the suppression of the Jesuits in 1773, the university had re-established a collection of over 4,000 works. Interestingly, though, this collection now had a significant component of works published in Poland–Lithuania: books not only from the Jesuit press, but from Warsaw and Kraków.[33] Thanks to the ever-increasing rate of publishing throughout Europe, the destruction of a library was decreasingly potent as a weapon, since library collections could be rebuilt so much more easily.

The Jesuits pursued their mission with dogged resilience, to which their adversaries, Catholic and Protestant, were forced to offer a grudging respect. The Jesuits were also not afraid to take the battle to the heart of darkness, Europe's new Protestant states. In the early seventeenth century, the Jesuits opened a covert mission in Leeuwarden, flinty stronghold of Calvinism in the Dutch Republic's northern province of Friesland. Here, in pursuit of their mission work, they gathered a collection of more than 1,200 volumes, mainly composed of Catholic theology.[34] Throughout the Dutch Republic, Catholics maintained a smooth supply of the necessary devotional literature, not least thanks to booksellers who were happy to work across confessional lines in pursuit of profit.

Never slow to recognise a weakness in their opponents' lines of defence, the Jesuits bombarded the Dutch Republic with Catholic devotional works, often by Jesuit authors. The four Jesuit colleges in the contested borderlands at Maastricht, Den Bosch, Roermond and Breda functioned as advanced observation posts. The Dutch conquest of Den Bosch cost the Jesuits their most active printing press, but this was a very temporary setback. Often Jesuit books were printed in the Republic itself, though the publishers were usually respectful enough to disguise their work with a false imprint of Antwerp or Cologne, two safely Catholic foreign cities.[35]

In England, Catholics were subject to harsh punitive laws, and Jesuits were particularly feared and despised for their association with plots against the life of Queen Elizabeth, and the Gunpowder Plot against James VI and I. Henry Garnet, the English Jesuit Superior, was among those executed in 1606 in the wake of the failed attempt to blow up the king and the Houses of Parliament. Despite this, in the course of the seventeenth century the Jesuit mission in England built a most remarkable network of clandestine libraries. The library at Cwm in Herefordshire held 336 volumes, drawn from the major centres of European Catholic printing. The library at Holbeck Woodhouse in Nottinghamshire was twice as large.[36] Both were confiscated in the wave of anti-Catholic hysteria at the time of the alleged Popish Plot to kill King Charles II in

1678, although presumably the existence of both had been known to the authorities well before this.

Weapons of war come in all shapes and sizes. Some make their presence felt through terrifying impact, others by stealth. So it was with the library wars of the seventeenth and eighteenth centuries. Libraries could be destroyed through pillage, or through the inadvertent impact of the savage fires that often accompanied the sack of a city. Frequently, libraries were targets for deliberate appropriation, most famously in the removal of the library of the University of Heidelberg, Germany's most illustrious medieval library, to the Vatican in 1622.[37] With its 5,000 printed books and an astonishing 3,500 manuscripts, Heidelberg was the greatest prize, though, as we have seen, Swedish thoroughness ensured that for sheer quantity this could be matched many times over. The Pilgrim Fathers relied on what could be carried on the tiny vessels of their first fleet throughout several cold winters, being a community that valued every single text. The Jesuits of England gathered their libraries more discreetly: mission sometimes thrived when its purpose was not shouted from the rooftops. The relatively fortunate Catholics of the Dutch Republic could feast openly on the abundance of the Amsterdam book market. What we learn most from this story of conflict, confrontation and purposeful construction was that the people of Europe recognised books for the incendiary objects they were: beacons of faith or pollutants of the body politic. Yet we also learn, from the eager appropriation of Jesuit books for Protestant libraries, and vice versa, how much of the cultural capital of the era was held in common. Intellectuals of all faiths valued the classics, the Church Fathers, the grammars and dictionaries that supplied the most substantial tomes in any collection. That was why the victors would rather work their way round the shelves of a conquered library than pick through the ashes.

PART FOUR

BETWEEN PUBLIC AND PRIVATE

Chapter Ten

GRAND DESIGNS

If James Kirkwood, a staunch Presbyterian minister in Bedford-shire, had visited Paris in the 1680s, it is unlikely that he would have secured access to its great scholarly libraries. Kirkwood, a Scotsman, was eking out a living in exile, for many religious refugees often the ideal time to bury themselves in book collecting, so long as they had sufficient resources or could find a new patron. Kirkwood was unusual, however, in that his energies went not into building his own private place of solace, but a grand plan for bringing enlightenment and learning to all parts of his native Scotland by planting a public library in every parish. This sense of the unlimited possibilities brought by books was something he shared with the greatest collector of France, Cardinal Jules Mazarin, who created one of the most stupendous libraries yet seen in Europe. Both men had a vision of the future of the library; one, of a series of libraries, curated by the church, which would be a major theological resource in many of Scotland's smaller habitations; the other, of an Alexandrian collection open to visiting scholars. It is a mark of the influence of such scholars that Mazarin's library would be by far the better known.

Mazarin's view of the public was, as one might expect, aristocratic and elitist.[1] As with the great men of the Roman Empire, the library was an instrument (one of many) with which to build a personal following and secure a legacy: a display of wealth, power and taste (though in this case the taste was very largely that of his librarian, Gabriel Naudé). It was also a monument to the rapacity of the great ministers who had come to dominate European politics. The gifts, lands and emoluments that came to them through the king's favour allowed his principal counsellors to build and collect on a scale to outshine the highest ranks of the nobility. When their power weakened, the libraries of statesmen like Mazarin would be a natural target for the anger of the populace, often with the tacit support of the great men they had eclipsed.

Kirkwood's vision was very different. The Reformation had proclaimed the instruction of the people as a central goal of the new evangelical movement. The Elizabethan Church had famously prescribed that each parish church should have a copy of *Foxe's Book of Martyrs* and the Gospel paraphrases of Erasmus. These small parochial libraries would replace the collection of Mass books gathered by the Catholic churches of the medieval era. Yet Kirkwood and his friend, Thomas Bray, were well aware that two centuries of Protestant preaching, catechising and religious instruction had not turned this vision of access to libraries into reality. Rather Scotland and England, like the Netherlands and northern Germany, had developed a patchwork of church, school and town libraries largely depending on the pious lay donors who had established them. Others had grown quickly as repositories of redundant church books confiscated from the dissolved monasteries, most of which were irrelevant to the needs of their anticipated patrons. It was as patently insufficient a vision of the public library as Mazarin's lofty and limited invitation to scholars of the Republic of Letters to inspect the treasures he had assembled in his library in Paris. Neither would have an enduring future.

A Contested Inheritance

The origins of the town library can be traced to the era of Charlemagne.[2] In 802, the Synod of Aachen had made parish churches responsible for keeping a minimal number of liturgical books. Books were required for worship and the dispensing of the sacraments, for biblical exposition, and sermons: a church with twenty or thirty books could therefore be considered very well equipped. However, clergy were also expected to increase the book possessions passed on to them.[3] This was an ambitious prescription, and one difficult to police effectively, but it did establish a paradigm of library building firmly centred on the parish church. Before the invention of printing, the local church library would have been the largest, if not the only, library in many European communities.

The idea that such libraries could and should be of use to the whole community arose only around the fourteenth and fifteenth centuries. Bequests aimed at benefitting the general public were naturally given to parish churches, because they were a regularly used space available to the entire community. They also provided the most favourable conditions for storage and preservation, administration and public accessibility, as funds were rarely available for a separate library building. Examples of pastors or wealthy citizens who made bequests of their book collections to their communities can be found in most parts of Europe. In 1309, Pastor Jordanus left the eighteen books in his possession to his parish of St Andrew in Braunschweig in central Germany. One of his successors bequeathed some forty volumes a hundred years later. Another century passed before Gerwin of Hameln, the council scribe of Braunschweig, deposited 336 books in the library while still living.[4] Such generosity was prompted by pride in one's community, to satisfy the wish to be praised by one's peers, or by a general desire to leave material possessions in the world after one's departure.

The tradition of bequeathing books to the community increased with the invention of printing, as more and more citizens were able to amass substantial collections of books. Yet their increasingly diverse range of subject material meant that sometimes the local church no longer made an appropriate destination for such bequests. In the sixteenth and seventeenth centuries, we find an increasing number of collectors leaving their libraries to the town, with the specific instruction to establish a municipal or public library. However, it required substantial financial incentives to effect the transformation from a personal library to a municipal institution. The Flemish priest Frans Potens bequeathed his book collection to the town of Kortrijk in 1564; on his deathbed, Potens appointed two burgomasters and aldermen as executors, but after his death the magistrates proved reluctant to fulfil the terms of the legacy.[5] Disappointing this may be, but Frans Potens was far from the only book collector to have their carefully thought-out will ignored in this manner.

The burden of caring dutifully for someone else's books was great enough, but to develop them as a public resource often proved an unsurmountable challenge. In Catholic regions, it remained far more convenient to deposit book collections in ecclesiastical institutions, monastic houses or the new seminaries. In Protestant Europe, attempts to set up civic institutions were further complicated by the fact that the most expedient source of books from which to build such collections were the holdings of abolished monastic libraries. This filled the new institutions with collections of outdated scholastic theology of marginal interest even to the local ministers. It was no wonder that so many of these collections were quickly consigned to the church attic, out of public view.

One community that did manage to develop a popular town library was the large, rich and fiercely independent port city of Hamburg. Here the municipal library flourished, thanks to relatively generous conditions of access. From 1651 onwards, it was open for four hours each day, and fifty years later it even allowed citizens of the city to borrow books. The collection grew from 25,000 volumes in 1704 to 100,000 volumes by the end of the eighteenth century.[6] In the great cities of the Swiss cantons, Zurich and Basel, the destruction of church property accompanying the Reformation hindered attempts to set up municipal libraries; yet here too, civic pride ultimately prevailed.[7] The Zurich *Burgerbibliothek* was founded in 1629 as a private initiative by four young merchants. It expanded thanks to donations from generous citizens, most notably through objects from their cabinets of curiosities.[8] Basel, too, accumulated a remarkable collection of such objects, including the famous Erasmus chest, where Erasmus reputedly stored the gifts brought to his door by admirers and supplicants for his goodwill.[9]

Outside these large cities, it proved much more difficult to establish flourishing libraries. Since they frequently consisted of texts from the abolished Catholic monasteries, it was difficult to justify the expense of curating a collection of hundreds or thousands of old books, mostly in Latin, for a non-existent public. Without the injection of civic energy that was evident in the great free German cities, monastic book collections were dumped in the

nearest convenient location or left in situ. In small towns the ultimate destination for these libraries was often the local school, itself
attached to the newly consecrated Protestant church. In the first
days of the Reformation, Martin Luther had made an eloquent call
for the establishment of schools to educate German youth, and his
message was heeded. When a territory accepted Lutheranism, the
new *Kirchenordnungen*, the ecclesiastical ordinances, made provisions for the new schools to be equipped with libraries, for the use
of students and teachers alike. This proved a useful excuse to hoard
antiquated book collections from churches and monasteries, once
the titles penned by the most vehement Catholic apologists had
been removed.

By the eighteenth century, many German school libraries had
as many as 10,000 books, magnificent scholarly collections, but
not very useful to young students. Far more appropriate were the
small parish libraries, stocked with recent German devotional literature, that were established later in the seventeenth or eighteenth
centuries. The church libraries of Mecklenburg–Pomerania generally comprised between fifty and 200 books, the result of carefully
considered purchases or donations by the local minister; or, as in
Salzwedel, Saxony, the bequests of burgomasters.[10] The success of
these libraries ultimately depended on the degree of access, as well
as the enthusiasm of local ministers and schoolmasters. If they
were prepared to treat the library as a genuine public resource,
rather than an adjunct to their personal collection, then a parish
or school library could flourish.

If the narrative of the early public library in the German lands
is a story of mixed fortunes, that of the Netherlands is a sorry tale.[11]
The flourishing mercantile centres of the Netherlands had a rich
history of parish and monastic libraries before the Reformation;
the town of Gouda alone had no fewer than eleven. All were badly
affected by the tribulations of the Revolt that ended with the independence of the Dutch Republic and the acceptance of Calvinism
as the acknowledged state religion. The town library of Zutphen,
in the east of the country, was first opened in the 1560s, shortly
before the outbreak of the conflict. It was plundered five times
between 1572 and 1591, and its collection declined from 357 works

to barely a hundred. The desperate librarian at one point tried to cement up the door of the library, but he found that this was no serious obstacle to soldiers on a quest for the gilded clasps that adorned the bindings in the collection.

By the 1590s, Protestantism was entrenched in all the provinces that made up the Dutch Republic, and monastic property in each town was quickly turned over for use by the state as Protestant churches, orphanages, schools, arsenals or warehouses. Libraries increasingly became part of this programme of renovation, by necessity as much as by desire: city councils and the Reformed ministers soon realised that they had substantial monastic collections on their hands, built up over centuries, that needed to be put to use.

What resulted was a remarkably energetic programme of library building accomplished in the four decades between 1580 and 1620. With the rhetoric of providing 'a library for public service' or 'a library for common use', the former monastic holdings were transformed into new city libraries. Most contained 200 to 300 books, although invariably the best books had been plundered or taken by the monks when they were expelled. The councillors realised that building an adequate library required additional purchases, and in most towns substantial funds were made available to augment the collections. In Deventer, a library of forty-six books grew to some 600 within two decades. The council of Alkmaar spent 800 guilders at two auctions in 1601 and 1607 to purchase books for the library. Donations were also solicited from distinguished members of the community, as in Utrecht, where two major bequests saw the library grow by 3,000 volumes. Such large bequests, it should be said, were uncommon. The family of one of the Utrecht donors, Huybert van Buchell, were aghast that he had given away his books in his will, rather than allow the family to sell them at auction.

Limited acquisition budgets were often consumed by prestige purchases, multi-volume atlases or polyglot Bibles, as was the case in Deventer, Nijmegen, Utrecht and Amsterdam. The spirit of competition played its part in ambitious acquisitions of this nature: Amsterdam, for instance, spent 400 guilders on acquiring the *Oceanus Juris*, twenty-eight Latin folio volumes filled with a compendium of jurisprudential knowledge, printed in Venice in the 1580s; the librarian at Gouda auctioned off books from the collection in order to buy more volumes of atlases, and to complement the two Blaeu globes that the library had purchased earlier; and when the Rotterdam admiral Cornelis Matelief returned from a voyage to the East Indies in 1608, he donated a manuscript Qur'an to the local library, given to him by the ruler of Malacca.

The city fathers clearly believed that such luxurious items were a necessary accoutrement of a city library. If anything, the libraries imitated academic libraries in form and function, as repositories of reference works. This ensured that the municipal institutions were bound to remain dominated by books in Latin. The library of Amsterdam, celebrated by the city council in two lavishly published catalogues, possessed only a few books in Dutch and German. An alternative seems never to have been considered. For the same price of the *Oceanus Juris*, some 300 vernacular works could have been purchased for the library, which would certainly have appealed to a larger proportion of the community. Instead, the municipal libraries of the Netherlands remained sources of civic pride, unused but admired.

Because the city libraries had been padded with relatively new, expensive books, curators were much less likely to open their doors freely to local citizens. Some of the municipal libraries had begun with relatively generous terms of access. Zutphen had distributed sixty keys to leading members of the city, but after the Dutch Revolt these were ordered to be returned. In most towns, terms of access were never specified clearly and were thus entirely at the discretion of the minister, councillor or schoolmaster who had been appointed as the librarian. Gouda had one of the few libraries where access was carefully regulated: upon paying the fee of 6 guilders, or donating books equivalent to the same sum, 'honourable men' of the town could use the library. Women and children were expressly forbidden from entering the library.[12] The librarian at Gouda, recognising that the library contained many old monastic books that might offend Protestant readers, warned users that they were not allowed to cross out passages in the books that they disagreed with.

Security concerns also prompted city councils to invest significant funds on chaining books to lecterns or desks. This traditionalist architecture (that can still be observed today in the former town library of Zutphen in the St Walburgis Church) was adopted partly out of reverence to an older ecclesiastical model of book collecting. While the towns had rejected Catholic monasticism, they appropriated monastic ideals of intensive devotional study, focused on a single book at a time: this had serious consequences for the growth of the town libraries, due to the space required for the lecterns to which the books were chained. Nor were these books, or the reading conditions, likely to attract readers, since the libraries were invariably unheated and often ill lit. As a result, local government soon lost interest, and there is little evidence of library growth after the 1620s. The Deventer library did not grow at all between 1602 and 1710. In 1698, a German visitor, describing the library as 'very bad', still had a better experience than the foreign nobleman who was shown the town library of Alkmaar in 1704 and had to have his clothes washed afterwards because of the layers of dust and dirt.

The English Parish Library

England's patchwork of early public libraries emerged later than in Germany or the Netherlands. Here too the libraries were heavily influenced by local clergy, and especially charismatic local preachers. A case in point, the fine library at Ipswich was established tentatively from the last years of the sixteenth century, though it only found a proper home in 1617.[13] The initiative for its foundation came from William Smarte, draper, member of parliament and local hero: Smarte was briefly imprisoned for having prevented the export of Suffolk bacon to the Earl of Leicester's forces in the Low Countries, local patriotism trumping duty to country. His bequest for a library also became snarled in legal issues and competing claims for the books and manuscripts, a contest won by the University of Cambridge. So it was only with the arrival of Samuel Ward as town preacher that the library became reality. Ipswich, the birthplace of Cardinal Wolsey, who for over a decade was the influential first minister to King Henry VIII, was already in a highly privileged position with a distinguished grammar school. The council minute ordering Ward and his colleagues to 'make view in the hospital for some convenient rooms there for the placing of a library' comes at the end of a discussion of scholarships for local boys to attend Cambridge under the terms of the contested Smarte bequest.

Ward's priority was more conventional – establishing a working library for himself and other Suffolk preachers – and he hit on the clever idea of encouraging monetary donations rather than gifts of books. Ward's charismatic leadership ensured a cascade of giving, with over a hundred local citizens giving money before 1650. All the books bought were marked with a printed label naming the donor. Thanks to Ward's lobbying, the council set aside space at the north end of Taylors Hall, which was renovated and glazed at public expense after the receipt of the books. Animated by the energy of a respected local preacher and fuelled by civic pride, the collection reflects this dual purpose: a mixture of stately Protestant commentaries for the use of the clergy, and pious literature in English for the sober citizens. Significantly, the books were unchained, stored on shelves along the walls.

The county of Suffolk spawned a remarkable network of parish libraries in its prosperous wool towns, radiating out from the two major market towns at opposite ends of the county, Ipswich and Bury St Edmunds.[14] We know of fifteen, of which, rather miraculously, eight are still more or less intact. Leaving aside the town library at Ipswich, the greatest by far was that of St James's church (now cathedral) at Bury, which consisted of some 481 books, the majority in Latin. The surviving catalogue of gifts records the names of 117 individuals who donated books to the library between 1595 and 1764, predominantly gentry, clergy, physicians and schoolmasters, with the occasional tradesman. The inscriptions added to these books neatly illustrate the conflict of purpose playing out in the libraries of provincial England. When Anthony Rous, rector of Hessett, gave a valuable Basel folio of 1526 to the Bury library in 1595, he indicated that this was for the use of theological students, *'in usum theologiae studiosorum'*. The Royalist High Master of the grammar school in 1639 had a rather wider constituency in mind, '*in usum republicae literariae*', though it might be said that the book, an edition of the Pauline epistles, would have appealed mostly to the clergy.[15] Many of the other Suffolk libraries were the gift of individual donors for the use of the local minister: some, indeed, were housed in the parsonage rather than the church. Sometimes these donations seem rather ill advised. In the early eighteenth century, two tiny villages a mile apart near Lavenham received separate donations amounting to 3,500 books. A bewildering burden to their incumbents, they would have been a more suitable adornment to the great wool church at Lavenham. It is perhaps no coincidence that both disappeared, leaving scarcely a trace, at the beginning of the nineteenth century.

As these examples from Suffolk demonstrate, most of these new libraries were attached to parish churches and kept under the control of the local clergy. The local vicar was often appointed as the librarian. They were also generally theological in content, and very Latinate. They were bequeathed by both ministers and secular collectors for the spiritual health of the community, and to memorialise a life that would otherwise sink into obscurity. When in 1681, John Tregonwell left his books to establish a church library at Milton Abbas in Dorset, this was 'a thankful acknowledgement of God's wonderful mercy in his preservation, when he fell from the top of this church'.[16] This providential escape secured a notable collection for a small Dorset village.

Surprisingly, given that it was the location of almost all of the English publishing industry, London was exceptionally poorly served by public libraries. In the middle of the seventeenth century, the only libraries were those at Westminster Abbey, St Paul's and Sion College.[17] Perhaps conscious of this, in 1684, Thomas Tenison, later Archbishop of Canterbury, founded a library for clergy in St Martin-in-the-Fields in London. According to John Evelyn,

> He [Tenison] told me there were thirty or forty young men in orders in his parish, either, governors to young gent[lemen]: or chaplains to noble-men, who being reprov'd by him upon occasion, for frequenting taverns or coffee-houses, [said]

they would study and employ their time better, if they had books.[18]

Yet this library would be far less substantial than the library of some 8,100 books and pamphlets that in 1704, Thomas Plume, vicar of Greenwich and archdeacon of Rochester, bequeathed to his native town of Maldon, in Essex, to be kept in the old St Peter's church in the town centre. This he established 'for the use of the minister and clergy of the neighbouring parishes who generally make this town their place of residence on account of the unwholesomeness of the air in the vicinity of their churches'.[19] Yet how many well-qualified and sufficiently intellectually curious ministers were there around Maldon to take advantage of such a rich bequest? The truth is that a national network that developed in this way, through the idiosyncratic decisions of private collectors, was hardly likely to meet the more urgent need for libraries in the places where they would have been most useful. It seems that many library builders prioritised their own desire – to leave a monumental presence in their community – over careful consideration of the future users of their bequest.

Collectors always find it difficult to conceive that what they have curated, at great expense and effort, may hold little value to others. For that reason, few private collections donated by men such as Plume in Maldon or Francis Trigge in Grantham, Lincolnshire, left a lasting legacy as public libraries.[20] Those who did succeed, like Johannes Thysius in Leiden and Humphrey Chetham in Manchester, were immensely rich. A library was their life's work, and a monument to their taste or piety; but they had to leave a significant estate to pay the costs of upkeep for the library to be of future use to the public.[21] Chetham's was different from most English public libraries because it was given over to trustees rather than to a parish or city council. This decision saved the library from the neglectful administration that sealed the fate of many of the smaller parish and town libraries.[22] It was only at the end of the seventeenth century that two men of great vision and tenacity, James Kirkwood and Thomas Bray, would conceive a national network of libraries, intended to seed an efflorescence of public collections.

Scottish Alexandria

By 1700, there were parish, school and city libraries dotted all over Europe. Some were founded by individual donors, by groups of friends, or by the local authorities. There were few which were truly satisfactory, but that was no impediment to ambitious plans for a future in which public libraries served a broad public in towns and the countryside. In 1699, the Reverend James Kirkwood presented to the world one of the most comprehensive library programmes ever conceived: to establish a public library in every parish in his native Scotland.

Kirkwood's vision emerged partially from the widely shared perplexity at the sheer scale of the expanding book stock of Europe. This rung true especially on the periphery of the book world, where there was little domestic printing, and where books were naturally more expensive and more difficult to come by. By establishing libraries all over Scotland, Kirkwood mused, it would be

> the first and the only nation for a while, that shall have this regular and useful plenty of books ... Hereby all sort of learning will mightily increase and flourish amongst us, and though we be not a great or a rich people, yet we may be a wise and a learned people. Yea further, these libraries in two or three hundred years will be so full and compleat, that the most famous and magnificent libraries in the world, shall not outdo the meanest library in any parish of this kingdom.[23]

A source of Scottish patriotism, the new libraries would also keep bright young men at home, rather than have them spend all their money abroad at foreign universities. Anticipating future public library campaigners in the nineteenth century, Kirkwood argued that a good local library would have a moral function, encouraging men to spend less time gambling and drinking, and more time reading.

To persuade his fellow countrymen, Kirkwood published a twelve-point plan in a short, easily digestible pamphlet. The proposals stretched towards the utopian: Kirkwood demanded that every

Scottish minister should donate all of his own books to his local parish, before sending a copy of the catalogue of the collection to a central 'principal' library in Edinburgh. Every book would then be valued, so that ministers could be compensated. After the catalogues of all the parish libraries had been scrutinised, a list would be drawn up of the books that each parish library should have, or at least be available in every presbytery. These would be purchased or bartered with other parishes. Finally, and most radically, every parish library would receive a copy of every book printed. This would be funded with £72,000 Scots of public money, financed by landholders in every parish and deductions from the salaries of ministers. A central office was to be set up to check regularly which books were printed in Europe, so that copies of the books could be acquired, or reprinted in Scotland, at a special new printing house devoted entirely to providing books for the parish libraries.

Like all pilgrims searching for the lost library of Alexandria, Kirkwood was hopelessly idealistic. The idea that ministers should surrender all their own books against the hope of future compensation was naive, to say the least, and since ministers were crucial to the whole cataloguing enterprise, it ensured that the scheme would make no progress. Kirkwood's plan was ignored by the church assembly of Scotland. Not easily discouraged, the persistent library reformer proposed a more modest plan in 1702. This second programme was meant to establish libraries only in the Highlands, the part of Scotland least well served by large personal book collections or educational institutions.[24] This time Kirkwood succeeded, but only by emphasising to fellow Protestants the threat of Catholic missionaries roaming the Highlands, persuading book-poor clergymen and lay folk to return to the bosom of Rome.[25] His clarion call had especial resonance in London, where many wealthy Protestants had sympathy for Kirkwood's evangelical cause and a healthy fear of Jacobite agitation. Through dogged campaigning, over £1,300 was raised, in addition to many private book donations. More than 5,000 volumes would be shipped from London to Scotland, and between 1704 and 1708 seventy-seven libraries were founded across the Highlands and Islands, open to all local inhabitants.

12. The oldest lending library in Scotland, at Innerpeffray, Perthshire.
The library was first housed in a small upstairs room in the chapel
(right), before it was moved in 1762 (to the building on the left), with the
collection upstairs and accommodation for the librarian downstairs.

This was a significant achievement, yet its success was also its undoing. Planted in areas where the local population were at best indifferent to Protestantism, the libraries were mistrusted as covert Presbyterian enterprises. When Kirkwood died in 1709, the initiative of the library movement died with him, and without further financial contributions from landowners in the Highlands it was difficult to maintain the libraries. By 1730, many Kirkwood libraries had disappeared; two were already lost in 1715, when Jacobite rebels seized and destroyed the libraries at Alness in Ross-shire. The executor of the estate of Thomas Chisholm, the librarian at Kilmorack in Inverness-shire (a predominantly Catholic area), sold the parish books by weight for snuff wrappers.[26] By the early nineteenth century there was barely a trace left of the libraries founded a hundred years earlier.

Despite its failure, the need Kirkwood identified was very real. In rural areas, it was vital for library users to take books home because trips to the local church could be few and far between.

Anyone who lived up to twenty miles away from their Kirk-wood library could borrow a small book for up to a fortnight, while substantial tomes could be borrowed for a longer period. Lending rights were equally crucial to the success of the public library established at Innerpeffray, a hamlet in Perthshire, founded by Lord David Drummond of Madertie in 1680 'for the benefit and encouragement of young students'. Drummond's substantial bequest ensured the library's survival: this collection of some 3,000 volumes is still in existence today, and a recognised treasure of Scottish library culture. Located four miles from the nearest town, the library at Innerpeffray served as a centre of spiritual and recreational literature for a community spread among the foothills of the Highlands. A lending register for the second half of the eighteenth century shows that 287 borrowers of all social classes, including eleven women, borrowed books 1,483 times.[27] The library had a significant scholarly profile (Drummond had been a fashionable collector), but the books that were borrowed most were English-language devotional and historical works. The key to success for the public library, as many library founders failed to realise, was to make available books that users truly wanted to read.

Thomas Bray's Grand Design

Kirkwood's cognate in England was the Reverend Thomas Bray; indeed, he and Kirkwood were friends, and mutually supportive of each other's ventures. In 1698, Bray had established the Society for Promoting Christian Knowledge, the SPCK.[28] He focused on providing small library collections for parish churches in rural communities, as outlined in his 1709 *Proposals for Erecting Parochial Libraries in the Meanly Endowed Cures throughout England* which was similar in spirit, though less directive, than Kirkwood's contemporary scheme. All the parishes favoured by this gift received a chest of books, each with a catalogue and a copy of the 1708 Parochial Libraries Act, in which Bray had played an instrumental role, pasted inside the lid.

The Bray libraries, some fifty-two in these early years, and rising to 140 after his death, generally contained between sixty-two and seventy-two volumes, delivered in oak carrying cases.[29] Each library cost £20, paid partly by trustees of the SPCK, though the parish that was to receive the library was required to contribute £5. The recipients were carefully chosen. In Suffolk, already well favoured with libraries, All Saints in Sudbury was the only recipient. Still, the prestige of this library in 1903 was enough to persuade the rector of Milden to donate his parish library of over 2,000 volumes to Sudbury's Bray library, a far smaller collection (in 1813 comprising only thirty-nine titles).[30] Gratefully received in Sudbury, the most valuable items were promptly sold to buy new books.[31]

Bray's SPCK libraries were really meant for clergymen rather than parishioners. Their impact was reduced by the fact that it was at precisely this moment, between 1680 and 1720, that many communities were accumulating their own, far more substantial libraries. This, as we have seen, was often the result of bequests of individual book collectors, but sometimes the town council would take a more instrumental role. In Maidstone, the council had ordered their chamberlain to buy Walton's six-volume Polyglot Bible and place it in the church vestry for the use of any inhabitant in 1658. By 1716, there were thirty-two books in the church, and these books could also be borrowed by citizens. In 1731, the town council bought the remains of the private library of the recently deceased Thomas Bray, some 559 titles, also for the church library. Thanks to the borrowing records of the library, we know that clergymen accounted for only half the users. In libraries like this, we see prototypes of more genuinely public libraries: the church was simply an appropriate location to house the books.[32]

The evangelism of rural England represented only half of Bray's ambitious mission field. In 1696, Bray had caught the eye of the Bishop of London, Henry Compton. Compton was anxious for the future of the Anglican Church in the American colonies, and appointed Bray as his agent to bring order and succour to these far-flung communities.[33] In 1699, Bray set sail for America. In Maryland, he established thirty parishes endowed with seventeen parish libraries, though his endeavours on behalf of the church were soon mired in colonial politics, which also painfully delayed the payment of his promised salary. Nothing daunted, Bray

13. A bookplate for the Society for the Propagation of the Gospel in Foreign Parts (1704). The Protestant minister, proudly bearing a book at the bow of a ship, greets the indigenous inhabitants destined to be instructed in the Christian faith. It is safe to say that such dreams were not always realised.

returned to England, where he pursued the foundation of a new society for the Propagation of the Gospel in Foreign Parts, closely allied to the SPCK. He also continued energetically raising funds for his American libraries, netting the considerable sum of £5,000 for the purchase of books. Bray proposed that in addition to his parochial libraries, each colony should have a provincial library and a series of laymen's libraries, a stock of Bibles and improving literature, to be housed in the church for lending to members of the congregation.

All told, Bray collected funds to establish thirty-eight parochial, five provincial and thirty-seven laymen's libraries in the American colonies. The most considerable, in Annapolis, Maryland, was sent more than a thousand books, though the parochial libraries sometimes consisted of no more than ten volumes. Their recipients were not always grateful. In Bath, North Carolina, the library was utterly dissipated within nine years of its arrival, as reported by a local Anglican minister: 'The books are all unbound and have served for some time as waste paper.' Even the books destined for the parochial and laymen's libraries could be misappropriated:

'Madame Hyde, the wife of the governor, sold me all the books committed to her care for butter and eggs.'[34] By the end of the revolutionary wars most of the Bray libraries had disappeared altogether; the Annapolis library today is reduced to a mere 211 of the original 1,095 volumes.

What most endured from these endeavours was not the libraries but the SPCK. In the next two centuries the society would distribute millions of tracts, in the mill towns of industrial England and to all corners of the British Empire. The society recognised, as many Victorian idealists did not, that if the new industrial classes were to be brought to God, then it was necessary to bring the books to the people, rather than insisting that the people came to the libraries. This was an implicit recognition of the failure of the earlier generations of parochial, laymen's or town libraries to address the needs of any but the clergy and a limited civic elite. The age of the public library still lay some way in the future.

Chapter Eleven

CARDINAL ERRORS

There were few statesmen whose power rivalled that of Cardinal Richelieu, chief minister of King Louis XIII of France. For close to two decades, the cardinal directed the government of one of the most powerful countries in the world. That he was able to do so without ending his career in disgrace, or with his head on a block, was a remarkable feat, especially so for a man from the minor nobility, who made his fair share of enemies and amassed extraordinary wealth for himself and his family. Richelieu was the most successful figure of a new generation of statesmen, the great ministers, who, throughout Europe, were responsible for a rapid expansion of the power of the state and the instruments of government. They exercised this role in the name of kings and queens, but the reliance of monarchs on the great ministers riled the old orders, especially members of the aristocracy, whose superior bloodline had always granted them a position at the heart of court. The great ministers could be nobles by birth, but they generally assumed their position thanks to their juridical or clerical training. Their weapon was the pen, rarely the sword.

Cardinal Richelieu's accumulation of wealth and power was matched by his assiduous attention to the growing bureaucracy of government. To fulfil their duties, great ministers had increasing need for large reference collections of working papers, law books and ordinances. Richelieu also required scholars, erudite men who could trawl through books for legal precedents, correspond with librarians abroad and acquire new volumes for their patron's use.[1] Out of these dynamic working collections developed ever larger libraries. Books also found their way to ministers of state in much the same way as they did to monarchs, as gifts, presented by scholars keen to find themselves in the employ of a great statesman. The dizzying heights of power also presented other opportunities. After Richelieu subdued the rebellious Protestants of La Rochelle in 1628, King Louis XIII granted him the entire town library as a reward. By the end of this life, Richelieu had a library of over 6,000 volumes, especially rich in Greek, Hebrew and Arabic manuscripts. His great rival, Gaspar de Guzmán, the Count-Duke of Olivares and chief minister of Spain, had an equally distinguished library, with over 5,000 printed volumes and 1,400 manuscripts.[2]

The size of these collections indicates that the great ministers were not only passive collectors. They spent substantial resources on building impressive libraries, remarkable for the rarity of their choicest volumes and the encyclopaedic scope of their holdings. These were multifunctional libraries: a supplement to the minister's working archive, but also a means of display, and, to a limited extent, a public resource. The statesman's library was implicitly public in the sense that it was operating in a public context; many of the great collections were also built with public funds. Two centuries earlier, Renaissance cardinals and statesmen had prided themselves on their small and secretive *studioli*, like that of Duke Federico of Urbino, intimate spaces designed to impress a small number of guests. The seventeenth- and eighteenth-century libraries of cardinals and ministers of state were entirely different: large, ostentatious and accessible to those with the right connections. Modelled, perhaps unconsciously, on the imperial libraries of Rome, they functioned as gathering places for artists and writers who would play their part in elevating the reputation of the patron, protecting him against rivals at court and countering the crude jokes overheard on the streets. The great libraries of antiquity, which served a similar role as a fount of patronage, were reborn at the heart of Europe's expanding bureaucratic states.

Hushed insults and tavern rumours had to be taken seriously by the great ministers, for their hold on power was always precarious. Their new status required lavish expenditure and grandiose display beyond the resources of rivals at court, and they spent freely on palaces, gardens, art collections, an extensive household and a loyal guard. King James VI and I of Scotland and England, viewing Audley End in Essex, the newly built house of his lord high treasurer, Thomas Howard, is said to have remarked that it was sufficient for a minister in such high office but too big for a king. This shaft of wit demonstrates the perspicacity of this shrewd monarch, who understood but also enjoyed the dangerous tightrope act performed by those who served him, yet neglected to ensure that they did not serve themselves too much in the process.

Richelieu died in 1642, at the height of his power. In his will he bequeathed his personal library to the French public, to indicate that his collecting had always been undertaken for the benefit of the people.[3] This should have catapulted France to the forefront of the movement to create great libraries open to the public. Contemporaries talked of three great public libraries: Thomas Bodley's Oxford library, and two Catholic libraries founded in Italy, the Ambrosiana in Milan and the Angelica in Rome. Sadly for France, Richelieu's collection was not destined to join this pantheon. The University of Paris, the Sorbonne, was to administer Richelieu's collection, but was instructed to leave the books in their present location at the late cardinal's residence. Many of the most prized items in the collection, the Greek manuscripts, went missing during several rounds of examination while an inventory was prepared. In 1660 the Sorbonne asserted its right over the collection and demanded that the books be moved to their premises. This was somewhat perverse, since there was little room on the shelves of the existing library for a collection of this size. Richelieu's books were simply removed to storage, and over time many volumes were disposed of. As new men plotted their rise to the summit of power, new libraries were assembled. Those who scrambled to put on Richelieu's mantle were too busy with their own ambitious plans to pay much attention to the plundered collection of books mouldering in storage.

Buying by the Foot

Shortly before his death, Cardinal Richelieu had recalled from Italy a fellow Frenchman, Gabriel Naudé, to organise and expand his book collection. Naudé was a man very much in demand, the living epitome of the new professional librarian, employed by the great to establish or build a library. Characteristically, this new breed of librarian–consultants were scholars from a humbler background who could devote themselves to their patron's ambition with a zeal that did not come naturally to those of more elevated ranks. The precocious second son of a modest but respectable Parisian household, Naudé had first distinguished himself as the librarian of Henri II de Mesmes, one of the presidents of the Paris Parlement. Under his watch, the Mesmes library served as a meeting place for the intellectual elite of the capital, and Naudé, then in his early twenties, was able to become the familiar of the greatest scholars of the Paris intelligentsia. After curating and cataloguing the 8,000-volume-strong collection, the young librarian thanked his patron by writing a short tract, entitled *Advis pour dresser une bibliothèque* (Advice on Establishing a Library). Published in 1627, this was the first guide addressed directly to would-be book collectors, explaining what they should collect and how they should arrange their library.[4]

The *Advis* was Naudé's calling card to the cultural elite of France. Praising the tasteful collecting of his patron was akin to praising his own skills as a librarian. Naudé's decision to write in French, rather than Latin, also hints at the intended audience of the work: not fellow scholars, who would be Naudé's rivals for employment, but wealthy noblemen and diplomats, potentially even more distinguished patrons than Henri de Mesmes. Naudé understood that to this elite, a library was more important as a social space than as a storehouse for books. Attracting luminaries to one's library was a crucial step towards elevating one's influence and reputation. To ram this message home, Naudé mused at great length on the absence of great public libraries, and the necessity of powerful magnates to establish them: and, implicitly, to employ learned librarians like himself.

What sort of library should the great magnate of Naudé's dreams create? Naudé was not radically innovative in his advice, wrapping contemporary collecting practice in a blanket of ancient authority. He urged his patron to consider carefully what books should adorn his library, as a reflection of his erudition, but at the same time he suggested that a great library should be universal in scope and include all the traditional faculties of scholarship. Naudé built on these established models by encouraging the collector to include heretical books, a tradition that was already pronounced in Protestant countries but often eschewed by Catholic collectors. Most controversial was Naudé's endorsement of the collecting of ephemera, 'such as satires, broadsides, [university] theses, scraps, [printing] proofs and the like', precisely the sort of material that Sir Thomas Bodley was so keen to keep out of the Oxford library. Naudé's recommendation came with a sensible qualification, that ephemeral material should be carefully sorted and bound to make it truly useful. Most important of all was to let the world know that you were a collector: that way gifts would inevitably flow into your hands. The best way to announce your credentials as a library builder was to purchase a complete collection from a distinguished owner, or their heirs. One could always sell off unwanted books or duplicates later.

This knowledgeable pragmatism was a breath of fresh air in the book world, and word of Naudé's expertise spread rapidly. Several years after publishing the *Advis*, his reputation won him recommendation to an influential Italian cardinal, Guidi di Bagno, whom he had met in Paris. As his secretary and librarian, Naudé accompanied Bagno back to Rome, where he spent ten years. Italy, with its rich profusion of libraries, was a cornucopia of delights; it was also a useful location from which one could maintain social credit with powerful patrons back home. From Rome, Naudé was able to hunt down desired texts for collectors in France and present himself as resourceful and connected. Thus, in 1642, when Cardinal Richelieu desired a librarian, Naudé was a natural candidate.

Richelieu's death, several months after Naudé's appointment, was a blow, but one that was immediately made good by Richelieu's successor as chief minister, Cardinal Jules Mazarin. In Mazarin, Naudé had found the ideal patron: a man with unlimited resources who still had to prove his worth to the French state, and justify the immense power inherited from Richelieu. An Italian by birth, Mazarin would also have to demonstrate his loyalty to France, and one of the ways in which he set about this task was to build a library that would be the richest and most complete in Europe.[5]

Naudé had to work fast: Mazarin's staff were already hard at work constructing a magnificent library in the Palais-Cardinal, the substantial property that had been the residence of Cardinal Richelieu. Naudé swiftly recognised that the solution to his patron's demands lay in the block purchases of books by weight, rather than the careful selection that the librarian had called for in his *Advis*. The 150 bookstores of Paris provided him with 6,000 titles. Naudé then snapped up a great Parisian library, which secured another 6,000 books, at the cost of 22,000 livres (ten times Naudé's annual income).

With these accessions secured, the Bibliothèque Mazarine was thrown open to the public every Thursday. By 30 January 1644 the bi-weekly Paris *Gazette* could already report that Cardinal Mazarin had turned his library, then double the size of the royal book collection, into 'an academy for all the learned and curious, who flock there on Thursdays, from morning till night, in order to peruse his beautiful library'. Yet Naudé's task was far from finished. In April 1645 he left for Italy, where he purchased stock by the yard – and drove a hard bargain with the booksellers in the process. According to a friend, Gian Vittorio Rossi, the bookseller would attempt to strike a good deal,

> but in the end it is Naudé who by insisting, by bullying, by blustering and finally by sheer gall, gets his way so that he carries off the very best volumes cheaper than if they were pears or lemons, while the merchant, reflecting on this transaction, complains later that a spell was cast over his eyes and his hand forced, because he could have gotten a far better price for these books from the spice merchants for wrapping incense or pepper, or from the grocers for wrapping up butter or fish in sauce, and other pickled items.[6]

Pitiless in the face of such lamentations, Naudé pursued this wholesale pillage in Florence, Mantua, Padua and Venice. Within eight months he had assembled eighty-six bales of books. 'Nothing disgusts him,' according to Ismaël Boulliau, a bibliophile who

GABR. NAVDÆVS PARIS. E. CARD.
MAZARINI BIBLIOTH. Æ. A. XLIX

14. Gabriel Naudé, the energetic librarian who bought books by the
yard to fulfil the dreams of his patron, Cardinal Mazarin. Although he
announced himself through his theoretical musings on library building,
it was his strong-willed pragmatism that secured his reputation.

witnessed several of these forays: 'He finds everything good,
especially books by unknown authors.' By the time Naudé had
ransacked the bookshops of Venice, Boulliau was worried there
would be nothing left, and the local inhabitants would be reduced
'to primers and books of hours'.

The indefatigable librarian arrived back in Paris with 14,000
books, for which the cardinal was required to stump up only
12,000 livres, which included Naudé's personal expenses. After
two years of frantic travel, through France, Switzerland, Germany,
England and the Netherlands, Naudé had furnished the cardinal
with a library of breathtaking size – estimated at 40,000 printed
books and 850 volumes of manuscripts. The total cost amounted
to 65,000 livres, though Naudé recouped 4,000 livres by selling
duplicates back into the Parisian market.

On the open days of the Bibliothèque Mazarine, between eighty and 100 scholars worked in the library. Even if one does not believe Naudé's boast that foreign scholars cried in amazement when they discovered books from their own country that they had never seen before, one can understand that the unprecedentedly liberal access to such an enormous collection won many admirers. For a few years, the Mazarine library was the greatest public library the world had thus far seen.

Sadly, this was not to last: within a few years Cardinal Mazarin was on the run, forced to flee Paris by the Fronde rebellion, a complex protest against economic hardship and the rule of Mazarin and the Queen Regent, Anne of Austria, rumoured to be his lover. Naudé and others fought a long rearguard action to save the great library; initially, with some success. Although Mazarin's goods and property were declared confiscated by the Parlement of Paris in 1648, the library was padlocked and the contents remained intact. It was as if even his most urgent critics, who would eagerly have sacrificed the cardinal, recognised the cultural significance of what he and his librarian had created. Even the young king, Louis XIV, was enlisted to save the library. But on 29 December 1652, towards the end of the insurrection, the Frondeurs finally ordered the sale of the contents of Mazarin's palaces.

News of the dissolution of the library spread rapidly abroad, not least because rival collectors were licking their lips at the prospect of cheap acquisitions from Mazarin's collection. In England, a plea by Naudé to the Parlement of Paris was translated and issued in print. He had urged the councillors to save 'the most beautiful, and the best furnished of any library now in the world'.

> Can you permit, Gentlemen, the public to be deprived of a thing so useful and precious? ... When this loss has been suffered, there will not be a man in the world ... that will be able to repair it. Believe me, if you please, that the ruin of this library will be more carefully marked in all histories and calendars, than the taking and sacking of Constantinople.[7]

A heartbroken Naudé did his best to save the collection, even to the extent of investing his own money in purchasing some of the books, but when it was clear that he could do nothing more, the faithful librarian accepted an invitation to move to Stockholm, to be royal librarian to Christina, Queen of Sweden.[8]

Politics moves fast. By 1653, Cardinal Mazarin was back, and the call went out to Naudé to return and repair the damage. Naudé set off from Sweden but died before he reached Paris. It now fell to a more worldly wise political operator to see what could be done to restore France's greatest library: Jean-Baptiste Colbert. For the last ten years of the cardinal's life, Colbert was Mazarin's financial intendant and when the minister returned to power, the restoration of the library was an important priority. Mazarin allowed Colbert a generous budget for this purpose, but Colbert, a shrewd merchant's son and a master of accounting, was always prudent. A number of those who had made purchases at the auction of Mazarin's first library were very amenable to the suggestion that Mazarin might let past offences slide if they returned them. Three councillors charged with supervising the sale, who had helped themselves generously to the cardinal's books, had their entire libraries confiscated. With this demonstration of *force majeure*, and through judicious use of the cardinal's budget, the library was soon restored to some 29,000 volumes.[9] This time, however, the cardinal did not open his library to an ungrateful public.

The Imitation Game

The ignoble fate of the Mazarine library had serious repercussions in France. After Cardinal Mazarin's death in 1661, Colbert passed smoothly into the service of the king. Now he could think about building his own fortune, family and estate: naturally, a library formed part of this agenda. But first there was one obstacle to be removed: Nicolas Fouquet, the dominant government minister, and the man who had expected to be appointed to Mazarin's place. Fouquet came from a family of jurists. His father, François, had a fine library in the customary style of his profession; Nicolas, as a barrister of the Parlement of Paris, moved easily within a class of monied jurists who collected books as a matter of course.

With his appointment to Mazarin's inner circle, Fouquet seized the opportunity to build a library that reflected his new eminence. First, he followed Naudé's advice and bought a number of opulent collections. A librarian, Pierre de Carcavi, was appointed to curate a collection that, like Mazarin before him, Fouquet intended to open to the public. All of this came to naught when Fouquet was arrested and imprisoned, a victim of the conspicuous display that had aroused the king's suspicions. For six years the library, a stunning collection of some 27,000 volumes, lay locked and bolted while the vultures circled.[10]

Once it became clear that Fouquet's disgrace was permanent, the professors of the Collège Royal proposed that their institution would be the appropriate home for Fouquet's library. This was a legitimate request, given the historic connection between the college and the monarchy. But Colbert, now the king's intendant of finances in succession to Fouquet, had other plans. First 1,000 works of Italian history were removed to the royal collection, until this point substantially smaller than the library of both Mazarin and Fouquet and closed to the public. The 10,000 livres required for this purchase went to satisfy Fouquet's creditors. This caution reflected the fact that in the absence of a definitive condemnation (Fouquet's trial lasted three years and became an international cause célèbre), the king was cautious of outright confiscation of the minister's properties. Fouquet's former librarian, de Carcavi, was appointed to select other items for the royal collection before, in 1673, Madame Fouquet was finally permitted to sell the remainder to finance repayment of her husband's debts.

It is interesting that Colbert here passed up the opportunity to pillage Fouquet's library to augment his own substantial collection: the subtle minister had a different plan. By installing his brother as librarian of the royal collection, he had ensured his access there; he may also have judged, correctly, that conspicuous opulence had played a large part in Fouquet's downfall. In any case, Colbert intended to create for his royal master's service a very different sort of library: a working collection of documentary resources to support the public administration of the realm. The years of Colbert's ministry would be dominated by Louis XIV's efforts to expand the territories of France. All of these acquisitions required legal justification, and this in turn required a search for precedents, charters and genealogies. Colbert's agents fanned out through France, burrowing through archives and making copies. The ever-vigilant Colbert provided guidance on the type and size of paper they should use for these copies, to facilitate binding into files. This was not the peacock display of the great collector, but a potent instrument of the administrative state.[11] Thanks to Colbert, the royal library rapidly grew into a collection of 36,000 printed books and over 10,000 manuscripts; the minister's own collection expanded to close to 30,000 volumes. Colbert developed an encyclopaedic system of catalogues and indices to navigate these files, and as long as he could use the library to its full potential, he had no need for public adulation.

Colbert's shrewd understanding of the power of the library, and the dangers of conspicuous display, was not necessarily passed on to other statesmen. Long after his death, Cardinal Mazarin's ambitious library programme would inspire many noblemen, diplomats, cardinals and bishops to build their own grand collections, and open them to the public; the librarians they would employ would be humanist scholars like Naudé, instead of astute administrators like Colbert. That the tribulations of such flamboyance were easily forgotten was largely the result of a persistent culture of emulation. None of the collectors wished to be outshone by their rivals: this competitive spirit was actively encouraged by librarians, who urged the collector to examine carefully what other great collectors owned. Naudé had advised that the collector should copy and improve upon other collections by acquiring copies of their book catalogues.[12] Emulation was made possible because great collectors were eager to show off their libraries to visitors; on diplomatic missions and on the grand tour, famous libraries became an essential destination for cultured envoys, bishops and young noblemen, keen to make their impression upon the world. Contacts made on foreign trips would also play an important role when the collector had returned home; a trusted correspondent who could seek out and acquire art, curiosities and books for their patron was a vital requirement for any serious collector.[13]

Gaining access to a great library generally depended on one's social credit. This was an age, however, during which information on libraries became easily accessible; through catalogues, many of them now printed, as well as guidebooks that smoothly integrated the great libraries into the itineraries of the affluent tourist. One of Naudé's close friends was Louis Jacob, a Carmelite friar, who, like Naudé, became librarian to a cardinal, Jean François Paul de Gondi. In 1644, with the encouragement of Naudé, Jacob published the *Traicté des plus Belles Bibliothèques* (Account of the Most Beautiful Libraries).[14] The essence of this work was a descriptive list of hundreds of contemporary libraries, public and private, primarily those of France. Proud owners could write to Jacob to have their library included, as long as they had a minimum of 3,000 books. That this was a patriotic work was without doubt:

> My book will above all serve as a guide to libraries here in the French kingdom, where there are more today than in all the other kingdoms of the world. Why, I am able to state that the city of Paris alone has many more libraries than the whole of Germany and Spain, as one can see for himself by the enumeration I have made.[15]

This particular remark infuriated German scholars, but Jacob's work was ultimately successful in framing France as the European home of sophisticated literary culture. One element that stood out in the guidebook was the importance of aristocratic collections in provincial French towns. By the seventeenth century, the scions of noble houses had decisively shaken off their reputation as illiterate warriors: they attended universities, mostly to study jurisprudence, and competed not only for positions at court, but also in local government. Their book collections, rich in books of law, history and classics, played a fundamental role in maintaining the prestige of towns like Aix-en-Provence, home to one of France's highest law courts, the *parlements*.[16]

Jacob's guidebook went through several editions, and its style would be much imitated, most successfully by a Dutch schoolmaster, Johannes Lomeijer. In 1669, Lomeijer's *De Bibliothecis* (On to acquire rare or important books from numerous Italian monasteries. He generally did pay for them, but at cut-throat rates, and not always with the consent of their intimidated custodians. On one trip, the Pope issued an edict to the Neapolitan Franciscans which forbade them to sell any books from their collections unless they first offered them to Francesco Barberini and his librarian. Because the Pope had the right to confiscate the books of all priests who died without making a will, his nephew would regularly receive substantial donations to augment the already enormous Barberini collection.

The power structures in Catholic Europe made this sort of rapacious library building possible: from the days of Poggio Bracciolini, the greatest of the fifteenth-century book hunters, unfortunate monks had found that the church took away as often as it gave. In Protestant countries, after the windfall of the dissolution of the monasteries, similar opportunities did not present themselves as often. The unsuccessful attempt by Adriaen Pauw, for several decades chief minister of the Dutch Republic, to create a public library, offered a telling reminder of the difficulties of collecting in a society that frowned upon ostentatious display.[20] Pauw was an admirer of Mazarin, and although he was a devout republican, he was also devoted to aristocratic splendour. His friendliness to French foreign policy, exacerbated by his love for French taste, helped precipitate his removal from office in 1636.

During his spell in political exile, Pauw built up a library of some 16,000 books. Once he was restored to prominence in the 1640s, he used every political opportunity to acquire more: as Dutch negotiator at the peace congress in Münster, he acquired a valuable medieval manuscript of the works of Plautus. When, in 1649, he was sent over as extraordinary envoy to London to plead for the life of King Charles I, Pauw scandalised his hosts by offering to purchase the late king's library after Charles had been executed. His bid was rejected, but three years later he tried again; this time, when news of the attempted purchase became known, widespread outrage in the Netherlands prompted Pauw to back down.

Political setbacks were compounded by a disobedient family. Although Pauw had instructed his heirs to keep his book collection

Libraries) offered a sweeping survey of modern European librar but only, in the author's words, 'the more famous ones'.[17] Lome recognised that libraries were omnipresent, but that some sto out for their size, beauty, the rarity or richness of their conter and the illustrious name of the patron: these were the libraries t deserved close attention.

Lomeijer's work was remarkable for two reasons. He p dutiful but cursory attention to the libraries of antiquity, wh had thus far always been the key inspiration for Renaissance coll tors. His tract made clear that the modern collector should look the likes of Thomas Bodley and Cardinal Mazarin for emulati rather than Emperor Augustus. This was the work of an armch traveller: Lomeijer was able to compose his work without e leaving the Netherlands. There was now so much informati available in print that Lomeijer could gather copious amounts detail on over a hundred modern libraries. Without even pack their bags, readers could open the doors of the great collections the world.

At least in one respect Lomeijer was more traditional. Unl Louis Jacob, he paid most attention to Italian libraries, as throu; out Europe, Italy was still considered the birthplace of learning high culture and sophistication. All grand tours incorporated Italian cities as their destination, chief among them the Eter City, Rome. Five years before Lomeijer published his work, t Italians, Giovan Pietro Bellori and Fioravante Martinelli, provid information on no fewer than ninety-eight great libraries in Ro in their booklet *Nota delli Musei*.[18] The greatest collectors in t illustrious list were the Barberini family. The election of Maf Barberini as Pope Urban VIII in 1623 demanded a demonstrati of cultural power to sanctify the greatness of a family which serv the church with one pope and three cardinals. In 1627, Cardi Francesco Barberini, the favourite nephew of Urban VIII, attract Lucas Holste, a peripatetic German scholar and gifted linguist, his librarian.[19] With virtually unlimited financial resources at disposal, Holste created a library that would almost rival the fi Mazarine library in size.

Holste, unlike Naudé, could use his relationship with the Po together and open it to the public after his death, his less bookish children considered that their family name would be better honoured by building a magnificent family mausoleum in Pauw's domain of Heemstede, and his library was sold two years later, in 1656. Yet one collector's misfortune is another's gain. One of the prominent buyers at the Pauw library auction in The Hague was a reclusive German princeling, August of Braunschweig-Lüneburg.

The wealthy sovereign of a modest north German principality, Duke August was Europe's most successful bibliophile statesman.[21] He maintained permanent agents – publishers, art dealers, merchants and diplomats – in almost twenty centres of commerce: one of their daily activities was to ensure that the duke acquired as many newly printed books as could be crammed into the available book barrels. Other agents, like Lieuwe van Aitzema in The Hague, bought for him at auction, while another Dutchman, Abraham de Wicquefort, copied manuscripts and books for him from Parisian libraries, including the Mazarine. Wicquefort ultimately sent the duke some 400 volumes of transcribed tracts, all bound in exquisite red morocco leather. Despite rarely leaving the small town of Wolfenbüttel, August acquired a library of 31,000 printed volumes and 3,000 manuscripts – a truly universal collection, housing a complete range of classical works set alongside religious staples of all denominations, and all the most recent works of medicine, law and history. August was also partial to collecting more ephemeral items, from political pamphlets and news sheets to funeral sermons and wedding poetry.

In his collecting practices, the duke followed Naudé's school of thought, which was beginning to attract many followers. Yet August was unique in one major respect that distinguished him from other statesmen-collectors of his era: he was his own librarian. He collected extensively but never bought entire libraries. He acquired because he actively desired books for their own sake, rather than to impress visitors, whom he kept to a minimum. Every day, August could be found opening book barrels and cataloguing titles. He compiled all his own catalogues and had a massive bookwheel constructed to hold the six-folio volume master list, covering 7,200 pages. Although the duke grudgingly allowed scholars access

15. Duke August of Braunschweig-Lüneburg, pictured here in his favourite space, his library. A true bibliophile, August preferred to be his own librarian, and never let anyone access his catalogue.

to his library, he never shared the key to its resources: this magnificent catalogue. In an age of imitation, secrecy could be a powerful tool. Like so many other collectors, the duke had little control over the tastes of his descendants. Unlike Fernando Colon, in this respect he was fortunate, in that his heirs recognised his Herculean efforts for what they were, and preserved the library, curating it as a monument to its first founder. The immortality that was so often desired by great collectors but rarely realised, did materialise in little Wolfenbüttel. The library still stands there today, as a centre of scholarship, but also as reminder that some bibliophilic dreams do come true.

Baroque Glories

On 22 May 1729, Robert Howard, bishop of the Irish diocese of Killala and Achonry, complained to his brother Hugh that 'a great number of books, unless one hath very convenient room for them, are a greater plague than I ever imagined'.[22] Howard was not the only collector to express such sentiment. In the age of the great cardinal collectors, libraries had grown to enormous size; this was inevitable if they were to stand out from the book collections of professional men who themselves often owned thousands of books. The creation of so many libraries, in castles, palaces and town houses all over Europe, also called for new design solutions. No statesman could keep 20,000 books in chests: even if they could, they had no wish to do so. If great collectors opened their collection to their friends or the wider public, they had to pay considerable attention to the architecture, decorations and fittings of the room where their books were kept.

Before the seventeenth century, most libraries, great and small, had occupied spaces which were not originally constructed as rooms for books. So it was a purposeful statement when a grandiose hall was constructed to house exclusively a collection of books. Constructing a physical library incurred significant expense, and could therefore help distinguish the libraries of the great collectors from those of lawyers and physicians who had to keep their books at home. These aristocratic libraries were designed not only for the housing of large numbers of books, but as a social space, where one could receive visitors and conduct business, all the while impressing upon guests the host's erudition and wealth. Even libraries that were not open to the public, such as the magnificent collection of Cardinal Bernardino Spada in Rome, were adorned with frescoes and paintings by some of the greatest artists of the age. The construction of prominent library buildings marked a return to the ideals of classical Rome: writers on libraries, from stoic philosophers to polemical Jesuits, all agreed that the great libraries of their age should mimic classical architecture, albeit enhanced with baroque paintings, statues and portraits. Some library builders went to extraordinary lengths in their quest for the perfect aesthetic. While it took only two years to erect a brand new building for the Sapienza library in Rome, as well as gather together a collection of thousands of books, the decoration of the frescoes on the ceiling took another four years.[23]

The Jesuit professor Claude Clement was at the forefront of the visual transformation of the library.[24] In 1628, a year after Naudé published his *Advis*, Clement produced his own tract on library building. It differed from Naudé's in two significant ways: it was published in Latin, targeting an international Catholic audience, and it devoted most of its space not to books but to architecture. Clement recognised that the baroque library, sumptuously decorated, could be at the heart of Catholic revival, as an aesthetic manifestation of the power and wealth of its owner and their rank in the social (often ecclesiastical) hierarchy, while also paying dutiful tribute to the glories of God. Central to this concept was the redesign of library space so that it resembled a church, a temple of wisdom, rather than a room for actual study.

There were a few voices, mostly in Protestant northern Europe, who baulked at this baroque turn. Naudé had insisted that a collector should not care for lavish ornamentation, but instead spend the money saved to buy books. Duke August of Wolfenbüttel had kept his magnificent library, divided between two floors, directly above his stables. Yet what all of these libraries – sober and lavish alike – shared, was a general rearrangement of the books themselves.[25] Libraries throughout Europe abandoned the basic fittings of the medieval college and church libraries, dominated by reading lecterns and low central bookcases. Instead they remodelled library rooms to resemble great halls, in which books were placed, spines out, in great vertical bookcases along the walls. Although this was not entirely unprecedented (Fernando Colon had already experimented with a similar design, as had King Philip II of Spain), it now became the standard, and those who had ample financial resources available employed it to great effect.

In a lectern library, the books themselves were crucial to the visual attraction of the library: they were immediately in the eye of the beholder, ready to be opened, read and studied. In the baroque hall library, the books disappeared into the décor. It was only in their mass, their enormous volume, that they were impressive. The creation of a vast empty space in the centre of the hall emphasised the grandeur of the room, as the eye could roam freely over a marbled floor, surrounded on all sides by rows upon rows of neatly bound volumes, decreasing in size as one moved from the floor to the domed ceiling. To guide the by now deeply impressed visitor, the space between and above shelves was richly decorated, often in gold, cream, blues and soft pinks. Frescoes covered the ceiling, while cases, arranged by strict classifications, were adorned with portraits of Church Fathers, philosophers and famous authors. The Ambrosiana in Milan had no fewer than 306 portraits of illustrious writers installed between 1609 and 1618.[26]

Nowhere was this architectural trend so transformative as in the monasteries of the remaining German Catholic lands, in southern Germany, Austria and Bohemia.[27] Unlike their Italian neighbours, many of the German monasteries had fallen on hard times during the upheavals of the Reformation.[28] In the eighteenth century, they underwent a programme of architectural rejuvenation, as much to invigorate the monks themselves as to restore the monasteries' former reputation as centres of spirituality, learning and education. The abbots of the great monasteries were not unlike the cardinal ministers of Paris: they were, in effect, ecclesiastical princes, who could compete with many secular rulers in terms of wealth, land and status. The transformation of the libraries into lavish showrooms emphasised the continued role of the church in scholarship and erudition. It was also a means to justify the continuing power of the clergy, influence that was increasingly under fire during the course of the eighteenth century even in Catholic lands.

Many monastic libraries did genuinely require some revitalisation. In 1722, the prior of Sankt Polten complained that he must take the library in hand, since in its current state it was 'an almost completely ridiculous thing', nearly devoid of books. Some of his idle monks had converted it into a billiards room.[29] It was especially embarrassing to the prior because it was a common courtesy in many monasteries to grant visiting monks and dignitaries a tour of the grounds and buildings, and visitors often asked to see the library. In medieval Europe, the scriptorium and library might be entered towards the end of the visit, as these rooms were naturally located in the quietest, most secluded areas of the monastic complex. The eighteenth century dramatically altered this layout. As the prior of Sankt Polten argued, the new library should be at the entrance of the abbey, where 'it appears more beautiful to guests and visitors, not having to be sought out in a corner as previously'.

Visual decoration, in the form of frescoes, paintings and sculptures, was vital to the baroque monastic library. These were rich with biblical and classical allegories, beautiful but not always easily understood. A prior at Sankt Florian provided a helpful handbook in 1747 for his fellow monks, because 'our canonry is frequently examined by guests, [who ask] what story, fable, or allusion lies hidden under the schema of this or that picture'.[30] Others had the emblematic meanings written on a table or sheet displayed in the library for all to read. In the most ambitious architectural schemes, no expense was too much to achieve the desired effect: at Seitenstetten, all books in the library were rebound in white leather to harmonise with the new marble. The process took thirty years.[31]

The building of a new library was not always completed as quickly as the Sapienza in Rome. At Roggenburg, in Swabia, a new library was planned in the 1730s, constructed in the 1760s and finished in the 1780s. Then, when all the books were placed on the shelves during the 1790s, it was discovered that the new library was too small. On the other hand, some libraries were rebuilt on such a grand scale that the monks possessed enough books to fill only a small portion of the space. At Altenburg Abbey, in Lower Austria, the library was modelled closely on the form and shape of the Vienna court library, which had grown to some 200,000 books. The monks owned only a fraction of this number, leaving a room equipped with only a few bookcases. The space itself, 48 metres (157 feet) long and three storeys high, was nevertheless deemed to be extremely impressive: today Altenburg is still considered one of the finest baroque abbeys, and its pristine marbled, stuccoed and frescoed library room is its great treasure.

The baroque library was a visual delight, but one that sacrificed study space for beauty, and relegated books to the same function as lavish wallpaper. The ordinary needs of readers – desks or lecterns for study – were sacrificed to accommodate marvellous objects that epitomised the wonders of inquiry. The baroque library room that opened at the monastery of St Gallen in 1758 included an Egyptian sarcophagus; more commonly, libraries might showcase antique statues, mathematical instruments, globes, architectural models, or cabinets filled with coins, gems and natural curiosities. Duke August of Wolfenbüttel owned at least seventy clocks and watches, sundials, astrolabes, telescopes and a cabinet of curiosities. From one piece of correspondence we know that it contained 'a pair of

Turkish boots, a leather conjuring bag, an Indian sword of ebony, a model of a Turkish galley, a hunting horn made of tortoise shell', as well as a dissected deer's head, which could be opened by a concealed mechanism. This last piece arrived in Wolfenbüttel with its antlers broken.[32] Objects such as these were meant to elicit intellectual reflection on the part of the owner and cries of amazement from each visitor who was allowed to admire them. This process could now take place in halls of exceeding beauty, where all the knowledge of the world could be accessed – if only one could find a desk.

From Royal Library to Library of State

All Saints' Day, 1755, saw the destruction of one of Europe's great capital cities. Lisbon was devastated by a massive earthquake, followed by fire and a tsunami. Tens of thousands died, and along with them perished the library of King John V, one of the finest collections in Europe. Located in the great royal palace, on the riverfront in Lisbon, nothing remained of the library. The king, a sickly but fiercely intellectual man, had died five years earlier, and luckily did not have to see the sad fate of his life's work. He was a true bibliophile in every sense of the word. Whereas for Duke August of Wolfenbüttel, his library allowed him to turn away from the turbulence of German politics in the age of the Thirty Years' War, for the young king of Portugal it was a means to learn about the wider world, in which he was unable to travel because of ill health. Often, King John would not lunch until four in the afternoon because he was in the library, engrossed in his reading.[33]

This private retreat, by some accounts comprising 70,000 volumes, was amassed at exorbitant cost, with books acquired from all the great centres of collecting. John's ambassadors were frequently ordered to put aside other duties to visit bookshops and book auctions, bidding for their king. This could be a frustrating process, because exchanging letters from Paris, The Hague or Rome to Lisbon and back could take weeks, and often the king's decision on a purchase arrived after a book had been sold. The king would be bidding against other monarchs, dukes and great ministers of state, like Eugene of Savoy, the King of Poland or agents of the Tsar of Russia. At one auction, King John bought 6,000 books from the library of Cardinal Guillaume Dubois, chief minister of Louis XV of France.[34] Thus immense quantities of books circulated from one grand collector to another. By the eighteenth century, it was recognised that monarchs and sovereign princes could no longer be without a library. As the personification of the state, they were required to demonstrate a love for learning, education and enlightenment. Even if they cared little for such concepts, books increasingly came their way, not least thanks to their chief ministers, statesmen and clerics. As books circled up the social hierarchy, multiplying along the way, a road was paved towards the foundation of the first national libraries.

Chapter Twelve

THE ANTIQUARIANS

Institutional collections assembled over many decades inevitably found themselves with more than one copy of some donated texts. Sometimes it made sense to dispose of the duplicates: certainly, this appealed to the Dominican friars of Frankfurt, who at various points in the seventeenth century sold books from their library to local bookbinders. These were used as 'binder's waste', thickening the bindings of books, or as loose covers and wrappings. What seems extraordinary to us was that many of these books were incunabula, books from the first age of print, the fifteenth century. The Dominican convent at Frankfurt had flourished precisely around the time that printing was invented in nearby Mainz, so the library had over 1,000 incunabula, many of them printed on parchment. Today, these books would be sold for phenomenal prices. To the Dominicans they were worth no more than the reuse value of the parchment.

After many years of this commerce, gradually depleting their collection, the friars were pleasantly surprised when, in 1718, they were able to sell four incunabula to a foreign buyer, an Englishman, who offered 90 guilders, probably ten times the waste value of the books.[1] The buyer, an agent named George Suttie, was an expert hunter of manuscripts and rare books. Exiled from England due to a penchant for gambling, he travelled on commission around the European continent, producing lists of valuable books for Europe's wealthiest collectors. This was no latter-day Poggio Bracciolini, sneaking into monasteries and appropriating their treasures at dead of night; on this occasion he was hunting books for Robert Harley, First Earl of Oxford, one of the great statesmen of England and a noted patron of the arts. Harley's son, Edward, was also an avid collector, whose library numbered over 7,000 manuscripts and 50,000 printed volumes at his death in 1741; it would later provide one of the foundation stones of the collections of the British Museum, now the British Library.

Since the days of Gutenberg, the book trade had recognised one universal truth: books did not accrue additional value just because they were old. At best they kept their value, if the content was still relevant; at worst they could be sold for the value of the paper or parchment. Books could be recycled in this way for myriad purposes: as wallpaper, bookbinding supports, wrapping paper or toilet paper. Misprinted sheets and obsolete books were found on butcher's counters to wrap meat, with spice merchants and in the shops of lace makers. In the eighteenth century, Amsterdam would be home to 'book lotteries', disposing of enormous quantities of unwanted books and old paper to wholesalers.[2]

That anyone would begin to pay large sums for old books just because of their antiquity was a new development, and a disruptive one. Gabriel Naudé had advised his readers not to offer large sums for lavishly illustrated or 'antique books', but by 1720 there were collectors who had the confidence to ignore such advice. Two years after Suttie acquired the four Mainz incunabula, an early Mainz Bible was sold in The Hague for 1,200 guilders, twice the average annual household income of the day. It made Suttie's purchase look like a bargain. In 1722, a Gutenberg Bible was sold at auction in The Hague for the extraordinary sum of 6,000 guilders.[3]

Such prices were shocking because in the seventeenth century, high prices were rarely paid for incunabula. At the auction of Gaspar Fagel's library in 1689, where substantial sums were paid for his collection of modern works of jurisprudence, one could pick up two incunabula for a tenth of a guilder. In 1646, a 1477 Cologne Bible went under the hammer in Leiden for 3 guilders, a fifth of the price of a new folio Bible.[4] In 1680, the Oxford bookseller Moses Pitt donated to the Bodleian Library a volume of four editions published by William Caxton, England's first printer. The volume had failed to sell at auction, and Pitt could not find a buyer anywhere else. By 1810, a bookseller could ask 5 guineas, a month's wages for most artisans, for a fragment of a Caxton.[5] In the space of a hundred years, the sale of early printed books had become part of a sophisticated antiquarian market.

This was a development with momentous consequences for the future of the library. The eighteenth century saw the rise of new scientific modes of thought, of Enlightenment philosophy and secularism. This intellectual upheaval decreased the allure of building huge libraries, filled with as many books as possible on as wide a range of subjects. A new generation of collectors opted for a select library that marked them out as men of the new learning. Yet at the same time there emerged a second type of collector, often of noble extraction or with noble aspirations, who did not interest themselves as much in the content as in the aesthetics, the form and the age of the book. Many of these collectors still acquired new books, and built up libraries of thousands of volumes, but within these libraries they devoted most effort to finding *'livres rares et curieux'*, as booksellers began to advertise them. The distinction of a fine library depended increasingly on books that were precious because of their illustrations, their date of publication, their binding, or even their printer.

This was a trend first established by the English aristocracy. England had played a peripheral part in the production of books in the first centuries of print; now its collectors, buoyed by the growing power of the English economy and its global trade, came to the fore. By taking their purses abroad, and spending liberally, they established a new market for old books. These collectors created new roles within the trade for brokers and agents, and also for professors and scholars who could guide the taste of rich but naive collectors and point them in the direction of the best copies. These skills were forged in the most competitive and volatile sector of the book trade, in the service of some of Europe's most demanding customers: those engaged in the hunt for manuscripts.

Lock Up Your Manuscripts

On the morning of 7 June 1650, the central Dam square of Amsterdam was its usual self, a hub of activity. The hustle and bustle was especially pronounced outside one popular bookshop, 'The

Burning Column'. A book auction would start that morning and occupy most of the week. By this point book auctions were commonplace, but that morning the mood was different. Up for sale was the library of a reclusive lawyer, poet, bibliophile and renowned thief.[6]

Suffridus Sixtinus had amassed during his life over 2,000 volumes, a large but not extraordinary library, but one characterised by an extremely choice selection of classical editions.[7] Most tantalising, Sixtinus possessed numerous manuscripts that no scholar had been able to lay their eyes on for decades. Unlike other scholars, who freely shared and indeed boasted of the treasures of their collections, Sixtinus had hidden his books from the world since he arrived in Amsterdam in 1627. Many knew the reason for this secrecy: Sixtinus was widely believed to have acquired his most precious manuscripts through burglary.

In 1622, Sixtinus had broken into the house of Janus Gruter, a distinguished humanist scholar and professor at Heidelberg. Gruter's library was his pride and joy, as well as his chief source of fame, but he had been forced to flee town before the anticipated onslaught of Habsburg troops. Sixtinus took his chance before the soldiers arrived and removed the most valuable items. After the theft, Gruter, exiled in Tübingen, wrote to a friend despairing of the violence that Sixtinus inflicted upon his books: 'Every day I hear the most appalling things of Suffridus. They say that he has deflowered my library to satisfy his own lusts.'[8] Sixtinus could have argued that he rescued the most priceless pieces: after his theft, Habsburg soldiers plundered Gruter's house, and whatever books were left were dispatched, along with the great Palatine library, to the Vatican. When Gruter returned home in the spring of 1625 he found only trampled remnants of a once proud library: 'the sight would make even a stone burst into tears'.

The manuscripts taken by Sixtinus had not been seen since. One can imagine that news of his death in 1649 spread like wildfire throughout the international Republic of Letters. The books did not come to the market immediately: it took some time to identify the heir to the estate. Luckily the man in question, a Geldrian nobleman, turned out to be keen to sell the books. This was an event not to be missed, but the demands of work and expense of travel prevented some prominent scholars from attending. As was usual, they asked friends or agents to bid on their behalf. Mutual trust, and respect, governed the relationships of the scholarly community. Yet here, too, greed got the better of decorum. Three leading scholars – Johann Friedrich Gronovius, Nicolaas Heinsius and Isaac Vossius – each entrusted the philologist Franciscus Junius to buy for them at auction. Prices were high, as was expected, but in his report on the proceedings of the auction, Junius was vague as to his success. Gronovius and Heinsius had no idea what he had managed to buy for them. The third scholar, Isaac Vossius, knew better. Junius was his uncle and allowed him to take first pick of what he had bought. When Gronovius realised what had happened, he complained that Vossius 'shall keep the books he has a mind to, but the books he does not care for, are for us'.[9] Gronovius ended up with only three.

Yet even sly Vossius was disappointed. The manuscript he had longed for most, a copy of Julius Caesar's *De Bello Gallico* (Commentaries on the Gallic War), had been bought for a considerable sum by the rich collector Jan Six. Written in the monastery of Fleury in the ninth or tenth century, this manuscript was the oldest known extant version of Caesar's chief work.[10] It had come into the possession of Janus Gruter only through the generosity of a friend, who allowed Gruter to borrow it because he was working on a new edition of Caesar. The friend died, and Gruter, wilfully or accidentally, still had the text when Sixtinus laid his hands on it.

We can learn much from this sordid tale of self-interest, trust betrayed and stolen manuscripts. Sixtinus was certainly an eccentric, a drunkard too, according to Vossius, but as the story reveals, he was not the only collector guilty of misappropriating books, only the most brazen. These rare codices were the lifeblood of classical scholarship; scholars could make their name publishing new editions of classical texts based on close study of the best early manuscripts. This had been a central tenet of humanist scholarship since Boccaccio investigated the ruins of the library at Monte Cassino. Despite the scientific revolutions taking place in the seventeenth century, classical philology had lost none of its allure. Manuscripts were also still valued for their theological significance. A professor of theology at Utrecht, Gisbertus Voetius, instructed his students to look far and wide for manuscripts and early editions of theological texts, in order to withstand the 'dangerous wave of purging' executed by the Catholic Church, 'the result of the barbaric, evil plans of the fathers and censors of the Council of Trent'.[11]

With the exceptions of the Bodleian Library and the University of Leiden, large institutional collections of manuscripts were still unusual in the seventeenth century. Scholars like Gruter, Heinsius, Gronovius or Vossius had to assemble their own collections. In the rough and tumble world of acquisition and attribution, this required a steely determination to take advantage of the opportunities afforded to them as the foremost scholars of their day. Isaac Vossius was a true polymath: he wrote on topics ranging from ballistics, optics and air pressure to geography and biblical chronology. He made substantial contributions to classical philology and at one felicitous moment of his career was employed simultaneously by the States of Holland, King Charles II of England and King Louis XIV of France. Born into a distinguished scholarly family, he travelled as a young man for three years through England, France and Italy. He met scholars, obtained references, visited libraries, but above all, bought manuscripts. By the age of twenty-seven he had already acquired 400.

His erudition, as much as his collecting, caught the eye of one of Europe's richest monarchs, Christina, the Queen of Sweden. In 1648, Vossius left Amsterdam to join Christina in Stockholm, invited to settle at court as her private tutor, for which he would enjoy a salary of 2,000 rijksdaalders a year, five times the salary of the foremost professors in the Dutch Republic. In Stockholm he joined an illustrious and increasingly competitive circle of other scholars, ornaments of a court that Christina envisioned as the new cultural centre of Europe. To achieve this she laid out lavish sums on attracting the intellectually eminent to Stockholm, though given the distance of her court from most centres of learning and the harshness of the Swedish winter, this proved a dangerous temptation. René Descartes died at her court from complications of a cold, while Claude Saumaise was rarely able to leave his bed while in Stockholm due to illness. Hugo Grotius, too, paid the price for obeying Christina's siren call, shipwrecked on a return journey from Sweden.

Christina could attract such renowned names because she had inherited a considerable windfall income from the booty accumulated by Swedish armies in Germany during the Thirty Years' War. It was this cultural loot, in the form of thousands of books, that attracted Vossius to her court. Very soon he was not only tutoring the queen, but also working as her librarian. He helped unpack the thirty-one barrels of books taken from the castle of Rudolf II in Prague in 1648, including the Codex Argenteus, a sixth-century Gothic translation of the Gospels. Christina shared Vossius's passion for the classics, and for manuscripts, but the war booty was not enough. Vossius was dispatched on book-buying trips to Paris to augment the royal collections and given free rein with the purse of state. On one trip he purchased 2,000 manuscripts in one transaction.[12] These he examined back in Sweden, though he much preferred reading the rare codices to cataloguing them: 'such work was fit for Germans', he declared to a friend.[13]

Christina's library was now one of the finest in Europe, unrivalled for its collection of manuscripts. However, the queen's primary interest turned out to be spending money on acquisitions, rather than having a library to show off to visitors (crowned heads were more reluctant to visit Stockholm than impecunious scholars). Christina's loss of interest in her library would turn out to Vossius's advantage. She had not paid his extremely high salary for several years, so instead resolved to pay his arrears in books.

This offer Vossius gladly accepted, especially when it became clear that Christina would abdicate her throne. Vossius rushed through the library, picking out many items he had bought with Christina's money. Manuscripts from Prague also came into his possession, including the Codex Argenteus, and several shipments were dispatched to Amsterdam. Upon arrival there, the classical scholar Johann Georg Graevius wrote

By Jove! What a splendid library! How ample, and how rich in valuable items! Almost all of the best Latin authors are

represented several times in manuscript, besides the Greek,
French and German ones, and very special, rare editions of all
kinds. Those who know about these matters assure me there
is no public library in Holland which can compare with it.[14]

Swedish courtiers were, understandably, less delighted. Their precious war booty had now been plundered, not by feat of arms, but
by subterfuge and the unscrupulous charm of a scholar who knew
the collection intimately.

Back home in the Netherlands, Vossius had come into so many
books that he decided to hold two auctions from his own library,
selling off 3,500 books in all.[15] It is unlikely he needed money;
space for his books was a far more pressing concern. Luckily, he
was a practical man, and enjoyed making bookcases. Possibly to
pacify his former hosts, he did sell the Codex Argenteus back to
Sweden, but for the sum of 1,250 guilders. Vossius lived for books,
but he was unsentimental about the value of individual pieces. To
him manuscripts had always remained tools of scholarship, to be
studied and collated, but he knew how to exploit their mystical
appeal in a commercial market-place: having assembled one of the
finest manuscript libraries in Europe thanks to the Swedish treas-
ury and the whims of a young queen, he was now ready to cash in.

Although Vossius was certainly more liberal than the sordid
Sixtinus when it came to access to his precious manuscripts, an air
of mystery shrouded his collection for the rest of his life. When
he died in 1689, he stipulated in his will that his library should
be offered for sale as one lot to one of four institutional libraries: Oxford, Leiden, Cambridge or Amsterdam. The Bodleian was
keen to acquire the library, and bid 30,000 guilders on condition
that no manuscripts were removed by the heir. Vossius's nephew
then turned to Leiden with the Bodleian offer, which Leiden
promptly raised to 33,000 guilders. Today the Vossius collection,
which added close to 800 manuscripts to Leiden's library in 1690,
is regarded as one of the great treasures of the university. But when
the books first arrived at their new home, the professors rightly
suspected that the nephew had kept some of the most valuable
items and called in local booksellers, who valued the books at a

third of the price paid.[16] The ensuing court case dragged on for fifteen years before all parties were satisfied.

This protracted saga, involving some of the most respected figures in the scholarly world, demonstrated what dangerous forces were unleashed when books were no longer valued according to the set system of principles that had traditionally governed the book trade. The growing market for manuscripts, dominated by commercially minded scholars and librarians, paved the way for the formation of a volatile antiquarian market.

Creating the Canon

On 7 June 1675, the Amsterdam bookseller Andreas Frisius wrote to the librarian of the Medici library in Florence with his assessment of three local book collectors. One, his favourite customer, was a man 'who really has a comprehensive knowledge of which books are good'. The second was an alderman of the city, 'who bought more to acquire reputation and indulge in ostentation', while the last, a collector born into great wealth, had no judgement of quality at all. He bought books, pictures and porcelain without discrimination, simply on the basis that they cost a great deal.[17]

Frisius, a publisher of significant scholarly works, found all this rather beneath him, yet between 1650 and 1750, the history of collecting was completely reshaped by men like his second and third customers. As the number of personal libraries grew, a collection of several hundred or even a thousand books was no longer anything to boast about. It was natural that some collectors, who wished to equip themselves with elegant books as much as fine porcelain, paintings and upholstery, looked for books which by their expense, beauty, rarity or typographical sophistication marked the collection out as special.

Manuscripts clearly fitted the category of books that could elevate the distinction of a library. But many collectors could not afford manuscripts nor had the expertise to find them at affordable prices. Printed books with manuscript annotations by famous scholars were similarly collectable and could command high prices at auction; but these were in short supply. Most were already in university libraries or in the collections of other famous scholars like Isaac Vossius. Instead, a burgomaster, judge or merchant could focus on creating a library which was composed chiefly of the best printed editions available. But how could one determine what was the best edition of a work? Initially this was not a question of age. The venerable qualities of time, the particular allure of the first printed edition of a text (known as the *editio princeps*), was rarely espoused before the eighteenth century. In fact, more recent editions were generally preferred, especially in scholarly and institutional collections. When the Third Folio of Shakespeare's works appeared, the Bodleian duly sold its First Folio (incidentally, today one of the most prized books in any library).[18]

Gradually there emerged a more discerning collector, who recognised, sometimes nudged by scholars or dealers, the superior quality of the work of particular printers and exquisite typography. Books by Aldus Manutius, inventor of the italic or cursive typeface and one of the most successful Venetian printers around 1500, had been prized when they first appeared. The elegance of his classical editions was much imitated by later publishers in France and the Netherlands, some of whom entered the typographical canon more by luck and business acumen than innate superiority. The Dutch publishing house of the Elzeviers, active in Leiden and Amsterdam, was extremely successful in marketing their editions as modern successors to Aldus Manutius, even if their design was easily matched by many other contemporary print shops.[19]

By the second half of the seventeenth century, a canon of the most distinguished printers – Italian, French, German and Dutch – was largely established. Auctioneers began to expand the descriptions of books by listing the names of renowned printers: Aldus Manutius, Christophe Plantin, the families Wechel, Estienne, Blaeu and Elzevier. From this period onwards we begin to find that some personal libraries, like that of the Leiden schoolmaster Paulus Junius, were largely made up of works by these printing houses. One of the most refined personal libraries of the period was owned by Samuel van Huls, a burgomaster of The Hague, whose books were auctioned in 1730.[20] Van Huls could not read a word of Latin or Greek, yet he had put together a collection of over 5,000 volumes, mostly in Latin, including fifty folio Bibles and almost all the work of celebrated printers.

Collectors like Van Huls were frequently lampooned. Already in 1710, Joseph Addison had presented to the readers of *The Tatler* the collecting habits of a man named Tom Folio, who had 'a greater esteem for Aldus and Elzevir, than for Virgil and Horace'.[21] Twenty years later Alexander Pope mocked one noble collector for his antiquarian interests:

His Study? With what Authors is it stor'd?
In Books, no Authors, curious is my Lord;
For Lock or Milton 'tis in vain to look,
These Shelves admit not any Modern Book.[22]

The fascination with typography advanced interest in the early history of printing. This fitted neatly into the broader currents of antiquarian scholarship, the interest in ancient objects and physical remains as historical sources: in this context, early printed books were valued as sources for the study of history.[23] Patriotic scholars, especially in Germany and the Netherlands, also had a point to prove by studying the earliest printed books: both vied for the honour of declaring their homeland the birthplace of print. Although evidence was increasingly available to demonstrate the rightful claim of Gutenberg's Mainz, Dutch scholars clung to the notion that Gutenberg had really stolen the art of printing from Laurens Jansz Coster of Haarlem.

As interest in early printed books took hold, commercial agents took note. In 1688 a Dutch bookseller, Cornelius à Beughem, produced a little handbook of some 200 pages called *Incunabula typographiae*.[24] This was the first attempt to provide a wishlist for collectors, but the most assiduous book buyers would already have compiled their own lists, which they could refer to when writing to correspondents abroad and scouring auction catalogues for noteworthy items. Interest in incunabula and other rare books was eagerly stoked by booksellers, auctioneers and book agents. In 1742, a bookseller from The Hague, Pierre Gosse, prepared a catalogue in which he had annotated lots with an ascending number of asterisks based on their supposed rarity: one asterisk for 'books which I know are not common', two for 'those which I believe to be more rare' and three for 'those which I believe to be of great rarity'.[25] Such rhetoric, as his colleague Prosper Marchand noted, was widespread and entirely useless, obscuring all sense of real value.[26] Exaggerations of this sort nevertheless persisted, not least because there were plenty of less sophisticated buyers who could be lured by such false precision. When Isaac Vossius sold part of his library at auction, he added exaggerated descriptions in the sale catalogues to some of the items, which, according to his nephew, on one occasion earned him twenty times the value of the book.[27]

As the vogue for rarity gathered pace, so did the shamelessness of selling practices. In 1757, an English bookbroker based in Amsterdam was found guilty of altering the year of publication on early printed books to make them appear to be incunabula.[28] The dupe of this crime was another book dealer, Pieter van Damme, who traded exclusively in rare books, and held auctions devoted solely to incunabula. He could afford to specialise so narrowly because by the middle of the eighteenth century there was a sufficiently large clientele for precisely this specialism.

The best profits were to be made when dealers were closest to the sources of many of these incunabula, the monastic heartlands of Germany and Italy. Monks and friars could be handed substantial sums for some of their early printed books before the same were sold on for far higher prices in France, England or the Dutch Republic. The banker Joseph Smith, a renowned art and book dealer, based himself in Venice in 1700, where he represented the English government as consul. From there he travelled around the Italian countryside, collecting for himself, and on commission for English noblemen.[29] By 1751 he had assembled a library of some 12,000 volumes, and he produced extensive catalogues to advertise his collection for sale. The catalogues devoted a specific section to Smith's incunabula, the pride of his library, which was accompanied by 280 pages of prefatory matter. This was indeed a library fit for a king: Smith sold it to King George III of England.

Illiberal Enlightenment

In the late eighteenth century, the new bookbrokers, who supplied the libraries of England, the Dutch Republic and France with antiquarian books, profited much from the general disintegration of monastic libraries in the heartlands of Catholicism. This process, conducted under the banner of Enlightenment, unleashed a flood of manuscripts and antique books on to the market, often at very low prices. It would turn out to be the most destructive purge of libraries until the Second World War.

The first major blow was struck with the dissolution of the Jesuit Order, a process that had been underway since the 1750s but was formally concluded by papal brief in 1773. The global network of Jesuit colleges and schools had always been important centres of learning. With the dissolution, the libraries, very often the largest in the surrounding area, were plundered, carted off, sold or left to rot in derelict buildings. In 1773, the books from the Jesuit college in Brussels were appropriated for the royal collection. Because the royal library had no space, the books were kept in the Jesuit church, which, it turned out, had an infestation of mice. The secretary of the local literary society was appointed to find a solution: he duly made a selection of 'useful books' which he placed on the shelves in the middle of the nave, and the remainder were strewn on the floor, so as to distract the mice with easily accessible food.[30]

In many towns, other religious orders were allocated the Jesuit books, or simply helped themselves to the library. At least here they found a new purpose, but the books were generally not safe for long. Monastic communities were a prime target for the agendas of modernising governments, enthralled by the possibilities of social and economic reform inspired by the Enlightenment. Nowhere were the ideals of Enlightenment in greater fashion than at the courts of the so-called 'enlightened despots', the monarchs of Prussia, Russia and Austria, who saw in rational philosophy the means to strengthen their grip on power and turn their territories into modern states. In contrast to the English noblemen who hunted for antique books, these rulers had little interest in antiquarianism, and even less respect for the inherited traditions. One of the supreme ambitions of the eighteenth-century

Enlightenment was to liberate knowledge from the grip of the past. The new Enlightenment library was to consist of useful books, not those that reaffirmed traditional academic or ecclesiastical hierarchies. This placed the monastic libraries, at this point still the largest repositories of books in most Catholic lands, directly in the firing line.

The greatest catastrophe unfolded in Austria. In the 1780s, Emperor Joseph II embarked on one of the most radical programmes of social reform ever attempted. Under the spell of rational philosophy, Joseph introduced a series of ambitious policies that aimed to modernise the social structures of the Habsburg Empire, including the abolishment of serfdom, the weakening of craft guilds, universal compulsory education and the subjugation of the Catholic Church. The numerous monasteries of the Austrian territories, rich in lands and libraries, were a natural target for the modernising monarch. Around 700 monasteries were dissolved by Joseph between 1782 and 1787, a third of the total.[31]

The libraries of these monasteries were intended first to be added to the Habsburg court library, but this proved impractical given the sheer quantity of books involved. Instead, all dissolved institutions were ordered to send their books to the nearest university or college of their province. Now the academies were flooded with books, most for which they had no use. 'Useless prayer books' were pulped, while those deemed to be insignificant 'old editions from the fifteenth century' or books said 'only to show off imagined or self-indulgent learning' were sold or cast aside.[32]

The Strahov monastery, outside Prague, suffered multiple lootings throughout its long history, including a ferociously efficient visit from the Swedes in 1648. This time the monks were determined to save their library from the destructive forces unleashed by their own ruler. They were successful, but only by acquiring thousands of books from less privileged monasteries in the Habsburg lands. They promptly organised these books under the assignation of a 'philosophical library', to match the grand 'theological library' already present at the monastery. For good measure they installed a bust of Joseph II in the new hall. The Emperor, delighted that the monks should show such reverence for the cause of Enlightenment, declared the Strahov monastery library too useful to destroy.[33]

Today the library at Strahov is one of Prague's great tourist attractions, yet it is a collection built on the corpses of many other, less fortunate institutions. The library of the Dominicans at Bolzano had possessed 6,400 volumes, including 300 incunabula. The books were destined for the Innsbruck lyceum, but the school was only interested in 335 volumes. The rest were sold to a local tavern-owner for a pittance. The most valuable books from the monastery at Ardagger, including ninety-four incunabula, were put up for auction, and the rest were sold to a cheesemaker for wrappers. The auction was attended by two people, a priest and the librarian of a nearby monastery. The librarian secured them all for a month's salary, and promptly sold one of the ninety-four incunabula for half that amount. Clearly not all librarians were naive and unworldly, and would have been well aware of the rise of interest in such items; but then we know that already from Vossius's sly dealings.

Of these sorts of speculations fortunes could be made, especially as English and French bookbrokers, working for patrons at home, cast their nets wide. It was now without question that they should first seek out precious manuscripts and incunabula. A visitor to the library at Waldhausen, founded in 1147, despaired of the sight that he found in 1806.

> The library looks as if the Russians had lived there: almost everything is mutilated. Now the mice and rats are there, eating up everything. Because so many people have already picked out the better things for themselves, it is pure luck if you find a splendid tenth- or eleventh-century manuscript left in a corner.[34]

After the spoils of Austria's monasteries had been distributed, the golden age of antiquarian collecting only gathered speed. The French Revolution, followed by a lengthy period of warfare, prompted many monasteries to realise the now inflated value of their best manuscripts. In 1798, Alexander Horn, the Scottish librarian of the Benedictine monastery of St James in Regensburg, supplied the Earl of Spencer with several pieces from the library, including a 1457 Mainz psalter.[35]

The greatest convulsions were yet to come. The outbreak of revolution in France in 1789 saw all monastic property confiscated by the state. France had thus far been spared the destruction of their monastic libraries, with the result that some collections were extremely large. In Paris, the abbey of St Geneviève had 60,000 volumes in 1789, while that of St Germain-des-Prés had 50,000.[36] These libraries, like all others throughout France, were now ordered to be handed over to the local municipality, so that they could become tools of edification for the liberated French public.

With so many books to be dealt with at a time of revolutionary excitement and heightened emotions, this could not be an orderly process. There were many cases of vandalism and wanton destruction, of soldiers ransacking libraries, 'lighting their pipes and stoking cooking fires' with paper ripped from books.[37] But many town councils took their mission seriously, even if they did not follow the instructions from the National Assembly strictly. Theological books or those that supported the institutions of royalty or aristocracy were not supposed to be preserved; after all, these had little role to play in educating the revolutionary public. Any book with an armorial binding was also to be destroyed, as an unwanted memorial to a discredited nobility. The local authorities quickly realised that this was an impossible task, arduous and self-defeating, and in many cases, they incorporated monastic libraries in their entirety into new *bibliothèques municipales*. Once one added the libraries of émigrés and members of the nobility condemned to death, the new municipal libraries were extremely large. In the wake of the revolution, Amiens had 40,000 volumes in its library and Marseille and Rouen had 50,000 each.[38] Whether these were books that the public actually wanted to read was a problem that would preoccupy them for much of the nineteenth century.[39]

Revolutionary France also eagerly embraced an ideological mission to civilise other European states, something that would begin by making Paris the unrivalled cultural centre of the world. In the words of the President of the Comité d'Instruction Publique, writing in 1794: 'The monuments which slaves have erected for our enemies will acquire in our midst that glory which a despotic government can never confer on them.'[40] The French government adopted the most centralised and efficient system of looting libraries thus far known. Commissioners were given free rein to gather for France the rarest books that the occupied territories had to offer. These commissioners were real antiquarian experts, librarians or bookbrokers. Individuals who had bought manuscripts from monasteries for resale before the revolution now worked on salary for the French government and appropriated books by threat of force. The commissioners worked with determined speed. In 1794, Belgium was occupied by French armies in one of the early campaigns of the French Revolutionary Wars. Two months after the occupation, the librarian of the Bibliothèque Mazarine reported that he had visited eight libraries and selected 8,000 books for removal. Five thousand had already been packed and dispatched, including 929 manuscripts from the old Burgundian library. The commissioners were especially keen on targeting old royal or aristocratic collections, or those of former monasteries. Sometimes they confiscated libraries *en masse*, but in most cases they worked swiftly through the collection, separating out manuscripts and incunabula for immediate dispatch to Paris.

As the first French Revolutionary War neared its end, in 1796 and 1797, French tactics changed. Their successful conquests in Italy, with its myriad principalities and extremely rich libraries, offered new opportunities. Instead of forcing their way into the libraries, the number of manuscripts that each state had to give up to France was written into the terms of the armistice. The Duke of Modena surrendered 70; the Venetian republic and the papacy were marked up for 500 each. Bologna lost 506 manuscripts and 94 incunabula. The French left no major library of distinguished medieval heritage unscathed: Milan, Urbino, Pavia, Verona, Florence and Mantua all suffered losses. Commissioners arrived with carefully prepared lists, their taste prepared by a century of antiquarian collecting. Some, like the keeper of printed books of the national library in Paris, Joseph-Basile-Bernard van Praet, 'hardly ever chose a book printed after 1500, unless it was on vellum'. The libraries that suffered most were those which had good catalogues. The commissioner's list for the books to be taken from Nuremberg city library even had shelf marks.[41] In the aftermath of France's defeat at Waterloo (1815), France was compelled to return some of these, but van Praet ensured that some of the most valuable manuscripts were hidden, or claimed that they were lost. In other cases, he substituted inferior copies for the incunabula that had been stolen.

Before the French Revolution, books had a spiritual and ethical value: as symbols of learning, of social distinction and of religious belief. The antiquarian craze of the eighteenth century had created a new form of historical capital, turning books into symbols of national prestige. The greatest irony was that these antiquarian books, in their content, often espoused precisely those philosophies that the intellectual revolutionaries of the period had sought to overthrow. This irony was lost, however, on the bookbrokers, auctioneers, opportunistic librarians and rich collectors who had commodified these books, and now dictated their price.

This was a process that would continue in other countries into the nineteenth century. Portugal and Spain dissolved their monasteries in the 1830s, and Italy followed by the 1860s. Numerous Polish monasteries vanished under Russian rule in the same period. Yet again, impoverished monks and friars sold their libraries to survive. Early printed books flooded the market to grace both the homes of gentlemen and the shelves of institutional libraries, mostly in Britain and the United States, where they could be repackaged as symbols of ancient learning and civilisation.

The Book Madness

In 1748, the Earl of Chesterfield passed on some useful advice to his son:

> Buy good books and read them; the best books are the commonest, and the last editions are always the best, if the editors are not blockheads; for they may profit of the former. But take care not to understand editions and title-pages too well.

of bibliomania, rich private collectors offered these superfluous volumes a temporary place of safety until the revolutionary fervour of the Enlightenment began to recede. When these fugitives re-emerged from country-house and aristocratic collections in the late nineteenth and twentieth centuries, they did so in a context when all books from the first era of print could attract high prices on the auction market. And that has not changed today.

PART FIVE

FICTIONS

CHAPTER THIRTEEN

ORDERLY MINDS

In the autumn of 1727, a group of friends in Philadelphia, Pennsylvania, gathered to discuss subjects of mutual interest drawn from their reading. This was not the cream of Philadelphia society. Three of the group were workers at the same print shop; others included a glazier, a surveyor, a joiner and a merchant's clerk. They were bound together by enquiring minds and a restless desire for self-improvement, and this was especially true of the man who was the driving force behind their common endeavour, Benjamin Franklin.[1] Franklin suggested they should pool their books into a single collection, so they would be freely available to all. By 1731, Franklin was prepared to go a step further and open this society to a larger group of Philadelphia citizens: each would pay a joining fee and annual subscription to allow the creation of a library for their mutual use. Thus was born the Library Company of Philadelphia, the world's first subscription library. Unlike many such ventures, the Library Company flourishes to this day.

In the next hundred years, subscription libraries proliferated in the American colonies, Britain and continental Europe. Meanwhile the world, and the world of books, changed out of all recognition. Both Europe and the United States experienced huge increases in population, along with a steady rise in rates of literacy. New methods of transportation brought isolated communities together, creating reading nations. Steam-powered presses made available a multitude of new reading materials: books, magazines and newspapers. Political reform, the spirit of enterprise and industrialisation transformed the social and political expectations of peoples demanding an increasing stake both in decision-making and the wealth created by their labour. All this had consequences for the development of the library. The new reading classes were largely shut out of the comfortable middle-class sociability of the subscription libraries. They relied instead on a new tier of commercial circulating libraries that served up fiction and escapist literature for readers to while away their precious hours of leisure away from the loom or the factory floor.

These new, more democratic, circulating libraries were initially run by booksellers and functioned as an adjunct to their regular business. By the mid nineteenth century, the most successful of the circulating libraries had grown into huge institutions, matching the subscription libraries for size and influence. They were also very different in character. The subscription libraries, though sometimes very large, served a defined membership, their books carefully chosen by a committee of trustees who continued the worthy principles of self-improvement first advanced by the Library Company of Philadelphia. Their manifestos and catalogues emphasised improving literature: history, science, agriculture, maps and atlases. They offered their members some lighter reading but did not boast about it. It was only with the arrival of the circulating libraries that the reading public could fully indulge their taste for the books they read for leisure. This preference was overwhelmingly for fiction: novels, detective stories and romance, with a few true-life travel adventures thrown in.[2]

All of this represented a quantum shift in the previously rather staid, disciplined world of the library. Until the middle of the eighteenth century, book collecting was still the preserve of a relatively narrow range of society. Nobles and crowned heads, bishops and religious orders, universities and their graduates, professional men who built their own working collections: the privileged few who had money for books and time to read them. The vast proportion of the new millions joining the reading nation, men and women, had little or no access to these collections; even if they had access, they had no influence over their contents. The subscription libraries, and their brash junior cousins the circulating libraries, gave customers for the first time real control over the books available to them, either because members of the subscription libraries chose them for themselves, or because the proprietors of the circulating libraries put economic considerations first, and gave their customers what they wanted.

This caused considerable ructions in the library world. Collectors of books and custodians of the established institutional libraries would not easily surrender their traditional roles as gatekeepers of knowledge and arbiters of taste. How far the public should be indulged in their pleasures, rather than be given what was good for them, was the subject of tortured debate throughout the eighteenth and nineteenth centuries. For all that, beyond the fire and fury over the place of fiction, newspapers or magazines in their collections, there was little doubt that by the end of the nineteenth century, libraries had changed out of all recognition.

First, and most decisively, the library had finally said farewell to the long supremacy of Latin. The books ordered by Franklin for the new library in Philadelphia were all in English, and this would be a common pattern for most of the subscription libraries and all stock of the commercial circulating libraries. The study of Latin still played a role in the schoolroom, and books in the classical languages still filled many yards of shelving in academic libraries. Yet even here, from the nineteenth century onwards, the urgent need for curriculum modernisation, and the growth of scientific and technical education, eroded the traditional dominance of humanist learning.

This major change was accompanied by the beginnings of another significant evolution as the library began to slip its moorings in the European continent. The United States played an increasingly important part in the development of the library, with the innovation of the subscription library a prime example. In the nineteenth century, the US would play a leading role in promoting the rebirth of the public library: its precociously democratic reading nation, and the rapid development of an industrialised and increasingly diverse population, helped redefine the nature of 'public'. Imperial expansion of the European mother countries also helped plant an embryonic European library culture in other parts of the world and offered the first frail shoots of the later globalisation of library provision.[3]

With the rapid growth of subscription and circulating libraries, for the first time borrowing books became a plausible alternative to ownership. This, too, was a crucial development. Of course, in every age, those who wished to read or study had borrowed books from their friends, yet before the eighteenth century, borrowing was essentially a mutual courtesy between collectors, those who had their own libraries. Now, thanks to the new library institutions offering easy affordable access to books, readers could read avidly, without cluttering their homes with books they might never want to read again. As a result, the link between book ownership and reading was weaker in the nineteenth century than it would be at any point before or since.

All of this – the huge increase in the availability of books and the enormously increased numbers of readers – might seem to have offered much-needed impetus for the growth of public libraries. There was certainly a strong sense of the importance of reaching a wide public: witness the presence of 'public' in the name of many libraries that in fact had more limited access or charged fees for membership. But if we treat the 'public library' in the modern understanding of the term – a taxpayer-funded facility freely avail- able to all local inhabitants, where books can be borrowed free of charge – then this concept made only halting progress until the very end of the nineteenth century. In many respects the success of the subscription and circulating libraries retarded rather than encouraged the development of free libraries; patrons either pre- ferred the social ambiance of the more exclusive subscription libraries, or found in the circulating libraries, unpatrolled by dis- approving librarians, more of the sort of literature they wanted to read. For much of this period it was far from clear that the public library had a future, or whether it would share the fate of other equally well-intentioned ventures such as the parish library move- ment of the seventeenth century.

For promoters of the educative value of books and reading, this became an increasingly urgent question. For bubbling away below the surface was a large substratum of reading matter which libraries considered beneath them, but which was taking up an increasing portion of the energies of the publishing industry and generating a large proportion of booksellers' sales.[4] In the nineteenth century, fiction for the new industrial masses became an industry in itself, with quickly penned tales of crime, passion and punishment sold cheaply and then discarded.[5] This 'dime fiction' or 'penny dreadfuls' generated problems for libraries: their determination to keep such materials away from their patrons matched the equal determination of the reading public to have access to them. This tension between improvement and entertainment, and more nuanced debates distinguishing what was trivial in fiction from what was morally degrading, would preoccupy library trustees and the new cohort of professional librarians right through to the twentieth century.

Subscription Libraries

The artisan friends who gathered with Benjamin Franklin for earnest discussions in Philadelphia would not be typical of the membership of the subscription libraries. Most of the social libraries in North America were sponsored by town elites, who provided the bulk of the first shareholders and therefore established the tenor of association life; they also patrolled the boundaries of acceptable book stock. Not surprisingly, the most extensive growth of libraries took place in the former Puritan colonies of New England. This had been, since the first settlements, a bookish society. It also had the densest network of towns and, in Boston, with Harvard just across the river, two of the principal beacons of American culture.

In 1733, two years after the foundation of the Philadelphia Library Company, eight citizens of Durham, Connecticut, came together to establish a library, motivated by their desire to enrich their minds 'with useful and profitable knowledge by reading'.[6] A further five Connecticut communities established libraries before the foundation, in 1747, of the Redwood library in Newport, Rhode Island. This was made possible by a generous bequest of £500 from Abraham Redwood, providing a second model for the establishment of community libraries: a gift from a rich local inhabitant. Both of the first libraries in Boston, the Price library and the New England library, established in 1758, were similarly built with money from the bequest of Thomas Price. The citizens of Portsmouth, New Hampshire, raised money by a third route, a public lottery. By 1780, fifty-one townships in New England had established a library.[7]

Library building resumed after the conclusion of the revolutionary wars, with 576 new libraries in the period between 1786 and 1815; another 465 would be added before 1850. Some catered for more select communities: libraries for children or young men, the agricultural library in Concord, Massachusetts, and the influential Mechanics' and Apprentices' Libraries. Collectively these libraries undoubtedly made a significant contribution to fostering a culture of improvement and the development of polite society.

It would be wrong, however, to overestimate the role of these libraries as institutions of democratic empowerment. In most cases the membership remained small, largely limited to the local commercial elites, bolstered by the professional classes who had been collecting their own books since the seventeenth century. A pooled resource was all the more attractive in America because, until well into the nineteenth century, all but the most mundane publications had to be imported from London, greatly adding to the expense. In consequence, the collections owned by these social libraries remained small. Only eighty-one of the 1,045 libraries are known to have had more than 1,000 volumes, a collection that would have been well within the reach of a lawyer or minister in the seventeenth-century Dutch Republic. To many, the main attraction of membership of social libraries was their provision of congenial space in which to read newspapers and meet other of the town's leading citizens. This easy sociability would be disrupted by the furious political contention of the Jacksonian era, when, for instance, the Democratic faction in Portsmouth, New Hampshire, opened their own reading room in competition to the Portsmouth Athenaeum.[8] The presence of more than one social library in many New England towns by 1850 facilitated this sort of partisan separation.

Like the Democratic reading room in Portsmouth, not all of these libraries were particularly long-lived, and many could scarcely be maintained beyond the lifetime of their founding subscribers. Only 13 per cent of the early New England libraries were still in business fifty years after their foundation.[9] It is perhaps inevitable that the subscription libraries should be defined for us by these rare survivors: the Philadelphia Library Company, the New York Society Library or the Boston Athenaeum. Outside the north east, the Charleston Library Society was established in 1748 by the pooling of funds 'to collect such new pamphlets and magazines as should occasionally be published in Great Britain'.[10] It would be another century before the development of the American publishing industry would create a reliable supply of home-grown literature and finally sever this umbilical cord.

That subscription libraries were rather slower to take off in England may partly be attributed to a rich hinterland of alternative institutions. Coffee houses, which became all the rage in the early eighteenth century, offered a wide range of newspapers but some also accumulated substantial libraries. These consisted largely of pamphlets and verse satires on contemporary political issues, precisely the sort of reading material that would appeal to the news-savvy clientele that gathered in the London coffee houses clustered around the Inns of Court or the City. They were open to regular users for a subscription as little as one shilling, but they could also be available to drop-in customers. This James Boswell experienced to his delight when, disappointed in his hope of finding one of his own publications at his publisher's, he was directed round to the Chapter Coffee House where he located it with ease.[11]

Coffee houses offered easy access to contemporary literature without the responsibilities of association life that came with membership of a subscription library, or even the more ephemeral book clubs. These book clubs have largely disappeared from the library story, but there seem to have been many hundreds if not thousands of them in Georgian England.[12] The book clubs flourished especially in smaller towns where local readers felt starved of the intellectual intercourse they imagined would be theirs in large cities or the county town. Book clubs generally consisted of between six and twelve friends, who met either in each other's homes or in a local tavern. The books purchased with the subscription funds were disposed of at the end of the year: there was no intention to build a permanent collection. The book clubs were

16. One of the reading rooms of the Portico library, a subscription library opened in Manchester in 1806 and still in existence today. The library soon enrolled 400 subscribers, who had access to a collection of some 20,000 books, mostly non-fiction, although the library eschewed works of theology, to respect the varied spiritual allegiances of its members.

also far more welcoming to female participants than the coffee houses.

Mention should be made of the newspaper reading societies, even more informal arrangements where a group of neighbours clubbed together to afford a newspaper. Popular particularly in the first decades of the nineteenth century, these newspaper reading clubs left little footprint in the wider history of the library, but they did offer yet another form of competition to the more expensive subscription libraries, many of whose members would make far more use of the newspapers and periodicals than the collections of books.

For all this, the subscription library became a significant force in the century between 1750 and 1850, particularly in the rapidly emerging northern industrial towns and port cities of England. In 1758, the newly established Liverpool library advertised its attractions 'for gentlemen and ladies who wish to promote the advancement of knowledge'. By 1800, there were a hundred such libraries spread around England: a far smaller number than in colonial America, but still a substantial contribution to an increasingly self-confident civic culture. The Portico library, established in 1806, was funded from an appeal that attracted 400 subscribers, allowing for the building of a fine neo-classical building in the centre of Manchester. It was with some justice that, in 1814, a local newspaper suggested that choosing not to join the Portico was to place oneself 'outside the circle of Manchester cultured society'.[13] The reformer Richard Cobden was an early member, and William Gaskell, husband of the novelist Elizabeth Gaskell and a Unitarian minister, its longest-serving chair. Its first secretary, Peter Mark Roget, began his famous *Thesaurus* in the Portico reading room. Robert Peel, twice prime minister, was a member, as was Hugh Hornby Birley, who led the deadly cavalry charge at Peterloo in 1819. A particularly important presence was the liberal MP James Heywood, a sponsor of the first Public Libraries Act in 1850.

As this example suggests, libraries in the major industrial cities attracted a large membership, allowing them to build considerable collections. The Liverpool library had 893 members in 1800, at which point it was obliged to close its list. This prompted the foundation of the Liverpool Athenaeum, which recruited a further 502 members by 1820. Many of the libraries issued printed catalogues, both for the convenience of their members and to advertise their collections. Frustratingly, few of these catalogues survive, but we do know that the Liverpool library had 21,400 books in 1830 and the Bristol Library Society already had 5,000 by 1798. Today, the Portico in Manchester has a collection of 25,000 books, almost all from the nineteenth century.

Many of the larger subscription libraries were in the fast-growing northern industrial towns, marking their new prosperity with new institutions and civic buildings. Elsewhere, in county towns like York, Shrewsbury or Lancaster, subscription libraries brought a gloss of metropolitan sophistication to the established rhythms of agrarian life. These libraries attracted a different sort of member: country gentlemen, for whom the library was an agreeable place to rest their feet when in town; military men and retired naval officers; the usual spread of country lawyers and many members of the Anglican clergy. This inevitably had its impact on the collections, with many more works of divinity and volumes of sermons than the libraries of the industrial cities, where the strength of Methodism and the dissenting churches made this contentious territory. The county libraries were also especially welcoming to women members. Women made up between 10 and 20 per cent of the membership of subscription libraries, and many more undoubtedly borrowed books through male relatives. In the eighteenth century, female readers were fast becoming a major force in the expanding book world.

Rise Up!

Subscription libraries in England went through a difficult period at the end of the eighteenth century, and again during the radical agitation at the end of the Napoleonic Wars. Fear that the contagion of radicalism might spread to England from France cast membership of private associations under suspicion, and this seems also to have embraced book clubs and libraries. Many prudently resigned their membership, though numbers revived in the 1820s. However, libraries were not made the object of any special measures, and the rigorous scrutiny of the book selection sub-committee was generally thought sufficient proof against revolutionary sentiment. The situation was very different in continental Europe, where subscription libraries were regarded as potential hotbeds of liberal agitation for political reform.

The French *cabinets de lecture* fell somewhere between the anglophone subscription libraries and circulating libraries run by booksellers. The *cabinets* normally charged an annual fee (though with some provision for walk-in visitors) and provided clients with a reading room. Some of the grander *cabinets* had separate rooms for newspapers and books. But they differed from English subscription libraries in that the proprietor, often a member of the book trade, was entirely responsible for the selection of the book stock. Patrons could also take away books to read at home.

The years between the restoration of the monarchy in 1815 and the revolution of 1848 provided France with much-needed respite from war. However, politically, the atmosphere remained febrile, and there was little inclination to relax the firm controls on the press decreed by Napoleon. Any tradesman wishing to establish a *cabinet de lecture* was obliged to seek police permission, as the belief that *cabinets* could incubate opposition prompted close scrutiny by the police authorities. In 1818, the local prefect in Caen, Normandy, reported the manager of a *cabinet* for circulating seditious works: not through any radical sentiments, he conceded, but purely from economic necessity. A list of the disapproved titles was appended. In Stendhal's novel *Lucien Leuwen*, a young officer is severely reprimanded for patronising a *cabinet* in Nancy, which his colonel believed to be a hotbed of Jacobinism. In fact, the unlucky officer had been reading a review of Mozart's *Don Giovanni*.[14]

Of course, a novelist like Stendhal would deplore any restriction on reading. But the publisher Alexandre-Nicolas Pigoreau was also forced to warn his clients that 'the *cabinets de lecture* are under the most acute police surveillance. They are determined to purge the book trade of novels.' This would have been a considerable task, as the stock of the *cabinets* comprised mostly literary fiction, generally a mixture of popular and serious literature. Artists, students and professional people were among the most frequent users. Sustaining the *cabinets*, as with the subscription and circulating libraries in England, was the high price of fiction, putting ownership of novels beyond the reach of the majority of readers. This was exacerbated in the French case by the conservatism of publishers, and their unwillingness to invest in new cost-saving technologies. The number of *cabinets* consequently increased very rapidly, from thirty-two in Paris in 1820 to 226 in 1850. There were at least another 400 in the French provinces.[15] A number of unregulated operations served a more diverse clientele who could afford to rent the occasional novel at 10 centimes a volume.

The eighteenth century was also a difficult time for library culture in Germany. The continued existence of 355 small and middle-sized states militated against the creation of an integrated market, or the national reform of the libraries as was so frequently attempted in France.[16] The activity of a number of celebrity scholar librarians (among them Goethe, successively supervisor of the great Ducal libraries in Weimar and Jena) rather disguised the lack of energy in the library world as a whole.[17] The collections of the universities and princely courts remained inaccessible to most readers; town libraries were weighed down by the burden of inherited collections, and there was little impetus for renovation of this book stock.

The most potent instruments for widening access were the *Lesegesellschaften*, reading societies, in the eighteenth century, and circulating libraries in the nineteenth. Reading societies first appeared in the 1720s and became a mass phenomenon from the middle of the century. By 1800, there were at least 600 in German-speaking lands, with a total of 250,000 members.[18] The reading societies were generally small, and served a wide variety of different constituencies. Some were essentially circulating libraries, managed by a bookseller; others concentrated exclusively on journals. The wealthier literary societies rented rooms or purchased their own property. The interest of many of their more enlightened members in contemporary politics inevitably attracted the suspicions of the authorities, though the reading societies do not seem to have been especially active politically. Their most important role was to miti-gate the frustrations of the rising middle class at the inaccessibility of the larger aristocratic and princely collections.

Since the reading societies remained relatively exclusive, the field was clear for the establishment of commercial circulating libraries. As elsewhere, this term covers a wide variety of institu-tions, with some, towards the top end, maintaining their own premises with a reading room, exhibition space for new titles and even a café or music room. Many issued catalogues, which reveal here as elsewhere the inexorable onward march of the novel. These catalogues also show a steady shift in public taste from vestigial chivalric tales, through Dumas and Sir Walter Scott, to the begin-nings of the crime novel.[19] In 1777, Hofmeister in Zurich offered 1,600 works in 4,617 volumes. These included a section of '*Amuse-ment pour les dames*' and the charmingly titled 'Adventures and Robinsons', a whole genre of literature inspired by the success of *Robinson Crusoe*.[20] This creeping influence of anglophone literature was especially evident in the catalogues of the German circulating libraries, though Sir Walter Scott also had a considerable follow-ing in France. As the nineteenth century wore on, an increasing proportion of French and English authors were offered to German customers in their original languages: foreign authors accounted for a quarter of the stock presented by Dirnböck in Vienna in 1882.

Very Proper to Debauch All Young Women

The British and American subscription library, the German reading societies and the French *cabinets* were generally held in high esteem. This could not be said of their raucous alter ego, the circulating libraries. As citizens fretted over what might fall into the hands of their wives and daughters, apprentices and servants or impressionable youths, the circulating libraries found themselves in the eye of a storm: a storm exacerbated by the vast increase in the market for reading. Circulating libraries were denounced as purveyors of pornography and books of brain-rotting triviality. When in the nineteenth century, the libraries recognised their new responsibilities as gatekeepers of morality, they were equally denounced as prudes and censors. This was especially the case in England in the second half of the century, when the market for quality literature was wholly dominated by two remarkable Victorian entrepreneurs, Charles Edward Mudie and W. H. Smith. The influence of these two library proprietors on the book market provides one of the most extraordinary episodes in the history of the library, and one that deserves to be better known.

Although we can find instances of booksellers loaning out books or charging customers a small fee to read in their shop from at least 1661, the honour of establishing the first documented circulating library falls to Allan Ramsay, poet of Edinburgh. In 1725, Ramsay opened his lending library, charging an annual subscription, Sir John Clerk of Penicuik being invoiced the sum of 10 shillings in 1726, for 'annual readings'.[21] Books could also be borrowed overnight. In 1740, Ramsay sold his shop to John Yair, establishing a pattern that would be typical of circulating libraries: although we can identify hundreds of libraries, spread the length and breadth of Britain, many were relatively short-lived, and their stock was frequently recycled into new ventures. For all that, from the mid century onwards, they would have a transformative impact on reading habits.

The real age of the circulating library began at about the time of Ramsay's retirement, when a group of established London booksellers each opened a circulating library. Not coincidentally, this was also the beginning of a huge upsurge in the publication of novels: at least 800 new titles between 1750 and 1779.[22] A number of the proprietors of the circulating libraries were themselves publishers, most famously the brothers Francis and John Noble, who between 1744 and 1789 published at least 200 novels, most of which found their way into the circulating libraries.

Many of the Nobles' publications made no pretensions to be great literature. When it was suggested to Fanny Burney that she should change the end of *Cecilia*, she offered this withering response: 'The last page in any novel in Mr Noble's circulating library may serve for the last page of mine, since a marriage, a reconciliation and some sudden expedient for great riches, concludes them all alike.'[23] The literary reviews were equally acid. *The Way to*

Lose Him, published by the Nobles in 1773, was dismissed by the *London Magazine* as 'written solely for the use of the circulating libraries, and very proper to debauch all young women who are still undebauched'.[24] Henry Mackenzie, himself a novelist, equally denounced 'that common herd of novels (the wretched offspring of circulating libraries) ... which are despised for their insignificance, or proscribed for their immorality'.[25]

The perceived pernicious influence of the circulating libraries led calls for regulation of their stock, or even that they should be closed altogether. In 1773 it was suggested that 'An Act of Parliament is soon to be passed, by which Circulating Libraries are to be suppressed, and by which the owners of them are to be declared, like ... players, rogues and vagabonds, and debauchers of morals, and the pest of society.'[26] Circulating libraries were routinely compared to brothels and gin shops. This moral panic was entirely due to their close association, in the public mind, with the circulation of fiction. In 1789 the prolific author Maria Edgeworth wrote that 'though I am as fond of novels as you can be, I am afraid [that] they act on the constitution of the mind as drams do on that of the body'.[27] Yet if we scrutinise the catalogues published by circulating libraries, fiction accounts for a surprisingly small proportion of the stock. The catalogue of Thomas Lowndes, bookseller on the Strand in 1755, offered several thousand titles, including a section of works in Italian and French. Works of history, bibliography and divinity were as numerous as novels, poetry and plays. The writings of the Greek and Roman authors were also reasonably abundant, though now always in English translation.

The major London circulating libraries, which frequently carried a stock of between 5,000 and 10,000 copies, could expect their metropolitan clients to have diverse and sophisticated reading tastes. Their proprietors were also well aware of the shrill criticism of their licentiousness, so the advertisement of a wide range of non-fiction titles was a sensible precautionary measure. However, we should not necessarily assume that these flew off the shelves as regularly as did the novels. Nor were the circulating libraries likely to accession twenty-five or more copies of the non-fiction titles, as we know they routinely did for novels. Lowndes also took care, on

the title-page of this same catalogue, to reassure subscribers that
he would also supply 'all new novels and other books of entertainment that have hitherto been published'.[28]

Some, like William Ward's circulating library in Sheffield in the
1760s, made a conscious appeal to a more high-minded and ambitious readership, but in general it can be said that the smaller the
library and the smaller the community they served, the more absolute was their reliance on novels. When, in 1793, Professor James
Beattie visited a bookshop in Dundee and expressed his surprise
at finding 'merely a circulating library of novels', the booksellers
acknowledged that 'nothing else was read in Dundee'.[29]

The London proprietors certainly enjoyed a privileged position in the trade, able to manage income and cash flow between
their bookselling, publishing and circulating library. They also
derived extra profit by acting as wholesalers to the network of
circulating libraries that spread rapidly through the English provinces, first to the spa towns and seaside resorts, then to the county
towns. We know of at least ten circulating libraries at some point
in eighteenth-century Shrewsbury, and twenty-two in York. The
stately subscription libraries of the northern industrial cities, with
their refined clientele and collections, were no proof against the
appeal of circulating libraries: we can identify forty-one in Manchester, forty-six in Birmingham and an astonishing eighty-eight
in Liverpool.[30] Here is sufficient explanation why, with weasel
words and careful self-justification, subscription libraries would
also stock fiction. The Literary Society of Leicester relied on the
sanctification of age before admitting such works: 'No novel or
play shall be admitted into the library but such as have stood the
test of time, and are of established reputation.'[31] Ironically, this
would allow members access to works, like Fielding's *Tom Jones*,
that would not pass scrutiny in public libraries at the end of the
nineteenth century.

The librarians of spa towns like Bath had no hesitation in supplying their patrons with a wide range of diverting literature, and
circulating libraries soon took their place in the roster of fashionable entertainments. Inscribing one's name in the list of subscribers
was as effective as a calling card in announcing one's arrival (and

an opportunity to check who else was in town). The libraries of Bath, Margate and Scarborough were often large, gracious facilities where patrons would linger to read and gossip; in 1782, Shrimpton of Bath offered separate reading rooms for ladies and gentlemen. The libraries provided a home for exiles from London club-land and an adequate substitute for the subscription libraries; in 1780, Pratt and Clinch offered their patrons thirteen London papers and twenty-two from the provinces.[32] Competition was not particularly cut-throat: in the 1770s, the Bath circulating libraries all raised their prices from 3 to 4 shillings per quarter, following the example of seven major London libraries, who in 1767 had agreed to harmonise their annual subscription at 12 shillings.[33] For those exiled to the provinces, the London libraries also offered a postal service. Books were sent down by carriage in locked boxes; the libraries supplied the boxes, but subscribers had to meet the costs of carriage.[34]

An insight into the reading life of these far-flung corners of the English book world is provided by the bookshop of Samuel Clay of Warwick.[35] Clay's surviving records of 1770–72 are particularly useful because we can compare the business of his bookshop with the contents of his small circulating library. These confirm the widespread assumption that readers borrowed rather than purchased fiction. The stock of the bookshop consisted largely of books for children and other chapbooks. Women did borrow novels, but so did men; and none read so voraciously as to confirm suspicions of the addictive properties so often attributed to novels. Indeed, several borrowers found them so unappealing that they gave up after the first volume: novels in this period were characteristically published in two or three volumes, adding greatly to their cost. Servants and apprentices, frequently cited as at-risk groups, are not very evident in Clay's register of borrowers, the major patrons of his circulating library being the gentry and professional classes who had made up the familiar core of the book world for more than two centuries.

What we do see in this period is an enormous transformation in the overall size of the market for recreational reading. At the other end of the scale from Clay's tiny library in Warwick, the

London library of Bell (the grandly titled British Library) boasted 100,000 volumes by the end of the eighteenth century. This now outstripped the largest personal collections by a considerable margin as well as almost all institutional libraries. Circulating libraries with 5,000 or 10,000 books, which would have been a very large collection for a subscription library, were now common-place. This was a significant shift in the economic centre of gravity of the British book industry, and one that would not be reversed.

Mudie

The development of circulating libraries in Britain soon found its echo in the American colonies. In 1762, William Read, book-seller in Annapolis, offered a circulating library to customers in Maryland for the sum of 27 shillings per annum. His stock was small, 150 titles, but represented a well-judged selection of proven bestsellers. Read's venture failed, but this did not deter others from chancing their arms. Within five years circulating libraries had been established in Charleston, New York, Boston and Phila-delphia, and shortly thereafter in Baltimore. All were attached to bookshops. This had the great advantage that circulating libraries could be open throughout bookshop hours, a sharp contrast to the early social libraries, which often only permitted borrowing for four hours on a Saturday afternoon.

From the beginning it was clear that as in Britain, novels would be the cornerstones of their business. Circulating libraries also encouraged female subscribers. Overall, eleven circulating librar-ies were established in the seventeen years before the American Revolution, most of relatively short duration. The end of the war then brought a new wave of foundations, thirty-nine in nineteen different cities from New Hampshire to Georgia. To one enthu-siastic observer, this seemed to be the future of the library, with profound social consequences:

> It is scarce possible to conceive the number of readers with
> which even every little town abounds. The common people
> are on a footing, in point of literature, with the middle ranks

in Europe. They all read and write and understand arithmetic. Almost every little town now furnishes a circulating library.[36]

This was acutely observed, though in terms of circulating libraries over-optimistic when written in 1789. It appeared in a book published in London, neatly illustrating the principal obstacle to the rapid growth of the circulating libraries: the continuing need to import almost all book inventory from England. The golden age of the American circulating libraries would be the first half of the nineteenth century, when the capacities of the American publishing industry grew exponentially. This also provided a major new opportunity for American authors, although none yet challenged the invincible Sir Walter Scott, as popular in America as he was in France and Germany. For the first time also in this period, libraries were owned by female proprietors, like Mary Sprague of Boston, who added a library to her millinery store, and Hannah Harris of Salem. Circulating libraries were also established in quintessentially American locations such as riverboats on the Mississippi and barges on the Erie Canal.

Circulating libraries declined after the end of the American Civil War, destroyed not by the advance of public libraries, but by the drop in book prices which made ownership more attractive than borrowing for their core middle-class clientele. At this point the experience of readers in Britain and America diverged, for in England this was the great age of the circulating libraries: or at least, this was the age of Mudie. Not since the iron rule of the Stationers' Company, the association of London publishers who had acted as the industry's regulatory body in the sixteenth and seventeenth centuries, had a single commercial institution exercised influence over a nation's reading equal to that of Mudie's circulating library. For the fifty years between 1844 and 1894, the golden age of Victorian prose writing, Mudie possessed a quasi-monopoly over the supply of quality fiction.

Charles Edward Mudie was the son of a London stationer, who also loaned out books for a penny a volume. At the age of twenty-two, Charles Edward opened his own shop, where in 1842 he established a circulating library, moving to larger quarters on

17. A typical Mudie's library label, pasted on the front cover of a copy
of Robert Louis Stevenson's *Letters to his Family and Friends, Vol. 1*
(London: Methuen, 1900). Rarely had a single commercial library exerted
such influence on one of the largest literary markets in the world.

the corner of New Oxford Street in 1852. Rapidly outgrowing
these second premises, in 1860 he built a new book emporium,
opened in the presence of most of London's literati. Between 1853
and 1862, he added an astonishing 960,000 volumes to his stock.[37]
According to one awestruck reporter, who visited the New Oxford
Street headquarters in 1863, in comparison the collection 'of the
famous Bodleian sinks into the shade, and that of the Vatican
becomes dwarfish, as far as quantity is concerned'. According to
The Times, by the end of the century Mudie's had acquired over
7 million books, many of them still stored in his cavernous vaults
despite frequent sales at heavily discounted prices of titles that had
run their course.[38]

Mudie was an entrepreneur, the key to his success lying largely
in his willingness to order new titles in exceptionally large quantities. In 1855, he purchased 2,500 copies of the newly published
volumes 3 and 4 of Macaulay's *History of England*. He also benefited from the spectacular wave of talented writers at work, from
Dickens and Thackeray, to Trollope, Mrs Gaskell, George Eliot
and Disraeli. For all that, the foundation stone of Mudie's business

model was the pricing structure for new fiction, sustained at his insistence at an astonishingly high level for the entire half-century when he ruled the English market.

The years between 1780 and 1830 had seen a steady increase in the price of new fiction, exacerbated by the pressure on the industry caused by the French Revolutionary Wars, and the post-war depression. The extraordinary popularity of the historical fiction of Sir Walter Scott allowed prices to reach new heights. New novels by Scott came to the market at a guinea and a half (31*s* 6*d*), a price that placed them outside the range of all but the wealthiest customers. Furnishing these new works to customers unwilling to wait a year for a 6-shilling reprint became the staple of the circulating libraries, which by the 1840s could charge 4 to 6 guineas for an annual subscription.

Mudie boldly joined this market offering an annual subscription of only one guinea, which allowed him to gather new subscribers very rapidly. In 1864, Mudie's became a public company, financing further growth. By this point Mudie was in the position to make his own terms with publishers, insisting that he would only take novels in the traditional three-volume format, for which the cover price remained 31*s* 6*d*, even for authors far less lustrous than Sir Walter Scott.

This was an arrangement that brought benefits to all parties. Readers got for their guinea-a-year as many books as they could read for less than the price of one new novel, and publishers secured a guaranteed sale, since Mudie would take the bulk of the first edition. An edition of 500 copies could secure for the publisher a decent profit, and Mudie would order 1,500 of an established author. Pre-publication correspondence with Mudie could help establish the print run and take most of the risk out of the enterprise. Mudie's regular lists of recommended new titles also spared publishers the expense and effort of promotion. Authors also benefited: a publisher could take on a new project without much risk, so many new authors could bring their books to market. For his part, Mudie insisted on deep discounts, seldom paying more than 18 shillings for the three-volume set. The three volumes, crucially, would be loaned out separately, guaranteeing Mudie a profit three times as great as for a novel in one volume. In effect, Mudie had secured himself a national monopoly on the publication of new fiction. What he chose not to take would not be published.

Mudie did pass up one major opportunity when in 1858 he declined an invitation from W. H. Smith to operate a network of railway libraries on Smith's behalf. After the chaotic decade of railway competition in the 1840s, Smith had emerged with a dominant role in the distribution of newspapers from London. It made sense also to establish a network of railway bookstalls, selling newspapers and cheap recreational literature. As journeys became longer and more frequent, there was growing demand for more substantial reading matter, and Smith now saw the potential of attaching circulating libraries to his bookstands. Books not available to the browsing customer could be ordered from a central depot, and brought down by rail for when the client next passed through.[39]

When Mudie declined his offer, Smith decided to run the new circulating libraries himself, thus starting a national institution that would persist until 1961. This caused no real tension with Mudie. Although he also had an expanding national network, served by satellite libraries in the major cities and the delivery of his trademark iron-cornered chests to country clients, the two enterprises were not really in competition. Railway customers preferred the easily portable one-volume reprints available from about a year after publication (the equivalent of the modern paperback), so Mudie's monopoly of the three-decker remained intact. Besides, the two men were cut from the same cloth, both being deeply religious philanthropists, living embodiments of the civic virtues of Victorian commerce. Smith would pursue a career in politics, culminating in his appointment as First Lord of the Admiralty (famously satirised in Gilbert and Sullivan's *HMS Pinafore*).[40] Both took their role as custodians of Victorian morality very seriously, and since they were now chief arbiters of the nation's reading tastes, this would put an increasing strain on their cosy relationship with authors and publishers.

Mudie's insistence on the three-volume format was undoubtedly responsible for the verbosity of many nineteenth-century novels, as authors went to extraordinary efforts to pad their texts to the required length. While a seasoned professional like Anthony Trollope mastered the required skill, writing his daily quota of words before work, many struggled to maintain inspiration and dramatic tension for the required 200,000 words, 66,000 words per volume. If we wonder why so many nineteenth-century novels lose themselves in a convoluted (though chaste) love story between two marginal characters in the novel's middle passage, we should blame Charles Edward Mudie: this was the problem of the difficult second volume. If all else failed and authors came in short, publishers resorted to large typefaces and wide margins to disguise the deficit.

Edgy authors pressing the boundaries of Victorian taste found Mudie an increasingly preposterous figure. According to George Moore, a bitter and frequent critic, 'The literary battle of our time lies not between the romantic and realistic schools of fiction, but for freedom from the illiterate censorship of a librarian.'[41] Wilkie Collins exploded when Mudie asked his publisher to alter the title of *The New Magdalen*: 'Nothing will induce me to modify the title. His proposal would be an impertinence if he was not an old fool ... But the serious side of this affair is that this ignorant fanatic holds my circulation in his pious hands.'[42] Collins was an established figure, who had other avenues for his work, such as the serial publication in magazines pioneered by Charles Dickens. But for those making their way, adoption by Mudie was a necessity of life. Authors and publishers altered their writing timetable to accommodate Mudie's plans, rather as authors had to do when writing for the next Frankfurt Fair in the sixteenth century. Correspondence flowed back and forth between publishers and Mudie, pleading their author's case and fighting, usually in vain, Mudie's demands for discounts. Many did not fight too hard, because they were themselves shareholders in Mudie's company.

W. H. Smith was if anything more censorious. When in 1896 the Bishop of Wakefield denounced Thomas Hardy's recently published *Jude the Obscure*, Smith withdrew copies from circulation.[43] This was censorship every bit as insidious as that practised by the public libraries, without any of the agonising. Mudie and Smith prevailed partly because of their financial muscle, but also because their judgements matched the sensibilities of their subscribers. Mudie saw to it that they never read anything likely to shock them.

This has gone down badly with later generations, as it did with radical authors at the time, but Mudie and Smith between them performed one critical service which must be recognised: they decontaminated English fiction. In 1794, commentators from the traditional reading classes were seriously advocating banning circulating libraries. One hundred years later, when Mudie's son abandoned his defence of the three-decker, fifty years of his one-guinea subscriptions had brought the novel safely home to the respectable shelves of the library. That, for all the longueurs of the difficult second volume, was a remarkable achievement.

CHAPTER FOURTEEN

BUILDING EMPIRES

In 1844, a publicist for the British New Zealand Company, a commercial charter spearheading the settlement of New Zealand, was seeking to recruit emigrants. He was at pains to demonstrate that New Zealand was no penal colony or dingy commercial trading station, but a community of cultured men who sought to model the world they now inhabited upon the best of what they had left behind. One of the crucial elements in this societal transplantation was the library:

> A well-conducted colonist is of necessity a reading man: debarred from the more frivolous amusements of the mother country, he has no other resource but in books, or the debasing influence of the tavern – the bane and antidote of colonial life. None but they who have resided in a new colony can appreciate the value of a new book; and we are happy to bear testimony, that in no colony is literature more appreciated than in New Zealand: as might be expected from the very superior class of men who have migrated to our favourite colony.[1]

The reference to the rampant alcoholism that plagued many a colony, trading post or settlement indicated that, even in New Zealand, all was not necessarily well. What was undeniable, however, was the strong connection that was understood to exist between books and civilisation, which was emphasised by colonial recruiters and borne out by the desires and aspirations of colonial communities. Between the signing of the Treaty of Waitangi between the British crown and the Māori chiefs of the North Island in 1840 and 1914, New Zealand's settler population expanded from a few thousand to just over 1 million. In the same period, 769 libraries were founded in the colony. In 1878, there was one library for every 1,529 people. Virtually all these foundations followed the model of the subscription library, much preferred in nineteenth-century colonial society, as it encouraged personal collections to be pooled for communal benefit. In the outposts of New Zealand, a couple of hundred books might be one of the few physical links to the motherland, and a crucial resource with which to pass the time, face the inevitable hardships and dream of a prosperous future.

We have seen how European books were carried on the first voyages to the Americas, and how books were found among the most treasured possessions of English Puritans and Spanish Jesuits.[2] For those that carried them, books were a totem of civilisation as much as tools to plant European culture in their new homes. Acquiring relevant up-to-date books was rarely straightforward, but books would necessarily accumulate in colonial posts as there were few places for them to go when their owners died. Thus a shrewd collector like Joachim von Dessin (1704–61), the overseer of auctions of goods of the deceased in Cape Colony, South Africa, could acquire almost 4,000 books. This collection he donated to a local church in Cape Town upon his death, with instructions to make them available to the public. Books could be borrowed and inspected on site once a week.[3] The local pride that inspired a minister to donate his books to the community in Scotland or Germany was equally applicable to the Cape, Australia or Canada.

The English slaving post at Cape Coast (present-day Ghana) had a substantial library for the officers in the castle. The presence of English literature, histories and books of law, serving as a reminder of the polite civility to which these men apparently aspired, forms a strange contrast to the brutality of their everyday business.[4] At the same time, eighteenth-century Christian missionaries who evangelised in the Cape and the Caribbean tried to build their own libraries which they could use to spread the word of God. Some, like the Protestant Moravian Brethren, made specific efforts to teach enslaved people to read and write, a process that brought them all too often into conflict with plantation owners.[5] For the enslavers, literacy was deemed to be a dangerous path towards subversion, and ultimately liberation. Enslaved people, though from a different perspective, also believed in the liberating power of books: in Cape Colony, many of those freed bought books at auction, and gathered together their own libraries as a powerful symbol of their free status.[6]

After the abolition of slavery in the middle of the nineteenth century, tensions over access to books did not dissipate. In South Africa, black activists saw in library provision a key tool for emancipation, but were persistently frustrated by a government which had little sympathy for their cause.[7] In the Dutch East Indies, on the other hand, the colonial government was an active sponsor of libraries, and created no fewer than 2,500 public libraries between 1918 and 1926, stocked with literature in the vernacular languages specifically designed for the Malay, Javanese and Sundanese populations. These proved exceptionally popular and facilitated real strides in the advance of literacy. To the Dutch colonial government, they were a tool to inculcate support for colonial rule and western values; in this they were only partially successful, given that the indigenous populations, once exposed to western notions of liberty, self-determination and democracy, were determined to apply these principles to themselves.[8]

The nineteenth century, the great age of empire, was a critical era in the global development of the library. Attempts to export European culture overseas accelerated with the expansion of empire and the global migration of European people. The transplanting of European libraries to Canada, India and Australia would not be without difficulties, and the result rarely matched up to the library culture found in London or Paris. At the same time, the glories of empire were lauded in new national libraries, substantial collections erected to celebrate the cultural and literary achievements of each European nation. The size of these libraries, a source of repeated international rivalry, would mark them out as behemoths of their day; they were the first institutional libraries that outmatched even the finest personal collections. Yet this did not deter a new breed of library builder, the robber barons of the rapidly industrialising United States of America, from chasing their own dreams as princes of sophistication. This was book collecting as reputation laundering, building a cultural legacy to expunge the memory of their rapacious business practices.

Shipwrecked Novels

The period between 1757 and 1818 saw the British East India Company transformed from a merchant corporation with a few coastal trading posts into the dominant power on the Indian subcontinent. As British officers settled into their roles as administrators over this vast territory, they encountered a country with rich literary traditions and a history of great royal libraries. Since the days of Akbar I (1542–1606), the Mughal emperors had always surrounded themselves with orators and poets, and assembled thousands of manuscripts at their imperial libraries, mostly written on palm leaves.[9] These collections were predominantly made up of works in Arabic, Persian and Urdu; many items were richly illuminated by court painters, often with celebratory portraits of the ruler and his entourage. Works of poetry and literature from the imperial library would generally be read out for the enjoyment of the ruler and his court; Emperor Akbar himself never learned to read or write. The library programme of the Mughals was without doubt exclusive, and the art of printing never enticed these great rulers. Their chief experience with print was to observe the somewhat clumsy but determined efforts of missionaries at the trading post at Goa to produce Catholic books for India's vast population. The typographical complexities of this venture were considerable, given the range of languages and scripts encountered by the missionaries. Some royals, like Maharaja Serfoji II of Tanjore (1777–1832), did collect European printed books out of curiosity: he possessed a library of 30,433 palm leaf manuscripts and 6,426 printed European books, the result of 300 years of collecting by his dynasty.

Another great library, that of the Sultan of Mysore, was seized by the British after his defeat at Seringapatam (1799), and the spoils divided between Oxford, Cambridge and Fort William college in Calcutta (now Kolkata). This was one of many Indian collections to be appropriated by Britain in the age of empire; the remains of the imperial Mughal library also fell into British hands in 1859, but only after it had been much diminished by a century and a half of plunder and neglect. Sending these books home was a demonstration of triumph, not unlike Swedish plunder of Catholic libraries in the seventeenth century, but also part of a determined effort to build comprehensive collections of Asian works in Oxford, Cambridge and London, to help scholars and administrators engage with the culture of people who lived under British dominion abroad. Not all libraries were seen as appropriate for such anthropological purposes. The great library of the Augustinian friars in Goa, some 10,000 volumes, did not impress Sir James Mackintosh, chief judge at Bombay (now Mumbai): 'I did not know before that the world had produced 10,000 such useless and pernicious books, or that it had been possible to have formed a large library with so curious an exclusion of whatever is instructive or elegant.'[10]

Undoubtedly fuelled by anti-Catholic sentiments, this was a rather unfair dismissal of a library assembled in the face of considerable difficulties over the course of several centuries. Yet Mackintosh's outburst was made in the context of a pressing need to provide 'instructive or elegant' books for the increasingly numerous British soldiers, officers, administrators and traders in India.[11] Books had long been accumulated at company forts and missions, mostly through the personal collections of company employees, bolstered by the dispatch of Bibles and prayer books from London. Concern over the well-being of British soldiers, and therefore their military effectiveness, required a more systematic approach. British troops in India were the first in the world to be provided with permanent libraries, some two decades before their colleagues in Britain received the same. By the 1820s, every European regiment in India had the benefit of the services of a schoolmaster, a reading master and writing master, two assistant schoolmasters, a librarian and a schoolmistress for children.[12]

These generous provisions, it was frequently emphasised in reports home, were necessary due to the heat, which made recreational activity requiring physical exertion impracticable. The chaplain of Dinapore station remarked in 1832 that

> I should say generally that the minds of those soldiers who
> use the library are better regulated and their conduct more
> becoming them as men and as Christians than it would have
> been had they been left to their own resources, and their very
> limited means of finding useful occupation for the many
> leisure hours which the European soldier in India has at his
> own disposal.[13]

When dedicated library buildings were erected at each major
station, and librarians instructed how to deal with the voracious
white ants that plagued the books, officers and chaplains made
clear that the libraries should allow provision for lending books,
rather than insist they be consulted in the often crowded library
room. The libraries were used more frequently, and the mood of
the men improved considerably, if they were granted permission
to borrow books and read them in the quiet hours in their own
barracks. On the question of content, the military libraries were
also a step ahead of their time: they were among the first institutional libraries to fill their shelves with fiction. The novelist
Maria Edgeworth argued that British soldiers and sailors should
read tales of heroism, adventure and hardship likely to instil virtue
(presumably her own titles being considered particularly suitable).
Accounts of shipwreck and arduous voyages were also to be recommended, 'beginning with *Robinson Crusoe*, the most interesting of
all stories, and one which has sent many a youth to sea'.[14]

This was not just the self-interested claim of a bestselling novelist: company officers in India agreed wholeheartedly. The shelves
of military libraries were filled with fiction, including Defoe's *Robinson Crusoe*, the novels of Sir Walter Scott, and Shakespeare. Even
the chaplains in India noted that spiritual fare alone was not good
for the morale of the men; although religious works were found in
every library, they sat largely unread, providing nourishment for
the ants.

The value of books exported from Britain to India rose dramatically between 1791 and 1810, from £8,725 to £66,180; by the early
1860s this had grown to £313,772.[15] Military libraries were responsible for only a portion of this market, as numerous private initiatives

were launched in the leading cities of the empire: Calcutta (now Kolkata), Madras (now Chennai) and Bombay (now Mumbai). There were five commercial circulating libraries in Calcutta by 1831, mostly serving the white population of some 12,000 people, a third of whom were British.[16] Here, too, fiction reigned supreme. All these books had been supplied from London, though more were dispatched from the home country than ever reached their destination. In 1835, the travel writer Emma Roberts declared that 'At the Cape of Good Hope, the beach is said sometimes to be literally strewn with novels; an occurrence that takes place upon the wreck of a ship freighted from the warehouses of Paternoster Row'.[17]

The 1830s also saw the emergence of two great subscription libraries, in Bombay (1830) and Calcutta (1836). Both bore the name of 'public library', and although both charged fees for membership, these were kept deliberately low. The Calcutta library was free for poor students, while the Bombay library resolved that 'it should be open to all ranks, classes and castes without distinction; a decorous demeanour, and a strict adherence to the rules, constituting the only requisites for admission'.[18] These policies suggested that the collections would be available to members of the Indian population as well as the colonial elite. The radicalising impact of literature feared in the Caribbean was here of less concern than the need to promote the growth of a capable westernised class of Indians who could assist the colonial administration. Both libraries rapidly accumulated stock, especially Calcutta's, as it received all the European books from the dismantled Fort William college in 1854. The libraries also attracted many donations from local patrons, British and Indian alike: Indian subscribers represented some 20 per cent of the members in the second half of the nineteenth century.[19] Crucially, Indian members were also on the library committee. While subscription libraries, such as that of the Asiatic Society, were also valued by a more exclusive membership, it was the more inclusive 'public' libraries that would grow substantially during the nineteenth century. The British Raj demonstrated its esteem for the Calcutta library when it became the nucleus of the public imperial library in 1903, the direct forerunner of the modern National Library of India.

The pattern of library growth in India was replicated in the other colonies of the British Empire.[20] What stood out was the reliance on private initiative, often backed by government subsidy and support. In Cape Town, a government-funded public library, opened in 1822, was turned into a subscription library seven years later as the funding source, a duty on the wine trade, was withdrawn.[21] By 1833, it had a stock of 26,000 volumes, at that stage one of the largest libraries in the British colonies. Cape Town could accumulate a substantial library of this sort relatively quickly, as it remained a busy way station for shipping to the East.

In Canada, subscription libraries were actively encouraged by the colonial administration, and liberally funded. Montreal was served by four subscription libraries, the largest of which had a stock of 3,800 volumes.[22] By 1858 there were 143 private library associations receiving aid from the government, mostly through funds to buy books from Britain. In Quebec and Montreal, the libraries were seen as means to instil British values in otherwise entirely French regions, whereas in the gold fields of British Columbia, it was hoped that libraries could bring order, culture and respectability to rough frontier posts.[23] In neither instance were these ventures entirely successful. French inhabitants of Montreal and Quebec City banded together to establish their own French libraries, while the miners of British Columbia did not always value the tone with which local authorities sought to publicise libraries as 'surrogate families' for these young working men. Another challenge in British Columbia, also seen in the gold rush era in California, was that thousands of migrants would settle in one locality for a few months or years, but then pack up again, moving on to the next field, leaving libraries in their wake.

The library was a ubiquitous concept in rural Canada by the middle of the nineteenth century, but few libraries had staying power. In small communities, the survival of the local subscription library was often dependent on the energy of a few individuals. Anne Langton, who struggled to operate a library for settlers near Lake Sturgeon, Ontario, reflected in 1842 that 'I think I shall be obliged to accept a pound of butter or a few eggs in payment [for the subscriber's fee], and put the sixpence into the bag myself. I am afraid that I shall have to be perpetually dunning [chasing] one subscriber or another.'[24] In New Zealand, which saw the greatest boom of subscription libraries of all colonies in the British Empire, one third of the libraries founded before 1914 survived less than twenty years. This fragility was exacerbated by the isolation of many small communities. In Maungakaramea, in North Auckland, a library was founded in 1878, twenty years after the first settler arrived, with twenty-six subscribers. This number of subscribers declined into single figures, but in 1938 the library was still active, with eighteen members and 2,050 volumes.[25] Throughout the period of its activity there were never more than 350 people in the community.

Until 1929, private subscription libraries were financially supported by the New Zealand authorities. Despite their limitations, there was a profound sense that these libraries provided a welcome public service. Library societies actively promoted this reputation, and were successful in attracting funding from government, not least because its civil servants were among the likely pool of subscribers. In the great cities of the empire, the largest subscription libraries would later form the basis of public or national libraries. In Singapore and Australia, ironically, this led to the expunging of the novels and light literature that had made these libraries popular in the first place.[26] Nevertheless, it was fiction that finally alerted publishers in Britain to the potential of the market overseas. Knowing that libraries in Australia or India were well out of reach of the tyrannical hold of Mudie's, publishers could afford to drop their prices by a shilling a book and ship out enormous quantities of new novels. Between 1870 and 1884 there was a fourfold increase in British books exported to Australia; shipping times were also reduced to just forty days.[27]

The opportunities afforded by the colonial market were fully exploited by the publishers Macmillan, founded by two Scottish brothers in 1843. In 1886, Macmillan launched their Colonial Library, a series of titles that were only allowed to be sold in the British market overseas. Within thirty years, the Colonial Library, dressed in a recognisable livery of uniform bindings, comprised 680 titles, of which 632 were fiction.[28] Not surprisingly, an encomium from the *Times of India* which trumpeted their virtues was gleefully circulated by the publishers.

> For an expenditure of two or three pounds every upstation can now start a library of sterling worth, with the certainty that a little further outlay, every now and then, will keep it abreast of the times. To messes, clubs, school libraries, and native book-clubs, the 'Colonial Library' should be simply invaluable, and we honestly commend it as the best endeavour we have ever seen to give English readers out here the same advantages that are enjoyed at home by those who live close to one of Mudie's agencies, or one of W. H. Smith's bookstalls.[29]

The publishers were keen to stress that their colonial readers were valued as much as those in Britain and treated with equal courtesy. This was largely true: Macmillan did not use the Colonial Library as a means to dump old or unsellable stock. They also quickly realised that the novels that sold well in Britain did not always resonate with the colonial public. The first two titles in the Colonial Library – Mary Anne Barker's *Station Life in New Zealand* and *A Year's Housekeeping in South Africa* – sold poorly. These household and travel accounts, although of some interest to the European expatriate community, held little attraction for the much larger Indian population. It also soon became clear that the dominant themes in English realist fiction did not appeal in India, the largest colonial market, as they did not reflect the realities of Indian readers. Instead these readers favoured fiction that emphasised themes like moral virtue, struggle, oppression and liberation; most strikingly the novels of George W. M. Reynolds, many of which centred around social injustice in nineteenth-century London.

Although Reynolds has found little favour with literary critics, Macmillan knew their business, and their target audience. Their success did not go unnoticed. By 1895, there were eight other British publishing houses who had special 'colonial series', all dressed, like Macmillan, in a uniform design, and selling for a shilling less than at home. Not coincidentally, the period between 1886 and 1901 saw a rapid increase in the number of circulating and subscription libraries in India: from 49 to 137 in the Bengal presidency and from 13 to 70 in the Bombay presidency. Some were founded by and catered specifically for the emerging Indian professional classes.[30] These proliferating libraries articulated a growing self-confidence that would play an important role in the independence movements of the twentieth century.

A Library for the Nation

In 1753, the president of the Royal Society, Sir Hans Sloane, offered his life's work to the British nation. In his will, Sloane gave the state the opportunity to purchase his library, 40,000 printed books and over 3,500 manuscripts, for the comparatively low sum of £20,000. The collection also included his unrivalled collection of antiquities, medals and curiosities, and botanical, zoological and mineralogical specimens. This was an opportunity not to be missed. Although London had become one of the greatest cities of the world, it lacked a cultural attraction that could match its global renown. Its libraries, although not insignificant in number, paled in comparison to the Bodleian in Oxford, never mind the famous Bibliothèque du Roi in Paris.

Parliament appointed a forty-one-member committee of trustees to oversee Sloane's collections and organise a public lottery to gather the necessary funds. The lottery was successful, raising over £100,000. This sum allowed for the purchase of a generous endowment, in the form of Bank of England annuities, in addition to a permanent location for the collections, Montagu House, at the heart of Bloomsbury. Despite the necessity of extensive renovation, funds were still left to acquire the Harleian manuscripts, some 8,000 items collected by the earls of Oxford. Two smaller, but no less distinguished collections, already in the possession of the crown, were conveniently added, before the king, George II, decided to present his royal library, comprising at least 9,000 volumes, to the nation.[31]

In 1759, the British Museum opened its doors. Entry was free, but required a ticket, which had to be requested days in advance. Tour groups soon graced the halls of Montagu House, while a motley band of scholars worked in the reading room, which by all accounts was beset by intolerable damp. They also grumbled, in unison with the fifteen members of staff, about the hustle and bustle of the gawping visitors who marvelled at Sloane's curiosities, ranging from exotic footwear and weaponry to remarkable pieces of coral. The tension between the two glories of the museum, its library and its natural and antique collections, always simmered below the surface. It was the proper habit of a gentleman-collector to gather both books and a cabinet of curiosities in one place, and Sloane's extraordinary collections were testament to his encyclopaedic ambitions.[32] To him, the books and specimens informed one another. In practice, the two sides of the museum grew steadily apart, as the demands of the library user differed from that of the museum visitor. Yet the two were also imperative to each other's success: the number of day visitors maintained the popular profile of the collections, while the books bestowed on the institution an air of intellectual distinction. The trustees and staff evidently found themselves more often than not on the side of the books: it was on the library that most effort and funding was expended. Many of Sloane's famous taxonomical specimens, on the other hand, were incinerated in the early nineteenth century, as the stink of putrefaction seeping from the catacombs of Montagu House became increasingly unbearable for readers.[33]

Despite these teething problems, the foundation of the British Museum was a remarkable success. It would remain the host of the national library collection until the foundation of the British Library in 1973: and only in 1998 was the collection moved to its own purpose-built building at St Pancras, finally separating the books from the antiquities. It was the first collection of its sort to be conceived as a national resource, and one that was regarded by its readers and visitors as the embodiment of the confidence, prestige and ambition of the British people. Libraries had long been seen as symbols of cultural distinction, but that this concept could be tied directly to the nation state was a particular nineteenth-century development.[34]

Although the British Museum was admired from abroad, few other countries emulated the principle of a conjoined library and museum. This was partly an issue of legacy and resources: there were few collectors who collected on the scale of Hans Sloane. In contrast, most states could identify an old collection of books that had some claim to belonging to the nation, not least through the remnants of royal libraries. These collections provided a strong basis for national libraries, not necessarily because of their size but through the lustre of their former owners, and often the richness of their manuscript collections.

It was, however, through the acquisition of distinguished personal libraries that national libraries increased their collection. This was the case in the Netherlands and Belgium, where small royal collections were expanded by tens of thousands of volumes from private collectors, who either donated freely or sold cheaply to the crown. Royal support for a national library also helped: in Britain, King George III bought a collection of 30,000 newspapers and pamphlets from the English Civil War era for the British Museum (these were described laconically under a single entry in the first published catalogue of the library), while his son, George IV, later presented his father's library, 65,000 volumes and 20,000 pamphlets, to the museum in the 1820s. More humble, but no less welcome, was a steady trickle of donations from patriotic citizens. Between 1759 and 1798, the British Museum received over 1,000 gifts of books, often one or two valuable items, sometimes small collections.[35]

Another source of books, exploited especially ruthlessly by Catholic states, was the appropriation of the contents of monastic and church libraries. The French Bibliothèque du Roi, although already one of the largest libraries in Europe, expanded by half a million books during the French Revolution to at least 800,000 volumes, albeit rebaptised as the Bibliothèque Nationale.[36] A similar story unfolded in Portugal, and in the comparatively younger state of Greece. Established in 1828, the year of Greece's independence, the Greek national library opened with 1,844 volumes, generously deposited by friends of the revolution. This tiny collection was soon enhanced by a decree stating that all valuable manuscripts and books to be found in the libraries of the country's Orthodox monasteries, churches and other libraries on Greek territory were to be deposited in the new national collection.[37] In the 1860s, Risorgimento Italy, a remarkably disunited new country, settled on no fewer than seven national libraries; the stock of which was bolstered by, and in one case entirely based on, books from recently suppressed convents.[38]

If one could not plunder one's own libraries, one might as well appropriate the book stock of another nation. In 1794, when Russia played its part in the third partition of Poland–Lithuania, its armies returned from Warsaw with the famous Zaluski library. Assembled painstakingly by two Polish brothers and opened to the public in 1747, the Zaluski library was one of the greatest libraries of Europe, with some 300,000 volumes. It had come into the formal possession of the last king of Poland, Stanisław II Augustus (1732–98); as Russia dismantled the Polish state, the library was considered an appropriate basis for the new Imperial Public Library of St Petersburg.[39] Despite the fact that poor transportation arrangements resulted in the loss of at least 40,000 volumes between Warsaw and St Petersburg, Russia had, in one fell swoop, acquired the second-largest library in Europe.

The rapacity of the Russian Empire was fuelled by a sense of cultural inferiority with western Europe, one that could only be repaired through aggressive collecting.[40] Yet rivalry permeated all national libraries because these libraries were supposed to embody the intellectual ambitions of the nation itself. This competition expressed itself not through the contents of the libraries, but predominantly through their size. For the first time in history, institutional libraries had become decisively larger than the best private collections.[41] The librarian of the British Museum, Antonio Panizzi (1797–1879), declared before the House of Commons in 1835 that the size of the British Museum paled in comparison with the great libraries of France and Germany. 'Paris must be surpassed' became the rallying cry that saw Parliament vote additional funding for acquisitions.[42] Ironically, the fact that Panizzi was Italian by birth also ruffled feathers: how could the principal librarian of the British Museum be a foreigner?

It was Panizzi, however, who best articulated the role that a national library should play. It was not enough to have a collection of books that belonged to the nation in name: it should reflect the cultural values of that nation, and most of all, collect and preserve its literature. A national library should aspire to be a universal collection of a nation's books: those printed in the country, written by all authors of that nationality, written in the language of that nation, or dealing with its language and culture. Crucially, these were principles that resonated with the nationalist movements of the nineteenth century. Even those states which did not acquire independence established their own national libraries along these lines. In nineteenth-century Transylvania, under the rule of the Austrian Habsburg Empire, the three disparate linguistic communities of Germans, Hungarians and Romanians each developed their own 'national' library.[43]

In the British Museum, Antonio Panizzi also articulated the vision that the British Library, as the greatest library of the greatest empire in the world, should possess the best collections of foreign-language works of any library. Panizzi hoped that 'the library of the British nation will not be suffered to sink into a collection of common volumes. The very name given to the institution implies a collection of rare and curious objects.'[44] A national library should be universal in ambition as a repository, but selective when acquiring antiquarian volumes, because it was here that the reputation of a library was made.[45] Despite the widely shared vogue for manuscripts and early printed books, national libraries were among the first institutional libraries to value works in the vernacular tongue over scholarly languages such as Latin and Greek. Although the catalogues of the collections continued to be published with Latin title-pages and prefaces, the national library would actively pursue the accumulation of works in the vernacular; it would also, by necessity, accession newspapers and periodicals. The Russian imperial library, its foundation collection purloined from abroad, faced particular challenges in this respect. When, in 1808, the librarian Aleksei Olenin undertook a survey to investigate the contents of the library, he discovered that among its 238,632 printed volumes and 12,000 manuscripts, there were only eight books in Russian or

Church Slavonic, the liturgical language of the Russian Orthodox Church.[46]

Tied to the collecting policies of the national libraries was the notion of generous accessibility. Libraries of state in most countries had long been available to the friends of the king's librarian, or notables of the court. When Elector Frederick William of Brandenburg–Prussia made his court library available to the public in 1661, it was housed in the top room of his castle: not an approachable destination for an average citizen of Brandenburg.[47] At the British Museum, the demands of formal registration as reader posed similar challenges to those unused to polite society. Yet when the museum's collections expanded in the early nineteenth century, with illustrious trophies such as the Rosetta Stone, the Elgin marbles and many other Greek, Roman, Egyptian and Assyrian antiquities, the popularity of the institution increased so much that hundreds of thousands of visitors passed through its building each year. Despite grumbling about 'persons of low education' and their 'idle curiosity', there emerged the notion that the national library could help 'improve the vulgar class', in the words of one member of parliament.[48]

The origins of national libraries ensured that fulfilling any of these ambitions was a constant struggle. Personal libraries from the seventeenth and eighteenth centuries, never mind monastic libraries, rarely met the aspirations of those such as Panizzi. Relatively few libraries were like the Bibliothèque Nationale in Paris and the British Museum in being encyclopaedic in their collections, and even they had notable gaps. Only steady acquisitions and the enforcement of legal deposit rights could remedy the situation. National governments proved relatively reluctant, however, to grant a regular acquisitions budget. Until the end of the nineteenth century, most national libraries did without; the best they could hope for were grants for specific purchases. In London, Parliament was comparatively generous with its funding, voting an annual grant of £10,000 for book purchases in 1845.[49] In countries with lesser means, such as Argentina, funds remained elusive. Although a national library was established in 1810, when the country declared independence, it languished in neglect for most of the nineteenth century.[50] Legal deposit rights, although granted by many governments to their national libraries, in practice proved difficult to enforce. Since the earliest days of printing, authorities had tried to force publishers to relinquish copies of their books to institutional collections, rarely with success. The practice was much resented by the book trade, and when confronted by persistent noncompliance, the authorities usually gave way. In Britain, Panizzi, despairing of the failure of the scheme, asked that the legal authority to pursue publishers be transferred directly to him. When this was done, and he embarked on a crusade against recalcitrant publishers, the tide slowly turned.

Success breeds its own challenges. As national libraries attracted donations and secured copyright deposits, the quantity of books entering its stacks grew unmanageable. How could one put in order the mass of books swamping these collections? The royal library in Copenhagen acquired over 100,000 volumes between 1820 and 1848; the British Museum library grew from 125,000 volumes in 1823 to 374,000 in 1848. Three years later, another 100,000 volumes had been added to its collections.[51] Chaos could only be avoided through rapid construction. Between 1823 and 1857 the British Museum resembled a building site, as Montagu House was torn down in stages and replaced by a grandiose neoclassical palace, the main structure of which is still admired by visitors today. The crowning glory of the building was the circular reading room and stacks, built in a dome modelled on the Pantheon, that occupied the previously empty quadrangle of the museum. Iron bookstacks surrounding the reading room were designed to house some 1.5 million volumes.[52] In the summer of 1857, when the circular reading room opened, 62,000 people toured it during evening hours to marvel at the gracious palace erected to house the nation's books.

Great construction projects, in the nineteenth century as today, attract funding more easily than book cataloguing. While the new reading room of the British Museum could accommodate 300 readers, these readers had to jostle for the single copy of the reading-room catalogue that allowed them to request books. There was no published catalogue of all the book collections of the British Museum. Panizzi advocated strongly for an alphabetical catalogue to replace the more traditional method of classifying books by subject, as the mass of books was too overwhelming to classify consistently and adequately by genre. While he eventually prevailed, he would not live to see the project completed. The alphabetical catalogue was first proposed in 1834, when it was thought that the project would take five or six years to complete. By 1880, a year after Panizzi's death, it was still unfinished, with 160,000 entries requiring revision. Printing nevertheless went forward, and in 1905, there was a complete catalogue, of 397 parts and 44 supplements with some 4.5 million entries and cross-references.[53] For some readers, this came far too late, not least those who had abandoned the library to establish their own subscription library, the London Library, where they could be assured of more satisfactory provision.

The cataloguing delays experienced in London were by no means unique. Many libraries prioritised specialist sub-catalogues, covering incunabula and manuscripts, over cataloguing the mass of books in the entire collection. This was the preferred approach of Aleksei Olenin in St Petersburg, until the Russian minister of education ordered him to produce an alphabetical catalogue.[54] For ten years, the staff of the library laboured away, until the minister was replaced and the whole venture was quietly dropped.

It may not come as a surprise that uncatalogued collections are a fine target for book thieves, an unwelcome but unavoidable presence in the freely accessible national collections. None were as bold, however, as the Bavarian theologian Alois Pichler (1833–74), who was employed as extraordinary librarian at the imperial library in St Petersburg.[55] Between August 1869 and March 1871, Pichler removed some 4,500 books and manuscripts from the library. His method, as suspicious as it was efficient, was to hide them in his bulky overcoat, which he never removed. When caught, and placed on trial, he admitted that a scholar in Munich had shown him how to construct a cloth sack to attach to the inside of his coat. Pichler was convicted and sentenced to exile in Siberia. Prison sentences and hard labour were similarly imposed on many less celebrated book thieves in London: because they stole from a national library, their crimes were considered against the nation itself.

The symbolic association between the nation and its library has ensured that the concept of a national library continues to be of some relevance. Yet its strong association with the nation, its people, culture and language, not to mention its prominent location in its capital city, also marks it out as a prime target. The national library of Peru, founded thirty days after independence in 1821, was entirely destroyed by the Chilean army in the War of the Pacific in 1879.[56] In more recent years, the national library of Bosnia was deliberately firebombed by Serbian troops in 1992 during the Bosnian War, while the national library of Iraq was partially burned and looted during the early days of the invasion of 2003. A country under threat has more to fear than Dr Pichler and his coat pockets.

Book Tycoons

The development of the great national libraries was regarded with admiration and envy from the other side of the Atlantic. Nevertheless, it took most of the nineteenth century for the United States of America to develop its own. Partisan politics, driven by the rift concerning the relative power of the federal government and over the issue of the abolition of slavery, curtailed efforts to establish a library that, in name and contents, could serve all Americans. Supporters of a national library did see a hopeful future for the Library of Congress. When it moved to Washington DC in 1800, Congress acquired a library of some 3,000 volumes, mostly works on jurisprudence and politics, to serve congressmen in their work. This library was torched by British troops in 1814, while its replacement, which included Thomas Jefferson's personal collection, was partially destroyed in 1851 by fire. These setbacks were exacerbated by the insistence that the library, because it served Congress, must remain bipartisan, and therefore could not build up a comprehensive selection of books and periodicals, including the great number devoted to the debate on slavery.[57]

The American Civil War (1861–5) put an end to much of the

squabbling over the role of the library, and the decades afterwards saw the Library of Congress assume the role as the national library of the United States.[58] A series of extremely capable librarians, generous funding and an enforced legal deposit saw the library grow at a frightening pace, spilling out of the rooms of the Capitol building. In 1897, a monumental library structure located behind the Capitol, filling an entire block, was ready to house the collections. Its design was inspired by the British Museum building and its panoptic reading room; the interior of the dome featured a mural entitled 'The Evolution of Civilization', which presented America as the final incarnation of scientific and cultural progress.

The rapidity with which the United States could build the most expensive library building in the world, and its confident presentation of American destiny, was characteristic of the Gilded Age, the final decades of the nineteenth century. This was an era of unbridled growth, and the seemingly unlimited expansion of American wealth. As the country was transformed, through rail, steel, oil and immigration, new metropoles rose up. There was unease, however, that economic success lacked a cultural complement, one that paid tribute to the achievements of American determination and ingenuity.

This was a task ideally suited to those builders, investors and speculators who amassed fortunes during the Gilded Age. American industrialists and financial magnates wanted their homeland to equal if not surpass Europe in sophistication. Although the robber barons, as they were derided in the press, were frequently attacked for their greed, their patronage was of immense value in announcing America as a cultural leader of the world. Universities, museums, galleries and libraries were among the favoured beneficiaries of the American magnates. The first decades of the twentieth century saw a host of great research libraries rise in Chicago (the Newberry), New York (the Morgan), San Marino, California (the Huntington) and Washington DC (the Folger). A striking factor is that these libraries, with the exception of the Newberry, were composed of the personal libraries of the founders themselves.[59] None were as sizeable as the libraries of state, nor as universal in content; instead they resembled the fine libraries of

18. A library fit for a new global power: the Library of Congress, pictured here in 1902. Inside, a mural heralded America as the latest brilliant civilisation to be brought forth by the world.

Renaissance princes, filled with items of great value, lavish colour, and most of all, rarity. Informed by the antiquarian fashions for manuscripts, incunabula, first editions and other rare books, the great American collectors competed against one another for the most outstanding collections. Access to their libraries was similarly exclusive. Although lauded by the political elite for providing America with unrivalled public collections, the libraries were available only to a socially restricted class of gentlemen scholars. The oil executive Henry Folger (1857–1930), when discussing provisions for the reading room in his library in Washington DC, wanted only five reading tables. When architects suggested an increase to eight, he responded that

It will not be a reading-room in the way reading-rooms are used generally, nor even as a room for study, because our library is too special in its character, and the contents are so costly and limited in scope – Our collection should not be offered freely to all comers, and the library should not be looked upon as a reading-room nor a comfortable rest-room.[60]

Folger's great rival, the rail tycoon Henry E. Huntington (1850–1927), had his research library built on his 600-acre estate in San Marino, California, a stone's throw from his mansion; also a location which was not intended to draw large crowds.[61] Huntington and Folger were particularly reticent about opening up their collections, because they were true bibliophiles. They read and studied their books, and they loved them to the extent that they could not bear to see them dispersed. Housing them in a public building, with a generous endowment for the future, was the only solution.

There were nevertheless differences between the two collectors. Huntington collected widely and quickly. He amassed some 150,000 volumes, thanks in no part to buying, in their entirety, 200 personal libraries. Henry Folger and his wife Emily, on the other hand, had one particular passion: William Shakespeare's writings, as printed through the ages, and books commenting on his world and his legacy.[62] The couple collected with single-minded purpose. They remained childless; Folger was reported to refer to his books as 'the boys'. Although extremely rich, Folger gave rarely to charity, and did not act as patron of hospitals, colleges, theatres or other civic ventures. While the executive meetings of Standard Oil would rarely be interrupted, if they were it was because Henry Folger was on the hunt for another Shakespeare copy that had surfaced in an English castle. He corresponded with some 600 booksellers and spent evenings with Emily poring over catalogues and newspaper clippings, looking for a bargain, or news that a famous collection might come up for auction.

Folger was in debt for much of his life, continually taking loans, secured by his stocks in oil, to finance his book buying. The Folgers did not own a home until 1928, two years before Henry's death; instead they occupied relatively modest rented lodgings in Brooklyn. They held few fancy dinners, owned no extravagant cars, or indulged in any other luxuries appropriate to an oil magnate – and this did attract some attention. Although books were an accepted form of luxurious expenditure, they were only so if combined

19. The Folger Shakespeare Reading Room, with a copy of one of its eighty-two First Folios on show. The room is decked out in Elizabethan glory, a stark contrast to the neoclassical art deco of the library's exterior.

with other indulgences. J. D. Rockefeller once asked Folger if, as he had read in the paper, Folger had really spent $100,000 (close to his annual salary) on a volume of Shakespeare. Folger responded that it had been much less; which was necessary reassurance, as Rockefeller explained:

Well, I'm glad to hear you say that, Henry. We – that is, my
son and I and the board of directors – were disturbed. We
wouldn't want to think that the president of one of our major
companies would be the kind of man foolish enough to pay
$100,000 for a book.[63]

Folger had not lied, but he did regularly spend over $10,000 on
an exceptional or rare copy, and occasionally over $40,000 or
even $50,000. The result of this extravagance was, however, truly
unmatched in its field. The Folgers accumulated 1,400 different
copies of the collected works of Shakespeare, including 200 from
the seventeenth century. Eighty-two of these were copies of the
famous First Folio (1623), some of them previously owned by
kings, queens and illustrious individuals such as Samuel Johnson
and William Pitt. Ironically, the First Folio is not a very rare book:
over 200 copies are still in existence today. Yet the fact that Folger
was able to acquire more than a third of those was exceptional.

The key to Folger's success was to diverge from the accepted
standard of fashionable collectors to own 'clean' books, unblemished by any mark. J. P. Morgan, the New York banker, despaired
of imperfect copies as 'lepers of a library'. This led to a deplorable but widespread nineteenth-century practice of 'washing' rare
books to remove any trace of marginalia or previous ownership.
Folger, swimming against the tide in this as in so much else, bought
these 'dirty books' gratefully.[64] Furthermore, Folger was exceedingly secretive. When, in 1901, the scholar Sidney Lee sought
to undertake the first survey of Shakespeare First Folios, Folger
did not respond to any of his three questionnaires. When it was
published, Folger did use the Lee survey to his own advantage:
he now knew where he could buy more. He sent letters to thirty-
five owners of First Folios in England, asking them to name their
price. All rebuffed him, but Folger persisted, successfully in many
cases. When the books entered the Folger collection, they were
kept hidden from the world. Folger never allowed any scholar
access to his library, most of which was kept in vaults. This made
the inauguration of the Folger Shakespeare Library in Washington
DC in 1932, two years after Henry Folger's death, an unmissable

society event; President Hoover was among those who attended. Yet here too subterfuge had played an important role. The Folgers had desired a prime location for their library. They settled on a block of residential housing, a street across from the Library of Congress. They then spent the next nine years secretly buying up fourteen adjoining houses, which they then demolished to erect their monument to Shakespeare.

When the library was ready, the books were transported from New York in a convoy of armoured trucks. Those passers-by on the street would have thought that the vehicles, manned by guards armed with rifles, machine guns and tear-gas canisters, contained gold or diamonds. Inside there was indeed a fortune: a legacy of collecting, pursued doggedly, with no concerns for expense. Of that the stuff of libraries is made.

CHAPTER FIFTEEN

READING ON THE JOB

If there is one figure who we associate with the success of public libraries then it must be Andrew Carnegie (1835–1919), the proud son of Dunfermline, Scotland. After emigrating to America as a schoolboy, Carnegie made a fortune by developing a quasi-monopoly on the supply of steel at precisely the time that the United States became the world's economic powerhouse. He made many friends through his philanthropy, and a lot of enemies with his way of doing business: labour organisations regarded him with such loathing that they lobbied local communities not to accept his donations.[1] But it has to count for something that rather than building a princely book collection for himself, to be enjoyed in the company of friends from America's new business aristocracy, he embarked on a carefully considered programme of grants to small and middle-sized communities to build a library for the use of all. The money came with strings. Carnegie would only give if the town authorities agreed to commit, in perpetuity, to matching 10 per cent of the value of his donation for maintenance of the building and staff wages. Nor did he provide the books. He did, however, offer a range of architectural designs, which provided for elegant but serviceable space. There were none of the Doric columns and sweeping staircases with which the new American Medici decorated the public libraries in Boston, New York and elsewhere: as much statements of civic pride as repositories of books. Carnegie would have none of that. His designs were square squat buildings, with good sight-lines for a librarian to preside over the patrons as they went about their business of browsing and taking out books.

Carnegie brought little romance to the business of libraries, but much of the clear-minded rationality with which he had made

20. The greatest founder of public libraries: the Scot Andrew
Carnegie, pictured here among his books in 1913. Unlike many other
magnates of his era, Carnegie did not collect for himself but for
millions of other people, thanks to his 3,000 Carnegie libraries.

his business fortune: when he sold out to John Pierpont Morgan in
1901 to devote himself entirely to philanthropy, he was the richest
man in America. This sense of purpose was precisely what the
public library movement needed at the time Carnegie was most
active, between 1880 and 1919. Libraries proliferated during the

nineteenth century, responding to the rapidly growing demand for books, a product of radical social and technological change. Books became cheaper and more abundant, and more men and women were looking to read, for recreation, information and social advancement. Yet abundance brought its own challenges: if books became cheaper, the imperative to borrow, rather than own, which had sustained the subscription and circulating libraries in the eighteenth century and the first decades of the nineteenth, fell away. The public library had to find a motive, a clientele, and a niche in the library world. Until the arrival of Carnegie, it was by no means certain that it had succeeded.

The Halfpenny Rate

On 14 February 1850, Mr William Ewart rose from his seat in the British Parliament to introduce his bill 'for enabling town councils to establish public libraries and Museums'.[2] This is seen, quite rightly, as a critical moment in the history of the public library movement, though the process of actually putting its provisions into effect would be agonisingly slow. In moving his motion, Ewart appealed not only to his colleagues' better nature, but also to their patriotism. Compared to Germany, France or Italy, and even the United States, he suggested, England was very inadequately served by libraries. On the European continent, no major town was without a library: in cities like Amiens, Rouen and Marseille, the working classes patronised these institutions in great numbers. This, as we will see, rather exaggerated the appeal of these French municipal libraries, but it concurred with the evidence presented to the parliamentary select committee of enquiry that had paved the way for this milestone legislation. Influential, too, was the statistical survey of libraries in Europe and the United States undertaken in 1848 by a reclusive employee of the British Museum, Edward Edwards, which demonstrated that outside the British Museum and the libraries of Oxford and Cambridge, Britain hardly features in a list of 310 European towns with major library collections.[3]

The establishment of public libraries was not driven entirely by this sense of international competition (though it helped). As

Britain grew into a global superpower, statesmen and campaigners also turned their attention to the dark underbelly of this success: the dreadful conditions of work and abject poverty of many industrial workers, and the need to educate these new citizens to follow the rational, civilising pursuits enjoyed by the prosperous middle classes. Given the scope of this ambition, the provisions of the bill today seem remarkably modest. Its purpose was entirely permissive. Any municipal or borough council could, if they wished, incorporate into local taxation a halfpenny levy on property values to pay for establishing a library. None of this could be used to purchase books. Presuming the municipality would make available suitable premises, the sum raised would go for maintenance and staffing. To the surprise of its proponents, even this modest measure met vociferous opposition. We can perhaps excuse Colonel Sibthorp, member for Lincoln, who opposed any increase in taxation. Besides, 'he did not like reading at all, and hated it at Oxford'. Others opposed the measure, including the members for Oxford and Cambridge universities, partly because it made no provision for the purchase of books; libraries thus established would have to rely on donations, as did the parish and town libraries of old. It was also argued that the main beneficiaries of such libraries would likely be middle-class users who could afford to buy their own books without burdening the poor with further taxation.[4] The bill passed, but only with two crucial and debilitating amendments: one limiting the Act to communities of 10,000 inhabitants or more; the other requiring the support of two thirds of ratepayers at a public meeting.

Thus amended, the Act was bound to be very limited in its application. Norwich and Winchester swiftly obtained the required permission from their ratepayers. Brighton obtained a private act that allowed them to raise a more generous fourpenny rate: for a seaside resort, a library had obvious utility. Altogether, twenty-five councils had adopted the Act by 1860, assisted by an amending bill of 1855 that somewhat loosened the restrictive terms of the original act. Among them were the great northern cities of Manchester and Birmingham. Both could rely on local civic pride and philanthropy to stock the library's shelves. The Manchester library opened in 1852, in a ceremony graced by the novelists Charles Dickens and William Thackeray, with a collection of 25,000 volumes. In its first year, the lending department was patronised by 4,841 persons, borrowing an average of twenty volumes each during the course of the year.[5]

Manchester, though, is a very exceptional case, which might soon have had its own library even without the help of the legislation: the first libraries were almost all, as here, in the large cities whose parliamentary representatives had supported the bill, or prosperous county towns. Elsewhere, proposals to adopt the rate were resoundingly defeated, including in Bath, Glasgow and Hastings. Opposition was particularly intense in the working-class districts of London that had been at the heart of the argument that libraries would bring succour and enlightenment to the working man. In Lambeth, the first attempt to adopt the Act in 1866 was howled down in a boisterous meeting held, perhaps unwisely, at the Horns Tavern. It was not until 1886 that the rate could be carried, and then only for a halfpenny, rather than the full penny rate now permitted. Even so, it required an enormous donation of £10,500 from Jemima Durning Smith to build the library – the very Durning library that campaigners have been struggling since the 1990s to keep open.[6]

The port city of Bristol offers a useful indication of the strength of the current against which proponents of the public library were struggling. Bristol had an educated middle class, wealthy philanthropists and civic pride, yet still did not take advantage of the 1850 Act to establish a public library. A combination museum and library building was erected in 1871, but made little impact on the community. A timorous library committee raised only half the permitted rate. The problem in Bristol, and in many other such places, was that the public library had to compete for funds and clientele with an increasingly wide range of institutionally sponsored leisure attractions: municipal baths, playgrounds, temperance societies, church missions, evening classes, music festivals and exhibitions. The growth of organised sport and the music hall represented further challenges to reading as a preferred leisure activity. The ideal of 'liberal culture', so important to proponents of the library, motivated only a small minority.[7]

The situation in the industrial north was rather different, but equally emblematic of why the public library movement made such slow progress. Halifax and Huddersfield, two towns in the West Riding of Yorkshire, would have no public library until 1882 and 1898 respectively. This was not because of any lack of interest in reading: rather these two booming mill towns, citadels of industrious working-class culture, were already teeming with libraries. The Mechanics' Institutes, founded to teach science to working men, became the cornerstone of adult education and important centres of sociability. The institutes in both Halifax and Huddersfield had substantial libraries, along with separate reading rooms for journals and newspapers. The Halifax institution had a separate juvenile library, and Huddersfield a collection exclusively for the use of female members. The Co-operative Movement, founded in nearby Rochdale, also sponsored local libraries, not only in the two towns, but also in many of the industrial villages of the valley. The Halifax library opened in 1872 with a collection of 3,000 volumes, and a number of local employers sponsored factory libraries.[8]

In the second half of the nineteenth century, the established subscription libraries, serving the needs of local professional classes, spawned a variety of literary and scientific societies, some with considerable collections: 20,000 volumes in the case of the Halifax Literary and Philosophical Society. Huddersfield had a law library, a medical library and a library devoted exclusively to works in foreign languages. These more learned institutions were also forced to confront the insatiable demand for fiction, often by taking out a corporate subscription to Mudie's or W. H. Smith's. At the other end of the market, numerous sometimes short-lived commercial libraries offered a generous range of recreational reading. Some of the more successful were run by local printers, like William Milner, who turned out massive cheap reprints of the works of Burns, Byron and Longfellow, or William Nicholson, publisher of the no doubt bestselling *Poems by a Halifax Cheesemonger*.

If we add to this list school libraries, the libraries of Sunday Schools (an essential instrument of working-class literacy before free primary education became ubiquitous), along with the numerous libraries run by church institutions and the libraries of the local colleges, we see industrial communities in which reading was recognised as critical both to economic improvement and political empowerment. The presence of numerous newspaper reading rooms, and at least one coffee shop with subscriptions to the radical papers, further diminished the appeal of a ratepayer-funded public library.

Although the United States was also cited in the 1850 parliamentary debate as a source of emulation, here too the development of public libraries was patchy at best. Decisions on taxpayer support lay in the hands of the states and municipalities, so local culture played a crucial role in determining the success or otherwise of the library movement. Once again, the campaign for libraries would be in the hands of two influential groups: those who favoured libraries as a shield against vice ('the cheapest police force that could ever be established', in the words of one British parliamentarian), and those who believed that libraries were an essential marker of a cultured society. This motive was particularly strong in the United States: the emerging superpower needed libraries, just as it needed theatres, opera houses and museums. The question was whether these should necessarily be funded by the taxpayer.

It is not surprising that the public library should have had its strongest appeal in New England. There the principal of common ownership of books had been established in the first settlements, and a conviction of the moral force of reading remained strong throughout the nineteenth century. Concord, Massachusetts, had a collection of books owned by the town in 1672, of which sadly little more is known, so whether this amounted to a public library is hard to say. The multiple parish libraries funded by the initiative organised by Thomas Bray brought chests of books to many communities, though not all cherished them.[9] The honour of establishing the first truly public library, funded by local taxation with free access to its citizens, is generally assigned to the small New Hampshire town of Peterborough, which chose in 1833 to divert a sum provided for the development of local schools to the creation of a library.[10] The most important institutional step in this era of library development was the opening in 1854 of the Boston Public Library. This was thirteen years in the making, building on a proposal by a visiting French showman, Nicholas Vattermare, that a library on the French model could be created by merging several local libraries into one public institution. An authorisation to this effect was enacted in 1848, though a failed attempt to merge this proposal with the established Athenaeum library would frustrate completion for another six years.

The Boston project would be given further impetus by the gift, in 1848, from John Jacob Astor to the city of New York of $400,000 to establish a public library. The Brahmins of Boston had no wish to be outdone by their noisy commercial rival, and while the Astor plan would mutate into a distinguished reference library, the free-access public library in Boston would rise triumphant as the nationwide model of emulation. For the next forty years, philanthropy and civic pride would be the twin motors of library building in the United States: Enoch Pratt provided a fine library for Baltimore in 1882 (with six branch libraries), and one of Andrew Carnegie's first substantial donations provided a library network for Philadelphia. A local property tax underwrote the costs of a public library for San Francisco in 1878; Seattle had a public library in 1891, and when this burned down ten years later, it was swiftly replaced by a magnificent new Carnegie library. How powerful this culture of emulation, not to say rivalry, could be was demonstrated by the campaign for a public library in Los Angeles, a relative latecomer to the party. When a bond issue was proposed to fund a fine new building in 1921, proponents of the ballot measure did not hold back. 'Grow up, Los Angeles. Own your own public library and take your place with progressive cities!' 'Mr Average Taxpayer, pay 50 cents a year and remove this stigma from Los Angeles's name.' A flier set out the case with a direct comparison with the other major cities of the West Coast. 'Every self-respecting city owns its own library home. San Francisco and Seattle make us look like a village with their own fine library homes, best proof of their culture and development.' The bond issue passed with 71 per cent approval.[11]

Sons of Toil

In 1890, Fritz Baedeker dispatched the editor of his English-language editions, James F. Muirhead, to gather information for the first edition of his travel guide to the United States. Muirhead made a scrupulously compendious survey, though giving most attention to the East Coast and Midwest. Only one man-made structure rated Baedeker's coveted two-star ranking: the Capitol building in Washington. Among the more numerous attractions awarded one star were sixteen libraries. The libraries of New York, with twenty-six enumerated, and Massachusetts with eleven, merited the most attention, but only half of the sixteen starred libraries were public institutions. In New York, Muirhead picked out the Astor and Lenox libraries, and the New York state library in Albany.[12] Astonishingly, the opening of the famous New York Public Library building on 42nd Street, the quintessential encapsulation of the United States as a library giant, still lay twenty years in the future.

In Baedeker's fascination with libraries we can see both the powerful influence of the library on civil society, and the reasons for the continuing slow development of the public library movement. Apart from civic pride, New York really did not need one central taxpayer-funded public library, given the plethora of other large and powerful institutions with excellent library facilities. Some admitted members of the public, though these were not necessarily public libraries as we would understand the term. In the eighteenth century, a library might be 'public' in much the same way as a public house (tavern) or public conveyance (bus, tram). Anyone could use it, but only on payment of a fee for the service offered. Other libraries provided services only for a defined membership, often united by a shared interest or profession. The Boston ideal, of libraries offered free to all citizens for the greater good of society as a whole, had to struggle against the engrained practice of a commercially minded society entering a golden age of prosperity and international influence.

To examine these competing visions of public duty and public utility, New York provides a perfect laboratory. In 1796, when the state legislature passed the new nation's first law governing public libraries, permitting citizens to form associations to purchase and share collections of books, New York was a city of some 33,000 inhabitants. This population was in ethnic terms homogenous, English and Dutch, though not particularly bookish. In the eighteenth century, John Sharpe had grumbled that 'the genius of the people [is] so inclined to merchandise that ... letters must be in a manner forced upon them not only without their seeking, but against their consent'.[13] Boston and Philadelphia were the new nation's major cultural centres.

By 1850, New York had half a million inhabitants; by 1876, one million. This rate of growth was unprecedented in the history of humanity. The population was diverse in almost every respect, with a business class as wealthy as any in the world, and vast numbers of impoverished immigrants crowded into filthy tenements. By the middle of the century, nearly half of the city's inhabitants were foreign born and the bourgeoisie began their flight up Manhattan. The masses might be downtrodden, but they were not silent. In 1822, the state constitution had granted the franchise to all adult white males, and the spirit of Jacksonian democracy did not smile on institutions like the New York Society Library, founded in 1754 by three ambitious young Whig lawyers.[14] The spirit of the times was expressed more by the Apprentices' Library established by the General Society of Mechanics and Tradesmen, and the Mercantile Library Association, both founded in 1820. By 1855, this last was the most extensive and popular circulating library in the city, with 42,000 volumes, and a membership of 4,600 readers. In 1870, the Mercantile Library had the highest circulation of any library in the United States and the fourth-largest collection.

This, however, was the tipping point. Events moved with dizzying rapidity in nineteenth-century New York. By the last quarter of the century the libraries that had been established in south Manhattan in the 1850s were abandoned by their prosperous readers in the stampede north. The quintessential institution of the last quarter of the century was the Cooper Union, established by a visionary philanthropist industrialist, which had a large well-supplied reading room with a small reference library. The Cooper Union, open every day between 8.30 a.m. and 10 p.m., recorded

219,710 visitors in 1860, 403,685 in 1880, and 516,986 in 1900. It provided them, free of charge, with subscriptions to 436 periodicals, including 84 dailies from across the United States and 31 foreign-language periodicals. Librarians recorded three daily groups of users. In the early morning the unemployed checked the newspapers for situations vacant. The daytime places were given over to the chronically unemployed and those with financial means, replaced by an evening shift of serious students, clerks and businessmen who made use of the reference collection. The Cooper Union was never publicly funded, but it did provide many of the functions that in other places would be undertaken by the city library and its branches: a warm place to sit as much as access to books.

The mid nineteenth century was the heyday of the Mechanics' Institutes: in his landmark *Manual of Public Libraries in the United States*, William Rhees reported twenty-three Apprentices' Libraries and thirty-four Mechanics' Institutes.[15] This represented the transportation of an influential development in the European library scene, though in England, in particular, one born of a very different political context. Three years before all adult males in New York were granted the franchise, a crowd in Manchester that had gathered to demand parliamentary reform was charged by cavalry, the infamous Peterloo massacre. Working men were excluded from the franchise reform of 1832, prompting the tenacious but ultimately fruitless Chartist movement. Two years later, six agricultural workers from Dorset were sentenced to transportation after joining together to protest the decline of agricultural wages.

For liberal reformers like Henry Brougham, adult education was a critical weapon in the fight to raise up the new industrial poor. The Mechanics' Institute, with its improving lectures and evening classes, seemed the ideal vehicle. By 1850, there were 702 Mechanics' Institutes; the 610 in England had a combined membership of 102,000. Their libraries collectively owned 700,000 books. Upholders of the political status quo viewed these new institutions as potential hotbeds of sedition, but their worries were overdrawn. Working men, for whom the libraries were intended, soon found themselves driven out by a different class of reader. As early as 1840, the Yorkshire Union of Mechanics' Institutes reported that no more than one in twenty of their members was a true working man. All the rest were 'connected with the higher branches of handicraft trades, or are clerks in offices, and in many instances, young men connected with liberal professions'.[16] In truth, the programme of lectures was often pitched more at the level of university students than for men who had just concluded a twelve-hour day of work. As one observed, 'You must remember we have masters all day long, and we don't want 'em at night'.[17]

Many working men and women preferred to patronise circulating libraries, to while away their precious leisure hours with the increasingly ubiquitous cheap fiction, although, as we have seen, many less affluent readers also purchased plenty of cheaper reprints of *Robinson Crusoe*, Dickens and the poems of Burns and Byron. Engagement with good literature was not confined to the rich or expensively educated. Even so, rather than submit to the judgement of their social superiors, working people found their reading needs could often best be met by banding together to establish their own institutions of sociability and instruction. The most powerful institutional manifestations of this development were the libraries of the Mining Institutes created in the coalfields of South Wales.[18] These were entirely funded by voluntary contributions from the miners themselves, so members could choose the books they wanted to read. Fiction predominated, but miners also read a range of key texts in political and social policy. The tradition of self-reliance was strong enough for the village of Penrhiwceiber to turn down the offer of support in 1903 from Andrew Carnegie, who did so much to expand the network of public libraries in Britain as well as the United States. Local government support was also rebuffed, to the frustration of those seeking to build a comprehensive network of public libraries in Wales.

A similar feature of the German library scene was the network of workers' libraries, built and maintained by the trade union movement. By the end of the nineteenth century they offered an impressive alternative to public libraries, offering relatively small collections (1,000–5,000 books) to workers in accessible locations.

By 1911–12, the Social Democratic Party and trade unions between them maintained 547 libraries, including no fewer than fifty-seven in the city of Leipzig, an industrial and proletarian stronghold.[19] These offered a variety of ideologically improving literature, along with a decent range of novels. Again, though, the expectations of well-meaning (or paternalistic) patrons proved ill founded: in the Döbeln library in 1910, the 187 books on politics and socialism were loaned out only sixty times. The 106 books on trade unionism were borrowed on only three occasions. Meanwhile, the 361 books of literature and drama were checked out 1,633 times.[20]

If this suggests that workers were more interested in relaxation than ideological improvement, at least these books, from the point of view of the founders of the libraries, would have been more edifying than cheap pamphlet fiction, American detective stories and exotic adventures, the 'penny dreadfuls' that sold millions of copies at the beginning of the twentieth century. The popularity of penny dreadfuls, which could be obtained from any kiosk or tobacco shop along with illustrated newspapers and mass-circulation magazines, rattled the library community. 'Is it not a disgrace', wrote Erich Schultze, 'that in Germany and Austria some twenty million among the "people of thinkers and poets" obtain their intellectual nourishment from 45,000 penny-dreadful colporteurs.' This is a reference to the practice of employing house-to-house sales representatives to sell sensational stories in 10-pfennig instalments around the villages and small towns of Germany. This trade in 'colporteur' novels, which flourished briefly in the second half of the nineteenth century, could be astonishingly lucrative. The sales of one such title, *Der Scharfrichter von Berlin* (The Executioner of Berlin), was reckoned to have made its publisher 3 million marks.[21] Cultural commentators struggled to understand the appeal of these undemanding fictions, which might extend to over 150 instalments before a rambling tale reached its conclusion. Dresden's librarian Walter Hoffmann could only lament that 'we are better informed about the living conditions of half-savage African peoples than the lower classes among our own people'.[22]

The consequences of this passion for recreation were laid bare to leaders of the socialist movement in 1918, when the collapse of the German monarchy offered the opportunity to build a socialist state. Yet the workers did not grasp this. According to one jaded intellectual, 'The overwhelming majority of the German workers could not imagine life clearly in a socialist state, in spite of the fifty years' existence of German Social Democracy'; and, one might add, the existence of fifty years of workers' libraries.[23]

Tomb of Books

When scholars and social reformers from Britain and the United States were seeking to promote the building of public libraries, they often looked for inspiration to France and Germany. The scions of American business families undertaking their obligatory tours of Europe were astonished by the size of libraries on the European continent, and enthralled by the treasures that were laid out for their admiration. When, in Britain, the House of Commons Parliamentary Committee heard the evidence that would lead to the passage of the 1850 Public Libraries Act, sympathetic members were seriously embarrassed by the comparative size of continental collections: of the ducal and university libraries in Germany, and the unrivalled network of municipal libraries established by the French Revolution. This was somewhat ironic, because in many respects these French libraries were working models of exactly what public libraries should not be. True, in terms of size they were impressive. A survey of 1828 registered 117,000 books in the Bibliothèque Municipale of Lyon, 110,000 in Bordeaux and 80,000 in Aix-en-Provence. For the mid nineteenth century these were stupendous numbers, and a further twelve provincial libraries had collections of at least 40,000 books.[24] But they were often poorly run, poorly maintained and abysmally badly catalogued. Most of all, they were filled with books that very few of their local citizens would want to read.

This was the poisoned inheritance of the French Revolution. As we have seen, thanks to the abolition of the monasteries, the state suddenly found itself the curator of a dispersed collection of several million ancient volumes. Most of these were, in principal, destined for destruction. But as the carts of books piled up, local librarians found this process impossible to manage; and in truth, it went against the grain with any scholar to destroy beautiful and valuable books simply because they did not accord with the principles of a secular revolutionary movement. Happily, from their point of view, the moment of revolutionary fervour proved fleeting. Less happily, in times of war, economic catastrophe and intellectual turmoil, few municipal elites were prepared to make the creation of the new public library a priority. The books were eventually found a home and shelved, but the public did not come. Books assembled for the use of monasteries proved, as they had done in the seventeenth century, an insufficient basis for a genuinely public library. They became the refuge of a local scholarly elite and the occasional visitor, and librarians got used to a gentle life largely undisturbed by the press of eager readers.

The extent to which these libraries fell short of an acceptable standard of curatorial care was vividly exposed by one of the most sordid scandals in the history of libraries, plunder accomplished by a leading scholar operating with an almost flagrant disregard for consequences. The Libri affair resonated through Europe, drawing in a distinguished cast of characters including the French first minister, François Guizot, most of the Parisian beau monde, and international bookmen of unblemished reputation such as Antonio Panizzi of the British Museum.[25]

Jean Aymon, known as Libri, was an Italian who spent most of his adult career in France. A considerable scholar, who published important work in the field of mathematics, Libri developed his taste for rare books early in life, when he had been placed in charge of a learned library in Florence, from which he absconded with 300 books. Perhaps it was the ease of this discreditable act that emboldened him to the behaviour that revealed both the scale of the treasures residing in French municipal libraries and the negligent manner in which they were maintained. In France, Aymon was appointed to two professorial positions, but the monotony of teaching paled beside the lure of rare books. He got his chance when, thanks to the patronage of Guizot, he was appointed to one of the many official commissions charged with the investigation of the moribund provincial libraries. With licence to roam, and librarians anxious not to have their negligence exposed, Aymon made some discoveries of real importance, not least 900 ancient manuscripts uncatalogued in the collection at Troyes. He publicised his findings in the prestigious *Journal des Savants*, while simultaneously calling for more stringent security in the libraries. Many of his most luminous discoveries he would bring to Paris, to exhibit to literary friends. What only gradually became clear was that he was selling other interesting books and manuscripts on the open market.

The first hints of impropriety circulated in Paris in 1842, but Aymon could rely on the protection of powerful friends. When questioned, local curators would naturally deny that anything was missing from their collections: since they scarcely knew what their collections contained, this was by far the safest option. In 1845, Aymon prepared a dazzling sales catalogue of almost 2,000 manuscripts. Had they been able to match his asking price, this would have been bought by the British Museum; instead, the British Lord Ashburnham paid £8,000 (200,000 francs) for the entire catalogue, the foundation of one of the greatest collections in Europe.

A catalogue of printed books in 1847 brought further suspicion, and these could be traced more easily by the libraries. In 1848 Libri fled to London, taking advantage of the turbulence of this revolutionary year to join both his ministerial patron Guizot and King Louis Philippe in exile. From London, he waged a vigorous pamphlet campaign, alleging a plot by jealous rivals. His friends, including Panizzi and the novelist Prosper Mérimée (whose mistress, in a characteristically French touch, was the wife of the police chief who had exposed Libri), rallied to his aid. It was only in 1883 that Léopold Delisle, librarian of the Bibliothèque Nationale, exposed the full extent of the deception, and some years later the Ashburnham manuscripts were discreetly returned to Paris, where they remain today.

Aymon was unique in his exploitation of the negligence of the municipal libraries, but he exposed a systemic problem: beautiful and stuffed with rare treasures though they were, they had utterly failed in their original purpose to build a collection for the people of their cities. After many commissions of enquiry,

multiple reorganisations and endless exhortation to the municipal
authorities (but no substantial offers of cash), French governments resolved to address the problem by building two parallel
structures. These consisted of 3,000 so-called 'popular' libraries,
which would offer the cheap vernacular books that the municipal
libraries did not possess, and, particularly for rural areas, small collections held by schools but open to local adults.[26] This proved to
be a serious misstep, for all manner of reasons. First, the existence
of the popular libraries liberated the municipal libraries from any
obligation to modernise or improve their service. Visitor numbers
remained small. Second, the existence of parallel tiers of libraries meant that scarce resources were even more stretched. After
a promising start, particularly in laying out a network of libraries
throughout Paris, money to replace books ran out. The same was
true of the school libraries, which remained very small, and were
usually committed to the care of a schoolteacher who regarded it
as an unwelcome additional chore. Local adults had soon read any
book in the collection that interested them and there were few
new additions. As a result, the French municipal libraries receded
into a half-life of neglect and irrelevance. This would continue up
to and beyond the Second World War, awaiting the radical renovation that would transform them into the vibrant, well-stocked and
inviting Médiathèques they are today.

Carnegie

What France badly needed was not further ministerial direc-
tives, but a figure of the vision and resources of Andrew Carnegie.
The transformation of the public library network in the United
States and Britain in the last decades of the nineteenth century
demonstrated the difference that a powerful and clear-minded
entrepreneur could make. In 1880, Andrew Carnegie had returned
to Scotland to admire his first benefaction to the town of his birth,
Dunfermline, the swimming baths built with a donation of £5,000.
By this point Andrew Carnegie was forty-five years old and already
a very rich man, feeling his way towards the programme of philanthropy that would dominate the last three decades of his life. In

the course of discussions with the civic elders, Carnegie offered another £5,000, so long as the city would adopt the Library Act – that is, levy a tax rate to support a new library. The council readily agreed, and in 1884 Dunfermline opened the first of what would become 3,000 Carnegie libraries.[27]

The Dunfermline design reflected the somewhat experimental character of Carnegie's vision of the public library. By 1904, it was already too small and had to be remodelled and expanded. A children's library was substituted for the ladies' reading room (women, on the whole, tended to prefer the general reading room), and the space previously allocated to the librarian's flat was incorporated into the floor plan. The library still thrives, thanks in part to a recent extension capitalising on the library's magnificent position overlooking the cathedral, while preserving the historic core of Carnegie's building. Carnegie would give another forty libraries to his native Scotland, including five in Dundee, and £250,000 for a free public library in Edinburgh. Equally generous provision for England, including a whole branch network for Birmingham and Manchester and libraries in many county towns, would bring the total of Carnegie libraries in Britain and Ireland to 660.

For the fifteen years after the opening of the Dunfermline library, Carnegie's involvement was largely limited to other places with which he had a close personal connection, including a workers' library for one of his steel mills. When the city fathers of Pittsburgh rebuffed his first offer, unwilling to commit the matching funds on which Carnegie insisted, he turned instead to Allegheny City, Pennsylvania, where he had famously devoured books as a teenager in the personal library of Colonel Anderson. This cathedral of books, in a strange mock-Romanesque style, reflected the embryonic state of American library design. When in 1889 the chastened Pittsburgh council invited Carnegie to renew his offer, he bore no grudges. The library was incorporated into the Carnegie Institute on which he lavished $5 million.

An astonishing gift in 1899 of a further $5.2 million to the New York Public Library system to build a network of sixty-seven branch libraries indicated that Carnegie was prepared to take his giving to a different level. The terms of the award provided for thirty-nine libraries in Manhattan, the Bronx and Staten Island, twenty-one in Brooklyn and seven in Queens. In return, the city government undertook to provide sites for the libraries, along with sufficient funds to employ staff to maintain the buildings, which were to remain open between 9 a.m. and 9 p.m. every day except Sunday. Carnegie had now found the model that would shape his negotiations with potential beneficiaries. In 1899 he extended his giving to thirty-one cities in Pennsylvania. Between 1901 and 1903 he offered 460 grants, including a substantial sum to the city of Philadelphia, whose librarian somewhat diffidently requested support for thirty new libraries that would create a branch system to rival that of New York. He believed the required cost would be between $20,000 and $30,000 per branch. Carnegie disagreed. He did not think this would be enough:

> You should have lecture rooms in these Branch Libraries and our experience in Pittsburgh is that we have not spent enough upon them ... I think, therefore, that it would be well for you to spend fifty thousand dollars for these branch library buildings, and it would give me pleasure to provide a million and a half dollars.

Providing, that is, that the city agreed to maintain the libraries 'at a cost of not less than $150,000 a year'.[28]

Small towns received $10,000, reflecting both the needs of the community and their ability to provide the required matching funds ($1,000 per annum) in maintenance. It is in small cities and towns across the American continent that a Carnegie library would have the most transforming impact on a community's cultural life and self-respect.[29] Between 1900 and 1920, seventeen new Carnegie libraries were erected in Montana. A huge territory of mining and difficult farming country (at least before irrigation), Montana had been granted statehood only in 1889. In the next thirty years, stimulated by the discovery of mineral deposits and the coming of the railways, its population doubled. Towns grew rapidly, and without much regard for planning. The town elites soon identified a library as a necessary civilising influence. The

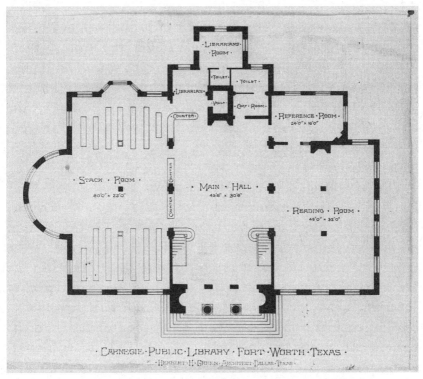

21. The floor plan for the Carnegie library, Fort Worth, Texas (*c.*1900), one of the sparser Carnegie plans, providing for a single reading room adjoining the main hall. Larger Carnegie libraries often included a separate children's reading room.

problem of social control featured frequently in correspondence with James Bertram, Carnegie's secretary, and by now the driving force behind the library plan: 'the fact that this is a railroad center ... brings to the city a large number of unmarried men who desire good books to read and a place in which to read them'.[30] None of these letters promoted the library as an intellectual force: a Carnegie library was a symbol of the community's coming of age.

This latter wave of small libraries also played a critical role in the development of a distinctive style of library architecture. Up to this point, library buildings reflected the idiosyncratic desires of a local donor or echoed the monumentalism of the great libraries of the north-east. Philanthropists could cast themselves as the benevolent fathers of the community, and architects were given carte blanche to effect this vision. Some, as in the Winn library of Woburn, Massachusetts, created a cathedral style with high ceilings and recessed alcoves of books in the 'nave'. Clearly there was no way readers could be supervised in such space, and climate control was an insuperable problem. Most large city libraries would follow either the Italian *palazzo* effect of Boston, or the monumental classicism of New York. The interiors, with high ceilings, splendid staircases and spacious porticos, put grandeur ahead of the effective use of space.

This would not do for the 'wholesale' stage of Carnegie library building, as James Bertram made clear in his *Notes on the Erection of Library Buildings*, condensing the experience of two decades of negotiation with city councils on both sides of the Atlantic.[31] The model architectural designs presented with these notes laid the emphasis on the maximum use of space, and the most effective supervision of readers browsing the shelves. A relatively modest building could still make room for a lecture theatre and a children's room, as well as a boiler room in the basement (all Carnegie libraries were heated), by sacrificing the rhetorical flourishes so beloved by donors, such as a large portico or fireplaces. Bertram was also a great enemy of decorative columns on the frontage, a patently useless expense. These designs were not prescriptive: Bertram recognised that the nature of the site and size of the collection would be different in each case. But he did make possible a new pragmatic, democratic library architecture that put the needs of readers and librarians ahead of the glorification of donors and trustees.

In 1909, Baedeker issued a new version of its guidebook to the United States. Twenty-four libraries had now earned their star, including the Carnegie libraries in Pittsburgh, Allegheny and Atlanta. The New York Public Library was even awarded a star in anticipation of its opening two years later. Perhaps more significant was the almost offhand remark that New York now had about 350 'more or less' public libraries.[32] This was very largely the achievement of Carnegie, not just the funding of libraries emulating the grand central buildings in New York and Boston, Manchester and Birmingham, but in bringing libraries to the working-class quarters and sprawling middle-class suburbs of the growing industrial

22. The Carnegie Public Library in Bryan (2014), established in 1902.
One of thirteen Carnegie libraries in Texas still in existence of thirty-
two originally built. Carnegie's energetic secretary James Bertram
disliked grand neoclassical fronts, but many town councils favoured such
embellishment to highlight the prestige of their new local library.

conurbations. In this clear-minded, sustained and sympathetic
campaign, Carnegie truly inaugurated the golden age of the public
library.

Falling in Love with Fiction

The public library movement offered the opportunity for a further
extended skirmish in the interminable war on fiction. Almost since
the invention of print, the campaign to turn reading into an instrument of moral purpose had concentrated its fire on fiction. In the
sixteenth century, the Spanish authorities had banned the export
of chivalric romances to the Americas, albeit with little success,
and almost every generation of library development had fought to
exclude the pernicious instruments of light entertainment likely to
turn heads and addle brains: Sir Thomas Bodley's 'idle books and
riffe raffes'. It was not that critics could present tangible evidence

of fiction's noxious impact, although some tried. In 1840, the New York Lyceum circulated a pamphlet claiming that the reading of novels was 'one of the standing causes of insanity' citing 'reports of some French hospitals for lunatics'.[33] This, it must be said, was a weak source of authority, particularly when used, as here, as part of an advertising campaign for a library that would exclude all works of fiction 'except those of a religious or moral character'.

Despite such absurdities, belief in the adverse consequences of reading fiction remained powerful, even as novels became the absolute cornerstone of the publishing industry in the nineteenth century. This complex relationship, between a taste for fiction and a continuing sense of its harmful effects, is beautifully captured in the works of Jane Austen, where the female protagonists most addicted to novels are those drawn to shallow men, and most likely to elope with ensigns in handsome uniforms. Yet Austen cared deeply whether the public read her novels, and also patronised the more upmarket circulating libraries.[34]

The circulating libraries had little compunction in trading works of fiction, since these were their lifeblood and raison d'être. London institutions like Mudie's could be more discriminating, favouring not only history, travel literature and the classics, but also writers whose elevation to the literary canon saved them from the taint of vulgarity. Mudie was quite happy to function as the moral gatekeeper of polite letters, through the economic power he held over the industry. More difficult was the expanding world of the penny dreadful and dime novel, over which he had no influence.

There was no doubt, however, that all classes of readers wished to delve more deeply into the imaginative works of their own age, and defences gradually crumbled. The trustees of the subscription libraries justified the purchase of fiction as a means of inculcating the habit of reading, hoping that neophyte readers would then move on to more serious books. This optimistic prognosis was frequently repeated, even when all evidence was to the contrary. The annual report of the Mechanics' Institute of New York would frequently suggest a declining demand for fiction, with no supporting statistical evidence. But then membership began to decline, and in

1871 the library purchased no fewer than 700 copies of *Lothair*, the fashionable new novel by Benjamin Disraeli.

As taxpayer-funded institutions, public libraries were to some extent insulated from immediate economic pressures. Between 1870 and 1920 the war on fiction moved inexorably towards its climax, with the new national professional bodies of librarianship, the Library Association in Great Britain, the American Library Association (ALA) and the *Association des Bibliothécaires de France*, leading the charge. The members of these bodies were not the world's natural warriors. On the eve of the First World War, when the ALA was celebrating forty years of annual meetings, Burton E. Stevenson thought of it as

a humdrum professional organisation, wrapped around with tradition, settled in its habits of thought, and chiefly occupied with matters of technical detail. Its members were quiet, inoffensive, well-behaved people, cherishing the same hobby and agreeing upon everything except whether a large circulation was a merit or a disgrace.[35]

So although in principle public libraries continued to favour serious works of history, geography and comprehensible technical and scientific books, by the 1890s, public libraries reported that between 65 and 90 per cent of books borrowed were works of fiction.[36] This was too strong a tide to be ignored. Librarians switched their attention to directing patrons towards the right sort of fiction. Librarians recognised the difference between the trivial, which could be tolerated, and the 'vicious', well represented in the explosion of publishing of cheap, sensational novels that proved so popular with readers in Europe and the United States.

In 1893, the ALA offered the first of a series of guides for small libraries, consisting of 5,000 recommended titles. Only 803 were works of fiction. The recommended titles included some contemporary writers like Sir Arthur Conan Doyle and George Alfred Henty, but excluded older favourites such as Horatio Alger and Ouida. The classics also came under scrutiny: Fielding and Sterne were included; Richardson and Smollett were not.[37] In

England, the great fiction debate was closely bound up with the move from closed stacks to open access. Many readers found the need to choose from a catalogue before presenting their choices to the circulation desk deeply intimidating – the power to browse was liberating. Librarians regretted the dilution of their custodial function; they also feared that, left to themselves, readers would choose nothing but fiction. One solution, widely practised, was to allow access to the non-fiction, while keeping fiction in the stacks. Another, more devious, was to mix the two, so at least the search for a novel would involve exposure to more demanding titles.[38] In the United States, librarians routinely kept the more controversial titles in the central library but declined to circulate them to the branches.[39]

One key difference between the library communities in England and the United States was a growing disparity between their staff. In the United States, the sudden proliferation of libraries in small communities saw a wave of appointments of female librarians. At the outbreak of the First World War, 85 per cent of the staff employed in American libraries were women, whereas in England the proportions were exactly reversed. It is certainly true that many women were employed in subordinate positions (and were paid less than men), but not always: the public library in Los Angeles was presided over by a remarkable sequence of seven female librarians between 1880 and 1905. When the last of these, Mary Letitia Jones, the first librarian of Los Angeles to have graduated from library school, was ordered to resign to make way for a man, she refused. Her case brought national support and a demonstration by the women of Los Angeles. The impasse was broken only when Jones left to become librarian at Bryn Mawr College in Pennsylvania.[40]

How did this great influx of female librarians impact on the public libraries? Certainly, some leading figures in the library community muttered that the atmosphere of the library had been feminised, largely in the context of anxieties over whether libraries had been too warmly welcoming to the homeless and the unemployed. In 1894, Josephus Larned, president of the ALA, asked whether those who came to libraries to read newspapers ever read anything else: 'Are they not, for the most part, a vagrant and mal-odourous class, whose presence in the reading room repels many who would receive more benefit from it?'[41] But the leading question of the 1894 ALA survey, 'Do you deprecate the reading of fiction to the extent now practiced?', was posed by a woman, Ellen Coe, head of the New York free circulating library. While female librarians can be credited with a leading role in bringing children's books (and rooms in which to read them) into the library, they seem to have been every bit as firm as their male counterparts in deploring unsuitable fiction.

Successive editions of the ALA guide chopped and changed. Thomas Hardy, Henry James and Émile Zola were all excluded in 1904, but *The Red Badge of Courage* and H. G. Wells's *The War of the Worlds* were reprieved in 1908. Sometimes calls for censorship came from readers, and this would increasingly be the case as the librarians' own approach to fiction became more relaxed. Providing fiction for the troops in the First World War demolished many taboos, and the post-war challenge of communism moved the spotlight on to non-fiction titles. The red menace, pornography and sexual licence seemed, in the twentieth century, to be much greater threats than the Sherlock Holmes novels of Sir Arthur Conan Doyle.

It was only after the First World War that the library shed its nineteenth-century identity as an instrument of social reform, and tentatively embraced a new role, as much a part of the entertainment industry as it was a source of enlightenment, improvement and redemption. This was even before it began to grapple with the new threats of the age of telecommunication: radio, cinema and ultimately television. All would offer tempting alternatives to reading for leisure time. As the twentieth century wore on, it gradually became clear that fiction was in fact the main defence of libraries against obsolescence. Falling in love with fiction was the key to survival.

PART SIX

THE WAR ON BOOKS

CHAPTER SIXTEEN

SURVIVING THE TWENTIETH CENTURY

When the United States of America declared war on Germany on 6 April 1917, the American library community threw off three years of uncomfortable neutrality and devoted itself to the nation's cause. The library became an engine of war, vying with other agencies in the fervour of its patriotic engagement. Librarians took a practical role in ensuring citizens had access to books explaining the causes of the war. Pro-German titles were discreetly withdrawn from circulation, as a general assault unfolded on German language, literature and even foodstuffs: sauerkraut became liberty cabbage, Frankfurters, liberty sausage.[1] Everett Perry, appointed head of the Southwest Division of the Library War Council, directed his librarians to root out any books that 'sing the praises of German Kultur'.[2] As prominent public buildings, libraries paid their full part in promoting war bonds, recruiting for the Red Cross and pointing the way towards the nearest recruiting office. For the American Library Association, war was a major opportunity to prove its worth. By November 1918, with the cooperation of the YMCA and Carnegie Foundation, the association had built and stocked libraries in each of the stateside training camps, and shipped over a million books to the American Expeditionary Force in France.[3]

In 1941, the Japanese attack on Pearl Harbour produced a similar outpouring of patriotic bibliophilia. Althea Warren, chief librarian of Los Angeles, took four months' leave to run the Victory Book Campaign, a nationwide drive to gather books for army reading rooms, military hospitals and training camps.[4] By April 1942, 6 million titles had been collected and sorted for distribution. These efforts were acknowledged when President Roosevelt provided a keynote address for the ALA convention in

1942. England's librarians had been similarly engaged in both wars. Opening hours were extended to accommodate new shift-working patterns, and troops stationed away from home were issued with temporary reading cards. Even fines for late return, a sacred duty in the library profession, were sometimes forgiven or forgotten for those in uniform.

In times of war, especially for those outside the immediate theatres of conflict, a sense of powerlessness can be as corrosive as fear. Libraries helped channel the boundless energies of populations committed to a patriotic cause, as the economic and human demands of total war brought radical change to the rhythms of life. In these unsettling times, books were a familiar anchor, a source of both comfort and escape.

Hitler, too, had his eye on libraries. One of his first acts on coming to power in 1933 was to announce a new public libraries programme, focused particularly on small towns and villages. Until this point German public libraries had relied mostly on gifts and local grants to build their collections, which were often out of date and unappealing. Now a major infusion of public funds transformed the face of the public library. In 1934, Germany had 9,494 libraries. By 1940, that number had risen to 13,236.[5]

Of course, all this had a clear ideological purpose. Unsuitable books or books by disapproved authors such as Erich Maria Remarque (*All Quiet on the Western Front*) were removed from circulation, though the extent to which such instructions were followed depended on the zeal of the local librarian, and how well they knew their stock.[6] It was easier, when war came, to throw themselves into the task of gathering books for fighting men. In the autumn of 1939, public libraries in Germany packed up and dispatched 8 million books for the troops. The Luftwaffe opened over 1,000 new libraries on airbases, and all of those had to be stocked. While the tide of war ran in Germany's favour, directors of the major libraries were seconded to scour the libraries of conquered Europe for representative texts of German culture to be repatriated to the libraries of the Reich. The cultural treasures of groups marked out for extinction were rooted out and obliterated.

The industrialised warfare of the twentieth century would

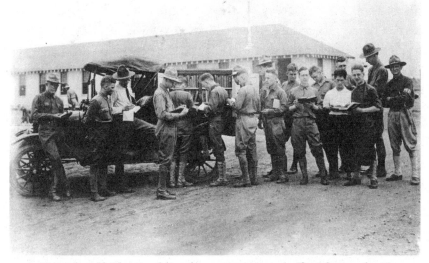

23. Providing books to soldiers became a national effort during the First World War. Millions of books were supplied to military libraries, hospitals and truck libraries, like that pictured here, in Texas around 1917.

ultimately take a terrible toll on the library stock of continental Europe. But before we count the cost of bombing and more targeted destruction, it is as well to remember this: libraries were not only the victims of war, but were active participants in the conflict. This was especially true of the technical and scientific libraries of universities and laboratories. Protecting these collections was a war priority, as was limiting the international flow of scientific data. What in peacetime represented the normal commerce of scientific exchange now became closely guarded state secrets.[7] The public libraries did their bit, the peerless map collections of the New York Public Library and the British Museum scoured for every scrap of relevant data as the Allies prepared their counter-attacks on North Africa, Italy and France.

Most of all, libraries played a critical role in preparing the population for war and strengthening their resolve to fight. In July 1939, the German Reich library service ordered that thirteen books on Poland's German minorities were to be procured by public libraries. In the same year instructions went out that 'writings about England and France are to be to checked to determine whether the books contain what encourages the strength to carry on and the will to victory on the German side'.[8] Marxist and pro-Soviet texts purged after the Nazi takeover were quietly returned to circulation after the signature of the Ribbentrop–Molotov Pact in August 1939 (albeit briefly). It would be wrong to think that such measures were imposed on a reluctant library community or provoked widespread protests from readers. In 1917, American librarians competed to demonstrate a robust detestation of Bolshevism and eradicate any hint of socialist sentiment on their shelves.[9] The same active patriotism would be evident, more controversially, during the Cold War.

War brought both a relaxing of boundaries and a coarsening of taste; this, too, was reflected in the wartime history of libraries. Whereas at the beginning of the wars, patrons sought out works of history, by 1943 German librarians were noting an overwhelming demand for light fiction, 'books with cheerful content'. As the bombs rained down, books were a means of escape from current woes, a desperate means to banish care, if only for a brief interval before being forced once again to confront reality. The heightened emotions of war brought peaks of elation, triumph, horror and catastrophe. The library community shared in all these experiences and played a crucial role in stoking the emotions that moved both fighting men and those who supported them at home to deeds of which, in peacetime, they would scarcely have been capable. Libraries were never just the innocent victims of war: they were themselves weaponised. At a time of total war, their role became more important than ever.

Total War

Libraries had always been a target of conquering armies, but it was the advances in military technology in the nineteenth century that first introduced civilian populations to the horrors of total war. A public library was created in the French–German city of

Strasbourg relatively early, when in 1765 Jean-Daniel Schoepflin gave his personal collection to the use of the community. This library was considerably augmented, as elsewhere in French territory, by confiscations during the French Revolution.[10] By 1846, the collection had grown to 80,000 books, and it would grow further when amalgamated with the university library; when both collections were moved to new premises in the Temple-Neuf church, the library comprised 300,000 works, including 5,000 incunabula and 1,600 manuscripts. The collection of the Protestant seminary, also housed in the church, numbered another 100,000 volumes, including a priceless collection of pamphlets from the Reformation era. On the night of 24 August 1870, all three libraries were completely destroyed by incendiary bombs fired by German artillery.[11]

Until annexed by Louis XIV in 1681, Strasbourg had always been a German city, indeed one of the greatest cities of the Holy Roman Empire and a leading centre of German book production and intellectual life. Its recovery from France was one of the primary war aims of the Franco-Prussian War of 1870–71. So while the Prussian armies bludgeoned French armies into defeat at Sedan and Metz, Strasbourg was placed under siege. Such sieges had been a common feature of warfare since the Middle Ages; what was new was the power of industrialised weaponry to wreak havoc on civilian populations. When Prussian forces trained their high-calibre artillery on the centre of the medieval town, this marked a decisive change in military strategy.

There would be many such lessons in the century that followed, in which the industrialised nations of Europe fought brutal wars of attrition. Whole cities were reduced to rubble, and, alongside the inhabitants, libraries also suffered. Such destruction was never entirely random or purposeless. When France surrendered in 1871, Alsace and Lorraine were ceded to Prussia. Strasbourg University was re-established as the Kaiser Wilhelm University, and its library installed in a new building in 1895. Already by 1875, 2,700 institutions and individuals, almost all German, had answered the call for books and funds, donating a total of 400,000 books. A generous annual book budget ensured that by the time Alsace and Lorraine were returned to France in 1918, the library

had expanded to a collection of over a million books. This was
an entirely German library, a tangible seal of their claim of right
to Strasbourg. This re-Germanisation programme was largely successful: by 1918 only a quarter of the population of Alsace could
read French. This stimulated an equally determined campaign
after 1918 to render Alsace francophone, initiated with the creation of 800 new French-language libraries. By 1927, this Oeuvre
du Livre Français had supplied 200,000 books to 2,275 libraries.[12]
Such library politics in the service of state building was the inevitable fate of a contested border zone.

The mechanised nature of the First World War meant that it
was unavoidable that towns close to the front line would suffer
devastation. Repeated artillery barrages destroyed or seriously
damaged a string of libraries in northern France, including those
in Arras, Béthune, Montdidier, Ham, Roye, Péronne, Mézières,
Saint-Quentin, Soissons, Compiègne, Rethel, Noyon, Pont-à-
Mousson and Reims. Most cruelly, Nancy university library lost
155,000 books just ten days before the armistice.[13] By far the most
notorious casualty, which became an international cause célèbre,
was the library of the University of Louvain in Belgium. The viola-
tion of Belgian neutrality by the advancing German army caused
an international outcry, amplified by the horror at the destruction of the medieval city of Louvain on 25 August 1914. Flames
consumed the entire university library, one of the oldest and most
distinguished in Europe.[14]

When the guns finally fell silent in 1918, the reconstruction of
Louvain university library became a symbol of hope that war could
now be banished for ever. The provisions of the Treaty of Versailles
required the defeated Germans to replace the books destroyed,
and within three years 450,000 books had been collected, 210,000
from Germany. Each book was supplied with a bookplate acknowl-
edging German reparations. Donations poured in from all over
the world, particularly from America. The new university library
was designed by an American architect and built with American
money. A proposed inscription on the balustrade, 'demolished by
German fury, reconstructed with American gifts', was thwarted by
the university administration, conscious that the Germans were

still their neighbour.[15] This act of diplomatic self-restraint would count for little when German armies returned in 1940.

But while, to the battered survivors, the First World War must have seemed the war to end all wars, collateral damage was largely limited to towns and cities close to the front line. The Second World War would introduce damage of a whole new order. This was the war of the bomber, raining down death from the skies. For the populations trapped beneath, this brought nightly terror, exhaustion and death. The carpet bombing of cities made little distinction between houses and factories, railroads and civic buildings, ports and libraries.

Europe received a first taste of what was in store with the German invasion of Poland. On 1 September 1939, while German troops streamed across the border, the undefended town of Wieluń was destroyed by dive-bombers. The national library in Warsaw sustained serious damage. Interwar strategies recognised the near impossibility of preventing the bombers from reaching their targets. Cultural institutions in France, Belgium, Britain and the Netherlands began discreetly moving their most valuable items to places of safety. At first, these protective measures concentrated mostly on priceless works of art. It was in any case widely realised that with families divided by war service, and alternative forms of recreation restricted, libraries would play an important role in maintaining civilian morale. So in fact little had been done to protect the bulk of library stock when in May 1940 the German Wehrmacht unleashed its assault in the west.

In the Netherlands, the first air raids consumed the library of the port city of Middelburg, and laid waste the entire old centre of Rotterdam. On 16 May 1940, the library at Louvain was again reduced to ashes: this time, a million books were lost. In 1914, the Germans had blamed a Belgian sniper for provoking the artillery barrage that destroyed the library: ninety-three prominent German scientists, artists and intellectuals were cajoled into signing a letter supporting this and endorsing Germany's right of reprisal. In 1940, a German commission of enquiry blamed the retreating British for torching the library. Neither justification made much impact on international opinion.[16]

24. The facade of the library of the Dutch city of Middelburg, ruined but still standing, after a bombardment in 1940. Destruction by bomb and fire would be the sad fate of many great libraries of Europe during the Second World War, by far the most destructive epoch in the history of the library.

The German descent into France claimed the municipal libraries at Beauvais and Tours, a major communication centre on the Loire. The bombing of Caen inflicted losses to the city and university libraries amounting to half a million books. The French government saved the priceless libraries of the capital by declaring Paris an open city. The chaotic French retreat in fact demonstrated the hazards of sending books to places of safety, since several shipments got lost on roads hopelessly clogged by refugees fleeing south. The speed of the French surrender limited the damage to French libraries in this stage of the war: much worse was to follow in the years of occupation.[17]

With France defeated, Hitler could turn his attention to the conquest of Britain. The German Luftwaffe was ordered first to destroy the defensive capacity of the Royal Air Force; it was only gradually that attention shifted to targets in London and the major industrial cities and ports. The destruction of Coventry in November 1940, an iconic event that did much to harden British opinion to later acts of cruelty towards the German cities, destroyed 150,000 books in the city library, and its extensive collection of technical scientific literature. The Minet library in Lambeth, another creation of Victorian philanthropy, was destroyed with its 18,000 books, as was the library at Camberwell. Hampstead library lost 25,000 books when its reference room was destroyed. Outside London, the entire stock of the Manchester Literary and Philosophical Society, 50,000 books, was lost when the city centre sustained serious damage.[18] The most serious disaster of this first winter of bombing was the destruction of the warehouses of the publishing industry crammed together in Paternoster Row, by St Paul's Cathedral. The entire stock of seventeen publishing houses, comprising more than five million books, was engulfed in flames. With limited access to imported wood pulp for paper, this was a grievous blow.[19]

The Battle of Britain took a terrible toll on Britain's limited military resources, already seriously depleted by the loss of equipment in the evacuation of Dunkirk. But it did succeed in its primary objective in persuading Hitler to abandon his planned invasion. In the context of the times, faced with the apparent invincibility of German armies, this was just enough. The valour of the aircrews, famously saluted by Winston Churchill in the House of Commons, was presented to a grateful nation in a timely pamphlet account of the Battle of Britain. The hunger for good news ensured that this would be a runaway bestseller. The initial print run of 50,000 sold out in a few hours; 300,000 extra copies were quickly ordered. An illustrated version, with action photographs and explanatory diagrams, sold 700,000 copies. By April 1942, *The Battle of Britain, August–October 1940* had been published in forty-three editions in twenty-four languages and serialised in newspapers around the globe. It shaped this desperately close-run battle as a defining triumph for the embattled underdog for both the domestic market and world opinion (as well as demonstrating that Britain knew a thing or two about propaganda).[20]

For all this, German bombing continued unabated. No town in England was more than an hour's flying time from German-held airfields in France and the Low Countries, and many suffered grievously. The battering of Plymouth, an essential naval base on the south coast, consumed its city library in April 1941, along with its complete stock of 100,000 books. In May, the destruction of the Liverpool central library cost the city 200,000 books. The British Museum library was hit eight times by high explosives and numerous times by incendiaries; it is astonishing that the losses – 230,000 books – were not much more severe. In 1942, the bombers returned, in the infamous Baedeker raids, so called for singling out cathedral cities and other places of especial beauty. In May, the city library of Exeter was destroyed, along with over a million documents and books.

Libraries adapted. Book drives produced millions of donated books for salvage, and to stock war-damaged libraries and new libraries for British troops around the globe. Every night when the sirens sounded, millions of Londoners made their way down to their new subterranean sanctuaries, many in disused stations of the underground railways. Here the authorities laid on bunks and bedding, food stations and small mobile libraries to while away the long hours until the all clear. St Marylebone had collections of 50–350 books in forty-nine shelters, while Bethnal Green provided

25. The library at Holland House in Kensington, London, damaged
by a German firebomb (1940). Although the estate, previously
the home of the statesman Charles James Fox, was almost entirely
destroyed, most of the library remained intact. Here three users browse
among the ruin, in what was an officially circulated propaganda
photo, encapsulating the sang froid of the home front.

a considerable library of 4,000 volumes serving a nightly clientele
of 6,000 people.[21] Other libraries that survived the bombing functioned as rallying points for those bombed out.

As the tide turned against Germany after Stalingrad, 1943
offered something of a respite on the home front, before a new
wave of bombing with V1 self-propelled bombs (prototype drones)
and especially the potent V2 rockets launched in September 1944.
More than 1,400 V2 rockets were launched against London before
March 1945, causing 2,000 civilian casualties and a new wave of
destroyed libraries. Many of the bombs aimed at London fell short,
leading to heavy destruction in Kent and south London. The libraries in Streatham, Kingston-upon-Thames and Croydon all suffered
devastating raids, this phase of the conflict collectively costing England's public libraries somewhere over 2 million books.[22]

The success of the V2, enormously corrosive of civilian morale at a time when many were daring to hope for a return to peace, goes some way towards appreciating the importance attached by the British high command to attacks on German institutes of technology and their library resources. Inevitably, given their connection to universities, many of these were in city centres. There was also the legitimate fear that if Germany did win the race to develop an atomic bomb, victory could be snatched away by the terrible consequences of its use. This fear was not without some foundation. In the interwar years Germany, and particularly the University of Göttingen, had cemented its reputation as the world-leading centre of research in theoretical physics: until 1933, the United States had won only eight Nobel prizes, while Germany had won thirty-three. Embarrassingly for the Nazi mind, a high proportion of its most eminent scientists were Jewish. Many would end up in the United States, making their own substantial contribution to the American war effort.[23]

Libricide

This, then, was the collateral damage of Blitzkrieg. As the tide turned, the Americans, British and Russians would in turn wreak havoc on the libraries of Germany. Yet this terrible destruction of libraries in fact accounts for only a relatively small proportion of the churning of book stock during this global war. The ideologies of the thousand-year Reich had more ambitious plans for books and libraries, and these were pursued with an extraordinary tenacity until the very last days of the war. The first strand was the wholesale destruction of the entire written record of groups singled out for obliteration: this assault on culture, to wipe memory from the face of the earth, has been described as libricide, the genocide of books. Second, in paradoxical opposition to this policy, was the systematic collecting in Nazi Germany of huge collections of the books of enemy ideologies, so that even in the perennial rule of National Socialism, these evils – Bolshevism, Socialism, Judaism, Freemasonry – could be studied.

The discovery, selection, sorting, transportation and

re-cataloguing of these books and archives generated a huge bureau-cracy, employing thousands of troops, freight trains and enslaved labourers, as well as academic specialists to identify key titles and separate the wheat from the chaff. Many librarians and archivists gave themselves willingly to this cause, either because they were ideologically committed to the purposes of National Socialism, or because the pleasures of handling such extraordinary materials easily overcame any moral scruples at the wholesale appropriation of Europe's cultural capital. Some no doubt welcomed a relatively safe berth cataloguing books when the alternative was almost certain death on the eastern front. But the library profession generated its share of true believers, and, of course, librarians are natural collectors.

There had been no other time in history when this collect-ing urge could be indulged with such licence, and without fear of reprisal. Even so, the eagerness with which existing German librar-ies – universities, public libraries and state institutions – competed to obtain their share of the spoils piled up in Nazi warehouses around Europe presents an unedifying spectacle. Sometimes this plunder could be disguised as a sale, with Jewish owners or dealers offered a fraction of the market value as they hurried to liquidate assets before fleeing the country. At other times, German librar-ies received without charge bulk consignments of the books not required in the new Nazi research institutions, sometimes to replace books destroyed by bombing. At the end of the war, as the Allied victors and surviving library staff sorted through the ruins of shattered library buildings, and explored the Aladdin's caves of valuables hidden away, the book stock of much of Europe was damaged beyond restitution. Very little of this looted stock has found its way back to its original home in the seventy-five years since the war's end. Often there were none of the original owners left to receive the recovered books.

It was in Poland that the full impact of the Nazi racist ideology would be most systematically exposed. The German conquer-ors came with a prepared list of 60,000 leaders of Polish society who would be rounded up and shot, including politicians, union leaders, army officers and professors. The Poles were envisaged as a subject people of agricultural workers and a reduced industrial proletariat; Jews, meanwhile, were to be eliminated altogether.

Cutting away the roots of Polish culture also required attention to the nation's books. In December 1939, the new German government decreed that all book collections other than those owned by German nationals should be surrendered. St Michael's church in Poznań was set aside for the reception of confiscated libraries; at one point, over a million books were piled up there, including much of the collection of Poznań university library. Some of the church's contents were sent for pulping, what remained being destroyed in an air raid of 1944. The major national institutional libraries were largely closed to local inhabitants, except those of German extraction. Research materials of use to the occupying power were consolidated into appropriate collections in Warsaw, the rest marked for destruction, including the contents of most of the nation's public libraries and libraries in schools.

The consequences were devastating. It is reckoned that school and public libraries lost 90 per cent of their stock, private and specialised libraries some 80 per cent. Even the spectre of annihilation at the hands of the advancing Red Army could not deflect the German occupying forces from their work of destruction. The famous Zaluski library, stolen by Russia in 1794, but partially returned in the 1920s, was destroyed during the Warsaw Uprising in October 1944: of a collection of 400,000 books, only 10 per cent survived. The early printed books in the national library of Poland were also destroyed. Even as the Germans prepared to evacuate Warsaw in January 1945, troops with flamethrowers were sent into the stacks of the main public library to ensure that nothing remained.

These *Brennkommandos* had been practising their trade on Jewish collections since 1939. In Poznań and Będzin the arson squads burned both the synagogues and their books. The destruction of Jewish libraries in Kraków began almost immediately after the arrival of German troops on 6 September 1939. Kraków was one of the historical centres of Polish culture, and the Jewish community, one quarter of the population, lay at the heart of its intellectual life. The first commercial lending library in Kraków was established in 1837 by the Jewish merchant and city council-man Abraham Gumplowicz, and the city was also the seat of an early Jewish public library, the Ezra library, opened in 1899. More specialist libraries included the Jewish socialist library and the people's library, in addition to libraries attached to synagogues and an extended network of libraries attached to Jewish schools.[24]

In the course of two years, all these libraries were systematically ransacked, plundered or destroyed. The two Gumplowicz libraries, holding 45,000 volumes, were closed and the books disappeared: presumably German soldiers made free with the English, French and German titles. When Jewish schools were closed, their librar-ies were destroyed; the Germans also closed all Jewish cultural, educational and political organisations, and with them their librar-ies. The contents of the Ezra library and the Jewish collections in the Jagiellonian university library were both appropriated for a new state library for German use. Desperate attempts to save the sacred scrolls of the synagogues, many of which were burned to the ground immediately after the German occupation, were thwarted when the places the scrolls had been hidden were discovered after the liquidation of the ghetto in 1943. All were destroyed.

The systematic destruction of Jewish culture in Kraków was echoed in all of Poland's Jewish communities from Poznań to Vilnius.[25] In 1941, the great Talmudic collection of the Jewish theological library in Lublin, one of the largest in Europe, was con-signed to the flames. The crushing of the uprising in the Warsaw ghetto in 1943 culminated in the ceremonial dynamiting of the Great Synagogue. Since this had been used since its closure as a warehouse for the city's confiscated Jewish books, all perished in the destruction. The commander of the engineers who carried out this assignment later recalled his thrill at this moment of triumph.

> What a marvellous sight it was. A fantastic piece of theatre. My staff and I stood at a distance. I held the electronic device which would detonate all of the charges simultaneously ... After prolonging the suspense for a moment, I shouted 'Heil Hitler' and pressed the button. With a thunderous, deafen-ing bang and a rainbow burst of colours, the fiery explosion

soared toward the clouds, an unforgettable tribute to our triumph over the Jews.[26]

The Germans well understood the power of such Wagnerian moments. The destruction of the theological seminary in Lublin provided the opportunity for another public celebration of annihilation.

> We threw the huge Talmudic Library out of the building and carried the books to the market-place, where we set fire to them. The fire lasted for twenty hours. The Lublin Jews assembled around and wept bitterly, almost silencing us with their cries. We summoned the military band, and with joyful shouts the soldiers drowned out the sounds of the Jewish cries.[27]

The distraught Jewish observers well understood the significance of what they had witnessed. This was an existential struggle between two great cultures, both of which valued books. As Chaim Kaplan, a Jewish teacher in Warsaw, 1939, recognised. 'We are dealing with a nation of high culture, with a "people of the book". Germany has become a madhouse – mad for books ... The Nazi has both book and sword, and this is his strength and might.'[28] The Nazis, in the words of Michal Bušek, librarian of the Jewish museum in Prague, 'knew how important books were to the Jews. Reading makes you into a human being. They wanted to destroy the Jews by robbing them of what was most important to them.'[29] At this moment the Nazis did indeed command both book and sword: it lay within their power to eradicate the written records of Judaism through much of Europe. That they did not was also to some extent a matter of choice, the contradictory desire to retain for future study the written record of enemy ideologies. This became the grand design of Alfred Rosenberg, Hitler's chief ideologue, and the accidental saviour of much of the cultural heritage of European Jewry.

Rosenberg's Vision

Alfred Rosenberg was born in Reval, now Tallinn in Estonia, in 1893. He studied in Moscow before settling in Germany and joining the Nazi party. As a member of the dispersed German ethnic community in the east he had more reason than most to embrace the Nazi concept of *Lebensraum* (living space). The publication of his exposition of Nazi racial theory, *The Myth of the Twentieth Century*, in 1930, reinforced his claim to be regarded as the chief ideologue of the movement, a position in which he was formally confirmed by Hitler in 1934.[30]

With the coming of war and the easy conquests of 1939 and 1940, Rosenberg began planning for the perpetuation of Nazi rule throughout Europe. Crucial to this was the development of a new educational system for the next generation of the Nazi elite. A new cohort of Adolf Hitler schools formed the base of an educational pyramid topped by the planned Hohe Schule der NSDAP, a Nazi finishing school to be established on the shores of the Chiemsee. To service the academic work of Nazi social science, Rosenberg proposed a network of research institutes, each devoted to one part of Nazi ideology: an Institute of Racial Studies in Stuttgart, the Institute of Ideological Colonial Research in Hamburg, ten in all. Only the Institute for Research on the Jewish Question in Frankfurt would be built during the war; the rest, including the Hohe Schule, would wait for war's end. But in 1940 Hitler charged Rosenberg with necessary preparatory work, 'especially in the way of research and the setting up of the library'.[31]

This laconic phrase would spawn a massive plundering of books from Europe's libraries on the desired themes, together with a vast bureaucracy created by Rosenberg, the Einsatzstab Reichsleiter Rosenberg (ERR). By the end of the war the ERR had more than 5 million books in vast depots in Berlin, Frankfurt and Ratibor: many were still in the packing cases when the Germans surrendered.

Since the ERR was only tasked with this work in 1940, it missed out on the looting of Poland: that fell to other units, such as the Sonderkommando Paulson, led by the former professor of history at Berlin, Peter Paulson. Rosenberg too recruited his share

of academics to sift through the collections of institutional libraries
and confiscated private libraries. Some, such as the Jewish libraries
in Amsterdam, Ets Haim and the Bibliotheca Rosenthaliana, were
removed in their entirety. The same fate awaited the distinguished
émigré libraries in Paris, the Alliance Israélite Universelle, the Bibliothèque Russe Tourguéniev and the Bibliothèque Polonaise.[32] In
Rome the Biblioteca del Collegio Rabbinico Italiano was shipped
to Frankfurt; the other major Jewish collection, the Biblioteca
della Comunità Israelitica vanished en route.

The ERR was thorough: 29,000 raids in the Netherlands,
mostly of the houses of prosperous Jews, harvested 700,000 books.
In France the ERR confiscated 723 libraries, a total of 1.7 million
books.[33] They also worked quickly. This was increasingly necessary,
since Rosenberg's organisation faced plenty of competition.[34] The
most serious threat came from Himmler's secret police, the RSHA,
who had been collecting books since their early years in Munich.
The Dutch International Institute of Social History (IISH), which
had assembled a remarkable collection of the archives of left-wing
institutions, was the focus of an unedifying four-way struggle for
possession. The local Nazi ruler, Arthur Seyss-Inquart, wanted
it to remain in the Netherlands, whereas Robert Ley, leader of
the Nazi labour movement, thought that his organisation would
be the most appropriate home. Rosenberg also faced off against
Reinhard Heydrich bidding on behalf of the RSHA. The ERR
triumphed by right of possession, having appropriated the IISH
building in Amsterdam as their local headquarters.

It is hard to visualise so many books wending their way across
Europe to Germany, where they were received in four main depositories: in Frankfurt for the new Jewish Institute, the Hohe Schule
in the south, and two depots in Berlin, the RSHA's library in the
former Freemasons' lodge on Eisenachstrasse and the ERR's Ost-
bucherei. By 1943, all four had received between 1 and 3 million
books each, and the Frankfurt Institute had the finest Jewish
library in Europe. A further 2 million books were subsequently
accumulated at a new sorting station at Ratibor in Silesia, established to cope with the flood of books from the east.[35]

In the latter stages of the war, Rosenberg turned his attention increasingly to the eastern front. Here the booty was so enormous that priority was given to public collections, the living witness to the ideology of Bolshevism. Vilnius, the heart of eastern Jewry, sometimes known as the 'Jerusalem of the North', received special attention. Here the two principles of selection and annihilation were merged. The library of YIVO, the Yiddish Scientific Institute, was packed up and dispatched to Germany. The Strashun library, donated to the Vilnius Jewish community in 1885, was carefully examined by a small team of Jewish prisoners working under the Strashun's own librarian. Forty thousand books were selected to go to Germany; the rest were pulped. Meanwhile, in the streets outside, the Vilnius Jewish community was liquidated.[36]

'For the obvious reason that Herr Goldschmidt was a Jew'

The libraries of Germany also made increasing use of enslaved labour as the war went on: sorting and carting the crates, rescuing books from burning buildings during air raids.[37] But the work of the ERR would not have been possible without the willing participation of scholars and members of the German library profession. After the fall of France, the head librarian of the Bibliothèque Nationale, Julien Cain, a Jew, was summarily dismissed. His position was taken by the collaborationist intellectual Bernard Faÿ, but now working under a cadre of library bureaucrats seconded from Germany – Hugo Andres Krüss, director of the state library (*Staatsbibliothek*) in Berlin, his colleague Hermann Fuchs, and Ernst Wermke, director of the Breslau library. The libraries of Strasbourg and Alsace were once again reintegrated into the Reich, under the supervision of Peter Borchardt, seconded from Berlin.[38]

Scholars also worked directly for the ERR, including the young historian Dr Wilhelm Grau, and the Hebraist Johannes Pohl. Pohl, who had previously worked in the Jewish division of the Frankfurt city library, was by far the most travelled, acting as Rosenberg's plenipotentiary in Amsterdam, Paris, Rome, Thessalonica and Vilnius. Although Rosenberg would be executed for his crimes, his agents got off remarkably lightly. Grau and Pohl both found a safe berth in the German publishing industry. The Baltic

German Gottlieb Ney, who worked to build up the library for the Hohe Schule, was employed after the war as an archivist in Lund, Sweden.

Library colleagues left behind in Germany also found ways to profit from the cornucopia of books brought to Germany. Both the Berlin state library and Freiburg University obtained considerable quantities of books from France: French scholars reckon the total loss of book stock as being between 10 and 20 million volumes. The Berlin state library also requested 30,000 volumes of works relating to Jews or Judaism from the ERR.[39] The librarian at Königsberg acknowledged that the confiscation of the Catholic seminary at Plock had enriched his collection by some 50,000 volumes.[40] In Berlin, those books not required for the new institutes were turned over to the *Reichstauschstelle*, where libraries could make their bids; Hamburg obtained 30,000 books from former Jewish collections to begin rebuilding after the ruinous Allied bombing of 1943.[41] In the same year, the Berlin city library applied to the *Städtische Pfandleihanstalt*, the city pawnbroker, for 40,000 books. They hoped to be given them at no charge, but the agency insisted on a payment of 45,000 reichsmarks, the proceeds of which, they informed the library, would be contributed to the efforts 'to solve the Jewish question'. It is inconceivable that the library hierarchy, which made generous use of enslaved labour at this stage of the war, would not have known what this meant. They took the books and paid. The library was still cataloguing these books on 20 April 1945, when the Russian army opened a ferocious artillery assault on the city centre. Cataloguing would continue after the war, though instead of describing these as Jewish books, the ledgers would record them as 'gifts'.[42]

A more insidious form of exploitation was the pre-war acquisition of bargains from distressed Jewish owners having to liquidate their assets prior to flight. Relations between library directors, collectors and book dealers were often close, so the librarians had a clear idea of both the real value of the books and their owners' vulnerability. One example here may stand for many. Arthur Goldschmidt was heir to a business manufacturing cattlefeed, though his passion was for collecting books. By 1932, he had created a unique collection of seventeenth- and eighteenth-century illustrated almanacs, some 2,000 in all. The jewel of this well-known collection was a number of almanacs published by Goethe, of obvious interest to the Anna Amalia library in Weimar, the city where Goethe made his home. The director of the library, Hans Wahl, sensed an opportunity. Goldschmidt valued the collection at 50,000 reichsmarks; Wahl regretted that the library could offer no more than one reichsmark per volume. Announcing his triumph, Wahl recognised that this had been 'an unusually advantageous affair ... for the obvious reason that Herr Goldschmidt was a Jew'.[43]

At the end of the war Wahl, a Nazi party member, smoothly transferred his loyalty to the new Soviet regime. It says a great deal for the universal reluctance of the German library community to face up to its legacy of stolen books that this correspondence only came to light in 2004, after a major fire in the Anna Amalia library promoted a fundamental review of the surviving stock. Goldschmidt's heirs eventually received €100,000 for this priceless family heirloom. The staff of the Berlin city library, now rehoused and rebranded, made use of the forty years after the war to remove marks of ownership from the suspect books. Only 500 of their many thousands of stolen books have made their way back to Jewish owners.

The Reckoning

By 1943, the tide was turning, and the book stock of Germany became vulnerable to Allied retribution. In the early years of the war, many German libraries had done little to move their treasures to places of safety. Official guidance in 1939 was extremely restrictive, listing only manuscripts, incunabula and unique early printed books as priorities for evacuation. Besides, Air Marshal Goering had promised that not a single bomb would fall on Berlin, and to have acted prematurely might have brought official disfavour. This was not an era of dynamic library management. Call-up to the front hollowed out the library staff; many of those who remained were in poor health or elderly. Some of the more able librarians, as we have seen, were seconded to service abroad. When an attack on Kassel in September 1941 destroyed 87 per cent of the stock of the provincial library, 400,000 books, a news blackout was declared: according to the erstwhile head of the German library association, Georg Leyh, 'Nothing is supposed to be published in the *Zentralblatt* [the library trade paper] about the bombing damage in libraries'.[44]

The intensification of bombing in 1943 meant that it was no longer possible to conceal the extent of the damage. In July, the firestorm in Hamburg consumed the university library, and the distinguished Commerzbibliothek. Eight hundred thousand volumes were destroyed in Munich; in Leipzig the stock of almost the entire publishing industry went up in flames. Libraries now made urgent attempts to move their stock to safety – wherever that could be found. Sometimes the decision on what to send could be distinctly quixotic. Darmstadt, home to one of the world's great music collections, sent to storage a year's worth of gardening, cookery and fashion journals, while priceless autograph manuscripts of Handel, Mozart, Vivaldi and Beethoven were left to take their chances. On 11 September 1944 the library was destroyed, with the loss of 400,000 books.[45] By this point even the most ideologically committed could see the writing on the wall: 1 million books from Rosenberg's Frankfurt Institute were sent away to Hungen, 31 miles north, where they were divided between thirty-eight storage depots. It was there that the Americans found them in 1945.

In January 1944, the Berlin state library closed its doors to users; a skeleton staff continued to work in the ruins, processing new acquisitions. Director Krüss took up residence in the cellar, where on 27 April 1945, with the Russians approaching, he committed suicide. His library's books had by this point been scattered between twenty-nine separate depositories, mostly remote castles or deep mines. Because the American and British bombers came from the west, the books were generally sent east. This dramatically reduced the chance that they would ever return. The creation of a Soviet zone of occupation in what became Communist East Germany (the DDR), and the adjustment of Polish borders westwards, meant that many books were now in areas where repatriation

1. Illumination depicting Mark the Evangelist in the Codex Caesareus, an exquisite Bible written for Emperor Henry III in Echternach, around 1050. The Bible was made for the Emperor's new cathedral in Goslar, where the book remained until Goslar was occupied by Swedish forces in the 1630s. Like many other German books, it made its way to Sweden, although it remained in private hands until 1805. Today it resides in Uppsala university library, home to spoils from many German, Czech and Polish libraries.

2. The main hall of Admont Abbey library, Austria: the library has become a baroque temple, designed for pure magnificence. Above all, the redesigned monastic libraries of Germany, Austria and Bohemia were laid out to impress their visitors and made little provision for desks where the books might be consulted.

3. With the rise of antiquarian tastes, the book auction was easily mocked as a place where bibliophiles squandered their fortunes. In this print (*c.*1810), the potential buyers size each other up as a book is displayed in the central ring.

4. Circulating libraries were the target of much derision for providing light literature to a female audience. In *Beauty in Search of Knowledge* (1782), a fashionable young lady displays her choice, whereas in *The Circulating Library* (1804), the viewer's eye is drawn to the empty shelves of 'novels', 'romances' and 'tales', while the shelf of sermons is fully packed.

BEAUTY in SEARCH of KNOWLEDGE.

London, Printed for R Sayer & I Bennett, Map, Chart & Printsellers N.º 53, Fleet Street, 30.ª Dec.ª 1782.

THE CIRCULATING LIBRARY.

"Pray, my dear M.ª Page," cried a pretty lisper, looking over a Catalogue "will you let me have that dear Man of Feeling, I have so long waited for: Well, this will do for one. N.º 1889, Cruel Disappointment, for another, Reuben, or Suicide, higho! N.º 1746, I suppose he killed himself for love. Seduction, yes, I want that more than any thing, Unguarded Moments, ah we all have our unguarded moments. True Delicacy, N.º? that must be a silly thing by the title. School of Virtue, heaven knows mamma gives me enough of that, Test of Filial Duty, at any rate she puts me to that test pretty often. Mental Pleasures, worse & worse! I'll look no longer, Oh! stay a moment. Mutual Attachment, Assignation, Frederick or the Libertine, just add these M.ª Page, & I shall not have to come again until the day after to-morrow." _____ Published Oct. 22, 1804, by LAURIE & WHITTLE, 53, Fleet Street, London.

Bücherſaal der neuen Bibliothek im Britiſchen Muſeum zu London. Originalzeichnung von C. Saumann.

5. Two views of the British Museum library, displaying the grand circular reading room, here busily frequented, and the metal stacks around its exterior. The combination of a palatial classical dome and innovative shelving practices were the source of much admiration, a welcome distraction from the concerns raised about the unfinished catalogue.

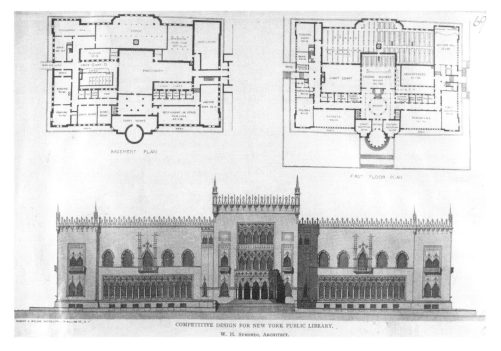

BASEMENT PLAN

FIRST FLOOR PLAN

COMPETITIVE DESIGN FOR NEW YORK PUBLIC LIBRARY.
W. H. SYMONDS, ARCHITECT.

6. One of eighty-eight competitive designs for the New York Public Library (1897), and the building that it became, as seen from across the intersection of East 42nd Street and Fifth Avenue (1915).

7. 'The Empire: British Robbery and Treachery', the title of this 1941 Nazi work on the evils of Great Britain, as told through a selection of the stamps of its colonies. Under the Third Reich, the holdings of public libraries were completely given over to propagandistic literature of this type.

8. Three Mills & Boon titles, from 1977, 1983 and 1989. Initially destined mainly for circulating libraries, the publisher developed a dominant grip on the market in romantic fiction. Librarians only reconciled themselves to supplying such books to their readers when it became necessary to justify continued funding.

9. 'Reading is a man's obligation', reads this Communist poster by Sergei Ivanovich Ivanov from around 1919. The Soviet government indeed attached great importance to the provision of libraries in a country which, before the Bolshevik Revolution, had very low literacy rates.

10. When architectural visions clash with the demands of library users, architecture often wins: the atrium of the main branch of the San Francisco Public Library, pictured in 2009, some fifteen years after hundreds of thousands of books were removed without consultation.

11. The ubiquitous threat to the library, in this as every age: fire trucks
battle the fire that engulfed the Los Angeles central library in 1986.

was out of the question. Of the twenty-nine shelters used for the books of the Berlin state library, twelve were in the Soviet zone, eleven in Poland and one in Czechoslovakia.[46] In the post-war years, after counting the cost of years of German occupation and 25 million dead, the Russians were not inclined to be magnanimous. Russian scholars reckon that their libraries lost up to 100 million books. In compensation, many millions of books were now shipped east from occupied Germany, along with other cultural booty and industrial machinery. The 2 million books at the depot in Ratibor were easy targets, as were the gradually revealed underground storehouses.[47] The Berlin state library, which, like the city library, now found itself in the Soviet zone, reckoned to have lost 2 million books to Russia. The city library had also evacuated large parts of its collection to Poland and Czechoslovakia, little of which came back. They at least could rebuild their collection from the 'unowned' books gathered out of the ruins of private houses and the many libraries of the Nazi ministries.

The Soviet trophy battalions did a thorough job: so thorough indeed, that they had no immediate use for the millions of books now removed from Germany. Many of these, of course, had been previously looted from western Europe, as well as from Russia itself and from Jewish owners throughout the continent. Russia and the successor states since the collapse of the USSR have not been inclined to recognise these fine distinctions: all the books recovered in Germany are regarded as inadequate reparation for what was lost.[48] The brief period of Glasnost after 1989 brought the startling revelation that 2.5 million books, unsorted since the war, had simply been piled up in a church in Uzkoye. By this time they had degenerated into unreadable mush. Since this brief period of openness, the Russian libraries have once again been less forthcoming. In 2009 the Berlin state library began for the first time to list the books lost to Russia and Poland in its own catalogue, together with their present locations. But the locations of many millions of books that made their way east are still unknown today.[49]

Books in libraries and depots in the British or American zones could sometimes be repatriated very quickly, particularly if they had never left their crates. Ets Haim and the Bibliotheca Rosenthaliana made their way back to Amsterdam, and the library of the Alliance Israélite Universelle to Paris. Overall, the Americans sent back over 2.5 million books from their depot in Offenbach, while the British returned half a million from their depot at Tanzenberg.[50] The Soviets were less concerned about such issues. Thirty tons of books from the main Jewish libraries that had not been destroyed in Vilnius at war's end were unceremoniously pulped. Sixty thousand books from the Turgenev library in Paris had somehow made their way to the Red Army Officers Club in Legnica. In the mid 1950s orders came from Moscow that they should all be burned.[51]

In some respect, this was not the most urgent library problem exercising the occupying powers. Equally important was that the surviving libraries should be purged again, this time of the ideologies of Nazism. There was much discussion about how this could be achieved. The Americans in particular were anxious not to be seen as the destroyers of books; against this, there were real doubts whether sensitive decisions could be left to German librarians about what should be removed.[52] A compromise was to issue an indicative list of the sorts of books to be removed; in practice, many librarians had already removed these and many more. In the event, German public libraries were stripped of around 4 million volumes, or half their stock. About a million volumes, including a compendious collection of Nazi propaganda, was appropriated for the Library of Congress in Washington DC. By 1945, libraries were widely recognised as important agencies of national security; stocking up for the future seemed the prudent choice.[53]

Sixty Million Books and the Library that Never Was

The fact that so much damage could be done to a thousand years of cultural heritage, so much of it deliberate, shook something fundamental in the European perception of the viability of their civilisation. Faced with shattered buildings, absent or smouldering collections, and displaced and starving populations with far more urgent priorities than books, many wondered whether such a cultural heritage was even worth restoring. As well as the destruction, millions of books had been displaced far from their original homes – vanished with their owners, plundered, or sent to places of safety, many now in the hands of new rulers. Difficulties securing their return and squabbles over ownership added new layers of bitterness and recrimination in the post-war years. Even in 2013, a summit between Russia and Germany was almost derailed by debates over cultural restitution.

Some problems were so intractable that they could only be resolved by the intervention of a neutral broker. This was the role that UNESCO hoped to play, and its intervention in the reconstruction of Germany's battered libraries was well prepared and thoughtful. Sensibly, the western powers quickly ruled out reparations: as Edward J. Carter, head of the libraries division at UNESCO, argued, 'A harsh reparations policy of restocking British or French libraries by seizures from Germany and Italy will be disastrous.'[54] UNESCO also made it clear that their priority was not simply to return books to their previous locations: 'A library should not automatically have a claim to international benevolence because it has been destroyed. The test must be its place in the present and future library system.' Standing somewhat aside from the immediate concerns of the occupying powers, UNESCO could take a longer view, recognising, for instance, the dangers posed by the new politics of divided Europe.

> What Hungary has lost during the Second World War is less important than the fact that ... the output of the cultural life in the democratic countries, as expressed in books and reviews, had mostly failed to reach the country. English, American and foreign books are needed in hundreds and thousands of copies.[55]

That was all very true, but the concentration on the English language, though popular with readers, raised fears of a new imperialism. There was also the intractable problem posed by orphaned Jewish books. Left in the hands of the American and British occupying forces were over a million books, whose owners could not be located, often because the entire family had been wiped out. Existing protocol would suggest that such books should be returned to the country of the family's residence. Where the owners were Jewish, and the home Germany, this was morally and politically inconceivable. This dilemma provided the context for a well-meaning plan that the orphaned books should form the basis of a world Jewish library. Amsterdam and (more insistently) Copenhagen offered themselves as the potential location. Those who supported this plan at UNESCO were somewhat surprised at the vehemence of the reaction. Opponents saw Denmark and UNESCO as trying to wrest control of books away from Jewish organisations. The Czechs made clear that they would send their books to Palestine or nowhere, and eventually 100,000 books were transported to Israel from central and eastern Europe. In the event, the plans for a world Jewish library shrivelled and died: the orphaned books mostly ended up either in Israel or the United States.

The passions raised by this well-intentioned but ultimately abortive proposal demonstrate the continuing difficulties posed by library politics to the book stock of most of Europe after ten years of turmoil. Russia had lost 100 million books, France 20 million, Poland two thirds of its entire book stock. Even in England, the year 1943 alone reputedly saw the destruction of 60 million books – an astonishing number, considering that this was after the end of the Blitz and before the coming of the V1 and V2 bombing campaign. Few bombs fell on Britain in 1943, so how could 60 million books have been destroyed in this year?

The answer is that almost all were books gathered up in a salvage campaign – voluntarily offered by their owners for reuse and recycling as part of the war effort.[56] Salvage trucks brought the books to marquees or halls, where volunteers gave them a rapid inspection to see what could usefully be saved to replenish the stock of war-damaged libraries or dispatched to the forces abroad. The previous year King George VI had set the appropriate patriotic example by contributing a ton of waste paper, consisting of 'a large consignment of old books and manuscripts from the royal library'.[57] What this all brings home is the sheer quantity of books, magazines and newspapers then in circulation in Europe. The losses of irreplaceable copies of rare or unique books from the sixteenth and seventeenth centuries were a grievous blow to libraries and scholars, but for the vast bulk of the reading public, what they most wanted could easily be replenished. Once paper supplies were restored, buildings repaired, and life returned to normal, the libraries could resume the role that they had created for themselves in the pre-war years, secure in the knowledge that, as we shall see in the following chapter, the conditions of war had turned many additional millions into avid readers.

CHAPTER SEVENTEEN

WRESTLING WITH MODERNITY

Given the extent of the damage wreaked by industrialised warfare on Europe's libraries, it seems somewhat paradoxical to suggest that the period 1880–1960 was simultaneously the great age of the public library. Books and libraries were never more valued than during the Second World War. Men on active service, far from home, often turned to books, and enormous logistical effort went into keeping them supplied. On the home front, the blackout and long evenings at home or on war duty made books both an essential source of solace and respite from ever-present anxieties. It was in this period, too, that the network of libraries truly reached beyond its European and American heartland to serve populations in every continent.

It was only after the war that the pleasures and plenty of peace challenged the role of the library. From the 1960s and 1970s onwards, a slowdown in post-war industrial growth brought governments and civic authorities to question seriously whether lavish public provision of reading matter was affordable, or an urgent social priority. This crisis of identity occurred long before the digital challenge that has consumed attention more recently: the appeal of television certainly loomed large in contemporary explanations of the crisis of reading in the age of mass literacy. But the seeds of decay were evident long before this, even as the public libraries consolidated their network in the first half of the twentieth century, and reached out to previously under-served groups of women, children and rural readers. This too involved an uncomfortable brush with new technology.

Throughout the nineteenth century and well into the next, books, magazines and newspapers were both critical instruments of

modernity and its chronicler. The great nineteenth-century innovations in communication, the telegraph and telephone, seemed as
if they would be likely to reinforce the supremacy of print. And so
it proved. Innovations in production and distribution, the steam
press and the railways, multiplied the quantity of books available
and helped bring printed matter to its new consumers. The telegram and telephone brought immediacy to the news for the first
time in history, to the great excitement of readers, while stirring
cut-throat competition between rival newspapers for the scoop,
stop-press or breaking news. The railways transported books to
customers outside the metropolitan centres, while commuting to
work and holiday journeys created new opportunities for reading,
not least thanks to the ubiquitous railway bookstalls.

For all the huffing and puffing about the unsuitability or triviality of much of this reading matter, print, it seemed, would always
continue to play the central role in keeping humans informed and
entertained, and drawing them ever closer together. In 1919, even
after the most destructive war ever witnessed, the author Sher-
wood Anderson could rhapsodise:

> Books, badly imagined and written though they may be in
> the hurry of our times, are in every household, magazines cir-
> culate by the millions of copies, newspapers are everywhere.
> In our day a farmer standing by the stove in the store in his
> village has his mind filled to overflowing by the words of
> other men. The newspapers and the magazines have pumped
> him full. The farmer by the stove is brother to the men of the
> cities, and if you listen you will find him talking as glibly and
> as senselessly as the best city man of us all.[1]

This neatly captures not only the sense of new frontiers, but also
the patronising tone of cultural elites towards this new reading
public. Yet even now, times were changing; and in the next fifty
years, for the first time since Gutenberg, cultural commentators
began to doubt whether books could hold their own.

The twentieth century, it soon became clear, would be different. From the first days of radio and then cinema these were real

competitors, not just for much-valued leisure time, but also for possession of the imaginative world once shaped primarily by print. This, rather than the fascination for new technology that characterised Europe and North America throughout this century, was probably the most potent challenge to the supremacy of the book and thus to the long-term viability of the library. Treasured library books could populate the waking mind, and dreams, with distant worlds and adventures. But with radio you could hear the voices, and at the movies you could see King Kong's massive bulk. These were multimedia experiences. The addition of a skilful soundtrack trained the regular radio listener or moviegoer to a whole range of emotional responses; a vastly more appealing audioscape than the noise of squabbling siblings jolting you back from Mandalay when curled up for evening reading.

Lights, Camera, Panic

The early years of both radio and film were exhilarating, experimental and at times chaotic. Key decisions had to be taken, not least over who should have ownership and control over quality and output. With radio we see a tantalising glimpse of the road not travelled, for many of the early exponents saw radio as a form of private person-to-person communication, a more versatile alternative to the telephone. Ultimately it fell to government to decide whether radio would be developed by individual members of the public, radio hams, or by corporations on its behalf. The decisive voice was that of the powerful radio manufacturing industry which saw a massive new market opening up. Their lobbying spurred in the United States a decisive intervention from the secretary of commerce, Herbert Hoover, squashing the hopes of the radio amateurs. Radio hams retreated to the garage to lick their wounds, while the family radio, resplendent in a modish wooden cabinet, took pride of place in the living room. Families would huddle around the set, where they might have once sat around the kitchen table, reading their books.

Of all modern technological innovations, radio developed with the most astonishing speed. The first commercial radio station was established in the United States in 1921. Two years later there were 556, run by a variety of electrical goods manufacturers, corporations, churches, schools and department stores. By the end of the decade, with this cacophony of voices brought into some sort of order by the Radio Act of 1927, a radio could be found in 55 per cent of American homes, growing to 81.5 per cent in 1939. In 1924, the purchase of radios accounted for a third of American spending on furniture: in 1934, Americans owned 42 per cent of all the radios in the world.

This phenomenal growth could not be matched elsewhere, though in Europe, the British Broadcasting Corporation (BBC) offered a powerful alternative model, as a state corporation with a virtual monopoly of the airwaves. This experiment was watched closely in America but rejected on the grounds that a regulated monopoly provider would be too close to government. There was some truth in this, not least in the early years under the autocratic rule of its first director general, Sir John Reith, an austere Scottish Presbyterian who felt that pleasure should be taken in small doses.[2]

Having adopted in its mission statement the goal to 'inform, educate and entertain', many observers thought that the BBC placed far too little emphasis on the last of these three objectives. This could certainly not be said of the more raucous American broadcasters, who bombarded their listeners with a freewheeling menu of music, variety entertainers and advertising. In Britain, radio owners were obliged by law to support the BBC with a 10-shilling annual licence fee. Forced to establish their own income base, American radio turned to those with products to sell. By 1938, a third of airtime was devoted to advertisements, and radio was draining serious money away from the newspapers. The BBC, with its income secure, was able to eschew advertising altogether.

The BBC also had money to spend on programming, and much of this went on supporting orchestral and band music, and radio plays. The BBC broadcast its first radio play in 1922, and from that point forward radio drama would be a staple of its consumption. A further inducement to the book-reading classes was the introduction of two regular, long-lived weekly publications, *The Radio Times* (1923) and *The Listener* (1929). The American response was the soap opera, a made-for-radio medium that encouraged a regular pattern of listening, particularly for women at home during the working day. In neither case was there much place for news and current affairs, though for rather different reasons: in America because news was not a popular feature of their output, in Britain because nervous newspaper proprietors had required the BBC to foreswear a regular news service. Though this embargo was to some extent eroded during the General Strike of 1926, it was only with the outbreak of war in 1939 that radio began to play a critical role in the provision of news. In America, radio also launched the career of a number of radio evangelists, a development made for America with its fissiparous multiplicity of faiths.

Like all media innovations, radio attracted its fair share of doom-merchants and naysayers. For those to whom books played an important recreational role, the radio was initially disorientating in its offer of a prescribed schedule of entertainment. Against the versatility of opening a book in odd moments of leisure, radio output could only be caught at the appointed hour; and if concentration wavered, there was no turning back a few pages to recap. The Dutch historian Johan Huizinga, visiting America in 1926, was unimpressed. Radio, he felt, demanded strong but superficial attention, 'completely excluding reflexion, or what I might call reflective assimilation'.[3] Radio, with its kaleidoscope of fast-changing fare, and numerous advertising breaks, was blamed for a national collapse of concentration, much as the iPhone would be eighty years later. Here, intellectuals made common cause with newspapermen, initially terrified at radio's assault on their own love affair with the public (and their advertising revenue).

Yet if radio disturbed the naturally bookish, they soon integrated the new medium into a recreational life where reading and listening could easily coexist. This was not true of cinema, where the assault on the senses was if anything even more traumatic. Long before Al Jolson astonished audiences in the first talking picture, *The Jazz Singer*, in 1927, Americans had been obsessed by the movies. The success of the nickelodeons, which offered a primitive moving picture through peepholes, or projected on to walls, pointed to the potential of the new medium. By the time the first

movie companies had set up shop in Hollywood in 1912, an estimated 10 to 20 million Americans visited the movies regularly. In
1919, a study of the entertainment culture of Toledo, Ohio, revealed
that an average of 45,000 moviegoers attended the city's forty-nine
theatres every week. In 1924, Muncie, Indiana (population 26,000)
had nine movie theatres, showing films continuously from 1 p.m.
until 11 at night. Even in the silent era, the movies had become the
preferred recreation of young America.[4] The move to Hollywood,
and the creation of the major film companies, gave America its first
superstars, Charlie Chaplin, Mary Pickford and Rudolph Valen-
tino; and it generated a cottage industry of film magazines and
endless copy for the newspapers.

The introduction of sound was technically difficult and ruinously expensive, but enthusiastically embraced by audiences.
The purists were inconsolable: 'an art has been exterminated at
the zenith of its power', keened one critic, but the paying public
never looked back.[5] The new technology helped cushion customers through the pain of the Depression, and by 1938 cinemas were
patronised by 85 million moviegoers a week. In 1940, the last full
year before America entered the war, Hollywood turned out 450
major films.

This extraordinary efflorescence created a new vocation, that
of the screenwriter. During the Depression, Hollywood became a
magnet for writers keen to make a new career. Those at some point
employed to craft scripts for the insatiable Hollywood machine
included most of the literary giants of the era: F. Scott Fitzgerald,
William Faulkner, Lillian Hellman and Dorothy Parker. Faulkner
had been working on a fishing boat while writing *The Sound and
the Fury*; now he could pad his bank balance with a six-month
assignment earning 'more money than I have ever seen'. The English
comic writer P. G. Wodehouse paid a visit in 1931 and left 'dazed':
'I cannot see what they engaged me for. They were extremely nice
to me and gave me $104,000 for no reason.'[6] This was all the more
astonishing because the celebrity authors did not always adapt well
to the collective enterprise of screenwriting. Few boasted of their
lucrative efforts or fought for a scriptwriting credit in the finished
product.

Once again, it was left to journalists, less fastidious and more resilient, to fill the breach. Just as they had by penning cheap novels in the nineteenth century, journalists found it easier to apply their facility with words (and their experience of writing as a collective enterprise) to screenwriting.[7] Herman Mankiewicz, Ben Hecht and Billy Wilder were all former journalists who flourished in Hollywood: Hecht is credited with inventing the gangster film, Jean-Luc Godard later saluting him as a genius 'who invented 80 per cent of what is used in Hollywood';[8] Mankiewicz survived working with Orson Welles to secure a screen credit for *Citizen Kane*; Wilder, born Shmuel Vildr, fled Hitler's Germany in 1933, and although English was his fourth language, this did not prevent him from scripting a series of Hollywood classics including *Sunset Boulevard* and *Some Like it Hot*.

The triumph of the movies was the most profound change in recreational culture in modern times, a democratic medium for all ages and all social classes. The knock-on effects had to be severe. As we have seen, newspapers initially feared the lure of radio, and the squeeze on advertising revenue did cause some newspapers to close. The passion for movie going had a disastrous effect on live theatre, so much so that Broadway probably only survived because a high proportion of new plays were underwritten by Hollywood companies looking for new material that could subsequently be filmed. When we couple this with the scriptwriting bonanza, Hollywood appears less of a threat to literature than a huge infusion of new capital.[9]

Libraries, too, could feed off the new media. Demand for books that had been filmed increased exponentially, and the new genre of celebrity biographies brought additional patrons through the library doors. Libraries were also the indirect beneficiaries of the new income streams that gave literary authors like Faulkner the freedom to write full time. Even so, there was no doubting that the library looked staid and conservative alongside the new Leviathans of twentieth-century culture. This was not necessarily to their disadvantage. To many, and not just disconnected intellectuals, change on this scale, and at this pace, was profoundly disorientating. 'Novelties crowd the consciousness of modern man,' wrote the influential media critic Walter Lippmann: 'The press, the radio, the moving picture, have enormously multiplied the number of unseen events and strange people with which he has to be concerned ... He finds it increasingly difficult to believe that through it all there is order, permanence and connecting principle.'[10] Those living in Europe and North America faced innovation in every area of life, not least electrification, with all its concomitant effects on the length of the working day and leisure time. For city dwellers, underground and overground (sometimes overhead) trains dramatised the restless pace of modern life. Technology was empowering, but it also made those who could not afford a fridge or new automobile acutely aware of their inferiority. For those bent on self-improvement, libraries might hold the key, an aspirational goal epitomised by the huge success of Dale Carnegie's *How to Win Friends and Influence People* (1936). To others, libraries were havens of peace in an ever more demanding society, a familiar, reassuring presence.

Libraries also flourished because rising prosperity prevented consumers from having to choose between their modes of entertainment. The library became one more generous amenity in a land of plenty, a reassuringly familiar presence in a whirlwind of the new.[11] Yet the book industry itself was changing, feeding the needs and desires of this voraciously ambitious age. Ironically, for all the fear of the new media, the main challenges to the library came from within the print industry itself, from magazines, book clubs, and the ever greater affordability of books.

Reading in an Age of Consumption

Periodicals had long been a staple of the library, a tradition passed to the public library by the subscription libraries and gentlemen's clubs of the nineteenth century. The titles regularly accessioned included the worthy literary reviews born in the Enlightenment such as *Blackwood's* and the *Edinburgh Review*, a genre refreshed by the gentle humour of newcomers like *Punch*, a British weekly magazine famous for its beautifully drawn topical cartoons.[12] The proliferation of magazines, aimed at all levels of the reading market, posed difficult choices for libraries, particularly as readers insisted

equally on a well-stocked newspaper reading room. Some libraries carried an extraordinary range: in 1897, Whitechapel public
library, in an inner-city area of London, stocked twenty-seven
daily newspapers, seventy-seven weekly periodicals and twenty-
nine monthlies.[13] For many patrons, newspapers and periodicals
were as important a draw as the book stock.

Libraries functioned best when they offered readers what they
could not easily buy for themselves; but the consumer revolution
of the early twentieth century created a more affluent and better-
educated readership who could well afford to purchase their own
recreational reading matter. The publishing industry was revolu-
tionised by the potential of this new market, and in return, helped
mould new reading and buying tastes. Along with bestselling books
that might sell hundreds of thousands of copies, the discerning
reader could now enjoy a range of well-targeted periodicals which
elbowed aside the fusty literary reviews. First came *Reader's Digest*
(1922), a pre-digested miscellany of stories of generally uplifting
content. Then in 1923, Henry Luce launched *Time*, a weekly digest
of political news with punchy, well-illustrated text. This first wave
was completed by the *New Yorker* (1925), a magazine of stylish
variety and puck-like humour, also famous for its dryly ironic cartoons. These were periodicals that were cheap and entertaining
enough to justify taking out a regular subscription, and they soon
found many imitators.

Traditionally the magazine market was littered with optimistic new titles with a short lifespan, but these had staying power.
Time was selling half a million copies by 1934, most subscribers,
significantly, reading it cover to cover. *Esquire* (1933), an upmarket
journal of men's fashion, was selling 700,00 copies a week within
four years.[14] But none would match the extraordinary circulation
of *Life*, a photojournal launched with prescient timing in 1936. Its
superbly framed photographs, chronicling both American life and
the evolving European crisis, had attracted 20 million readers by
1938 (sharing 3 million copies), a figure that represented one in
every five Americans over the age of ten. *Picture Post*, launched in
the wake of *Life* in 1938, would play an equally influential role in
shaping self-perceptions of Britain during the war.

All of these journals, with the partial exception of *Reader's Digest*, were aimed at the growing class of sophisticated urbanites and the new generation of upwardly mobile, often now college-educated householders. They were an advertiser's dream and highly profitable. Meanwhile, established stables of the library reading room, such as the *Literary Digest* or *Scribner's*, withered and died. The *Literary Digest* had 250,000 subscribers when it closed its doors, but virtually no paid advertising. When *Women's World* closed in 1940, it left behind a circulation of 1.5 million, but its wholesome diet of 'home, church and patriotism', served up mostly to women beyond the great metropoles, had little interest to advertisers, and that spelled its end.

The readers of these new upmarket journals were not necessarily buying magazines instead of books. They read the bestsellers and subscribed to *Time* but had no great pretensions to literary taste. As first-generation refugees from small-town America, they enjoyed Sinclair Lewis's sly takedown of the stuffy values of middle America in *Main Street*. But then they, and their wives, equally enjoyed James Hilton's exotic romance, *Lost Horizon*, and *Anthony Adverse* (1933), a rollicking tale of the Napoleonic era.[15]

A feature of these bestselling titles, many of which would top a million sales, is the extent to which they benefited from cross-media promotion. *Lost Horizon* was selling slowly until promoted on a popular radio show. Dale Carnegie's *How to Win Friends and Influence People* took off after a favourable review in *Reader's Digest*. The film version of *Anthony Adverse* garnered four Oscars in 1936, the year *Gone with the Wind* sold 1.5 million copies. These were novels with real staying power – even Zane Grey, the author of a conveyer belt of formulaic novels, would rack up lifetime sales of 19 million.[16]

All told, 110 million copies of books were printed in the United States in 1933, a figure that had more than doubled by 1943. New readers needed help to separate the wheat from the chaff, or at least the talked about from the ignored.[17] This was the role of institutions like the Book of the Month Club (1926) and the more obviously aspirational Literary Guild. These and a host of imitators catering to more niche markets had by 1946 a collective membership of

3 million, and the Book of the Month Club alone distributed 11.5 million books in this year. Its main monthly recommendation was an automatic bestseller: in its heyday the Book of the Month Club exercised a power in the market-place that would only be matched by Oprah's Book Club at the end of the century.[18]

While book clubs provided for the needs of neophyte collectors, bestseller lists, and the cascade of books that could sell hundreds of thousands of copies, reshaped the book market in ways that made it difficult for public libraries to respond. Should they follow popular taste or continue to pursue their improving mission of promoting good literature, at the risk of subjecting their staff to angry patrons, clamouring for the title of the moment? Often, they fell between two schools. In 1935, the St Louis public library had 1,897 copies of the works of Mark Twain and only thirty books by Hemingway. Hemingway, despite his celebrity, had a hard job establishing himself in the public library: in 1933 he lost out to Sinclair Lewis by a margin of 472 copies to thirty in St Louis, and 290 to three in Boston.[19] Buying bulk copies of the current bestsellers depleted budgets and left libraries with the problem of having to dispose of them a few years later to make space for the newly fashionable (a problem that still exercises librarians today). But the failure to cater sufficiently to public taste risked losing readers to commercial rental libraries, which experienced a significant revival during the 1930s. In America this was partly a reaction to the decline of public library budgets in the Depression, but both these commercial libraries and the so-called 'Tuppeny Libraries' in Britain represented a vote of no-confidence, particularly from readers who felt their tastes for detective novels and adventure stories were not well catered for in public institutions.[20]

All this was evident even before the arrival of paperbacks in the 1930s. Here, the most significant milestone was the launch of Penguin Books in 1935, building on the example of a less successful German prototype, Albatross Books. Allen Lane's gamble that he could interest the public in quality books in cheap formats was richly rewarded: the new series, clearly branded with the appealing Penguin and colour coded for genre, sold one million copies within ten months. The model was swiftly imitated by the

American Pocket books, which entered the market in 1939 with an eclectic list of ten titles, all priced at 25 cents, including works by Agatha Christie and Dorothy Parker, along with Thornton Wilder's *Bridge of San Luis Rey* and Hilton's *Lost Horizon*.

Paperbacks posed yet another problem for public libraries, as they were smart enough to be collectable for the home library, but not sufficiently resilient for repeated reading. None of these challenges proved terminal. In the financial year 1961–2, public libraries in the UK spent £6 million on new books, a creditable increase of 10 per cent on the previous year. This represented 9.8 per cent of total domestic book sales. The previous year libraries had recorded 441 million issues, from a total stock of 75 million volumes, an increase of 25 per cent over the past ten years.[21] Public libraries, it was clear, had survived their encounter with competing media, which by the 1960s also included television, seen by many commentators as yet another existential threat. For television offered consumers the best of both worlds: enjoyed, like radio, in the home, with the potent visual appeal of cinema. But again, as with radio, the book world would profit from the obvious crossover opportunities afforded by new editions of books dramatised on television, epitomised by the unlikely success of John Galsworthy's *Forsyte Saga* (1906–21), a set of which would decorate the shelves of millions of homes after a twenty-six-part serialisation by the BBC in 1967. Documentaries and comedy series proved equally lucrative sources of spin-off titles, which boosted the revenues of the BBC and increasingly dominated the UK bestselling lists by the 1980s.[22]

It was not competing media then, but rather the economic tribulation of the 1960s and the oil shocks of the 1970s that squeezed public finances and caused the first sustained downturn in the fortunes of the public library. Opening hours were trimmed, buildings went unrepaired, book budgets declined. At first, public reaction to these economies was muted. Now that libraries were in serious competition with other public services for diminishing funds, many of those who would have been expected to support their case for public funds were no longer regular users. In 1960s Britain, a quarter of the population held a library card, but society's influencers, who preferred to display their neat rows of paperbacks on their living-room shelves to borrowing books, were not those who relied on libraries for their reading material. As the public library movement celebrated its first century, the library reading rooms were already beginning their evolution from an essential institution for the promotion of learning and civilising values, to a branch of the social services.

Enter the Bookmobile

The challenges of new technology were by no means the only concern of library professionals in the first half of the twentieth century. As ever, the contents of the collections – what could be stocked and how much could be afforded – dominated discussions between the growing band of trained library professionals who manned the public library networks of Europe and North America. This was also an era in which, for the first time, librarians systematically addressed the needs of women, children, and citizens who lived outside the metropolitan hubs that had dominated the public library movement in the nineteenth century. Only with female readers were libraries successful in adjusting library provision to patron needs. Libraries struggled to understand the rapidly changing priorities of adolescents and what would later be called teenagers: the urge to offer children what was good for them remained strong. And the challenge to provide adequate library services to far-flung rural communities remained daunting, despite well-intentioned efforts to offer all readers at least some books.

When it came to building library provision for rural areas, America once again leads the story, partly because it had by far the largest rural hinterland of the countries that were approaching universal literacy by the twentieth century. France also had a profound sense of its rural identity, but to some extent evaded the issue by offering villagers access to school libraries. However, for the United States extending library access to the rural hinterland was a task of almost religious importance, a true mission handed down by the Founding Fathers. Alabama club women felt their

26. The bookmobile served a dual role as travelling branch libraries in cities and in delivering library services to rural readers. This picture shows a book van in Tompkins County, in the north-west of New York State, in 1930.

efforts to bring books to the people brought them 'in touch with the spirit of Thomas Jefferson'.[23] Very often, as here, the most imaginative initiatives were pursued by women's clubs and a cohort of pioneering women librarians, in the same way that women propelled the movement to offer more adequate services to younger readers. This was no surprise. As the first generation of male leaders in the library profession passed on, the connections with the urban patriarchal elites were loosened. The consequences of this for the library movement were profound.

The first major initiatives to meet the needs of rural readers came with the establishment of a network of travelling libraries: boxes of around thirty to 100 books sent out to be deposited in post offices, schoolrooms, general stores or even private houses, where they were made available to the local community by volunteer managers. First proposed for upstate New York in 1893, travelling libraries were energetically adopted in Michigan through the advocacy of Mary Spencer, and most famously by Lutie Stearns in

Wisconsin. Elsewhere, as in the Dakotas and Texas, women's clubs in the sparsely populated towns took the lead in promoting travelling libraries. At the time that travelling libraries were established in South Dakota in 1913, 80 per cent of the state's population lived outside the reach of a public library. By 1920, 251 travelling libraries were in circulation, in boxes economically constructed by the state carpenter.[24]

The New York initiative was the work of Melvil Dewey, one of the most influential library leaders of his day, not least through his invention of the Dewey decimal cataloguing system. With characteristic showmanship, Dewey had promised that travelling libraries would offer 'the best reading for the largest number at the least cost'.[25] Arguably, none of these objectives were really feasible. In far-flung tiny communities the scheme inevitably reached comparatively few people, was expensive to run, and the collection of books was too small and infrequently refreshed to represent 'the best reading'. However carefully selected, fewer than one hundred books could not meet the needs of rural communities whose reading interests were no less diverse than those of city dwellers. This was particularly the case when valuable space was consumed with improving literature dealing with 'missions, temperance, good citizenship and Sunday school work', as demanded by the Kansas Travelling Library Commission.[26] One early proponent backed the power of travelling libraries 'to make the libraries and the books the centres of interest in isolated and sordid communities and to bring the people into personal touch with the outer world'.[27] This sort of lofty paternalism often went down poorly with its intended beneficiaries. In the memorable words of one farmer, 'folks down to the State House think because I'm a farmer I want to spend my nights reading about fertilizers'.[28] It turned out that rural readers did not want to be improved, but to be offered some respite from back-breaking work in their hard-won hours of rest.

Each state demanded a different approach. Foreign-language material was essential in areas populated by German or Swedish immigrants, as were sensitivities to the strongly held views of religious communities. The scheme had its successes. 'Perhaps only a pioneer in this vast portion of the west can so fully appreciate the value of even one book', was the generous response of Nellie Vis, of Pennington County, South Dakota, though as her homestead played host to a travelling library, she had access to many more than one. By the 1920s, with the establishment of networks of county libraries, travelling libraries were beginning to be phased out, though they lived on through the Depression in the devastated Plains States. The Depression was a good age generally for libraries, a place of solace in hard times, warm and dry and useful and free. In Los Angeles, after the stock market crash, book circulation rose by 60 per cent and the number of patrons doubled, even though the public library's budget was cut by 25 per cent.[29] Federal funding programmes of the New Deal era also brought some money for libraries, not least the packhorse librarians' unit established by the Works Progress Administration (WPA) to serve mountain communities in Kentucky in 1936: a service that might well have been more useful for photo opportunities than as a real public amenity.

By this time the birth of the automobile era had brought new, more cost-efficient opportunities to serve the needs of rural readers. This was applying new technology to refresh an older idea: the first bookmobile was a horse-drawn wagon of books which travelled around Washington County, Maryland, in 1905.[30] The provision of a book van allowed the system to reach far more readers, since it carried far more books than the single book box of the travelling library, and was not anchored to one place. And whereas the travelling library box remained static until being returned to the library, often months later, the bookmobile could bring along requested books the following week. The travelling librarian, assisted by the driver in two-person teams, could also pop in a few extra titles that they knew might interest regular clients – and most patrons of this service were regulars. This was also a service that was strongly orientated towards women, who could break off their chores when the bookmobile arrived. The bookmobile staff became as much a friend as the travelling butcher, fishmonger or general store.

The bookmobile soon became as familiar a sight throughout the United States as the mobile library in rural England, driving into small communities, once a week on the appointed day,

27. Where the bookmobile could not reach, there were packhorses. Here four
packhorse librarians are pictured in the Appalachian Mountains (1937).

through the middle decades of the twentieth century.[31] In places
like Texas, the bookmobile represented the only practical means
to meet the needs of citizens spread over a vast, sparsely populated
territory. The first Texas bookmobile, in 1930, carried about 1,400
volumes; the New Deal WPA project provided another thirty-
three bookmobiles. The bookmobile movement crested in Texas,
as elsewhere, in the post-war years. Despite this, the rural library

service remained poor, exacerbated by the flight to the cities caused by the growing Texas oil boom. Ironically, it was Cold War anxieties of Soviet technological superiority that spurred a concerted effort to improve library provision in rural areas through the Library Services Act of 1956. As the state librarian put it, one hopes with more opportunism than conviction, 'In library books, as well as guided missiles, the United States lags behind other countries of the world. An informed, enlightened, intelligent and alert America is really essential to our defense and freedom.'[32]

The truculence of the Cold War era also made trouble for the evangelicals of library provision. Not all citizens welcomed the bookmobile, as became clear when, in 1950, the Wisconsin Library Board established an experimental service for the two rural counties of Door and Kewaunee. To those involved the initiative was a huge success, but after the two-year trial period, continuation was narrowly rejected in a local referendum. Children had embraced the scheme, accounting for 88 per cent of the borrowings; but children do not vote, and adults were more sceptical, particularly the men, who were usually off at work when the bookmobile dropped by.[33] Many rural voters disapproved of public spending on non-essentials such as books, and worried about the books pressed into their children's hands. This extended equally to school libraries. The list of recommended texts regularly issued by state boards were carefully scrutinised by parent groups, which campaigned vociferously against those of which they disapproved. Catholic schools, which were not taxpayer supported, chose their own library content. The 1942 edition of the influential *Standard Catalogue for High School Libraries* included annotations against seventy titles which stated that these were not recommended for Catholic schools. They included Daphne du Maurier's *Rebecca*, and *Westward Ho!* by Charles Kingsley (presumably anathema because the sixteenth-century English sailor hero was tortured by his Spanish jailors in a vain attempt to persuade him to convert to Catholicism).[34]

Bookmobiles were phased out entirely in Texas in the 1970s. But there were still over a thousand operating in the United States in 2015, and 650 in 2018.[35] This remains a popular form of library service in many parts of the developing world: in India and South

East Asia, Kenya and Trinidad, as well as north European countries like Norway and Finland with large rural hinterlands.[36] By the last third of the twentieth century, the mobile library had become a very visible symbol of the globalisation of library culture. The Biblioburro donkey library of Colombia, the iRead mobile library of Nigeria and BiebBussen (converted shipping containers) are only the most colourful examples of the ingenuity of the library profession in bringing books and information services to widely dispersed and economically disadvantaged communities.[37] Whether they will survive the shift to worldwide digital access is an open question; for the moment, readers continue to welcome their regular visits, not least those of the BookyMcBookFace library on the islands of Orkney, also a popular Twitter phenomenon with 70,000 followers.

Keeping Up with the Kids

Given how important children have become in these diverse modern-day library services, it is strange to recall that it was only in the twentieth century that the needs of young readers began to be systematically addressed by library professionals.[38] Part of the problem was deciding what children were, and whether they should even by allowed through the door. Nineteenth-century libraries concentrated most of their attention on young adults, principally young men embarking on the first steps of a profession or career in trade. The network of Mechanics' Institutes and mercantile libraries that sprang up across the US and western Europe offered these young men a range of lectures, reading material and opportunities to build personal connections for their professional lives. Many of these institutions, as we have seen, built library collections of very considerable size.

The success of the mercantile libraries presented the new public libraries with one compelling model of how to serve younger patrons, though not necessarily a helpful one. Many of the posed pictures of the newly opened children's rooms in public libraries show a sprinkling of sober young men and some girls, all rather formally dressed, the young men complete with jacket and tie like junior bank clerks on their lunch break. The atmosphere of studious silence depicted here was a great deal more attractive to library trustees than to actual children. Noise, running in the stairs, grubby fingers damaging books: all posed a threat to the good order and decorum expected if the library was to function as an extension of the Victorian family. Some American libraries responded by placing the children's room next to the entrance, so young readers would have no need to stray further into the building. In Britain, many libraries banned children under the age of twelve altogether.[39]

There was indeed a serious debate to be had over whether public libraries were the most appropriate place to nurture the habit of reading. Legislation mandating compulsory primary education brought an ever higher proportion of the populations of the major industrial nations into the schoolroom, where they would be taught reading and arithmetic. Here, teachers could guide the developing reading taste of their young charges. As we have seen, this was the path followed more or less systematically in France, where the public libraries remained repositories of their mouldering revolutionary inheritance of antiquarian books.

The first children's library was not opened in France until 1924. Instead, considerable effort was devoted to ensuring that all primary and secondary schools had a collection of books. While these school libraries doubtlessly played a key role in helping many children make the first steps in imaginative reading, the drawbacks of relying exclusively on the schoolroom were clear. Some schoolteachers were reluctant librarians, and libraries would be closed during school holidays. There was a danger too, that for many children books would always be associated with the humiliations and punishments of the schoolroom. Most of all, the collections were too small. Though successive French ministers of education made heroic efforts to persuade local authorities to provide books for every school, these collections were only intermittently refreshed. The books became dog-eared through overuse, and for the avid reader, soon utterly insufficient. While some secondary schools, especially the privileged English independent schools, built extensive library collections, it was soon evident that schools could not bear this burden alone.

The public libraries therefore took up the charge, with a greater or lesser degree of reluctance. Some blessed with empathetic and energetic librarians (often female) built collections of real merit, helped in this by a rapid expansion of writing for young adults. These adventure stories help draw the youthful reader away from the sort of disapproved gore and sensation that had populated the lower rungs of the nineteenth-century penny-dreadful market-place.[40] Even so, libraries remained intimidating and unattractive to many children, too redolent of the schoolroom to be a first choice for valued leisure time. To obtain a library card one needed the sponsorship of a parent, and libraries generally discouraged children from browsing the shelves. Borrowing a book required exposing your choice to a formidable and probably disapproving adult; the brittle confidence of a young person exercising independent judgement was easily bruised, and a rebuff might militate against a return visit. It was, in the last resort, far more fun to read one of the many boys' or girls' magazines, available for a few pence and easily traded with school friends. These children's papers, with their recurring characters and stories continued from week to week, were well adapted to a few minutes of reading on the street corner. For many children, the library was far more relevant to their parents' aspirations than their own fast-changing world.

We must at least give credit to local councils and library boards for opening their doors to children and allocating an increasing amount of resources to children's books. There was a danger, however, that while embracing children they were losing young adults. By the first half of the twentieth century the Mechanics' Institutes and mercantile libraries had lost their crucial role in the educative and social world of the professional classes. Many closed their doors; others merged their collections with other libraries. Changing patterns of work were partly responsible for their decline, but larger social changes also played their role. The first half of the twentieth century was particularly challenging for young adults, and those recognised, in the new psychology, as adolescents. The First World War, the Depression and the Second World War were all crises in which young adults bore the brunt of decisions taken by their elders.[41] Many lost their jobs, their lives, or suffered life-changing mental and physical injuries. Children,

28. Children enjoy themselves in a reading room at the public library in Buffalo, New York (*c.*1900). Few children were lucky enough to find a dedicated room for their interests before the First World War.

too, found themselves in the front line, through bombing or, in the case of the child soldiers of the Third Reich, pressed into service to man the defences. By the end of 1933, 3 million had joined the Hitler Youth, a figure that grew to 8 million when membership became compulsory for boys over the age of ten. Totalitarian regimes controlled every area of the child's life from the school-room to quasi-military exercises, including the cinema and reading matter. Even a sedentary, herbivorous occupation like stamp col-lecting was not safe from ideological appropriation, as with the denunciation of British imperial oppression illustrated by stamps of all the British colonies. The public libraries of Germany were so thoroughly Nazified that at war's end half of the surviving stock was deemed unfit for the transition to democracy.

Reading could be dangerous, as the First World War had already demonstrated. A seventeen-year-old working-class Londoner, Vic Cole, could not wait to enlist: 'I wanted to be in the army with gun in hand like the boys I had so often read about in books and magazines'.[42] The young men of France and Germany hurtled with equal fervour towards the front, and died in the barbed wire of no man's land. Disillusionment brought a retreat from ideology and a plunge into hedonism. The depleted generation of the 1920s found jobs easily; with money to spend, consumerism offered them a route to social inclusion in societies still stratified by class and education. Clothes, the cinema and the dance hall became the new markers of peer respect, pursued with a fervour that paid little attention to the largely discredited parental ideologies of discipline and self-restraint. In the 1930s, 28 million American adolescents visited cinemas at least weekly. Europe embraced the new heroes of Hollywood with equal passion. And this was a pattern of living that, for the first time, embraced young women from working-class backgrounds on equal terms. In 1933, a young English shop girl set out her weekly budget, significantly in a letter to a film magazine.

> Wages 32 *s*[hillings] – Board and lodging 25*s* 2*d* – Saturday visit to cinema 1*d* [one penny] – Monday visit 7*d* – Thursday visit 7*d* – that makes 27*s* 2*d*. Then there is threepence for *Film Weekly* and three shillings for dress allowance ... When I get a rise in salary, I shall be able to afford another night at the pictures.[43]

The Depression put something of a dent in this consumer boom: to the young adult now deprived of the keys to consumer society it was, in the words of one middle-class youngster, like being 'de-princed'. War conditions would revive the reading habits of the adult population, but the young were harder to convince. Called into factory work aged as young as fourteen, girls and women left alone on the home front shaped consumer choice. Of twenty-seven city girls surveyed for a pioneering survey of *Girls Growing Up* in 1941, few read books. Wages were laid out on cosmetics and romance magazines like *Girls' Crystal* and *Glamour*.[44] Dancing and going to the pictures were overwhelmingly the entertainments of choice: the radio was tolerated only when it was playing dance music. To a large extent, the young people of the war generation were taking their cues from contemporaries, rather than from their elders. The generation that witnessed exponential growth in high school education (there was an eightfold increase in high school graduates between 1914 and 1939 in America) had also grown minds of their own. 'Keeping up with the kids' was a problem to which libraries, with their stiff civic virtues and ruling committees of local worthies, were not well attuned. Gratefully they turned their attention to shipping out books to the boys at the front. This at least they understood, while their own boisterous, independent young were increasingly a mystery.

The Power of Love

When in 1937 Penguin Books launched its non-fiction strand, Pelican, the first title was George Bernard Shaw's *The Intelligent Woman's Guide to Socialism, Capitalism, Sovietism and Fascism.* This, as the title suggests, was a controversial choice. When first published in 1929, as Shaw's response to his sister-in-law's request for a pamphlet explaining Socialism, it provoked an immediate and blistering reply from a reader who objected to its patronising tone: Lilian Le Mesurier's *Socialist Woman's Guide to Intelligence.*[45] The point was well made, but not enough to discourage Allen Lane from the Pelican reprint, updated to reflect the new threats of the era.

In fairness to Shaw, it must be noted that condescending attitudes in the literary world were not uniquely male, as rural readers found to their cost in the urgent evangelism of the promoters of travelling book libraries. But it remained the case that in the early years of the public library movement, librarians and legislators did not quite know how to accommodate the needs of female patrons. The early public libraries had been shaped by a model established by institutions of male sociability and professional education: the subscription library, the Mechanics' Institute and the university. The women of these urban elites had seemed largely content with their own parallel structures, and their book clubs played a vital role in promoting the establishment of public libraries outside the main metropolitan centres. The public library movement was initially far more concerned with issues of class than gender, integrating the expanding working class into the civilising pleasures of reading.

Nevertheless, a good proportion of the first generation of public libraries in England were supplied with a separate ladies' reading room. This was not generally the case in the United States, and there is no clear indication of why Britain chose to go in a different direction. It may in part have been a response to an argument made during parliamentary debate on the 1850 Public Libraries Act, that ladies might be deterred from using the library by the malodorous company in the main reading room. If so, this was an expensive way to parry one of the ragbag of claims made on behalf of a losing cause.

There is no evidence that English women lobbied for separate accommodation, but they must have been pleasantly surprised by what they found. The ladies' room in the library of Hull, Yorkshire, was 'finished in walnut with comfortable tables and chairs, while in the chimney piece is a fine piece of beautifully figured onyx'.[46] This offered a fair approximation of the imagined drawing room of a middle-class home, and suggests that ladies' reading rooms were not expected to play a significant role in the 1850 Act's avowed intent of encouraging reading among the 'lower orders'. The reading rooms were also supplied with a very decent range of periodicals. Some, like *Queen, Gentlewoman, Lady's Pictorial, Lady* and *Lady's Realm*, would only appear in the ladies' reading room; others would have to be duplicated in the general reading room. A significant number of titles, such as *The Englishwoman's Review* and suffragette titles, were probably donated.[47] Interestingly, it was generally not thought necessary to supply the ladies' room with newspapers.

It is striking that in the United States, where women's groups played such an important role in promoting public libraries, ladies' rooms were very uncommon. The model designs provided by the Carnegie Foundation for small town and branch libraries sometimes made room for a children's room, but no separate accommodation for women. In Dunfermline, Carnegie's prototype in Scotland, the library opened with a generously proportioned ladies' room, but in the first refit this disappeared to make room for a children's room. This proved to be a general pattern. There were strong arguments against duplication of resources, not least periodicals, in segregated reading rooms. But the most pressing reason for the disappearance of separate ladies' accommodation was the need to create a room for children in buildings where there were usually neither funds nor space for a significant extension. The removal of ladies' rooms in British libraries took place mostly in the two decades before and after the 1919 Public Libraries Act, which made possible a significant extension of library provision into the shire counties. It is probably not a coincidence that this is also when women were granted the vote in Britain, and when the library profession was becoming increasingly feminised: a consequence of women filling the places of men drafted into the armed forces during the First World War. The 'gentleman's agreement' that they would immediately vacate these positions on war's end was far less scrupulously observed in librarianship than in other professions.[48]

The new generation of female librarians directed much of their efforts to organising children's reading rooms, as had their colleagues across the Atlantic. Here, as in curating the stock of the adult library, female librarians were also every bit as likely to uphold the wholesome values of improving literature. The influence of Christian publishing remained strong, not least because so much of the book and periodical stock was provided by donation. There were also significant external pressures, prejudices strongly articulated by Sir Frederick Banbury, MP for the City of London, on the debate on the Public Libraries Act of 1919:

> My experience is that public libraries are places where, if the weather is cold, people go in and sit down and get warm, while other people go in to read novels. I do not believe, generally speaking, that public libraries have done any good. On the contrary, they have done a great deal of harm, because the books read, as far as my information goes, are chiefly sensational novels, which do no good to anybody.[49]

It was too late at this stage to turn back the tide on fiction.[50] But this did not mean that librarians, on either side of the Atlantic, were any less convinced of their obligation to distinguish good literature from works that had no place in a public library collection. The American Library Association had issued its first list of texts appropriate for the core collection of a public library in 1893. This had some surprising omissions on grounds of taste, excluding some genuinely literary texts such as Stephen Crane's *The Red Badge of Courage*. Successive editions of this list, relied on very heavily by smaller libraries, offer a barometer of American taste and propriety.[51]

In the first half of the twentieth century, public libraries would only go so far in stocking books outside the literary canon, unless consecrated by large sales and consequent high demand from patrons for particular titles. But the books many women wished to read did not fall into this category. These readers sought a particular genre, light, sentimental tales of love, yearning, heartbreak and reconciliation, all in the space of 250 pages: romance. This was the sort of book that found few advocates in the public libraries, so instead they looked elsewhere, to commercial subscription libraries, and to an unlikely pair of champions, Gerald Mills and Charles Boon.

The firm of Mills & Boon was established in 1908 as a general fiction publisher by two disgruntled employees of the publishing house Methuen. It sailed along in the slipstream of the publishing giants, without achieving consistent profits, until in the 1930s it established the niche market that would make Mills & Boon a famous name as a publisher of romance.[52] Charles Boon, the driving force after the death of his partner in 1928, found the formula for success: a large list of titles, published in a uniform, highly recognisable format, distinctive brown bindings and highly coloured jackets. By 1939, Mills & Boon had 450 novels in print, all published in editions of 3,000 to 8,000 copies. Most of all, Boon had discovered the golden secret of brand loyalty. The endpapers of their novels in the 1930s ended not with a puff for other particular titles but with a recommendation of the whole list:

The Fiction Market is overburdened with new novels, and the ordinary reader finds it most difficult to choose the right type of story either to buy or to borrow. Really the only way to choose is to limit your reading to those publishers whose lists are carefully selected, and whose fiction imprint is a sure guarantee of good reading. Mills & Boon issue a strictly limited Fiction List, and the novels they publish all possess real story-telling qualities of an enduring nature.[53]

To many inexperienced readers, bewildered by the cornucopia poured out before them, this was excellent advice.

Many readers of romance consumed voraciously, a book every three days. Until the 1960s, Mills & Boon published exclusively in hardback, and at 7s 6d their titles would have been beyond the means of many readers of romance. Readers turned instead to the commercial libraries, enjoying something of a renaissance in the interwar period. Whereas the 'tuppenny libraries' catered mostly to the taste of less affluent readers, the established giant W. H. Smith offered a wide range of literature, including light recreational fiction. In 1898, it was joined by a new competitor, the Boots Booklovers Library, a venture that would outlast both Smith's and the ailing Mudie's (which closed its doors in 1937).[54]

Boots Booklovers Library was the inspiration of Florence Boot, the wife of the founder of the well-known chain of pharmacy stores. At its zenith, libraries would be attached to around 460 of their branches. In the 1950s, Boots issued approximately 50 million books a year to its members, for whom subscriptions started at 10s 6d a year.[55] This was good value for the overwhelmingly female subscribers who, though they preferred not to rub shoulders with the more diverse clientele of the public library reading rooms, still had to cope with a strict domestic budget.

There is something very appropriate about the synergy of a book club with a pharmacy, always through history the repository of a community's secrets. Arriving at the book club service desk, members would be ushered through to a discreet book-lined reading room, where they would be able to browse undisturbed and unobserved except by other members. It was a winning formula, both for the members and for Mills & Boon, who relied on the book clubs for the disposal of a high proportion of their first printing. Boots would normally take between 300 and 500 copies of each title, and wholesalers like Argosy and Sundial took 700 for distribution to the tuppenny libraries. A Mills & Boon for tuppence a time was possible for many working-class housewives, and the sturdy brown books could survive the attentions of many readers. On average, a Mills & Boon novel would be issued 165 times, though one Taunton proprietor recorded 740 borrowers for a 1935 title, *Anchor at Hazard*.

Romance also made money for its authors, many of them romance readers who had decided to try their hand at writing. Mills & Boon promised they would read any script submitted to them, a pledge that brought in some of their most prolific writers. Mary Burchell, who wrote forty-one novels, netted around £1,000 per annum, a considerable sum that could be further augmented by serialisation in the weekly women's magazines. This was lucrative work, but demanding. Editors made clear what they wanted. According to one Mills & Boon author, editors at the Dundee firm D. C. Thomson, publishers of *My Weekly* and *The People's Friend*, ran a tight ship. 'If at the end of Chapter Three [the heroine] had had a second sherry, I would get a telegram saying, "Cut out the sherry".'[56]

Mills & Boon authors earned a good living but no celebrity: an average reader would have no idea who had written the book they had just finished. They bought the brand rather than a bestselling name like Barbara Cartland, a giant in the romance industry, who never wrote for Mills & Boon. In contrast, Mills & Boon authors were actively encouraged to write under a variety of different aliases. This helped circumvent the rule of the Boots Booklovers Library that only two books by the same author could be bought in any year.

In the 1960s, the circulating libraries faded in importance, not least because public libraries were gradually yielding to pressure from their readers to stock more romantic fiction. The death of the circulating libraries (Smith's in 1961 and Boots in 1966) led to an adjustment of the Mills & Boon business model, and in 1958 they made a tentative step into the paperback market. This proved hugely successful: in 1992, Mills & Boon still held a dominant market share as a publisher of romantic fiction, a staggering 85 per cent of the market. The paperbacks were initially intended for the North American market, distributed by Harlequin, a Toronto-based company founded in 1949. By 1964, the company was publishing exclusively novels originated by Mills & Boon, and in 1971 Harlequin bought the company outright. By 1982, Harlequin were selling 182 million copies a year.[57]

In December 1979, the American academic Janice Radway made contact with Dorothy Evans, author of an influential newsletter review of romantic fiction. Evans introduced Radway to a group of her subscribers who were prepared to share their experiences of romantic fiction and explain the part it played in their lives. To some, reading was something of a guilty pleasure: moments stolen from household chores while the children were at school. Husbands sometimes resented them reading. But prodded and encouraged by others in the group, the subscribers revealed themselves as both fierce defenders of the romance genre and demanding in their expectations.

Romantic fiction works to a formula: an independently minded female protagonist encounters a flawed but ultimately impressive man. Having paid good money for their hard-won escape from the stresses of the everyday, readers require their expectations to be fulfilled. They resent authors or publishers playing tricks, such as clothing a book that does not obey the conventions of this form of literature in a standard romance cover. Sudden plot shifts and surprising revelations are deplored. The death of the heroine is inconceivable. The happy ending may be pre-ordained, but readers expect a gradual progress to mutual understanding between the heroine and the initially brusque or disdainful hero.

Readers often insulated themselves from unpleasant surprises by re-reading old favourites. Sometimes, to make sure a new title would suit, readers read the ending first. Of course, it is much easier to have a peep towards the back in a library than under the disapproving eye of a bookseller. It is also easier to abandon an unsatisfactory story if money has not been expended on it in the first place. Libraries have now made their peace with romance. Online articles offer library staff advice on how to promote romance titles, usually prominently displayed in their own sections of shelves or bespoke stands.[58] Go into any branch library and you will see the familiar paperback livery of Mills & Boon or Harlequin, borrowed by the handful by a devoted, and now somewhat older clientele, to be exchanged for another bundle the following week.[59]

Romance has never attracted much admiration or attention from literary critics, yet in one respect it represents a remarkable triumph for female agency, pursued with the dogged devotion of the novels' own plucky heroines, in the face of critical and official disdain. The romance would eventually emerge triumphant as libraries realised they need the readers of romances as much as the readers need the libraries. Millions of regular readers now rely increasingly on libraries for a rapid turnover of titles. And libraries, fearful of constant retrenchment, are grateful for any clients who continue to come through their doors.

CHAPTER EIGHTEEN

LIBRARIES, BOOKS AND POLITICS

All libraries are the product of a process of judicious selection. This we take for granted as a natural part of library building, a constant throughout the history of collecting. On the other hand, external constraints defining what books are acceptable and what books should be censored are generally deplored. In the astute observation of the historian Robert Darnton, the difficulty of the issue of censorship is 'that it looks so simple: it pits the children of light against the children of darkness'.[1] So it bears emphasis that throughout the twentieth century, issues of selection, discrimination and exclusion continued to preoccupy the library world, from the first lists of recommended content issued to libraries by their national library associations at the beginning of the century, to the Patriot Act in 2001. This Act required libraries in the United States to provide the department of Homeland Security with access to readers' borrowing cards on request.[2] Over the course of the twentieth century the library community sometimes resisted official interference, while at other times the views of librarians have coincided with the prevailing orthodoxy. Whatever the case, librarians have never doubted their vocation to shape the contents of their collections, and with that to mould public taste.

Censorship was most acute in totalitarian states, but we see many instances also in western democracies and in the emerging library cultures of the developing world. The problems of discrimination, choice and official interference were as acute in the second half of the twentieth century as at any point in history. Living in the shadow of nuclear annihilation, libraries could provide either a respite from everyday worries, or a storehouse of ideological reinforcement for the verities of East or West. These were difficult times for those charged with building, curating and preserving library collections; not least in demonstrating their continued relevance to societies where citizens sat glued to their television screens as the world teetered on the brink of nuclear catastrophe. The proper role of books in banishing anxiety or promoting patriotism were issues of particular contemporary urgency, but they had their roots in the unresolved tensions between private desires and public duty, laid bare by the ideological confrontations of the twentieth century. To many, censorship was not a dirty word, but the defence of essential values relentlessly threatened by sedition, bad literature and the weak curation of public library collections.

Big Bill

On the night of Sunday 8 October 1871, a fire began in Chicago that would change the face of the city. At this point Chicago was fast emerging as one of the wonders of the new industrial world, a nodal point of the transcontinental transport network and the food distribution centre of a hungry continent. A tough city, and magnet for immigrants from all over Europe, the wealth of the Chicago elite was nevertheless expended to supply the customary accoutrements of metropolitan sophistication: churches and civil buildings, the Chicago Academy of Sciences, the Chicago Historical Society (home to a collection of more than 165,000 books) and the Illinois Library Association. The fire, which raged unchecked through all of Monday, swept all of this away, along with 17,450 homes, rendering 95,000 people homeless. Almost incidental to this enormous human suffering were the losses to the libraries: contemporary estimates, incorporating fifty fine private libraries, suggested losses of up to 3 million volumes, and this may be conservative. The lost stock of the Chicago booksellers was valued at $1 million. The premises of the publishers of nine daily newspapers and over a hundred periodicals were also laid waste.[3]

The extinction of Chicago, through this single savage act of fate, touched off an enormous wave of sympathy on both sides of the Atlantic. English efforts focused on the creation of a new free public library for Chicago, something which to this point had been lacking. The campaign, chaired by Thomas Hughes, a member of parliament and the author of *Tom Brown's Schooldays*, gathered 8,000 books, with donations from Prime Minister Gladstone, his great adversary Benjamin Disraeli and Queen Victoria. Disraeli's presence in the list of sponsors is particularly noteworthy, since as a popular author he had suffered grievously from the American disregard for British copyright law. All the English donations were accompanied by a neat book label making reference to this humane act of solidarity, all the more remarkable since England was simultaneously contributing to the reconstruction of the Strasbourg library after German bombardment. The books proved a great success with Chicago's library-goers, and especially collectors of book plates, since of the original 8,000 books only 300 now survive; unless as the first historian of the library tactfully suggests, they were all 'worn out in general use'.[4]

If these proud Victorians patriarchs thought they had earned the lasting gratitude of the citizens of Chicago, they had reckoned without Big Bill Thompson. A vehement critic of prohibition and proud friend of the gangster Al Capone, Big Bill blazed an eccentric trail through Chicago politics as the city's mayor. Forced out of office once, in 1927 Big Bill planned his comeback with a novel rallying cry. Should the King of England visit Chicago, he pledged, Big Bill would punch him on the nose. The inoffensive George V had no plans to visit the United States, so the threat was somewhat moot, but the pledge struck a sufficient chord with Chicago's electorate and Big Bill returned triumphant to City Hall.[5]

King George's nose remained intact, but Mayor Thompson's one-sided feud was not over. He now announced that the city library must be purged of pro-British literature. Since the mayor was simultaneously engaged on hounding out of office the supervisor of schools, this task was delegated to one of his appointees, Urbine 'Sport' Herrmann. The director of the public library, Carl Roden, offered only tepid resistance. Noting that identifying all books expressing anti-American sentiment would be a huge task, he offered instead to remove them from general circulation to the safety of the library's closed reserve. In the event, the books were saved by Herrmann's indolence. Having checked out four books

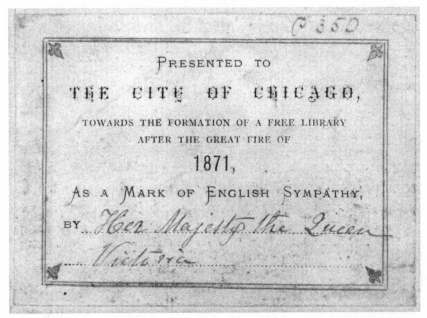

29. The generosity of the English nation after the Great Fire of Chicago of 1871 was memorialised in these elegant bookplates. Many were appropriated by collectors before Big Bill Thompson turned his fire on the remainder.

flagged up by the Patriots League, he found the task of locating the offensive passages beyond his capacities, and tamely returned them the following day.

This and subsequent attempts to purge the Chicago library collection emphasised the need for a more robust statement of the library's commitment to free speech.[6] The result was a terse document, drafted by the American Library Association, rather sententiously titled the Library Bill of Rights, affirming first and foremost the librarian's inalienable right to choose what books should enter the collection. Published in 1939, as storm clouds gathered over Europe, and revised frequently since, it offered a fragile defence for the idea that libraries should be the sanctuary for literature representing all strands of opinion. Not all librarians were destined to be the heroic defenders of this principle. Carl Roden, who had frankly acknowledged in 1927 that he would surrender disapproved books if ordered to do so, was the following year elected chair of the ALA. His colleague, Frederick Rex of the

Chicago municipal reference library, went one better, personally purging the collection of all material of a pro-British character. Now, he announced proudly, 'I have an America-First Library'.[7]

After 1945, the speedy dissipation of the euphoria of victory, and the onset of Cold War anxieties, created a toxic environment for librarians. In 1950, Ruth Brown, the long-serving librarian of Bartlesville, Oklahoma, was dismissed, ostensibly for harbouring subversive material in her collection, in reality because she made no secret of her sympathy for the local African-American community.[8] The ALA made little attempt to save her; apparently the matter fell between the jurisdiction of two of its committees, the Intellectual Freedom Committee and the Board on Personnel Administration. Most of the ALA's energies were at this point directed to fending off the implications of President Truman's introduction of a loyalty oath for those in public service. With evidence that senior officials had been involved in trading nuclear secrets to Russia, news that the Soviets had the atom bomb and the outbreak of the Korean War, most citizens saw no problem in asking public figures to give assurance of their loyalty to American values.[9] When the Los Angeles county librarian was slow to sign the pledge, one library commissioner wondered aloud whether 'our librarian ... is free of those liberal thoughts that we don't like in the head of our library'.[10]

The loyalty pledge split the ALA, with some influential figures supporting it. In truth, while some librarians were bold ambassadors for plurality, most reflected the wider values of the communities they served, and in the age of Joe McCarthy, paranoia over Communist infiltration was rampant. In a 1958 survey, two thirds of librarians acknowledged an instance when controversy about a book or author resulted in a decision not to buy. This rather bears out the jaundiced conclusion that librarians insisted on 'stereotypes of democratic freedom of expression and diversity of opinion' but counted 'with close attention the political costs of exercising those rights in their own institutions'. It was left to that unlikely liberal President Eisenhower to calm the waters, advising the graduating class at Dartmouth not to join the book burners. 'Do not be afraid to go into your library and read every book, so long as any document does not offend our own ideas of decency.'[11]

Where the boundaries of decency lay, was of course a matter of debate, one that in the United States would be decided (or not) by the nine august gentlemen of the Supreme Court. Forced to uphold or quash bans on printed material that would certainly not have been welcome in their own homes, they decided that Congress could only ban material 'utterly without redeeming social importance', or in other words, 'whether to the average person, applying contemporary community standards, the dominant theme of the material taken as a whole appeals to the prurient interest'. Such judicial equivocation counted for nothing against citizen activism, still strong in the Kennedy years. In 1961, both *Catcher in the Rye* and Steinbeck's classic *Of Mice and Men* came under sustained attack by parent groups; *1984* and *Brave New World* were removed from high school reading lists in Florida on the strength of one anonymous phone call.[12]

While the Supreme Court hummed and hawed, in Britain the issue of censorship on the grounds of indecency was effectively settled in six days of comedy at the High Court in London.[13] When in 1960, Penguin Books announced their intention to publish D. H. Lawrence's *Lady Chatterley's Lover*, they had the very good fortune to be charged under the Obscene Publications Act. D. H. Lawrence had obtained considerable celebrity in the 1920s for his dark depiction of working-class life, though his reputation had declined steadily since, thanks in no small measure to Stella Gibbons' cheerful parody of dark, brooding bucolic characters in *Cold Comfort Farm*.[14] *Lady Chatterley's Lover* had never been published in Britain in an unexpurgated version, and the diminishing band of those who wished to read its graphic tale of the bored wife of a war-wounded landowner's affair with her husband's gamekeeper had to source an edition published in Paris or Florence. Now the cream of literary London lined up to testify to its towering literary merit; to no one's surprise, there were few willing to take to the witness stand to testify that they had been debauched and depraved by reading the book. When prosecution counsel invited the jury to consider whether this was a book they would wish their wives and servants to read, the game was up: the defence of the book was now a defence of modern Britain. Penguin was acquitted and within a month had an edition of 200,000 copies on the street. This was the most widely publicised book publication until the Harry Potter series, and the edition sold out in two days. The trial is widely credited with having helped usher in the era of permissiveness sometimes badged the Swinging Sixties. Even so, it would be another eleven years before E. M. Forster's *Maurice*, a semi-autobiographical tale of homosexual love, first written in 1913–14, found its way into print.

The issue of segregation in the American South posed the greatest challenge to the American Library Association, and one it conspicuously failed to meet. The southern states had always lagged behind the rest of America in the provision of public libraries, and the vast majority would not admit black patrons. Those who presented themselves at their counters would be brusquely shown the door.[15] In many jurisdictions the already discredited principle of 'separate but equal' was further dishonoured by the provision of a single, badly equipped building in the black quarter, often paid for by philanthropic donation. Desegregation came slowly to the libraries of the American South.[16] It is a story which reflected no great credit on anyone in authority during the period, not least the American Library Association, which consistently put professional solidarity (not to say an easy life) over any attempt to enforce social justice for African-American readers.

In the ALA, segregation was largely a silent subject. In 1959, it was decided 'not to take any action on the question'. The chair of the Intellectual Freedom Committee reported with exasperation, 'I am personally much concerned over the efforts of a few people to make an issue where there is none.' In March 1960 the society declared that it could not 'intrude on local jurisdiction'. An editorial in the society's *Bulletin* later that year stated that the ALA 'exists to further the development of libraries, not to regulate the manner in which they are operated'.[17]

In fairness, all of these statements were contested, with an increasing sense of outrage, by rank and file members of the ALA. But it would be a long hard struggle to obtain acceptance, even when the libraries of the south reluctantly opened their doors to black patrons. What that eventual transformation meant to young black men and women can be summed up in the story of Eric Motley, a precocious child brought up in Madison Park, a close-knit community founded by formerly enslaved people outside Montgomery, Alabama. In 1985, when Eric was twelve, his father began driving him up to the city each Saturday to spend the day in the library. One day he found himself sitting next to a fragile-looking old man in a wheelchair. This was George Wallace, former governor, former presidential candidate, and the symbol in the 1960s of southern white opposition to desegregation. A few years earlier, Eric would not have been able to enter the library.[18]

Gulags of the Mind

In May 1961, at the height of the Cold War, an excited group of American librarians were given an extensive tour of the Russian library system. No expense was spared, and they were duly impressed.

> The number and size of bookstores in the USSR, and the number of customers – not window shoppers – per square inch are as impressive as the number of libraries and their patrons. Ninety million books are reported to be sold annually in Moscow alone, through 170 major bookstores and 340 bookstands.[19]

Visiting carefully selected public libraries, the American visitors noted the long opening hours, the presence of volunteer assistants in every department, and the high rate of occupancy in reading rooms. True, the correspondent was disappointed by the absence of recent American literature on the shelves, and the physical surroundings were spartan by American standards. But clearly, the delegation had been impressed by the carefully choreographed display. 'Yes, Ivan reads' was the excited first report penned on the flight back from Moscow.

It is doubtful whether many Soviet citizens would have shared this particular pair of rose-tinted spectacles. All western visitors acknowledged that this was a nation of readers: every Russian they encountered on buses, in the metro, or taking the air in the park, seemed to have their heads deep in a book or newspaper. And the crowds at the bookstores were genuine. Yet at the same time, many Soviet citizens complained that there was nothing to read.[20] Authors tolerated by the state provided dull, cautious fare. This could stand for those not only in the USSR, but in its unwilling satellites, in Poland, Hungary, Czechoslovakia and Communist East Germany (the DDR).

Nonetheless, they read. The key to this paradox lies in the fact that, even in highly controlled societies, reading is an individual activity. Reading offered escape from the pressures of the everyday, not least of crowded home living space. It also offered a means of establishing some sort of intellectual autonomy, in a life where every step of personal development was carefully monitored. The ideological theorists of Communism were well aware that reading was a double-edged sword and put in place mechanisms to mitigate its dangers. For many readers, this regime of inspection and control was one of the most stultifying aspects of life under Communism.

Libraries were always at the centre of the Soviet project. As dawn broke after the storming of the Winter Palace in 1917, Lenin impressed on the newly appointed Commissar for Education that libraries would be a key weapon in the fight for hearts and minds.

> Try to pay attention to libraries in the first instance. We must borrow from progressive bourgeois countries all those methods they have developed for making library books widely available. We must make books accessible to the masses as soon as possible. We must try to make our books available all over Russia, in as large a quantity as possible.[21]

Despite the devastation of the old Czarist libraries in the civil war that followed, Lenin's objectives were largely realised, accompanied by a huge increase in literacy across the Russian population. In 1917, just 19.7 per cent of the overall population and 8.6 per cent of the female population could read. Yet by 1940, Soviet Russia was reckoned to have a quarter of a million libraries, with over 450 million books. It was an astonishing transformation, achieved in just over twenty years.[22] Then came the German invasion. The devastation created by the German advance and bitter retreat took a terrible toll on the Russian population and its cultural institutions. Thousands of libraries were burned, shelled or pillaged, often as a deliberate act of spite as the German armies withdrew. Russian libraries lost well over 100 million volumes: the libraries of Belorussia were utterly destroyed.

The rebuilding of Soviet library stock after the war was both painful and angry. Millions of books were removed from Germany as reparations, including treasures from the first age of print. A large proportion remained hidden away for decades, uncatalogued and unused. Only after 1989 was there some tentative rapprochement between Russian library staff and the former owners: the catalogue of the Berlin state library now lists 700,000 of its former possessions under the locations of their new Russian homes.

None of these trophy books, almost exclusively in German or Latin, were at all relevant to the needs of modern Soviet citizens: the public library network had to be completely rebuilt. In little more than a decade, miracles had been achieved. By 1961, and the visit of the American librarians, Russia could boast forty-one university libraries with 50 million volumes serving 300,000 students and staff. This was the capstone of a cascading system which by 1973 numbered 360,000 libraries, including 128,000 public libraries, 58,000 scientific and technical libraries and 170,000 school libraries.[23] Those serving the needs of the population included soldiers' libraries, trade union and factory libraries, and motorised libraries for the rural population. There were libraries in prisons and even in the Gulags, though in truth these pitiful collections only served to emphasise the privations of the bookish political prisoners condemned to live there.[24]

Even for those who did not fall foul of the system, reading was fraught with difficulties, particularly for those who wished to go beyond the ideological agenda imposed by the state. Modelling Soviet libraries on those he admired in the west, Lenin had insisted on open-access shelving, but in 1933 this was withdrawn. Books were only accessible through a card catalogue, and by application to a librarian. This provided many opportunities to mould reader behaviour. The obligatory readers' cards grew to more substantial documents, with extensive personal information, including on occasions the contents of personal home libraries. Young readers successfully nudged from an early infatuation with adventure stories to more improving literature had this approvingly noted on their cards. Especially in the larger libraries, only a portion of the stock would be represented in the catalogue in the reading room, to the frustration of researchers who would from time to time be told that a now disfavoured author had in fact never existed.[25]

Librarians were placed in an invidious situation, serving as the public face of book censorship, obliged on fear of dismissal to report requests for disapproved material. Access to library records was a powerful tool of state security, which is why US Homeland Security insisted on this power in the 2001 Patriot Act. Some Russian librarians colluded with their readers, bravely entering false titles on readers' cards, but most complied. The result was a gradual erosion of professional self-respect.[26] In the 1980s, Russian readers gradually turned away from the public libraries. This, as we have seen, was not a phenomenon particular to the Communist bloc, but even after 1989 readers were slow to return. With few resources available to renovate stock, or even restore dangerously dilapidated buildings, readers turned instead to informal subscription libraries offering the texts that had previously been denied them.

The difficulties of managing reading in a controlled society were only multiplied in the 'fraternal' European states allocated to Soviet control at the end of the Second World War. Poland, Czechoslovakia and Hungary were all highly sophisticated central European societies with long histories of literacy, book production and library building. The shattered remnant of north-eastern Germany, shorn of much of the old Prussian state, was rechristened the German Democratic Republic, and only gradually recovered from the devastation of war and Soviet reparations. Shaping these nations to the new imperatives of Marxist ideology was a testing task, and for both readers and book producers, often traumatic.

During the war, Poland had lost most of its book stock, and the library community initially welcomed the new regime's commitment to rebuilding the public library network. This was, in many respects, a remarkable success. Between 1946 and 1949, the number of public libraries increased from 426 to almost 4,000, with a total book stock of 6.5 million volumes.[27] But it soon became clear that the management of these collections would be very different. Part of this stock came from the appropriation of private and corporate collections.[28] The first list of banned books to be removed from the libraries was circulated as early as October 1945. Pre-war librarians who chafed under this new regime were gradually expelled.

Among the titles condemned were 'sensational and mystery books or sentimental romances'. If western librarians would not necessarily have demurred, they would not have condemned them for the reason that 'such works were full of bourgeois ideals, snobbery and the cult of lazy good-for-nothings'. Communist societies were nothing if not thorough. In 1948, an association of satirists vowed to eschew any sign of 'bourgeois discontent'. Instead, they promised to offer satire ridiculing 'manifestations of the capitalist mentality and surviving traces of aristocratic behaviour'.[29]

In Czechoslovakia after the Communist takeover, 27.5 million books were removed from public libraries, and about 85 per cent of publisher's stock was destroyed when private ownership of publishing firms was abolished. This provided a huge opportunity to local authors, not least because a high proportion of the Czech intelligentsia had supported the Communist takeover. Though the number of available titles declined, print runs were sometimes six times greater than the pre-Communist norm.[30] Ultimately, more authors would renounce the official sphere of publishing in Czechoslovakia than in Hungary or East Germany, many in the wake of the brutal destruction of the tentative liberalisation of 1968 known as the Prague Spring. The subsequent repression reached into all areas of intellectual life: twenty-five literary magazines were closed, half of all journalists and 80 per cent of publishing house editors were dismissed. Many took solace in the exchange of poetry and prose in typescript. Duplicated with the help of carbon copies and poorly paid female secretaries, this became the celebrated *samizdat* underground, although it is true that many bad books were published as *samizdat* that would have been winnowed out by the normal workings of the commercial market. Significantly, the surge in demand for books prohibited under Communism evaporated very quickly as the market normalised after 1989.

For better or worse, the official market supplied the book needs of the vast proportion of Czechs, Hungarians and Poles. In Prague, long queues would form outside bookshops on a Thursday morning, when new books were released. Readers followed the publishers' lists closely, necessarily so, since bookshops sold their books over the counter, often in pre-wrapped packages. This ban on browsing created a new opportunity for second-hand bookshops, which flourished. Most distinctive of these years was the crucial importance of private libraries in sustaining intellectual life. Many Czech and Hungarian households assembled collections of several hundred books, and these private libraries could not easily be purged when authors fell out of favour. Milan Kundera's *The Joke* sold 119,000 copies in the years following its publication in 1967, but then was banned on his expulsion from the Communist party in 1970. Copies were removed from public libraries, but this still left 100,000 copies in private hands. Private libraries, with their mix of escapist fiction and books banned since 1968, sustained Czech literary culture through the drab years of 'normalisation'. Public libraries necessarily toed the party line, but readers took their revenge, by leaving books by Russian authors untouched on the shelves.[31]

The collapse of Communism in 1989 inspired a greedy demand for anything western. This caused enormous turbulence in the publishing industry and rendered public libraries largely irrelevant. Although Czechs honoured their intellectuals – the writer Václav Havel served fourteen years successively as president of Czechoslovakia and then the Czech Republic – with rare exceptions they eschewed earnest works of literature in favour of cookery, crime and tales of the American West, a sobering lesson for the veterans of the *samizdat* underground. Czechs also devoured mountains of guidebooks, dictionaries and self-help manuals. Television, freed of the stultifying voice of socialist worthiness, also left less room for reading. Doom-laden newspaper headlines predicted 'A Farewell to Books' or mourned 'A National Shame'.[32] This rather missed the point. Czech publishing took a battering because it had rejected international investment. In Hungary and to a lesser extent Poland, foreign capital helped the publishing industry to ride out the storm. Today, these nations, along with the liberated Baltic republics, have more libraries per head of population than any of the nations of western Europe.[33]

In Communist East Germany, the fall of the Berlin Wall exposed a stark difference between the very different status of public libraries in the East and West. In 1989, the DDR supported 13,535 public libraries for a population of 16 million. West Germany had only 4,988 public libraries, albeit with larger collections, for a population four times as large. Conversely, West Germany spent three times as much on its academic libraries, especially sixty university libraries, as on public libraries. In East Germany academic libraries received less funding than the public library network.[34] Many reasons may be advanced for this disparity, not least the fact that the citizens of West Germany had far more disposable income to buy their own books, and many more to choose from. In East Germany, the lack of hard currency, as well as the disinclination to supply texts not consistent with socialist ideology, also inhibited the growth of academic collections. The result was that after unification, 80–90 per cent of DDR university collections were declared functionally obsolete.

Public libraries also could not escape a painful purge. The city library of Frankfurt an der Oder de-accessioned a third of its collection. In Wittenberg, the contents of the town library were simply piled on barrows on the street for passers-by to take away.[35] Publishers in the DDR were left with a mountain of unsaleable stock: much was pulped, or simply tipped into landfill. In this ignominious grave, editions of Shakespeare, Zola and Tolstoy nestled with the collected speeches of the deposed leader Erich Honecker. It was as if, in the words of one observer, 'by simply throwing things away, the employees of bookstores and publishing houses were trying to dispose of the DDR's past'.[36] This, too, is one way libraries die.

New Frontiers

While the liberated peoples of eastern Europe were consigning the contents of their libraries to the municipal tip, in many parts of the world a public library network was emerging for the first time. We may appreciate the irony that the public library became a global phenomenon at precisely the moment that the West was predicting its extinction. In the event, neither the hopes of the developing world nor the baleful predictions of the West would be fully realised. In the West, the library would cling to life through the storms of media change, while despite the best intentions of home governments, philanthropists and non-governmental organisations, the public library movement is yet to realise its full potential in the developing world.

In India, as elsewhere in the former British colonies, libraries were initially intended to serve the needs of the European governing elite. With the passage of time, these facilities were shared with the growing class of educated Indians, so long as they adhered to the values of the colonial rulers. In time, these Indian readers established their own circulating libraries, though these were still largely populated with the same imported English books favoured by expatriates. Attempts to create an Indian literature in local languages were carefully monitored for evidence of sedition.[37] Given the need to train a new administrative class, the primary task was the provision of libraries for the universities established in Mumbai, Kolkata and Chennai. By 1947, the year of independence, there were nineteen universities and 636 colleges in India, with a total enrolment of 106,000.[38] The provision of libraries for the general public lagged behind, notwithstanding an extraordinary initiative of the Maharaja of Baroda, who established a whole network of public libraries in his state. This was overseen by William Alanson Borden, librarian of the Young Men's Institute in New Haven, and from 1910 the agent of the Maharaja's grand design. By the time Borden left the state, Baroda had a central library of 40,000 volumes, and libraries had been established in thirty-six of the thirty-eight towns and 216 of the principal villages. This network depended entirely on the Maharaja's beneficence; after his death in 1936 it could not be sustained.

That the most impressive development of public libraries depended entirely on the patronage of what in eighteenth-century Europe would have been called an enlightened despot, boded ill for the future of library provision with the coming of independence. The problems facing the new nations of India and Pakistan were mountainous: poverty, the legacy of colonialism, lack of basic health provision, national security and the conflict between the two nations were all more pressing political priorities. It was hard to give libraries priority, since in a nation of chronically low literacy, this was bound to be of limited utility to the broad mass of the population. In 1931, as revealed by the national census, only 15.6 per cent of men and 2.9 per cent of women could read. Male literacy reached 56 per cent in 1981, but female literacy still lagged badly behind. Even in 2011, and after a significant upward revision of the raw data, three out of ten women still could not read.

In these circumstances it made perfect sense that the establishment of schools and the training of teachers should be the major resource priority. In 1952, as in nineteenth-century France, it was optimistically suggested that school libraries, defined as collections of fifty books or more, should also be made available to the local population. For the most part, a full public library service was confined to the larger cities. The flagship system in Delhi, in 1997 consisted of a central library and seventy-three branches. Collectively these libraries held 1.4 million volumes, curated by 451 staff. Yet only 64,000 had enrolled as library members, a figure that included 22,000 children.[39] The history of library provision in India is largely written as a sequence of enabling legislation, enacted by the Indian states: the necessary resources to make this a reality were not always forthcoming. A survey published in 2008 concludes with the still hopeful call for more resources: 'a massive investment in public libraries is needed to make them true information resource centres for the layman'.[40]

The post-war drive to establish libraries in the developing world received considerable impetus from the new world institutions promoting peace, principally UNESCO, the cultural arm of the United Nations. UNESCO's public libraries manifesto, issued in 1949, was largely written by the French public intellectual

André Maurois. The library, he maintained, was an instrument of peace that should be free from propaganda and prejudice; with this, Maurois deftly sidestepped plentiful evidence to the contrary within the last ten years. The public library, he went on, was a product of democratic aspiration and would itself help spread (western) democracy around the globe. For ten years, such a programme would be pursued with an almost evangelical fervour, redolent of the missionary efforts of the colonial era, in this new manifestation promoting not Christianity but the secular value of 'modernity'.

Like much of what we associate with UNESCO, these documents let their eyes dwell on sunlit uplands with little regard for the grimmer realities facing a major programme of library building. Most countries outside Europe were not democracies, and faced more imminent problems, of poverty, low levels of literacy and the integration of competing racial and ethnic groups struggling for supremacy, along with corruption in government agencies. The flaws in the UNESCO approach were well demonstrated by the establishment of three model libraries, first and most successfully in India (1950, Delhi), then Colombia (1954, in Medellín, later home to the notorious drug cartel founded by Pablo Escobar) and Nigeria (1957). These were intended as beacons of the best practice of European libraries, without much sensitivity to local circumstances in the countries in which they were placed. In the Nigerian library, most of the users were locally based Europeans: literacy rates in the indigenous population were below 10 per cent. Siting the library in Enugu, in south eastern Nigeria, was also controversial, since this was home to the Igbo, resented for their prosperity and influence in the newly independent Nigerian state. In 1967, Enugu became the capital of the short-lived Republic of Biafra, bombed and starved into submission in an ugly war while the rest of the world averted its eyes. In the harsh world of realpolitik, the need for Nigerian oil trumped the civilising influence of libraries.[41]

Even beyond Biafra, the legacy of library provision in the post-colonial Cold War era was a tangled web of vaunting ambition, naivety and tragic disappointment. There was no doubt that in some circumstances, libraries provided the weapons of intellectual empowerment for nationalist movements. The Indian librarian S. R. Ranganathan explicitly saw the library in these terms. But elsewhere, as for instance in Vietnam and Cambodia, libraries were all too easily part of the collateral damage of great power conflict.[42] In Africa, library provision often became one more field of competition for influence among the post-colonial powers.[43] The statistics of book production point out the sobering data of global imbalance. In 1970, the developed world, with just 29 per cent of the world's population, still produced 87 per cent of the copies, and 93 per cent of book titles.

Libraries are Great, Mate!

It was an open question whether books would catch up with the world before progress caught up with books. Australia was one of the first to face up to these issues. As in India or Canada, libraries were initially a marker of transposed European values. The coastal metropolitan cities were soon served by an impressive array of libraries, while the scattered communities of the vast interior offered a more challenging environment. Despite a sustained effort to offer universal provision, by the 1970s there was a clear sense that libraries were losing their way. Prime Minister Gough Whitlam asked a commission of enquiry, headed by the respected librarian Allan Horton, to come up with solutions, which he did in the endearingly titled report, *'Libraries are great mate!' But they could be greater*.

Horton recommended that central government should bear more of the burden, but in return, libraries should become real community hubs, with a range of responsibilities, recreational, informational and advisory. Citizens should look to libraries, as before, as a source of recreational material for reading, listening and viewing. But they should also be a point of reference for information and advice, which included pointing the way towards the correct group or organisation to solve any problem. Libraries should also stock materials supporting life-long education and vocational continuing education.[44] If this sounds eerily familiar, it is because Horton had identified, back in 1976, exactly the crisis of purpose that we associate with the digital age. His case to the Australian taxpayer was not so very different to that put by the citizens of Lambeth we met at the beginning of this book, pleading for the future of the Durning library in Kennington. The Australian library could survive, but only as a community hub.

There is no doubt that library strategists have a daunting task. They need to serve the current generation of users, while at the same time anticipating future need in an ever-changing media environment in which consumer habits constantly evolve. That was evident in 1976 with the first generation of audio and film libraries; it would become more challenging with the arrival of the video cassette, the CD-ROM and digital technologies. Libraries need to move with the times, but too confident a step in the wrong direction can lead to calamity. A famous, notorious example was the decision of leading libraries to first film, then jettison, their collections of historic newspapers. The advantage was obvious, as newspapers take up enormous space and tend to degrade; but the chosen rescue technology, microfiche, proved equally transitional. Within a few decades the microfiches were functionally unusable, and the newspapers long gone. Eventually the microfiche readers were themselves removed from the reading rooms, tomorrow's technology now redundant.[45]

Most of all, in the rush to anticipate and adapt, librarians can all too easily ignore the evident, solid value of existing technologies, that is books. Despite their somewhat herbivorous reputation, many librarians are ambitious for their community, evangelical about education, and, at the top end of the profession, keen to leave a permanent legacy. Those who reach the top of the tree are also often agile politicians, comfortable in the company of elected officials, and aware of their susceptibility to grand plans. The opportunity to present a new concept of information technology, ideally with a shiny new building attached, often proves irresistible. Nowhere has this been more disastrously demonstrated than with the new library of San Francisco, a remarkable story of hubris, misjudgement and maladministration, all to build an architectural monument to the new digital age.

San Francisco had long contemplated replacing its ageing

central library, but when the city librarian suggested an upgrade to the dilapidated Old Main, a fine period building though showing its age, the board of trustees decided instead to build a striking new structure. The San Francisco library had already gone through hard times, destroyed entirely in the earthquake of 1906, while the earthquake of 1989 dumped 500,000 books from the shelves, leading to months of expensive restoration work. Building of the replacement began in 1993, and three years later the high-tech New Main opened its doors.[46]

There is little doubt that the new library provides an awesome visitor experience. Twice the size of the old library, built around a honeycombed central atrium leading to a towering central roof window, the library brings to mind a rocket installation packed with cutting-edge technology. There are all the computer terminals, meeting spaces and breakout rooms one could ever want. The problem was that the design made totally inadequate provision for the library's collection of 3 million books. With the Old Main needing to be emptied so that it could be repurposed as a museum, the collection was unceremoniously removed to temporary warehousing, while an unspecified proportion of the books were simply dumped in landfill: some estimate 200,000 books, others half a million.

This operation was on too large a scale to be concealed, not least from horrified library staff. The problem was compounded by the abandonment of the old card catalogue, so no one could say which books had been discarded, or how they had been chosen. The panicked administrators now invited protestors to rescue what they could from the skips; revealing that many of the books destined for destruction were the only copies held in the San Francisco library system. The city librarian, a true believer in the post-book information age, was obliged to resign. When interviewed some years later by the author Nicholas Basbanes, neither he nor other senior colleagues could give a clear view of how many books had been destroyed: 'I don't know, okay? Because I didn't count the books, and there are no records of what was discarded.'[47]

Where to start? It is axiomatic in good library practice that a de-accessioning programme should never be undertaken during a major building project. Certainly, you need to know what books are being discarded, and why, and secure genuine support from the community. Secrecy, bad faith, chaos and panic characterised the San Francisco fiasco, driven forward by senior management who no longer believed that books were central to the purpose of the library. If this is the price of progress, then what are the benefits?

To answer this question, we need to turn to France, a good news story towards the end of this roller-coaster journey through 2,000 years of creation, disaster and destruction, malice and commitment, and the occasional piece of illiterate foolishness. For most of the era since the birth of the public library, French libraries had been a byword for dereliction and neglect. France indeed had been in the first wave of public library formation, when the confiscations of the Revolution had been turned over to local magistrates. This inheritance had been more of a curse than a blessing: by 1860, the French Bibliothèques Municipales made little pretence of any aspiration to serve the public. This all changed in an astonishing wave of creativity, beginning in 1975, when the French state intervened to promote, and largely fund, a total renovation of the dilapidated public libraries.

The result was a new generation of Médiathèques, often beautifully designed new buildings in the heart of the city, ably repurposed for community need, and anticipating the needs of the developing future. The siting of the new-built libraries demonstrates the amount of civic pride invested in the project: the Médiathèque at La Rochelle looks out towards the harbour, that of Nîmes over the city's Roman remains. Other communities have opted for a sensitive renovation of a classic building; in Aix-en-Provence, for example, a converted match factory. The historic collection, the *patrimoine*, is not forgotten. Each library has a well-equipped rare book room, often in close proximity to the children's library, the music library and the general collection. Here the many ages of the book, and the several generations of the library community, coexist in harmony. Most of all, these libraries are busy, a true and vital reflection of their communities. In 2019, France supported some 16,500 libraries, an increase of 400 over the figure recorded two years earlier. Collectively they supply 280 million loans to an active user community: 76 per cent of French citizens continue to believe that libraries are a useful part of the social fabric. In an age when libraries throughout Europe plan anxiously for a future of ever-diminishing resources, library use in France has increased by 23 per cent in the last fifteen years.[48]

READING WITHOUT BOOKS

So we circle back to Alexandria, and the spectacular building that encapsulates so many of the contradictory impulses of the twenty-first-century library movement: honouring the historical heritage, impatient to embrace the future. In the twenty years since its foundation, the new Alexandria library has settled into its role as a major cultural institution, host to conferences, seminars, concerts, theatrical performances and the Alexandria International Book Fair. Its fifteen permanent exhibitions and striking architecture draw a steady stream of visitors, 1.5 million a year before its temporary closure in the 2020 coronavirus pandemic. Its book collections remain stable at about 2 million copies, well below the 8 million capacity, as the Bibliotheca Alexandrina, like other libraries, shifts its focus towards serving a worldwide community of readers through digital access to its collections.

Most of all, the Bibliotheca Alexandrina serves as a symbol: of a worldwide commitment to the value of education as a means of empowerment, and the place of information at its heart. It also acts as a powerful manifestation of the place of the global south in the future history and development of the library. In the last twenty years this movement has received powerful impetus from the engagement of one of the world's best-known digital pioneers, Bill Gates. Since 1997, the Bill and Melinda Gates Foundation has poured billions of dollars into libraries, first with a programme to offer free Wi-Fi in all American public libraries, a programme then extended to over fifty countries. The Global Libraries Foundation fixed on public libraries as natural community hubs, often the only places where those with a yearning for education could find an accommodating space, together with a trained and sympathetic staff. This was not a new Carnegie programme of library build-ing, but a refit of existing infrastructure to provide modern digital resources and to train first-time users. From Botswana and Bul-garia to Chile, Colombia, Mexico and Vietnam, the Foundation also rewarded existing local programmes, recognising the impor-tance of inspirational leadership in integrating developmental opportunities into the digital future.[1] The project also embraced a transformation of the library ideal characteristic of the age of democratic choice: where once libraries had expressed the elite purpose of improving its users, power had now shifted decisively towards the users themselves.

It is hard to see the Global Libraries project as anything other than an unmitigated good. Elsewhere, the engagement of the book world with digital giants has been far more fraught. Publishers watched the growth of Amazon with the appalled fascination of a French aristocrat catching their first glimpse of the guillotine. It did not help that Amazon's founder, Jeff Bezos, reputedly told employees to approach small publishers the way a cheetah would a sickly deer.[2] Meanwhile, Google, riding the tide of positive pub-licity that attended the growing dominance of its search engine, became embroiled in a bitter ten-year battle with the book world over its plan to digitise the whole book stock of the world. Inter-estingly, both Amazon and Google claimed inspiration from the ancient library of Alexandria. Amazon's artificial intelligence virtual assistant, Alexa, was named after the great library, while the vaulting ambition of Alexandria to encompass the world's knowledge – specifically cited by Google's founders as their plan to digitise every book in the world – ran into choppy waters.

It is important to remember that when Larry Page and Sergey Brin unveiled their plan to unlock 500 years of the world's printed heritage, the library world reacted with enthusiasm. By 2010, Google had calculated, with vainglorious precision, that 129,864,800 books had been published since Gutenberg. Google wanted them all, and they found willing partners in the world's greatest libraries. Michigan, Harvard, Stanford, Oxford and the New York Public Library all signed up; even now, Antwerp, Ghent, Amsterdam and the British Library continue to cooperate with

Google. For Google, this was both a staggering investment and a monumental logistical exercise. In all, some 20 million books, including many of the world's oldest, were filmed.

Soon, however, the doubts set in.[3] Leading libraries pondered whether it was really wise to consign the world's knowledge to a single corporation. Then there was the issue of copyright. Google believed that they had solved this problem by presenting Google Books more as a search engine, a giant encyclopaedia of content, than as a place people would read texts: this represented 'fair use', a critical legal defence of the appropriation of creative work. Authors were not persuaded, and in 2005 initiated a class action to protect their property. A provisional settlement, which would have seen Google paying $125 million for the right to exploit this material commercially, was initially accepted but then collapsed.

Ultimately the Google case rests on an issue of trust: can we entrust our precious heritage of books to a digital future which is still so uncertain? What happens if Google disappears behind a paywall, or just disappears; or, alternately, decides to share some titles with users and withhold others? Are we prepared to have a single corporation patrol the boundaries of acceptable writing? To turn to more mundane issues, how will authors make a living if their works are shared in an uncontrolled environment, replicating the carnage in the music industry? More fundamentally, are books just too slow for the modern world, where our mindscape is dominated by the smartphone, a small rectangular electronic box which we consult incessantly during the day? A study in 2016 concluded that we touch our cell phones 2,617 times a day.[4] The real problem, it is argued, is not the assault on the medium of the book, but the attack on our attention span.[5] But then, this was said also with radio and the television: in the sixteenth century, real bookmen deplored the pamphlet. A more potent criticism of the smartphone is that its addictive features are not an accidental by-product, but deliberately programmed to create dependence; a dependence that leaves little space for reflective reading.

Dousing the Flames

On 29 April 1986 a fire broke out in the Los Angeles county library, by now a familiar enough story to readers of this book. By the end of the day, 400,000 books had perished, and another 700,000 were damaged by water, smoke, or both. This was the library catastrophe that nobody knew. On the day the library burned, western news agencies learned for the first time the extent of the damage to a nuclear power station in the Soviet Union: Chernobyl. Unsurprisingly, the world's newspapers followed the larger story: the exception was *Pravda*, official organ of the Soviet Communist Party, which since it was ignoring Chernobyl had plenty of space for the travails of Los Angeles.[6]

Library fires are in fact not uncommon: there are 200 fires reported every year in libraries in the United States. Antiquated electrics are responsible for many of the most serious. In 1982, faulty wiring destroyed the North Hollywood branch library, and in 2004, a similar cause carried off much of the priceless collection of the famous Anna Amalia library in Weimar, Germany. The city library in Norwich, England, burned down in 1994, along with its collection of 350,000 books, while a fire begun in the newspaper section of the Russian Academy of Sciences in St Petersburg destroyed 400,000 items in 1988.[7]

Until relatively recently we liked to think of libraries as sanctuaries: a place where books, once safely stowed, will be protected. As it turns out, this safe refuge is only provisional. Books leave libraries all the time: occasionally as a result of one of the catastrophic events that have captured our attention in this book, but also in the normal run of a librarian's work. Books are removed because they are no longer read, and to make room for new accessions; worn copies are replaced. 'Weeding' is a core part of the librarian's job, and undertaken with seriousness while applying careful protocols. The authors of this present book have benefited greatly from the opportunity to pick up a considerable number of these superfluous titles, recycled into the academic community through the not-for-profit Better World Books.[8]

Sometimes books are stolen, particularly from the larger collections where the sheer quantity of books poses serious security problems. One patron of the Los Angeles collection ran a successful second-hand business for forty years exclusively with books stolen from the library. Occasionally librarians will abuse their own position of trust: as lovers of books, with a clear perception of both their rarity and value, the temptations are obvious, though mostly they are removed for private enjoyment rather than sold on. In 1982 a Los Angeles library clerk, confronted with the 10,000 library books found in his home, confessed meekly that he was a bit of a hoarder, before surrendering his stash and tendering his resignation.[9] A more egregious case unfolded relatively recently, when the director of the Girolamini Library in Naples was convicted of presiding over the systematic plunder of his own collection, feeding up to 4,000 rare and precious books into the market through a range of crooked book dealers.[10] The presence of copies of Copernicus's masterwork in many poorly protected collections in eastern Europe has made this not only one of the most valued of early texts, but the most stolen. At least seven copies disappeared in the last decades of the twentieth century.[11]

Such cases are, thankfully, extremely rare. More culpable are the more deliberate acts of destruction performed not by unbalanced or larcenous individuals, but by library administrations.[12] Often these are undertaken in the service of modernity. Librarians become futurologists, eager to get ahead of the curve, to provide the most modern, forward-looking facilities. If all else fails, a desired outcome can simply be described as inevitable, and no one can stand in the way of progress. Thus Michael Schuyler, an electronics systems librarian, writing in *Computers in Libraries*: 'The paradox in libraries, particularly public ones, is that there are some people who grew up thinking books were sacred ... They don't want to throw away any, no matter how dated they are ... Technology, including its ugly side, is going to win anyway.'[13]

Space has to be found for banks of computers, meeting space, new media. Often removing books has been the only solution. Card indexes and catalogues were an early casualty of this process, condemned as redundant though often containing material that cannot easily be replicated from online searches. One such catalogue, happily retained in Amsterdam university library, provided us with data on thousands of seventeenth-century books not available through any online resource.[14]

The extent to which the library profession has become dominated by the jargons of modernity can be followed in the ever-changing title of one of its most influential periodicals, founded in 1966 as *The Journal of Library History*. In 1988, *The Journal of Library History* morphed into *Libraries & Culture*: 'an interdisciplinary journal that explores the significance of collections of recorded knowledge – their creation, organization, preservation and utilization – in the context of cultural and social history, unlimited as to time and space.' The first article in the reconfigured journal was a discussion of the microcard, an opaque microform. This sufficed until 2006 when the title evolved once more to *Libraries & the Cultural Record*. So that readers understood that this was no mere distinction without a difference, the editor, David B. Gracy II, offered a new manifesto. 'Under its new title the journal will give voice to historical exploration, single and in concert, of libraries and librarianship, archival and records enterprise, museums and museum administration, and preservation and conversation – those fields uniting in the Information domain and joined in the stewardship of the cultural record.'

This extended note made clear that this relatively modest change was carefully considered and reflected a determination to address changing priorities in the discipline of librarianship: indeed, the editorial board regarded it as so urgent that it occurred halfway through volume 41. Perhaps, in retrospect, the most significant part of this manifesto statement was the last clause, and the imperative capitalisation of 'Information'. For after only six years, *Libraries & the Cultural Record* became *Information & Culture*, finally banishing libraries from its title. The editor, William Aspray, was at pains to point out that scholarship on libraries would still find a home, but it would be shared with exponents of the 'iSchool' movement. This is true, up to a point. One can imagine 'Use of Books in the Ohio Valley before 1850' being welcome in the periodical in any of its manifestations. This is less true of 'Playpens for Mind Children', 'Normalising Soviet Cybernetics', 'The World as Database' and 'The Performance of Information Flows in the Art of Stephen Willats': all titles from the first volume of *Information & Culture.*

Going all-in on digital is not a choice without dangers for the library community. Libraries are in effect betting the store on a technology that will soon be so ubiquitous that libraries could become irrelevant to it. In ten years, it may well be technically possible to throw Wi-Fi clouds over whole cities, even whole countries. Amazon has a plan for 3,236 satellites that would provide high-speed internet anywhere in the world.[15] Why then would people head to the library for these digital resources? For 500 years books have been central to the purpose of the library. Free Wi-Fi as the key to the library's future is unlikely to last out this decade.

In 1986, the Los Angeles central library loaned out 900,000 books; 700,000 people passed through their doors. Many of them came to ask questions of the well-informed staff: in 1986 staff answered 6 million questions on a magnificent range of subjects.[16] Staff would willingly sit on this desk for years, accruing an encyclopaedic knowledge worthy of Mr Memory in John Buchan's *Thirty-Nine Steps* (a character, incidentally, absent from the novel but added for the film versions). Now we have Wikipedia, Google and Alexa: the 6 million questions asked of the reference desk can now be answered without schlepping across town. Indeed in 2019, Amazon's Alexa answered 500 million questions *a day* from customers in more than eighty countries.[17]

Most of all, by empowering the digital revolution, librarians have given up the one unique selling point which they defended so tenaciously for almost as long as we have had libraries: the right to apply their knowledge, taste and discrimination to assisting the choice of their patrons. This has been the key to understanding so much in this book: the first booksellers' catalogues, Gabriel Naudé's manifesto, the ALA guide to a model library collection, the book club: the idea that in an age of plenty there will always be helpmates to assist readers in making the right choice of book. Can the internet, in all its enormous variety, ever replace this reflective process of deliberation, the slow choosing, the eager anticipation, the slow unfolding of plot? The internet, it is true, is the perfect tool for an impatient age; we love the convenience of same-day delivery, but we complain more and more of the stress of the relentless pace of life. And it will only get worse: the research firm IDC has predicted that globally, within the next five years the average person will interact with connected devices every eighteen seconds.[18] Libraries and books encourage reflective thought. We cannot delegate the whole burden of returning balance to our lives to classes and therapeutic groups. A book creates a mindfulness class of one.

Surviving

In that spirit, let us take a deep breath and reflect on what we still have. According to the International Federation of Library Associations and Institutions, in 2020 there were still more than 2.6 million institutional libraries worldwide, including 404,487 public libraries.[19] Almost all of them still have books. New libraries are still built. The example of France quoted in the last chapter is quite unique in Europe, but Europe has its fair share of spectacular new libraries: the national library of Copenhagen (the Black Diamond), an inspiration for the new Latvian national library in Riga. The destroyed Norwich library has been replaced by a fine community hub, while Manchester has recently completed a sensitive regeneration of the central library, one of the oldest public libraries in England. The renovated library is now replete with the appropriate levels of convivial meeting space, and with a whole wing allowing patrons to combine a trip to the library with the opportunity to see council officers about housing and passport issues. New York recovered from the abandonment of the Foster redesign for the New York Public Library with a spectacular new branch library on 53rd street.[20]

Technology moves with lightning speed. The distance in time between the beginning and domestication of innovation shortens exponentially with each era. But the death of the book, predicted with great confidence with each new communication invention, just refuses to happen. In 1979, the head of the RAND corporation announced that libraries would soon be obsolete.[21] A good-natured wall chart of technological extinction predicted

2019 as the year the last library would close its doors.[22] Yet these tattered, battered heritage technologies refuse to expire, and sometimes, for those who have attempted to get ahead of technology, the future turns out to be very temporary: witness the rise, and discreet departure, of the CD-ROM, very much yesterday's future of books. The e-reader, Amazon's Kindle, seems likely to follow.[23] At least one futurologist is beginning to have second thoughts about libraries. 'I thought they'd go virtual and that librarians would be replaced with algorithms. Apparently not.' Why have they survived? 'Libraries are slow-thinking spaces away from the hustle and bustle of everyday life.'[24]

The book too lives on, for precisely the reason Jeff Bezos, looking for the right product, fixed upon books at the core of Amazon. Books do not spoil, they are easily transported, they come in relatively uniform sizes, and customers have a good idea of what they want.[25] You could add, perhaps of less benefit to a tech entrepreneur looking for repeat sales, they are sturdy and resilient, they do not require servicing or replacement parts, and they provide cultural capital: either to be admired as an adornment of the home or office, or to be shared, loaned or cherished.

This is well understood in the library profession, at least by those who interact on a daily basis with library patrons. In the course of researching and writing this book, we have spoken to many librarians and worked in many types of library buildings in over twenty countries. It is possible to discern a real difference between the library assistants, the foot soldiers of the institutions, who still see the point of books, and the managers who want to stay ahead of modernity and seem quite attracted to libraries without books. Hearing these zealots talking of the inevitability of change, and a new inclusive future of endless digital resources, it is hard not to be reminded of the first generation of humanists, who talked of the future, but really had mostly in mind a better supply of texts for people like themselves. Available online is a revealing promotional video for Bibliotech, the first all-digital public library, in San Antonio, Texas.[26] The library offers a well laid out, well-lit array of computer stations enjoyed by a cheerful clientele, all completely at home in their environment. Almost all are young, dressed uniformly in tee shirt and slacks. Most of the clients are high school or college kids. They are generation digital, sharing their membership of this elite group, as ethnically diverse as the quarterdeck of the Starship *Enterprise* but otherwise utterly the same. What has been forgotten here is the young parent taking their infants to the children's library, where the handling of the books is as crucial to cognitive development as the texts, or the pensioner exchanging one handful of novels for another. These remain the everyday clients of the public library and its branch networks.

Let us imagine a different scenario – not a provision of more of these new-build, state-of-the-art digital experiments, but a world in which our present town, city and branch libraries just gave up their books to create more space for all the other things they do: classes, group meetings, computers, social services. Would that still be a library? Take out the books and it is hard to see what marks these institutions out from other public community spaces or government offices. They would soon lose much of their clientele. For books have one key characteristic that differentiates these users from any of the other groups who meet in library space. Anyone who wishes may join the community of book readers at any point in their lives, and they may equally leave or suspend their membership (a characteristic libraries share with organised religion). Many people use libraries intensively for parts of their life – as college students or mothers with young children – and then possibly never again. They may start using the library for the first time when they retire.

This voluntary, incidental, intermittent character which defines the reading life for many men and women is very different from the focused purpose of those who use the library building for a meeting or class. Those who pass through the door of any of the 400,000 public libraries open on any given day throughout the world to read, borrow or consult books, do not necessarily have any other interests, needs or social characteristics in common. Those with shared problems, political views, hopes or aspirations are far more likely to have found each other elsewhere, most likely online. It is good that libraries have now reached out to such groups and provide them with places where they can be together on a regular basis. But such gatherings by definition exclude those who do not share this one thing in common.

In the first century of the public library, from the 1880s onwards, this was very different. Those who entered the library did share one vital characteristic, in that they were by and large aspirational: the library was an instrument of social or personal improvement. It is the continuation of this tradition that ensures the vitality of the library in parts of the world where public provision is relatively novel. In the west, were it not for books, the repurposing of the library as a meeting point might leave us with a spectrum of niche groups, performing a valuable social service for all of them, but without much interaction. It is the randomness of books, of taste and curiosity that ensures that libraries remain a place where a broad cross-section of society can drop in, wander, browse, and leave when they like. It is randomness that marks out the library from other public shared space; and the search for something uplifting, whatever it may be.

Browsing is key to the success of the institutional library, and a key difference between this and personal collections. Since digital resources began to develop new models of selling, a great deal of ingenuity has been invested in trying to replicate the experience of browsing. The results are impressive, if a little creepy, in the recommendations by association in both the search results ('if you bought this, you may also like this') and the micro-targeted paid advertising. But what if we want something different, rather than more of the same? What if we do not know that we want something different, but a chance encounter sparks our interests? Digital has not found a way either to replicate this unplanned event, or indeed the tactile rhythm of turning the page, of marking the hours, of progressing through a text. To be the ideal customer for digital services, humans have themselves to become much more robotic, predictable, limited, docile.

It is hard not to think that the health of the library will remain connected to the health of the book. The book, the artefact, has proved exceptionally resilient through the centuries: surviving the collapse of the Roman Empire, the media change from manuscript to print, the Reformation and the Enlightenment, carpet bombing and numerous attempts to limit access to unacceptable texts. Most recently it has seen off many of the technological pall-bearers sent to conduct it to the crematorium: microfilm, the CD-ROM, and now the e-reader. The sheer tangibility of the book is a key element of its success, and its versatility: as manual, totem, encyclopaedia and source of entertainment. And the library, as location and concept, has shared this mutability.

ACKNOWLEDGEMENTS

In the course of this and other projects, the two authors have worked, together or separately, in over 300 libraries and archives. So our first, fundamental debt is to librarians: the special collections librarians who fetched for us sometimes hundreds of books; the library assistants in small branch libraries who shared their impressions on the shifting working regimes of the modern library; and the senior librarians who have discussed with us the challenges of a fast-changing media landscape. They have been generous with their time and shrewd in their guidance.

With this particular project, we owe the library community a second major debt: for their published works on the history of libraries and readers. No one knows a collection as well as the librarian or archivist who curates it. Many have shared the benefit of this access in the published works that have been an essential part of the literature we have consulted, particularly for the second half of this book. In most cases this work has been published as articles in scholarly journals: librarians do not have the luxury of academics with time set aside in their contracts for research. To all of them, and to the editorial boards of the dozen or more journals devoted to libraries and information culture that we have combed through in preparation for the writing of this book, along with other contextual literature, we express our profound gratitude.

We also need to thank one institution on the fringe of the library world: Better World Books. It will not come as a surprise to many readers of this book to learn that when a book reaches the shelves of a public or university library it is not necessarily there to stay. The endless conundrum of new stock and limited shelf-space requires disposal: indeed the careful assessment of whether a book should be retained is one of the everyday tasks of librarians. Many of these de-accessioned books are passed to dealers like Better World Books and sold on. Completing this text, during a year when most research libraries were closed for much of the time, the ability to source many necessary texts through various second-hand sellers like Better World Books or AbeBooks was something of a lifeline. Between us we now own texts from more than fifty public and academic libraries, often with their borrowing log intact. This has been a virtual world tour that has greatly enhanced our enjoyment of the writing process of this book.

The research that underpins this work was happily completed before the Covid-19 pandemic changed the research environment so radically in the spring of 2020. We are grateful for fellowships in the Herzog August Bibliothek Wolfenbüttel, the libraries of Leiden University, the Free University of Amsterdam and Trinity College Dublin, that allowed us to pursue critical literature before the shutdown. We were able to share our ideas on the history of the library with audiences in Wolfenbüttel, Tallinn and London. Further engagements in Riga, Philadelphia, Toronto and New York fell victim to the pandemic. Two cohorts of students at St Andrews who took the course we offered on the history of the library also provided valuable feedback on chapters of this text as they were developed.

Our text has also been greatly enhanced by the kindness of the friends who read the entire book in draft: Jacob Baxter, Jessica Dalton, John Sibbald, Peter Truesdale and Fran der Weduwen. Their perceptive remarks and suggestions for additional material greatly enhanced the final product. Jane Pettegree and Fran der Weduwen supported the authors through the whole process of researching and writing this book, and Megan and Sophie Pettegree provided many happy memories of library visits together, in Britain and all over France. We conceived and wrote this book in the supportive environment of the University of St Andrews, and especially of our own book history research group. This text has profited in a huge number of ways from the opportunity of discussion on a day-to-day basis with talented colleagues and graduate students in the book project team. We owe a particular obligation to Dr Graeme Kemp, deputy director and project manager of the Universal Short Title Catalogue, for the skill with which he has kept up with the constant flow of new data into the project and his imaginative visualisation of future possibilities. The USTC in its current manifestation is very much his creation. We should also acknowledge the help of Arjan van Dijk of Brill publishing and Farhana Hoque at ProQuest, not least for helping us with access to their two superb digital resources, Book Sales Catalogues Online and Early European Books.

Before submission the manuscript was given a vigorous workout by our editor at Profile, Cecily Gayford. We owe a profound debt to Cecily for her editorial rigour and imaginative suggestions for re-shaping some of our material. Thanks are also due to Penny Gardiner for her precise and sensitive copy-editing, and to Samantha Johnson for the superb cover design. Another critical influence was our agent, Felicity Bryan. It was Felicity who encouraged us to expand our canvas and embrace the whole scope of library history. We fixed on the title in a conversation by telephone with Felicity from beneath the ramparts of Prague Castle. It was the sort of issue on which she was both meticulous and uncompromising, and it was of course through Felicity that we were first introduced to Profile and Cecily Gayford.

Felicity Bryan, MBE, died on 21 June 2020. We dedicate this book to her memory, in thankfulness and respect for her enormous influence on the world of books.

St Andrews
December 2020

LIST OF ILLUSTRATIONS

Colour plates

Section One

1. Interior of the new Library at Alexandria, 2018. Wikimedia Commons, © Cecioka.
2. Facade of the Roman Library of Celsus (Ephesus). Wikimedia Commons, © Benh Lieu Song.
3. Miniature depicting Ezra the scribe in front of a book cupboard (armarium), from the Codex Amiatinus (early eighth century). Florence, Biblioteca Medicea Laurenziana, MS Amiatinus 1 / Wikimedia Commons.
4. Miniature of Vincent of Beauvais in a copy of his *Miroir historial*, written in Bruges *c.*1478–80, from the collection of King Edward IV. © British Library Board: Royal MS 14 E I vol. 1.
5. A fifteenth-century Book of Hours written in France. Ville de Nantes, Bibliothèque municipale: ms22.
6. Portrait of Federico da Montefeltro and his Son Guidobaldo (*c.*1475). Wikimedia Commons, © Galleria nazionale delle Marche, Urbino / VIRan.
7. Parmigianino, *Portrait of a Collector* (*c.*1523). Heritage Images/Hulton Archive/Getty Images.
8. Quentin Metsys, *Erasmus of Rotterdam* (1517). Imagno/Hulton Archive/Getty Images.
9. A trade card for Liebig's beef extract (1912), featuring a highly fictionalised travelling book merchant. Culture Club/Hulton Archive/Getty Images.
10. The interior of Duke Humphrey's library. Wikimedia Commons, © Diliff.
11. Georg Balthasar Probst, *Bibliotheca Büloviana Academiae, Georgiae Augustae donata Göttingae* (*c.*1742–1801). Rijksmuseum, Amsterdam: RP-P-2015-26-1573.
12. Library of the monastery of San Francisco in Lima, Peru, founded in 1673. De Agostini Picture Library/De Agostini/Getty Images.

Section Two

1. Illumination depicting Mark the Evangelist in the Codex Caesareus (*c.*1050). Uppsala university library: C 93.
2. The main hall of Admont Abbey library. Wikimedia Commons, © Jorge Royan.
3. Thomas Rowlandson, *A Book Auction* (*c.*1810). Print Collector/Hulton Fine Art Collection/Getty Images.

4. *Beauty in Search of Knowledge* (London: Robert and John Bennett Sayer, 1782). Rijksmuseum, Amsterdam: RP-P-2015-26-946; *The Circulating Library* (London: Laurie & Whittle, 1804). Rijksmuseum, Amsterdam: RP-P-2015-26-1356.

5. *Büchersaal der neuen Bibliothek im Britischen Museum zu London* (Leipzig: Johann Jacob Weber, 1869). Rijksmuseum, Amsterdam: RP-P-2015-26-1362; Fortunino Matania, *Reading Room in the British Museum, London* (1907). DEA/Biblioteca Ambrosiana/De Agostini/Getty Images.

6. W. H. Symonds, Competitive design (one of eighty-eight submitted) for the New York Public Library (1897). Library of Congress, Washington DC: LC-DIG-ds-06530; The New York Public Library Main Branch as seen from across the intersection of East 42nd Street and Fifth Ave (1915). Library of Congress, Washington DC: LC-USZ62-133258.

7. Curt Wunderlich, *Das Empire. Britischer Raub und Verrat* (Berlin: Ernst Staneck Verlag, 1941). Private Collection, Andrew Pettegree.

8. Three romantic titles from the Mills & Boon range, from 1977, 1983 and 1989. Private Collection, Andrew Pettegree.

9. 'Reading is a man's obligation'. Communist poster by Sergei Ivanovich Ivanov (St Petersburg, *c.*1919). Poster Plakat.com, PP 764.

10. The atrium of the main branch of the San Francisco Public Library (2009). Wikimedia Commons, © Joe Mabel.

11. Fire trucks battle the fire that engulfed the Los Angeles central library in 1986. Ben Martin/Archive Photos/Getty Images.

Illustrations

1. James Gillray, *Tales of Wonder!* (1802). Library of Congress, Washington DC: LC-USZ62-139066.

2. Miniature depicting St Benedict handing down his Rule to his followers, in a copy of the Rule written during the second quarter of the twelfth century. © British Library Board: Add MS 16979.

3. Plan of St Gallen, early ninth century. Stiftsbibliothek Sankt Gallen, Ms 1092.

4. Books chained to a lectern at the library of Hereford Cathedral. Epics/Hulton Archive/Getty Images.

5. Interior of the library of San Marco, Florence, designed by Michelozzo. Leemage/Universal Images Group/Getty Images.

6. Verso of a leaf from the Gutenberg Bible. It contains Sirach (Ecclesiasticus) 43:25–45:2. Wikimedia Commons / Miami University Libraries.

7. Coenraet Decker, *View of the Ruins of the Cloister Koningsveld, near Delft* (1680). Rijksmuseum, Amsterdam: RP-P-1905-5697.

8. Frontispiece of an edition of the *Index librorum prohibitorum* (1758). Library of Congress: LC-USZ62-95166.

9. Hendrik Bary, *Portrait of the Dutch theologian Jacobus Taurinus (1576–1618)* (*c.*1657–1707). Rijksmuseum, Amsterdam: RP-P-1894-A-18220.

10. *Catalogus variorum et insignium librorum Pauli Johan: Resenii* (Copenhagen: Henrici Gödiani, 1661). Det Kongelige Bibliioteket, Copenhagen.

NOTES

Prologue: Curating the Ruins

1. Quoted in Anthony Hobson, *Great Libraries* (London: Weidenfeld & Nicolson, 1970), p. 143.
2. *Advis pour dresser une bibliothèque* (Paris: François Targa, 1627). Gabriel Naudé, *Advice on Establishing a Library*, ed. Archer Taylor (Berkeley, CA: University of California Press, 1950).
3. See chapter 12.
4. Kristian Jensen, *Revolution and the Antiquarian Book: Reshaping the Past, 1780–1815* (Cambridge: Cambridge University Press, 2011).
5. For a nice selection, see Christopher de Hamel, *Meetings with Remarkable Manuscripts* (London: Allen Lane, 2016).
6. See chapter 14.
7. W. B. Stevenson, 'The Selection of Fiction for Public Libraries', in Raymond Astbury (ed.), *The Writer in the Market Place* (London: Clive Bingley, 1969), p. 148.
8. Andrew Pettegree and Arthur der Weduwen, *The Bookshop of the World: Making and Trading Books in the Dutch Golden Age* (London and New Haven: Yale University Press, 2019), pp. 172–94.
9. Rebecca Knuth, *Burning Books and Leveling Libraries: Extremist Violence and Cultural Destruction* (Westport, CT: Praeger, 2006), pp. 80–86.
10. Michael Kevane and William A. Sundstrom, 'The Development of Public Libraries in the United States, 1870–1930: A Quantitative Assessment' *Information & Culture*, 49 (2014), pp. 117–44.
11. John Carey, *The Intellectuals and the Masses: Pride and Prejudice among the Literary Intelligentsia, 1880–1939* (London: Faber & Faber, 1992), pp. 3–19.
12. Jonathan Rose, 'A Conservative Canon: Cultural Lag in British Working-Class Reading Habits', *Libraries & Culture*, 33 (1998), pp. 98–104.

1. A Confusion of Scrolls

1. Beverley Butler, *Return to Alexandria: An Ethnography of Cultural Heritage, Revivalism and Museum Memory* (Walnut Creek, CA: Left Coast Press, 2007).
2. See chapter 5.
3. Jeremy Black, 'Lost Libraries of Ancient Mesopotamia', in James Raven (ed.),

Lost Libraries: The Destruction of Great Book Collections since Antiquity (Basingstoke: Palgrave, 2004), pp. 41–57, here p. 41.

4. William V. Harris, *Ancient Literacy* (Cambridge, MA: Harvard University Press, 1989).

5. Lionel Casson, *Libraries in the Ancient World* (London and New Haven: Yale University Press, 2001), p. 22.

6. Rory MacLeod (ed.), *The Library of Alexandria: Centre of Learning in the Ancient World* (London and New York: I. B. Tauris, 2000).

7. See chapter 2.

8. Bernard Lewis, 'The Arab Destruction of the Library of Alexandria: Anatomy of a Myth', in Mostafa El-Abbadi and Omnia Fathallah (eds.), *What Happened to the Ancient Library of Alexandria?* (Leiden: Brill, 2008), pp. 213–17.

9. T. Keith Dix, '"Public Libraries" in Ancient Rome: Ideology and Reality', *Libraries & Culture*, 29 (1994), pp. 282–96, here p. 283.

10. T. Keith Dix, 'Pliny's Library at Comum', *Libraries & Culture*, 31 (1996), pp. 85–102.

11. Felix Reichmann, 'The Book Trade at the Time of the Roman Empire', *Library Quarterly*, 8 (1938), pp. 40–76, here p. 73. P. White, 'Bookshops in the Literary Culture of Rome', in William A. Johnson and Holt N. Parker (eds.), *Ancient Literacies: The Culture of Reading in Greece and Rome* (Oxford: Oxford University Press, 2009), pp. 268–87.

12. Anthony J. Marshall, 'Library Resources and Creative Writing at Rome', *Phoenix*, 30 (1976), pp. 252–64. On Cicero's library see especially T. Keith Dix, '"Beware of Promising Your Library to Anyone": Assembling a Private Library at Rome', in Jason König, Katerina Oikonomopoulou and Greg Woolf (eds.), *Ancient Libraries* (Cambridge: Cambridge University Press, 2013), pp. 209–34.

13. Lorne Bruce, 'Palace and Villa Libraries from Augustus to Hadrian', *Journal of Library History*, 21 (1986), pp. 510–52, here pp. 544–5.

14. Sandra Sider, 'Herculaneum's Library in 79 AD: The Villa of the Papyri', *Libraries & Culture*, 25 (1990), pp. 534–42.

15. Reichmann, 'Book Trade', p. 43.

16. Victor M. Martínez and Megan Finn Senseney, 'The Professional and His Books: Special Libraries in the Ancient World', in König, *Ancient Libraries*, pp. 401–17.

17. Vivian Nutton, 'Galen's Library', in Christopher Gill, Tim Whitmarsh and John Wilkins (eds.), *Galen and the World of Knowledge* (Cambridge: Cambridge University Press, 2009), pp. 18–36. Susan P. Mattern, *The Prince of Medicine: Galen in the Roman Empire* (Oxford: Oxford University Press, 2013).

18. See chapters 2, 3 and 4.

19. See chapter 7.

20. George W. Houston, *Inside Roman Libraries: Book Collections and Their Management in Antiquity* (Chapel Hill, NC: University of North Carolina Press, 2014).

2. Sanctuary

1. Cited in J. Berthoud, 'The Italian Renaissance Library', *Theoria: A Journal of Social and Political Theory*, 26 (1966), pp. 61–80, here p. 68.

2. A concise narrative is found in Dom Romanus Rios, 'Monte Cassino, 529–1944', *Bulletin of the John Rylands Library*, 29 (1945), pp. 49–68, an article written in the aftermath of the most recent destruction of the monastery during the Second World War.

3. For a particularly pertinent case study, see Adrian Papahagi, 'Lost Libraries and Surviving Manuscripts: The Case of Medieval Transylvania', *Library & Information History*, 31 (2015), pp. 35–53.

4. King James Version, II Timothy 4:13.

5. John Barton, *A History of the Bible: The Book and Its Faiths* (London: Allen Lane, 2019).

6. Herman A. Peterson, 'The Genesis of Monastic Libraries', *Libraries & the Cultural Record*, 45 (2010), pp. 320–32.

7. Cited in James Westfall Thompson, *The Medieval Library* (New York, NY: Hafner, 1957), p. 34.

8. Bruce L. Venarde (ed.), *The Rule of Saint Benedict* (Cambridge, MA: Harvard University Press, 2011), chapter 48, pp. 161–3.

9. Cited in Jacob Hammer, 'Cassiodorus, the Savior of Western Civilization', *Bulletin of the Polish Institute of Arts and Sciences in America*, 3 (1945), pp. 369–84, p. 380.

10. L. D. Reynolds and N. G. Wilson, *Scribes and Scholars: A Guide to the Transmission of Greek and Latin Literature* (Oxford: Oxford University Press, 1968), pp. 34–5.

11. Reynolds and Wilson, *Scribes and Scholars*, p. 76.

12. Thompson, *The Medieval Library*, p. 35.

13. Sven Meeder, *The Irish Scholarly Presence at St. Gall: Networks of Knowledge in the Early Middle Ages* (London: Bloomsbury, 2018).

14. Yaniv Fox, *Power and Religion in Merovingian Gaul: Columbanian Monasticism and the Frankish Elites* (Cambridge: Cambridge University Press, 2014).

15. Rosamond McKitterick, *Charlemagne: The Formation of a European Identity* (Cambridge: Cambridge University Press, 2008), p. 306.

16. Rosamond McKitterick, *The Carolingians and the Written Word* (Cambridge: Cambridge University Press, 1989).

17. McKitterick, *Charlemagne*, p. 316.

18. James Stuart Beddie, 'The Ancient Classics in the Mediaeval Libraries', *Speculum*, 5 (1930), pp. 3–20.

19. McKitterick, *Charlemagne*, pp. 331–2.

20. Donald Bullough, 'Charlemagne's court library revisited', *Early Mediaeval Europe*, 12 (2003), pp. 339–63, here p. 341.

21. Laura Cleaver, 'The circulation of history books in twelfth-century Normandy', in Cynthia Johnston (ed.), *The Concept of the Book: The Production, Progression and Dissemination of Information* (London: Institute of English Studies, 2019), pp. 57–78.

22. Thompson, *The Medieval Library*, p. 628.

23. Ibid, pp. 51, 618. See also more broadly, Florence Edler de Roover, 'The Scriptorium', in the same, pp. 594–612, and see Cynthia J. Cyrus, *The Scribes for Women's Convents in Late Medieval Germany* (Toronto: University of Toronto Press, 2009), pp. 18–47.

24. Thompson, *The Medieval Library*, p. 606.

25. Cyrus, *The Scribes for Women's Convents*, especially pp. 48–89, 132–65.

26. Christopher Given-Wilson, *Chronicles: The Writing of History in Medieval England* (London: Hambledon, 2004).

27. Johannes Duft, *The Abbey Library of Saint Gall* (St Gallen: Verlag am Klosterhof, 1985).

28. For some of the general architectural developments, see John Willis Clark, *The Care of Books: An Essay on the Development of Libraries and Their Fittings, from the Earliest Times to the End of the Eighteenth Century* (Cambridge: Cambridge University Press, 1901), Henry Petroski, *The Book on the Bookshelf* (New York, NY: Knopf, 1999) and K. Sp. Staikos, *The Architecture of Libraries in Western Civilization: From the Minoan Era to Michelangelo* (New Castle, DE: Oak Knoll Press, 2017).

29. For what follows, see most notably Eva Schlotheuber and John T. McQuillen, 'Books and Libraries within Monasteries', in Alison I. Beach and Isabelle Cochelin (eds.), *The Cambridge History of Medieval Monasticism in the Latin West* (Cambridge: Cambridge University Press, 2020), pp. 975–97.

30. Edward T. Brett, 'The Dominican Library in the Thirteenth Century', *The Journal of Library History*, 15 (1980), pp. 303–308, here p. 305.

31. Cited in Staikos, *Architecture of Libraries*, pp. 248–9.

32. Schlotheuber and McQuillen, 'Books and Libraries', p. 981.

33. See also chapter 3.

34. K. W. Humphreys, 'The Effects of Thirteenth-century Cultural Changes on Libraries', *Libraries & Culture*, 24 (1989), pp. 5–20.

35. N. R. Ker, 'The Beginnings of Salisbury Cathedral Library', in his *Books, Collectors and Libraries: Studies in the Medieval Heritage*, ed. Andrew G. Watson (London and Ronceverte: Hambledon, 1983), pp. 143–74, and see also his 'Cathedral Libraries', in the same, pp. 293–300.

36. Richard H. Rouse, 'The early library of the Sorbonne', *Scriptorium*, 21 (1967), pp. 42–71. J. O. Ward, 'Alexandria and Its Medieval Legacy: The Book, the Monk and the Rose', in Roy MacLeod (ed.), *The Library of Alexandria: Centre of Learning in the Ancient World* (London and New York: I. B. Tauris, 2000), pp. 163–79, here p. 171.

37. N. R. Ker, 'Oxford College Libraries before 1500', in his *Books, Collectors and Libraries*, pp. 301–20.

38. Ibid, p. 302.

39. Staikos, *Architecture of Libraries*, p. 253.

40. Burnett Hillman Streeter, *The Chained Library: A Survey of Four Centuries in the Evolution of the English Library* (London: Macmillan, 1931).

41. S. K. Padover, 'German libraries in the fourteenth and fifteenth centuries', in Thompson, *The Medieval Library*, pp. 453–76, here p. 455.

42. Anthony Hobson, *Great Libraries* (London: Weidenfeld & Nicolson, 1970), p. 22.
43. See chapter 3.
44. Phyllis Goodhart Gordan, *Two Renaissance Book Hunters: The Letters of Poggius Bracciolini to Nicolaus de Niccolis* (New York, NY: Columbia University Press, 1974). See also chapter 3.
45. Ibid, pp. 188–9.
46. Ibid, p. 192.
47. Ibid, pp. 42, 46.
48. Ibid, p. 99.
49. Ibid, pp. 100, 102.

3. Little Monkeys and Letters of Gold

1. Richard H. Rouse and Mary A. Rouse, 'The Commercial Production of Manuscript Books in Late-Thirteenth-century and Early-Fourteenth-century Paris', in Linda L. Brownrigg (ed.), *Medieval Book Production: Assessing the Evidence* (London: Red Gull Press, 1990), pp. 103–15, here p. 103.
2. See chapter 4.
3. For a good example, see Adrian Papahagi, 'The Library of Petrus Gotfart de Corona, Rector of the University of Vienna in 1473', *The Library*, 7th series, 20 (2019), pp. 29–46, p. 39.
4. Graham Pollard, 'The pecia system in the medieval universities', in M. B. Parkes and Andrew G. Watson (eds.), *Medieval Scribes, Manuscripts and Libraries: Essays Presented to N. R. Ker* (London: Scolar Press, 1978), pp. 145–61.
5. Nikolaus Weichselbaumer, '"Quod Exemplaria vera habeant et correcta": Concerning the Distribution and Purpose of the Pecia System', in Richard Kirwan and Sophie Mullins (eds.), *Specialist Markets in the Early Modern Book World* (Leiden and Boston: Brill, 2015), pp. 331–50, here p. 343.
6. Richard H. Rouse and Mary A. Rouse, *Manuscripts and Their Makers: Commercial Book Producers in Medieval Paris, 1200–1500* (London: Harvey Miller, 2000).
7. A phenomenal study is Frits Pieter van Oostrom, *Court and Culture: Dutch Literature, 1350–1450* (Berkeley, CA: University of California Press, 1992).
8. Eamon Duffy, *Marking the Hours: English People and Their Prayers, 1240–1570* (London and New Haven: Yale University Press, 2006).
9. Roger S. Wieck, *Time Sanctified: The Book of Hours in Medieval Art and Life* (New York, NY: George Braziller, 2001), p. 39.
10. Christopher de Hamel, *Meetings with Remarkable Manuscripts* (London: Allen Lane, 2016), pp. 376–425.
11. Georges Dogaer and Marguerite Debae, *La Librairie de Philippe le Bon* (Brussels: Bibliothèque royale, 1967), p. 1.
12. Godfried Croenen and Peter Ainsworth (eds.), *Patrons, Authors and Workshops: Books and Book Production in Paris around 1400* (Leuven: Peeters, 2006).
13. Hanno Wijsman, *Luxury Bound: Illustrated Manuscript Production and Noble and Princely Book Ownership in the Burgundian Netherlands (1400–1550)* (Turnhout: Brepols, 2010), p. 23.

14. This is now in the British Library as Add MS 18850.

15. Alessandra Petrina, *Cultural Politics in Fifteenth-century England: The Case of Humphrey, Duke of Gloucester* (Leiden: Brill, 2004), pp. 153–258.

16. See chapter 6.

17. For a case study, see Andrew Taylor, 'Manual to Miscellany: Stages in the Commercial Copying of Vernacular Literature in England', *The Yearbook of English Studies*, 33 (2003), pp. 1–17.

18. Dogaer and Debae, *La Librairie de Philippe le Bon*. Wijsman, *Luxury Bound*, pp. 244–53.

19. Hanno Wijsman, *Handschriften voor het hertogdom. De mooiste verluchte manuscripten van Brabantse hertogen, edellieden, kloosterlingen en stedelingen* (Alphen: Veerhuis, 2006).

20. James P. Carley (ed.), *The Libraries of King Henry VIII* (London: British Library, 2000), p. 3.

21. Duffy, *Marking the Hours*, p. 25.

22. Ibid, p. 22.

23. Dora Thornton, *The Scholar in His Study: Ownership and Experience in Renaissance Italy* (London and New Haven: Yale University Press, 1997).

24. Ibid, p. 32.

25. Ibid, p. 4.

26. Cited in ibid, pp. 133–4.

27. See chapter 2.

28. For a good example, see David Rundle, 'A Renaissance Bishop and His Books: A Preliminary Survey of the Manuscript Collection of Pietro del Monte (*c.*1400–57)', *Papers of the British School at Rome*, 69 (2001), pp. 245–72, here p. 256.

29. See chapter 1.

30. R. J. Mitchell, 'A Renaissance Library: The Collection of John Tiptoft, Earl of Worcester', *The Library*, 4th series, 18 (1937), pp. 67–83.

31. Albinia C. de la Mare, 'Vespasiano da Bisticci, Historian and Bookseller' (PhD thesis, London University, 1966). Idem, 'Vespasiano da Bisticci as Producer of Classical Manuscripts in Fifteenth-century Florence', in Claudine A. Chavannes-Mazel and Margaret M. Smith (eds.), *Medieval Manuscripts of the Latin Classics: Production and Use* (London: Red Gull Press, 1996), pp. 166–207. Most recently: Ross King, *The bookseller of Florence* (London: Chatto & Windus, 2021).

32. De la Mare, 'Vespasiano da Bisticci, Historian and Bookseller', p. 214.

33. Ibid, pp. 215–16.

34. Vespasiano da Bisticci, *Renaissance Princes, Popes and Prelates: The Vespasiano Memoirs – Lives of Illustrious Men of the XVth Century*, trans. William George and Emily Waters (New York, NY: Harper & Row, 1963).

35. Ibid, pp. 102–104.

36. Thornton, *The Scholar in His Study*, p. 120. K. Sp. Staikos, *The Architecture of Libraries in Western Civilization: From the Minoan Era to Michelangelo* (New Castle, DE: Oak Knoll Press, 2017), pp. 316–19.

37. Vespasiano da Bisticci, *Renaissance Princes, Popes and Prelates*, pp. 114–15, 118, 155–6, 171, 237.

38. The whole story is expertly told in Berthold L. Ullman and Philip A. Stadler, *The Public Library of Renaissance Florence: Niccolò Niccoli, Cosimo de' Medici and the Library of San Marco* (Padova: Editrice Antenore, 1972).

39. De la Mare, 'Vespasiano da Bisticci, Historian and Bookseller', p. 219.

40. Vespasiano da Bisticci, *Renaissance Princes, Popes and Prelates*, p. 221.

41. Ullman and Stadler, *The Public Library of Renaissance Florence*, p. 28.

42. Elias Muhanna, *The World in a Book: Al-Nuwayri and the Islamic Encylopedic Tradition* (Princeton, NJ: Princeton University Press, 2018).

43. Arnold H. Green, 'The History of Libraries in the Arab World: A Diffusionist Model', *Libraries & Culture,* 23 (1988), pp. 454–73. Ribhi Mustafa Elayyan, 'The History of the Arabic-Islamic Libraries: 7th to 14th Centuries', *International Library Review*, 22 (1990), pp. 119–35.

44. Brent D. Singleton, 'African Bibliophiles: Books and Libraries in Medieval Timbuktu', *Libraries & Culture*, 39 (2004), pp. 1–12.

45. Paul E. Walker, 'Literary Culture in Fatimid Egypt', in Assadullah Souren Melikian-Chirvani (ed.), *The World of the Fatimids* (Toronto: Aga Khan Museum, 2018), pp. 160–75. Johannes Pedersen, *The Arabic Book* (Princeton, NJ: Princeton University Press, 1984), pp. 118–19, and, more broadly, pp. 113–30.

46. Kuang Neng-fu, 'Chinese Library Science in the Twelfth Century', *Libraries & Culture,* 26 (1991), pp. 357–71. On Japan, see Peter Kornicki, *The Book in Japan: A Cultural History from the Beginnings to the Nineteenth Century* (Honolulu: University of Hawai'i Press, 2001), pp. 363–412.

47. Mark Kurlansky, *Paper: Paging through History* (New York, NY: W. W. Norton, 2016), pp. 76–97.

48. Kai-wing Chow, *Publishing, Culture and Power in Early Modern China* (Stanford, CA: Stanford University Press, 2004). C. J. Brokaw, 'On the history of the book in China', in C. J. Brokaw and Kai-wing Chow (eds.), *Printing and Book Culture in Late Imperial China* (Berkeley, CA: University of California Press, 2005), pp. 3–55.

49. See the *International Dunhuang Project*, co-hosted by the British Library: http://idp.bl.uk/.

50. On a recent and highly authoritative perspective, see Joseph P. McDermott and Peter Burke (eds.), *The Book Worlds of East Asia and Europe, 1450–1850: Connections and Comparisons* (Hong Kong: Hong Kong University Press, 2015). See also chapter 4.

4. The Infernal Press

1. Cited in Eric Marshall White, *Editio Princeps: A History of the Gutenberg Bible* (London and Turnhout: Harvey Miller, 2017), p. 23.

2. Ibid, pp. 23–4. See more broadly Albert Kapr, *Johann Gutenberg: The Man and His Invention* (Aldershot: Scolar Press, 1996).

3. Andrew Pettegree, *The Book in the Renaissance* (London and New Haven: Yale University Press, 2010), pp. 21–62. Susan Noakes, 'The Development of

the Book Market in Late Quattrocento Italy: Printers' Failures and the Role of the Middleman', *The Journal of Medieval and Renaissance Studies*, 11 (1981), pp. 23–55.

4. Mary A. Rouse and Richard H. Rouse, 'Backgrounds to print: aspects of the manuscript book in northern Europe of the fifteenth century', in their *Authentic Witnesses: Approaches to Medieval Texts and Manuscripts* (Notre Dame, IN: University of Notre Dame Press, 1991), pp. 449–66.

5. Elizabeth L. Eisenstein, *Divine Art, Infernal Machine: The Reception of Printing in the West from First Impressions to the Sense of an Ending* (Philadelphia, PA: University of Pennsylvania Press, 2011), p. 13.

6. For an excellent case study, see Paul Saenger, 'Colard Mansion and the Evolution of the Printed Book', *Library Quarterly*, 45 (1975), pp. 405–18.

7. Falk Eisermann, 'A Golden Age? Monastic Printing Houses in the Fifteenth Century', in Benito Rial Costas (ed.), *Print Culture and Peripheries in Early Modern Europe* (Leiden: Brill, 2012), pp. 37–67, here p. 41.

8. Ibid, p. 63.

9. Melissa Conway, *The Diario of the Printing Press of San Jacopo di Ripoli, 1476–1484* (Florence: Olschki, 1999), pp. 28, 56–61.

10. Eisermann, 'A Golden Age?', p. 37.

11. Lotte Hellinga, 'Book Auctions in the Fifteenth Century', in her *Incunabula in Transit: People and Trade* (Leiden and Boston: Brill, 2018), pp. 6–19, here p. 6.

12. White, *Editio Princeps*, p. 49.

13. Eisermann, 'A Golden Age?', p. 37.

14. Curt F. Bühler, *The Fifteenth-century Book: The Scribes, the Printers, the Decorators* (Philadelphia, PA: Philadelphia University Press, 1960), p. 41.

15. Hannes Kleineke, 'The Library of John Veysy (d. 1492), Fellow of Lincoln College, Oxford, and Rector of St James, Garlickhythe, London', *The Library*, 7th series, 17 (2016), pp. 399–423. Wolfgang Undorf, 'Print and Book Culture in the Danish Town of Odense', in Costas (ed.), *Print Culture and Peripheries*, pp. 227–48.

16. N. R. Ker, 'Oxford College Libraries in the Sixteenth Century', in his *Books, Collectors and Libraries: Studies in the Medieval Heritage* (London and Ronceverte: Hambledon, 1985), pp. 379–436, here p. 395.

17. Filippo de Strata, *Polemic against Printing*, ed. Martin Lowry (Birmingham: Hayloft Press, 1986).

18. See chapters 13 and 15.

19. Vespasiano da Bisticci, *Renaissance Princes, Popes and Prelates*, p. 104.

20. Albinia C. de la Mare, 'Vespasiano da Bisticci as Producer of Classical Manuscripts in Fifteenth-century Florence', in Claudine A. Chavannes-Mazel and Margaret M. Smith (eds.), *Medieval Manuscripts of the Latin Classics: Production and Use* (London: Red Gull Press, 1996), pp. 166–207, here p. 206.

21. Berthold L. Ullman and Philip A. Stadler, *The Public Library of Renaissance Florence: Niccolò Niccoli, Cosimo de' Medici and the Library of San Marco* (Padova: Editrice Antenore, 1972), pp. 46–7.

22. Marcus Tanner, *The Raven King: Matthias Corvinus and the Fate of His Lost Library* (London and New Haven: Yale University Press, 2008).

23. Hanno Wijsman, 'Philippe le Beau et les livres: rencontre entre une époque et une personnalité', in his *Books in Transition at the Time of Philip the Fair: Manuscripts and Printed Books in the Late Fifteenth and Early Sixteenth Century Low Countries* (Turnhout: Brepols, 2010), pp. 17–92, here pp. 88, 91.

24. Hanno Wijsman, 'Une bataille perdue d'avance? Les manuscrits après l'introduction de l'imprimerie dans les anciens Pays-Bas', in his *Books in Transition*, pp. 257–72, here p. 263.

25. Hanno Wijsman, *Luxury Bound: Illustrated Manuscript Production and Noble and Princely Book Ownership in the Burgundian Netherlands (1400–1550)* (Turnhout: Brepols, 2010), pp. 337–8.

26. Marguerite Debae, *La Librairie de Marguerite d'Autriche* (Brussels: Bibliothèque royale, 1987).

27. Roger Chartier, *The Cultural Uses of Print in Early Modern France* (Princeton, NJ: Princeton University Press, 1987), p. 150.

28. Julia Boffey, *Manuscript and Print in London, c.1475–1530* (London: British Library, 2012), pp. 1–2.

29. James P. Carley (ed.), *The Libraries of King Henry VIII* (London: British Library, 2000).

30. See chapter 6.

5. Coming of Age

1. Noel L. Brann, *The Abbot Trithemius (1462–1516): The Renaissance of Monastic Humanism* (Leiden: Brill, 1981), pp. 4–53.

2. An English translation is available: Johannes Trithemius, *In Praise of Scribes*, trans Elizabeth Bryson Bongie (Vancouver: Alcuin Society, 1977).

3. USTC 749471.

4. Trithemius, *In Praise of Scribes*, p. 4.

5. Anthony Grafton, *Worlds Made by Words: Scholarship and Community in the Modern West* (Cambridge, MA: Harvard University Press, 2009), chapter 3.

6. A career now beautifully evoked in Edward Wilson-Lee, *The Catalogue of Shipwrecked Books: Young Columbus and the Quest for a Universal Library* (London: Harper Collins, 2018).

7. Mark P. McDonald, *Ferdinand Columbus: Renaissance Collector* (London: British Museum, 2005).

8. Klaus Wagner, 'Le commerce du livre en France au début du XVIe siècle d'après les notes manuscrites de Fernando Colomb', *Bulletin du bibliophile*, 2 (1992), pp. 305–29.

9. The USTC has seven editions, published in Barcelona, Valladolid, Rome, Basel and Antwerp. There was also an Italian versification, by Giuliano Dati. See Martin T. Davies, *Columbus in Italy* (London: British Library, 1991).

10. Egbertus van Gulik, *Erasmus and his Books* (Toronto: University of Toronto Press, 2018).

11. Wilson-Lee, *Catalogue of Shipwrecked Books*, pp. 314–16.

12. Henry Harrisse, *Excerpta Colombiniana: Bibliographie de 400 pièces du 16e siècle; précédée d'une histoire de la Bibliothèque colombine et de son fondateur* (Paris: Welter, 1887).

13. Andrew Pettegree, *Foreign Protestant Communities in Sixteenth-century London* (Oxford: Oxford University Press, 1986).

14. The largest portion are in the university library in Groningen.

15. Ladislaus Buzás, *German Library History, 800–1945* (Jefferson, NC: McFarland, 1986), p. 16.

6. Reformations

1. Andrew Pettegree, *Brand Luther: 1517, Printing, and the Making of the Reformation* (New York: Penguin, 2015).

2. Drew B. Thomas, 'Circumventing Censorship: the Rise and Fall of Reformation Print Centres', in Alexander S. Wilkinson and Graeme J. Kemp (eds.), *Negotiating Conflict and Controversy in the Early Modern Book World* (Leiden and Boston: Brill, 2019), pp. 13–37.

3. Karl Schottenloher, 'Schicksale von Büchern und Bibliotheken im Bauernkrieg', *Zeitschrift für Bücherfreunde*, 12 (1909), pp. 396–408. Ladislaus Buzás, *German Library History, 800–1945* (Jefferson, NC: McFarland, 1986), pp. 31–85. S. K. Padover, 'German libraries in the fourteenth and fifteenth centuries', in James Westfall Thompson (ed.), *The Medieval Library* (New York, NY: Hafner, 1957), pp. 453–76, here pp. 475–6.

4. Schottenloher, 'Schicksale von Büchern', p. 399.

5. Martin Germann, 'Zwischen Konfiskation, Zerstreuung und Zerstörung: Schicksale der Bücher und Bibliotheken in der Reformationszeit in Basel, Bern und Zürich', *Zwingliana*, 27 (2000), pp. 63–77, here p. 65.

6. Schottenloher, 'Schicksale von Büchern', p. 398.

7. Padover, 'German libraries', p. 476.

8. Germann, 'Zwischen Konfiskation', p. 65.

9. Ibid, p. 70.

10. See chapters 8 and 10.

11. Nigel Ramsay, '"The Manuscripts Flew about Like Butterflies": The Break-up of English Libraries in the Sixteenth Century', in James Raven (ed.), *Lost Libraries: The Destruction of Great Book Collections since Antiquity* (Basingstoke: Palgrave, 2004), pp. 125–44, here p. 126.

12. Ronald Harold Fritze, '"Truth Hath Lacked Witness, Tyme Wanted Light": The Dispersal of the English Monastic Libraries and Protestant Efforts at Preservation, ca. 1535–1625', *Journal of Library History*, 18 (1983), pp. 274–91, here p. 276. Ramsay, '"The Manuscripts Flew about Like Butterflies"', p. 125.

13. Mark Purcell, *The Country House Library* (London and New Haven: Yale University Press, 2017), p. 59.

14. See chapter 12.

15. Purcell, *Country House Library*, p. 76.

16. Ramsay, '"The Manuscripts Flew about Like Butterflies"', p. 129.

17. C. E. Wright, 'The Dispersal of the Monastic Libraries and the Beginnings of Anglo-Saxon Studies: Matthew Parker and His Circle', *Transactions of the Cambridge Bibliographical Society*, 1 (1951), pp. 208–37, here p. 211.

18. Ibid.

19. Cited in Fritze, '"Truth Hath Lacked Witness, Tyme Wanted Light"', p. 282.

20. James P. Carley, 'The Dispersal of the Monastic Libraries and the Salvaging of the Spoils', in Elisabeth Leedham-Green and Teresa Webber (eds.), *The Cambridge History of Libraries in Britain and Ireland, vol. I: To 1640* (Cambridge: Cambridge University Press, 2006), pp. 265–91, here p. 268.

21. Wright, 'The Dispersal of the Monastic Libraries', p. 210.

22. Carley, 'The Dispersal of the Monastic Libraries', pp. 274–5.

23. Cited in Ramsay, '"The Manuscripts Flew about Like Butterflies"', p. 131.

24. James P. Carley (ed.), *The Libraries of King Henry VIII* (London: British Library, 2000), p. lxxvii.

25. Sarah Gray and Chris Baggs, 'The English Parish Library: A Celebration of Diversity', *Libraries & Culture*, 35 (2000), pp. 414–33, p. 416.

26. Cited in Ramsay, '"The Manuscripts Flew about Like Butterflies"', p. 133.

27. Kristian Jensen, 'Universities and Colleges', in Leedham-Green and Webber, *The Cambridge History of Libraries in Britain and Ireland*, pp. 345–62, here p. 350.

28. J. C. T. Oates, *Cambridge University Library, a History: From the Beginnings to the Copyright Act of Queen Anne* (Cambridge: Cambridge University Press, 1986), p. 70.

29. N. R. Ker, 'Oxford College Libraries in the Sixteenth Century', in his *Books, Collectors and Libraries: Studies in the Medieval Heritage*, ed. Andrew G. Watson (London and Ronceverte: Hambledon, 1985), pp. 379–436, here p. 389.

30. See chapter 8.

31. Cited in Renaud Adam, 'The profession of printer in the Southern Netherlands before the Reformation: Considerations on professional, religious and state legislations (1473–1520)', in Violet Soen, Dries Vanysacker and Wim François (eds.), *Church, Censorship and Reform in the Early Modern Habsburg Netherlands* (Turnhout: Brepols, 2017), pp. 13–25, here p. 13.

32. Grantley McDonald, '"Burned to Dust": Censorship and repression of theological literature in the Habsburg Netherlands during the 1520s', in ibid, pp. 27–45, here pp. 29–31.

33. Pierre Delsaerdt, 'A Bookshop for a New Age: The Inventory of the Bookshop of the Louvain Bookseller Hieronymus Cloet, 1543', in Lotte Hellinga, et al. (eds.), *The Bookshop of the World: The Role of the Low Countries in the Book-Trade, 1473–1941* ('t Goy-Houten: Hes & De Graaf, 2001), pp. 75–86.

34. César Manrique Figueroa, 'Sixteenth-century Spanish Editions Printed in Antwerp Facing Censorship in the Hispanic World: The Case of the Antwerp Printers Nutius and Steelsius', in Soen, Vanysacker and François, *Church, Censorship and Reform*, pp. 107–21, here pp. 116–18. See more broadly Clive Griffin, *Journeymen-Printers, Heresy, and the Inquisition in Sixteenth-century Spain* (Oxford: Oxford University Press, 2005).

35. Federico Barbierato, *The Inquisitor in the Hat Shop: Inquisition, Forbidden Books and Unbelief in Early Modern Venice* (Farnham: Ashgate, 2012), p. 59.

36. George Haven Putnam, *The Censorship of the Church of Rome and its Influence upon the Production and Distribution of Literature* (2 vols., New York, NY: Benjamin Blom, 1967). Jesús Martínez de Bujanda, Francis M. Higman and

James K. Farge (eds.), *Index de l'Université de Paris* (Geneva: Droz, 1985), and others in this series of modern editions of the sixteenth-century indices.

37. Paul F. Grendler and Marcella Grendler, 'The Survival of Erasmus in Italy', *Erasmus in English*, 8 (1976), pp. 2–22.

38. Work is currently undertaken by the RICI project in Italy (*Ricerca sull'Inchiesta della Congregazione dell'Indice dei libri proibiti*) to document this survey.

39. Idalia García Aguilar, 'Before We are Condemned: Inquisitorial Fears and Private Libraries of New Spain', in Natalia Maillard Álvarez (ed.), *Books in the Catholic World during the Early Modern Period* (Leiden: Brill, 2014), pp. 171–90.

40. Paul F. Grendler, *The Roman Inquisition and the Venetian Press* (Princeton, NJ: Princeton University Press, 1977).

41. Ian Maclean, *Episodes in the Life of the Early Modern Learned Book* (Leiden: Brill, 2020), chapters 1 and 2.

42. Roger Kuin, 'Private library as public danger: the case of Duplessis-Mornay', in Andrew Pettegree, Paul Nelles and Philip Conner (eds.), *The Sixteenth-century French Religious Book* (Aldershot: Ashgate, 2001), pp. 319–57, here p. 325.

43. For a detailed case study, see Barbierato, *The Inquisitor in the Hat Shop*, pp. 295–334.

7. The Professionals

1. Ann Blair, *Too Much to Know: Managing Scholarly Information before the Modern Age* (London and New Haven: Yale University Press, 2010). R. J. W. Evans and Alexander Marr (eds.), *Curiosity and Wonder from the Renaissance to the Enlightenment* (Aldershot: Ashgate, 2006).

2. David Rundle, 'English Books and the Continent', in Alexandra Gillespie and Daniel Wakelin (eds.), *The Production of Books in England, 1350–1500* (Cambridge: Cambridge University Press, 2011), pp. 276–91.

3. R. J. Fehrenbach and E. S. Leedham-Green, *Private Libraries in Renaissance England: A Collection and Catalogue of Tudor and Early Stuart Book-Lists* (9 vols., Binghamton, N.Y: Medieval & Renaissance Texts & Studies, 1992–), III, pp. 36–44. E. S. Leedham-Green, *Books in Cambridge Inventories: Book Lists from Vice-Chancellor's Court Probate Inventories in the Tudor and Stuart Periods* (2 vols., Cambridge: Cambridge University Press, 1986), I, pp. 492–508; II, pp. 839–42.

4. Leedham-Green, *Cambridge Inventories*, I, pp. 508–22; *Private Libraries*, IX.

5. Leedham-Green, *Cambridge Inventories*, I, pp. 102–104, II, p. 316.

6. Andrea Finkelstein, 'Gerard de Malynes and Edward Misselden: The Learned Library of the Seventeenth-Century Merchant', *Book History*, 3 (2000), pp. 1–20.

7. Andrew Pettegree and Arthur der Weduwen, *The Bookshop of the World: Making and Trading Books in the Dutch Golden Age* (London and New Haven: Yale University Press, 2019).

8. And occasionally leave their bag behind. See Arthur der Weduwen and Andrew Pettegree, *The Dutch Republic and the Birth of Modern Advertising* (Leiden: Brill, 2020), pp. 176–7 for various mislaid valuables.

9. Pettegree and der Weduwen, *Bookshop of the World*, p. 305. See also, William Bouwsma, 'Lawyers and Early Modern Culture', *American Historical Review*, 78 (1973), pp. 303–27.

10. Norbert Furrer, *Des Burgers Bibliothek. Personliche Buchbestände in der stadt Bern des 17. Jahrhunderts* (Zurich: Chronos Verlag, 2018).

11. For examples of some early auctions see Lotte Hellinga, 'Book Auctions in the Fifteenth Century', in her *Incunabula in Transit: People and Trade* (Leiden: Brill, 2018), pp. 6–19.

12. For examples of the distribution of catalogues abroad, see Arthur der Weduwen and Andrew Pettegree, *News, Business and Public Information: Advertisements and Announcements in Dutch and Flemish Newspapers, 1620–1675* (Leiden: Brill, 2020), pp. 616–17.

13. For examples, see Forrest C. Strickland, 'The Devotion of Collecting: Ministers and the Culture of Print in the Seventeenth-Century Dutch Republic' (PhD thesis, University of St Andrews, 2019), p. 76.

14. See the enormous list of booksellers who owed money to Daniel Elzevier on his death in 1681, reproduced in B. P. M. Dongelmans, 'Elzevier addenda et corrigenda', in B. P. M. Dongelmans, P. G. Hoftijzer and O. S. Lankhorst (eds.), *Boekverkopers van Europa* (Zutphen: Walburg Pers, 2000), pp. 53–8.

15. See chapter 12.

16. *Bewys dat het een predicant met zyn huysvrouw alleen niet mogelijck en is op vijfhondert guld eerlijck te leven* [Proof that it is impossible for a minister and his wife to live on 500 guilders a year] (Delft: Pieter de Menagie, 1658), USTC 1839412.

17. Hellinga, 'Book Auctions in the Fifteenth Century', pp. 10, 14–17, 18–19.

18. Urs B. Leu, and Sandra Weidmann, *Huldrych Zwingli's Private Library* (Leiden: Brill, 2019). The Luther imprints are nos. A120–A144.

19. Urs B. Leu, Raffael Keller and Sandra Weidmann, *Conrad Gessner's Private Library* (Leiden and Boston: Brill, 2008).

20. Strickland, 'The Devotion of Collecting'.

21. Ibid, pp. 65–6.

22. Henriëtte A. Bosman-Jelgersma, 'De inventaris van een Leidse apotheek uit het jaar 1587', *Leids Jaarboekje*, 86 (1994), pp. 51–68, here pp. 54–5.

23. Caroline Duroselle-Melish and David A. Lines, 'The Library of Ulisse Aldrovandi (†1605): Acquiring and Organizing Books in Sixteenth-century Bologna', *The Library*, 7th series, 16 (2015), pp. 133–61. Angela Nuovo, 'Private Libraries in Sixteenth-Century Italy', in Bettina Wagner and Marcia Reed (eds.), *Early Printed Books as Material Objects* (Berlin and New York: De Gruyter Saur, 2010), pp. 231–42.

24. Dresden, Sächsisches Hauptstaatsarchiv, Bestand 10088 Oberkonsistorium, Loc. 1979, fol. 1015r. The authors thank our St Andrews colleague Professor Bridget Heal for this reference.

25. Lisa T. Sarasohn, 'Thomas Hobbes and the Duke of Newcastle: A Study in the Mutuality of Patronage before the Establishment of the Royal Society', *Isis*, 90 (1999), pp. 715–37. Mark Purcell, *The Country House Library* (London and New Haven: Yale University Press, 2017), pp. 89–90.

26. John Harrison and Peter Laslett, *The Library of John Locke,* 2nd edn (Oxford, Clarendon Press, 1971).

27. Marcella Grendler, 'A Greek Collection in Padua: The Library of Gian Vincenzo Pinelli (1535–1601)', *Renaissance Quarterly,* 33 (1980), pp. 386–416. Idem, 'Book Collecting in Counter-Reformation Italy: The Library of Gian Vincenzo Pinelli (1535–1601)', *Journal of Library History,* 16 (1981), pp. 144–51.

28. Paulo Gualdo, *Vita Joannis Vincentii Pinelli, Patricii Genuensis: In qua studiosis bonarum artium, proponitur typus viri probi et eruditi* (Augsburg: Markus Welser, 1607). USTC 2040570.

29. The story is well told in Anthony Hobson, 'A Sale by Candle in 1608', *The Library,* 5th series, 26 (1971), pp. 215–33. See also Angela Nuovo, 'The Creation and Dispersal of the Library of Gian Vincenzo Pinelli', in Giles Mandelbrote, et al. (eds.), *Books on the Move: Tracking Copies through Collections and the Book Trade* (New Castle, DE: Oak Knoll Press, 2007), pp. 39–68.

30. See chapter 10.

31. Duroselle-Melish and Lines, 'The Library of Ulisse Aldrovandi'.

32. Geoffrey Davenport et al (eds.), *The Royal College of Physicians and its Collections* (London: James & James, 2001).

33. *Critical Review,* 55 (1783), pp. 391–2. Harrison and Laslett, *The Library of John Locke.*

34. Jan Pirozynski, 'Royal Book Collections in Poland during the Renaissance', *Libraries & Culture,* 24 (1989), pp. 21–32. Peter H. Reid, 'Patriots and Rogues: Some Scottish Lairds and Their Libraries', *Library & Information History,* 35 (2019), pp. 1–20.

35. Purcell, *The Country House Library,* offers a definitive survey of aristocratic collecting. See also chapter 12.

8. Idle Books and Riff Raff

1. Mary Clapinson, *A Brief History of the Bodleian Library* (Oxford: The Bodleian Library, 2015), p. 7.

2. Ian Philip, *The Bodleian Library in the Seventeenth and Eighteenth Centuries* (Oxford: Clarendon Press, 1983), pp. 1–22.

3. Cited in ibid, p. 3.

4. J. Dirks, 'Aanteekeningen van Z.C. von Uffenbach gedurende zijn verblijf in Friesland in 1710', *De Vrije Fries,* 6 (1853), pp. 305–90, here p. 344.

5. Clapinson, *A Brief History,* p. 32.

6. Clapinson, *A Brief History,* p. 14.

7. Cited in Anna E. C. Simoni, 'The librarian's *cri de coeur*: rules for readers (1711)', *Quaerendo,* 32 (2002), pp. 199–203.

8. For Harvard, see chapter 9.

9. Richard W. Clement, 'Librarianship and Polemics: The Career of Thomas James (1572–1629)', *Library & Culture,* 26 (1991), pp. 269–82.

10. Located today in the national library of Hungary, Budapest, under call number 627.947.

11. Carolyn O. Frost, 'The Bodleian Catalogs of 1674 and 1738: An Examination

in the Light of Modern Cataloging Theory', *Library Quarterly*, 46 (1976), pp. 248–70.

12. On the Mazarine library, see chapter 11.

13. John Harrison and Peter Laslett, *The Library of John Locke*, 2nd edn (Oxford: Clarendon Press, 1971).

14. Elaine Gilboy, 'Les exemplaires interfoliés du catalogue de la Bodléienne', in Frédéric Barbier, Thierry Dubois and Yann Sordet (eds.), *De l'argile au nuage, une archéologie des catalogues* (Paris: Éditions des Cendres, 2015), pp. 274–80.

15. John Warwick Montgomery, *A Seventeenth-century View of European Libraries: Lomeier's De Bibliothecis, Chapter X* (Berkeley, CA: University of California Press, 1962), p. 51.

16. See chapter 9.

17. See chapter 10.

18. Jens Bruning and Ulrike Gleixner (eds.), *Das Athen der Welfen: Die Reformuniversität Helmstedt, 1576–1810* (Wiesbaden: Harrassowitz, 2010), pp. 248–83.

19. Thomas Hendrickson, *Ancient Libraries and Renaissance Humanism: The 'De Bibliothecis' of Justus Lipsius* (Leiden: Brill, 2017).

20. Christian Coppens, 'Auspicia bibliothecae: donators at the foundation of the Central Library in Louvain (1636–9)', *Quaerendo*, 34 (2004), pp. 169–210.

21. Clapinson, *A Brief History*, p. 9.

22. David McKitterick, 'History of the Library', in Peter Fox (ed.), *Cambridge University Library: The Great Collections* (Cambridge: Cambridge University Press, 1998), pp. 5–32, here p. 15. Jayne Ringrose, 'The Royal Library: John Moore and his books', in the same, pp. 78–89.

23. Ringrose, 'The Royal Library', p. 84.

24. P. C. Molhuysen, *Bronnen tot de geschiedenis der Leidsche universiteit 1574–1811* (7 vols., Den Haag: Martinus Nijhoff, 1913–24), II, p. 59.

25. P. G. Hoftijzer, 'A Study Tour into the Low Countries and the German States: William Nicolson's *Iter Hollandicum* and *Iter Germanicum*, 1678–1679', *Lias*, 15 (1988), pp. 73–128, here p. 93.

26. E. Hulshoff Pol, 'What about the library? Travellers' comments on the Leiden Library in the 17th and 18th centuries', *Quaerendo*, 5 (1975), pp. 39–51, especially pp. 44, 46–7.

27. Some examples in J. Vallinkoski, *The History of the University Library at Turku. I, 1640–1722* (Helsinki: University Library at Helsinki, 1948), p. 119.

28. O. S. Lankhorst, 'De Bibliotheek van de Gelderse Academie te Harderwijk – thans te Deventer', in J. A. H. Bots, et al. (eds.), *Het Gelders Athene. Bijdragen tot de geschiedenis van de Gelderse universiteit in Harderwijk (1648–1811)* (Hilversum: Verloren, 2000), pp. 95–118, here p. 101.

29. For some figures see Arvo Tering, 'The Tartu University Library and Its Use at the End of the Seventeenth and the Beginning of the Eighteenth Century', *Libraries & Culture*, 28 (1993), pp. 44–54 and Paul Raabe, 'Bibliothekskataloge als buchgeschichtliche Quellen. Bemerkungen über gedruckte kataloge öffentlicher Bibliotheken in der frühen Neuzeit', in Reinhard Wittmann (ed.),

Bücherkataloge als buchgeschichtliche Quellen in der frühen Neuzeit (Wiesbaden: Harrassowitz, 1984), pp. 275–97, here pp. 295–7.

30. Robert S. Freeman, 'University Library of Tübingen', in David H. Stam (ed.), *International Dictionary of Library Histories* (2 vols., Chicago and London: Fitzroy Dearborn, 2001), pp. 793–5.

31. Manfred Komorowski, 'Bibliotheken', in Ulrich Rasche (ed.), *Quellen zur frühneuzeitlichen Universitätsgeschichte* (Wiesbaden: Harrassowitz, 2011), pp. 55–81, here pp. 58–9.

32. Zacharias Conrad von Uffenbach, *Merkwürdige Reisen durch Niedersachsen Holland und Engelland, Zweyter Theil* (Ulm: Johann Friederich Baum, 1753), II, p. 249. Albrecht von Haller, *Tagebücher seiner Reisen nach Deutschland, Holland und England 1723–1727*, ed. Ludwig Hirzel (Leipzig: Hirzel, 1883), p. 94. With thanks to Jacob van Sluis for these references.

33. Vallinkoski, *History of the University Library at Turku*, p. 44.

34. See chapter 11.

35. John Dury, *The Reformed Librarie-Keeper* (London: William Du-Gard, 1650), p. 16. See more broadly, Catherine J. Minter, 'John Dury's *Reformed Librarie-Keeper*: Information and Its Intellectual Contexts in Seventeenth-century England', *Library & Information History*, 31 (2015), pp. 18–34.

36. Cited in Jacob van Sluis, *The Library of Franeker University in Context, 1585–1843* (Leiden: Brill, 2020), pp. 217–18.

37. Ibid, pp. 185–90.

38. Tering, 'The Tartu University Library', pp. 44–54.

39. Andrew Pettegree, 'The Dutch Baltic: The Dutch book trade and the Building of Libraries in the Baltic and Central Europe during the Dutch Golden Age', in Arthur der Weduwen, Andrew Pettegree and Graeme Kemp (eds.), *Book Trade Catalogues in Early Modern Europe* (Leiden: Brill, 2021), pp. 286–316.

40. McKitterick, 'History of the Library', p. 24.

41. Kate Loveman, *Samuel Pepys and his Books: Reading, Newsgathering and Sociability, 1660–1703* (Oxford: Oxford University Press, 2015), p. 245.

42. Nicolas K. Kiessling, *The Library of Anthony Wood* (Oxford: Oxford Bibliographical Society, 2002).

43. Ibid, pp. xv–xx.

9. Mission Fields

1. Ian Morrison, 'The History of the Book in Australia', in Michael F. Suarez and H. R Woudhuysen (eds.), *The Oxford Companion to the Book* (Oxford: Oxford University Press, 2010), pp. 394–402, also now available as *The Book: A Global History* (Oxford: Oxford University Press, 2013).

2. Quoted in Lucien X. Polastron, *Books on Fire: The Destruction of Libraries throughout History* (Rochester, VT: Inner Traditions, 2004), p. 126. Michael Arbagi, 'The Catholic Church and the Preservation of Mesoamerican Archives: An Assessment', *Archival Issues*, 33 (2011), pp. 112–21.

3. Andrés de Olmos, *Arte de la lengua mexicana* (Mexico City: s.n., [1547]). USTC 351748. Alonso de Molina, *Aquí comiença un vocabulario en la lengua*

castellana y mexicana (Mexico City: Joan Pablos, 1555). USTC 344084. Arbagi, 'Catholic Church', p. 114.

4. Hortensia Calvo, 'The Politics of Print: The Historiography of the Book in Early Spanish America', *Book History*, 6 (2003), pp. 277–305, here p. 279.

5. Julie Greer Johnson, *The Book in the Americas: The Role of Books and Printing in the Development of Culture and Society in Colonial Latin America* (Providence, RI: John Carter Brown Library, 1988).

6. Magdalena Chocano Mena, 'Colonial Printing and Metropolitan Books: Printed Texts and the Shaping of Scholarly Culture in New Spain, 1539–1700', *Colonial Latin American Historical Review*, 6 (1997), pp. 69–90. Hensley C. Woodbridge and Lawrence S. Thompson, *Printing in Colonial Spanish America* (Troy, NY: Whitson, 1976).

7. Antonio Rodriguez-Buckingham, 'Monastic Libraries and Early Printing in Sixteenth-century Spanish America', *Libraries & Culture*, 24 (1989), pp. 33–56, here p. 52. Valentina Sebastiani, *Johann Froben, Printer of Basel: A Biographical Profile and Catalogue of His Editions* (Leiden: Brill, 2018).

8. On the printing press, which served a similar role to that of Mexico City, see Pedro Guibovich, 'The Printing Press in Colonial Peru: Production Process and Literary Categories in Lima, 1584–1699', *Colonial Latin American Historical Review*, 10 (2001), pp. 167–88.

9. Teodoro Hampe-Martínez, 'The Diffusion of Books and Ideas in Colonial Peru: A Study of Private Libraries in the Sixteenth and Seventeenth Centuries', *The Hispanic American Historical Review*, 73 (1993), pp. 211–33.

10. Allan P. Farrell, *The Jesuit Code of Liberal Education* (Milwaukee, WI: Bruce, 1939).

11. Quoted in Mark L. Grover, 'The Book and the Conquest: Jesuit Libraries in Colonial Brazil', *Libraries & Culture*, 28 (1993), pp. 266–83, p. 268. Brendan Connolly, 'Jesuit Library Beginnings', *Library Quarterly*, 30 (1960), pp. 243–52.

12. Grover, 'The Book and the Conquest', p. 271.

13. Michiel van Groesen, 'The Printed Book in the Dutch Atlantic World', in his *Imagining the Americas in Print: Books, Maps and Encounters in the Atlantic World* (Leiden: Brill, 2019), pp. 164–80, here p. 173.

14. Quoted in Louis B. Wright, 'The Purposeful Reading of Our Colonial Ancestors', *ELH: A Journal of English Literary History*, 4 (1937), pp. 85–111, here p. 91.

15. Jeremy Dupertuis Bangs, *Plymouth Colony's Private Libraries* (Leiden: American Pilgrim Museum, 2016).

16. Rendel Harris and Stephen K. Jones, *The Pilgrim Press: A Bibliographical and Historical Memorial of the Books Printed at Leyden by the Pilgrim Fathers* (Nieuwkoop: De Graaf, 1987).

17. Bangs, *Private Libraries*, p. 218.

18. There are 418 volumes, of which only eighty-four are separately enumerated.

19. David Cressy, 'Books as Totems in Seventeenth-century England and New England', *Journal of Library History*, 21 (1986), pp. 92–106.

20. Joe W. Kraus, 'Private Libraries in Colonial America', *Journal of Library History*, 9 (1974), pp. 31–53, here p. 31.

21. W. H. Bond and Hugh Amory, *The Printed Catalogues of the Harvard College Library, 1723–1790* (Boston: Colonial Society of Massachusetts, 1996).
22. Conversations reported by Thomas Hollis at the New England Coffee-House in London. Bond and Amory, *Printed Catalogues*, p. xxx.
23. Bond and Amory, *Printed Catalogues*, p. xv.
24. From 1578 to 1621, we know of close to thirty editions of *Lettere del Giapone* or *Litterae Japonicae* produced mainly on Italian presses, but also frequently in the southern Netherlands and France, and in several languages. These are often described as the 'Annual Letters of Japan', produced there by Jesuit missionaries. They commented not only on Japan, but also on China and other parts of East Asia. Individual volumes in USTC. For context, see Ronnie Po-chia Hsia (ed.), *A Companion to Early Modern Catholic Global Missions* (Leiden: Brill, 2018).
25. Quoted in Paul Begheyn, *Jesuit Books in the Dutch Republic and its Generality Lands, 1567–1773* (Leiden: Brill, 2014), p. 17.
26. Emma Hagström Molin, 'To Place in a Chest: On the Cultural Looting of Gustavus Adolphus and the Creation of Uppsala University Library in the Seventeenth Century', *Barok*, 44 (2016), pp. 135–48, here pp. 142–5.
27. Emma Hagström Molin, 'The Materiality of War Booty Books: The Case of Strängnäs Cathedral Library', in Anna Källén (ed.), *Making Cultural History: New Perspectives on Western Heritage* (Lund: Nordic Academic Press, 2013), pp. 131–40.
28. Molin, 'Materiality of War Booty Books', p. 131.
29. Molin, 'To Place in a Chest'. Idem, 'Spoils of Knowledge: Looted Books in Uppsala University Library in the Seventeenth Century', in Gerhild Williams, et al. (eds.), *Rethinking Europe: War and Peace in the Early Modern German Lands* (Leiden: Brill, 2019). See also her forthcoming *Plundered Books and Documents in Seventeenth-century Europe* (Leiden: Brill, 2022).
30. Józef Trypućko, *The Catalogue of the Book Collection of the Jesuit College in Braniewo Held in the University Library in Uppsala* (3 vols., Warsaw: Biblioteka Narodowa/Uppsala: Universitetsbibliotek, 2007). The Riga catalogue will be published in 2021.
31. Jan Pirozynski, 'Royal Book Collections in Poland during the Renaissance', *Libraries & Culture*, 24 (1989), pp. 21–32, here pp. 25, 27.
32. Alma Braziuniene, '*Bibliotheca Sapiehana* as a mirror of European culture of the Grand Duchy of Lithuania', in Ausra Rinkunaite (ed.), *Bibliotheca Sapiehana. Vilniaus universiteto bibliotekos rinkinys katalogas* (Vilnius: Lietuviu literaturos ir tautosakos institutas, 2010).
33. The catalogue is a manuscript now held in the university library at Vilnius. See http://www.virtus.mb.vu.lt/en/.
34. H. Oldenhof, 'Bibliotheek Jezuïetenstatie Leeuwarden', in Jacob van Sluis (ed.), *PBF. De Provinsjale Biblioteek fan Fryslân, 150 jaar geschiedenis in collecties* (Leeuwarden: Tresoar, 2002), pp. 75–80.
35. See Begheyn, *Jesuit Books in the Dutch Republic*, pp. 10–12, for a useful list.
36. Hannah Thomas, '"Books Which are Necessary for Them": Reconstructing a Jesuit Missionary Library in Wales and the English Borderlands, ca. 1600–1679', in Teresa Bela et al. (eds.), *Publishing Subversive Texts in Elizabethan*

England and the Polish-Lithuanian Commonwealth (Leiden: Brill, 2016), pp. 110–28. Hendrik Dijkgraaf, *The Library of a Jesuit Community at Holbeck, Nottinghamshire (1679)* (Cambridge: LP Publications, 2003).

37. Jill Bepler, '*Vicissitudo Temporum*: Some Sidelights on Book Collecting in the Thirty Years' War', *Sixteenth Century Journal*, 32 (2001), pp. 953–68.

10. Grand Designs

1. See chapter 11.
2. See chapter 2.
3. Ladislaus Buzás, *German Library History, 800–1945* (Jefferson, NC: McFarland, 1986), pp. 97–100.
4. Ibid, p. 98.
5. Theodoor Sevens, 'Bibliotheken uit vroeger tijd. I: Eene openbare Bibliotheek te Kortrijk in de 16ᵉ eeuw', *Tijdschrift voor Boek- en Bibliotheekwezen*, 1 (1903), pp. 196–8.
6. Buzás, *German Library History*, pp. 208, 215.
7. See chapter 6.
8. Christian Scheidegger, 'Buchgeschenke, Patronage und protestantische Allianzen: Die Stadtbibliothek Zürich und ihre Donatoren im 17. Jahrhundert', *Zwingliana*, 44 (2017), pp. 463–99.
9. Elisabeth Landolt, *Kabinettstücke der Amerbach im Historischen Museum Basel* (Basel: Historisches Museum, 1984).
10. Robert Zepf (ed.), *Historische Kirchenbibliotheken in Mecklenburg-Vorpommern* (Rostock: Universitätsbibliothek Rostock, 2019). Renate Stier-Meinhof, 'Die Geschichte der Bibliothek der St. Katharinenkirche in der Neuen Stadt Salzwedel', in Uwe Czubatynski, Adolf Laminski and Konrad von Rabenau (eds.), *Kirchenbibliotheken als Forschungsaufgabe* (Neustadt an der Aisch: Degener, 1992), pp. 47–68. Joachim Stüben and Falk Eisermann (eds.), *Rundblicke: Kirchenbibliotheken und Reformation im kulturellen Kontext* (Schwerin: Thomas Helms, 2019).
11. What follows is largely drawn from the essays in Ad Leerintveld and Jan Bedaux (eds.), *Historische Stadsbibliotheken in Nederland* (Zutphen: Walburg Pers, 2016).
12. J. W. E. Klein, *Geen vrouwen ofte kinderen, maer alleenlijk eerbare luijden: 400 jaar Goudse librije, 1594–1994* (Delft: Eburon, 1994), p. 34.
13. John Blatchly, *The Town Library of Ipswich, Provided for the Use of the Town Preachers in 1599: A History and Catalogue* (Woodbridge: Boydell, 1989).
14. John Fitch et al., *Suffolk Parochial Libraries: A Catalogue* (London: Mansell, 1977).
15. Ibid, p. xii.
16. Cited in Thomas Kelly, *Early Public Libraries: A History of Public Libraries in Great Britain before 1850* (London: The Library Association, 1966), p. 69.
17. Ibid, p. 76.
18. E. S. de Beer (ed.), *The Diary of John Evelyn*, IV (Oxford: Clarendon Press, 1955), pp. 367–8.

19. W. J. Petchey, *The Intentions of Thomas Plume* (Maldon: Trustees of the Plume Library, 2004).

20. John Glenn and David Walsh, *Catalogue of the Francis Trigge Chained Library* (Cambridge: Brewer, 1988).

21. Esther Mourits, *Een kamer gevuld met de mooiste boeken: De bibliotheek van Johannes Thysius (1622–1653)* (Nijmegen: Vantilt, 2016).

22. Matthew Yeo, *The Acquisition of Books by Chetham's Library, 1655–1700* (Leiden: Brill, 2011). Kelly, *Early Public Libraries*, p. 77.

23. James Kirkwood, *An overture for founding and maintaining of bibliothecks in every paroch throughout this kingdom* (S.I.: s.n., 1699), pp. 14–15.

24. James Kirkwood, *A copy of a letter anent a project, for erecting a library in every presbytery, or at least county, in the Highlands* (Edinburgh: s.n., 1702).

25. Keith Manley, 'They Never Expected the Spanish Inquisition! James Kirkwood and Scottish Parochial Libraries', in Caroline Archer and Lisa Peters (eds.), *Religion and the Book Trade* (Newcastle-upon-Tyne: Cambridge Scholars, 2015), pp. 83–98, here pp. 90–91.

26. Ibid, pp. 96–7.

27. Paul Kaufman, 'Innerpeffray: Reading for all the People', in his *Libraries and Their Users* (London: Library Association, 1969), pp. 153–62.

28. William D. Houlette, 'Parish Libraries and the Work of the Reverend Thomas Bray', *Library Quarterly*, 4 (1934), pp. 588–609. Samuel Clyde McCulloch, 'Dr. Thomas Bray's Commissary Work in London, 1696–1699', *William and Mary Quarterly*, 2 (1945), pp. 333–48.

29. Sarah Gray and Chris Baggs, 'The English Parish Library: A Celebration of Diversity', *Libraries & Culture*, 35 (2000), pp. 414–33. David Allan, *A Nation of Readers: The Lending Library in Georgian England* (London: British Library, 2008), p. 167.

30. Allan, *Nation of Readers*, p. 172.

31. Fitch, *Suffolk Parochial Libraries*, p. xv.

32. Gray and Baggs, 'English Parish Library', pp. 423–6.

33. Charles T. Laugher, *Thomas Bray's Grand Design: Libraries of the Church of England in America, 1695–1785* (Chicago, IL: American Library Association, 1973).

34. Laugher, *Thomas Bray's Grand Design*, pp. 35, 40.

11. Cardinal Errors

1. For a good case study, see Erik Thomson, 'Commerce, Law and Erudite Culture: The Mechanics of Théodore Godefroy's Service to Cardinal Richelieu', *Journal of the History of Ideas*, 68 (2007), pp. 407–27.

2. Jeremy Lawrance, Oliver Noble Wood and Jeremy Roe (eds.), *Poder y saber. Bibliotecas y bibliofilia en la época del conde-duque de Olivares* (Madrid: Centro de Estudios Europa Hispánica, 2011).

3. Jacqueline Artier, 'La bibliothèque du Cardinal de Richelieu', in Claude Jolly (ed.), *Histoire des bibliothèques françaises, II: Les bibliothèques sous l'Ancien Régime, 1530–1789* (Paris: Electre, 2008), pp. 158–66.

4. For a modern English translation, see Gabriel Naudé, *Advice on Establishing a*

Library, ed. Archer Taylor (Berkeley, CA: University of California Press, 1950). On Naudé himself see Jack A. Clarke, 'Gabriel Naudé and the Foundations of the Scholarly Library', *Library Quarterly*, 39 (1969), pp. 331–43.

5. Yann Sordet, 'Reconstructing Mazarin's Library / Libraries in Time and Space', *Quaerendo*, 46 (2016), pp. 151–64.

6. Clarke, 'Gabriel Naudé', p. 338.

7. Gabriel Naudé, *News from France. Or, a description of the library of Cardinall Mazarini: before it was utterly ruined* (London: Timothy Garthwait, 1652).

8. See chapter 12.

9. E. Stewart Saunders, 'Public Administration and the Library of Jean-Baptiste Colbert', *Libraries & Culture*, 26 (1991), pp. 283–300, here p. 287. Sordet, 'Reconstructing Mazarin's Library', p. 153.

10. E. Stewart Saunders, 'Politics and Scholarship in Seventeenth-century France: The Library of Nicolas Fouquet and the College Royal', *Journal of Library History*, 20 (1985), pp. 1–24.

11. Jacob Soll, *The Information Master: Jean-Baptiste Colbert's Secret State Intelligence System* (Ann Arbor, MI: University of Michigan Press, 2009).

12. Naudé, *Advice*, p. 11.

13. Heiko Droste, 'Diplomacy as Means of Cultural Transfer in Early Modern Times – the Swedish Evidence', *Scandinavian Journal of History*, 31 (2006), pp. 144–50. Marika Keblusek and Badeloch Vera Noldus (eds.), *Double Agents: Cultural and Political Brokerage in Early Modern Europe* (Leiden: Brill, 2011).

14. John Warwick Montgomery, *The Libraries of France at the Ascendency of Mazarin: Louis Jacob's Traicté des plus belles Bibliothèques* (Bonn: Verlag für Kultur und Wissenschaft, 2015).

15. Ibid, p. 35.

16. Donna Bohanan, 'The Education of Nobles in Seventeenth-Century Aix-en-Provence', *Journal of Social History*, 20 (1987), pp. 757–64.

17. John Warwick Montgomery, *A Seventeenth-century View of European Libraries: Lomeier's De Bibliothecis, Chapter X* (Berkeley, CA: University of California Press, 1962).

18. Giulia Martina Weston, 'Universal Knowledge and Self-Fashioning: Cardinal Bernardino Spada's Collection of Books', in Annika Bautz and James Gregory (eds.), *Libraries, Books, and Collectors of Texts, 1600–1900* (Abingdon: Routledge, 2018), pp. 28–47. Margaret Daly Davis, 'Giovan Pietro Bellori and the *Nota delli musei, librerie, galerie, et ornamenti di statue e pitture ne' palazzi, nelle case, e ne' giardini di Roma* (1664): Modern libraries and ancient painting in Seicento Rome', *Zeitschrift für Kunstgeschichte*, 68 (2005), pp. 191–233.

19. Peter Rietbergen, 'Lucas Holste (1596–1661), Scholar and Librarian, or: the Power of Books and Libraries', in his *Power and Religion in Baroque Rome: Barberini Cultural Politics* (Leiden: Brill, 2006), pp. 256–95.

20. Herman de la Fontaine Verwey, 'Adriaan Pauw en zijn bibliotheek', in his *Uit de Wereld van het Boek*, IV ('t Goy: HES, 1997), pp. 183–96.

21. Helwig Schmidt-Glintzer (ed.), *A Treasure House of Books: The Library of Duke August of Brunswick-Wolfenbüttel* (Wiesbaden: Harrassowitz, 1998).

22. Cited in Margaret Connolly, 'A Plague of Books: The Dispersal and

Disappearance of the Diocesan Libraries of the Church of Ireland', in James Raven (ed.), *Lost Libraries: The Destruction of Great Book Collections since Antiquity* (Basingstoke: Palgrave, 2004), pp. 197–218, here p. 209.

23. Peter J. A. N. Rietbergen, 'Founding a University Library: Pope Alexander VII (1655–1667) and the Alessandrina', *Journal of Library History*, 22 (1987), pp. 190–205, here p. 192.

24. Mathilde V. Rovelstad, 'Claude Clement's Pictorial Catalog: A Seventeenth-century Proposal for Physical Access and Literature Evaluation', *Library Quarterly*, 61 (1991), pp. 174–87. Idem, 'Two Seventeenth-century Library Handbooks, Two Different Library Theories', *Libraries & Culture*, 35 (2000), pp. 540–56.

25. Frédéric Barbier, István Monok and Andrea De Pasquale (eds.), *Bibliothèques décors (XVIIe–XIXe siècle)* (Paris: Éditions des Cendres, 2016). André Masson, *Le Décor des Bibliothèques du Moyen Age à la Révolution* (Geneva and Paris: Droz, 1972).

26. Guy le Thiec, 'Dialoguer avec des hommes illustres. Le rôle des portraits dans les décors de bibliothèques (fin XVe–début XVIIe siècle)', *Revue française d'histoire du livre*, 130 (2009), pp. 7–52, here p. 22.

27. Eric Garberson, *Eighteenth-century Monastic Libraries in Southern Germany and Austria: Architecture and Decorations* (Baden-Baden: Valentin Koerner, 1998). Rolf Achilles, 'Baroque Monastic Library Architecture', *Journal of Library History*, 11 (1976), pp. 249–55.

28. See chapter 6.

29. Garberson, *Eighteenth-century Monastic Libraries*, p. 12.

30. Ibid, p. 104.

31. Ibid, pp. 86–7.

32. Wolf-Dieter Otte, 'The Unknown Collector: Duke August and his Cabinet of Art and Curiosities', in Schmidt-Glintzer (ed.), *A Treasure House of Books*, pp. 173–92, here pp. 187–8.

33. Angela Delaforce, *The Lost Library of the King of Portugal* (London: Ad Ilissvm, 2019), p. 23.

34. Ibid, pp. 59–60.

12. The Antiquarians

1. Lotte Hellinga and Margaret Nickson, 'An Early-Eighteenth-Century Sale of Mainz Incunabula by the Frankfurt Dominicans', in Lotte Hellinga, *Incunabula in Transit: People and Trade* (Leiden: Brill, 2018), pp. 353–60.

2. Daniel Bellingradt, 'Book Lotteries as Sale Events for Slow-Sellers: The Case of Amsterdam in the Late Eighteenth Century', in Shanti Graheli (ed.), *Buying and Selling: The Business of Books in Early Modern Europe* (Leiden: Brill, 2019), pp. 154–77.

3. Herman de la Fontaine Verwey, 'Grolier-banden in Nederland', in his *Uit de Wereld van het Boek*, IV ('t Goy: HES uitgevers, 1997), pp. 155–82, here pp. 158–9.

4. These instances are derived from the auctions of the libraries of Gaspar Fagel

(1689) and Adriaen Smout (1646). Both are available via Brill's *Book Sales Catalogues Online*.

5. Kristian Jensen, *Revolution and the Antiquarian Book: Reshaping the Past, 1780–1815* (Cambridge: Cambridge University Press, 2011), pp. 79–80.

6. The story of Sixtinus is told in Herman de la Fontaine Verwey, 'The history of the Amsterdam Caesar codex', *Quaerendo*, 9 (1979), pp. 179–207.

7. The library, as sold at auction, is listed in *Catalogus Bibliothecae Viri Clarissimi, D. Suffridi Sixtini J. V. D.* (Amsterdam: Johannes Colom, 1650).

8. De La Fontaine Verwey, 'The history of the Amsterdam Caesar codex', p. 188.

9. F. F. Blok, *Isaac Vossius and his Circle: His Life until his Farewell to Queen Christina of Sweden, 1618–1655* (Groningen: Egbert Forsten, 2000), p. 339.

10. It now resides at the university library of Amsterdam, as Codex Amstelodamensis 73.

11. Jos van Heel, 'Gisbertus Voetius on the Necessity of Locating, Collecting and Preserving Early Printed Books', *Quaerendo*, 39 (2009), pp. 45–56, here p. 56.

12. Blok, *Isaac Vossius*, p. 329.

13. Ibid, p. 356.

14. Ibid, p. 453.

15. Astrid C. Balsem, 'Collecting the Ultimate Scholar's Library: The *Bibliotheca Vossiana*', in Eric Jorink and Dirk van Miert (eds.), *Isaac Vossius (1618–1689): Between Science and Scholarship* (Leiden: Brill, 2012), pp. 281–309.

16. Christiane Berkvens-Stevelinck, *Magna Commoditas: Leiden University's Great Asset* (Leiden: Leiden University Press, 2012), pp. 102–109.

17. Cited in Ian Maclean, 'Andreas Fries (Frisius) of Amsterdam and the search for a niche market, 1664–1675', in his *Episodes in the Life of the Early Modern Learned Book* (Leiden: Brill, 2020), chapter 5.

18. Mary Clapinson, *A Brief History of the Bodleian Library* (Oxford: The Bodleian Library, 2015), pp. 31, 118–19. See also chapter 14.

19. Andrew Pettegree and Arthur der Weduwen, *The Bookshop of the World. Making and Trading Books in the Dutch Golden Age* (London: Yale University Press, 2019), chapters 1 and 11.

20. *Bibliotheca Hulsiana* (The Hague: Johannes Swart and Pieter de Hondt, 1730).

21. *The Tatler*, No. 158. Thursday 13 April 1710.

22. Cited in Jensen, *Revolution and the Antiquarian Book*, p. 117.

23. Theodor Harmsen, *Antiquarianism in the Augustan Age: Thomas Hearne, 1678–1735* (Bern: Peter Lang, 2000).

24. Cornelius à Beughem, *Incunabula typographiae* (Amsterdam: Joannes Wolters, 1688).

25. Otto Lankhorst, 'Dutch auctions in the seventeenth and eighteenth centuries', in Robin Myers, Michael Harris and Giles Mandelbrote (eds.), *Under the Hammer: Book Auctions since the Seventeenth Century* (New Castle, DE: Oak Knoll Press, 2001), pp. 65–87, p. 76. *Bibliotheca universalis vetus et nova* (The Hague: Pierre Gosse, 1740).

26. Christiane Berkvens-Stevelinck, '"Rarus, rarior, rarissimus" ou de la qualification exagérée des livres dans les catalogues de vente', in J. van Borm and

L. Simons (eds.), *Het oude en het nieuwe boek: De oude en de nieuwe bibliotheek* (Kapellen: DNB/Pelckmans, 1988), pp. 235–40.

27. Balsem, 'Collecting the Ultimate Scholar's Library', p. 281.

28. Herman de la Fontaine Verwey, 'Pieter van Damme, de eerste Nederlandse antiquaar', in his *Uit de Wereld van het Boek*, IV ('t Goy: HES uitgevers, 1997), pp. 197–220, here pp. 197, 203.

29. Lotte Hellinga, 'Buying Incunabula in Venice and Milan: The Bibliotheca Smithiana', in her *Incunabula in Transit*, pp. 370–92.

30. Anthony Hobson, *Great Libraries* (London: Weidenfeld & Nicolson, 1970), p. 15.

31. Friedrich Buchmayr, 'Secularization and Monastic Libraries in Austria', in James Raven (ed.), *Lost Libraries: The Destruction of Great Book Collections since Antiquity* (Basingstoke: Palgrave, 2004), pp. 145–62. Derek Beales, 'Joseph II and the Monasteries of Austria and Hungary', in N. Aston (ed.), *Religious Change in Europe, 1650–1914* (Oxford: Oxford University Press, 1997), pp. 161–84.

32. Buchmayr, 'Secularization and Monastic Libraries in Austria', p. 151.

33. Ibid, p. 156.

34. Ibid, p. 146.

35. Jensen, *Revolution and the Antiquarian Book*, pp. 58–9.

36. Andrew Pettegree, 'Rare Books and Revolutionaries: The French Bibliothèques Municipales', in his *The French Book and the European Book World* (Leiden: Brill, 2007), pp. 1–16.

37. Pierre Riberette, *Les Bibliothèques françaises pendant la révolution (1789–1795)* (Paris: Bibliothèque Nationale, 1970), pp. 10–11, 40.

38. Pettegree, 'Rare Books and Revolutionaries', p. 7.

39. See chapter 15.

40. Anthony Hobson, 'Appropriations from foreign libraries during the French Revolution and Empire', *Bulletin du bibliophile*, 2 (1989), pp. 255–72, here p. 257.

41. Hobson, 'Appropriations from foreign libraries', p. 269. Jensen, *Revolution and the Antiquarian Book*, p. 11.

42. Cited in Mark Purcell, *The Country House Library* (London and New Haven: Yale University Press, 2017), pp. 100–101.

43. Jensen, *Revolution and the Antiquarian Book*, p. 130.

44. Cited in Shayne Husbands, 'The Roxburghe Club: Consumption, Obsession and the Passion for Print', in Emma Cayley and Susan Powell (eds.), *Manuscripts and Printed Books in Europe, 1350–1550: Packaging, Presentation and Consumption* (Liverpool: Liverpool University Press, 2013), pp. 120–32, here p. 122. See also Idem, *The Early Roxburghe Club, 1812–1835: Book Club Pioneers and the Advancement of English Literature* (London: Anthem Press, 2017).

45. E. J. O'Dwyer, *Thomas Frognall Dibdin: Bibliographer and Bibliomaniac Extraordinary, 1776–1847* (Pinner: Private Libraries Association, 1967). See more recently John A. Sibbald, 'Book Bitch to the Rich – the Strife and Times of the Revd. Dr. Thomas Frognall Dibdin (1776–1847)', in Shanti Graheli (ed.),

Buying and Selling: The Business of Books in Early Modern Europe (Leiden: Brill, 2019), pp. 489–521.

46. Jensen, *Revolution and the Antiquarian Book*, p. 186.

47. Owen Chadwick, 'The Acton Library', in Peter Fox (ed.), *Cambridge University Library: The Great Collections* (Cambridge: Cambridge University Press, 1998), pp. 136–52, p. 139.

13. Orderly Minds

1. Margaret Barton Korty, 'Benjamin Franklin and Eighteenth-century American Libraries', *Transactions of the American Philosophical Society*, 55 (1965), pp. 1–83.

2. See the revealing subject division in Ronald F. Batty, *How to Run a Twopenny Library* (London: John Gifford, 1938).

3. See chapter 14.

4. Richard D. Altick, *The English Common Reader: A Social History of the Mass Reading Public, 1800–1900* (Chicago: University of Chicago Press, 1957; 2nd edn, Columbus, OH: Ohio State University Press, 1998).

5. Robert K. Webb, *The British Working Class Reader, 1790–1848: Literacy and Social Tension* (London: Allen & Unwin, 1955). Louis James, *Fiction for the Working Man, 1830–1850* (Oxford: Oxford University Press, 1963).

6. J. H. Shera, *Foundations of the Public Library: The Origins of the Public Library Movement in New England 1629–1855* (Chicago, IL: University of Chicago Press, 1949), pp. 32–3.

7. Mark Towsey and Kyle B. Roberts (eds.), *Before the Public Library: Reading, Community and Identity in the Atlantic World, 1650–1850* (Leiden: Brill, 2018).

8. Michael A. Baenen, 'A Great and Natural Enemy of Democracy? Politics and Culture in the Antebellum Portsmouth Athenaeum', in Thomas Augst and Kenneth Carpenter (eds.), *Institutions of Reading: The Social Life of Libraries in the United States* (Amherst, MA: University of Massachusetts Press, 2007), pp. 73–98.

9. Shera, *Foundations*, p. 73.

10. Korty, 'Benjamin Franklin', p. 24. James Raven, *London Booksellers and American Customers: Transatlantic Literary Community and the Charleston Library Society, 1748–1811* (Columbia, SC.: University of South Carolina Press, 2002).

11. Markman Ellis, 'Coffee-House Libraries in Mid-Eighteenth-century London', *The Library*, 7th series, 10 (2009), pp. 3–40. Hyder Abbas, '"A fund of entertaining and useful information": Coffee Houses, Early Public Libraries, and the Print Trade in Eighteenth-century Dublin', *Library & Information History*, 30 (2014), pp. 41–61.

12. David Allan, *A Nation of Readers: The Lending Library in Georgian England* (London: British Library, 2008), pp. 24–61.

13. Allan, *Nation of Readers*, p. 71.

14. Harry Earl Whitmore, 'The "Cabinet De Lecture" in France, 1800–1850', *Library Quarterly*, 48 (1978), pp. 20–35, here pp. 27–8.

15. James Smith Allen, 'The "Cabinets de Lecture" in Paris, 1800–1850', *The Journal of Library History*, 16 (1981), pp. 199–209, here p. 201.

16. Chapter 15.
17. Charles F. Gosnell and Géza Schütz, 'Goethe the Librarian', *Library Quarterly*, 2 (1932), pp. 367–74.
18. Uwe Puschner, 'Lesegesellschaften', in Bernd Sösemann (ed.), *Kommunikation und Medien in Preussen vom 16. Bis zum 19. Jahrhundert* (Stuttgart: Franz Steiner, 2002), pp. 194–205.
19. Alberto Martino, *Die Deutsche Leihbibliothek* (Wiesbaden: Harrassowitz, 1990). Georg Jäger, Alberto Martino and Reinhard Wittmann, *Die Leihbibliothek der Goetheziet* (Hildesheim: Gerstenberg, 1979).
20. Jäger, Martino and Wittmann, *Die Leihbibliothek der Goetheziet*, pp. 383–4.
21. K. A. Manley, *Books, Borrowers and Shareholders: Scottish Circulating and Subscription Libraries before 1825* (Edinburgh: Edinburgh Bibliographical Society, 2012), pp. 9–10.
22. James Raven, 'The Noble Brothers and Popular Publishing', *The Library*, 6th series, 12 (1990), pp. 293–345, here p. 303.
23. Hilda M. Hamlyn, 'Eighteenth-century Circulating Libraries in England', *The Library*, 5th series (1946–1947), pp. 197–222, here p. 204.
24. Raven, 'Noble Brothers', p. 308.
25. Allan, *Nation of Readers*, p. 134.
26. Raven, 'Noble Brothers', p. 308.
27. Maria Edgeworth, *Letters for Literary Ladies* (London: J. M. Dent, 1993), p. 15.
28. Norbert Schürer, 'Four Catalogues of the Lowndes Circulating Library, 1755–66', *Papers of the Bibliographical Society of America*, 101 (2007), pp. 327–57.
29. Manley, *Books, Borrowers and Shareholders*, pp. 2–3.
30. Allan, *Nation of Readers*, p. 124.
31. Ibid, p. 105.
32. Hamlyn, 'Eighteenth-century Circulating Libraries', pp. 220–21.
33. Schürer, 'Four Catalogues', p. 344.
34. Hamlyn, 'Eighteenth-century Circulating Libraries', p. 215.
35. Jan Fergus, 'Eighteenth-century Readers in Provincial England: The Customers of Samuel Clay's Circulating Library and Bookshop in Warwick, 1770–72', *Papers of the Bibliographical Society of America*, 78 (1984), pp. 155–213. See also her *Provincial Readers in Eighteenth-century England* (Oxford: Oxford University Press, 2007).
36. David Kaser, *A Book for a Sixpence: The Circulating Library in America* (Pittsburgh, PA: Phi Beta Mu, 1980).
37. Guinevere L. Griest, *Mudie's Circulating Library and the Victorian Novel* (London: David & Charles, 1970).
38. Guinevere L. Griest, 'A Victorian Leviathan: Mudie's Select Library', *Nineteenth-Century Fiction*, 20 (1965), pp. 103–26, here pp. 108, 113.
39. Charles Wilson, *First with the News: The History of W. H. Smith, 1792–1972* (London: Jonathan Cape, 1985).
40. Sullivan denied this, though Disraeli would refer to his own minister as 'Pinafore Smith'.
41. George Moore, 'A New Censorship of Literature', *Pall Mall Gazette*, 10 December 1884, a conflict renewed in a pamphlet *Literature at Nurse*. See

Pierre Coustillas (ed.), *George Moore, Literature at Nurse: A Polemic on Victorian Censorship* (Brighton: EER, 2017).

42. Griest, *Mudie's Circulating Library*, pp. 75, 83.
43. Ibid, p. 61.

14. Building Empires

1. J. E. Traue, 'The Public Library Explosion in Colonial New Zealand', *Libraries & the Cultural Record*, 42 (2007), pp. 151–64, here p. 154.
2. See chapter 9.
3. Adrien Delmas, '*Artem Quaevis Terra Alit*: Books in the Cape Colony during the Seventeenth and Eighteenth Centuries', in Natalia Maillard Álvarez (ed.), *Books in the Catholic World during the Early Modern Period* (Leiden: Brill, 2014), pp. 191–214, here p. 203.
4. William St Clair, *The Grand Slave Emporium: Cape Coast Castle and the British Slave Trade* (London: Profile, 2007), pp. 67–8.
5. Katharine Gerbner, *Christian Slavery: Conversion and Race in the Protestant Atlantic World* (Philadelphia, PA: University of Pennsylvania Press, 2018).
6. Archie Dick, *The Hidden History of South Africa's Books and Reading Cultures* (Toronto: University of Toronto Press, 2012), pp. 12–53.
7. Alan G. Cobley, 'Literacy, Libraries, and Consciousness: The Provision of Library Services for Blacks in South Africa in the Pre-Apartheid Era', *Libraries & Culture*, 32 (1997), pp. 57–80.
8. Elizabeth B. Fitzpatrick, 'The Public Library as Instrument of Colonialism: The Case of the Netherlands East Indies', *Libraries & the Cultural Record*, 43 (2008), pp. 270–85.
9. Kalpana Dasgupta, 'How Learned Were the Mughals: Reflections on Muslim Libraries in India', *The Journal of Library History*, 10 (1975), pp. 241–54. A. K. Ohdedar, *The Growth of the Library in Modern India, 1498–1836* (Calcutta: World Press, 1966).
10. Cited in Ohdedar, *The Growth of the Library in Modern India*, p. 10.
11. Sharon Murphy, 'Imperial Reading? The East India Company's Lending Libraries for Soldiers, c. 1819–1834', *Book History*, 12 (2009), pp. 74–99. Idem, *The British Soldier and his Libraries, c. 1822–1901* (London: Palgrave Macmillan, 2016).
12. Murphy, 'Imperial Reading?', p. 78.
13. Sharon Murphy, 'Libraries, Schoolrooms, and Mud Gadowns: Formal Scenes of Reading at East India Company Stations in India, c. 1819–1835', *Journal of the Royal Asiatic Society*, 21 (2011), pp. 459–67, here p. 459.
14. Murphy, 'Imperial Reading?', p. 76.
15. Dora Lockyer, 'The Provision of Books and Libraries by the East India Company in India, 1611–1858' (PhD thesis, Fellowship of the Library Association, 1977), pp. 183–8. Priya Joshi, *In Another Country: Colonialism, Culture, and the English Novel in India* (New York, NY: Columbia University Press, 2002), p. 39.
16. Ohdedar, *The Growth of the Library in Modern India*, p. 57.
17. Cited in ibid, pp. 117–20.

18. Ibid, p. 141.
19. Joshi, *In Another Country*, p. 56.
20. Lara Atkin, et al., *Early Public Libraries and Colonial Citizenship in the British Southern Hemisphere* (London: Palgrave Macmillan, 2019).
21. Ibid, p. 9.
22. Lorne D. Bruce, 'Subscription Libraries for the Public in Canadian Colonies, 1775–1850', *Library & Information History*, 34 (2018), pp. 40–63, here pp. 53–4.
23. Heather Dean, '"The persuasion of books": The Significance of Libraries in Colonial British Columbia', *Libraries & the Cultural Record*, 46 (2011), pp. 50–72.
24. Cited in Bruce, 'Subscription Libraries', p. 52.
25. Traue, 'The Public Library Explosion', p. 160.
26. Atkin, *Early Public Libraries*, pp. 82–7.
27. Paul Eggert, 'Robbery Under Arms: The Colonial Market, Imperial Publishers and the Demise of the Three-Decker Novel', *Book History*, 6 (2003), pp. 127–46, here p. 135.
28. An excellent treatment is found in Joshi, *In Another Country*, pp. 93–138.
29. Text inserted in H. B. Vogel, *A Maori Maid* (London: Macmillan, 1898).
30. Joshi, *In Another Country*, p. 47.
31. P. R. Harris, *A History of the British Museum Library, 1753–1973* (London: British Library, 1998). Giles Mandelbrote and Barry Taylor, *Libraries within the Library: The Origins of the British Library's Printed Collections* (London: British Library, 2009).
32. See also chapter 11.
33. James Delbourgo, *Collecting the World: The Life and Curiosity of Hans Sloane* (London: Allen Lane, 2017), p. xxv.
34. Arundell Esdaile, *National Libraries of the World: Their History, Administration and Public Services*, 2nd edn (London: Library Association, 1957). Ian R. Willison, 'The National Library in Historical Perspective', *Libraries & Culture*, 24 (1989), pp. 75–95.
35. Harris, *A History of the British Museum Library*, pp. 15, 20.
36. Paul M. Priebe, 'From Bibliothèque du Roi to Bibliothèque Nationale: The Creation of a State Library, 1789–1793', *The Journal of Library History*, 17 (1982), pp. 389–408, here p. 394.
37. Esdaile, *National Libraries*, p. 185.
38. Elizabeth A. Dean, 'The Organization of Italian Libraries from the Unification until 1940', *Library Quarterly*, 53 (1983), pp. 399–419.
39. Mary Stuart, *Aristocrat-Librarian in Service to the Tsar: Aleksei Nikolaevich Olenin and the Imperial Public Library* (Boulder, CO: East European Monographs, 1986).
40. Mary Stuart, 'Creating Culture: The Rossica Collection of the Imperial Public Library and the Construction of National Identity', *Libraries & Culture*, 30 (1995), pp. 1–25, here pp. 1–5.
41. A useful contemporary overview is provided in Edward Edwards, 'A Statistical View of the Principal Public Libraries in Europe and the United States

of North America', *Journal of the Statistical Society of London*, 11 (1848), pp. 250–81.

42. Harris, *A History of the British Museum Library*, p. 104. Willison, 'The National Library', p. 75.

43. James P. Niessen, 'Museums, Nationality, and Public Research Libraries in Nineteenth-century Transylvania', *Libraries & the Cultural Record*, 41 (2006), pp. 298–336.

44. Cited in Harris, *A History of the British Museum Library*, p. 133.

45. See chapter 12.

46. Stuart, *Aristocrat-Librarian*, pp. 37–62.

47. Esdaile, *National Libraries*, p. 98.

48. Delbourgo, *Collecting the World*, pp. 333, 337.

49. Harris, *A History of the British Museum Library*, p. 147.

50. Esdaile, *National Libraries*, p. 327.

51. Harris, *A History of the British Museum Library*, p. 180.

52. Ibid, pp. 187–90.

53. Ibid, pp. 84, 322, 389–90.

54. Stuart, *Aristocrat-Librarian*, pp. 90–95.

55. Mary Stuart, 'The Crimes of Dr Pichler: A Scholar-Biblioklept in Imperial Russia and his European Predecessors', *Libraries & Culture*, 23 (1988), pp. 401–26.

56. Esdaile, *National Libraries*, p. 346.

57. Carl Ostrowski, 'James Alfred Pearce and the Question of a National Library in Antebellum America', *Libraries & Culture*, 35 (2000), pp. 255–77, here pp. 267–8.

58. John Y. Cole, 'The Library of Congress Becomes a World Library, 1815–2005', *Libraries & Culture*, 40 (2005), pp. 385–98.

59. Albert L. Hurtado, 'Professors and Tycoons: The Creation of Great Research Libraries in the American West', *Western Historical Quarterly*, 41 (2010), pp. 149–69. On the Newberry, see Paul Finkelman, 'Class and Culture in Late Nineteenth-century Chicago: The Founding of the Newberry Library', *American Studies*, 16 (1975), pp. 5–22.

60. Stephen H. Grant, *Collecting Shakespeare: The Story of Henry and Emily Folger* (Baltimore, MD: Johns Hopkins University Press, 2014), p. 156.

61. Donald C. Dickinson, *Henry E. Huntington's Library of Libraries* (San Marino, CA: Huntington Library, 1995).

62. Grant, *Collecting Shakespeare*. Andrea Mays, *The Millionaire and the Bard: Henry Folger's Obsessive Hunt for Shakespeare's First Folio* (New York, NY: Simon & Schuster, 2015).

63. Grant, *Collecting Shakespeare*, p. xii.

64. Ibid, p. 120.

15. Reading on the Job

1. David Nasaw, *Andrew Carnegie* (London: Penguin, 2006).

2. John Minto, *A History of the Public Library Movement in Great Britain and Ireland* (London: George Allen & Unwin, 1932).

3. Edward Edwards, 'A Statistical View of the Principal Public Libraries in Europe and the United States of North America', *Journal of the Statistical Society of London*, 11 (1848), pp. 250–81.
4. Stanley M. Max, 'Tory Reaction to the Public Libraries Bill, 1850', *Journal of Library History*, 19 (1984), pp. 504–24.
5. 'The Manchester Free Library', *The Spectator*, 12 November 1853.
6. Ken Severn, *The Halfpenny Rate: A Brief History of Lambeth Libraries* (London: Lambeth Archives, 2006).
7. H. E. Meller, *Leisure and the Changing City, 1870–1914* (London: Routledge, 1976).
8. Linda Jean Parr, 'The History of Libraries in Halifax and Huddersfield from the Mid-Sixteenth Century to the Coming of the Public Libraries' (PhD thesis, University College London, 2003).
9. See chapter 9.
10. J. H. Shera, *Foundations of the Public Library: The Origins of the Public Library Movement in New England 1629–1855* (Chicago, IL: University of Chicago Press, 1949).
11. Susan Orlean, *The Library Book* (London: Atlantic Books, 2018), pp. 177–8.
12. Harold M. Otness, 'Baedeker's One-Star American Libraries', *Journal of Library History*, 12 (1977), pp. 222–34.
13. Tom Glynn, *Reading Publics: New York City's Public Libraries, 1754–1911* (New York, NY: Fordham University Press, 2015), p. 2.
14. Ibid, pp. 17–42.
15. William J. Rhees, *Manual of Public Libraries, Institutions and Societies in the United States and British Provinces of North America* (Philadelphia, PA: J. B. Lippincott, 1889).
16. Richard D. Altick, *The English Common Reader: A Social History of the Mass Reading Public* (Chicago, IL: University of Chicago Press, 1957; 2nd edn, Columbus, OH: Ohio State University Press, 1998), p. 192. Edward Royle, 'Mechanics' Institutes and the Working Classes, 1840–1860', *Historical Journal*, 14 (1971), pp. 305–21.
17. Altick, *The English Common Reader*, p. 192.
18. Chris Baggs, '"The Whole Tragedy of Leisure in Penury": The South Wales Miners' Institute Libraries during the Great Depression', *Libraries & Culture*, 39 (2004), pp. 115–36. See also his 'The Miners' Institute libraries of south Wales 1875–1939', in Philip Henry Jones, et al. (eds.), *A Nation and Its Books: A History of the Book in Wales* (Aberystwyth: National Library of Wales, 1998), and 'How Well Read Was My Valley? Reading, Popular Fiction, and the Miners of South Wales, 1875–1939', *Book History*, 4 (2001), pp. 277–301.
19. John Phillip Short, 'Everyman's Colonial Library: Imperialism and Working-Class Readers in Leipzig, 1890–1914', *German History*, 21 (2003), pp. 445–75. Hans-Josef Steinberg and Nicholas Jacobs, 'Workers' Libraries in Germany before 1914', *History Workshop*, 1 (1976), pp. 166–80.
20. Steinberg and Jacobs, 'Workers' Libraries', pp. 172–3.
21. Ronald A. Fullerton, 'Creating a Mass Book Market in Germany: The Story

of the "Colporteur Novel", 1870–1890', *Journal of Social History*, 10 (1977), pp. 265–83.

22. Short, 'Everyman's Colonial Library', pp. 452–453.

23. Steinberg and Jacobs, 'Workers' Libraries', p. 177.

24. J. L. A. Bailly, *Notices historiques sur les bibliothèques anciennes et modernes* (Paris: Rousselon, 1828).

25. Barbara McCrimmon, 'The Libri Case', *Journal of Library History*, 1 (1966), pp. 7–32. P. Alessandra Maccioni Ruju and Marco Mostert, *The Life and Times of Guglielmo Libri (1802–1869)* (Hilversum: Verloren, 1995).

26. Graham Keith Barnett, 'The History of Public Libraries in France from the Revolution to 1939' (PhD thesis, Fellowship of the Library Association, 1973).

27. Nasaw, *Carnegie*, pp. 193, 204.

28. Nasaw, *Carnegie*, p. 607.

29. George S. Bobinski, 'Carnegie Libraries: Their History and Impact on American Public Library Development', *American Library Association Bulletin*, 62 (1968), pp. 1361–7.

30. Daniel F. Ring, 'Carnegie Libraries as Symbols for an Age: Montana as a Test Case', *Libraries & Culture*, 27 (1992), pp. 1–19, here p. 7. See also his 'Men of Energy and Snap: The Origins and Early Years of the Billings Public Library', *Libraries & Culture*, 36 (2001), pp. 397–412, for an example of local philanthropy.

31. Abigail A. Van Slyck, *Free to All: Carnegie Libraries & American Culture, 1890–1920* (Chicago, IL: University of Chicago Press, 1995), pp. 35–40.

32. Karl Baedeker, *The United States, with excursions to Mexico, Cuba, Porto Rico and Alaska* (Leipzig: Karl Baedeker, 1909), p. 25.

33. Glynn, *Reading Publics*, p. 5.

34. Lee Erickson, 'The Economy of Novel Reading: Jane Austen and the Circulating Library', *Studies in English Literature, 1500–1900*, 30 (1990), pp. 573–90.

35. Quoted in Arthur P. Young, *Books for Sammies: The American Library Association and World War I* (Pittsburgh, PA: Beta Phi Mu, 1981), p. 10.

36. Altick, *The English Common Reader*, p. 231.

37. Evelyn Geller, *Forbidden Books in American Public Libraries, 1876–1939* (Westport, CT: Greenwood, 1984), pp. 54–5. Esther Jane Carrier, *Fiction in Public Libraries 1876–1900* (New York, NY: Scarecrow Press, 1965).

38. Robert Snape, *Leisure and the Rise of the Public Library* (London: The Library Association, 1995), pp. 56–7.

39. Geller, *Forbidden Books*, p. 84.

40. Orlean, *The Library Book*, pp. 130–32, 141–4.

41. Geller, *Forbidden Books*, pp. 42–3. See also Charles Johanningsmeier, 'Welcome Guests or Representatives of the "Mal-Odorous Class"? Periodicals and Their Readers in American Public Libraries, 1876–1914', *Libraries & Culture*, 39 (2004), pp. 260–92.

16. Surviving the Twentieth Century

1. Erik Kirschbaum, *Burning Beethoven: The Eradication of German Culture in the United States during World War I* (New York, NY: Berlinica, 2015).

2. Susan Orlean, *The Library Book* (London: Atlantic Books, 2018), p. 176. Wayne Wiegand, *"An Active Instrument for Propaganda": The American Public Library during World War I* (New York, NY: Greenwood, 1989).

3. Arthur P. Young, *Books for Sammies: The American Library Association and World War I* (Pittsburgh, PA: Beta Phi Mu, 1981).

4. Orlean, *The Library Book*, p. 202.

5. Margaret F. Stieg, 'The Second World War and the Public Libraries of Nazi Germany', *Journal of Contemporary History*, 27 (1992), pp. 23–40. See also her *Public Libraries in Nazi Germany* (Tuscaloosa, AL: University of Alabama Press, 1992).

6. *All Quiet on the Western Front*, 1929, was the most notable of the anti-war books generated by the First World War. As a decorated veteran of this conflict, Hitler's detestation of this book was visceral.

7. Pamela Spence Richards, 'German Libraries and Scientific and Technical Information in Nazi Germany', *Library Quarterly*, 55 (1985), pp. 151–73. Idem, 'Aslib at War: The Brief but Intrepid Career of a Library Organization as a Hub of Allied Scientific Intelligence 1942–1945', *Journal of Education for Library and Information Science*, 29 (1989), pp. 279–96.

8. Stieg, 'Second World War', p. 27.

9. Wayne Wiegand, 'In Service to the State: Wisconsin Public Libraries during World War I', *Wisconsin Magazine of History*, 72 (1989), pp. 199–224. Daniel F. Ring, 'Fighting for Their Hearts and Minds: William Howard Brett, the Cleveland Public Library, and World War I', *Journal of Library History*, 18 (1983), pp. 1–20.

10. Graham Keith Barnett, 'The History of Public Libraries in France from the Revolution to 1939' (PhD thesis, Fellowship of the Library Association, 1973), pp. 352–3.

11. Sarah Wentzel, 'National and University Library of Strasbourg', in David H. Stam (ed.), *International Dictionary of Library Histories* (2 vols., Chicago and London: Fitzroy Dearborn, 2001), pp. 459–61.

12. Barnett, 'Public Libraries', pp. 353–4, 603–4.

13. Ibid.

14. Margaret E. Parks, 'Catholic University of Louvain Library', in Stam, *International Dictionary of Library Histories*, pp. 244–7.

15. Chris Coppens, Mark Derez and Jan Roegiers (eds.), *Leuven University Library, 1425–2000* (Leuven: Leuven University Press, 2005), pp. 196–298.

16. It must be said that the ultimate work of vandalism inflicted on the suffering Louvain university was the result of Belgian politics. In 1968, the university was divided in two, with a new French university moving to Louvain-la-Neuve. The library was divided equally between them, by the simple though extraordinary expedient of having the odd class marks stay in Louvain, and the evens going with the French. Each got 800,000 books.

17. In the war as a whole, French provincial libraries lost approximately 2 million

books. Hilda Urén Stubbings, *Blitzkrieg and Books: British and European Libraries as Casualties of World War II* (Bloomington, IN: Rubena Press, 1993), pp. 235–69. Martine Poulain, *Livres pillés, lectures surveillées: Les bibliothèques françaises sous l'Occupation* (Paris: Gallimard, 2008).

18. Donal Sheehan, 'The Manchester Literary and Philosophical Society', *Isis*, 33 (1941), pp. 519–23. Stubbings, *Blitzkrieg*, pp. 313–15.

19. Valerie Holman, *Book Publishing in England, 1939–1945* (London: British Library, 2008), p. 30.

20. Henry Irving, '"Propaganda bestsellers": British Official War Books, 1941–1946', in Cynthia Johnston (ed.), *The Concept of the Book: The Production, Progression and Dissemination of Information* (London: Institute of English Studies, 2019), pp. 125–46.

21. Stubbings, *Blitzkrieg*, p. 320.

22. Dale C. Russell, '"Our Special Province": Providing a Library Service for London's Public Shelters, 1940–1942', *Library History*, 13 (1997), pp. 3–15. Stubbings, *Blitzkrieg*, p. 309.

23. Anders Rydell, *The Book Thieves: The Nazi Looting of Europe's Libraries and the Race to Return a Literary Inheritance* (New York, NY: Viking, 2015), pp. 86–7.

24. Marek Sroka, 'The Destruction of Jewish Libraries and Archives in Cracow during World War II', *Libraries & Culture,* 38 (2003), pp. 147–65.

25. Jacqueline Borin, 'Embers of the Soul: The Destruction of Jewish Books and Libraries in Poland during World War II', *Libraries & Culture,* 28 (1993), pp. 445–60.

26. Rydell, *Book Thieves*, p. 199.

27. Ibid, p. 197.

28. Borin, 'Embers', pp. 452–3.

29. Rydell, *Book Thieves*, p. 215.

30. Ernst Piper, *Alfred Rosenberg: Hitlers Chefideologe* (Munich: Karl Blessing, 2005).

31. Donald E. Collins and Herbert P. Rothfeder, 'The Einsatzstab Reichsleiter Rosenberg and the Looting of Jewish and Masonic Libraries during World War II', *Journal of Library History*, 18 (1983), pp. 21–36, here p. 23.

32. Patricia Kennedy Grimsted, *The Odyssey of the Turgenev Library from Paris, 1940–2002: Books as Victims and Trophies of War* (Amsterdam: IISH, 2003).

33. Patricia Kennedy Grimsted, *Library Plunder in France by the Einsatzstab Reichsleiter Rosenberg: Ten ERR Seizure Lists of Confiscated French Libraries* (Amsterdam: IISH, 2017).

34. Reinhard Bollmus, *Das Amt Rosenberg und seine Gegner: Studien zum Machtkampf im nationalsozialistischen Herrschaftssystem* (Munich: Oldenbourg, 2006).

35. Poulain, *Livres pillés*. Patricia Kennedy Grimsted, 'Roads to Ratibor: Library and Archival Plunder by the Einsatzstab Reichsleiter Rosenberg', *Holocaust Genocide Studies*, 19 (2005), pp. 390–458.

36. David E. Fishman, *The Book Smugglers: Partisans, Poets and the Race to Save Jewish Treasures from the Nazis* (Lebanon, NH: ForeEdge, 2017).

37. Dov Schidorsky, 'Confiscation of Libraries and Assignments to Forced Labour: Two Documents of the Holocaust', *Libraries & Culture*, 33 (1998), pp. 347–88.

38. Poulain, *Livres pillés*.

39. Joshua Starr, 'Jewish Cultural Property under Nazi Control', *Jewish Social Studies*, 12 (1950), pp. 27–48, here p. 34. Cornelia Briel, *Beschlagnahmt, Erpresst, Erbeutet. NS-Raubgut, Reichstauschstelle und Preussische Staatsbibliothek zwischen 1933 und 1945* (Berlin: Akademie Verlag, 2013).

40. Marta L. Dosa, *Libraries in the Political Scene* (Westport, CT: Greenwood, 1974), pp. 84–7.

41. Jan L. Alessandrini, 'Lost Books of "Operation Gomorrah": Rescue, Reconstruction and Restitution at Hamburg's Library in the Second World War', in Flavia Bruni and Andrew Pettegree (eds.), *Lost Books: Reconstructing the Print World of Pre-Industrial Europe* (Leiden: Brill, 2016), pp. 441–61.

42. Rydell, *Book Thieves*, p. 20.

43. Ibid, pp. 51–6.

44. Dosa, *Libraries in the Political Scene*, p. 94.

45. Nicola Schneider, 'The Losses of the Music Collection of the Hessische Landesbibliothek in Darmstadt in 1944', in Anja-Silvia Goeing, Anthony T. Grafton and Paul Michel (eds.), *Collectors' Knowledge: What is Kept, What is Discarded* (Leiden: Brill, 2013), pp. 381–412.

46. Werner Schocow, *Bücherschicksale: die Verlagerungsgeschichte der Preussischen Staatsbibliothek; Auslagerung, Zerstörung, Rückführung* (Berlin: de Gruyter, 2003).

47. Grimsted, 'Roads to Ratibor'.

48. Patricia Kennedy Grimsted, 'The Road to Minsk for Western "Trophy" Books: Twice Plundered but Not Yet "Home from the War"', *Libraries & Culture*, 39 (2004), pp. 351–404.

49. Patricia Kennedy Grimsted, 'Tracing Trophy Books in Russia', *Solanus*, 19 (2005), pp. 131–45.

50. Rydell, *Book Thieves*, p. 272. Robert G. Waite, 'Returning Jewish Cultural Property: The Handling of Books Looted by the Nazis in the American Zone of Occupation, 1945 to 1952', *Libraries & Culture*, 37 (2002), pp. 213–28.

51. Grimsted, *The Odyssey of the Turgenev Library*.

52. Margaret Stieg Dalton, 'The Postwar Purge of German Public Libraries, Democracy and the American Reaction', *Libraries & Culture*, 28 (1993), pp. 143–64.

53. Alex Boodrookas, 'Total Literature, Total War: Foreign Aid, Area Studies, and the Weaponization of US Research Libraries', *Diplomatic History*, 43 (2019), pp. 332–52.

54. Miriam Intrator, *Books Across Borders: UNESCO and the Politics of Postwar Cultural Reconstruction, 1945–1951* (London: Palgrave Macmillan, 2019), p. 140.

55. Ibid, p. 62.

56. W. C. Berwick Sayers, 'Britain's Libraries and the War', *Library Quarterly*, 14 (1944), pp. 95–9. Henry Irving, 'Paper Salvage in Britain during the Second World War', *Historical Research*, 89 (2016), pp. 373–93. Sayers, followed by

the later literature, actually gives the figure as 600 million, but this seems impossibly large.

57. Peter Thorsheim, 'Salvage and Destruction: The Recycling of Books and Manuscripts in Great Britain during the Second World War', *Contemporary European History*, 22 (2013), pp. 431–52, here p. 448.

17. Wrestling with Modernity

1. Warren Susman, 'Communication and Culture', in Catherine L. Covert and John D. Stevens (eds.), *Mass Media Between the Wars: Perceptions of Cultural Tension, 1918–1941* (Syracuse, NY: Syracuse University Press, 1984), p. xxiv.
2. Ian McIntyre, *The Expense of Glory: A Life of John Reith* (London: Harper Collins, 1993).
3. Covert and Stevens, *Mass Media*, p. 209.
4. James D. Hart, *The Popular Book: A History of America's Literary Taste* (New York, NY: Oxford University Press, 1950), p. 228.
5. Alice Goldfarb Marquis, *Hopes and Ashes: The Birth of Modern Times* (New York, NY: Free Press, 1986).
6. Ibid, pp. 63–4.
7. For journalists as authors of 'dime novels' see Michael Denning, *Mechanic Accents: Dime Novels and Working-Class Culture in America* (London: Verso, 1987), pp. 18–24.
8. Tanya Gold, 'The Outsiders', *The Spectator*, 14 November 2020, pp. 50–51.
9. Marquis, *Hope and Ashes*, p. 86.
10. Covert and Stevens, *Mass Media*, p. xiii.
11. Alistair Black, *The Public Library in Britain, 1914–2000* (London: British Library, 2000).
12. Patrick Leary, *The Punch Brotherhood: Table Talk and Print Culture in Mid-Victorian London* (London: British Library, 2010). Frank E. Huggett, *Victorian England as Seen by Punch* (London: Book Club Associates, 1978).
13. Chris Baggs, '"In the Separate Reading Room for Ladies Are Provided Those Publications Specially Interesting to Them": Ladies' Reading Rooms and British Public Libraries 1850–1914', *Victorian Periodicals Review*, 38 (2005), pp. 280–306, here p. 281.
14. Marquis, *Hope and Ashes*, pp. 124, 127.
15. Hart, *Popular Book*, pp. 236, 261–3.
16. Ibid, pp. 219, 256, 261–3.
17. Ibid, p. 273. Megan Benton, '"Too Many Books": Book Ownership and Cultural Identity in the 1920s', *American Quarterly*, 49 (1997), pp. 268–97.
18. Janice A. Radway, *A Feeling for Books: The Book-of-the-Month Club, Literary Taste and Middle-Class Desire* (Chapel Hill, NC: University of North Carolina Press, 1997). Hart, *Popular Book*, p. 273.
19. Hart, *Popular Book*, pp. 237, 286.
20. Christopher Hilliard, 'The Twopenny Library: The Book Trade, Working-Class Readers and "Middlebrow" Novels in Britain, 1930–42', *Twentieth Century British History*, 25 (2014), pp. 199–220.

21. Ronald Barker, 'Book Distribution in the United Kingdom', *ALA Bulletin*, 57 (June 1963), pp. 523–7.

22. John Sutherland, *Reading the Decades: Fifty Years of the Nation's Bestselling Books* (London: BBC, 2002).

23. Joanne E. Passet, 'Reaching the Rural Reader: Traveling Libraries in America, 1892–1920', *Libraries & Culture*, 26 (1991), pp. 100–118, here p. 103.

24. Lisa Lindell, 'Bringing Books to a "Book-Hungry Land": Print Culture on the Dakota Prairie', *Book History*, 7 (2004), pp. 215–38.

25. Wayne Wiegand, *Irrepressible Reformer: A Biography of Melvil Dewey* (Chicago, IL: American Library Association, 1996).

26. Passet, 'Reaching the Rural Reader', p. 105.

27. Jennifer Cummings, '"How Can we Fail?" The Texas State Library's Travelling Libraries and Bookmobiles, 1916–1966', *Libraries & the Cultural Record*, 44 (2009), pp. 299–325, here, p. 301.

28. Passet, 'Reaching the Rural Reader', p. 111.

29. Susan Orlean, *The Library Book* (London: Atlantic Books, 2018), p. 195. Tanya Ducker Finchum and Allen Finchum, 'Not Gone with the Wind: Libraries in Oklahoma in the 1930s', *Libraries & the Cultural Record*, 46 (2011), pp. 276–94.

30. Deanna B. Marcum, 'The Rural Public Library in America at the Turn of the Century', *Libraries & Culture*, 26 (1991), pp. 87–99.

31. As one of the present authors can attest from rural Shropshire in the early 1960s.

32. Cummings, '"How Can we Fail?"', p. 312.

33. Male adults accounted for only 2 per cent of borrowings. Christine Pawley, *Reading Places: Literacy, Democracy and the Public Library in Cold War America* (Amherst, MA: University of Massachusetts Press, 2010), p. 121.

34. Ralph A. Wagner, 'Not Recommended: A List for Catholic High School Libraries, 1942', *Libraries & Culture*, 30 (1995), pp. 170–98.

35. https://www.pewtrusts.org/en/research-and-analysis/blogs/ stateline/2018/03/28/yes-bookmobiles-are-still-a-thing-we-checked.

36. Dane M. Ward, 'The Changing Role of Mobile Libraries in Africa', *International Information and Library Review*, 28 (1996), pp. 121–33.

37. https://www.aljazeera.com/features/2018/4/23/ for-the-love-of-books-mobile-libraries-around-the-world.

38. Ellis Alec, *Library Services for Young People in England and Wales, 1830–1970* (Oxford: Pergamon Press, 1971).

39. Ibid, p. 28.

40. F. J. Harvey Darton, *Children's Books in England: Five Centuries of Social Life* (London: British Library, 1999). Michael Denning, *Mechanical Accents: Dime Novels and Working-Class Culture in America* (London: Verso, 1987).

41. Jon Savage, *Teenage: The Creation of Youth Culture* (London: Pimlico, 2008).

42. Ibid, pp. 141–2.

43. Ibid, p. 301.

44. Ibid, pp. 353–4. Cynthia L. White, *Women's Magazines, 1693–1968* (London: Michael Joseph, 1970).

45. Thelma McCormack, '*The Intelligent Woman's Guide to Socialism and*

Capitalism by George Bernard Shaw', *American Journal of Sociology*, 91 (1985), pp. 209–11.

46. Baggs, 'Separate Reading Room', p. 282.

47. Ibid, pp. 286–7.

48. Sterling Joseph Coleman, '"Eminently Suited to Girls and Women": The Numerical Feminization of Public Librarianship in England, 1914–1931', *Library & Information History*, 30 (2014), pp. 195–209.

49. Ibid, p. 201.

50. Esther Jane Carrier, *Fiction in Public Libraries 1900–1950* (Littleton, CO: Libraries Unlimited, 1985).

51. Evelyn Geller, *Forbidden Books in American Public Libraries, 1876–1939* (Westport, CT: Greenwood, 1984), pp. 54–6, 93–7, 105–108.

52. Joseph McAleer, *Popular Reading and Publishing in Britain, 1914–1950* (Oxford: Oxford University Press, 1992), pp. 100–132. Idem, *Passion's Fortune: The Story of Mills & Boon* (Oxford: Oxford University Press, 1999).

53. McAleer, *Popular Reading*, p. 106.

54. See chapter 13.

55. Nicola Wilson, 'Boots Book-lovers' Library and the Novel: The Impact of a Circulating Library Market on Twentieth-century Fiction', *Information & Culture*, 49 (2014), pp. 427–49.

56. McAleer, *Popular Reading*, p. 114.

57. Janice A. Radway, *Reading the Romance: Women, Patriarchy and Popular Literature* (Chapel Hill, NC: University of North Carolina Press, 1984), p. 20.

58. http://publiclibrariesonline.org/2013/05/ promoting-romance-novels-in-american-public-libraries/.

59. Conversations with library staff in English and Scottish branch libraries.

18. Libraries, Books and Politics

1. Robert Darnton, 'Censorship, a Comparative View: France 1789 – East Germany 1989', *Representations*, 49 (1995), pp. 40–60, here p. 40.

2. Emily Drabinski, 'Librarians and the Patriot Act', *The Radical Teacher*, 77 (2006), pp. 12–14.

3. Gladys Spencer, *The Chicago Public Library: Origins and Backgrounds* (Boston, MA: Gregg Press, 1972).

4. Spencer, *Chicago Public Library* p. 344. Constance J. Gordon, 'Cultural Record Keepers: The English Book Donation, Chicago Public Library', *Libraries & the Cultural Record*, 44 (2009), pp. 371–4.

5. Dennis Thompson, 'The Private Wars of Chicago's Big Bill Thompson', *Journal of Library History*, 15 (1980), pp. 261–80.

6. Joyce M. Latham, 'Wheat and Chaff: Carl Roden, Abe Korman and the Definitions of Intellectual Freedom in the Chicago Public Library', *Libraries & the Cultural Record*, 44 (2009), pp. 279–98.

7. Thompson, 'Big Bill', p. 273.

8. Louise S. Robbins, *The Dismissal of Miss Ruth Brown: Civil Rights, Censorship and the American Library* (Norman, OK: University of Oklahoma Press, 2000).

9. Christine Pawley, *Reading Places: Literacy, Democracy and the Public Library in Cold War America* (Amherst, MA: University of Massachusetts Press, 2010). Lisle A. Rose, *The Cold War Comes to Main Street: America in 1950* (Lawrence, KS: University Press of Kansas, 1999).

10. Louise S. Robbins, *Censorship and the American Library: The American Library Association's Response to Threats to Intellectual Freedom, 1939–1969* (Westport, CT: Greenwood, 1996), p. 37. Idem, 'After Brave Words, Silence: American Librarianship Responds to Cold War Loyalty Programs, 1947–1957', *Libraries & Culture*, 30 (1995), pp. 345–65.

11. Robbins, *Censorship* pp. 71, 74.

12. Ibid, p. 122.

13. Christopher Hilliard, '"Is It a Book That You Would Even Wish Your Wife or Your Servants to Read?" Obscenity Law and the Politics of Reading in Modern England', *American Historical Review*, 118 (2013), pp. 653–78. H. Montgomery Hyde, *The Lady Chatterley's Lover Trial* (London: Bodley Head, 1990).

14. Whether this was aimed at Lawrence is contested, but it certainly hit the mark. Faye Hammill, 'Cold Comfort Farm, D. H. Lawrence, and English Literary Culture Between the Wars', *Modern Fiction Studies*, 47 (2001), pp. 831–54.

15. Michael Fultz, 'Black Public Libraries in the South in the Era of De Jure Segregation', *Libraries & the Cultural Record*, 41 (2006), pp. 337–59. Stephen Cresswell, 'The Last Days of Jim Crow in Southern Libraries', *Libraries & Culture*, 31 (1996), pp. 557–72.

16. A story beautifully told in Shirley Wiegand and Wayne Wiegand, *The Desegregation of Public Libraries in the Jim Crow South: Civil Rights and Local Activism* (Baton Rouge, LA: LSU Press, 2018).

17. Robbins, *Censorship*, p. 107. Wayne Wiegand, '"Any Ideas?": The American Library Association and the Desegregation of Public Libraries in the American South', *Libraries: Culture, History, and Society*, 1 (2017), pp. 1–22.

18. Eric L. Motley, *Madison Park: A Place of Hope* (Grand Rapids, MI: Zondervan, 2017), pp. 129–36.

19. Melville J. Ruggles and Raynard Coe Swank, *Soviet libraries and librarianship; report of the visit of the delegation of U.S. librarians to the Soviet Union, May–June, 1961, under the U.S.–Soviet cultural exchange agreement* (Chicago, IL: American Library Association, 1962). Rutherford D. Rogers, 'Yes, Ivan Reads: A First Report of the American Library Mission to Russia', *American Library Association Bulletin*, 55 (1961), pp. 621–4.

20. Jenny Brine, 'The Soviet Reader, the Book Shortage and the Public Library', *Solanus*, 2 (1988), pp. 39–57.

21. Quoted in Jennifer Jane Brine, 'Adult readers in the Soviet Union' (PhD thesis, University of Birmingham, 1986), p. 8. http://etheses.bham.ac.uk/1398/.

22. Ralph A. Leal, 'Libraries in the U.S.S.R', unpublished survey accessible at https://files.eric.ed.gov/fulltext/ED098959.pdf (last accessed 27 July 2020), p. 6.

23. Ibid, p. 12.

24. L. I. Vladimirov, 'The Accomplishments of University Libraries in the Soviet Union', *Library Trends*, 4 (1964), pp. 558–82. Ilkka Mäkinen, 'Libraries in Hell:

Cultural Activities in Soviet Prisons and Labor Camps from the 1930s to the 1950s', *Libraries & Culture*, 28 (1993), pp. 117–42.

25. Andrei Rogachevskii, 'Homo Sovieticus in the Library', *Europe-Asia Studies*, 54 (2002), pp. 975–88. Boris Korsch, 'The Role of Readers' Cards in Soviet Libraries, *Journal of Library History*, 13 (1978), pp. 282–97.

26. Boris Korsch, 'Soviet Librarianship under Gorbachev: Change and Continuity', *Solanus*, 4 (1990), pp. 24–49.

27. Marek Sroka, 'The Stalinization of Libraries in Poland, 1945–1953', *Library History*, 16 (2000), pp. 105–25.

28. Idem, '"Forsaken and Abandoned": The Nationalization and Salvage of Deserted, Displaced, and Private Library Collections in Poland, 1945–1948', *Library & Information History*, 28 (2012), pp. 272–88.

29. Sroka, 'Stalinization', pp. 113, 117.

30. Jiřina Šmejkalová, *Cold War Books in the 'Other Europe' and What Came After* (Leiden: Brill, 2011), p. 115.

31. Ibid, pp. 161, 196–8.

32. Ibid, p. 324.

33. The countries of eastern Europe and the Baltic region occupy all of the first eight places in the data supplied by the European Parliament lobby group, Public Libraries 2030. https://publiclibraries2030.eu/resources/eu-library-factsheets/.

34. Kathleen A. Smith, 'Collection Development in Public and University Libraries of the Former German Democratic Republic since German Unification', *Libraries & Culture*, 36 (2001), pp. 413–31.

35. As witnessed by one of the authors in 1991.

36. Smith, 'Collection Development', p. 422.

37. Priya Joshi, *In Another Country: Colonialism, Culture, and the English Novel in India* (New York, NY: Columbia University Press, 2002). Robert Darnton, *Censors at Work: How States Shaped Literature* (London: British Library, 2014).

38. Jashu Patel and Krishan Kumar, *Libraries and Librarianship in India* (Westport, CT: Greenwood, 2001), p. 52.

39. Ibid, p. 91.

40. Zahid Ashraf Wani, 'Development of Public Libraries in India', *Library Philosophy and Practice* (ejournal, 2008).

41. A. Dirk Moses and Lasse Heerten, *Postcolonial Conflict and the Question of Genocide: The Nigeria-Biafra War, 1967–1970* (London: Routledge, 2017). Chinua Achebe, *There Was a Country: A Personal History of Biafra* (London: Allen Lane, 2012).

42. Helen Jarvis, 'The National Library of Cambodia: Surviving for Seventy Years', *Libraries & Culture*, 30 (1995), pp. 391–408.

43. Mary Niles Maack, 'Books and Libraries as Instruments of Cultural Diplomacy in Francophone Africa during the Cold War', *Libraries & Culture*, 36 (2001), pp. 58–86.

44. Allan Horton, *'Libraries are great mate!' But they could be greater. A report to the nation on Public Libraries in Australia* (Melbourne: Australian Library Promotional Council, 1976).

45. Nicholson Baker, *Double Fold: Libraries and the Assault on Paper* (New York, NY: Random House, 2001).

46. Nicholas Basbanes, 'Once and Future Library', in his *Patience and Fortitude* (New York, NY: Harper Collins, 2001), pp. 386–424.

47. Basbanes, *Patience and Fortitude*, p. 401.

48. https://publiclibraries2030.eu/wp-content/uploads/2019/12/France-2019.pdf.

Postscript: Reading Without Books

1. https://www.gatesfoundation.org/what-we-do/global-development/global-libraries.

2. Brad Stone, *The Everything Store: Jeff Bezos and the Age of Amazon* (New York, NY: Little, Brown, 2013), p. 302.

3. Robert Darnton, *The Case for Books: Past, Present, and Future* (New York: Public Affairs, 2009), pp. 3–64.

4. Rana Foroohar, *Don't Be Evil: The Case Against Big Tech* (London: Allen Lane, 2019), p. 28.

5. Maryanne Wolf, *Reader, Come Home: The Reading Brain in a Digital World* (New York, NY: Harper, 2018).

6. Susan Orlean, *The Library Book* (London: Atlantic Books, 2018).

7. UNESCO report: 'Lost memory: libraries and archives destroyed in the twentieth century' (1996).

8. https://www.betterworldbooks.com/.

9. Orlean, *Library Book*, p. 87.

10. https://www.nytimes.com/2013/11/30/books/unraveling-huge-thefts-from-girolamini-library-in-naples.html.

11. https://www.latimes.com/archives/la-xpm-2000-feb-20-mn-762-story.html. Owen Gingerich, *The Book Nobody Read: Chasing the Revolutions of Nicolas Copernicus* (London: Heinemann, 2004), pp. 220–38.

12. For a passionate *cri de coeur*, see William H. Wisner, *Whither the Postmodern Library? Libraries, Technology, and Education in the Information Age* (Jefferson, NC: McFarland, 2000).

13. Nicholas Basbanes, *Patience and Fortitude* (New York, NY: Harper Collins, 2001), p. 405.

14. Our work with the apparatus Van der Woude is described in Andrew Pettegree and Arthur der Weduwen, 'What was published in the seventeenth-century Dutch Republic?', *Livre. Revue Historique* (2018), pp. 1–22.

15. Brian Dumaine, *Bezonomics: How Amazon Is Changing Our Lives and What the World's Best Companies Are Learning from It* (London: Simon & Schuster, 2020), p. 238.

16. Orlean, *Library Book,* p. 39.

17. Dumaine, *Bezonomics*, p. 110.

18. Ibid, p. 91.

19. https://librarymap.ifla.org/.

20. https://www.nypl.org/about/locations/53rd-street.

21. Orlean, *Library Book*, p. 157.

22. https://rossdawson.com/wp-content/uploads/2007/10/extinction_timeline. pdf.

23. 'The e-reader device is dying a rapid death', 11 November 2019. https:// justpublishingadvice.com/the-e-reader-device-is-dying-a-rapid-death/.

24. Richard Watson, *Future Files: A Brief History of the Next 50 Years*, 3rd edn (London: Nicholas Brealey, 2012).

25. Dumaine, *Bezonomics*, p. 39.

26. https://bexarbibliotech.org/. https://www.youtube.com/watch?v= QtvytxreYlc.

BIBLIOGRAPHY

Prologue & General Works

Buzás, Ladislaus, *German Library History, 800–1945* (Jefferson, NC: McFarland, 1986).

Crawford, Alice (ed.), *The Meaning of the Library: A Cultural History* (Princeton and Oxford: Princeton University Press, 2015).

Harris, Michael H., *History of Libraries in the Western World*, 4th edn (Metuchen, NJ: Scarecrow Press, 1995).

Hoare, Peter (ed.), *The Cambridge History of Libraries in Britain and Ireland* (3 vols., Cambridge: Cambridge University Press, 2006).

Hobson, Anthony, *Great Libraries* (London: Weidenfeld & Nicolson, 1970).

The Library Book (London: Profile, 2012).

Raven, James (ed.), *Lost Libraries: The Destruction of Great Book Collections since Antiquity* (Basingstoke: Palgrave, 2004).

Stam, David H. (ed.), *International Dictionary of Library Histories* (2 vols., Chicago and London: Fitzroy Dearborn, 2001).

Wiegand, Wayne A., and Donald G. Davis Jr. (eds.), *Encyclopedia of Library History* (New York and London: Garland, 1994).

1. A Confusion of Scrolls

Black, Jeremy, 'Lost Libraries of Ancient Mesopotamia', in James Raven (ed.), *Lost Libraries: The Destruction of Great Book Collections since Antiquity* (Basingstoke: Palgrave, 2004), pp. 41–57.

Boyd, Clarence Eugene, *Public Libraries and Literary Culture in Ancient Rome* (Chicago, IL: University of Chicago Press, 1915).

Bruce, Lorne, 'Palace and Villa Libraries from Augustus to Hadrian', *Journal of Library History*, 21 (1986), pp. 510–52.

Butler, Beverley, *Return to Alexandria: An Ethnography of Cultural Heritage, Revivalism and Museum Memory* (Walnut Creek, CA: Left Coast Press, 2007).

Casson, Lionel, *Libraries in the Ancient World* (London and New Haven: Yale University Press, 2001).

Dix, T. Keith, '"Public Libraries" in Ancient Rome: Ideology and Reality', *Libraries & Culture*, 29 (1994), pp. 282–96.

Dix, T. Keith, 'Pliny's Library at Comum', in *Libraries & Culture*, 31 (1996), pp. 85–102.

Dix, T. Keith, "'Beware of Promising Your Library to Anyone": Assembling a Private Library at Rome', in König, *Ancient Libraries*, pp. 209–34.

Dix, T. Keith, and George W. Houston, 'Public Libraries in the City of Rome: from the Augustan Age to the time of Diocletian', *Mélanges de l'École de Rome. Antiquité*, 118 (2006), pp. 671–717.

El-Abbadi, Mostafa, and Omnia Fathallah (eds.), *What Happened to the Ancient Library of Alexandria?* (Leiden: Brill, 2008).

Hanson, Carl A., 'Were There Libraries in Roman Spain?', *Libraries & Culture*, 24 (1989), pp. 198–216.

Harris, William V., *Ancient Literacy* (Cambridge, MA: Harvard University Press, 1989).

Hendrickson, Thomas, *Ancient Libraries and Renaissance Humanism: The 'De Bibliothecis' of Justus Lipsius* (Leiden: Brill, 2017).

Houston, George W., *Inside Roman Libraries: Book Collections and Their Management in Antiquity* (Chapel Hill, NC: University of North Carolina Press, 2014).

Johnson, William A., 'Libraries and Reading Culture in the High Empire', in König, *Ancient Libraries*, pp. 347–63.

König, Jason, Katerina Oikonomopoulou and Greg Woolf (eds.), *Ancient Libraries* (Cambridge: Cambridge University Press, 2013).

Lewis, Bernard, 'The Arab Destruction of the Library of Alexandria: Anatomy of a Myth', in Mostafa El-Abbadi and Omnia Fathallah (eds.), *What Happened to the Ancient Library of Alexandria?* (Leiden: Brill, 2008), pp. 213–17.

MacLeod, Roy (ed.), *The Library of Alexandria: Centre of Learning in the Ancient World* (London and New York: I. B. Tauris, 2000).

Marshall, Anthony J., 'Library Resources and Creative Writing at Rome', *Phoenix*, 30 (1976), pp. 252–64.

Martínez, Victor M., and Megan Finn Senseney, 'The Professional and His Books: Special Libraries in the Ancient World', in König, *Ancient Libraries*, pp. 401–17.

Mattern, Susan P., *The Prince of Medicine: Galen in the Roman Empire* (Oxford: Oxford University Press, 2013).

Nutton, Vivian, 'Galen's Library', in Christopher Gill, Tim Whitmarsh and John Wilkins (eds.), *Galen and the World of Knowledge* (Cambridge: Cambridge University Press, 2009).

Parsons, Edward Alexander, *The Alexandrian Library, Glory of the Hellenic World: Its Rise, Antiquities and Destruction* (Amsterdam: Elsevier, 1952).

Pinner, H. L., *The World of Books in Classical Antiquity* (Leiden: Sijthoff, 1958).

Posner, Ernst, *Archives in the Ancient World* (Cambridge, MA: Harvard University Press, 1972).

Reichmann, Felix, 'The Book Trade at the Time of the Roman Empire', *Library Quarterly*, 8 (1938), pp. 40–76.

Sider, Sandra, 'Herculaneum's Library in 79 AD: The Villa of the Papyri', *Libraries & Culture*, 25 (1990), pp. 534–42.

White, P., 'Bookshops in the Literary Culture of Rome', in William A. Johnson and Holt N. Parker (eds.), *Ancient Literacies: The Culture of Reading in Greece and Rome* (Oxford: Oxford University Press, 2009)

Woolf, Greg, 'Introduction: Approaching the Ancient Library', in König, *Ancient Libraries*, pp. 1–20.

2. Sanctuary

Barton, John, *A History of the Bible: The Book and Its Faiths* (London: Allen Lane, 2019).

Beddie, James Stuart, 'The Ancient Classics in the Mediaeval Libraries', *Speculum*, 5 (1930), pp. 3–20.

Berthoud, J., 'The Italian Renaissance Library', *Theoria: A Journal of Social and Political Theory*, 26 (1966), pp. 61–80.

Bischoff, Bernhard, *Manuscripts and Libraries in the Age of Charlemagne* (Cambridge: Cambridge University Press, 1994).

Brett, Edward T., 'The Dominican Library in the Thirteenth Century', *The Journal of Library History*, 15 (1980), pp. 303–308.

Bullough, Donald, 'Charlemagne's court library revisited', *Early Medieval Europe*, 12 (2003), pp. 339–63.

Christ, Karl, *The Handbook of Medieval Library History*, ed. and trans. Theophil M. Otto (Metuchen, NJ: The Scarecrow Press, 1984).

Clark, John Willis, *The Care of Books: An Essay on the Development of Libraries and Their Fittings, from the Earliest Times to the End of the Eighteenth Century* (Cambridge: Cambridge University Press, 1901).

Cleaver, Laura, 'The circulation of history books in twelfth-century Normandy', in Cynthia Johnston (ed.), *The Concept of the Book: The Production, Progression and Dissemination of Information* (London: Institute of English Studies, 2019), pp. 57–78.

Cyrus, Cynthia J., *The Scribes for Women's Convents in Late Medieval Germany* (Toronto: University of Toronto Press, 2009).

Duft, Johannes, *The Abbey Library of Saint Gall* (St Gallen: Verlag am Klosterhof, 1985).

Dunning, Andrew N. J., 'John Lakenheath's Rearrangement of the Archives of Bury St Edmunds Abbey, c.1380', *The Library*, 19 (2018), pp. 63–8.

Fox, Yaniv, *Power and Religion in Merovingian Gaul: Columbanian Monasticism and the Frankish Elites* (London and New Haven: Yale University Press, 2014).

Given-Wilson, Christopher, *Chronicles: The Writing of History in Medieval England* (London: Hambledon, 2004).

Goodhart Gordan, Phyllis, *Two Renaissance Book Collectors: The Letters of Poggius Bracciolini to Nicolaus de Niccolis* (New York: Columbia University Press, 1974).

Hamel, Christopher de, *A History of Illuminated Manuscripts,* 2nd edn (London, Phaidon, 1994).

Hammer, Jacob, 'Cassiodorus, the Savior of Western Civilization', *Bulletin of the Polish Institute of Arts and Sciences in America*, 3 (1945), pp. 369–84.

Hobson, Anthony, *Great Libraries* (London: Weidenfeld & Nicolson, 1970).

Humphreys, K. W., 'The Effects of Thirteenth-century Cultural Changes on Libraries', *Libraries & Culture*, 24 (1989), pp. 5–20.

Ker, N. R., *Medieval Libraries of Great Britain*, 2nd edn (London: Royal Historical Society, 1964).

Ker, N. R., *Books, Collectors and Libraries: Studies in the Medieval Heritage*, ed. Andrew G. Watson (London and Ronceverte: Hambledon, 1985).

Kibre, Pearl, *The Library of Pico della Mirandola* (New York, NY: Columbia University Press, 1936).

Labowsky, Lotte, *Bessarion's Library and the Biblioteca Marciana: Six Early Inventories* (Rome: Edizioni di storia e letteratura, 1979).

Martin, Henri-Jean, and Roger Chartier, *Histoire de l'édition francaise. Le livre conquerant. Du Moyen Age au milieu du XVIIe siècle* (Paris: Promodis, 1982).

McKitterick, Rosamond, *The Carolingians and the Written Word* (Cambridge: Cambridge University Press, 1989).

McKitterick, Rosamond, *Charlemagne: The Formation of a European Identity* (Cambridge: Cambridge University Press, 2008).

Meeder, Sven, *The Irish Scholarly Presence at St. Gall: Networks of Knowledge in the Early Middle Ages* (London: Bloomsbury, 2018).

Padover, S. K., 'German libraries in the fourteenth and fifteenth centuries', in James Westfall Thompson (ed.), *The Medieval Library* (New York: Hafner, 1957), pp. 453–76.

Papahagi, Adrian, 'Lost Libraries and Surviving Manuscripts: The Case of Medieval Transylvania', *Library & Information History*, 31 (2015), pp. 35–53.

Peterson, Herman A., 'The Genesis of Monastic Libraries', *Libraries & the Cultural Record*, 45 (2010), pp. 320–32.

Petroski, Henry, *The Book on the Bookshelf* (New York: Knopf, 1999).

Reynolds, L. D., and N. G. Wilson, *Scribes and Scholars: A Guide to the Transmission of Greek and Latin Literature* (Oxford: Oxford University Press, 1968).

Rios, Dom Romanus, 'Monte Cassino, 529–1944', *Bulletin of the John Rylands Library*, 29 (1945), pp. 49–68

Robothan, Dorothy M., 'Libraries of the Italian Renaissance', in James Westfall Thompson (ed.), *The Medieval Library* (New York: Hafner, 1957), pp. 509–88.

Rouse, Richard H., 'The early library of the Sorbonne', *Scriptorium*, 21 (1967), pp. 42–71.

Schlotheuber, Eva, and John T. McQuillen, 'Books and Libraries within Monasteries', in *The Cambridge History of Medieval Monasticism in the Latin West* (Cambridge: Cambridge University Press, 2020), pp. 975–97.

Staikos, K. Sp., *The Architecture of Libraries in Western Civilization: From the Minoan Era to Michelangelo* (New Castle, DE: Oak Knoll Press, 2017).

Streeter, Burnett Hillman, *The Chained Library: A Survey of Four Centuries in the Evolution of the English Library* (London: Macmillan, 1931).

Thompson, James Westfall, *The Medieval Library* (New York: Hafner, 1957).

Thornton, Dora, *The Scholar in His Study: Ownership and Experience in Renaissance Italy* (London and New Haven: Yale University Press, 1997).

Ullman, Berthold Louis, *The Humanism of Coluccio Salutati* (Padua: Antenore, 1963).

Venarde, Bruce L. (ed.), *The Rule of Saint Benedict* (Cambridge, MA: Harvard University Press, 2011).

Ward, J. O., 'Alexandria and Its Medieval Legacy: The Book, the Monk and the Rose', in Roy MacLeod (ed.), *The Library of Alexandria: Centre of Learning in the Ancient World* (London and New York: I. B. Tauris, 2000), pp. 163–79.

3. Little Monkeys and Letters of Gold

Alexander, J. J. G. (ed.), *The Painted Page: Italian Renaissance Book Illustration, 1450–1550* (London: Prestel, 1994).

Baswell, Christopher (ed.), *Medieval Manuscripts, Their Makers and Users: a special issue of Viator in honor of Richard and Mary Rouse* (Turnhout: Brepols, 2011).

BenAicha, Hedi, 'The Mosques as Libraries in Islamic Civilization, 700–1400 AD', *Journal of Library History*, 21 (1986), pp. 252–60.

Berthoud, J., 'The Italian Renaissance Library', *Theoria: A Journal of Social and Political Theory*, 26 (1966), pp. 61–80.

Bisticci, Vespasiano di, *Renaissance Princes, Popes and Prelates: The Vespasiano Memoirs – Lives of Illustrious Men of the XVth Century*, trans. William George and Emily Waters (New York, NY: Harper & Row, 1963).

Brokaw, C. J., 'On the history of the book in China', in C. J. Brokaw and Kai-wing Chow (eds.), *Printing and Book Culture in Late Imperial China* (Berkeley, CA: University of California Press, 2005), pp. 3–55.

Brown, Cynthia J., *The Queen's Library: Image-Making at the Court of Anne of Brittany, 1477–1514* (Philadelphia, PA: University of Pennsylvania Press, 2011).

Brown, Cynthia J. (ed.), *The Cultural and Political Legacy of Anne de Bretagne: Negotiating Convention in Books and Documents* (Woodbridge: Boydell and Brewer, 2010).

Bühler, Curt F., *The Fifteenth-century Book: The Scribes, the Printers, the Decorators* (Philadelphia, PA: Philadelphia University Press, 1960).

Buringh, Eltjo, *Medieval Manuscript Production in the Latin West* (Leiden: Brill, 2010).

Buringh, Eltjo, and Jan Luiten Van Zanden, 'Charting the "Rise of the West": Manuscripts and Printed Books in Europe, a Long-Term Perspective from the Sixth through Eighteenth Centuries', *Journal of Economic History*, 69 (2009), pp. 409–45.

Carley, James P. (ed.), *The Libraries of King Henry VIII* (London: British Library, 2000).

Cayley, Emma, and Susan Powell (eds.), *Manuscripts and Printed Books in Europe, 1350–1550: Packaging, Presentation and Consumption* (Liverpool: Liverpool University Press, 2013).

Chow, Kai-wing, *Publishing, Culture and Power in Early Modern China* (Stanford, CA: Stanford University Press, 2004).

Croenen, Godfried, and Peter Ainsworth (eds.), *Patrons, Authors and Workshops: Books and Book Production in Paris around 1400* (Louvain: Peeters, 2006).

Dasgupta, Kalpana, 'How Learned Were the Mughals: Reflections on Muslim Libraries in India', *Journal of Library History*, 10 (1975), pp. 241–54.

De la Mare, Albinia C., 'Vespasiano da Bisticci, Historian and Bookseller' (PhD thesis, London University, 1966).

De la Mare, Albinia C., 'New Research on Humanistic Scribes in Florence', in A.

Garzelli (ed.), *Miniatura fiorentina del Rinascimento 1440–1525, un primo censimento* (Florence: Giunta Regionale Toscana, 1985), I, pp. 393–600.

De la Mare, Albinia C., 'Vespasiano da Bisticci as Producer of Classical Manuscripts in Fifteenth-century Florence', in Claudine A. Chavannes-Mazel and Margaret M. Smith (eds.), *Medieval Manuscripts of the Latin Classics: Production and Use* (London: Red Gull Press, 1996), pp. 166–207.

Dogaer, Georges, and Marguerite Debae, *La Librairie de Philippe le Bon* (Brussels: Bibliothèque royale, 1967).

Duffy, Eamon, *Marking the Hours: English People and their Prayers, 1240–1570* (London and New Haven: Yale University Press, 2006).

Elayyan, Ribhi Mustafa, 'The History of the Arabic-Islamic Libraries: 7th to 14th Centuries', *International Library Review*, 22 (1990), pp. 119–35.

Green, Arnold H., 'The History of Libraries in the Arab World: A Diffusionist Model', *Libraries & Culture,* 23 (1988), pp. 454–73.

Hamel, Christopher de, *Meetings with Remarkable Manuscripts* (London: Allen Lane, 2016).

Hunt, R. W., and A. C. de la Mare, *Duke Humfrey and English Humanism in the Fifteenth Century* (Oxford: Bodleian Library, 1970).

Hunwick, John O., *The Hidden Treasures of Timbuktu: Historic City of Islamic Africa* (London: Thames & Hudson, 2008).

Kibre, Pearl, 'The Intellectual Interests Reflected in Libraries of the Fourteenth and Fifteenth Centuries', *Journal of the History of Ideas*, 7 (1946), pp. 257–97.

King, Ross, *The Bookseller of Florence* (London: Chatto & Windus, 2021).

Kornicki, Peter, *The Book in Japan: A Cultural History from the Beginnings to the Nineteenth Century* (Honolulu: University of Hawai'i Press, 2001), pp. 363–412.

Kurlansky, Mark, *Paper: Paging through History* (New York: W. W. Norton, 2016).

McDermott, Joseph P., and Peter Burke (eds.), *The Book Worlds of East Asia and Europe, 1450–1850: Connections and Comparisons* (Hong Kong: Hong Kong University Press, 2015).

McKendrick, S., 'Lodewijk van Gruuthuse en de librije van Edward IV', in M. P. J. Martens (ed.), *Lodewijk van Gruuthuse. Mecenas en Europees Diplomaat ca. 1427–1492* (Bruges: Stiching Kuntsboek, 1992), pp. 153–9.

Mitchell, R. J., 'A Renaissance Library: The Collection of John Tiptoft, Earl of Worcester', *The Library*, 4th series, 18 (1937), pp. 67–83.

Neng-fu, Kuang, 'Chinese Library Science in the Twelfth Century', *Libraries & Culture,* 26 (1991), pp. 357–71.

Oostrom, Frits Pieter van, *Court and Culture: Dutch Literature, 1350–1450* (Berkeley, CA: University of California Press, 1992).

Overty, Joanne Filippone, 'The Cost of Doing Scribal Business: Prices of Manuscript Books in England, 1300–1483', *Book History*, 11 (2008), pp. 1–32.

Papahagi, Adrian, 'The Library of Petrus Gotfart de Corona, Rector of the University of Vienna in 1473', *The Library*, 7th series, 20 (2019), pp. 29–46.

Pedersen, Johannes, *The Arabic Book* (Princeton: Princeton University Press, 1984).

Petrina, Alessandra, *Cultural Politics in Fifteenth-century England: The Case of Humphrey, Duke of Gloucester* (Leiden: Brill, 2004).

Pollard, Graham, 'The pecia system in the medieval universities', in M. B. Parkes and

Andrew G. Watson (eds.), *Medieval Scribes, Manuscripts and Libraries: Essays Presented to N. R. Ker* (London: Scolar Press, 1978), pp. 145–61.

Rouse, Mary A., and Richard H. Rouse, *Cartolai, Illuminators, and Printers in Fifteenth-century Italy: The Evidence of the Ripoli Press* (Los Angeles, LA: UCLA, 1988).

Rouse, Richard H., and Mary A. Rouse, 'The Commercial Production of Manuscript Books in Late-Thirteenth-century and Early-Fourteenth-century Paris', in Linda L. Brownrigg (ed.), *Medieval Book Production: Assessing the Evidence* (London: Red Gull Press, 1990), pp. 103–15.

Rouse, Richard H., and Mary A. Rouse, *Manuscripts and Their Makers: Commercial Book Producers in Medieval Paris, 1200–1500* (London: Harvey Miller, 2000).

Rundle, David, 'A Renaissance Bishop and His Books: A Preliminary Survey of the Manuscript Collection of Pietro Del Monte (c.1400–57)', *Papers of the British School at Rome*, 69 (2001), pp. 245–72.

Singleton, Brent D., 'African Bibliophiles: Books and Libraries in Medieval Timbuktu', *Libraries & Culture*, 39 (2004), pp. 1–12.

Staikos, K. Sp., *The Architecture of Libraries in Western Civilization: From the Minoan Era to Michelangelo* (New Castle, DE: Oak Knoll Press, 2017)

Taylor, Andrew, 'Manual to Miscellany: Stages in the Commercial Copying of Vernacular Literature in England', *The Yearbook of English Studies*, 33 (2003), pp. 1–17.

Thornton, Dora, *The Scholar in His Study: Ownership and Experience in Renaissance Italy* (London and New Haven: Yale University Press, 1997).

Ullman, Berthold L., and Philip A. Stadler, *The Public Library of Renaissance Florence: Niccolò Niccoli, Cosimo de' Medici and the Library of San Marco* (Padova: Editrice Antenore, 1972).

Weichselbaumer, Nikolaus, '"Quod Exemplaria vera habeant et correcta": Concerning the Distribution and Purpose of the Pecia System', in Richard Kirwan and Sophie Mullins (eds.), *Specialist Markets in the Early Modern Book World* (Leiden: Brill, 2015), pp. 331–50.

Wieck, Roger S., *Time Sanctified: The Book of Hours in Medieval Art and Life* (New York, NY: George Braziller, 2001).

Wijsman, Hanno, *Handschriften voor het hertogdom. De mooiste verluchte manuscripten van Brabantse hertogen, edellieden, kloosterlingen en stedelingen* (Alphen: Veerhuis, 2006).

Wijsman, Hanno, *Luxury Bound: Illustrated Manuscript Production and Noble and Princely Book Ownership in the Burgundian Netherlands (1400–1550)* (Turnhout: Brepols, 2010).

Woods, Marjorie Curry, *Weeping for Dido: The Classics in the Medieval Classroom* (Princeton, NJ: Princeton University Press, 2019).

4. The Infernal Press

Berkovits, Ilona, *Illuminated Manuscripts from the Library of Matthias Corvinus* (Budapest: Corvina Press, 1964)

Birrell, T. A., *English Monarchs and Their Books: From Henry VII to Charles II* (London: British Library, 1987).

Boffey, Julia, *Manuscript and Print in London, c.1475–1530* (London: British Library, 2012).

Booton, Diane E., *Manuscripts, Market and the Transition to Print in Late Medieval Brittany* (Farnham: Ashgate, 2009).

Bühler, Curt F., *The Fifteenth-century Book: The Scribes, the Printers, the Decorators* (Philadelphia, PA: Philadelphia University Press, 1960).

Carley, James P. (ed.), *The Libraries of King Henry VIII* (London: British Library, 2000).

Chartier, Roger, *The Cultural Uses of Print in Early Modern France* (Princeton, NJ: Princeton University Press, 1987).

Conway, Melissa, *The Diario of the Printing Press of San Jacopo di Ripoli, 1476–1484: Commentary and Transcription* (Florence: Olschki, 1999).

Cox-Rearick, J., *The Collection of Francis I: Royal Treasures* (New York, NY: Abrams, 1995).

Debae, Marguerite, *La Librairie de Marguerite d'Autriche* (Brussels: Bibliothèque Royale, 1987).

Eisenstein, Elizabeth L., *Divine Art, Infernal Machine: The Reception of Printing in the West from First Impressions to the Sense of an Ending* (Philadelphia: University of Pennsylvania Press, 2011).

Eisermann, Falk, 'A Golden Age? Monastic Printing Houses in the Fifteenth Century', in Benito Rial Costas (ed.), *Print Culture and Peripheries in Early Modern Europe* (Leiden: Brill, 2012), pp. 37–67.

Haemers, J., C. van Hoorebeeck and H. Wijsman (eds.), *Entre la ville, la noblesse et l'état: Philippe de Cleves (1456–1528), homme politique et bibliophile* (Turnhout: Brepols, 2007).

Hellinga, Lotte, 'Book Auctions in the Fifteenth Century', in her *Incunabula in Transit: People and Trade* (Leiden: Brill, 2018), pp. 6–19.

Hindman, Sandra, and James Douglas Farquhar, *Pen to Press: Illustrated Manuscripts and Printed Books in the First century of Printing* (College Park: University of Maryland, 1977).

Jensen, Kristian (ed.), *Incunabula and Their Readers: Printing, Selling and Using Books in the Fifteenth Century* (London: British Library, 2003).

Kapr, Albert, *Johann Gutenberg: The Man and His Invention* (Aldershot: Scolar Press, 1996).

Ker, N. R., 'Oxford College Libraries in the Sixteenth Century', in his *Books, Collectors and Libraries: Studies in the Medieval Heritage* (London and Ronceverte: Hambledon, 1985), pp. 379–436.

Kleineke, Hannes, 'The Library of John Veysy (d. 1492), Fellow of Lincoln College, Oxford, and Rector of St James, Garlickhythe, London', *The Library*, 7th series, 17 (2016), pp. 399–423.

Lowry, Martin, 'Two great Venetian libraries in the age of Aldus Manutius', *Bulletin of the John Rylands Library*, 57 (1974–5), pp. 128–66.

Neddermeyer, Uwe, 'Why were there no riots of the scribes? First results of a quantitative analysis of the book-production in the century of Gutenberg', *Gazette du livre medieval*, 31 (1997), pp. 1–8.

Noakes, Susan, 'The development of the book market in Late Quattrocento Italy:

printers' failures and the role of the middleman', *Journal of Mediaeval and Renaissance Studies*, 11 (1981), pp. 23–55.

Pettegree, Andrew, *The Book in the Renaissance* (London and New Haven: Yale University Press, 2010).

Pettegree, Andrew, 'The Renaissance Library and the Challenge of Print', in Alice Crawford (ed.), *The Meaning of the Library: A Cultural History* (Princeton: Princeton University Press, 2015), pp. 72–90.

Rouse, M. A., and R. H. Rouse, *Cartolai, Illuminators, and Printers in Fifteenth-century Italy* (Los Angeles, CA: UCLA, 1988).

Rouse, Mary A., and Richard H. Rouse, 'Backgrounds to print: aspects of the manuscript book in northern Europe of the fifteenth century', in their *Authentic Witnesses: Approaches to Medieval Texts and Manuscripts* (Notre Dame, IN: University of Notre Dame Press, 1991), pp. 449–66.

Saenger, Paul, 'Colard Mansion and the Evolution of the Printed Book', *Library Quarterly*, 45 (1975), pp. 405–18.

Scholderer, Victor, 'The petition of Sweynheym and Pannartz to Sixtus IV', *The Library*, 3rd series, 6 (1915), pp. 186–90.

Strata, Filippo de, *Polemic against Printing*, ed. Martin Lowry (Birmingham: Hayloft Press, 1986).

Sutton, Anne F., and Livia Visser-Fuchs, *Richard III's Books: Ideals and Reality in the Life and Library of a Mediaeval Prince* (Stroud: Sutton, 1997).

Tanner, Marcus, *The Raven King: Matthias Corvinus and the Fate of His Lost Library* (London and New Haven: Yale University Press, 2008).

Tedeschi, Martha, 'Publish and Perish: The Career of Lienhart Holle in Ulm', in Sandra Hindman (ed.), *Printing the Written Word: The Social History of Books, circa 1450–1520* (Ithaca, NY: Cornell University Press, 1991), pp. 41–67.

Undorf, Wolfgang, 'Print and Book Culture in the Danish Town of Odense', in Benito Rial Costas (ed.), *Print Culture and Peripheries in Early Modern Europe* (Leiden: Brill, 2012), pp. 227–48.

White, Eric Marshall, *Editio Princeps. A History of the Gutenberg Bible* (London and Turnhout: Harvey Miller, 2017).

Wijsman, Hanno (ed.), *Books in Transition at the Time of Philip the Fair: Manuscripts and Printed Books in the Late Fifteenth and Early Sixteenth Century Low Countries* (Turnhout: Brepols, 2010).

5. Coming of Age

Brann, Noel L., *The Abbot Trithemius (1462–1516): The Renaissance of Monastic Humanism* (Leiden: Brill, 1981).

Davies, Martin, *Columbus in Italy: An Italian Versification of the Letter on the Discovery of the New World* (London: British Library, 1991).

De Smet, Rudolf (ed.), *Les humanistes et leur bibliotheque. Humanists and their libraries* (Leuven: Peeters, 2002).

Grafton, Anthony, *Worlds made by Words: Scholarship and Community in the Modern West* (Cambridge, MA: Harvard University Press, 2009).

Gulik, Egbertus van, *Erasmus and his Books* (Toronto: University of Toronto Press, 2018).

Harrisse, Henry, *Excerpta Colombiniana: Bibliographie de 400 pièces du 16e siècle; précédée d'une histoire de la Bibliothèque colombine et de son fondateur* (Paris: Welter, 1887).

Hobson, Anthony, *Apollo and Pegasus: An Enquiry into the Formation and Dispersal of a Renaissance Library* (Amsterdam: Van Heusden, 1975).

Hobson, Anthony, *Renaissance Book Collecting: Jean Grolier and Diego Murtado de Mendoza, their Books and Bindings* (Cambridge: Cambridge University Press, 1999).

Kibre, Pearl, *The Library of Pico della Mirandola* (New York, NY: Columbia University Press, 1936).

McDonald, Mark P., *Ferdinand Columbus: Renaissance Collector* (London: British Museum, 2005).

Molino, Paola, 'World bibliographies: Libraries and the reorganization of knowledge in late Renaissance Europe', in Anthony Grafton and Gless Most (eds.), *Canonical Texts and Scholarly Practices: A Global Comparative Approach* (Cambridge: Cambridge University Press, 2016), pp. 299–322.

Pérez Fernández, José Maria and Edward Wilson-Lee, *Hernando Colón's New World of Books: Toward a Cartography of Knowledge* (London and New Haven: Yale University Press, 2020).

Sherman, William H., 'A New World of Books: Hernando Colón and the *Biblioteca Colombina*', in Ann Blair and Anja-Silvia Goeing (eds.), *For the Sake of Learning: Essays in Honor of Anthony Grafton* (2 vols., Leiden: Brill, 2016), pp. 404–14.

Trithemius, Johannes, *In Praise of Scribes*, tr. Elizabeth Bryson Bongie (Vancouver: Alcuin Society, 1977).

Wagner, Klaus, 'Le commerce du livre en France au début du XVIe siècle d'après les notes manuscrites de Fernando Colomb', *Bulletin du bibliophile*, 2 (1992), pp. 305–29.

Wilson-Lee, Edward, *The Catalogue of Shipwrecked Books: Young Columbus and the Quest for a Universal Library* (London: Harper Collins, 2018).

6. Reformations

Aguilar, Idalia García, 'Before We are Condemned: Inquisitorial Fears and Private Libraries of New Spain', in Natalia Maillard Álvarez (ed.), *Books in the Catholic World during the Early Modern Period* (Leiden: Brill, 2014), pp. 171–90.

Barbierato, Federico, *The Inquisitor in the Hat Shop: Inquisition, Forbidden Books and Unbelief in Early Modern Venice* (Farnham: Ashgate, 2012).

Carley, James P., 'The Dispersal of the Monastic Libraries and the Salvaging of the Spoils', in Elisabeth Leedham-Green and Teresa Webber (eds.), *The Cambridge History of Libraries in Britain and Ireland, vol. I: To 1640* (Cambridge: Cambridge University Press, 2006), pp. 265–91.

Delsaerdt, Pierre, 'A bookshop for a new age: the inventory of the bookshop of the Louvain bookseller Hieronymus Cloet, 1543', in Lotte Hellinga, et al. (eds.), *The Bookshop of the World: The Role of the Low Countries in the Book-Trade, 1473–1941* ('t Goy-Houten: Hes & De Graaf, 2001), pp. 75–86.

Fritze, Ronald Harold, '"Hath Lacked Witness, Tyme Wanted Light": The Dispersal of the English Monastic Libraries and Protestant Efforts at Preservation, ca. 1535–1625', *Journal of Library History*, 18 (1983), pp. 274–91.

Germann, Martin, 'Zwischen Konfiskation, Zerstreuung und Zerstörung. Schicksale der Bücher und Bibliotheken in der Reformationszeit in Basel, Bern und Zürich', *Zwingliana*, 27 (2000), pp. 63–8.

Gray, Sarah, and Chris Baggs, 'The English Parish Library: A Celebration of Diversity', *Libraries & Culture*, 35 (2000), pp. 414–33.

Grendler, Paul F., *The Roman Inquisition and the Venetian Press* (Princeton, NJ: Princeton University Press, 1977).

Grendler, Paul F., 'The Destruction of Hebrew Books in Venice, 1568', *Proceedings of the American Academy for Jewish Research*, 45 (1978), pp. 103–130.

Grendler, Paul F., *Culture and Censorship in late Renaissance Italy and France* (London: Variorum, 1981).

Grendler, Paul F., and Marcella Grendler, 'The Survival of Erasmus in Italy', *Erasmus in English*, 8 (1976), pp. 2–22.

Griffin, Clive, *Journeymen-Printers, Heresy, and the Inquisition in Sixteenth-century Spain* (Oxford: Oxford University Press, 2005).

Jensen, Kristian, 'Universities and Colleges', in Elisabeth Leedham-Green and Teresa Webber (eds.), *The Cambridge History of Libraries in Britain and Ireland, vol. I: To 1640* (Cambridge: Cambridge University Press, 2006), pp. 345–62.

Ker, N. R., 'Oxford College Libraries in the Sixteenth Century', *Bodleian Library Record*, 6 (1957–61), pp. 459–513, reprinted in his *Books, Collectors and Libraries: Studies in the Medieval Heritage* (London and Ronceverte: Hambledon, 1985).

Kuin, Roger, 'Private library as public danger: the case of Duplessis-Mornay', in Andrew Pettegree, Paul Nelles and Philip Conner (eds.), *The Sixteenth-century French Religious Book* (Aldershot: Ashgate, 2001), pp. 319–57.

Leedham-Green, Elisabeth, 'University libraries and book-sellers', in Lotte Hellinga and J. B. Trapp (eds.), *The Cambridge History of the Book in Britain. III: 1400–1557* (Cambridge: Cambridge University Press, 1999), pp. 316–53.

Mattioli, Anselmo, and Sandra da Conturbia, 'The Ecclesiastical Libraries in Italy: History and Present Situation', *Libraries & Culture*, 25 (1990), pp. 312–33.

Mittler, Elmar, *Bibliotheca Palatina: Katalog zur Ausstellung von 8. Juli bis 2. November 1986* (Heidelberg: Braus, 1986).

Oates, J. C. T., *Cambridge University Library: A History from the Beginnings to the Copyright Act of Queen Anne* (Cambridge: Cambridge University Press, 1986).

Padover, S. K., 'German libraries in the fourteenth and fifteenth centuries', in James Westfall Thompson (ed.), *The Medieval Library* (New York, NY: Hafner, 1957), pp. 453–76.

Pettegree, Andrew, *Brand Luther: 1517, Printing, and the Making of the Reformation* (New York, NY: Penguin, 2015).

Purcell, Mark, *The Country House Library* (London and New Haven: Yale University Press, 2017).

Putnam, George Haven, *The Censorship of the Church of Rome and its Influence upon the Production and Distribution of Literature*, 2 vols. (New York, NY: Benjamin Blom, 1967).

Ramsay, Nigel, '"The Manuscripts Flew about Like Butterflies": The Break-up of English Libraries in the Sixteenth Century', in James Raven (ed.), *Lost Libraries: The Destruction of Great Book Collections since Antiquity* (Basingstoke: Palgrave, 2004), pp. 125–44.

Schottenloher, Karl, 'Schicksale von Büchern und Bibliotheken im Bauernkrieg', *Zeitschrift fur Bücherfreunde*, 12 (1909), pp. 396–408.

Smidt, Tom de, 'An elderly, noble lady. The old books collection in the library of the Supreme Court of the Netherlands', in J. G. B. Pikkemaat (ed.), *The Old Library of the Supreme Court of the Netherlands* (Hilversum: Verloren, 2008), pp. 39–68.

Soen, Violet, Dries Vanysacker and Wim François (eds.), *Church, Censorship and Reform in the Early Modern Habsburg Netherlands* (Turnhout: Brepols, 2017).

Thomas, Drew B., 'Circumventing Censorship: the Rise and Fall of Reformation Print Centres', in Alexander S. Wilkinson and Graeme J. Kemp (eds.), *Negotiating Conflict and Controversy in the Early Modern Book World* (Leiden: Brill, 2019), pp. 13–37.

Wright, C. E., 'The dispersal of the monastic libraries and the beginnings of Anglo-Saxon studies: Matthew Parker and his circle', *Transactions of the Cambridge Bibliographical Society*, 1 (1951), pp. 208–37.

Wright, C. E., 'The dispersal of the Libraries in the Sixteenth Century', in Francis Wormald and C. E. Wright (eds.), *The English Library before 1700* (London: Athlone Press, 1958), pp. 148–75.

7. The Professionals

Blair, Ann, *Too Much to Know: Managing Scholarly Information before the Modern Age* (London and New Haven: Yale University Press, 2010).

Bosman-Jelgersma, Henriëtte A., 'De inventaris van een Leidse apotheek uit het jaar 1587', *Leids Jaarboekje*, 86 (1994), pp. 51–68.

Collins, Brenda, 'Family Networks and Social Connections in the Survival of a Seventeenth-century Library Collection', *Library & Information History*, 33 (2017), pp. 123–42.

Davenport, Geoffrey, et al (eds.), *The Royal College of Physicians and its Collections* (London: James & James, 2001).

Delsaerdt, Pierre, *Suam quisque bibliothecam. Boekhandel en particulier boekenbezit aan de oude Leuvense universiteit, 16de – 18de eeuw* (Leuven: Universitaire Pers Leuven, 2001).

Duroselle-Melish, Caroline, and David A. Lines, 'The Library of Ulisse Aldrovandi (†1605): Acquiring and Organizing Books in Sixteenth-century Bologna', *The Library*, 7th series, 16 (2015), pp. 134–61.

Evans, R. J. W., and Alexander Marr (eds.), *Curiosity and Wonder from the Renaissance to the Enlightenment* (Aldershot: Ashgate, 2006).

Fehrenbach, R. J., and E. S. Leedham-Green, *Private Libraries in Renaissance England: A Collection and Catalogue of Tudor and Early Stuart Book-lists* 9 vols. (Binghamton, NY: Medieval & Renaissance Texts & Studies, 1992–).

Finkelstein, Andrea, 'Gerard de Malynes and Edward Misselden: The Learned Library of the Seventeenth-century Merchant', *Book History*, 3 (2000), pp. 1–20.

Furrer, Norbert, *Des Burgers Bibliothek. Personliche Buchbestände in der stadt Bern des 17. Jahrhunderts* (Zurich: Chronos Verlag, 2018).

Grendler, Marcella, 'A Greek collection in Padua: the library of Gian Vincenzo Pinelli (1535–1601)', *Renaissance Quarterly*, 33 (1980), pp. 386–416.

Grendler, Marcella, 'Book Collecting in Counter-Reformation Italy: The Library of Gian Vincenzo Pinelli (1535–1601)', *Journal of Library History*, 16 (1981), pp. 144–51.

Harrison, John, and Peter Laslett, *The Library of John Locke* 2nd edn (Oxford: Clarendon Press, 1971).

Hellinga, Lotte, 'Book Auctions in the Fifteenth Century', in her *Incunabula in Transit: People and Trade* (Leiden: Brill, 2018), pp. 6–19.

Hobson, Anthony, 'A sale by candle in 1608', *The Library*, 5th series, 26 (1971), pp. 215–33.

Lankhorst, Otto, 'Dutch auctions in the seventeenth and eighteenth centuries', in Robin Myers, Michael Harris and Giles Mandelbrote (eds.), *Under the Hammer: Book Auctions since the Seventeenth Century* (New Castle, DE: Oak Knoll Press, 2001), pp. 65–87.

Leedham-Green, E. S., *Books in Cambridge Inventories: Book Lists from Vice-Chancellor's Court Probate Inventories in the Tudor and Stuart Periods*, 2 vols. (Cambridge: Cambridge University Press, 1986).

Leu, Urs B., Raffael Keller and Sandra Weidmann, *Conrad Gessner's Private Library* (Leiden: Brill, 2008).

Leu, Urs B., and Sandra Weidmann, *Huldrych Zwingli's Private Library* (Leiden: Brill, 2019).

Martin, Henri-Jean, *The French Book: Religion, Absolutism and Readership* (Baltimore, MD: Johns Hopkins University Press, 1996).

Niedzwiedz, Jakub, 'The use of books in 16th-century Vilnius', *Terminus*, 15 (2013), pp. 167–84.

Nuovo, Angela, 'Gian Vincenzo Pinelli's collection of catalogues of private libraries in sixteenth-century Europe', *Gutenberg Jahrbuch* (2007), pp. 129–44.

Nuovo, Angela, 'The Creation and Dispersal of the Library of Gian Vincenzo Pinelli', in Giles Mandelbrote, et al. (eds.), *Books on the Move: Tracking Copies through Collections and the Book Trade* (New Castle, DE: Oak Knoll Press, 2007), pp. 39–68.

Nuovo, Angela, 'Private Libraries in Sixteenth-century Italy', in Bettina Wagner and Marcia Reed (eds.), *Early Printed Books as Material Objects* (Berlin and New York: De Gruyter Saur, 2010), pp. 231–42.

Pearson, David, 'Patterns of Book Ownership in Late Seventeenth-century England', *The Library*, 11 (2010), pp. 139–67.

Pettegree, Andrew, and Arthur der Weduwen, *The Bookshop of the World: Making and Trading Books in the Dutch Golden Age* (London and New Haven: Yale University Press, 2019).

Pirozynski, Jan, 'Royal Book Collections in Poland during the Renaissance', *Libraries & Culture*, 24 (1989), pp. 21–32.

Pollard, Graham, and Albert Ehrman, *The Distribution of Books by Catalogue from the Invention of Printing to AD 1800* (Cambridge: Roxburghe Club, 1965).

Purcell, Mark, *The Country House Library* (London and New Haven: Yale University Press, 2017).

Reid, Peter H., 'Patriots and Rogues: Some Scottish Lairds and Their Libraries', *Library & Information History*, 35 (2019), pp. 1–20.

Selm, Bert van, 'The introduction of the printed book auction catalogue', *Quaerendo*, 15 (1985), pp. 16–53, 115–49.

Sibbald, John A., 'The *Heinsiana* – almost a seventeenth-century universal short title catalogue', in Malcolm Walsby and Natasha Constantinidou (eds.), *Documenting the Early Modern Book World: Inventories and Catalogues in Manuscript and Print* (Leiden: Brill, 2013), pp. 141–59.

Strickland, Forrest C., 'The Devotion of Collecting: Ministers and the Culture of Print in the Seventeenth-century Dutch Republic' (PhD thesis, University of St Andrews, 2019).

Weduwen, Arthur der, and Andrew Pettegree, *The Dutch Republic and the Birth of Modern Advertising* (Leiden: Brill, 2020).

Weduwen, Arthur der, and Andrew Pettegree, *News, Business and Public Information: Advertisements and Announcements in Dutch and Flemish Newspapers, 1620–1675* (Leiden: Brill, 2020).

8. Idle Books and Riff Raff

Adams, R. J., 'Building a Library without Walls: the Early Years of the Bodleian Library', in A. Bautz and I. Gregory (eds.), *Libraries, Books, and Collectors of Texts, 1600–1900* (London: Routledge, 2018).

Beddard, R. A., 'The Official Inauguration of the Bodleian Library on 8 November 1602', *The Library*, 3 (2002), pp. 255–83.

Berkvens-Stevelinck, Christiane, *Magna Commoditas: Leiden University's Great Asset* (Leiden: Leiden University Press, 2012).

Clapinson, Mary, 'The Bodleian Library and its Readers, 1602–1652', *Bodleian Library Record*, 19 (2006), pp. 30–46.

Clapinson, Mary, *A Brief History of the Bodleian Library* (Oxford: Bodleian Library, 2015).

Clement, Richard W., 'Librarianship and Polemics: the career of Thomas James (1572–1629)', *Library & Culture*, 26 (1991), pp. 269–82.

Coppens, Chris, 'Auspicia bibliothecae: donators at the foundation of the Central Library in Louvain (1636–9)', *Quaerendo*, 34 (2004), pp. 169–210.

Coppens, Chris, Mark Derez and Jan Roegiers, *Leuven University Library, 1425–2000* (Leuven: Leuven University Press, 2005).

Finlayson, C. P., and S. M. Simpson, 'The History of the Library, 1580–1710', in Jean R. Guild and Alexander Law (eds.), *Edinburgh University Library, 1580–1980: A Collection of Historical Essays* (Edinburgh: Edinburgh University Library, 1982), pp. 45–7.

Fox, Peter (ed.), *Cambridge University Library: The Great Collections* (Cambridge: Cambridge University Press, 1998).

Frost, Carolyn O., 'The Bodleian Catalogs of 1674 and 1738: An Examination in the Light of Modern Cataloging Theory', *Library Quarterly*, 46 (1976), pp. 248–70.

Gilboy, Elaine, 'Les exemplaires interfoliés du catalogue de la Bodléienne', in Frédéric

Barbier, Thierry Dubois and Yann Sordet (eds.), *De l'argile au nuage, une archéologie des catalogues* (Paris: Éditions des Cendres, 2015), pp. 274–80.

Hamilton, Tom, *Pierre de l'Estoile and his World in the Wars of Religion* (Oxford: Oxford University Press, 2017).

Hampshire, Gwen, *The Bodleian Library Account Book, 1613–1646* (Oxford: Oxford Bibliographical Society, 1983).

Harrison, John, and Peter Laslett, *The Library of John Locke*, 2nd edn (Oxford: Clarendon Press, 1971).

Hendrickson, Thomas, *Ancient Libraries and Renaissance Humanism: The 'De Bibliothecis' of Justus Lipsius* (Leiden: Brill, 2017).

Hulshoff Pol, E., 'What about the library? Travellers' comments on the Leiden Library in the 17th and 18th centuries', *Quaerendo*, 5 (1975), pp. 39–51.

Kiessling, Nicolas K., *The Library of Anthony Wood* (Oxford: Oxford Bibliographical Society, 2002).

Komorowski, Manfred, 'Bibliotheken', in Ulrich Rasche (ed.), *Quellen zur frühneuzeitlichen Universitätsgeschichte* (Wiesbaden: Harrassowitz, 2011), pp. 55–81.

Lankhorst, O. S., 'De Bibliotheek van de Gelderse Academie te Harderwijk – thans te Deventer', in J. A. H. Bots, et al. (eds.), *Het Gelders Athene. Bijdragen tot de geschiedenis van de Gelderse universiteit in Harderwijk (1648–1811)* (Hilversum: Verloren, 2000), pp. 95–118.

Loveman, Kate, *Samuel Pepys and his Books: Reading, Newsgathering and Sociability, 1660–1703* (Oxford: Oxford University Press, 2015).

Lunsingh-Scheurleer, Th.H., et al. (eds.), *Leiden University in the Seventeenth Century: An Exchange of Learning* (Leiden: Universitaire Pers Leiden, 1975).

Miert, Dirk van, *Humanism in an Age of Science: The Amsterdam Athenaeum in the Golden Age, 1632–1704* (Leiden: Brill, 2009).

Minter, Catherine J., 'John Dury's *Reformed Librarie-Keeper*: Information and its Intellectual Contexts in Seventeenth-century England', *Library & Information History*, 31 (2015), pp. 18–34.

Nowak, Maria J., 'The History of the Jagiellonian Library', *Libraries & Culture*, 32 (1997), pp. 94–106.

Oates, J. C. T., *Cambridge University Library: A History from the Beginnings to the Copyright Act of Queen Anne* (Cambridge: Cambridge University Press, 1986).

Pettegree, Andrew (ed.), *Broadsheets: Single-Sheet Publishing in the First Age of Print* (Leiden: Brill, 2017).

Pettegree, Andrew, 'The Dutch Baltic: The Dutch book trade and the Building of Libraries in the Baltic and Central Europe during the Dutch Golden Age', in Arthur der Weduwen, Andrew Pettegree and Graeme Kemp (eds.), *Book Trade Catalogues in Early Modern Europe* (Leiden: Brill, 2021), pp. 286–316.

Philip, Ian, *The Bodleian Library in the Seventeenth and Eighteenth Centuries* (Oxford: Clarendon Press, 1983).

Raabe, Paul, 'Bibliothekskataloge als buchgeschichtliche Quellen. Bermerkungen über gedruckte kataloge öffentlicher Bibliotheken in der frühen Neuzeit', in Reinhard Wittmann (ed.), *Bücherkataloge als buchgeschichtliche Quellen in der frühen Neuzeit* (Wiesbaden: Harrassowitz, 1984), pp. 275–97.

Simoni, Anna E. C., 'The librarian's *cri de coeur*: rules for readers (1711)', *Quaerendo*, 32 (2002), pp. 199–203.

Sluis, Jacob van, *The Library of Franeker University in Context, 1585–1843* (Leiden: Brill, 2020).

Tering, Arvo, 'The Tartu University Library and Its Use at the End of the Seventeenth and the Beginning of the Eighteenth Century', *Libraries & Culture*, 28 (1993), pp. 44–54.

Tomalin, Claire, *Samuel Pepys: The Unequalled Self* (London: Viking, 2002).

Vallinkoski, J., *The History of the University Library at Turku. I, 1640–1722* (Helsinki: University Library at Helsinki, 1948).

9. Mission Fields

Amory, Hugh, and David D. Hall, *A History of the Book in America. I; The Colonial Book in the Atlantic World* (Cambridge: Cambridge University Press, 2000).

Bangs, Jeremy Dupertuis, *Plymouth Colony's Private Libraries* (Leiden: American Pilgrim Museum, 2016).

Begheyn, Paul, *Jesuit Books in the Dutch Republic and its Generality Lands, 1567–1773* (Leiden: Brill, 2014).

Bepler, Jill, '*Vicissitudo Temporum*: Some Sidelights on Book Collecting in the Thirty Years' War', *Sixteenth Century Journal*, 32 (2001), pp. 953–68.

Bond, W. H., and Hugh Amory, *The Printed Catalogues of the Harvard College Library, 1723–1790* (Boston, MA: Colonial Society of Massachusetts, 1996).

Bordsen, Alice L., 'Scottish Attitudes Reflected in the Library History of North Carolina', *Libraries & Culture*, 27 (1992), pp. 121–42.

Braziuniene, Alma, '*Bibliotheca Sapiehana* as a mirror of European culture of the Grand Duchy of Lithuania', in Ausra Rinkunaite (ed.), *Bibliotheca Sapiehana. Vilniaus universiteto bibliotekos rinkinys katalogas* (Vilnius: Lietuviu literaturos ir tautosakos institutas, 2010), pp. vii–xliii.

Calvo, Hortensia, 'The Politics of Print: the historiography of the book in early Spanish America', *Book History*, 6 (2003), pp. 277–305.

Connolly, Brendan, 'Jesuit Library Beginnings', *Library Quarterly*, 30 (1960), pp. 243–52.

Cressy, David, 'Books as Totems in Seventeenth-century England and New England', *Journal of Library History*, 21 (1986), pp. 92–106.

Diehl, Katharine Smith, *Printers and Printing in the East Indies to 1850. I. Batavia* (New Rochelle, NY: Aristide D. Cararzas, 1990).

Dijkgraaf, Hendrik, *The Library of a Jesuit Community at Holbeck, Nottinghamshire (1679)* (Cambridge: LP Publications, 2003).

Farrell, Allan P., *The Jesuit Code of Liberal Education* (Milwaukee, WI: Bruce, 1939).

Ferch, David L., '"Good Books are a Very Great Mercy to the World": Persecution, Private Libraries, and the Printed Word in the Early Development of the Dissenting Academies, 1663–1730', *Journal of Library History*, 21 (1986), pp. 350–61.

Finlayson, C. P., and S. M. Simpson, 'The History of the Library, 1580–1710', in Jean R. Guild and Alexander Law (eds.), *Edinburgh University Library, 1580–1980: A*

Collection of Historical Essays (Edinburgh: Edinburgh University Library, 1982), pp. 43–54.

Groesen, Michiel van, 'The Printed Book in the Dutch Atlantic World', in his *Imagining the Americas in Print: Books, Maps and Encounters in the Atlantic World* (Leiden: Brill, 2019), pp. 164–80.

Grover, Mark L., 'The Book and the Conquest: Jesuit Libraries in Colonial Brazil', *Libraries & Culture*, 28 (1993), pp. 266–83.

Guibovich, Pedro, 'The Printing Press in Colonial Peru: Production Process and Literary Categories in Lima, 1584–1699', *Colonial Latin American Historical Review*, 10 (2001), pp. 167–88.

Hampe-Martínez, Teodoro, 'The Diffusion of Books and Ideas in Colonial Peru: A Study of Private Libraries in the Sixteenth and Seventeenth Centuries', *The Hispanic American Historical Review*, 73 (1993), pp. 211–33.

Hannesdottir, Sigrun Klara, 'Books and Reading in Iceland in a Historical Perspective', *Libraries & Culture*, 28 (1993), pp. 13–21.

Harris, Rendel, and Stephen K. Jones, *The Pilgrim Press: A Bibliographical and Historical Memorial of the Books Printed at Leyden by the Pilgrim Fathers* (Nieuwkoop: De Graaf, 1987).

Johnson, Julie Greer, *The Book in the Americas: The Role of Books and Printing in the Development of Culture and Society in Colonial Latin America* (Providence, RI: John Carter Brown Library, 1988).

Kraus, Joe W., 'Private Libraries in Colonial America', *Journal of Library History*, 9 (1974), pp. 31–53.

Mena, Magdalena Chocano, 'Colonial Printing and Metropolitan Books: Printed Texts and the Shaping of Scholarly Culture in New Spain, 1539–1700', *Colonial Latin American Historical Review*, 6 (1997), pp. 69–90.

Molin, Emma Hagström, 'The Materiality of War Booty Books: The Case of Strängnäs Cathedral Library', in Anna Källén (ed.), *Making Cultural History: New Perspectives on Western Heritage* (Lund: Nordic Academic Press, 2013), pp. 131–40.

Molin, Emma Hagström, 'To Place in a Chest: On the Cultural Looting of Gustavus Adolphus and the Creation of Uppsala University Library in the Seventeenth Century', *Barok*, 44 (2016), pp. 135–48.

Molin, Emma Hagström, 'Spoils of Knowledge: Looted Books in Uppsala University Library in the Seventeenth Century', in Gerhild Williams, et al. (eds.), *Rethinking Europe: War and Peace in the Early Modern German Lands* (Leiden: Brill, 2019).

Morrison, Ian, 'The History of the Book in Australia', in Michael F. Suarez and H. R. Woudhuysen (eds.), *The Oxford Companion to the Book* (Oxford: Oxford University Press, 2010), pp. 394–402.

Oldenhof, H., 'Bibliotheek Jezuïetenstatie Leeuwarden', in Jacob van Sluis (ed.), *PBF. De Provinsjale Biblioteek fan Fryslân, 150 jaar geschiedenis in collecties* (Leeuwarden: Tresoar, 2002), pp. 75–80.

Pirozynski, Jan, 'Royal Book Collections in Poland during the Renaissance', *Libraries & Culture*, 24 (1989), pp. 21–32.

Rodriguez-Buckingham, Antonio, 'Monastic Libraries and Early Printing in Sixteenth-century Spanish America', *Libraries & Culture*, 24 (1989), pp. 33–56.

Shera, J. H., *Foundations of the Public Library: The Origins of the Public Library Movement in New England 1629–1855* (Chicago, IL: University of Chicago Press, 1949).

Thomas, Hannah, '"Books Which are Necessary for Them": Reconstructing a Jesuit Missionary Library in Wales and the English Borderlands, ca. 1600–1679', in Teresa Bela, et al. (eds.), *Publishing Subversive Texts in Elizabethan England and the Polish-Lithuanian Commonwealth* (Leiden: Brill, 2016), pp. 110–28.

Trypucko, Josef, *The Catalogue of the Book Collection of the Jesuit College in Braniewo held in the University Library in Uppsala* (3 vols., Uppsala: Universitetsbibliotek, 2007).

Wilkie, Everett C., '"Une Bibliothèque Bien Fournie": The Earliest Known Caribbean Library', *Libraries & Culture*, 25 (1990), pp. 171–93.

Woodbridge, Hensley C., and Lawrence S. Thompson, *Printing in Colonial Spanish America* (Troy, NY: Whitson, 1976).

Wright, Louis B., 'The purposeful reading of our Colonial Ancestors', *ELH*, 4 (1937), pp. 85–111.

10. Books in the Attic

Biemans, Jos A. A. M., *Boeken voor de geleerde burgerij. De stadsbibliotheek van Amsterdam tot 1632* (Nijmegen: Vantilt, 2019).

Blatchly, John, *The Town Library of Ipswich, Provided for the Use of the Town Preachers in 1599: A History and Catalogue* (Woodbridge: Boydell, 1989).

Comerford, Kathleen M., 'What Did Early Modern Priests Read? The Library of the Seminary of Fiesole, 1646–1721', *Libraries & Culture*, 34 (1999), pp. 203–21.

Dondi, Christina, and Maria Alessandra Panzanelli Fratoni, 'Researching the Origin of Perugia's Public Library (1582/1623) before and after *Material Evidence in Incunabula*', *Quaerendo*, 46 (2016), pp. 129–50.

Fitch, John, et al., *Suffolk Parochial Libraries: A Catalogue* (London: Mansell, 1977).

Fontaine Verwey, Herman de la, 'The City Library of Amsterdam in the Nieuwe Kerk, 1578–1632', *Quaerendo*, 14 (1984), pp. 163–205.

Glenn, John, and David Walsh, *Catalogue of the Francis Trigge Chained Library, St Wulfram's Church, Grantham* (Cambridge: Brewer, 1988).

Gray, Sarah, and Chris Baggs, 'The English Parish Library: A Celebration of Diversity', *Libraries & Culture*, 35 (2000), pp. 414–33.

Houlette, William D., 'Parish Libraries and the Work of the Reverend Thomas Bray', *Library Quarterly*, 4 (1934), pp. 588–609.

Kaufman, Paul, 'Innerpeffray: Reading for all the People', in his *Libraries and Their Users* (London: Library Association, 1969).

Kelly, Thomas, *Early Public Libraries: A History of Public Libraries in Great Britain before 1850* (London: Library Association, 1966).

Klein, J. W. E., *Geen vrouwen ofte kinderen, maer alleenlijk eerbare luijden. 400 jaar Goudse librije, 1594–1994* (Delft: Eburon, 1994).

Landolt, Elisabeth, *Kabinettstücke der Amerbach im Historischen Museum Basel* (Basel: Historisches Museum, 1984).

Laugher, Charles T., *Thomas Bray's Grand Design: Libraries of the Church of England in America, 1695–1785* (Chicago, IL: American Library Association, 1973).

Leerintveld, Ad, and Jan Bedaux (eds.), *Historische Stadsbibliotheken in Nederland* (Zutphen: Walburg Pers, 2016).

Manley, Keith, 'They Never Expected the Spanish Inquisition! James Kirkwood and Scottish Parochial Libraries', in Caroline Archer and Lisa Peters (eds.), *Religion and the Book Trade* (Newcastle-upon-Tyne: Cambridge Scholars, 2015), pp. 83–98.

McCulloch, Samuel Clyde, 'Dr. Thomas Bray's Commissary Work in London, 1696–1699', *William and Mary Quarterly*, 2 (1945), pp. 333–48.

Morgan, P., 'A 16th century Warwickshire Library: A Problem of Provenance', *Book Collector*, 22 (1973), pp. 337–55.

Mourits, Esther, *Een kamer gevuld met de mooiste boeken: De bibliotheek van Johannes Thysius (1622–1653)* (Nijmegen: Vantilt, 2016).

Murison, W. J., *The Public Library: Its Origins, Purpose, and Significance*, 3rd edn (London: Clive Bingley, 1988).

Petchey, W. J., *The Intentions of Thomas Plume* (Maldon: Trustees of the Plume Library, 2004).

Renting, A. D., and J. T. C. Renting-Kuijpers, *Catalogus Librije Zutphen, de kettingbibliotheek van de Walburgiskerk* (Groningen: Philip Elchers, 2008).

Roberts, Dunstan, 'The Chained Parish Library of Chirbury, with Reference to Herbert Family Provenances', *The Library*, 7th series, 19 (2018), pp. 469–83.

Scheidegger, Christian, 'Buchgeschenke, Patronage und protestantische Allianzen: Die Stadtbibliothek Zürich und ihre Donatoren im 17. Jahrhundert', *Zwingliana*, 44 (2017), pp. 463–99.

Schrijver, Emile, and Heide Warncke, *Ets Haim. The oldest Jewish library in the world* (Zutphen: Walburg Pers, 2018).

Sevens, Theodoor, 'Bibliotheken uit vroeger tijd. I: Eene openbare Bibliotheek te Kortrijk in de 16ᵉ eeuw', *Tijdschrift voor Boek-en Bibliotheekwezen*, 1 (1903), pp. 196–8.

Steiner, Bernard C., 'Rev Thomas Bray and his American Libraries', *American Historical Review*, 2 (1896), pp. 58–75.

Stier-Meinhof, Renate, 'Die Geschichte der Bibliothek der St. Katharinenkirche in der Neuen Stadt Salzwedel', in Uwe Czubatynski, Adolf Laminski and Konrad von Rabenau (eds.), *Kirckenbibliotheken als Forschungsaufgabe* (Neustadt an der Aisch: Verlag Degener, 1992), pp. 47–68.

Stüben, Joachim, and Falk Eisermann (eds.), *Rundblicke: Kirchenbibliotheken und Reformation im kulturellen Kontext* (Schwerin: Thomas Helms Verlag, 2019).

Yeo, Matthew, *The Acquisition of Books by Chetham's Library, 1655–1700* (Leiden: Brill, 2011).

Zauer, Christine, 'Reformation der Bücher: Die Gründung der Stadbibliothek als Folge des Anschlusses Nürnbergs an die neue Glaubenslehre', *Mitteilungen des Vereins für Geschichte der Stadt Nürnberg*, 104 (2017), pp. 101–36.

Zepf, Robert (ed.), *Historische Kirchenbibliotheken in Mecklenburg-Vorpommern* (Rostock: Universitätsbibliothek Rostock, 2019).

11. Cardinal Errors

Achilles, Rolf, 'Baroque Monastic Library Architecture', *Journal of Library History*, 11 (1976), pp. 249–55.

Barbier, Frédéric, Istvan Monok and Andrea De Pasquale (eds.), *Bibliothèques décors (XVIIe–XIXe siècle)* (Paris: Éditions des Cendres, 2016).

Bultmann Lemke, Antje, 'Gabriel Naudé and the Ideal Library', *Syracuse University Library Associates Courier*, 26 (1991), pp. 27–44.

Clarke, Jack A., 'Gabriel Naudé and the Foundations of the Scholarly Library', *Library Quarterly*, 39 (1969), pp. 331–43.

Clarke, Jack A., *Gabriel Naudé, 1600–1653* (Hamden, CT: Archon Books, 1970).

Davis, Margaret Daly, 'Giovan Pietro Bellori and the *Nota delli musei, librerie, galerie, et ornamenti di statue e pitture ne' palazzi, nelle case, e ne' giardini di Roma* (1664): Modern libraries and ancient painting in Seicento Rome', *Zeitschrift für Kunstgeschichte*, 68 (2005), pp. 191–233.

Delaforce, Angela, *The Lost Library of the King of Portugal* (London: Ad Ilissvm, 2019).

Fontaine Verwey, Herman de la, 'Adriaan Pauw en zijn bibliotheek', in his *Uit de Wereld van het Boek*, IV ('t Goy: HES, 1997), pp. 183–96.

Garberson, Eric, *Eighteenth-century Monastic Libraries in Southern Germany and Austria: Architecture and Decorations* (Baden-Baden: Valentin Koerner, 1998).

Jay, Emma, 'Queen Caroline's Library and its European Contexts', *Book History*, 9 (2006), pp. 31–55.

Jolly, Claude (ed.), *Histoire des bibliothèques françaises, II: Les bibliothèques sous l'Ancien Régime, 1530–1789* (Paris: Electre, 2008).

Keblusek, Marika, 'Books at the Stadholder's Court', in Marika Keblusek and Jori Zijlmans (eds.), *Princely Display: The Court of Frederik Hendrik of Orange and Amalia van Solms* (The Hague: Historical Museum, 1997), pp. 143–60.

Lawrance, Jeremy, Oliver Noble Wood and Jeremy Roe (eds.), *Poder y saber. Bibliotecas y bibliofilia en la época del conde-duque de Olivares* (Madrid: Centro de Estudios Europa Hispánica, 2011).

Lindorfer, Bianca, 'Aristocratic Book Consumption in the Seventeenth Century: Austrian Aristocratic Book Collectors and the Role of Noble Networks in the Circulation of Books from Spain to Austria', in Natalia Maillard Álvarez (ed.), *Books in the Catholic World during the Early Modern Period* (Leiden: Brill, 2014), pp. 145–70.

Masson, André, *Le Décor des Bibliothèques du Moyen Age à la Révolution* (Geneva and Paris: Droz, 1972).

Minter, Catherine J., 'John Dury's *Reformed Librarie-Keeper*: Information and its Intellectual Contexts in Seventeenth-century England', *Library & Information History*, 31 (2015), pp. 18–34.

Molino, Paola, *L'impero di carta. Storia di una biblioteca e di un bibliotecario (Vienna, 1575–1608)* (Rome: Viella, 2017).

Montgomery, John Warwick, *A Seventeenth-Century View of European Libraries: Lomeier's De Bibliothecis, Chapter X* (Berkeley, CA: University of California Press, 1962).

Montgomery, John Warwick, *The Libraries of France at the Ascendency of Mazarin:*

Louis Jacob's Traicté des plus belles Bibliothèques (Bonn: Verlag für Kultur und Wissenschaft, 2015).

Naudé, Gabriel, *Advice on Establishing a Library*, ed. Archer Taylor (Berkeley, CA: University of California Press, 1950).

Nelles, Paul, *The Public Library and Late Humanist Scholarship in Early Modern Europe: Antiquarianism and Encyclopaedism* (Ann Arbor, MI: University Microfilms, 1994).

Pirozynski, Jan, 'Royal Book Collections in Poland during the Renaissance', *Libraries & Culture*, 24 (1989), pp. 21–32.

Rietbergen, Peter J. A. N., 'Founding a University Library: Pope Alexander VII (1655–1667) and the Alessandrina', *Journal of Library History*, 22 (1987), pp. 190–205.

Rietbergen, Peter, 'Lucas Holste (1596–1661), Scholar and Librarian, or: the Power of Books and Libraries', in his *Power and Religion in Baroque Rome: Barberini Cultural Politics* (Leiden: Brill, 2006), pp. 256–95.

Rovelstad, Mathilde V., 'Claude Clement's Pictorial Catalog: A Seventeenth-century Proposal for Physical Access and Literature Evaluation', *Library Quarterly*, 61 (1991), pp. 174–87.

Rovelstad, Mathilde V., 'Two Seventeenth-century Library Handbooks, Two Different Library Theories', *Libraries & Culture*, 35 (2000), pp. 540–56.

Saunders, E. Stewart, 'Politics and Scholarship in Seventeenth-century France: The Library of Nicolas Fouquet and the College Royal', *Journal of Library History*, 20 (1985), pp. 1–24.

Saunders, E. Stewart, 'Public Administration and the Library of Jean-Baptiste Colbert', *Libraries & Culture*, 26 (1991), pp. 283–300.

Schmidt-Glintzer, Helwig (ed.), *A Treasure House of Books: The Library of Duke August of Brunswick-Wolfenbüttel* (Wiesbaden: Harrassowitz, 1998).

Soll, Jacob, *The Information Master: Jean-Baptiste Colbert's Secret State Intelligence System* (Ann Arbor, MI: University of Michigan Press, 2009).

Sordet, Yann, 'Reconstructing Mazarin's Library / Libraries in Time and Space', *Quaerendo*, 46 (2016), pp. 151–64.

Thiec, Guy le, 'Dialoguer avec des hommes illustres. Le rôle des portraits dans les décors de bibliothèques (fin XVe – début XVIIe siècle)', *Revue française d'histoire du livre*, 130 (2009), pp. 7–52.

Weston, Giulia Martina, 'Universal Knowledge and Self-Fashioning. Cardinal Bernardino Spada's Collection of Books', in Annika Bautz and James Gregory (eds.), *Libraries, Books, and Collectors of Texts, 1600–1900* (New York and Abingdon: Routledge, 2018), pp. 28–47.

12. The Antiquarians

Balsem, Astrid C., 'Collecting the Ultimate Scholar's Library: the *Bibliotheca Vossiana*', in Eric Jorink and Dirk van Miert (eds.), *Isaac Vossius (1618–1689) between Science and Scholarship* (Leiden: Brill, 2012), pp. 281–309.

Bellingradt, Daniel, 'Book Lotteries as Sale Events for Slow-Sellers: the Case of Amsterdam in the Late Eighteenth Century', in Shanti Graheli (ed.), *Buying* and Selling: *The Business of Books in Early Modern Europe* (Leiden: Brill, 2019), pp. 154–77.

Berkvens-Stevelinck, Christiane, '"Rarus, rarior, rarissimus" ou de la qualification exagérée des livres dans les catalogues de vente', in J. van Borm and L. Simons (eds.), *Het oude en het nieuwe boek: De oude en de nieuwe bibliotheek* (Kapellen: DNB/Pelckmans, 1988), pp. 235–40.

Berkvens-Stevelinck, Christiane, *Magna Commoditas: Leiden University's Great Asset* (Leiden: Leiden University Press, 2012).

Blok, F. F., *Isaac Vossius and his Circle: His Life until his Farewell to Queen Christina of Sweden 1618–1655* (Groningen: Egbert Forsten, 2000).

Buchmayr, Friedrich, 'Secularization and Monastic Libraries in Austria', in James Raven (ed.), *Lost Libraries: The Destruction of Great Book Collections since Antiquity* (Basingstoke: Palgrave, 2004), pp. 145–62.

Davies, David W., *The World of the Elzeviers* (Leiden: Nijhoff, 1954).

Dibdin, Thomas Frognall, *The Bibliomania or Book-Madness* (Richmond: Tiger of the Stripe, 2007).

Fontaine Verwey, Herman de la, 'The history of the Amsterdam Caesar codex', *Quaerendo*, 9 (1979), pp. 179–207.

Fontaine Verwey, Herman de la, 'Grolier-banden in Nederland', in his *Uit de Wereld van het Boek*, IV ('t Goy: HES, 1997), pp. 155–82.

Fontaine Verwey, Herman de la, 'Pieter van Damme, de eerste Nederlandse antiquaar', in his *Uit de Wereld van het Boek*, IV ('t Goy: HES, 1997), pp. 197–220.

Gatch, Milton M., 'John Bagford, bookseller and antiquary', *British Library Journal*, 12 (1986), pp. 150–171.

Harmsen, Theodor, *Antiquarianism in the Augustan Age: Thomas Herne, 1678–1735* (Bern: Peter Lang, 2000).

Hartz, S. L., *The Elseviers and their contemporaries: an illustrated commentary* (Amsterdam: Elsevier, 1955).

Heel, Jos van, 'Gisbertus Voetius on the Necessity of Locating, Collecting and Preserving Early Printed Books', *Quaerendo*, 39 (2009), pp. 45–56.

Hellinga, Lotte, *Caxton in Focus: The Beginnings of Printing in England* (London: British Library, 1982).

Hellinga, Lotte, *Incunabula in Transit: People and Trade* (Leiden: Brill, 2018).

Hobson, Anthony, 'Appropriations from foreign libraries during the French Revolution and Empire', *Bulletin du bibliophile*, 2 (1989), pp. 255–72.

Husbands, Shayne, 'The Roxburghe Club: Consumption, Obsession and the Passion for Print', in Emma Cayley and Susan Powell (eds.), *Manuscripts and Printed Books in Europe, 1350–1550: Packaging, Presentation and Consumption* (Liverpool: Liverpool University Press, 2013), pp. 120–32.

Husbands, Shayne, *The Early Roxburghe Club, 1812–1835: Book Club Pioneers and the Advancement of English Literature* (London: Anthem Press, 2017).

Jensen, Kristian, *Revolution and the Antiquarian Book* (Cambridge: Cambridge University Press, 2011).

Korsten, Frans, 'The Elzeviers and England', in Lotte Hellinga et al. (eds.), *The*

Bookshop of the World: The Role of the Low Countries in the Book-Trade, 1473–1941 ('t Goy-Houten: HES & De Graaf, 2001), pp. 131–43.

Kraye, Jill, and Paolo Sachet (eds.), *The Afterlife of Aldus: Posthumous Fame, Collectors and the Book Trade* (London: Warburg Institute, 2018).

Lankhorst, Otto, 'Dutch auctions in the seventeenth and eighteenth centuries', in Robin Myers, Michael Harris and Giles Mandelbrote (eds.), *Under the Hammer: Book Auctions since the Seventeenth Century* (New Castle, DE: Oak Knoll Press, 2001), pp. 65–87.

Maclean, Ian, *Episodes in the Life of the Early Modern Learned Book* (Leiden: Brill, 2020).

McKitterick, David, *The Invention of Rare Books: Private Interest and Public Memory, 1600–1840* (Cambridge: Cambridge University Press, 2018).

Morrison, Stuart, 'Records of a Bibliophile: the catalogues of Consul Joseph Smith and Some Aspects of his Collecting', *The Book Collector*, 43 (1994), pp. 27–58.

O'Dwyer, E. J., *Thomas Frognall Dibdin: Bibliographer and Bibliomaniac Extraordinary, 1776–1847* (Pinner: Private Libraries Association, 1967).

Pettegree, Andrew, 'Rare Books and Revolutionaries: The French Bibliothèques Municipales', in his *The French Book and the European Book World* (Leiden: Brill, 2007), pp. 1–16.

Potten, Edward, 'Beyond Bibliophilia: Contextualizing Private Libraries in the Nineteenth Century', *Library & Information History*, 31 (2015), pp. 73–94.

Purcell, Mark, *The Country House Library* (London and New Haven: Yale University Press, 2017).

Ramsay, Nigel, 'English Book Collectors and the Salerooms in the Eighteenth Century', in Robin Myers, Michael Harris and Giles Mandelbrote (eds.), *Under the Hammer: Book Auctions since the Seventeenth Century* (New Castle, DE: Oak Knoll Press, 2001), pp. 89–110.

Riberette, Pierre, *Les Bibliothèques Françaises pendant la Révolution (1789–1795)* (Paris: Bibliothèque Nationale, 1970).

Ricci, Seymour de, *The Book Collector's Guide* (Philadelphia and New York: Rosenbach, 1921).

Ricci, Seymour de, *English Collectors of Books and Manuscripts, 1530–1930* (New York: Burt Franklin, 1969).

Swift, Katherine, 'Poggio's Quintilian and the Fate of the Sunderland Manuscripts', *Quaerendo*, 13 (1983), pp. 224–38.

Swift, Katherine, 'Dutch Penetration of the London market for books, *c.*1690–1730', in C. Berkvens-Stevelinck, et al. (eds.), *Le Magasin de l'Univers: The Dutch Republic as the Centre of the European Book Trade* (Leiden: Brill, 1992), pp. 265–79.

West, Susie, 'An architectural typology for the early modern country house library 1660–1720', *The Library*, 7th series, 14 (2013), pp. 441–64.

Williams, Kelsey Jackson, *The Antiquary: John Aubrey's Historical Scholarship* (Oxford: Oxford University Press, 2016).

13. Orderly Minds

Abbas, Hyder, '"A fund of entertaining and useful information": Coffee Houses,

Early Public Libraries, and the Print Trade in Eighteenth-century Dublin',
   Library & Information History, 30 (2014), pp. 41–61.

Allan, David, 'Provincial Readers and Book Culture in the Scottish Enlightenment:
   The Perth Library, 1784–*c*.1800', *The Library*, 3 (2002), pp. 367–89.

Allan, David, *A Nation of Readers: The Lending Library in Georgian England*
   (London: British Library, 2008).

Allen, James Smith, 'The "Cabinets de Lecture" in Paris, 1800–1850', *Journal of
   Library History*, 16 (1981), pp. 199–209.

Altick, Richard D., *The English Common Reader: A Social History of the Mass
   Reading Public* (Chicago, IL: University of Chicago Press, 1957; 2nd edn,
   Columbus, OH: Ohio State University Press, 1998).

Baenen, Michael A., 'A Great and Natural Enemy of Democracy? Politics and
   Culture in the Antebellum Portsmouth Athenaeum', in Thomas Augst and
   Kenneth Carpenter (eds.), *Institutions of Reading: The Social Life of Libraries
   in the United States* (Amherst, MA: University of Massachusetts Press, 2007),
   pp. 73–98.

Carpenter, Kenneth E., 'Libraries', in Robert A. Gross and Mary Kelley (eds.),
   History of the Book in America, 2 (Chapel Hill, NC: University of North
   Carolina Press, 2010), pp. 273–85.

Coulton, Richard, Matthew Mauger and Christopher Reid, *Stealing Books in
   Eighteenth-century London* (London: Palgrave Macmillan, 2016).

Coustillas, Pierre (ed.), *George Moore, Literature at Nurse: A Polemic on Victorian
   Censorship* (Brighton: EER, 2017).

Ellis, Markman, 'Coffee-House Libraries in Mid-Eighteenth-century London', *The
   Library*, 7th series, 10 (2009), pp. 3–40.

Erickson, Lee, 'The Economy of Novel Reading: Jane Austen and the Circulating
   Library', *Studies in English Literature, 1500–1900*, 30 (1990), pp. 573–90.

Falconer, Graham, 'New light on the Bibliothèque Cardinal', *Nineteenth-century
   French Studies*, 41 (2013), pp. 292–304.

Fergus, Jan, 'Eighteenth-century Readers in Provincial England: The Customers of
   Samuel Clay's Circulating Library and Bookshop in Warwick, 1770–72', *Papers
   of the Bibliographical Society of America*, 78 (1984), pp. 155–213.

Fergus, Jan, *Provincial Readers in Eighteenth-century England* (Oxford: Oxford
   University Press, 2007).

Furlong, Jennifer, 'Libraries, Booksellers, and Readers: Changing Tastes at the New
   York Society Library in the Long Eighteenth Century', *Library & Information
   History*, 31 (2015), pp. 198–212.

Furrer, Norbert, *Des Burgers Buch. Stadtberner Privatbibliotheken im 18. Jahrhundert*
   (Zurich: Chronos Verlag, 2012).

Glynn, Tom, 'The New York Society Library: Books, Authority, and Publics in
   Colonial and Early Republican New York', *Libraries & Culture*, 40 (2005),
   pp. 493–529.

Gosnell, Charles F., and Géza Schütz, 'Goethe the Librarian', *Library Quarterly*, 2
   (1932), pp. 367–74.

Grenby, M. O., 'Adults Only? Children and Children's Books in British Circulating
   Libraries, 1748–1848', *Book History*, 5 (2002), pp. 19–38.

Griest, Guinevere L., 'A Victorian Leviathan: Mudie's Select Library', *Nineteenth-Century Fiction*, 20 (1965), pp. 103–26.

Griest, Guinevere L., *Mudie's Circulating Library and the Victorian Novel* (London: David & Charles, 1970).

Hamlyn, Hilda M., 'Eighteenth-century circulating libraries in England', *The Library*, 5th series, 1 (1946–7), pp. 197–222.

Jacobs, Edward H., 'Eighteenth-century British Circulating Libraries and Cultural Book History', *Book History*, 6 (2003), pp. 1–22.

Jäger, Georg, Alberto Martino and Reinhard Wittmann, *Die Leihbibliothek der Goetheziet* (Hildesheim: Gerstenberg, 1979).

James, Louis, *Fiction for the Working Man* (Oxford: Oxford University Press, 1963).

Kaser, David, *A Book for a Sixpence: The Circulating Library in America* (Pittsburgh, PA: Phi Beta Mu, 1980).

Kaufman, Paul, *Circulating Libraries and Book Clubs in the Eighteenth Century* (Philadelphia, PA: American Philosophical Society, 1961).

Kaufman, Paul, 'The Community Library: a chapter in English Social History', *Transactions of the American Philosophical Society*, 57 (1967), reprinted in his *Libraries and Their Users* (London: Library Association, 1969), pp. 188–222.

Korty, Margaret Barton, 'Benjamin Franklin and Eighteenth Century American Libraries', *Transactions of the American Philosophical Society*, 55 (1965), pp. 1–83.

Kraus, Joe W., 'Private Libraries in Colonial America', *The Journal of Library History*, 9 (1974), pp. 31–53.

Lewis, John Frederick, *History of the Apprentices' Library of Philadelphia, 1820–1920: The Oldest free Circulating Library in America* (Philadelphia, PA: Apprentices' Library Company, 1924).

Manley, K. A., *Books, Borrowers and Shareholders: Scottish circulating and subscription libraries before 1825: a survey and listing* (Edinburgh: Edinburgh Bibliographical Society, 2012).

Manley, K. A., *Irish Reading Societies and Circulating Libraries founded before 1825: Useful Knowledge and Agreeable Entertainment* (Dublin: Four Courts Press, 2018).

Manley, K. A., 'Booksellers, peruke-makers, and rabbit-merchants: the growth of circulating libraries in the eighteenth century', in Robyn Myers, Michael Harris and Giles Mandelbrote (eds.), *Libraries and the Book Trade* (New Castle, DE: Oak Knoll Press, 2000), pp. 29–50.

Martino, Alberto, *Die Deutsche Leihbibliothek* (Wiesbaden: Harrassowitz, 1990).

McKitterick, David, *Print, Manuscript and the Search for Order, 1450–1830* (Cambridge: Cambridge University Press, 2005).

McMullen, Haynes, *American Libraries before 1876* (Westport, CT: Greenwood, 2000).

Moore, Sean D., *Slavery and the Making of Early American Libraries: British Literature, Political Thought and the Transatlantic Book Trade, 1731–1814* (Oxford: Oxford University Press, 2019).

Olsen, Mark, and Louis-Georges Harvey, 'Reading in Revolutionary Times: Book Borrowing from the Harvard College Library, 1773–1782', *Harvard Library Bulletin*, 4 (1993), pp. 57–72.

Peterson, C. E., 'The Library Hall: Home of the Library Company of Philadelphia, 1790–1880', *Proceedings of the American Philosophical Society*, 95 (1951), pp. 266–85.

Puschner, Uwe, 'Lesegesellschaften', in Bernd Sösemann (ed.), *Kommunikation und Medien in Preussen vom 16. Bis zum 19. Jahrhundert* (Stuttgart: Franz Steiner, 2002), pp. 194–205.

Raven, James, 'The Noble Brothers and popular publishing', *The Library*, 6th series, 12 (1990), pp. 293–345.

Raven, James, 'Libraries for Sociability: the advance of the subscription library', in *Cambridge History of Libraries in Britain and Ireland*, II, pp. 241–63.

Raven, James, 'From promotion to proscription: arrangements for reading and eighteenth-century libraries', in Raven, Helen Small and Naomi Tadmor (eds.), *The Practice and Representation of Reading in England* (Cambridge: Cambridge University Press, 1996), pp. 175–201.

Raven, James, *London Booksellers and American Customers: Transatlantic Literary Community and the Charleston Library Society, 1748–1811* (Columbia, SC.: University of South Carolina Press, 2002).

Raven, James, *The Business of Books: Booksellers and the English Book Trade, 1450–1850* (London and New Haven: Yale University Press, 2007).

Schürer, Norbert, 'Four Catalogues of the Lowndes Circulating Library, 1755–66', *Proceedings of the Bibliographical Society of America*, 101 (2007), pp. 327–57.

Shera, J. H., *Foundations of the Public Library: The Origins of the Public Library Movement in New England 1629–1855* (Chicago, IL: University of Chicago Press, 1949).

St Clair, William, *The Reading Nation in the Romantic Period* (Cambridge: Cambridge University Press, 2004).

Stiffler, Stuart A., 'Books and Reading in the Connecticut Western Reserve: The Small-Settlement Social Library, 1800–1860', *Libraries & the Cultural Record*, 46 (2011), pp. 388–411.

Taylor, John Tinnon, *Early Opposition to the English Novel: The Popular Reaction from 1760 to 1830* (New York, NY: King's Crown Press, 1943).

Towsey, Mark, and Kyle B. Roberts, *Before the Public Library: Reading, Community and Identity in the Atlantic World, 1650–1850* (Leiden: Brill, 2018).

Webb, Robert K., *The British Working Class Reader, 1790–1848: Literacy and Social Tension* (London: Allen & Unwin, 1955).

Whitmore, Harry Earl, 'The "Cabinet de Lecture" in France, 1800–1850', *Library Quarterly*, 48 (1978), pp. 20–35.

Williams, Abigail, *The Social Life of Books: Reading Together in the Eighteenth-century Home* (London and New Haven: Yale University Press, 2017).

Wilson, Charles, *First with the News: The History of W. H. Smith, 1792–1972* (London: Jonathan Cape, 1985).

Wolf, Edwin, 'The First Books and Printed Catalogues of the Library Company of Philadelphia', *Pennsylvania Magazine of History and Biography*, 78 (1954), pp. 45–70.

Wolf, Edwin, *'At the Instance of Benjamin Franklin': A Brief History of the Library*

Company of Philadelphia, 1731–1976 (Philadelphia, PA: Library Company of Philadelphia, 1976).

14. Building Empires
Arduini, Franca, 'The Two National Central Libraries of Florence and Rome', *Libraries & Culture*, 25 (1990), pp. 383–405.

Atkin, Lara, et al., *Early Public Libraries and Colonial Citizenship in the British Southern Hemisphere* (London: Palgrave Macmillan, 2019).

Bruce, Lorne D., 'Subscription Libraries for the Public in Canadian Colonies, 1775–1850', *Library & Information History*, 34 (2018), pp. 40–63.

Cobley, Alan G., 'Literacy, Libraries, and Consciousness: The Provision of Library Services for Blacks in South Africa in the Pre-Apartheid Era', *Libraries & Culture*, 32 (1997), pp. 57–80.

Cole, John Y., 'The Library of Congress Becomes a World Library, 1815–2005', *Libraries & Culture*, 40 (2005), pp. 385–98.

Dasgupta, Kalpana, 'How Learned Were the Mughals: Reflections on Muslim Libraries in India', *Journal of Library History*, 10 (1975), pp. 241–54.

Davis, Donald G., 'The Status of Library History in India: A report of an informal survey and a selective bibliographic essay', *Libraries & Culture*, 25 (1990), pp. 575–89.

Dean, Elizabeth A., 'The Organization of Italian Libraries from the Unification until 1940', *Library Quarterly*, 53 (1983), pp. 399–419.

Dean, Heather, '"The persuasion of books": The Significance of Libraries in Colonial British Columbia', *Libraries & the Cultural Record*, 46 (2011), pp. 50–72.

Delbourgo, James, *Collecting the World: The Life and Curiosity of Hans Sloane* (London: Allen Lane, 2017).

Delmas, Adrien, '*Artem Quaevis Terra Alit*: Books in the Cape Colony during the seventeenth and eighteenth centuries', in Natalia Maillard Álvarez (ed.), *Books in the Catholic World during the Early Modern Period* (Leiden: Brill, 2014), pp. 191–214.

Dick, Archie, *The Hidden History of South Africa's Books and Reading Cultures* (Toronto: University of Toronto Press, 2012).

Dickinson, Donald C., *Henry E. Huntington's Library of Libraries* (San Marino, CA: Huntington Library, 1995).

Edwards, Edward, 'A Statistical View of the Principal Public Libraries in Europe and the United States of North America', *Journal of the Statistical Society of London*, 11 (1848), pp. 250–81.

Eggert, Paul, 'Robbery Under Arms: The Colonial Market, Imperial Publishers and the Demise of the Three-Decker Novel', *Book History*, 6 (2003), pp. 127–46.

Esdaile, Arundell, *National Libraries of the World: Their History, Administration and Public Services* (London: Grafton & Co., 1934).

Finkelman, Paul, 'Class and Culture in late nineteenth-century Chicago: the Founding of the Newberry Library', *American Studies*, 16 (1975), pp. 5–22.

Fitzpatrick, Elizabeth B., 'The Public Library as Instrument of Colonialism: The Case of the Netherlands East Indies', *Libraries & the Cultural Record*, 43 (2008), pp. 270–85.

Ghosh, Anindita, *Power in Print: Popular Publishing and the Politics of Language and Culture in a Colonial Society, 1778–1905* (New Delhi: Oxford University Press, 2006).

Grant, Stephen H., *Collecting Shakespeare: The Story of Henry and Emily Folger* (Baltimore, MD: Johns Hopkins University Press, 2014).

Harris, P. R., *A History of the British Museum Library, 1753–1973* (London: British Library, 1998).

Hopkins, Judith, 'The 1791 Cataloguing Code and the Origins of the Card Catalog', *Libraries & Culture*, 27 (1992), pp. 378–404.

Hurtado, Albert L., 'Professors and Tycoons: The Creation of Great Research Libraries in the American West', *Western Historical Quarterly*, 41 (2010), pp. 149–69.

Joshi, Priya, *In Another Country: Colonialism, Culture and the English Novel in India* (New York, NY: Columbia University Press, 2002).

Liebich, Susann, 'A Sea of Fiction: The Libraries of Trans-Pacific Steamships at the Turn of the Twentieth Century', *The Library*, 7th series, 20 (2019), pp. 3–28.

Lindell, Lisa, 'Bringing Books to a "Book-Hungry Land": Print Culture on the Dakota Prairie', *Book History*, 7 (2004), pp. 215–38.

Lockyer, Dora, *The provision of books and libraries by the East India Company in India, 1611–1858* (PhD thesis, Fellowship of the Library Association, 1977).

Mandelbrote, Giles, and Barry Taylor, *Libraries within the Library: The Origins of the British Library's Printed Collections* (London: British Library, 2009).

Matveeva, Irina G., 'Immigration and the Book: Foreigners as the Founders of the First Libraries in Russia', *Libraries & Culture*, 33 (1998), pp. 62–8.

Mays, Andrea, *The Millionaire and the Bard: Henry Folger's Obsessive Hunt for Shakespeare's First Folio* (New York, NY: Simon & Schuster, 2015).

Misra, Jagdish, *Histories of Libraries and Librarianship in Modern India since 1850* (Delhi: Atma Ram, 1979).

Murphy, Sharon, 'Imperial Reading? The East India Company's Lending Libraries for Soldiers, c. 1819–1834', *Book History*, 12 (2009), pp. 74–99.

Murphy, Sharon, 'Libraries, Schoolrooms, and Mud Gadowns: Formal Scenes of Reading at East India Company Stations in India, c.1819–1835', *Journal of the Royal Asiatic Society*, 21 (2011), pp. 459–67.

Murphy, Sharon, *The British Soldier and his Libraries, c.1822–1901* (London: Palgrave Macmillan, 2016).

Niessen, James P., 'Museums, Nationality, and Public Research Libraries in Nineteenth-century Transylvania', *Libraries & the Cultural Record*, 41 (2006), pp. 298–336.

Ohdedar, A. K., *The Growth of the Library in Modern India, 1498–1836* (Calcutta: World Press, 1966).

Ostrowski, Carl, 'James Alfred Pearce and the Question of a National Library in Antebellum America', *Libraries & Culture*, 35 (2000), pp. 255–77.

Patel, Jashu, and Krishan Kumar, *Libraries and Librarianship in India* (Westport, CT: Greenwood, 2001).

Priebe, Paul M., 'From Bibliothèque du Roi to Bibliothèque Nationale: The

Creation of a State Library, 1789–1793', *Journal of Library History*, 17 (1982), pp. 389–408.

Rose, Jonathan, 'The Global Common Reader', in Martin Hewitt (ed.), *The Victorian World* (London: Routledge, 2012), pp. 555–68.

Stuart, Mary, *Aristocrat-Librarian in Service to the Tsar: Aleksei Nikolaevich Olenin and the Imperial Public Library* (Boulder, CO: East European Monographs, 1986).

Stuart, Mary, 'Creating Culture: The Rossica Collection of the Imperial Public Library and the Construction of National Identity', *Libraries & Culture*, 30 (1995), pp. 1–25.

Sutherland, John, 'Literature and the Library in the Nineteenth Century', in Alice Crawford (ed.), *The Meaning of the Library: A Cultural History* (Princeton: Princeton University Press, 2015), pp. 124–50.

Traue, J. E., 'The Public Library Explosion in Colonial New Zealand', *Libraries & the Cultural Record*, 42 (2007), pp. 151–64.

Willison, Ian R., 'The National Library in Historical Perspective', *Libraries & Culture*, 24 (1989), pp. 75–95.

15. Reading on the Job

Altick, Richard D., *The English Common Reader: A Social History of the Mass Reading Public* (Chicago, IL: University of Chicago Press, 1957; 2nd edn, Columbus, OH: Ohio State University Press, 1998).

Baggs, Chris, 'The Miners' Institute Libraries of South Wales, 1875–1939', in Philip Henry Jones et al. (eds.), *A Nation and Its Books: A History of the Book in Wales* (Aberystwyth: National Library of Wales, 1998).

Baggs, Chris, 'How Well Read Was My Valley? Reading, Popular Fiction, and the Miners of South Wales, 1875–1939', *Book History*, 4 (2001), pp. 277–301.

Baggs, Chris, '"The Whole Tragedy of Leisure in Penury": The South Wales Miners' Institute Libraries during the Great Depression', *Libraries & Culture,* 39 (2004), pp. 115–36.

Baggs, Chris, '"In the Separate Reading Room for Ladies Are Provided Those Publications Specially Interesting to Them": Ladies' Reading Rooms and British Public Libraries 1850–1914', *Victorian Periodicals Review*, 38 (2005), pp. 280–306.

Barnett, Graham Keith, 'The History of Public Libraries in France from the Revolution to 1939' (PhD thesis, Fellowship of the Library Association, 1973).

Black, Alistair, 'Libraries for the Many: The Philosophical Roots of the Early Public Library Movement', *Library History*, 9 (1991), pp. 27–36.

Black, Alistair, *A New History of the English Public Library: Social and Intellectual Contexts, 1850–1914* (London: Leicester University Press, 1996).

Bobinski, George S., 'Carnegie Libraries: their history and impact on American Public Library Development', *American Library Association Bulletin*, 62 (1968), pp. 1361–7.

Brantlinger, Patrick, 'The Case of the Poisonous Book: Mass Literacy as threat in Nineteenth-century British Fiction', *Victorian Review*, 20 (1994), pp. 117–33.

Brantlinger, Patrick, *The Reading Lesson: The Threat of Mass Literacy in Nineteenth-century British Fiction* (Purdue: India University Press, 1998).

Brantlinger, Patrick, *Bread and Circuses: Theories of Mass Culture as Social Decay* (Cornell, NY: Cornell University Press, 2016).

Carrier, Esther Jane, *Fiction in Public Libraries 1876–1900* (New York, NY: Scarecrow Press, 1965).

Ditzion, Sidney, *Arsenals of a Democratic Culture: A Social History of the American Public Library Movement in New England and the Middle States from 1850 to 1900* (Chicago, IL: American Library Association, 1947).

Eddy, Jacalyn, '"We have become Tender-Hearted": The Language of Gender in the Public Library, 1880–1920', *American Studies*, 42 (2001), pp. 155–72.

Edwards, Edward, 'A Statistical View of the Principal Public Libraries in Europe and the United States of North America', *Journal of the Statistical Society of London*, 11 (1848), pp. 250–81.

Erickson, Lee, 'The Economy of Novel Reading: Jane Austen and the Circulating Library', *Studies in English Literature, 1500–1900*, 30 (1990), pp. 573–90.

Flint, Kate, *The Woman Reader* (Oxford: Clarendon Press, 1993).

Fullerton, Ronald A., 'Creating a Mass Book Market in Germany: The Story of the "Colporteur Novel", 1870–1890', *Journal of Social History*, 10 (1977), pp. 265–83.

Geller, Evelyn, *Forbidden Books in American Public Libraries, 1876–1939* (Westport, CT: Greenwood, 1984).

Glynn, Tom, *Reading Publics: New York City's Public Libraries, 1754–1911* (New York, NY: Fordham University Press, 2015).

Harris, Michael H., 'The Emergence of the American Public Library: a revisionist interpretation of history', *Library Journal*, 98 (1973), pp. 2509–14.

Hildenbrand, Suzanne, 'Revision versus Reality: Women in the History of the Public Library Movement, 1876–1920', in Kathleen M. Heim (ed.), *The Status of Women in Librarianship: Historical, Sociological, and Economic Issues* (New York, NY: Neal-Schuman, 1983), pp. 7–27.

Johanningsmeier, Charles, 'Welcome Guests or Representatives of the "Mal-Odorous Class"? Periodicals and Their Readers in American Public Libraries, 1876–1914', *Libraries & Culture*, 39 (2004), pp. 260–92.

Kaufman, Paul, *Libraries and Their Users* (London: Library Association, 1969).

Kelly, Thomas, *Books for the People: An Illustrated History of the British Public Library* (London: Andre Deutsch, 1977).

Kevane, Michael, 'The Development of Public Libraries in the United States, 1870–1930: A Quantitative Assessment', *Information & Culture: A Journal of History*, 49 (2014), pp. 117–44.

Lakmaker, Joosje, and Elke Veldkamp, *Amsterdammers en hun bibliotheek. OBA 1919–2019* (Amsterdam: Wereldbibliotheek, 2019).

Levine, Lawrence W., *Highbrow, Lowbrow: The Emergence of Cultural Hierarchy in America* (Cambridge, MA: Harvard University Press, 1988).

'The Manchester Free Library', *Spectator*, 12 November 1853, pp. 30–31.

Manley, K. A., 'Rural Reading in Northwest England: The Sedbergh Book Club, 1728–1928', *Book History*, 2 (1999), pp. 78–95.

Max, Stanley M., 'Tory Reaction to the Public Libraries Bill, 1850', *Journal of Library History*, 19 (1984), pp. 504–24.

McCrimmon, Barbara, 'The Libri Case', *Journal of Library History*, 1 (1966), pp. 7–32.

Meller, H. E., *Leisure and the Changing City, 1870–1914* (London: Routledge, 1976).

Minto, John, *A History of the Public Library Movement in Great Britain and Ireland* (London: George Allen & Unwin, 1932).

Nasaw, David, *Andrew Carnegie* (London: Penguin, 2006).

Oehlerts, Donald, *Books and Blueprints: Building America's Public Libraries* (Westport, CT: Greenwood, 1991).

Orlean, Susan, *The Library Book* (London: Atlantic Books, 2018).

Otness, Harold M., 'Baedeker's One-Star American Libraries', *Journal of Library History*, 12 (1977), pp. 222–34.

Passet, Joanne E., 'Men in a Feminized Profession: The Male Librarian, 1887–1921', *Libraries & Culture*, 28 (1993), pp. 385–402.

Pettegree, Andrew, 'Rare Books and Revolutionaries: The French Bibliothèques Municipales', in his *The French Book and the European Book World* (Leiden: Brill, 2007), pp. 1–16.

Rhees, William J., *Manual of Public Libraries, Institutions and Societies in the United States and British Provinces of North America* (Philadelphia, PA: J. B. Lippincott, 1889).

Ring, Daniel F., 'Carnegie Libraries as Symbols for an Age: Montana as a Test Case', *Libraries & Culture*, 27 (1992), pp. 1–19.

Ring, Daniel F., 'Men of Energy and Snap: The Origins and Early Years of the Billings Public Library', *Libraries & Culture*, 36 (2001), pp. 397–412.

Robson, Ann, 'The Intellectual Background of the Public Library Movement in Britain', *Journal of Library History*, 11 (1976), pp. 187–205.

Royle, Edward, 'Mechanics' Institutes and the Working Classes, 1840–1860', *Historical Journal*, 14 (1971), pp. 305–21.

Ruju, P. Alessandra Maccioni, and Marco Mostert, *The Life and Times of Guglielmo Libri (1802–1869)* (Hilversum: Verloren, 1995).

Sandal, Ennio, 'The Endowed Municipal Public Libraries', *Libraries & Culture*, 25 (1990), pp. 358–71.

Schidorsky, Dov, 'The Origins of Jewish Workers' Libraries in Palestine, 1880–1920', *Libraries & Culture*, 23 (1988), pp. 39–60.

Schidorsky, Dov, 'The Municipal Libraries of Tel Aviv during the British Mandate, 1920–1948', *Libraries & Culture*, 31 (1996), pp. 540–56.

Severn, Ken, *The Halfpenny Rate: A Brief History of Lambeth Libraries* (London: Lambeth Archives, 2006).

Shera, Jesse, *Foundations of the Public Library: The Origins of the Public Library Movement in New England 1629–1855* (Chicago, IL: University of Chicago Press, 1949).

Short, Hohn Phillip, 'Everyman's Colonial Library: Imperialism and Working-Class Readers in Leipzig', *German History*, 21 (2003), pp. 445–75.

Snape, Robert, *Leisure and the Rise of the Public Library* (London: The Library Association, 1995).

Some Impressions of the Public Library System of the United States of America (Edinburgh: Constable, 1927).

Stauffer, Suzanne M., 'In Their Own Image: The Public Library Collection as a Reflection of its Donors', *Libraries & the Cultural Record*, 42 (2007), pp. 387–408.

Steinberg, Hans-Josef, and Nicholas Jacobs, 'Workers' Libraries in Germany before 1914', *History Workshop*, 1 (1976), pp. 166–80.

Stielow, Frederick J., 'Censorship in the Early Professionalization of American Libraries, 1876 to 1929', *Journal of Library History*, 18 (1983), pp. 37–54.

Thompson, Alastair R., 'The Use of Libraries by the Working Class in Scotland in the Early Nineteenth Century', *Scottish Historical Review*, 42 (1963), pp. 21–9.

Valentine, Patrick M., 'Steel, Cotton, and Tobacco: Philanthropy and Public Libraries in North Carolina, 1900–1940', *Libraries & Culture*, 31 (1996), pp. 272–98.

Van Slyck, Abigail A., *Free to All: Carnegie Libraries & American Culture, 1890–1920* (Chicago, IL: University of Chicago Press, 1995).

Van Slyck, Abigail A., '"The Utmost Amount of Effectiv [sic] Accommodation": Andrew Carnegie and the Reform of the American Library', *Journal of the Society of Architectural Historians*, 50 (1991), pp. 359–83.

Vincent, David, *Literacy and Popular Culture, England 1750–1914* (Cambridge: Cambridge University Press, 1989).

Vincent, David, *The Rise of Mass Literacy: Reading and Writing in Modern England* (Cambridge: Cambridge University Press, 2000).

Webb, Robert K., 'Working Class Readers in Early Victorian England', *English Historical Review*, 65 (1950), pp. 333–51.

Webb, Robert K., *The British Working Class Reader, 1790–1848: Literacy and Social Tension* (London: Allen & Unwin, 1955).

Young, Arthur P., *Books for Sammies: The American Library Association and World War I* (Pittsburgh, PA: Beta Phi Mu, 1981).

16. Surviving the Twentieth Century.

Alessandrini, Jan L., 'Lost Books of "Operation Gomorrah": Rescue, Reconstruction and Restitution at Hamburg's Library in the Second World War', in Flavia Bruni and Andrew Pettegree (eds.), *Lost Books: Reconstructing the Print World of Pre-Industrial Europe* (Leiden: Brill, 2016), pp. 441–61.

Baez, Fernando, *A Universal History of the Destruction of Books: From Ancient Sumer to Modern-day Iraq* (London: Atlas, 2008).

Barnett, Graham Keith, 'The History of Public Libraries in France from the Revolution to 1939' (PhD thesis, Fellowship of the Library Association, 1973).

Beal, Peter, 'Lost: the destruction, dispersal and rediscovery of manuscripts', in Giles Mandelbrote et al. (eds.), *Books on the Move: Tracking Copies through Collections and the Book Trade* (New Castle, DE: Oak Knoll Press, 2007), pp. 1–16.

Bevan, Robert, *The Destruction of Memory: Architecture at War* (London: Reaktion, 2006).

Bollmus, Reinhard, *Das Amt Rosenberg und seine Gegner: Studien zur Machtkampt in nationalsozialistische Herrschaftsystem* (Munich: Oldenbourg, 2006).

Boodrookas, Alex, 'Total Literature, Total War: Foreign Aid, Area Studies, and the Weaponization of US Research Libraries', *Diplomatic History*, 43 (2019), pp. 332–52.

Borin, Jacqueline, 'Embers of the Soul: The Destruction of Jewish Books and Libraries in Poland during World War II', *Libraries & Culture*, 28 (1993), pp. 445–60.

Briel, Cornelia, *Beschlagnahmt, Erpresst, Erebeutet. NS-Raubgut, Reichstauchstelle und Preussische Staatsbibliothek zwischen 1933 und 1945* (Berlin: Akademie Verlag, 2013).

Bruni, Flavia, 'All is not lost. Italian Archives and Libraries in the Second World War', in Flavia Bruni and Andrew Pettegree (eds.), *Lost Books: Reconstructing the Print World of Pre-Industrial Europe* (Leiden: Brill, 2016), pp. 469–87.

Chamberlain, Russell, *Loot: the Heritage of Plunder* (New York, NY: Facts on File, 1983).

Collins, Donald E., and Herbert P. Rothfeder, 'The Einsatzstab Reichsleiter Rosenberg and the Looting of Jewish and Masonic Libraries during World War II', *Journal of Library History*, 18 (1983), pp. 21–36.

Coppens, Chris, Mark Derez and Jan Roegiers, *Leuven University Library, 1425–2000* (Leuven: Leuven University Press, 2005).

Dosa, Marta L., *Libraries in the Political Scene* (Westport, CT: Greenwood, 1974).

Fishman, David E., *The Book Smugglers: Partisans, Poets and the Race to Save Jewish Treasures from the Nazis* (Lebanon, NH: ForeEdge, 2017).

Grimsted, Patricia Kennedy, *The Odyssey of the Turgenev Library from Paris, 1940–2002: Books as Victims and Trophies of War* (Amsterdam: IISH, 2003).

Grimsted, Patricia Kennedy, 'The Road to Minsk for Western "Trophy" Books: Twice Plundered but Not Yet "Home from the War"', *Libraries & Culture*, 39 (2004), pp. 351–404.

Grimsted, Patricia Kennedy, 'Roads to Ratibor: Library and Archival Plunder by the Einsatzstab Reichsleiter Rosenberg', *Holocaust Genocide Studies*, 19 (2005), pp. 390–458.

Grimsted, Patricia Kennedy, 'Tracing Trophy Books in Russia', *Solanus*, 19 (2005), pp. 131–45.

Grimsted, Patricia Kennedy, *Library Plunder in France by the Einsatzstab Reichsleiter Rosenberg: Ten ERR Seizure Lists of Confiscated French Libraries* (Amsterdam: IISH, 2017).

Hill, Leonidas E., 'The Nazi attack on "Un-German" literature, 1933–1945', in Jonathan Rose (ed.), *The Holocaust and the Book* (Amherst, MA: University of Massachusetts Press, 2001), pp. 9–46.

Holman, Valerie, *Book Publishing in England, 1939–1945* (London: British Library, 2008).

Intrator, Miriam, *Books Across Borders: UNESCO and the Politics of Postwar Cultural Reconstruction, 1945–1951* (London: Palgrave Macmillan, 2019).

Irving, Henry, 'Paper salvage in Britain during the Second World War', *Historical Research*, 89 (2016), pp. 373–93.

Irving, Henry, '"Propaganda bestsellers": British Official War Books, 1941–1946', in Cynthia Johnston (ed.), *The Concept of the Book: The Production, Progression and Dissemination of Information* (London: Institute of English Studies, 2019), pp. 125–46.

Kirschbaum, Erik, *Burning Beethoven: The Eradication of German Culture in the United States during World War I* (New York, NY: Berlinica, 2015).

Knuth, Rebecca, *Libricide: The Regime-Sponsored Destruction of Books and Libraries in the Twentieth Century* (Westport, CT: Praeger, 2003).

Knuth, Rebecca, *Burning Books and Leveling Libraries: Extremist Violence and Cultural Destruction* (Westport, CT: Praeger, 2006).

Loss, Christopher L., 'Reading between Enemy Lines: Armed Services Editions and World War II', *Journal of Military History*, 67 (2003), pp. 811–34.

Nastulczyk, Tomasz, 'Two Centuries of Looting and the Grand Nazi Book Burning: The Dispersed and Destroyed Libraries of the Polish-Lithuanian Commonwealth', in Flavia Bruni and Andrew Pettegree (eds.), *Lost Books: Reconstructing the Print World of Pre-Industrial Europe* (Leiden: Brill, 2016), pp. 462–68.

Orlean, Susan, *The Library Book* (London: Atlantic Books, 2018).

Ovenden, Richard, *Burning the Books: A History of Knowledge Under Attack* (London: John Murray, 2020).

Piper, Ernst, *Alfred Rosenberg: Hitlers Chefideologe* (Munich: Karl Blessing, 2005).

Polastron, Lucien X., *Books on Fire: The Destruction of Libraries Throughout History* (Rochester, VT: Inner Traditions, 2007).

Poulain, Martine, *Livres pillés, lectures surveillées: les bibliothèques françaises sous l'occupation* (Paris: Gallimard, 2008).

Richards, Pamela Spence, 'German Libraries and Scientific and Technical Information in Nazi Germany', *Library Quarterly*, 55 (1985), pp. 151–73.

Richards, Pamela Spence, 'Aslib at War: The Brief but Intrepid Career of a Library Organization as a Hub of Allied Scientific Intelligence 1942–1945', *Journal of Education for Library and Information Science*, 29 (1989), pp. 279–96.

Ring, Daniel F., 'Fighting for Their Hearts and Minds: William Howard Brett, the Cleveland Public Library, and World War I', *Journal of Library History*, 18 (1983), pp. 1–20.

Russell, Dale C., '"Our Special Province": Providing a Library Service for London's Public Shelters, 1940–1942', *Library History*, 13 (1997), pp. 3–15.

Rydell, Anders, *The Book Thieves: The Nazi Looting of Europe's Libraries and the Race to Return a Literary Inheritance* (New York, NY: Viking, 2015).

Sayers, W. C. Berwick, 'Britain's Libraries and the War', *Library Quarterly*, 14 (1944), pp. 95–9.

Schidorsky, Dov, 'Confiscation of Libraries and Assignments to Forced Labour: Two Documents of the Holocaust', *Libraries & Culture*, 33 (1998), pp. 347–88.

Schliebs, Siegfried, 'Verboten, verbrannt verfolgt ... Wolfgang Herrmann und seine "Schwarze Liste. Schöne Literatur" vom Mai 1933 – Der Fall des Volksbibliothekars Dr. Wolfgang Hermann', in Hermann Haarmann, Walter Huder and Klaus Siebenhaar (eds.), *"Das war ein Vorspiel nur" – Bücherverbrennung Deutschland 1933: Voraussetzungen und Folgen* (Berlin and Vienna: Medusa Verlagsgesellschaft, 1983), pp. 442–4.

Schneider, Nicola, 'The Losses of the Music Collection of the Hessische

Landesbibliothek in Darmstadt in 1944', in Anja-Silvia Goeing, Anthony T. Grafton and Paul Michel (eds.), *Collectors' Knowledge: What is Kept, What is Discarded* (Leiden: Brill, 2013), pp. 381–412.

Schocow, Werner, *Bucherschicksale: die Verlagerungsgeschichte der Preussischen Staatsbibliothek; Auslagerung, Zerstörung, Rückführung* (Berlin: de Gruyter, 2003).

Sheehan, Donal, 'The Manchester Literary and Philosophical Society', *Isis*, 33 (1941), pp. 519–23.

Sroka, Marek, 'The Destruction of Jewish Libraries and Archives in Cracow during World War II', *Libraries & Culture,* 38 (2003), pp. 147–65.

Starr, Joshua, 'Jewish Cultural Property under Nazi Control', *Jewish Social Studies*, 12 (1950), pp. 27–48.

Stieg, Margaret F., *Public Libraries in Nazi Germany* (Tuscaloosa, AL: University of Alabama Press, 1992).

Stieg, Margaret F., 'The Second World War and the Public Libraries of Nazi Germany', *Journal of Contemporary History*, 27 (1992), pp. 23–40.

Stieg Dalton, Margaret, 'The Postwar Purge of German Public Libraries, Democracy and the American Reaction', *Libraries & Culture*, 28 (1993), pp. 143–64.

Stubbings, Hilda Uren, *Blitzkrieg and Books: British and European Libraries as Casualties of World War II* (Bloomington, IN: Rubena Press, 1993).

Thorsheim, Peter, 'Salvage and Destruction: The Recycling of Books and Manuscripts in Great Britain during the Second World War', *Contemporary European History*, 22 (2013), pp. 431–52.

Travis, Trysh, 'Books as Weapons and "The Smart Man's Peace": The Work of the Council on Books in Wartime', *Princeton University Library Chronicle*, 60 (1999), pp. 353–99.

Waite, Robert G., 'Returning Jewish Cultural Property: The Handling of Books Looted by the Nazis in the American Zone of Occupation, 1945 to 1952', *Libraries & Culture*, 37 (2002), pp. 213–28.

Wiegand, Wayne, *"An Active Instrument for Propaganda": the American Public Library during World War I* (New York, NY: Greenwood, 1989).

Wiegand, Wayne, 'In Service to the State: Wisconsin Public Libraries during World War I', *Wisconsin Magazine of History*, 72 (1989), pp. 199–224.

Young, Arthur P., *Books for Sammies: The American Library Association and World War I* (Pittsburgh, PA: Beta Phi Mu, 1981).

17. Wrestling with Modernity

Augst, Thomas, 'American Libraries and Agencies of Culture', *American Studies*, 42 (2001), pp. 5 –22.

Augst, Thomas, and Kenneth Carpenter, *Institutions of Reading: The Social Life of Libraries in the United States* (Amherst, MA: University of Massachusetts Press, 2007).

Baggs, Chris, '"In the Separate Reading Room for Ladies Are Provided Those Publications Specially Interesting to Them": Ladies' Reading Rooms and British Public Libraries 1850–1914', *Victorian Periodicals Review*, 38 (2005), pp. 280–306.

Benton, Megan, '"Too Many Books": Book Ownership and Cultural Identity in the 1920s', *American Quarterly*, 49 (1997), pp. 268–97.

Black, Alistair, *The Public Library in Britain, 1914–2000* (London: British Library, 2000).

Carrier, Esther Jane, *Fiction in Public Libraries 1900–1950* (Littleton, CO: Libraries Unlimited, 1985).

Coleman, Sterling Joseph, '"Eminently Suited to Girls and Women": The Numerical Feminization of Public Librarianship in England, 1914–1931', *Library & Information History*, 30 (2014), pp. 195–209.

Cummings, Jennifer, '"How can we Fail?" The Texas State Library's Traveling Libraries and Bookmobiles, 1916–1966', *Libraries & the Cultural Record*, 44 (2009), pp. 299–325.

Denning, Michael, *Mechanical Accents: Dime Novels and Working-Class Culture in America* (London: Verso, 1987).

Dugan, Sally, 'Boots Book-Lovers' Library: Domesticating the Exotic and Building provincial Library Taste', in Nicola Wilson (ed.), *The Book World: Selling and Distributing British Literature* (Leiden: Brill, 2016), pp. 153–70.

Ellis, Alec, *Library Services for Young People in England and Wales, 1830–1970* (Oxford: Pergamon Press, 1971).

Ellsworth, Ralph E., 'Library Architecture and Buildings', *Library Quarterly*, 25 (1955), pp. 66–75.

Escarpit, Robert, *The Book Revolution* (London: Harrap, 1966).

Finchum, Tanya Ducker, and Allen Finchum, 'Not Gone with the Wind: Libraries in Oklahoma in the 1930s', *Libraries & the Cultural Record*, 46 (2011), pp. 276–94.

Geller, Evelyn, *Forbidden Books in American Public Libraries, 1876–1939* (Westport, CT: Greenwood, 1970).

Hart, James D., *The Popular Book: A History of America's Literary Taste* (New York, NY: Oxford University Press, 1950).

Harvey Darton, F. J., *Children's Books in England: Five Centuries of Social Life* (London: British Library, 1999).

Hilliard, Christopher, 'The Twopenny Library: The Book Trade, Working Class Readers and "Middlebrow" Novels in Britain, 1930–42', *Twentieth Century British History*, 25 (2014), pp. 199–220.

Huggett, Frank E., *Victorian England as Seen by Punch* (London: Book Club Associates, 1978).

Leary, Patrick, *The Punch Brotherhood: Table Talk and Print Culture in Mid-Victorian London* (London: British Library, 2010).

Lindell, Lisa, 'Bringing Books to a "Book-Hungry Land": Print Culture on the Dakota Prairie', *Book History*, 7 (2004), pp. 215–39.

Marcum, Deanna B., 'The Rural Public Library in America at the Turn of the Century', *Libraries & Culture*, 26 (1991), pp. 87–99.

Marquis, Alice Goldfarb, *Hope and Ashes: The Birth of Modern Times* (New York: Free Press, 1986).

McAleer, Joseph, *Popular Reading and Publishing in Britain, 1914–1950* (Oxford: Oxford University Press, 1992).

McAleer, Joseph, *Passion's Fortune: The Story of Mills & Boon* (Oxford: Oxford University Press, 1999).

McCormack, Thelma, '*The Intelligent Woman's Guide to Socialism and Capitalism* by George Bernard Shaw', *American Journal of Sociology*, 91 (1985), pp. 209–11.

McIntyre, Ian, *The Expense of Glory: A Life of John Reith* (London: Harper Collins, 1993).

Orlean, Susan, *The Library Book* (London: Atlantic Books, 2018).

Passet, Joanne E., 'Reaching the Rural Reader: Traveling Libraries in America, 1892–1920', *Libraries & Culture*, 26 (1991), pp. 100–118.

Pawley, Christine, *Reading Places: Literacy, Democracy and the Public Library in Cold War America* (Amherst, MA: University of Massachusetts Press, 2010).

Radway, Janice A., *Reading the Romance: Women, Patriarchy and Popular Literature* (Chapel Hill, NC: University of North Carolina Press, 1984).

Radway, Janice A., *A Feeling for Books: The Book-of-the-Month Club, Literary Taste and Middle-Class Desire* (Chapel Hill, NC: University of North Carolina Press, 1997).

Savage, Jon, *Teenage: The Creation of Youth Culture* (London: Pimlico, 2008).

Susman, Warren, 'Communication and Culture', in Catherine L. Covert and John D. Stevens (eds.), *Mass Media Between the Wars: Perceptions of Cultural Tension, 1918–1941* (Syracuse, NY: Syracuse University Press, 1984).

Sutherland, John, *Reading the Decades: Fifty Years of the Nation's Bestselling Books* (London: BBC, 2002).

Valentine, Jolie, 'Our Community, Our Library: Women, Schools and Popular Culture in the Public Library Movement', *Public Library Quarterly*, 24 (2005), pp. 45–79.

Vincent, Ida, 'Public Libraries in New South Wales, 1935–1980: A Study in the Origins, Transformation, and Multiplication of Organizational Goals', *Library Quarterly*, 51 (1981), pp. 363–79.

Wagner, Ralph A., 'Not Recommended: A List for Catholic High School Libraries, 1942', *Libraries & Culture*, 30 (1995), pp. 170–98.

Ward, Dane M., 'The Changing Role of Mobile Libraries in Africa', *International Information and Library Review*, 28 (1996), pp. 121–33.

White, Cynthia L., *Women's Magazines, 1693–1968* (London: Michael Joseph, 1970).

Wiegand, Wayne, *Irrepressible Reformer: A Biography of Melvil Dewey* (Chicago, IL: American Library Association, 1996).

Wiegand, Wayne, *Main Street Public Library: Community Places and Reading Spaces in the Rural Heartland, 1876–1956* (Iowa City, IA: University of Iowa Press, 2011).

Wiegand, Wayne, *Part of Our Lives: A People's History of the American Public Library* (New York: Oxford University Press, 2015).

Wilson, Nicola, 'Boots Book-lovers' Library and the Novel: The Impact of a Circulating Library Market on Twentieth-century Fiction', *Information & Culture*, 49 (2014), pp. 427–49.

Winter, Jackie, *Lipsticks and Library Books: The Story of Boots Booklovers Library* (Dorset: Chantries Press, 2016).

18. Libraries, Books and Politics

Baker, Nicholson, *Double Fold: Libraries and the Assault on Paper* (New York, NY: Random House, 2001).

Basbanes, Nicholas, 'Once and Future Library', in his *Patience and Fortitude* (New York, NY: Harper Collins, 2001), pp. 386–424.

Brine, Jennifer Jane, 'Adult readers in the Soviet Union' (PhD thesis, University of Birmingham, 1986).

Brine, Jenny, 'The Soviet reader, the book shortage and the public library', *Solanus*, 2 (1988), pp. 39–57.

Cresswell, Stephen, 'The Last Days of Jim Crow in Southern Libraries', *Libraries & Culture*, 31 (1996), pp. 557–72.

Darnton, Robert, 'Censorship, a Comparative View: France 1789 – East Germany 1989', *Representations*, 49 (1995), pp. 40–60.

Darnton, Robert, *Censors at Work: How States Shaped Literature* (London: British Library, 2014).

Drabinski, Emily, 'Librarians and the Patriot Act', *The Radical Teacher*, 77 (2006), pp. 12–14.

Fultz, Michael, 'Black Public Libraries in the South in the Era of De Jure Segregation', *Libraries & the Cultural Record*, 41 (2006), pp. 337–59.

Gordon, Constance J., 'Cultural Record Keepers: The English Book Donation, Chicago Public Library', *Libraries & the Cultural Record*, 44 (2009), pp. 371–4.

Hammill, Faye, 'Cold Comfort Farm, D. H. Lawrence, and English Literary Culture Between the Wars', *Modern Fiction Studies*, 47 (2001), pp. 831–54.

Hilliard, Christopher, '"Is It a Book That You Would Even Wish Your Wife or Your Servants to Read?" Obscenity Law and the Politics of Reading in Modern England', *American Historical Review*, 118 (2013), pp. 653–78.

Horton, Allan, *'Libraries are great mate!' But they could be greater. A report to the nation on Public Libraries in Australia* (Melbourne: Australian Library Promotional Council, 1976).

Hyde, H. Montgomery, *The Lady Chatterley's Lover Trial* (London: Bodley Head, 1990).

Jarvis, Helen, 'The National Library of Cambodia: Surviving for Seventy Years', *Libraries & Culture*, 30 (1995), pp. 391–408.

Joshi, Priya, *In Another Country: Colonialism, Culture and the English Novel in India* (New York, NY: Columbia University Press, 2002).

Korsch, Boris, 'The Role of Readers' Cards in Soviet Libraries, *Journal of Library History*, 13 (1978), pp. 282–97.

Korsch, Boris, 'Soviet Librarianship under Gorbachev: Change and Continuity', *Solanus*, 4 (1990), pp. 24–45.

Latham, Joyce M., 'Wheat and Chaff: Carl Roden, Abe Korman and the Definitions of Intellectual Freedom in the Chicago Public Library', *Libraries & the Cultural Record*, 44 (2009), pp. 279–98.

Laugesen, Amanda, 'UNESCO and the Globalization of the Public Library Idea, 1948 to 1965', *Library & Information History*, 30 (2014), pp. 1–19.

Leal, Ralph A., 'Libraries in the U.S.S.R', unpublished survey accessible at https://files.eric.ed.gov/fulltext/ED098959.pdf (last accessed 27 July 2020).

Maack, Mary Niles, 'Books and Libraries as Instruments of Cultural Diplomacy in Francophone Africa during the Cold War', *Libraries & Culture*, 36 (2001), pp. 58–86.

Mäkinen, Ilkka, 'Libraries in Hell: Cultural Activities in Soviet Prisons and Labor Camps from the 1930s to the 1950s', *Libraries & Culture*, 28 (1993), pp. 117–42.

Motley, Eric L., *Madison Park: A Place of Hope* (Grand Rapids, MI: Zondervan, 2017).

Patel, Jashu, and Krishan Kumar, *Libraries and Librarianship in India* (Westport, CT: Greenwood, 2001).

Pawley, Christine, 'Blood and Thunder on the Bookmobile: American Public Libraries and the Construction of "the Reader", 1950–1995', in Thomas Augst and Kenneth Carpenter (eds.), *Institutions of Reading: The Social Life of Libraries in the United States* (Amherst, MA: University of Massachusetts Press, 2007), pp. 264–82.

Pawley, Christine, *Reading Places: Literacy, Democracy and the Public Library in Cold War America* (Amherst, MA: University of Massachusetts Press, 2010).

Pawley, Christine, and Louise S. Robbins, *Libraries and the Reading Public in Twentieth-Century America* (Madison, WI: University of Wisconsin Press, 2013).

Robbins, Louise S., 'Segregating Propaganda in American Libraries: Ralph Ulveling Confronts the Intellectual Freedom Committee', *Library Quarterly*, 63 (1993), pp. 143–65.

Robbins, Louise S., 'After Brave Words, Silence: American Librarianship Responds to Cold War Loyalty Programs, 1947–1957', *Libraries & Culture*, 30 (1995), pp. 345–65.

Robbins, Louise S., *Censorship and the American Library: The American Library Association's Response to Threats to Intellectual Freedom, 1939–1969* (Westport, CT: Greenwood, 1996).

Robbins, Louise S., *The Dismissal of Miss Ruth Brown: Civil Rights, Censorship and the American Library* (Norman, OK: University of Oklahoma Press, 2000).

Rogachevskii, Andrei, 'Homo Sovieticus in the Library', *Europe-Asia Studies*, 54 (2002), pp. 975–88.

Rogers, Rutherford D., 'Yes, Ivan Reads: A First Report of the American Library Mission to Russia', *American Library Association Bulletin*, 55 (1961), pp. 621–4.

Rose, Lisle A., *The Cold War Comes to Main Street: America in 1950* (Lawrence, KS: University Press of Kansas, 1999).

Ruggles, Melville J., and Raynard Coe Swank, *Soviet libraries and librarianship; report of the visit of the delegation of U.S. librarians to the Soviet Union, May–June, 1961, under the U.S.–Soviet cultural exchange agreement* (Chicago, IL: American Library Association, 1962).

Šmejkalová, Jiřina, *Cold War Books in the 'Other Europe' and What Came After* (Leiden: Brill, 2011).

Smith, Kathleen A., 'Collection development in Public and University Libraries of the former Democratic Republic since German Unification', *Libraries & Culture*, 36 (2001), pp. 413–31.

Spencer, Gladys, *The Chicago Public Library: Origins and Backgrounds* (Boston, MA:
     Gregg Press, 1972).
Sroka, Marek, 'The Stalinization of Libraries in Poland, 1945–1953', *Library History*,
     16 (2000), pp. 105–25.
Sroka, Marek, '"Forsaken and Abandoned": The Nationalization and Salvage of
     Deserted, Displaced, and Private Library Collections in Poland, 1945–1948',
     Library & Information History, 28 (2012), pp. 272–88.
Thompson, Dennis, 'The Private Wars of Chicago's Big Bill Thompson', *Journal of
     Library History*, 15 (1980), pp. 261–80.
Vladimirov, L. I., 'The Accomplishments of University Libraries in the Soviet Union',
     Library Trends, 4 (1964), pp. 558–82.
Wagner, Ralph D., 'Not Recommended: A List for Catholic High School Libraries,
     1942', *Libraries & Culture*, 30 (1995), pp. 170–98.
Wani, Zahid Ashraf, 'Development of Public Libraries in India', *Library Philosophy
     and Practice* (ejournal, 2008).
Wiegand, Shirley, and Wayne Wiegand, *The Desegregation of Public Libraries in the
     Jim Crow South: Civil Rights and Local Activism* (Baton Rouge, LA: LSU Press,
     2018).
Wiegand, Wayne, '"Any Ideas?": The American Library Association and the
     Desegregation of Public Libraries in the American South', *Libraries: Culture,
     History, and Society*, 1 (2017), pp. 1–22.

Postscript: Reading Without Books

Ari, Amro, 'Power, Rebirth and Scandal: A Decade of the Bibliotheca Alexandria',
     Jadaliyya, October 2012, https://www.jadaliyya.com/Details/27221.
Basbanes, Nicholas, *Patience and Fortitude* (New York, NY: Harper Collins, 2001).
Bhaskar, Michael, *The Content Machine: Towards a Theory of Publishing from the
     Printing Press to the Digital Network* (London: Anthem, 2013).
Bhaskar, Michael, *Curation: The Power of Selection in a World of Excess* (London:
     Piatkus, 2016).
Blummer, Barbara, 'E-Books Revisited: The Adoption of Electronic Books by
     Special, Academic and Public Libraries', *Internet Reference Services Quarterly*, 11
     (2006), pp. 1–13.
Bracken, Simon, 'Beyond the Book: A Whole New Chapter in the Role of Public
     Libraries', *Irish Times*, 6 June 2016, https://www.irishtimes.com/business/
     beyond-the-book-a-whole-new-chapter-in-the-role-of-public-libraries-1.2671826
Buschman, John, 'On Libraries and the Public Sphere', *Library Philosophy and
     Practice*, 11 (2005), pp. 1–8.
Butler, Beverley, *Return to Alexandria: An Ethnography of Cultural Heritage,
     Revivalism and Museum History* (London: Routledge, 2007).
Chepesiuk, Ron, 'Dream in the Desert: Alexandria's Library Rises Again', *American
     Libraries*, 31 (2000), pp. 70–73.
Darnton, Robert, 'The Library in the New Age', *New York Review of Books*, 12 June
     2008.
Darnton, Robert, *The Case for Books: Past, Present and Future* (New York, NY:
     Public Affairs, 2009).

Dumaine, Brian, *Bezonomics: How Amazon Is Changing Our Lives and What the World's Best Companies Are Learning from It* (London: Simon and Schuster, 2020).

Eisenstein, Elizabeth L., *Divine Art, Infernal Machine: The Reception of Printing in the West from First Impressions to the Sense of an Ending* (Philadelphia: University of Pennsylvania Press, 2011).

English, Charlie, *The Book Smugglers of Timbuktu* (London: William Collins, 2017).

EU Libraries factsheet, https://publiclibraries2030.eu/resources/eu-library-factsheets/.

Foroohar, Rana, *Don't Be Evil: The Case Against Big Tech* (London: Allen Lane, 2019).

Higginbotham, Barbra Buckner, 'The "Brittle Books Problem": A Turn-of-the-century Perspective', *Libraries & Culture*, 25 (1990), pp. 496–512.

Kiernan, Anna, 'The Growth of Reading Groups as a Female Leisure Pursuit: Cultural Democracy or Dumbing Down', in DeNel Rehberg Sedo (ed.), *Reading Communities from Salons to Cyberspace* (London: Palgrave Macmillan, 2011), pp. 123–39.

Kiernan, Anna, 'Futurebook Critics and Cultural Curators in a Socially Networked Age', in Robert Barry, Houman Barekat and David Winter (eds.), *The Digital Critic: Literary Culture Online* (New York: OR Books, 2017)

Linehan, Hugh, 'Culture Shock: Shh ... something strange is going on in the Library', *Irish Times*, 27 May 2016, https://www.irishtimes.com/culture/culture-shock-shh-something-strange-is-going-on-in-the-library-1.2663260.

Marcum, Deanna, 'Archives, Libraries, Museums: Coming Back Together?', *Information & Culture*, 49 (2014), pp. 74–89.

Nunberg, Geoffrey (ed.), *The Future of the Book* (Berkeley, CA: University of California Press, 1996).

Orlean, Susan, *The Library Book* (London: Atlantic Books, 2018).

Rabina, Debbie, and Lisa Peet, 'Meeting a Composite of User Needs amidst Change and Controversy: The Case of the New York Public Library', *Reference and User Services Quarterly*, 54 (2014), pp. 52–9.

Schnapp, Jeffrey, and Matthew Battles, *The Library Beyond the Book* (Cambridge, MA: Harvard University Press, 2014).

Schwartz, 'Rebirth of a Notion', *Wilson Quarterly*, 26 (2002), pp. 20–29.

Seed, Robert S., 'Impact of Remote Library Storage on Information Consumers: "Sophie's Choice?"', *Collection Building*, 19 (2000), pp. 105–109.

Sherman, Scott, *Patience and Fortitude: Power, Real Estate, and the Fight to Save a Public Library* (Brooklyn and London: Melville House, 2015).

Somers, James, 'Torching the Modern-Day Library of Alexandria', *The Atlantic*, April 2017, https://www.theatlantic.com/technology/archive/2017/04/the-tragedy-of-google-books/523320/.

'The State of America's Libraries, 2011', *American Libraries, Digital Supplement* (2011), pp. i–vi, 1–61.

Stone, Brad, *The Everything Store: Jeff Bezos and the Age of Amazon* (New York, NY: Little, Brown, 2013).

Striphas, Ted, *The Late Age of Print: Everyday Book Culture from Consumerism to Control* (New York, NY: Columbia University Press, 2009).

Watson, Richard, *Future Files: A History of the Next 50 Years* (London: Nicholas Brealey, 2009).

Watson, Richard, *Extinction Timeline*, https://www.rossdawsonblog.com/ extinction_timeline.pdf.

Weiss, Laura, *Buildings, Books and Bytes: Libraries and Communities in the Digital Age* (Washington, DC: Benton Foundation, 1996).

Wenzel, Sarah G., 'From Revolution to Evolution: The Transformation of the Bibliothèque Nationale into the Bibliothèque Nationale de France, through the Lens of Popular and Professional Reports', *Library Quarterly*, 69 (1999), pp. 324–38.

Wilkin, John P., 'Meanings of the Library Today', in Alice Crawford (ed.), *The Meaning of the Library: A Cultural History* (Princeton: Princeton University Press, 2015), pp. 236–53.

Wisner, William H., *Whither the Postmodern Library? Libraries, Technology, and Education in the Information Age* (Jefferson, NC: McFarland , 2000).

Wolf, Maryanne, *Reader, Come Home: The Reading Brain in a Digital World* (New York, NY: Harper, 2018).

INDEX

Andrew Pettegree, FBA, is professor of modern history at the University of St Andrews, where he directs the Universal Short Title Catalogue project. A leading expert on the history of book and media transformations, Pettegree is the award-winning author of several books on these subjects. He lives in Scotland.

Arthur der Weduwen is a historian and postdoctoral fellow at St Andrews. He is the author of several books on the history of newspapers, advertising, and publishing. He lives in Scotland.